The Economics
of Health
and Health Care

Third Edition

The Economics of Health and Health Care

Sherman Folland

Associate Professor of Economics
Oakland University

Allen C. Goodman

Professor of Economics
Wayne State University

Miron Stano

Professor of Economics and Management
Oakland University

Prentice
Hall

Upper Saddle River, NJ 07458

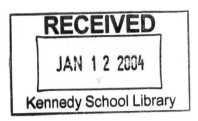
Library of Congress Cataloging-in-Publication Data

Folland, Sherman.
 The economics of health and health care / Sherman Folland, Allen C. Goodman,
Miron Stano.—3rd ed.
 p. cm.
 Includes bibliographical references and index.
 ISBN 0-13-012215-7

 1. Medical economics. I. Goodman, Allen C. II. Stano, Miron. III. Title.
RA410.F65 2001
338.4'33621—dc21

 00-037472

Vice President/Editorial Director: James Boyd
Editor-in-Chief: PJ Boardman
Senior Editor: Rod Banister
Managing Editor (Editorial): Gladys Soto
Editorial Assistant: Marie McHale
Assistant Editor: Holly Brown
Senior Marketing Manager: Lori Braumberger
Media Project Manager: Bill Minick
Production/Manufacturing Manager: Gail Steier de Acevedo
Production Coordinator: Maureen Wilson
Manufacturing Buyer: Natacha St. Hill Moore
Senior Prepress/Manufacturing Manager: Vincent Scelta
Cover Design: Bruce Kenselaar
Cover Art/Photo: PhotoDisc
Composition: BookMasters, Inc.

Prentice
Hall

10 9 8 7 6 5 4 3 2 1
ISBN 0-13-012215-7

Brief Contents

v

Contents

PART IV: INSURANCE AND ORGANIZATION OF HEALTH PROVIDERS

PART V: TECHNOLOGY

Preface

This is the third edition of a book that was conceived in 1990 and first published in 1993. To indicate how much the world of health economics has changed, the first edition made a single reference to "managed care," and that was in the context of monopoly power in the provision of health care. In addition, the debate on the Clinton health plan illuminated a large set of issues that invigorated the discipline of health economics.

This book was first written to assist health economics instructors in developing a clear, step-by-step understanding of health economics for their students. We also believe that it is important for instructors to show what health economics researchers are doing in theory and in empirical work. The book synthesizes contemporary developments around a set of basic economic principles, including maximization of consumer utility (or well-being) and economic profit, wishing to make these principles accessible to undergraduate students, as well as to graduate students. Rather than organizing the book around the institutions specific to the health care economy, we have used core economics themes as basic as supply and demand, as venerable as technology or labor issues, and as modern as the economics of information. Moreover, we have sought to improve accessibility to the book for the wide range of health services students and practitioners whose knowledge of economics may be more limited.

We have followed the philosophy that students must have a working knowledge of the analytical tools of economics and econometrics to appreciate the field of health economics. Some students may be ready to plunge directly into Cost-Benefit Analysis (chapter 4) or The Production of Health (chapter 5) upon completion of the introductory chapter 1. However, chapters 2 (Microeconomic Tools) and 3 (Statistical Tools) allow the students and their teachers to develop or to review the needed analytical concepts before tackling the core subject matter. In chapters 2 and 3, students with as little as one semester of microeconomics may review and study how economists analyze problems, using examples that are relevant to health economics. No calculus is needed.

Consistent with an emphasis on clarity of exposition, this book makes extensive use of graphs, tables, and charts. Discussion questions and exercises are provided to help students master the basics and to prompt them to think about the issues. Features on up-to-date applications of theory and policy developments are also included, as well as the occasional tidbit containing purely background information.

Finally, we caution that some of the chapters, such as those on insurance, although devoid of advanced mathematics, may still require considerable effort. No painless way

is available to appreciate the scope of the contributions that scholars have made in recent years. Sections or subsections that are more demanding and/or peripheral to the core material have been identified. These sections can be omitted without detracting from the flow of the book. More advanced students of the health care economy who wish to be challenged further can utilize a comprehensive references section, with more than 750 sources, so that their (and our) work can be enriched through referral to the original sources.

What's Changed in the Third Edition?

It is critical that this textbook contain the most current knowledge and address the needs of our readers. As with the second edition, almost every chapter is revised to incorporate significant developments in the field.

In response to the instructors and students who use this book, we have moved the chapter on cost-benefit analysis forward, so that it is now chapter 4. We have made major changes in the treatment of insurance and managed care. Also in response to user demand, we have broken up a single health insurance chapter into two components. Insurance (chapter 7), which looks at the individual determinants of insurance, now precedes Consumer Choice (chapter 8), as well as a set of chapters on important, related economic topics. The Organization of Health Insurance Markets (chapter 11), which looks at the development of health insurance markets (and asks the question "who pays?"), precedes the entirely rewritten and greatly expanded chapter on Managed Care (chapter 12). In this chapter, we make a major effort to link theoretical models and empirical findings.

The section on governmental actions regarding the health economy has been reorganized. Chapter 20 looks at conceptual issues regarding government intervention in health care markets; chapter 21 investigates the principal regulatory mechanisms, including antitrust policy. These are followed by an updated chapter 22, which includes information about the 1997 changes to Medicare and Medicaid.

Finally, we finish the book with two new chapters. Chapter 25 looks at economic "bads." Economists like to look at things that are good for us, but some things such as cigarettes are not. Chapter 26 is an entirely new chapter on pharmaceuticals. Rather than a simple "industry study," we look at those portions of the pharmaceutical industry with particularly novel economic contents. These include questions as to the optimal combinations of drug therapies and other economic technologies, the appropriate amount of patent protection that an industry (in this case the pharmaceutical industry) should enjoy, and price discrimination by pharmaceutical firms (or why drugs are cheaper in Mexico than in the United States).

Another change involves the emergence of Internet resources for students and scholars. Tables and charts that were once available only in book form, and then only after several years, are now available much more quickly, and are often available on the Internet long before they are available (if at all) in print. The downside to this explosion of information involves editorial oversight (not all sources are good ones) and frustrating tendencies for Internet sites to disappear. We have chosen to focus on governmental sites such as the following for references that we believe to be both long lasting and reliable.

National Institutes of Health (*http://www.nih.gov/*),
Health Care Financing Administration (*http://www.hcfa.gov/*),
Social Security Administration (*http://www.ssa.gov/*), and
Bureau of the Census (*http://www.census.gov/*).

Alternative Course Designs

As a developing field, the economics of health and health care has an evolving body of literature, and there is no single "correct" order for the course design. Economists (particularly U.S. economists) typically organize topics through markets, with government roles coming much later. Students and scholars of public health assign the governmental sector far more importance; it is "public" health. Unfortunately, a text is necessarily linear in that one chapter has to follow another.

The Economics of Health and Health Care offers instructors considerable flexibility. We have divided the 26 chapters into nine parts:

1. Basic Economic Tools (chapters 1–4)
2. Supply and Demand (chapters 5–8)
3. Information (chapters 9–10)
4. Insurance and Organization of Health Providers (chapters 11–12)
5. Technology (chapters 13–14)
6. Labor (chapters 15–16)
7. Hospitals and Nursing Homes (chapters 17–18)
8. Social Insurance (chapters 19–23)
9. Policy Issues and Analyses (chapters 24–26)

The categories are not entirely exclusive. Chapter 7, looking at the demand and supply of insurance, is as important to part 4 on insurance as it is to part 2 on demand and supply of goods.

From front to back, the organization follows an "economics" model in which consumers and firms are first analyzed in a world without government and governmental policies. As a result, explicit discussions of government policies do not come until chapter 19, although regulation, licensing, mandates, and the like are discussed in reference to other topics much earlier. Many economics instructors may wish to follow the chapters in the order of the book.

Other instructors, particularly those who are interested in public health and in governmental policies, may wish to "tool up" on some of the earlier analyses, and then skip directly to parts 8 and 9, in which we look at social insurance, health care regulation, and health care reform. After that, they may wish to browse selected topics. Although some analyses build on each other within chapters, we have sought to minimize cross-referencing among chapters.

New Instructional Materials

We are pleased to provide our users with two new features. Instructors and students will be able to log on to *http://www.prenhall.com/folland* where they will find occasional timely features, as well as links to useful health-related locations elsewhere on the Web. In addition, our new Instructor's Manual will provide instructors with teaching hints,

suggestions for discussion, and additional questions (with answers). With the increased use of our book for professional, as well as distance education, the manual will prove invaluable for teachers in both traditional and nontraditional settings. Instructors should contact their Prentice Hall sales representative for the user identification number and password to access the faculty resources.

Acknowledgments

Because this book emerges from years of classroom and professional interaction, we thank those students and colleagues who have discussed the economics of health and health care with us, and who have challenged our ideas. Perhaps our most significant debts go to Annie Todd, who suggested the endeavor and introduced us to each other, and to Tom McGuire, whose intellectual and collegial support convinced us that we could succeed. We have been blessed with outstanding editors—Jill Leckta edited the first edition, Leah Jewell edited the second, and Rod Banister and Gladys Soto have edited this third edition.

The staff at Prentice Hall has been outstanding in their support. Maureen Wilson has most capably managed production for this edition as she did for our second edition.

We have been helped all along by capable research assistants, including Kimberly Klett, Kalyani Velagapudi, and Daniel Armijo.

We are most grateful to instructors at more than 200 universities in the United States, Canada, and abroad, who have provided the market test for our work by adopting the book. Numerous professional colleagues were generous in offering their time and energy to read and critique various chapters. We thank:

- Carson Bays, East Carolina University
- James Burgess, Veterans Administration
- Frank Chaloupka, University of Illinois—Chicago
- Hope Corman, Rider College
- Merton Finkler, Lawrence University
- Andrew D. Foster, Brown University
- H. E. Frech, III, University of California—Santa Barbara
- Martin Gaynor, Carnegie Mellon University
- John Goddeeris, Michigan State University
- Warren Greenberg, George Washington University
- Michael Grossman, City University of New York
- Jack Hadley, Center for Health Policy Studies
- James Hamilton, Wayne State University
- Janet Hankin, Wayne State University
- Govind Hariharan, State University of New York—Buffalo
- Ronald Horwitz, Oakland University
- Harold Hotelling, Lawrence Technological University
- Paul Langley, University of Colorado
- William Low, University of Northern British Columbia
- Timothy McBride, University of Missouri—St. Louis
- Tom McCarthy, National Economic Research Associates
- Catherine McLaughlin, University of Michigan

- Eleanor Nishiura, Wayne State University
- Albert A. Okunde, University of Memphis
- Martin Pernick, University of Michigan
- Joann Richards, Oakland University
- John Rizzo, Yale University
- Ya-chen Tina Shih, University of North Carolina
- John M. Tilford, University of Arkansas
- Scott Vander Linde, Calvin College
- Rob Verner, Kent State University
- Kenneth Warner, University of Michigan
- Gerard Wedig, University of Pennsylvania
- Burton Weisbrod, Northwestern University
- William White, Yale University
- Barbara Wolfe, University of Wisconsin—Madison
- Michael Woolley, University of Southern California

We also thank the following colleagues who, with their classes, test-taught and test-learned parts of the text:

- Randall Ellis, Boston University
- Gail Jensen, Wayne State University
- Thomas McGuire, Boston University
- Lee Mobley, Oakland University
- Kathleen Possai, Wayne State University
- Richard Scheffler, University of California—Berkeley
- Nancy Wolf, Rutgers University

Yet again, we thank our wives and daughters who have patiently watched and supported their husbands and fathers in learning about health economics.

<div align="right">

S. F.
Rochester, Michigan

A. C. G.
Detroit, Michigan

M. S.
Rochester, Michigan

</div>

CHAPTER 1

Introduction

- The Relevance of Health Economics
- Economic Methods and Examples of Analysis
- Does Economics Apply to Health and Health Care?
- Is Health Care Different?
- New Challenges to Health Economists
- Conclusions

Health and health care are dominant economic and political issues in the United States and many other countries. Because most nations have experienced rapid rises in health care spending over the past 30 years, it is not surprising that health economics has emerged as a distinct specialty within economics. In a formal sense, health economics is the study of how resources are allocated to and within the health economy. The production of health care and its distribution across populations fall within this definition. Several examples will be introduced in this chapter to illustrate economic analysis of health care issues.

We also seek to demonstrate the magnitude and importance of the health sector. Various measures of size and growth will be used to establish the relevance of the health economy to both individual and national policy concerns.

The final goal of this chapter is to promote the theme that economics will help to explain how health care markets function. However, we will also stress the importance of recognizing features distinctive to health care markets so that appropriate modifications can be made to the economist's conventional analytical tools. Despite continuing controversy on most major issues, health economists have been able to provide answers to many questions of academic and policy interest.

The Relevance of Health Economics

The study of health economics proves important and interesting in three interrelated ways: (1) the size of the contribution of the health sector to the overall economy, (2) the national policy concerns resulting from the importance many people attach to the

1

economic problems they face in pursuing and maintaining their health, and (3) the fact that many other health issues have a substantial economic element.

THE SIZE AND SCOPE OF THE HEALTH ECONOMY

The health economy merits attention for its sheer size. It constitutes a large share of gross domestic product (GDP) in the United States, as well as other countries. It also represents a substantial capital investment and a large and growing share of the labor force.

Health Care's Share of GDP in the United States

Nearly one of every seven dollars spent on final goods and services in the U.S. economy goes to the health sector. To put this figure in perspective, as recently as 1980, the share of GDP devoted to health care was one dollar in eleven, and in 1960 it was just one in twenty.[1] Figure 1.1 tracks the health economy's share of GDP from 1950 to 1997. The conclusion? The health care sector is a large and growing portion of our economy.

In calculating the share of GDP spent on health care, both spending and GDP are measured in current dollars; thus, the effects of general inflation are netted out. Therefore, only three major possibilities exist to explain the substantially increased ratios shown in Figure 1.1:

1. People may be buying more health services. Patients may be consulting with health providers more frequently; doctors may be ordering more tests, or they may be prescribing more drugs.
2. People may be buying higher-quality health services, including products and services that previously were not available. Laser surgery, measles vaccines, and new treatments for burn victims have raised the quality of care since 1960. Economic theory suggests that people are willing to pay more for better quality.
3. Health care inflation may be higher than the general rate of inflation. Higher incomes and the increased prevalence of insurance, including large government programs such as Medicare and Medicaid, may have led to increased health care prices over time.

A major challenge is to understand these phenomena and their contributions to total spending. The study of demand, insurance, production, technology, and labor supply, among other topics, will help meet this challenge.

Health Care Spending in Other Countries

Examining the health economy of other countries will enhance our understanding of the U.S. health economy. Many countries have a large health care sector and share the same major issues of concern. Table 1.1 shows that in most countries the share of health care in the GDP grew rapidly between 1960 and 1980. However, unlike most other nations, the rate of increase in the United States continued to grow into the 1990s, although it has slowed somewhat in the last few years. The data also indicate the relative size of the U.S. health economy compared to that of other countries. For example, its share of GDP in the United States is approximately twice as large as its share in the United Kingdom—a country with national health insurance. Is care costlier in the

[1]GDP is the market value of final goods and services produced within the borders of a country in a year.

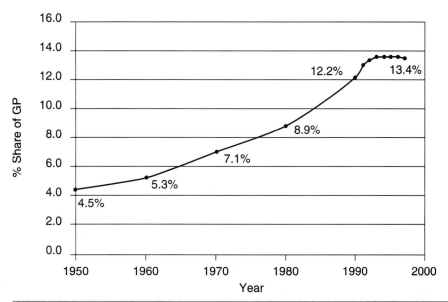

FIGURE 1.1 Health Expenditure Shares, 1950 to 1997.

Source: Health Care Financing Administration (1998).

United States? Is the care of higher quality, or is more simply being consumed? We will address such questions in chapter 23.

Importance of the Health Economy in Personal Spending

Because it accounts for such a large share of the national product, the size of the health economy is also reflected through other key indicators. Two of these are especially easy to relate to at the personal level: (1) share of income spent on medical care, and (2) number of jobs in the health economy.

Table 1.2 provides data on the ways in which U.S. consumers spend their disposable incomes. By 1992, medical care had supplanted food and tobacco as the largest category of expenditures. In 1997, consumers spent 17.4 percent of their budgets on medical care, as opposed to 15.1 percent on food and tobacco and 15.1 percent on housing. This represents a major shift in spending patterns. As recently as 1960, food represented about 25 percent of spending, housing about 15 percent, and medical care only 5 percent.

Importance of the Health Economy to the Labor Force

The flip side of spending is reflected through the jobs that have been created in the health economy. Table 1.3a shows that more than 11 million people, almost 9 percent of the labor force, worked at various health service sites in 1996; almost half of them worked in hospitals.

Table 1.3b indicates the considerable growth in health care personnel since 1970 for selected professions. In 1970, there were 290,862 physicians, or 143 per 100,000 population. By 1996, the number of physicians more than doubled, as had the number of registered nurses. The number of registered nurses per 100,000 population had also more than doubled from 369 to 815.

TABLE 1.1 Health Expenditures as Percent of GDP in Selected OECD Countries: (Selected Years)

	1960	1970	1980	1990	1997
Australia	4.9	5.7	7.3	8.3	8.3
Austria	4.3	5.3	7.7	7.2	7.9
Belgium	3.4	4.1	6.5	7.5	7.6
Canada	5.5	7.1	7.3	9.2	9.3
Czech Republic			3.8	5.4	7.0
Denmark	3.6	6.1	8.7	8.2	7.7
Finland	3.9	5.7	6.5	8.0	7.3
France	4.2	5.8	7.6	8.9	9.9
Germany	4.8	6.3	8.8	8.7	10.4
Greece	2.4	3.3	3.6	4.2	7.1
Hungary				6.1	6.5
Iceland	3.3	5.0	6.2	7.9	8.0
Ireland	3.8	5.3	8.7	6.7	7.0
Italy	3.6	5.2	7.0	8.1	7.6
Japan		4.4	6.4	6.0	7.3
Korea		2.1	2.9	3.9	4.0
Luxembourg		3.7	6.2	6.6	7.1
Mexico				3.6	4.7
Netherlands	3.8	5.9	7.9	8.3	8.5
New Zealand	4.3	5.2	6.0	7.0	7.6
Norway	2.9	4.5	7.0	7.8	7.4
Poland				4.4	5.3
Portugal		2.8	5.8	6.5	8.2
Spain	1.5	3.7	5.6	6.9	7.4
Sweden	4.7	7.1	9.4	8.8	8.6
Switzerland	3.1	4.9	6.9	8.3	10.2
Turkey		2.4	3.3	3.6	
United Kingdom	3.9	4.5	5.6	6.0	6.7
United States	5.3	7.1	8.9	12.2	13.4

Source: Organization for Economic Cooperation and Development Health Data 98.

Reflecting the increases in spending, the health care sector is increasingly a source of employment. Thus, cutbacks in spending on health care will typically mean cutbacks in employment opportunities.

Capital Investment in the Health Economy

In addition to labor, a substantial amount of capital has been drawn to the U.S. health care system. The number of nursing home beds increased from about 1.3 million in 1976 to 1.8 million in 1996 (beds per person, however, decreased slightly). The number of beds in more than 6,000 short-stay hospitals peaked in the late 1970s, but the total number remains on the order of 1 million. There are also considerable and growing amounts of other capital—such as diagnostic equipment—per bed.

TABLE 1.2 Total Personal Consumption Expenditures (in $ billions), by Type, 1997

	Total	*Percent*
Total	5,494	100.0
Food and Tobacco	832	15.1
Housing	830	15.1
Medical Care	957	17.4
Drugs/Sundries	98	1.8
Physicians	205	3.7
Dentists	53	1.0
Hospitals and Nursing Homes	408	7.4
Health Insurance	58	1.1
Other	135	2.5
Transportation	636	11.6
Household Operation	621	11.3
Recreation	463	8.4
Clothing	353	6.4
Personal Business	459	8.4
All Other	343	6.2

Source: U.S. Department of Commerce Survey of Current Business, August 1998, Table 2.4.

Other Resources

Data on expenses for health care and data on health care labor and capital inputs reflect only some of the inputs used by people to produce health. Inputs that are not bought and sold in the marketplace are also important, including a person's own contribution of time and effort. These inputs entail real costs to society. For example, when one's time is given over to producing better health, the cost to the individual and society is the value of the leisure that is foregone. Thus, the value of the inputs we use to produce and maintain our health is much greater than the measured costs of the health care that we buy.

TABLE 1.3a Employed Civilians at Health Services Sites: 1998

Category	*Total Employment (in thousands)*
All Employed Civilians	131,463
All Health Services Sites	11,504
Hospitals	5,116
Nursing and Personal Care Facilities	1,801
Offices and Clinics of Physicians	1,581
Offices and Clinics of Dentists	666
Offices and Clinics of Chiropractors	127
Other Health Services Sites	2,213

Source: U.S. Department of Health and Human Services, *Health United States,* 1999, Table 101.

| TABLE 1.3b Active Health Personnel and Number Per 100,000 Population (in parentheses) | | | | |
|---|---|---|---|
| *Profession* | *1970* | *1980* | *1990* | *1996* |
| Physicians | 290,862 (143) | 427,122 (190) | 567,611 (230) | 701,195 (264) |
| Dentists | 95,700 (47) | 121,240 (54) | 146,600 (59) | 159,500 (58) |
| Optometrists | 18,400 (9) | 22,300 (10) | 26,000 (10) | 29,500 (11) |
| Pharmacists | 112,750 (55) | 142,780 (63) | 161,900 (64) | 185,000 (69) |
| Podiatrists | 7,110 (4) | 8,880 (4) | 10,600 (4) | 10,300 (4) |
| Registered Nurses | 750,000 (369) | 1,272,900 (560) | 1,789,600 (714) | 2,161,700 (815) |

Source: U.S. Department of Health and Human Services, *Health United States,* 1998, Table 103, *Health United States,* 1999, Table 105.

Although we have stressed inputs, the contribution of health resources to the economy is ultimately a measure of the value of the output—health itself. The value of improvements to our health is measured both in consumption and production. This means that we value being healthy both for its own sake and for its contribution to the production of other goods.[2] The intrinsic value of being healthy is ultimately the value we attach to life and limb, which people commonly describe as infinite in certain circumstances and at least substantial in most circumstances. The value of health in the production of other goods is exemplified not just in reduced absenteeism rates but also in output per worker on the job. In both its consumption and production aspects, the output of the health sector makes a substantial contribution to the economy.

The Importance Attached to Economic Problems of Health Care Delivery

The health sector receives attention from policymakers because of its widely perceived problems. The substantial resources devoted to health care are reflected in a more meaningful way through the average level of this nation's spending for health care. Table 1.4 provides various measures of health care spending and its growth since 1960.

Table 1.4 shows how national health expenditures (NHE) have grown from $27 billion in 1960 to $1,088 billion in 1997. During that period, the U.S. population grew by 55 percent from 179 million to 278 million. Thus NHE per capita rose by a multiple of 27, from $143 in 1960 to $3,912 in 1997.

However, the real increase is what matters most. Prices, as measured by the broad-based consumer price index (CPI), rose 442 percent over the same period. After deflating by the CPI, we find that real expenditures per capita in 1997 were approximately five times the 1960 level—still a hefty increase.[3]

Inflation

Although we have deflated the spending values using the CPI, medical care prices have grown faster historically than prices overall. Table 1.4 also shows the pattern of health care inflation since 1960. Note that hospital and physician care prices have risen

[2]This idea was developed further in an essay by Fuchs (1972).
[3]This five-fold increase is determined by dividing $3,912 (1997 spending) by 160.5 (1997 CPI) and dividing the result by the corresponding ratio for 1960. National health spending updates are available at the Health Care Financing Administration's Internet site (*http://www.hcfa.gov/*).

TABLE 1.4 National Health Expenditures (NHE) and Other Data for Selected Years, 1960 to 1997 ($ billions)

Year	NHE	% Growth in NHE	GDP	NHE per capita	NHE % GDP	Price Indexes CPI	Hospital Rooms	Physician Services
1960	27.1	8.7	515	143	5.3	29.6	9.3	21.9
1970	73.2	13.1	1,035	346	7.1	38.8	23.6	34.5
1980	247.3	12.9	2,784	1,052	8.9	82.4	68.0	76.5
1990	699.5	11.0	5,744	2,691	12.2	130.7	175.4	160.8
1996	1,035.1	4.6	7,636	3,759	13.6	156.9	261.0	216.4
1997	1,088.2	4.7	8,111	3,912	13.4	160.5	N.A.	222.9

Source: U.S. Department of Health and Human Services, *Health United States,* 1998, Table 115, 118, and Levit et al. (2000).

much faster than the CPI—a phenomenon that is typical of other health care services and commodities as well.

Growing costs are a common problem for maintaining health programs, and they have spurred numerous cost-containment efforts by the government in the past two decades. Understanding and evaluating the effects of such regulatory measures are important tasks for the health economist.

Access

For many, the rising costs significantly reduce accessibility to health care. Financial affordability influences demand for most goods and services, and there are many reasons why some people do not have health insurance. What is clear is that the number of uninsured has risen in the United States; 44 million people now lack insurance. Many more are considered to have inadequate insurance. The problems of cost, inflation, and uninsured people have led to numerous proposals for some form of national health insurance. Later in this book, we will examine several broad groups of plans, as well as the national health insurance programs that exist in several other countries.

Quality

Increases in the quality of care contribute to increases in spending. Often, the focus is on ensuring quality through professional licensure and certification and, especially for hospitals, through quality-assurance programs. At the same time, concerns arise about access to high-quality care for those without insurance or with minimal insurance. Interestingly, some also are concerned that the quality of care in the United States is often excessive, especially for some forms of "high-tech" treatment. For such treatments, the costs of resources may exceed the benefits to patients. The interplay among insurance, technology, and consumption is of growing interest to economists.

THE ECONOMIC SIDE TO OTHER HEALTH ISSUES

Production, costs, and insurance are naturally issues that involve economics, but many other health issues have economic components, even though they may seem to be purely medical concerns. A few examples illustrate the point.

The choice of a health care treatment seems purely medical to many people, but physicians and other providers are increasingly aware that alternative treatments can be evaluated and compared on economic grounds. It is necessary to examine the costs of alternative techniques. Physicians are also increasingly sensitive to the economic side of the patient–physician relationship. The patient's preferences are considered valid in determining the appropriateness of a given treatment.

We also must explore the economic reasons behind people's choices about their health. People take care of themselves well at some times and poorly at other times. People's desired health status can be understood as a meaningful economic choice. Even addiction to a harmful substance can be understood better when analyzed as a possibly rational economic choice.

Other health issues clearly have an economic aspect: What role should the government play in health? What health care investments should a developing country make? Should cigarette advertising be banned? Questions like these are not solely economic, but they have an economic side.

Economic Methods and Examples of Analysis

We have already provided a formal definition of health economics as "the study of the allocation of resources to and within the health economy." From another perspective, however, economics is what economists actually do and how they apply economics to health. What economists do in practice is to use certain characteristic approaches to their analysis of the world.

FEATURES OF ECONOMIC ANALYSIS

Many distinctive features of economics might be exhaustively identified, but we emphasize only four:

- the assumption of rationality
- the use of abstraction
- the use of marginal analysis
- the use of models as metaphors.

Rational Decision Making

Economists typically approach problems of human economic behavior by assuming that the decision maker is a rational being. Rationality is effectively defined as "making choices that best further one's own ends given one's resource constraints." Some behaviors may appear irrational. However, when disputes over rationality arise, economists often attempt to point out, perhaps with some delight, that so-called irrational behavior often makes sense when the incentives facing the decision maker are properly understood.

Use of Abstraction

Most contemporary economic analyses draw the world abstractly. Whether models are too abstract is a matter of legitimate dispute, but it would be difficult for a first-time visitor to the New York Stock Exchange, for example, to understand the economics of financial markets from direct observation of the confusing flurry of activity on the floor of the exchange.

Similarly, a map serves as a model for abstractions. If you wanted to find the Library of Congress in Washington, D.C., a completely realistic aerial photo would not be useful, because you would have neither the street names nor the appearances of the buildings on the map. You would prefer an abstract drawing with the names clearly marked and the Library of Congress plainly indicated, perhaps in a different color. Abstraction in economics is the art of eliminating the nonessential detail in order to make the remaining model more useful to the purpose at hand. Abstraction is always necessary, but eliminating essential features (such as the location of the White House in a map of Washington) is an error in anybody's book.

Marginal Analysis

Mainstream economic analyses feature reasoning at the margin. To make an appropriate choice, decision makers must understand the cost as well as the benefit of the next, or marginal, unit. One could contemplate the appropriate total number of pounds of beef to buy, for example, by considering iteratively whether the next pound is worth the cost. Similarly, marginal analysis often entails the mental experiment of trading off the costs against the benefits at the margin. Trade-offs of this sort are ubiquitous in both economics and in the real world. Nobelist Milton Friedman once proposed that one could sum up economics with the following phrase: "There's no such thing as a free lunch."

Use of Models

Finally, economics characteristically develops models to depict its subject matter. The models may be described in words, graphs, or mathematics. This text features words and graphs. These models may be understood as metaphors for reality. We say, "This is the market for physician care," but what we mean is "this is *like* the market for physician care." Any metaphor can be pushed too far and must be tested against one's intuitive sense of reality and ultimately against the facts. Nonetheless, metaphors can be apt, and we can learn from them.

In economic analysis, the models are often abstract. Abstract models help to make sense of the world, in economics as in everyday life. A young child asking what the solar system is like will undoubtedly be shown the familiar drawing of the sun and planets in their orbits—an abstract model. The drawing is quickly grasped, yet no one supposes that the sky looks like this.

EXAMPLES OF HEALTH ECONOMICS ANALYSIS

What do economists do? Here are some examples of economic analysis. On the one hand, physicians, clinics, and hospitals use labor and machines just like other segments of the economy. They charge prices for their services, and they hope to earn at least enough to keep themselves from wanting to switch to other types of work. In this sense, the theories that tell us what firms do and how they combine resources to maximize profits may provide some insights into how the health care sector works.

On the other hand, the health sector is complicated. Consumers must often depend on health providers to tell them whether they are ill, and, if so, what they should do. Providers often prescribe treatments seemingly irrespective of their costs. Physicians may not only be entrepreneurs themselves, they may manage their own laboratories, control hospitals, or influence insurance companies that also affect the health care sector.

Some of the earliest work in health economics addressed several of these issues. Milton Friedman and Simon Kuznets, both of whom became Nobel laureates, studied the so-called physician shortage of the 1930s. They discovered that although physicians earned 32 percent per year more than dentists, their training costs were 17 percent higher. The remaining difference was still large, however, and Friedman and Kuznets (1945) attributed part of the higher returns on investment enjoyed by physicians to barriers to entry into the medical profession. Barriers to entry tend to lower the supply of physicians, hence raising physicians' incomes and raising the rate of return on their investment in their own education. The situation also meant that the value to society of producing one more physician exceeded the costs of producing one more physician.

Reuben Kessel addressed the practice common some years ago for physicians to charge different fees to different patients. The practice was often interpreted as an act of charity, for it was thought that physicians were charging lower fees to poorer patients. Kessel (1958) showed, however, that the practice of charging different fees could also be understood as a form of price discrimination that allowed physicians to increase their profits by charging more to those patients with greater ability to pay.

Kessel presented historical analysis supporting his case. He argued that physicians used the system of hospital privileges as a means of perpetuating price discrimination. Physicians, in order to practice, are usually affiliated with hospitals. Historically, those who adopted competitive economic practices were often branded as "unethical" and could be denied membership in county medical societies, access to specialty certification, or hospital privileges.

These examples also illustrate two features of health economics. The first is the interdisciplinary nature of health research. Economists must know how health care is delivered. This information comes from health care providers, as well as from members of other disciplines such as public health, sociology, and psychology, who study how organizations operate.

The second feature concerns the institutions in the health care system, including hospitals, insurers, or regulators. Examples of these include the following:

- relations of doctors to hospitals
- the organization and practices of the health insurance industry
- licensing and certification of health care providers

Such institutional concerns do not necessarily distinguish health economics from other forms of economic analysis, but the particular history and present form of health care institutions do set health economics apart from other fields. We must take care to describe the institutional characteristics of the health sector in order to devise appropriate models.

Does Economics Apply to Health and Health Care?

A frequent complaint by many who are exposed to applications of economics to health is that economics is irrelevant. This issue is raised often enough in serious contexts to require consideration. The complaint suggests a model of health care in which

health is considered to be primarily a technical issue of medical science, better left to experts. One gets sick, and one sees a doctor who provides the medically appropriate treatment.

On a most general level, the claim that economics does not apply to health care is untenable. If economics, as we have stated, studies how scarce resources are used to produce goods and services and then observes how these goods and services are distributed, then clearly economics applies. Certainly health care resources are scarce; in fact, it is their cost that concerns most people. There is no question that health care is produced and distributed.

Nevertheless, one can question whether the characteristic approaches of economics apply to health care. Are health care consumers rational? Do they calculate optimally at the margin? Imagine a loved one suffering cardiac arrest. Is there time or reasoning power left to calculate? Would anyone question the price of emergency services under such circumstances?

However, much of health care simply does not fit this emergency image. A considerable amount of health care is elective, meaning that the patient has and will perceive some choice over whether and when to have the diagnostics or treatment involved. Much health care is even routine, involving problems such as upper respiratory infections, back pain, and diagnostic checkups. The patient often has prior experience with these concerns. Furthermore, even in a real emergency, the consumer has an agent, the physician, to make or help make decisions on his or her behalf. Thus, rational choices can be made.

The primary objective of this text is to show that economics can help us understand how decision makers throughout the health economy make choices. It is, in fact, the special characteristics of health care markets and products that make the study of health economics both challenging and rewarding.

AN EXAMPLE: DOES PRICE MATTER?

To illustrate, does price matter? This question would not even be raised in the study of any other commodity. However, many have argued that health care is so different from other goods that consumers do not respond to financial incentives. These views have been justified by arguments that demand is based on need or arguments that patients leave decisions entirely to their providers, who are concerned with their own interests rather than how much patients have to pay.

Data from the Rand Health Insurance Experiment give an unequivocal answer to this question: Yes, economic incentives do matter to a considerable extent. Figure 1.2 describes results from the Rand study; amounts of health care consumed are measured along the horizontal axis. These amounts are scaled in percentage terms from zero to 100 percent, where 100 percent reflects the average level of care consumed by the group that used the most care on average. This group, not surprisingly, is the group with "free" care. The vertical axis measures the economic incentives as indicated by the coinsurance rate—the percentage of the bill paid out directly by the consumer. Thus, a higher coinsurance rate reflects a higher price to the consumer.

The curve shown in Figure 1.2 is similar to a demand curve in that it shows people consuming more care as the care becomes less costly to the consumer directly. More importantly, the curve demonstrates that economic incentives do matter.

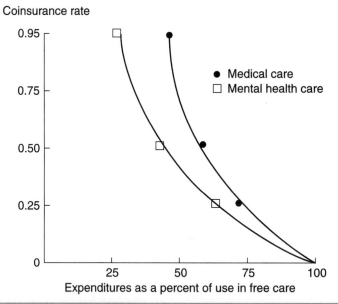

FIGURE 1.2 Demand Response of Ambulatory Mental and Medical Care in the Rand Health Insurance Experiment.

Sources: Keeler, Manning and Wells (1988) for mental health care; Keeler and Rolph (1988) for medical care.

Is Health Care Different?

Although economics certainly applies to health care, it is more challenging to answer the question of how directly and simply it applies. Is available economic theory so easily applicable that a special field of health economics is not even necessary? To the contrary, is health care so special as to be unique? Or is the truth somewhere in between?[4]

A reasonably satisfactory answer to these questions suggests that health care has many distinctive features, but that it is not unique in any of them. What is unique, perhaps, is the combination of features and even the sheer number of them. A review of these distinctive features serves the purpose of alerting the student to those salient features of health care that require special attention. In each case where health is distinctive in economic terms, a body of economic theory and empirical work can be found that illuminates the issue.

PRESENCE AND EXTENT OF UNCERTAINTY

When Nobelist Kenneth Arrow (1963) directed his attention to the economics of health, he helped establish health economics as a field. His theme stressed the prevalence of uncertainty in health care, on both the demand side and the supply side. Consumers are uncertain of their health status and need for health care in any coming period. This

[4]For further development of the following issues and for a variety of views, see Arrow (1963), Pauly (1978), and Fuchs (1972).

means that the demand for health care is irregular in nature from the individual's perspective; likewise, the demand facing a health care firm is irregular.

Uncertainty is also prevalent on the supply side. Standard economic analysis often assumes that products, and the pleasures that they bring, are well understood by the purchasers. The purchase of steak, milk, new clothes, or a ticket to a baseball game provides expected well-being that is easily known and understood. In contrast, several cases of product uncertainty exist in the health field. Consumers often do not know the expected outcomes of various treatments without their physicians' advice, and in many cases physicians themselves cannot predict the outcomes of treatments with certainty.

Arrow argued that uncertainty on both the supply and demand sides was such that markets for insurance for various risks would often fail to arise. These factors suggested a role for government. Although others disputed the conclusion, the point stands that uncertainty is a prominent feature in the field of health, and the tools of economic analysis of uncertainty and risk will need to be used to analyze health issues fully.

PROMINENCE OF INSURANCE

The fact of uncertainty and risk in health implies a role for insurance. Consumers purchase insurance to guard against this uncertainty. Because of health insurance, neither most Americans nor citizens of other countries pay directly for the full costs of their health care. Rather, the costs are paid indirectly through coinsurance and through insurance premiums that are often, although not always, purchased through participation in the labor force.[5]

Table 1.5 provides data on the sources of payment for personal health care services for selected years since 1960. In the 1960s, approximately 55 percent of all personal health care expenditures were paid out-of-pocket, meaning that 45 percent was paid by third-party payers (either private or government). By 1997, more than 80 percent was paid by third parties, with the increase due to the growth of both private insurance and public programs. Certainly, such separation from the direct payment must weaken some of the price effects that might be expected in standard economic analysis. Insurance changes the demand for care, and it potentially also changes the incentives of providers.

The possibility of changed provider incentives becomes more of a concern as the insurance portion of the bill increases. How the insurers pay the health care firm thus becomes a critical fact of economic life. Whether a procedure or a professional's services are accepted for coverage by insurers may determine whether providers use the procedure. Furthermore, changes in insurance payment procedures can substantially change provider behavior and provider concerns, as evidenced by Medicare's decision to change their hospital payment system during the 1980s in order to control costs more effectively.

PROBLEMS OF INFORMATION

The problem of uncertainty can in part be attributed to lack of information. Actual and potential information problems in health care markets raise many economic questions. Sometimes information is unavailable to all parties concerned. For example, neither the

[5]Analysts are becoming more concerned about the insurance coverage of those who are not in the work force, or those who are not covered through their jobs.

TABLE 1.5 Personal Health Care Expenditures ($ billion) by Source of Payment for Selected Years: 1960–1997

Year	Total	Out-of-Pocket	Private Health Ins.	Other Private	Gov't State/Loc	Total Federal	Total 3rd Party	Pct. 3rd Party
1960	23.6	13.1	5.0	0.4	3.0	2.1	10.5	44.7
1970	63.8	24.9	14.8	1.7	7.8	14.7	38.9	61.0
1980	217.0	60.3	62.1	7.8	23.7	63.4	156.7	72.2
1990	614.7	144.5	206.5	21.5	64.5	177.6	470.2	76.5
1997	969.0	188.0	313.0	35.9	95.0	337.2	781.0	80.6

Source: U.S. Department of Health and Human Services, *Health United States,* 1999, Table 120.

gynecologist nor her female patient may recognize the early stages of cervical cancer without a Pap smear. At other times, the information in question is known to some parties but not to all, and then it is the asymmetry of information that is problematic.

The problems of information mean that the careful economic analyst must modify standard methods of analysis. Standard analyses often assume that consumers have the necessary knowledge about the quality of the food or the clothing that they purchase. People purchase beef as opposed to fish, or cotton as opposed to nylon fabrics. They base their decisions on the characteristics of the goods, their prices, and their abilities to bring pleasure to the buyers.

The purchase of health goods and services departs substantively from this model. Consumers may not know which physicians or hospitals are good. They may not know whether they are ill or what should be done if they are. This lack of information often makes the consumer, sometimes referred to as the principal, dependent on the provider, as an agent, in a particular way. The provider offers both the information and the service, leading to the possibility of conflicting interests. Health economics must address the provision of health services in this context.

LARGE ROLE OF NONPROFIT FIRMS

A durable assumption of economic analysis is that firms maximize profits. Economic theory provides models that explain how businesses allocate resources in order to maximize profits. Yet many health providers, including many hospitals, insurers, and nursing homes, have nonprofit status.

What, then, motivates these nonprofit institutions, if they cannot enjoy the profits of their endeavors? The economist must analyze the establishment and perpetuation of nonprofit institutions, and understand the differences in their behaviors from for-profit firms.

RESTRICTIONS ON COMPETITION

Economists and policymakers generally laud the competitive market, because the entry of firms or providers in the face of high prices and/or profits will cause the other firms or providers to lower their prices. This entry and the resulting price reduction improve the well-being of consumers.

Nevertheless, the health sector has developed many practices that effectively restrict competition. These practices include licensure requirements for providers, re-

strictions on provider advertising, and standards of ethical behavior that enjoin providers from competing with each other. We must explain the forces that generated such practices and understand their potential benefits, but we must also understand their anticompetitive impacts and measure the magnitudes of the higher costs they may impose on society.

Regulation to promote quality or to curb costs also reduces the freedom of choice of providers and may have an impact on or restrict competition. There is often substantial interest in regulating the health care sector. The causes as well as the impacts of the regulations require considerable attention. There are industries, such as the pharmaceutical industry, that contend that patent protection is crucial for their financial stability. Economists must consider how regulations are developed, as well as who gains and who loses from them.

Other types of government intervention, particularly antitrust action, can serve to promote competition. Economic theory suggests that in the case of monopoly power, production may be restricted with a corresponding increase in price. Control of the monopolies or antitrust action to curb monopolistic practices may thus benefit the consumer.

ROLE OF EQUITY AND NEED

Poor health of another human being often evokes a feeling of concern that distinguishes health care from many other goods and services. Many advocates express this feeling by saying that people ought to get the health care they need regardless of whether they can afford it. In practice, need is difficult to define, and distributing care under certain definitions of need may cause more economic harm than good. Yet the word signals a set of legitimate concerns for analysis.

GOVERNMENT SUBSIDIES AND PUBLIC PROVISION

In most countries a major governmental presence can be felt in the provision of health services. Programs such as Medicare and Medicaid inject the government into the financing of and payment for services. In addition, under many circumstances governments provide health care services through clinics and hospitals. All told, government spending in the United States of $483 billion in 1996 accounted for almost 47 percent of total national health care spending of $1,035 billion.

New Challenges to Health Economists— Managed Care and Health Care Costs

From the mid-1960s into the early 1990s, the U.S. health care system grew resolutely. As we saw in Figure 1.1, health expenditures grew from 5.3 percent of the GDP in 1960 to 8.9 percent in 1980 and 12.2 percent in 1990. Buoyed by increased income, more generous insurance, and the new availability of state-of-the-art technology and high-cost treatments, consumers and their insurers increased their health care spending dramatically.

The "fee-for-service" (FFS) system that fed this increase was one that asked providers, mainly physicians and hospitals, how much they spent and then reimbursed them for their costs. The FFS system did not offer incentives for consumers to shop for less expensive care, nor did it foster cost-cutting competition among providers. Particularly for those with

health insurance, high-quality care (reflected by the frequent use of specialists and generously long hospital stays) was provided at a high price.

In the 1980s, the atmosphere began to change. Facing increased expenditures in its Medicare program, the federal government initiated a payment scheme based on Diagnostic Related Groups (DRGs) that *told* providers how much they would be paid and gave them the financial responsibility of cutting costs or losing money. This policy had a particularly strong impact on the length of hospitalization, which is one of the most expensive features of health care.

In addition, Health Maintenance Organizations (HMOs), which had comprised only a small portion of the health care sector, were encouraged by federal legislation as alternative, lower-cost providers of health care. Through selective contracting with hospitals and physicians and stricter review of service utilization, these HMOs and their subsequent variants provided alternative forms of less expensive health care. Their enrollments burgeoned.

This emergence of such "managed care" plans has led to substantial and sometimes heated debate. Do the less expensive HMO or PPO plans wring the waste out of the health care system, or do they provide inadequate care? Are patients discharged from hospitals "quicker but sicker?" The popular press has covered the debate in great depth on television, in magazines, and in newspapers, extending even to the cartoon pages. Some readers may remember puzzled Mike Doonesbury watching his physician and his insurance agent fighting over the proper diagnostic test on an injured knee.

Policy analysts and health care professionals have joined the debate. The September 1998 edition of *Health Affairs* featured an article by analysts from the Health Care Financing Administration (HCFA), the agency that finances Medicare and Medicaid, that projects health care shares of the national economy through 2007.[6] Although health expenditure shares leveled off in the mid-1990s at about 13.5 percent of the GDP, the HCFA analysts believe that shares are likely to resume their upward trend, rising to 16.6 percent by 2007. Their prediction is based on two fundamental beliefs:

1. The leveling off in the 1990s reflected the shift of a large portion of the population from FFS to the managed care sector, a change that provided a one-time decrease in expenditures. Little evidence suggests, however, that managed care costs grow less quickly than FFS costs. Hence, cost growth, which had been mitigated by a shift to lower-cost care, will resume because managed care costs also will grow.
2. As the year 2007 approaches, the large baby boom population (born from the late 1940s to the mid-1960s) will be moving into the 55- to 64-age cohort. This will signify higher health care costs for an increasingly large portion of the population.

In a subsequent (January 1999) edition of *Health Affairs,* others challenged the conclusions, asserting that managed care had fundamentally changed the health economy. Their challenges rest on speculation regarding the continued nature of managed care cost reductions. Does managed care provide one-time cost reductions, or will it also reduce the rate of spending growth over time? Will employers (who provide a large portion of the health insurance) pay for the increasing costs, or will they try to influence providers to hold down the costs?

[6]See Sheila Smith et al. (1998) for the full discussion.

To see how important these assumptions are, suppose that health care expenditures increase to "only" 15.6 percent of the GDP, which is one percentage point less than the 16.6 percent predicted by the HCFA researchers for 2007. How much is one percentage point? The 1998 GDP for the United States was $8.5 trillion. Assuming that GDP rises by 5 percent per year (real output plus inflation), we would expect a GDP in 2007 of approximately $13.2 trillion. A one-percentage-point difference in health expenditure share would be $132 billion that might be spent on items other than health care.

What is more important is not which projection is the correct one, but rather what we can do to understand the host of economic factors that underlie the projections. Economic analysis gives us insightful tools with which to examine, to project, to propose policies, and to act upon the health economy and its component parts.

Conclusions

The features of the health economy we have discussed are distinctive, but the health sector is not unique in these respects. Accounting for the features of the health sector falls well within the scope of economic inquiry. Uncertain events affect much of life including automobile safety, household security, and the fortunes of most businesses. Insurance programs cover many of these instances, and every financial decision entails an element of risk.

Much of health care arguably finds the consumer relatively well-informed. In instances where the physician is asymmetrically better informed, the case is often not unlike the information deficit faced by the typical purchaser of auto repair services or a complex camera.[7]

We commonly speak of needs for food and housing, and we have government programs to provide or subsidize the poor in these markets. Other professions are licensed in many states, and various industries are regulated. Nonprofit firms provide symphony music and college educations, as well as health care. Special tools of analysis are needed in all these cases, not just for health care.

Nevertheless, health and health care are unique in having this combination of distinctive features and perhaps in possessing the sheer number of them. It is not surprising that a distinctive field of economic inquiry with a distinctive set of questions has arisen regarding health.

The relevance of health economics hinges on its ability to inform, and possibly influence, the decisions of those who make health care policy. In his January 1996 presidential address to the American Economic Association, distinguished health economist Victor Fuchs concluded:

> In the past three decades economics has made a positive contribution to health and medical care, and I believe that future contributions will be even greater. Now that the basic ideas of economics are gaining acceptance, it will be more important than ever for economists to master many of the intricacies of health care institutions and technologies. We will also have to consider the problems

[7]See Pauly (1978) for a well-reasoned analysis of the differences between health care and other goods and services. He argues in particular that in many cases, information problems are no more severe for health care than for many other commodities.

of dissemination in order to ensure that when we agree on research results, these results are understood and accepted by all relevant audiences including the media, politicians, and health professionals (Fuchs, 1996, p. 20).

We believe that Professor Fuchs's optimistic statement represents a useful conclusion to this introductory chapter and an important point of departure for the chapters that follow.

Summary

1. Health care spending has grown rapidly in absolute and relative terms. It accounts for about one-seventh of the GDP in the United States, and its share of GDP is projected to continue to grow.
2. The growth in health care spending is attributable to more services, higher-quality services, and relative increases in the prices of health care services. A major goal of health economics is to determine the underlying causes of these phenomena.
3. The size of the health economy is also reflected through other measures such as the number of jobs in health care professions and amount of capital.
4. The health economy is considerably larger in the United States than in other countries.
5. There are significant policy concerns not only with the growth of spending but also with access and quality.
6. Economists use models to explain economic behavior. The models are abstract simplifications of reality.
7. Health economics is a relatively young and evolving field of study. As a result, health economists still disagree on some fundamental issues, such as the extent to which the competitive model applies to the health economy.
8. Health care services and the health economy are associated with a unique set of distinguishing features. The uniqueness of health care lies in the entire set rather than with individual distinctive features, such as the prevalence of uncertainty or insurance coverage.
9. Managed care has profoundly influenced the U.S. health care system in the 1990s. Analysts use economic models to predict its impact on health care spending.

Discussion Questions

1. Suggest several reasons why health care spending is higher in the United States than in other countries. Is the fact that the U.S. population spends more per capita on health care than people in any other developed country evidence of a failure of the U.S. system? What issues do you think are involved in answering the question?
2. Describe several key issues facing policymakers with regard to health care spending.
3. If greater health care spending leads to more jobs, why is there such concern about the rapid growth rates of spending?
4. Do consumers take the net price (including insurance and time) they face into consideration when choosing health care? What evidence suggests that "price matters"? Suggest real-life scenarios in which price may affect choices regarding health care.
5. What is meant by marginal analysis? Provide an example in which marginal analysis is useful in looking at policy questions.

6. Give three examples of quality of care in the provision of health services. Why might consumers be willing to pay more money to have each of them?

7. Describe the size of the health economy when measured by the quantities of capital and labor used to produce health care. What important inputs to the production of health are not being counted among these?

Exercises

1. Health care spending can be summarized by the following equation:

 $S = $ (Population size) \times (health care quantity per person) \times (price per unit of health care)

 a. Identify three factors that might lead to the rapid growth of health care spending.
 b. Compare health care spending to housing expenditures and to food expenditures. How are the sectors similar? How do they differ?

2. Identify five distinctive features of the health economy. Examine each one separately, and describe other commodities or sectors that share those features. Do any other commodities or sectors have all the features you listed?

3. In Table 1.1, calculate which country had the largest and smallest percentage increase in GDP share from 1960 to 1980. Compare these to similar calculations for the period 1980 to 1997. Discuss your results.

4. The United States, Canada, and the United Kingdom share the same language but have considerably different health care systems. Compare the three health shares of GDP from 1960 to 1997. What factors may explain the considerable differences among the three countries?

5. Table 1.4 provides indexes of the prices of health care inputs. Calculate the growth rates of the prices of hospital rooms and physician services. Compare them to the growth rate of the overall Consumer Price Index (CPI). Discuss your findings.

6. In Table 1.5, we see increases in out-of-pocket health expenditures by consumers, and in government expenditures. From year to year, which grew by a larger percentage? Over the entire period, which grew by a larger percentage?

2

Microeconomic Tools for Health Economics

- Scarcity and the Production Possibilities Frontier

- Practice with Supply and Demand

- Functions and Curves

- Consumer Behavior Theory: Ideas Behind the Demand Curve

- Individual and Market Demands

- Elasticities

- Production and Market Supply

- The Firm Supply Curve Under Perfect Competition

- Monopoly and Other Market Structures

- Welfare Losses

- The Edgeworth Box

- Conclusions

This chapter provides an explanation of the microeconomic tools that are used in the text by reviewing material that may be encountered at the introductory and intermediate levels of learning. These tools are useful for a deeper understanding of ideas in health economics. This review does not substitute for an introductory course in the principles of economics. Although the material is presented in a way consistent with more detailed and thus rigorous developments in a standard microeconomics course, mathematical detail is eliminated.

Health economics sometimes involves macroeconomic concepts such as gross domestic product (GDP) or the consumer price index (CPI). However, it deals primarily

with microeconomic concerns involving individual decision makers such as households and providers, and specific industries such as the health insurance and hospital industries. The behavior of individual decision makers is the focus and subject of microeconomics. Health economics also addresses the problem of the efficient use of scarce resources, which too is a microeconomic issue.

The chapter starts with the concept of scarcity and reviews supply-and-demand analysis. After these introductory treatments of supply and demand, the chapter returns separately to demand first and then to supply, developing the underlying ideas behind these tools. We then combine them into models of market structures, emphasizing those featured in health economics.

Scarcity and the Production Possibilities Frontier

A fundamental idea in economics is that there is no such thing as a free lunch. The fact that little if anything is free implies that to get something, one must usually give up something else, such as time or other resources. A helpful theoretical tool that illustrates this idea is the *production possibilities frontier* (PPF).

The production possibilities frontier is a curve drawn in a graph to illustrate the trade-offs between two categories of goods. The curve shows how our choices are constrained by the fact that we cannot have all of everything we want. The idea that we face resource constraints and must make trade-offs is central to the PPF, but similar ideas also apply to the individual firm or the individual consumer.

We begin the production possibilities problem with a table illustrating a classic dilemma. A classic PPF problem concerns society's trade-off between guns and butter. Table 2.1 shows data on the amounts of guns or butter that a hypothetical society could produce with its resources. Guns and butter are meant metaphorically to refer to all goods and services with a military use versus those that have a domestic consumption use. The PPF could in principle also be drawn in many dimensions. What is essential is that the goods represented exhaustively account for all the goods in the economy.

Table 2.1 contains many numbers but illustrates two central ideas. Note first that as the number of guns increases, the number for butter falls, indicating that to produce more of one good we must give up some of the other. The amount of butter given up in order to produce an extra 100 units of guns is called the opportunity cost of 100 units of

TABLE 2.1 Society's Trade-off Between Guns and Butter

Point	Butter	Guns	*Opportunity Cost: Butter Given Up to Produce 100 Units of Guns*
A	936	0	
B	891	100	45
C	828	200	63
D	732	300	96
E	609	400	123
F	444	500	165
G	244	600	200
H	0	700	244

guns. Opportunity cost can be measured per 100 units of guns as here, but more commonly we are interested in the opportunity cost of the single next unit of guns, called the marginal unit. In either case, the opportunity cost represents what is given up.

The opportunity cost column reporting the costs of each 100 units of guns in terms of butter foregone illustrates a second idea—that of increasing opportunity costs. As the number of guns increases, the opportunity cost gets larger. If society is to increase its production of guns, say from 200 to 300 units, it must transfer the resources, labor, and capital previously used in butter production to gun production. The idea that this is a frontier means that we are hypothetically representing society's best possible production. Thus, when we first shift butter resources toward gun production, we can arbitrarily choose to shift those resources relatively best suited to gun production first. By choosing laborers who are more handy at gun making than at butter making, we will gain the most guns per unit of butter we give up. As we shift more and more resources toward guns, we will necessarily have to dig deeper into our relatively good butter-producing resources, and hence give up greater quantities of butter. Increasing opportunity costs thus also illustrate the specialization of society's resources of labor and capital.

Graphing and its usefulness are illustrated by transferring the data in Table 2.1 into the graph in Figure 2.1. Note that if this society devotes all its labor and capital to butter production, the most butter it can produce is 936 units. The two numbers—936 units of butter and 0 units of guns—can be represented by point *A* in Figure 2.1. The other points are transferred in the same manner. We assume that the missing points between these data points will fit the same pattern, resulting in the PPF curve.

In the graph, the idea of no free lunch is illustrated by the downward slope of the PPF curve. In this example, increased gun production means we have to give up some butter production—hence, we get no free lunch. Second, the opportunity cost itself is

FIGURE 2.1 Society's Trade-Off Between Guns and Butter. Point *X* Is Inefficient; Point *Y* Is Infeasible.

illustrated in the slope of the curve. For example, the line between points *B* and *C* has a slope of 63 (the rise) over 100 (the run), and 63 units of butter per 100 units of guns is the opportunity cost we observed in the table.

The opportunity cost of one single unit of guns is virtually the slope of the PPF at a single point, which equals the slope of a line tangent at that point. Therefore, at point *E* the opportunity cost is identical to the slope of the tangent line to the PPF at *E*.

Finally, the idea of increasing opportunity cost is illustrated by the bowed-out shape of the PPF, showing its concavity to the origin. Recall that the slope is the opportunity cost. Thus, the slope becoming steeper means that the opportunity cost is increasing.

Society could choose any point on the PPF, but society can be at only one point at a time. How society makes and achieves its choice are other matters to discuss, but at present we have merely illustrated the best possible practices of some hypothetical society. An interior point such as *X* means that the particular society is not doing the best it can; it is inefficient. A point such as *Y* is unattainable because of insufficient resources to produce the indicated amounts of both guns and butter.

Although health economics applies primarily *micro*economic tools of analysis, the PPF concept bridges the gap between *micro* and *macro*. Before continuing with the *micro* tools, note that at least three additional concepts from *macro*economics, the study of economics in the "large," must also be understood when reading health economics. The GDP measures the total amount of goods and services produced in the country, not counting intermediate products (made for use in the production of some further products). When all final goods and services are added together, they are weighted by their prices, making GDP a "money-metric" concept. When current prices are used as the weights, the result is called *nominal* GDP. Newspapers and other sources typically report *real* GDP, which adjusts for changes in the general level of prices over time. This adjustment can be understood in two ways: (1) it weights the current products by the prices prevailing in an earlier, "base" year; or (2) it divides nominal GDP by an index of the general price level. Hence,

real GDP = nominal GDP/(GDP deflator)

where the deflator is the price index we have mentioned.

This logic is used for understanding microeconomic applications of price adjustments, as well. We will need to derive inflation indices for hospital care, physician and dental care, and so on. To illustrate, a hospital inflation index (or "deflator") similarly requires a base year as a reference. If 1982 were chosen, then hospital inflation in the current year would be *hospital inflation index = nominal hospital expenditures per patient/(real hospital expenditures per patient)*. Keep in mind that the denominator here uses the same logic as before: Real is the current hospital goods and services weighted by 1982 hospital prices. Note, finally, that the economist's responsibility in these calculations is to adjust accurately for quality changes. This is a notoriously difficult task. When the work described is completed, the result is called either the hospital inflation index or the "hospital price index." In principle, a price index for any collection of goods and services could be calculated by the same method. The best known of these is the Consumer Price Index (CPI), which evaluates price changes in the collection of goods that consumers typically buy, often called their "market basket."

Practice with Supply and Demand

The most familiar ideas in economics are probably supply-and-demand curves. We will illustrate supply-and-demand analysis for a hypothetical market for apples.

THE DEMAND CURVE AND DEMAND SHIFTERS

In Figure 2.2A, a demand curve illustrates the demand for apples in a hypothetical market for a given period of time, say one week. The demand curve drawn shows a quantity demanded in this market for this time period for each possible price. For example, at a price of $5.25 per bushel, the consumers would wish to buy a total of 345 bushels that week. The theory of demand suggests that quantity demanded would be less at higher prices—for example, 215 bushels at a price of $7.50. Some consumers may find that the price rise represents "the last straw" so that they buy none, while others may buy fewer apples than before, and yet others would not change their purchases. It is doubtful that anyone would use the occasion of a price rise as a reason to buy more.

This analysis is done *ceteris paribus,* meaning that we are assuming that all other things are held constant. The price of apples rises while people's tastes, perceptions, incomes, and so on stay the same. In life, it is common for two or more things to change at the same time. If, for example, the price of apples rises at the same time as tastes change, the result would be theoretically ambiguous, meaning that we cannot predict the direction of the change. In contrast, the demand curve depicts the behavior of consumers as price only changes.

As long as people buy less at higher prices, then the demand curve will be downward sloping. In statistical analysis, estimated demand curves are almost always downward sloping. The responsiveness of demand to price is measured by the elasticity. We will discuss elasticity in a later section.

Other variables also will affect the demand for apples. For example, the amount of various foods that people buy may depend on their incomes; richer people tend to buy more. Demand may be affected by the price of other substitutable goods. When any other

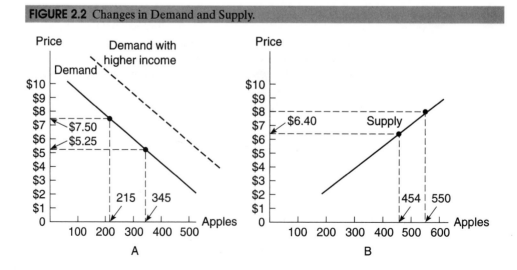

FIGURE 2.2 Changes in Demand and Supply.

variable affects demand, its effect will be shown as a shift in the curve. For convenience, we call such variables demand shifters. A list of demand shifters includes the following:

Income Generally, the quantity of a good that people wish to buy depends in part on their incomes. People with higher incomes tend to demand more of most goods. Such goods are called *normal* goods. But some goods, such as used clothing or generic brand goods, are purchased less often when people become richer. Such goods are called *inferior* goods. Let us assume that apples are normal goods. In Figure 2.2A, increased income in the community would tend to shift the demand curve outward.

Other Prices Prices of related goods also will affect demand. Related goods may be either substitutes or complements. If oranges are regarded as substitutes for apples, an increase in the price of oranges would cause the demand for apples to increase, shifting the demand curve to the right. In contrast, a complement is something that is used with apples, such as caramel. If the price of a complement rises, the demand for apples decreases or shifts left.

Insurance A variable that makes no sense for apples but that is essential on a list of demand shifters in health economics is insurance. Insurance reduces the price to the consumer at the point of service; given the lower price, a greater quantity of health care will be demanded. Although one can treat this as a movement down a given demand curve, we show in a later chapter that this is equivalent to a clockwise rotation in the original demand curve. Insurance plans have many complexities beyond changing the consumer's effective price, and these are addressed in a later chapter.

Tastes Many other shifters of demand may be grouped under the heading of tastes. Tastes can be literally what the word means, as when a new recipe increases interest in apples. The term can be less literal as well, as when we say that an older population has a greater demand for health care because it has a greater taste for health care.

THE SUPPLY CURVE AND SUPPLY SHIFTERS

Supply can be approached in a similar way. Figure 2.2B shows an upward-sloping supply curve for apples. It illustrates, for example, that apple growers would be willing to offer 454 bushels of apples for sale if the price were $6.40. At a higher price, say $8.00, more would be offered. Apple growers might be more willing to divert apples from cider production, to make greater efforts in harvest, or even to bring formerly unprofitable trees into production if the price were higher. Such reasons would suggest an upward-sloping supply curve such as the one shown.

We may likewise generate a list of supply shifters:

Technological Change As technology improves for producing a given product, the good becomes cheaper to produce. Certainly, technological changes that make products more costly without improving quality are ignored. As the product becomes cheaper to produce, suppliers are willing to offer more for sale at a given price. This increases supply, thus shifting the supply curve to the right.

Input Prices If the wages of apple pickers were to rise, this increase in an input cost would reduce suppliers' willingness to offer as much for sale at the original price. The supply would decrease, shifting the curve to the left.

Prices of Production-Related Goods The price of a good related in production, such as cider, also would be relevant. Because farmers can use raw apples for eating or for cider, generally a rise in cider prices will cause the apple supply to decrease, thus shifting the supply curve to the left.

Size of the Industry As more firms (in this case apple growers) enter a market, the supply of the product will be greater. Thus, entry of firms will cause supply to shift to the right.

Weather For a number of products, acts of God such as the weather will tend to affect production. The direction of the effect is obvious: Good weather increases supply.

EQUILIBRIUM

Under conditions of competition, the equilibrium in a market will be at the point where the demand and supply curves intersect. This is the point at which demanders' and suppliers' plans agree. In Figure 2.3, the equilibrium occurs at the price of $5.00 and at the quantity of 350 bushels. At higher prices, there will be excess supply, and suppliers who were unable to sell all their goods will be willing to bid prices down. At lower prices there will be excess demand, and demanders who went undersupplied will be willing to pay more and will tend to bid prices up.

COMPARATIVE STATICS

An equilibrium as depicted in Figure 2.3 is called a static equilibrium. It shows a picture of an unchanging equilibrium at a point in time. It is more interesting to assess how the equilibrium will change when the market is affected by some economic event. Figures 2.4A and B give two examples. Consider in Figure 2.4A what would happen to the market for coffee if there were a freeze in Brazil. This worsening of the weather would tend to shift supply to the left as shown. At the new equilibrium, the price of coffee is higher and the quantity consumed is lower.

FIGURE 2.3 Equilibrium where Demand Equals Supply.

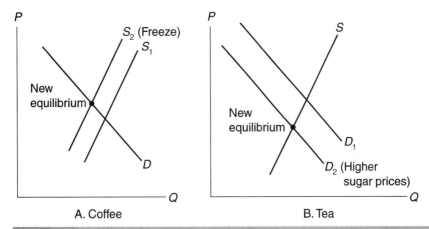

FIGURE 2.4 Market Effects of Supply-and-Demand Shifts.

Similarly, in Figure 2.4B, consider what happens to the market for tea when the price of sugar rises. Because sugar is a complement, this event causes a shift to the left in the demand for tea as shown. The new equilibrium will have a lower price and a lower quantity.

A few exercises help to generate experience with comparative statics and to demonstrate the applicability of this analysis:

1. A national health insurance proposal is passed that provides comprehensive health insurance to everyone. How would this affect the markets for health care in the short run?

 Answer: The competitive model is robust enough to give some guidance. Insurance coverage will probably increase on average, causing the demand for health care to increase, shifting the curve to the right. This will increase the equilibrium price of care, as well as the quantity consumed. The two results combined will increase the total money spent on health care. The analysis here is conducted *ceteris paribus.* If a successful cost control program were put into effect at the same time, the net result might be different.

2. A law is passed requiring that hospitals hire only nurses with baccalaureate degrees. How would this affect the market for hospital care?

 Answer: Hospital markets are not perfectly competitive, but the predictions of the competitive model would tend to hold. Such a law would increase an input price, thus shifting the supply of hospital care to the left. The equilibrium price of hospital care would tend to rise and quantity would fall.

3. Suppose the government lowers the reimbursement rates paid to physicians for Medicare patients. How would this affect the market for non-Medicare patients?

 Answer: The government action probably serves as a supply shifter because Medicare patients are a production-related good. Physicians would shift more time and other inputs into non-Medicare patient production, shifting the supply to the right, lowering equilibrium price, and raising quantity.

Functions and Curves

Most economic discussions consider how two or more economic variables are related to each other. For example, consider what we have theorized about the relationship of the price to the quantity demanded. We say that the quantity demanded is a function of the price. Mathematically, a function is an arrangement whereby we plug in the value of the independent variable, here the price, and the function generates the value of the dependent variable, here the quantity demanded. Alternatively, we can say that quantity demanded depends on price.

LINEAR FUNCTIONS

Before considering the writing of supply and demand in functional notation, consider the linear function. A linear function is that of a straight line and can be written as follows:

$$y = a + bx \tag{2.1}$$

where y is the dependent variable and x is the independent variable.

A linear function, no matter what idea it represents, has characteristic features: an intercept and a slope, both of which are constants. The y-intercept is the value of the function evaluated when x equals zero. Here the intercept is a.

The slope of a function is the rise over the run. To determine the slope of this particular function, examine this function drawn as a curve in Figure 2.5. We use the word *curve* for all functions, including the straight line. As noted, the y-intercept is a. Similarly, the function crosses the x-axis at a value of zero for y. Setting y to zero and solving for x yields a value of $x = -a/b$. Now, to find the slope divide the change in y, $-a$, by the change in x, $-a/b$, thus generating a value for the slope of b, the slope of this linear function. The value of b in this case must be negative, as the slope is downward.

DEMAND FUNCTIONS

The demand functions up to this point have been linear. In general, though, linear demand is only one special case. Even when demand is linear, there is a minor complication. Consider the following linear demand function:

$$Q_d = a - bP \tag{2.2}$$

where Q_d is quantity demanded and P is price.

A complication arises because economists customarily draw demand and supply curves with the independent variable, price, on the y-axis and the dependent variable, quantity demanded, on the x-axis. In standard mathematics, the dependent variable is usually drawn on the y-axis.

Most commonly, we will be considering cases where the dependent variable, such as quantity demanded, is a function of not one but several variables. For example, the quantity of spaghetti demanded, Q_d, may depend not only on the price of spaghetti, P_s, but also on the price of substitutes for spaghetti (such as other pastas), P_o, the individual's income, Y, and a taste factor, Z. Mathematically, using the general notation, the demand function for spaghetti would be written as follows:

$$Q_d = f(P_s, P_o, Y, Z) \tag{2.3}$$

FIGURE 2.5 Graph of the Function $y = a + bx$.

Here the notation $Q_d = f(\dots)$ is read, "Quantity demanded is a function of P_s, P_o, Y, and Z."

If the function in (2.3) also happens to be linear, its more specific form would have a characteristic linear look to it. Statisticians frequently use this case, and it is useful to look at an example. A linear spaghetti demand function, for example, might look like this:

$$Q_d = 500 - 10P_s + 5P_o + 20Y + 40Z \qquad (2.4)$$

Linear equations with several independent variables have some things in common with the simple linear equation in (2.1). An intercept constant is calculated by setting all the independent variables equal to zero; here the intercept is 500. The slope values in such linear cases will be the coefficients of the independent variables in question. For example, the slope value for the income variable Y is 20. The slope gives information regarding the contributions of changes in the independent variables to the value of the dependent variable.

Again, it is worthwhile emphasizing that functions in economics need not be linear. For example, the true spaghetti demand function might instead look like this:

$$Q_d = 7P_s^{-0.05} P_o^{0.002} Y^{0.8} Z^{0.01} \qquad (2.5)$$

which is not linear. Our theory says only a few things about a demand function: It is downward sloping in its own price, shifting rightward (leftward) with higher prices of substitutes (complements), shifting rightward (leftward) with income increases for normal (inferior) goods, and shifting rightward with a positive shift in tastes. Beyond these features, the demand function mathematically could take on many different forms.

Derived Demand

Demand by consumers for a final good or service may stimulate the provider of that service in turn to demand factors of production. There is no theoretical limit to how long this hierarchical chain can be, but in the health industry several good illustrations can be found. Individual consumers may wish to improve their health or the health of

family members. They may demand exercise equipment, healthful foods, and visits to a physician. These consumers generate a derived demand for factors. Considering just a clinic, the manager purchases electronics, technical equipment, drugs, and labor services, as well as the physician's time. The physician and other medically trained personnel, in anticipation of this, had a derived demand for medical education.

Consumer Behavior Theory: Ideas Behind the Demand Curve

Consumer theory examines how rational individuals make consumption choices when faced with limited resources. The limited resources determine what options a consumer can afford. From among these options, the consumer attempts to pick the best one. The theory has two parts. One is a description of what the consumer prefers—what he or she thinks is best; for this description, we use the ideas of utility and of indifference curves. The second part is a description of what the consumer can afford; for this part, we use the idea of budget constraints. The use of indifference curves and budget constraints together constitutes indifference curve analysis.

UTILITY

Consider a consumer, Kathy Richards. Let us suppose she is an experienced consumer who knows what her tastes are for kinds of houses to live in, cars to drive, food to eat, and books to read. She can't afford everything she would like to have, but she knows what she would prefer if she could afford everything.

In summarizing this information about Kathy's preferences, we suppose that she has a utility function. Utility is a measure of her level of satisfaction with various combinations of consumer goods. It includes a market basket filled with a combination of housing, food, transportation, and so on, with perhaps many different types of each. Bundles preferred over other bundles are given a greater value of utility. Because more utility, thus defined, is always better, Kathy will logically seek to maximize her utility subject to the constraint of what is affordable to her.

Using functions, we say that Kathy's utility is a function of the goods and services she consumes. In practice, the level of detail we use will vary. On some occasions, we must specify most of the detailed consumption of Kathy's life. Then we would describe her utility as a function of each good or service she buys, perhaps compiling hundreds of them. But in many cases, it is useful to abstract from this detail and describe Kathy's utility as a function of one or two goods of special interest, plus another general good representing all other goods she considers. At still other times, we will find it useful to describe Kathy's utility as a function of wealth. We will develop two examples in the following discussion.

Theories using the idea of utility may propose that utility is either cardinal or ordinal. Cardinal utility means a metric measure, like a measure of weight or volume. It is characteristic of cardinal measures that the difference as well as the ratio between two measurements has meaning. One can meaningfully say, for example, that five quarts is three more than two quarts and for that matter it is two and one half times two quarts. Under ordinal utility, to the contrary, only the ranking has meaning. Examples of ordinal numbers are first, second, third, and so on.

It is preferable to theorize that consumers' utility is ordinal. It is safer to assume that consumers can rank their preferences than to assume that they can both rank and scale them. It seems safer to suppose someone can say that he or she is happy to have gotten a raise, but it seems questionable to suppose that he or she is 1.07 times as happy. Most theories of demand assume only ordinality. In a few cases, such as the theory of behavior under risk and insurance, some degree of cardinality is assumed.

To illustrate ideas about utility, we should begin with the simplest case to draw. Figure 2.6 depicts Kathy's utility as a function of her wealth. The curve illustrates two ideas. First, the upward slope indicates that utility increases with wealth. Second, the bowed shape, concave from below, indicates that her utility increases with wealth at a decreasing rate.

Marginal utility is defined as the extra utility achieved by consuming one more unit of a good. Here the only good is wealth, so marginal utility is the extra utility Kathy gets from one more dollar of wealth. An extra convenience of drawing the function graphically is that the marginal utility is the slope of the curve at a given point. Starting at any point on the curve and adding a single dollar to Kathy's wealth leads to extra utility for that dollar, which we have just defined as marginal utility (MU).

If we understand marginal utility as the slope, the marginal utility of wealth for Kathy gets smaller as she gets wealthier. That is, the slope gets flatter. An extra dollar means more to Kathy when she is poorer than when she is richer. Does this notion apply to most people? That it might apply seems plausible to most students, but the notion also introduces an element of cardinal utility.

INDIFFERENCE CURVES

Often, we wish to depict the consumer's preferences over two or more goods. The most convenient case to draw is when there are only two goods. To capture the sense of the real world in a two-good drawing, let one of the two goods represent all other goods generally, as if they were a conglomerate. Call this conglomerate OG, meaning Other Goods. Suppose that the good of special interest is Food. Figure 2.7 depicts a graph with these two goods, OG and Food, on the axes. Any point in the space, such as *A*, represents a consumer bundle. The bundle *A* includes the combination of 8 units of Food and 4 units of Other Goods. Other bundles that are labeled include *B, C, D, E, F,* and *G,* but any other point in the space is also a bundle.

Suppose we focus on bundle *A* and that we hypothetically ask Kathy to identify all other bundles as well that for her are indifferent to *A* (that is, points that give her the

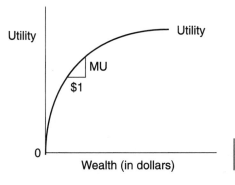

FIGURE 2.6 The Utility of Wealth.

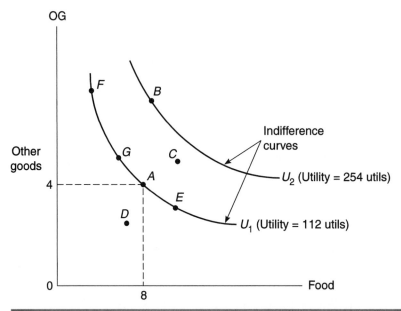

FIGURE 2.7 Indifference Curves between Food and Other Goods (OG).

same utility as *A*). The entire set of such points is labeled U_1; as noted in the graph, any point along U_1 affords Kathy 112 utils (we will call the units of utility *utils*).

This curve is downward sloping, as well as bowed toward the origin. Notice, for example, that Kathy did not choose point *C* as being indifferent to *A*. This seems plausible because *C* represents more of both goods, and as long as she is not satiated with these two goods, then she would prefer *C* to *A*. Likewise, she has not picked point *D* as indifferent to *A* because *D* has less of both goods. Instead, she has picked points such as *E*, which has more Food but less OG. Presumably, at *E* she has just balanced the loss of OG against the gain in Food. These considerations suggest that it is understandable that the indifference curve through *A* is downward sloping.

The curve is also convex to the origin. Consider that at point *F* Kathy has relatively a lot of OG and little Food. As Food is relatively scarce for her, she is willing to give up a lot of OG to get more Food. The rate at which she is willing to trade off the two goods is represented by the slope of the indifference curve, which is steep at point *F*. In contrast, as we move down the indifference curve, Kathy gains relatively more Food, and the more she gets the less ready she is to give up still further OG to gain yet more Food. Thus, the curve becomes flatter.

Indifference curves for Kathy summarize and represent her preferences. Every possible combination of goods will lie on some indifference curve so that in principle there would be an infinite number of indifference curves in Figure 2.7, with higher curves representing greater satisfaction.

BUDGET CONSTRAINTS

Indifference curve analysis uses preference maps and budget constraints. The budget constraint indicates the set of bundles the consumer can afford with a given income.

Suppose that Kathy Richards must allocate $30 of her family food budget per week between beef B and chicken C. If the price of beef is $2.00 per pound, and the price of chicken is $1.00 per pound, then she can afford any combination of B and C that costs less than or equal to $30, and her budget constraint is:

$$30.00 = 2.00B + 1.00C \qquad \text{(2.6)}$$

If we draw this constraint in Figure 2.8 with beef B on the vertical axis, then the budget constraint will start at 15 pounds of beef and proceed downward sloping to 30 pounds of chicken as the horizontal intercept.

It is convenient to demonstrate this pattern by examining the mathematical function. Equation (2.6) can be transformed using algebra so that B appears on the left-hand side and all other terms are on the right. Thus, the equivalent budget constraint is:

$$B = \frac{30}{2} - \frac{1}{2}C = 15 - 0.5C \qquad \text{(2.7)}$$

a linear function with an intercept of 15 and a slope of −0.5.

If, in Figure 2.8, the price of chicken were to rise, the amount that Kathy could buy, if she spent all $30 on chicken, would be less than before. If the price doubled, the chicken axis intercept would shift inward, permitting her to buy only 15 pounds of chicken rather than 30. The beef intercept is not affected when the price of chicken rises.

Consider instead an increase in the portion of her budget allocated to beef and chicken. A doubling to $60 would allow Kathy to increase the amount of beef from 15 to 30 pounds, or the amount of chicken from 30 to 60 pounds. As shown, the new budget constraint is parallel to the original budget constraint. Doubling the income in itself does not cause the prices to change. Because the slope of each budget constraint is the ratio of prices, the new constraint will be parallel. The intercepts will double.

CONSUMER EQUILIBRIUM

To maximize satisfaction given a budget constraint, the consumer will want to be on the highest attainable indifference curve. In Figure 2.9, the indifference curve U_1 is not the

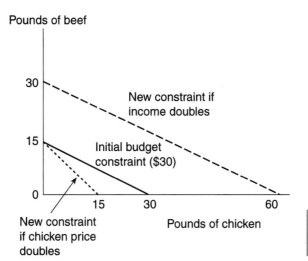

FIGURE 2.8 Changes in Budget Constraints Due to Changes in Price or Income.

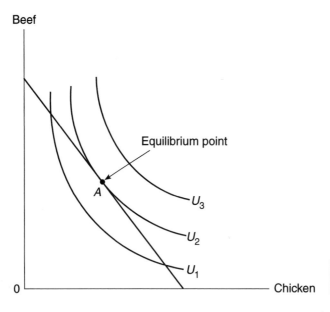

Beef

Equilibrium point

A

U_3

U_2

U_1

0

Chicken

FIGURE 2.9 The Consumer's Equilibrium.

best possible, while the indifference curve U_3 is unattainable. Rejecting such alternatives, the consumer will find that she maximizes utility at a point of tangency, shown as point A in the figure. At this point, the rate at which the consumer is willing to trade beef for chicken, the slope of the indifference curve is equal to the rate at which the consumer is able to trade the two goods at market prices—the slope of the budget constraint.

One can derive the equilibrium for different prices and/or for different values of income. For example, in Figure 2.10A, as the price of chicken rises consecutively, Kathy consecutively chooses points A, B, C, and D. The collection of such points is called the price offer curve. The information from these data points along the price offer curve can be used to generate her demand curve. For example, point A in Figure 2.10A represents her best choice for a given budget and set of prices. Suppose the price of chicken for budget constraint MN is P_0. Then, plotting P_0 together with the quantity demanded at A, namely F_0, in the graph at right generates point A'. In the same manner, data on price P_1 and the quantity demanded F_1, at point B, generate point B' in the graph at right. Repeating this process generates the demand curve.

Individual and Market Demands

The theory of consumer behavior focuses on the demand relationships of individual consumers. Many applications of demand theory, however, consider market demand. The extension from individual to market demand is straightforward. In Figure 2.11, health care demand is shown for two people who constitute a market for health care. For example, Mary demands 3 units at the price $p_H = 30$, and John demands 2 units. Market demand here at $p_H = 30$ is $(3 + 2)$ or 5 units. The market demand in panel C is derived by adding the quantities demanded at every price. The process can be extended to all of the consumers in the market, and it yields a market demand curve. If everyone's

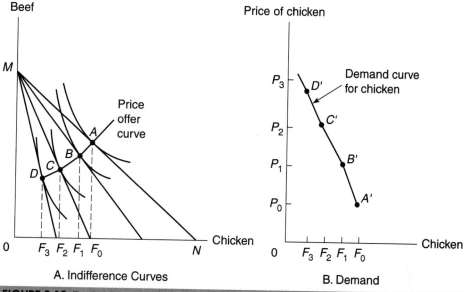

FIGURE 2.10 Derivation of the Consumer's Demand Curve.

demand curve conforms to the Law of Demand, the market demand curve must also be downward sloping.

Finally, note that as with individual demand functions, other variables such as income and the prices of related goods (the shift variable we discussed earlier) affect market demand. Thus, the market demand for some commodity X might be expressed in functional notation. Consider, for example

$$QD_x = f(P_x, Y, P_o, E) \qquad (2.8)$$

where Y represents income, P_o represents the prices of other goods, and E represents a socioeconomic variable such as average educational attainment (in years of schooling).

FIGURE 2.11 Derivation of a Market Demand Curve.

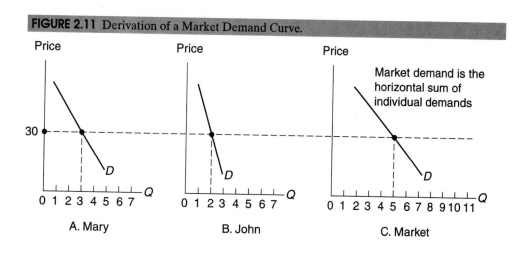

Elasticities

We are often particularly interested in the responsiveness of the quantity demanded to other variables. For example, if the price of health care rises, will the quantity demanded fall by a large amount or a small amount? Economists use the term *elasticity* to describe the responsiveness of *any* term y (in this case, quantity demanded of health care) to changes in some other variable x (here, price of health care).

Elasticity is defined as the percent change in the dependent variable resulting from a 1 percent change in the independent variable under study.[1] In the case of the price elasticity of demand, it is as follows:

$$E_p = (\text{\% change in quantity demanded})/(\text{\% change in the price})$$

or

$$E_p = \frac{\Delta Q/Q}{\Delta P/P} = \frac{\Delta Q}{\Delta P}\left(\frac{P}{Q}\right) \tag{2.9}$$

where Δ refers to change in the variable. The price elasticity is always algebraically negative because an increase in price leads to a decrease in quantity demanded. Other elasticities, such as the income elasticity of demand, are derived similarly.

$$E_y = (\text{\% change in quantity demanded})/(\text{\% change in income})$$

or

$$E_y = \frac{\Delta Q/Q}{\Delta Y/Y} = \frac{\Delta Q}{\Delta Y}\left(\frac{Y}{Q}\right) \tag{2.10}$$

Income elasticity may be positive (if a normal good) or negative (if an inferior good). If a variable elicits no response at all, then elasticity is 0.

Numerical values for price elasticities are often reported in absolute values, eliminating the minus sign. Absolute values for price elasticities indicate the responsiveness of demand to price in that the greater the elasticity is the greater the responsiveness is. Absolute values greater than 1 are considered relatively responsive and are called elastic. Elasticities less than 1 in absolute value are called inelastic. In the limiting cases, zero price elasticity means that the demand curve is perfectly vertical, while infinite price elasticity means that the demand curve is perfectly flat.

The importance of price elasticity to policy questions can be illustrated with an example regarding cigarettes, which are clearly a health concern. Suppose that a state were to add 50 cents per pack to its tax on cigarettes. Together with supply-and-demand analysis, our elasticity concepts help us identify the main policy issues. Lawmakers are hopeful that such a tax increase will curb smoking and bring in tax revenue, but these tend to be contradictory goals. The exact effects will be difficult to predict unless reliable estimates are available of the cigarette price elasticity. Were one to discover that demand is perfectly inelastic (D_1 in Figure 2.12), tax revenue would be at a maximum but with no effect on smoking or health. Alternative scenarios of increasingly elastic demand (D_2 and D_3) create bigger reductions in smoking but at the cost of decreasing

[1]Percentages allow us to "standardize" our measure. In particular, the use of percentages eliminates problems comparing various goods that may be measured in pounds, gallons, or feet. Here they are all measured in percent. For example, it becomes possible to compare demand elasticities for beef with automobiles, even though the price levels and quantities are different.

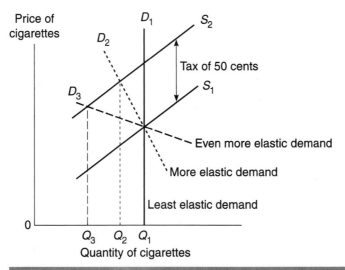

FIGURE 2.12 The Impact of a Cigarette Excise Tax.

tax revenues. Thus, the more elastic the response, the greater the effectiveness of an excise tax in inducing people to reduce their levels of smoking. Lewit and Coate (1982) indicate that teenagers, for example, are more responsive to cigarette prices than adults are. In such cases, taxes on cigarettes will be relatively more effective with teenagers.

Production and Market Supply

If market demand is one "blade of the scissors" in determining the price of a good, market supply by individual firms is the other. A typical firm will be faced with decisions on production levels, prices, production methods to be used, levels of advertising, and amounts of inputs to be purchased. The theory of the firm, much like the theory of consumer behavior for buyers, develops a framework for understanding how these choices are made.

The key assumption for most models of firm behavior is that the decision makers wish to maximize profits. It follows that the firm will try to minimize the costs of producing any given output and will undertake activities such as advertising only if they add to profits. Before examining such decisions, we will review production and cost relationships.

THE PRODUCTION FUNCTION

The production function shows the maximum sustainable output that can be obtained from all of the various possible combinations of inputs such as labor, materials, and machinery, with existing technology and know-how. It is useful to begin our discussion of production functions with a simple case—one in which there is just one input and one output. Suppose that food, perhaps in a hunter–gatherer society, were produced solely with labor. Let the production function be as shown in the top panel of Figure 2.13. The fact that the production function is rising indicates the idea that labor is productive;

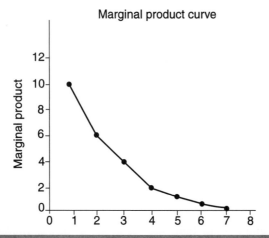

FIGURE 2.13 Output and Marginal Product of Labor.

more labor means that more food is produced. The bowed shape of the curve illustrates a second idea—the law of diminishing returns.

It is understood in Figure 2.13 that the production takes place during a specified period of time. Thus, the output axis represents a flow of output per unit of time. Likewise, the labor input represents labor services applied during a specified period of time.

The law of diminishing returns represents the idea that the marginal product (MP) of an input will eventually tend to fall as more is added. The marginal product (in this example, labor) is defined as the extra output that can be generated when one adds an additional hour of labor, holding all other inputs constant. In the figure, the food output increases from zero to 10 units when the first hour of labor is added. Thus, 10 units of food is the marginal product of the first unit of labor. When a second hour of labor is added, the output of food increases from 10 units to 16 units. The extra amount is thus 6 units, meaning that the marginal product of the second hour of labor is 6 units of food. The bottom panel of the graph illustrates the marginal product of consecutive hours of labor. The pattern of the marginal products in this illustration is clear: They tend to get smaller as more labor is applied. This illustrates the law of diminishing returns. Notice that total output need never fall during diminishing returns. That is, the

production curve itself never turns downward in this illustration, although it may in some applications.

PRODUCTION FUNCTIONS

In practice, production processes may involve several different inputs, not just labor. It is convenient to express the production relationship for a firm, or a unit of the firm, as follows:

$$Q = f(X_1, X_2, \ldots, X_n) \tag{2.11}$$

Here Q represents output; X_1, X_2, and so on are quantities of the various inputs.

The ultimate output of the health industry is health, and its related production issues are termed the "production of health," a phrase that applies to larger populations but also to the consumer's production of his or her individual health. When individuals seek to improve their family's health, they often purchase health care from hospitals, clinics, nursing homes, home health agencies, and so on. One step removed logically from health production, these elements of health care must themselves be produced, and much economic research and concern are directed at this production stage, too.

Consider, for example, the output of hospital X-ray services, which require the use of labor by technicians, nurses, and radiologists, and machinery such as X-ray machines, computers, and film. As with demand functions, production functions may take on many different mathematical forms. The theory of production functions specifies only certain patterns for these functions.

One commonly applied functional form that fits the theoretical patterns for such functions is called the Cobb-Douglas form. Historically, it was one of the earliest production functional forms to be studied and applied to firms. It derives its name from the two authors who developed it, mathematician Charles Cobb, and economist and later U.S. Senator Paul Douglas. Many other functional forms of production have since been investigated, but this form is still commonly used in the classroom to illustrate the mathematics of the production process.

If the production of X-ray services just discussed fits the Cobb-Douglas form, and if inputs of all kinds are grouped into the categories of capital, K, and labor, L, the production function actually estimated might look like this:

$$Q = L^{0.8}K^{0.2} \tag{2.12}$$

Here, as with any production function, there will be a unique level of maximum output for any combination of inputs.[2] For example, Table 2.2 shows values of output corresponding to changes in L, holding K constant at 5 units. The change in output associated with a one-unit change in L is the marginal product of labor. More L (e.g., technicians) with the same amount of K will typically produce more Q (hence, a positive marginal product of labor), but as the machines become crowded or break down, the marginal product may fall as L increases. Hence, the marginal product in Table 2.2 diminishes. This decreasing marginal product again illustrates the law of diminishing returns. The average output or average product (AP) for each worker is Q/L, as shown in the last column.

[2]There can always be less output if workers are shirking or if machines break down. As with the production possibilities frontier, there cannot be more than the maximum.

TABLE 2.2	Production Schedule for X-ray Services			
K	**L**	**Q**	**MP**	**AP**
5	0	0.00		
5	1	1.38	1.38	1.38
5	2	2.40	1.02	1.20
5	3	3.32	0.92	1.11
5	4	4.18	0.86	1.05
5	5	5.00	0.82	1.00
5	6	5.79	0.79	0.97
5	7	6.54	0.75	0.93

Alternatively, we can derive various input combinations needed to produce a given output level. Table 2.3 illustrates several combinations that produce ten units of output for the production function represented by equation (2.12). This method closely parallels the indifference curve analyses introduced in an earlier section, except that we actually observe and measure the quantities produced (in contrast to the levels of utility that could only be ranked). Combinations of inputs producing equal output levels lie on an *isoquant* (literally, "the same quantity"). The isoquant in Table 2.3 is illustrated graphically in Figure 2.14. The isoquant map, representing all possible values of Q, would be the geometric representation of a production function.

The negative slope to an isoquant indicates the possibility of substituting inputs in the production process and of the positive marginal product of the inputs. Consider, again, the example of X-ray services. The numerical value of the isoquant slope, indicating how much capital (X-ray machines, film, computers) must be given up per unit increase in labor (nurses, technicians, radiologists), is called the *marginal rate of technical substitution* of labor for capital (MRTS_{LK}).[3]

TABLE 2.3	An Isoquant Schedule	
Q	**L**	**K**
10	1	100,000.00
10	5	160.00
10	7	41.60
10	8	24.40
10	10	10.00
10	11	6.80
10	13	3.50
10	20	0.63

[3]Isoquants are typically convex to the origin (i.e., the numerical value of the slope diminishes as one moves to the right). This is consistent with a diminishing marginal rate of technical substitution.

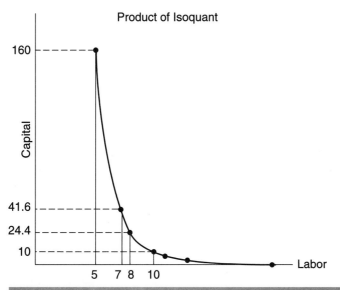

FIGURE 2.14 A Production Isoquant.

ISOCOST CURVES

In order for the X-ray unit to maximize profits, suppose that the unit wishes to minimize the costs of providing any given quantity of X rays. Suppose for the moment that it decides to produce a given level of X rays. Under the assumptions, it will want to minimize the cost of producing this output. Letting TC represent total costs, w the price (wages, salaries, fringe benefits) of labor, and r the cost of buying or renting machines for the production period, the total cost is as follows:

$$TC = wL + rK \qquad \qquad (2.13)$$

where L and K are the amounts of inputs used, labor and capital. For example, if $w = 50$, and $r = 20$, when the unit uses 30 hours of labor and 10 machines, TC $= 1,700 = (50 \times 30) + (20 \times 10)$. As with the consumer's budget problem, it is helpful to determine all of the combinations of L and K that cost a given amount, such as \$1,000. The equation for this isocost curve is

$$1,000 = 50L + 20K \qquad \qquad (2.14)$$

Again, as with the consumer example, we can rearrange the equation by placing capital (or labor) on the left-hand side, to yield

$$K = 50 - 2.5L \qquad \qquad (2.15)$$

which is a linear equation as shown in Figure 2.15. The isocost curve for TC $= 686$ is also shown.

More generally, equation (2.13) can be written as

$$K = TC/r - (w/r)L \qquad \qquad (2.16)$$

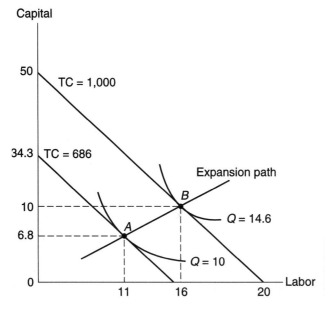

FIGURE 2.15 Cost Minimization (Output Maximization) Determining Efficient Combinations of Labor and Capital.

Equation (2.16) shows the impacts of changes in wages and/or rental rates on the costs of purchasing various amounts of labor and/or machinery.

COST MINIMIZATION OR OUTPUT MAXIMIZATION

In the example just given, the assumption that firms maximize profits requires that the X-ray unit select the least-cost method of producing its output. To produce Q^* units of output, the firm will wish to minimize the costs of that Q^* output, and hence be on the lowest possible isocost curve. The case where Q^* equals 10 units is illustrated in Figure 2.15. This will occur at point A, where the isocost curve is tangent to the isoquant representing 10 units of output. Higher isocost curves are unnecessarily wasteful; lower ones will not attain 10 units of output.

Suppose, on the other hand, that the firm has a budget of exactly $686 and wishes to maximize its output. It is easy to see from Figure 2.15 that the same equilibrium condition will hold, and that the most the firm can produce is 10 units. Cost minimization and output maximization in the manner described lead to the same results.

MARGINAL AND AVERAGE COST CURVES

By varying the production levels and finding the respective isocost curves, we can find the minimum cost of producing each output level. This is shown by the set of tangencies in Figure 2.15. The curve connecting these tangency points, A and B, is called the expansion path. Thus, the expansion path contains the information on the total cost and the average cost (cost/unit) of producing any output level.

If all inputs can be varied, then the long-run total cost and long-run average cost (LRAC) functions are generated. The LRAC curve is illustrated first in Figure 2.16. Total and average costs are related to the scale of the activity. If higher levels of production lead to improved ability to take advantage of specialization providing a better

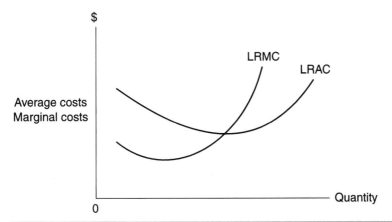

FIGURE 2.16 Long-Run Cost Curves for a Firm.

division of labor, it may be possible to reduce average costs; the case of decreasing long-run average costs is referred to as the case of economies of scale. If, on the other hand, the increased level of output leads to difficulties in managing and coordinating production activities, then long-run average costs may rise; this is referred to as the case of diseconomies of scale. Such issues are relevant for determining the optimal size for firms. For example, the socially optimal size and distribution of hospitals will depend on estimates of scale economies. As another example, it is clear that enough patient volume is needed to cover costs of such high-priced items as CAT scanners, a case of economies of scale. However, too many patients may lead to crowding of patients or to increased labor costs that could again increase costs, producing a case of diseconomies of scale.

In our specific Cobb-Douglas production function example, the LRAC will be a horizontal line reflecting constant average costs (about $68.60 per unit). This occurs simply because of the specific production function chosen as an example. Figure 2.16 shows the classical U-shaped relationship, which starts with economies of scale and then yields to diseconomies of scale. The long-run marginal cost (LRMC) curve shows the cost of producing an incremental unit when all inputs (both machinery and labor) can be varied. It will go through the minimum point of the LRAC.

The short run corresponds to a period where at least one input (typically machinery or plant) cannot be changed. This form is particularly applicable to big-ticket machinery items in hospitals, for example. In such cases, there are some fixed costs (the machine costs or plant costs) that cannot be changed in the short run. The other costs are called variable costs (e.g., labor costs).

The Firm Supply Curve Under Perfect Competition

The cost curves we have reviewed can be used to develop a theory of the supply curve for a firm, but to do so we must know something about the demand curve for the firm's product. In our earlier practice with supply and demand, the demand curve represented the market demand for the product. The demand for a single firm's product may be

different. To gain an idea of what a typical firm's demand curve will look like, we must know what type of market structure we are talking about.

Several market structures are of interest, either for the insights they provide to an idealized world or for their applicability to the real world. One defining principle that distinguishes the various market structures is the degree of control that individual firms have over the price that they get paid. Two cases define the extreme forms of market structure: the competitive and the monopoly cases. We will look first at the competitive model, then discuss market structure more generally, and finally follow that discussion with the monopoly case.

The competitive model is rarely seen in the world in its idealized form. It requires several assumptions that ensure perfect competition. The assumptions are as follows:

- A sufficient number of buyers and sellers of the good exist so that no single actor has any power over the price.
- The good is homogeneous; that is, all producers produce the exact same good so that the market cannot be segmented on the basis of difference of goods.
- Information is perfect. All buyers and sellers have information on all relevant variables such as prices and qualities.
- No barriers to entry or exit are present. A producer starts producing, buying necessary machinery, patents, or anything else on terms that are equivalent to those already in the industry.

These assumptions ensure that a short-run market equilibrium can be represented by the price and the quantity at which demand and supply curves intersect. Figure 2.17 illustrates the model. Under the assumptions of competition, the demand curve facing the firm will be flat, as shown by the curve $D = MR = P$. To understand this point, consider a mental experiment. Suppose that the market for wheat was competitive and that it had determined, by the actions of market demand and supply, some equilibrium price for wheat, say $3.50 per unit, as shown. Suppose now that a single firm determined to raise its price above $3.50. Would anyone buy its product? They would not because they know (perfect information) that they can buy an identical product (homogeneous product) elsewhere for $3.50. In theory, at even a slightly higher price, the quantity demanded would slide horizontally to zero. On the other hand, suppose that the farmer wished to double the output. Would the farmer have to lower the price in order to sell it all? This would not be necessary because the farmer's output is small relative to the whole market (numerous buyers and sellers); hence, the farmer could sell as much as he or she wanted at the going price of $3.50.

The demand curve for this firm is labeled $D = MR = P$ indicating that it represents demand, as well as the marginal revenue for the firm and the going market price. It is worth noting that the market price is identical to the firm's marginal revenue. Marginal revenue is defined as the extra revenue obtained by selling one more unit of product. Because this firm can sell all it wants at the going market price, it can sell the marginal unit at that price, as well. Thus, marginal revenue equals price in the competitive model. It is only in cases where a firm has some monopoly power that marginal revenue will differ from price.

The profit-maximizing output for this competitive firm can now be deduced. The firm will maximize its profits at that output where marginal revenue (the price) equals marginal cost; this occurs in the figure at output $Q*$. This output is called the firm's profit-

FIGURE 2.17 The Competitive Firm's Supply Curve.

maximizing output. The common sense of this seemingly technical proposition can be understood by examining a "wrong" output level—one that is not profit maximizing—for example, Q_1. Suppose a firm that is currently producing Q_1 units were to produce one more unit. The cost of this one extra unit would be A, by definition the point on the marginal cost curve at $Q = Q_1$. The revenue from this one extra unit would be B (which equals the price), the point on the marginal revenue curve at $Q = Q_1$.

The firm would increase its profits by producing that extra unit and would continue to increase its profits as long as the marginal revenue curve were above the marginal cost curve. Hence, maximum profits would occur only where $MR = MC$

The supply curve for a firm shows the firm's profit-maximizing output at each possible price. The competitive firm is producing at the output where price equals marginal cost. If the market price were to rise in steps, the firm's adjustment steps would just be to follow the marginal cost curve on up. The competitive firm's supply curve will be its marginal cost curve, as long as the price is sufficiently high to make it worthwhile to produce at all. Price must at least cover the firm's average variable cost (AVC).

The competitive market supply will be determined by the horizontal sum of the individual firm supply curves. This horizontal summing is done much in the manner in which we found market demand curves. The market supply curve in the competitive case, the sum of firm marginal cost curves, will also represent the industry marginal costs of production. In general, under competition the supply curve is the industry marginal cost curve.

What then determines the market price of a good? The answer is that combination of output and price at which market quantity demanded equals market quantity supplied, or the intersection of market demand and supply.

The assumption of free entry and exit, however, offers further insight into the workings of the competitive market. Suppose, for example, that the equilibrium price in the wheat market in the short run is high enough so that producers in the sector may earn attractive economic profits.[4] Any positive economic profit will be attractive to potential entrants. With perfect information and no barriers to entry, other suppliers will enter the market. This will increase market supply and drive down market prices. The entry process logically would continue in the long run until the prices have fallen enough to eliminate economic profits. In the long run, equilibrium profits will be zero, and price will be at the lowest point on each firm's long-run average cost curve.

However, if barriers to entry in the form of licensure or other restrictions exist, this adjustment process will be impeded. Sellers will be able to earn economic profits over long periods of time, perhaps indefinitely. Such a situation is not perfectly competitive even though the forces of demand and supply determine price at any moment. It is thus important to evaluate the extent to which *all* of the four conditions for competition stated at the beginning of this section are satisfied.

Monopoly and Other Market Structures

Firms in other market structures, unlike the perfect competitor, have market power, which is the ability to affect market price. These market structures entail the pure monopoly (and the natural monopoly version), monopolistic competition, and the several forms of oligopoly. In nearly all instances, the market power concept determines the characteristic of choice of optimal price or quantity. This concept is well illustrated by the pure monopolist.

A *pure monopoly* is an industry with a single seller who has no close substitutes. As such, the monopolist faces the whole market demand curve, which is usually downward sloping. Downward sloping demand and market power are synonymous concepts; this is because the monopolist, unlike the perfect competitor, will not lose all its customers when raising its price.

In health sectors, pharmaceutical firms that control patents for certain drugs may be pure monopolists. Individual physician practices are not pure monopolies, but because the numerous competitors of each are differentiated by reputation, patient loyalty, and patient/practice distance, each physician probably has some market power. Many economists treat physician markets as *monopolistically competitive*. Finally, when a town has only a few hospitals, each hospital also has some market power. There being few firms in that market, the hospitals would be considered an *oligopoly*.[5]

Equilibrium for the monopolist is illustrated in Figure 2.18. The demand curve facing the monopolistic firm is downward sloping because the monopolist faces the whole downward sloping market demand curve. With a downward sloping demand curve, the incremental, or marginal revenue, MR, is less than the demand price. Why is this the case? Suppose the monopolist were selling Q_0 units at price P_0. Total revenue, TR_0,

[4]Economic profits represent profits after considering all costs including opportunity costs. A "normal" level of profits is necessary to keep firms in the market, and is a factor payment to the entrepreneur, just like a factor payment to workers or to owners of machines or materials.

[5]Degree of monopoly power is a recurring theme in the discussion of market power and the need for regulation. We will return to this subject repeatedly.

FIGURE 2.18 The Monopolist's Equilibrium.

would be P_0Q_0. The monopolist would be selling to everyone who is at least willing to pay the price P_0. In order to sell one more unit of the good, the monopolist would have to induce more consumers to buy by lowering the price. It may be impossible to lower the price to extra consumers without also lowering to all previous consumers. In this case, because the monopolist must lower the price to everyone else, the marginal revenue will be the price of the extra unit of the good sold minus the loss of revenue from everyone else who now pays less.

To maximize profit, the monopolist produces where MC = MR, at Q_0 in Figure 2.18. The corresponding price is P_0 and total profit is the rectangle P_0ACB. If barriers to entry are persistent, the economic profits can be maintained and even increased through advertising, promotion, new product development, or other means.

The fact that the monopolist is earning excess profits suggests that the monopolist has reduced the amount produced from the competitive amount. The monopolist in the graph chooses point A on the demand curve. If the monopolist had acted like a competitor by setting a price equal to marginal cost, MC, it would have chosen point E, providing more output and charging a lower price. The induced scarcity caused by the monopolist necessarily raises the price to the consumer.

Welfare Losses

A major objective of economists is to compare different economic situations, or to examine the effects of different policies. In doing so, economists often use the concept of allocative efficiency. One of the most widely used examples to illustrate the problem of inefficient resource allocation is found in the comparison of monopoly and competitive equilibria.

Consider once again the case of monopoly. Figure 2.19 shows the long-run marginal cost curve in an industry with constant marginal costs. With demand curve D, the competitive market equilibrium is at P_c and Q_c. Suppose, somehow, that the providers are able to form a monopoly. If so, it will be in their interest to raise prices by withholding services from the market. The resulting monopoly will produce at quantity Q_m,

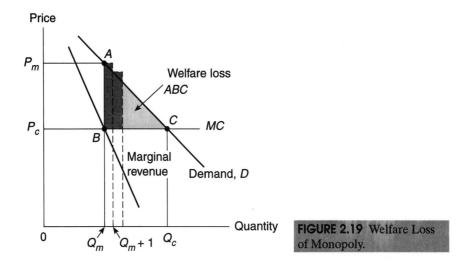

FIGURE 2.19 Welfare Loss of Monopoly.

consistent with price P_m, where price is higher than marginal cost. The result reflects a loss to the consumer due to the monopoly. The total loss is indicated by the triangle *ABC*, called the welfare loss.

Welfare loss can be better understood if we think in terms of marginals. Consider first that the demand curve measures the highest price that people are willing to pay for an extra unit of the good. The price they are willing to pay measures their marginal benefit.

Now consider what the consumer and society as a whole have to give up when they face a monopoly. The monopolist will choose output level Q_m. If we somehow could have produced one more unit of the good, the $(Q_m + 1)$th unit, we would have made a net gain for society. The benefit of that extra unit is Q_mA in the graph because by marginal benefit (here equal to the height of the demand curve) we mean the benefit of the extra unit. Similarly, the cost to the monopolist, and thus to society as well, of the extra unit is Q_mB. Because the marginal benefit is greater than the marginal cost, the extra unit yields society a net gain of the rectangular shaded area.

Reasoning iteratively, another unit again yields another net gain to society, this time somewhat smaller than the first net gain. Net gains will continue to occur until we reach the output at which society's marginal benefit (demand) intersects its marginal costs, which occurs at *C*. The total net gain to society from increasing output up to the point at *C* equals the triangular area labeled *ABC*.

The Edgeworth Box

The monopoly example applied methods of partial equilibrium analysis where one firm or industry is isolated from the rest of the economy. The example has clear implications and can be useful in many cases.

In many other applications, however, individual firms and markets exist with other firms and markets in a complex, interrelated economy. In an earlier example, we considered an excise tax on cigarettes and showed what would happen to cigarette consumption. We did not discuss the impact of the tax on the consumption of other goods; nor did we consider its impacts on the producers of cigarettes or the producers of other

goods, or the decrease in the need for health services because people are now healthier. For some policy issues, these may be important considerations.

The Edgeworth box is a useful tool to describe interrelated markets without complex mathematics. The box also is convenient for describing the mutual gains from trade and for defining the Pareto concept of efficiency.

Suppose that persons A and B, say Abner and Belinda, inhabit a desert island, forming a two-person economy. Further suppose that only two goods are available on the island: Food is gathered and is available in a fixed total amount, and medicine is likewise available in a fixed amount. Medicine consists of natural herbs and other medicinal plants.

To form the Edgeworth box, consider Figure 2.20. Abner's preference map is illustrated in the southwest corner. The only difference between this map and any others is that there is no reason to draw the axes out further than M_0 and F_0, which represent the total amounts of medicine and food available on the island. Belinda's preference map is similar to Abner's except that it starts at the northeast corner. It is also constrained by amounts M_0 and F_0.

Any point in the box represents a complete and exhaustive distribution of the island's endowment of food and medicine. For example, point A represents a distribution in which Abner has OM_A units of medicine and Belinda has M_0M_A units of medicine. Similarly at A, Abner has OF_A units of food while Belinda has F_0F_A units of food.

The economist Pareto defined an efficient (optimal) situation as one in which it is impossible to improve the lot of any one person without harming the lot of someone else. It would be inefficient to do anything less than apply and exhaust all possibilities for mutual gain.

Only when a society has exhausted all avenues for mutual gains among people will it be efficient. It follows that in a Pareto efficient situation, no further opportunities for mutual gain are left to exploit.

Under this definition, is point A a Pareto efficient distribution? It is *not*. This can be shown by example. Point B, within the "eye" formed by the two people's intersecting

FIGURE 2.20 Formulation of the Edgeworth Box.

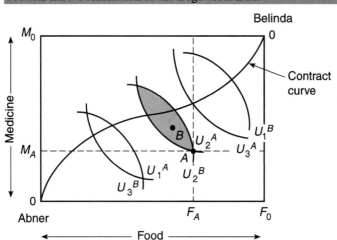

indifference curves, is at once a superior bundle for Abner and a superior bundle for Belinda. Thus, the two people would mutually gain by moving to B.

Point B also may not be Pareto efficient. Only when a distribution point is such that the two indifference curves are tangent with one another will the distribution be Pareto efficient.

There will be many alternative Pareto efficient points in the Edgeworth box. Every indifference curve of Abner's will have a point on it where an indifference curve of Belinda's is just tangent to it. The collection of all Pareto efficient points will tend to lie along a curve extending from one origin to the other. The resulting curve, the collection of all Pareto efficient points, is called the contract curve.

Conclusions

The microeconomic tools developed in this chapter consist of the production possibility frontier, demand-and-supply analysis, utility and indifference curve analysis, production and cost curves of a typical firm, firm behavior under competition and monopoly, the measure of welfare loss, and the Edgeworth box. The economic tools used later in the text are direct applications or extensions of the tools developed here. By learning these ideas, you will gain an understanding of the terminology used in health economics, as well as an understanding of the type of reasoning used.

Summary

1. The concept of scarcity underlies much economic thinking. Scarcity necessitates that decision makers make trade-off decisions at the margin. The production possibilities frontier represents these trade-offs, and its slope represents the opportunity cost of one good in terms of the other.

2. Supply-and-demand analysis of competitive markets is a basic tool of economics and provides insights that extend beyond the theoretical, perfectly competitive markets. Supply reflects sellers' offers as a function of price, and demand reflects buyers' offers as a function of price. The intersection of demand and supply describes the market equilibrium.

3. Comparative static analysis of demand and supply finds the new equilibrium after economic events shift either curve. Demand-increasing (-decreasing) events tend to raise (lower) equilibrium price, while supply-increasing (-decreasing) events tend to lower (raise) equilibrium price.

4. A relationship between one or more independent variables yielding a unique value for the dependent variable is called a function. The linear demand function, showing demand as a straight line, is only one special case of the many possibilities.

5. The utility function summarizes a consumer's preferences. Higher utility numbers are assigned to consumer bundles that provide higher levels of satisfaction, meaning that the consumer prefers these bundles.

6. Indifference curves are collections of points describing bundles that yield the same utility and hence the same level of satisfaction. Well-behaved indifference curves are downward sloping, continuous, and convex to the origin.

7. The budget constraint represents the combinations of goods that the consumer can afford given his or her budget. The budget constraint is downward sloping, and its slope is the negative of the ratio of prices.

8. In consumer theory, the consumer maximizes utility subject to a budget constraint. This means that the consumer picks the most preferred consumer bundle from among those he or she can afford. The equilibrium occurs at the tangency between the budget constraint and the highest attainable indifference curve.

9. Price elasticity depicts the responsiveness of demand to changes in price. It is defined as the ratio of the percentage change in quantity demanded to the percentage change in price. Each other elasticity also represents the ratio of a percentage change in a dependent variable to a percentage change in a given independent variable.

10. The production function describes the relationship of inputs to output. The marginal product of an input is the increase in output due to a one-unit increase in the input holding all others constant. That marginal product tends to decline as more input is added describes the law of diminishing marginal returns.

11. The average total cost curve of a firm shows the total cost per unit of output. The marginal cost curve shows the extra cost required to produce an additional unit of output.

12. The competitive firm in the short run produces that output where price equals marginal cost. The marginal cost curve is therefore the supply curve of the competitive firm.

13. In long-run equilibrium, entry by competing firms forces the typical competitive firm to produce an output level such that its price equals its minimum average cost. At this output, the competitive firm is producing the economically efficient output, and it is earning zero economic profits.

14. The pure monopolist faces the entire downward sloping market demand curve, and this implies that its marginal revenue lies below the demand curve. The monopolist restricts output, by comparison to the competitive case, and it charges a higher market price.

15. The pure monopoly case is one instance of a market in which a welfare loss occurs. A welfare loss, represented by an area under the demand curve and above the marginal cost curve, is an opportunity for mutual gains that is being foregone by the market.

16. The Edgeworth box for exchange represents compactly the indifference curves of the consumers in a two-person society. Pareto efficient points are those where all opportunities for mutual gain have (efficiently) been exhausted. The collection of Pareto efficient points in the box is called the contract curve.

Discussion Questions

1. Explain the difference between cardinal and ordinal utility.

2. If a consumer always prefers more to less, can the indifference curves between the two goods be upward sloping? Explain.

3. The law of diminishing marginal returns states that eventually the marginal product of an input will tend to fall as more input is added. Describe real-life scenarios, explaining why this is likely to happen.

4. Describe the long-run equilibrium of the competitive firm. Which of the assumptions of perfect competition are important in generating this result? Which are most important? Why do economists argue that in competitive markets, long-run profits should be normal, or "zero" profits? Is this necessarily the case in the short run?

5. What are the welfare losses due to monopoly? Do they mean that the monopoly does not earn profits?
6. What is a demand shifter? Use the concept to resolve the following: "The price of ice cream increased in the summer, yet quantity also increased. Therefore, the Law of Demand does not apply to ice cream."

Exercises

1. Draw the production possibilities frontier between guns and butter and show how it would change if there were an improvement in the technology of producing butter. Show the change if there were an increase in the available productive resources, capital and labor, in society.
2. Draw a production possibilities curve between health and all other goods. Insert a point in the drawing that illustrates an economy with an inefficient health system. Insert two additional points that illustrate two efficient economies but two that contrast in their relative emphasis on health care versus all other goods. Is there a cost to society of policies that lead to increases in health care? Explain.
3. Using a supply-and-demand graph and assuming competitive markets, show and explain the effect on equilibrium price and quantity of the following:
 a. A technological change that reduces the cost of producing X rays on the market for physician clinic services.
 b. Increased graduations of new doctors on the market for physician services.
 c. The virtual elimination of smoking in the population on the market for hospital services.
 d. A price ceiling placed on physician fees in the market for physician services.
4. Graph the following demand functions:
 a. $Q_d = 110 - 3.3P$
 b. $Q_d = 100P^{-1.3}$
5. What is the Other Goods (OG) axis intercept of a budget constraint? What is the x-axis intercept? How does the budget constraint shift if the consumer's income level and the two prices all double?
6. Calculate the price elasticity for a $1 change in price at initial price level $300 for the demand function $Q_d = 1,500 - 1.5P$.
7. What is the slope of the isoquant described by the data in Table 2.3 when evaluated from a labor input of 7 to 8?
8. Assume that a monopoly firm has a linear demand curve and a constant marginal cost curve. Graph this firm's optimal output choice before and after a per-unit excise tax is placed on the output. Does the equilibrium price rise by as much as the tax?
9. In prisoner-of-war camps during World War II, it was common for each prisoner to receive identical Red Cross packages containing cigarettes and other goods. Using an Edgeworth box for two prisoners, illustrate the Red Cross "endowment" of cigarettes and other goods. Are prisoners likely to trade? Using indifference curves, illustrate a trade from the initial endowment that makes both prisoners better off.
10. Using equation (2.4), what is the demand equation as a function of P_s if the price of other pastas (P_o) is $2, the individual's income (Y) in thousands is $25, and tastes ($Z$) are represented by 20? What happens if the individual's income increases to $30?

3

Statistical Tools
for Health Economics

- Hypothesis Testing

- Difference of Means

- Regression Analysis

- Multiple Regression Analysis

- The Identification Problem

- Discrete Choice Analysis

- Statistical Inference in the Sciences and Social Sciences

- Conclusions

The ideas from economic theory must be tested and measured according to the standards of real-world data. Statistical techniques applied to economics are collectively called econometrics. In Chapter 2, we discussed supply and demand, as well as the importance of price and income elasticities. Economic theory predicts that demand curves will slope downward, but it does not predict the degree of responsiveness of demand to price and other variables; it is the task of statistical analysis to estimate these magnitudes. When close substitutes are available for a good, theory predicts that demand will be more sensitive to price than if no close substitutes are available. Yet it is hard to know whether a 1 percent increase in price will decrease the quantity demanded of the good by 10 percent, 1 percent, or 1/10 of a percent, yielding elasticities of -10.0, -1.0, or -0.1, respectively. Measurements of the economic behaviors of both people and firms may be crucial in analyzing whether drug companies raise drug prices, whether income subsidies will cause people to buy more drugs, or whether mandated levels of health care are economically efficient.

This chapter considers statistical methods that econometricians use to draw inferences from data that are collected. Many students with natural science backgrounds are familiar with laboratory experiments, where the environment is held as constant as

possible and treatments are administered to experimental groups. The results are then compared to those of untreated control groups. One form of this design is called the *dose-response* model because the results or responses are generally related to the experimental treatment, or the dose.

Social science analysis of human behavior is rarely so fortunate as to find an experimental group that can be matched with a convenient control group. Social scientists, and economists among them, must usually collect information from people doing day-to-day activities. Using statistical methods, they try to control for the confounding differences among the people that they are analyzing. The more successful they are in controlling for such differences, the more reliable the analysis will be.

This chapter begins with discussions on how we form hypotheses. It then considers difference of means analysis as a way of introducing statistical inference. Most of the rest of the chapter concentrates on simple regression and multiple regression analyses that are most often used in economic and econometric analysis.

Hypothesis Testing

Economists who study health care have been confronted on occasion by statements that, while plausible, demand some validation:

"Twenty-year-old men have different cholesterol levels than 20-year-old women."

"Rich people spend more on health care than do poor people."

"Monopolists make more money than competitive firms."

These are all statements that either logic or casual observation would suggest to be true.

It would be useful, however, to have a rigorous method of determining whether the assertions are correct. Statistical methods suggest formulating these statements as hypotheses and collecting data to determine whether they are correct.

Take, for example, the first assertion about cholesterol levels for 20-year olds. We state clearly both the hypothesis we wish to disprove (the null hypothesis), as well as the hypothesis the theory suggests to be the case (the alternative hypothesis). The null hypothesis, H_0, presently is:

Men's levels (c_m) equal women's levels (c_w), or

$$H_0: c_m = c_w \tag{3.1}$$

against the alternative hypothesis H_1, that c_m does not equal c_w:

$$H_1: c_m \neq c_w \tag{3.2}$$

To indicate that 20-year-old men's levels are, in fact, different from their counterpart women's levels, it is necessary to show convincing evidence that c_m is different from c_w. Hypotheses that are designed to test for equality among two or more items are sometimes called simple hypotheses.

Consider the second hypothesis, which asserts that rich people spend more on health care than do poor people. If we define health care expenditures of the rich (poor) as E_r (E_p), then the null hypothesis is:

$$H_0: E_r = E_p \tag{3.3}$$

The alternative is:

$$H_1: E_r > E_p \tag{3.4}$$

In this analysis, it may not be enough just to show that E_r is different from E_p. Certainly, evidence that E_p is greater than E_r would not validate the hypothesis. Hypotheses that are used to test whether two or more items are greater (or less) than each other are sometimes called composite hypotheses. Having seen, then, how one might address the hypotheses in question, we now discuss how to test them.

Difference of Means

Let us return to the hypothesis about men's and women's cholesterol levels.[1] Some cholesterol is necessary to life; too much can be threatening, leading to coronary heart disease (CHD). Levels are measured in milligrams per deciliter (one-tenth of a liter). Levels typically range from 100 mg (extremely low) to 400 mg (extremely high). For individuals with levels between 240 mg and 300 mg, the likelihood of CHD is increased up to fourfold above that for individuals with levels below 200 mg.

Cholesterol levels depend on many factors. For example, those raised in more affluent families may have been better fed than those in poor families; poor children may have had diets higher in certain fats or starches. We would want to avoid bias in our results by making sure that our sample of women was not drawn primarily from one income level while the men were drawn from another.

We could attempt to avoid this sort of distortion by drawing our samples randomly from among all possible 20-year olds, called the universe of data. Alternatively, we may try to choose samples of 20-year-old men and women from the same general income group. A sample of college sophomores, for example, from the same location and with similar socioeconomic status may be a good group for holding many factors constant.

Even this example shows how difficult things may be to control. People of the same age (at the same college) may have had different prenatal care, birthweight, genetic composition, nutrition, vitamins, or exercise. The level exhibited at a given test may depend on what the subject ate that morning (physicians often ask for a "fasting" cholesterol test to avoid this problem).

To compare men's and women's cholesterol levels, we need a test that can determine the differences between two distributions of continuous data. Continuous data are natural measures that in principle could take on different values for each observation. Examples include height, weight, income, or price. Categorical data refer to arbitrary categories such as gender (male or female), race (black, white, or other), or location (urban or rural). In this chapter, unless we specify categorical data, our methods will refer exclusively to the analysis of continuous data.

Suppose at this point that the econometrician tests one woman and finds her cholesterol level to be 180 ($c_w = 180$). The first man tested has a level of 150 ($c_m = 150$). This provides evidence that women have higher levels than men, because $c_w > c_m$, or $180 > 150$. It is not very convincing evidence, however. The man, or woman, or either

[1]Sources for this discussion are U.S. Department of Health and Human Services (November 1990), and Rifkind et al. (1979).

may not be typical of the entire group. What if a different man and/or woman had been selected? Would the answer have been different?

It seems logical to test several men and to compute the mean or average level by summing the levels and dividing them by the total number of men tested. Suppose, for example, that there were 30 men, and that the mean, or average level, \bar{c}_m, was 163.3. Suppose also that there were 30 women, and that the average level, \bar{c}_w, was 173.5. The difference, $d = \bar{c}_w - \bar{c}_m$, then, is 10.2.

THE VARIANCE OF A DISTRIBUTION

Although a difference of the two means is improved evidence, the econometrician desires a more rigorous criterion. It could be that the true level for both men and women is 170, but our sample randomly drew a higher average level for women (173.5) than for men (163.3). Figure 3.1 plots each observation. Although the mean levels differ (women have higher levels than men), some men have higher levels than some women. Statisticians have found the variance of a distribution to be a useful way to summarize its dispersion. To calculate the variance of women's levels, we subtract each observation from the mean (173.5), square that term, sum the total, and divide that total by the number of observations, N. Hence, variance, V, equals:

$$V_w = \frac{(110 - 173.5)^2 + (125 - 173.5)^2 + ... + (215 - 173.5)^2}{30} \tag{3.5}$$

This term reflects the variance of any individual term in the distribution. If V is large, then the dispersion around the mean is wide and another woman tested might be far from our mean. If V is small, then the dispersion around the mean is narrow and another observation might be close to the mean.

STANDARD ERROR OF THE MEAN

The variance is often deflated by taking the square root to get the standard deviation, s, yielding:

$$s = \sqrt{V} \tag{3.6}$$

As with V, a large (small) value of s indicates a large (small) dispersion around the mean. Statisticians have shown that we can calculate the standard error of the mean itself by dividing s by the square root of the number of observations. Suppose, then, that the women's variance, V_w, equaled 587, so the standard deviation would equal the square root of 587, or 24.2. The standard error of the mean would then equal s_w divided by the square root of 30, or (24.2/5.5), which equals 4.4.[2]

A powerful theorem in statistics, the Central Limit Theorem, states that no matter what the underlying distribution, the means of that distribution are distributed like a normal, or bell-shaped, curve. Hence, we can plot the normal distribution of means of women's levels with a mean of 173.5 and a standard error of 4.4.

Statisticians have also shown that a little more than 68 percent of the area under the curve would be within one standard error, or between levels of 169.1 (173.5 − 4.4) and 177.9 (173.5 + 4.4), and that 95.4 percent would be within two standard errors. This

[2]Formally, in a sample, we calculate the standard error by dividing by $n - 1$. All calculations are rounded to the nearest tenth.

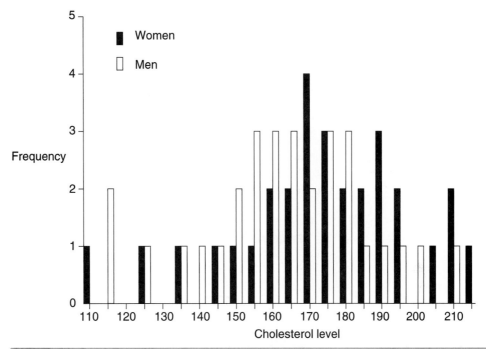

FIGURE 3.1 Distribution of Cholesterol Levels for Women and Men.

means that we could be about 95 percent sure that the true mean cholesterol level for 20-year-old women was between 164.7 [173.5 − (2 · 4.4)] and 182.3 [173.5 + (2 · 4.4)].

A similar calculation can be done for men, yielding a similar measurement. Intuitively, the further apart the means and the smaller the dispersions (standard errors), the more likely we are to determine that the average level for men is smaller than that for women. To test the hypothesis formally, we then construct a "difference of means" test. We wish to compare the measurement $d = (\bar{c}_w - \bar{c}_m)$ to 0, which was the original hypothesis.

Here $d = 10.2$. The variance of the difference is defined as the sum of the variances of the standard errors. If the standard error for women was 4.4 as we calculated it, and the standard error for men given the sample in Figure 3.2A was 4.1, then the standard error of the difference would be:

$$s_d = (4.4^2 + 4.1^2)^{0.5} = (19.36 + 16.81)^{0.5} = (36.17)^{0.5} = 6.02 \qquad \textbf{(3.7)}$$

The difference and its distribution also can be plotted.

The most probable value of the difference, as noted in Figure 3.2B, is 10.2. About 68 percent of the distribution lies between 4.18 (i.e., 10.2 − 1 · 6.02) and 16.22 (i.e., 10.2 + 1 · 6.02). About 95.4 percent of the distribution lies between −1.84 (i.e., 10.2 − 2 · 6.02) and 22.24 (i.e., 10.2 + 2 · 6.02).

This experiment would find good, although not absolutely conclusive, evidence that 20-year-old women have higher cholesterol levels than 20-year-old men. The probability that the difference of 10.2 would have been found, when the true difference is 0, is certainly less than 32 percent (100 percent less than the 68 percent figure); however, it is greater than 4.6 percent (100 percent less the 95.4 percent figure).

Frequency

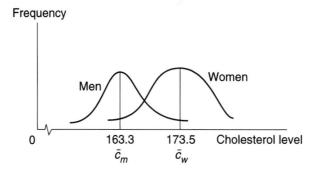

A. Means of Cholesterol Level

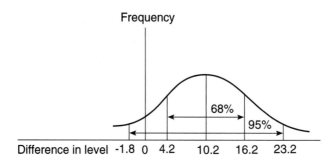

B. Difference of Means

FIGURE 3.2 Cholesterol Levels.

Alternatively, the *t*-statistic, comparing the numbers 10.2 and 0.0, equals 10.2/6.02, or approximately 1.69. Statisticians calculate tables of *t*-statistics, whose critical values are related to the size of the sample. With a sample of 30, a *t*-statistic of approximately 1.69 is statistically significant at approximately the 90 percent level. Still another way of phrasing this is to say that there is not more than a 10 percent chance that this difference of 10.2 between women and men was the result of a random draw from two distributions that have the same means.[3]

HYPOTHESES AND INFERENCES

This process illustrates the steps that are necessary to test hypotheses appropriately. The econometrician must do the following:

1. State the hypotheses clearly: $c_m = c_w$, against $c_m \neq c_w$.
2. Choose a sample that is suitable to the task of testing: a matched sample of men and women of the same age, in the same location.

[3]The difference in this example is approximately the difference found in Rifkind et al. (1979). Their standard errors are smaller because they have larger samples.

3. Calculate the appropriate measures of central tendency and dispersion: the mean and the standard error of the mean for both men and women, leading to the difference of the two means.

4. Draw the appropriate inferences: 20-year-old men have different cholesterol levels than 20-year-old women,[4] if we accept inferences at a 10 percent confidence level.

No matter how sophisticated the method used, good statistical analysis depends on the ability to address these four criteria and stands (or falls) on the success in fulfilling them.

There are, of course, measures of central tendency other than the mean. For example, analysts may worry that someone with a particularly high cholesterol count may influence the mean. A different measure, the median, calculates a statistic such that half of the observations are greater than the median and half are less. Thus, a median cholesterol level of 173.5 would imply that half of the sample was higher than 173.5, and half lower. The median is less sensitive to extreme values in the data (e.g., someone with a count of 400 would have no more effect on a median of 173.5 than does another with a count of 300). However, the use of the median presents some serious mathematical problems in hypothesis testing. Simple formulae for standard errors of medians are not available; hence, hypothesis testing is difficult.

Regression Analysis

The difference of means analysis is extremely useful in treating continuous data that can be broken up by categories, such as gender, race, or location.[5] Yet many interesting economic variables occur naturally as continuous variables. Health care expenses, physician visits, firm profits, as well as prices and/or incomes could take large numbers of values naturally, and are grouped into categories only with serious loss of information. If we have information on income, in terms of dollars per year, we can distinguish among households with incomes of $10,000, $20,000, $30,000, and so on. If we were to define high income as greater than $40,000, for example, thus separating all of the different incomes into two categories, we would then have no way of distinguishing between households with incomes of $10,000 and $20,000 (or, for that matter, between households with incomes of $50,000 and $100,000).

Regression analysis allows the econometrician to fit a straight line through a set of data points. Consider, for example, an economist who seeks to estimate consumer demand for aspirin (e.g., Bayer brand). Although one might argue that aspirin is not "chosen," it is clear that the amount of aspirin purchased is likely to be related to prices of substitutes, incomes of consumers, worries about side effects, and other factors. Using a carefully tested survey instrument, or observing consumer purchases at supermarkets and drugstores, the economist collects information about various determinants of demand. These include the amount of aspirin that is purchased each year, the price that is paid per box of aspirin, the prices of other types of medicines, whether there are any children in the household, and (usually last) the household's income.

[4]Econometricians often use more rigorous standards for hypothesis testing, requiring significance at the 5 percent or even the 1 percent levels.

[5]Although difference of means considers only two categories, analysis of variance methods allows the consideration of three or more categories. Newbold (1995) presents good discussions on this and other statistical topics.

No Link Between Childhood Cancer and Electromagnetic Fields

In 1979, Dr. Nancy Wertheimer and her assistant, Ed Leeper, reported that children who lived near power lines had twice the normal incidence of leukemia. The study was criticized because it was small and relied on indirect evidence rather than direct measurements of exposure to electromagnetic fields (EMFs). However, the report and its findings had major impacts. Parent of children with cancer sued power companies. Owners near power lines saw reductions in the values of their homes.

Scientists began to study the issue of power lines. While the studies tended to be small, and sometimes inferred exposure many years after the children had developed cancer, some did find associations between power lines and cancer.

In 1997, a new collaborative study between scientists at the National Cancer Institute and specialists from the nation's leading medical centers reported that there was no evidence showing that electric power lines cause leukemia in children. The study compared 636 children with acute lymphoblastic leukemia, the most common childhood cancer, to 620 healthy children who were matched to the cancer patients by race, age, and residential neighborhood. The researchers asked, "Did the children who developed leukemia have a higher exposure to magnetic fields produced by power lines?"

To answer the question, the researchers assessed the children's exposure to magnetic fields produced by power lines in their current and past residences, as well as where the mothers lived when they were pregnant. They measured the fields in the children's yards, schools, and day care centers and also had the children walk around with measurement devices. Investigators doing the measurements did not know which children had had cancer.

The research team, headed by Dr. Martha S. Linet of the National Cancer Institute, found that the children living in houses with the highest EMFs were about 24 percent more likely to develop leukemia than children in houses with the lowest EMFs. However, this difference was not statistically significant. Nonetheless, the fact that positive relationships exist over some range of the data is often misinterpreted as proof that definitive relationships exist.

Dr. Linet's group tested the hypothesis by relating the differences in means among groups, which were relatively small, to their variation, which was relatively large. This indicated that their measured effect was probably due to chance, rather than reflecting systematic differences. Their statistical test implied that we cannot confidently reject the null—that the true rates of leukemia were equal and unrelated to the level of EMFs.

Reference

Linet, Martha S., Elizabeth E. Hatch, Ruth A. Kleinerman, et al., "Residential Magnetic Field Exposures and Childhood Acute Lymphoblastic Leukemia," *New England Journal of Medicine* 337 (July 3, 1997): 1–7.

Assume that we have collected data where the unit of observation is the individual person. We have noted the amount of aspirin consumed for the year, and we have noted the price paid. By basing our estimates on such individual data, we can assume that our resulting estimates reflect the demand function.

Suppose that the economist wishes to relate the amount of aspirin purchased to the price of the aspirin. Even though other factors are likely to influence the quantity of aspirin purchased, it is useful to plot the quantity purchased against the price per box, as noted in Figure 3.3. Upon examination, the plot of points in Figure 3.3 looks like a higher price per box is related to lower purchases, and vice versa. We would like to know, however, how much they are related, or as we noted before, how responsive quantity demanded is to the price (the demand price elasticity). Recall that the price elasticity relates the percent change in quantity to the percent change in price. It would be useful to draw a straight line that would summarize the relationship.

ORDINARY LEAST SQUARES (OLS) REGRESSIONS

Two rules are commonly used to determine this line. The first rule is that the deviations (unless the line fits perfectly) from the line must sum to 0. Positive deviations must be offset by negative deviations. We can show, however (see Figure 3.3), that many lines have this characteristic. For example, dashed lines R_1 and R_2 both have 0 net deviations. It is necessary to have a second criterion by which to distinguish among the large number of lines where the sum of the deviations equals 0.

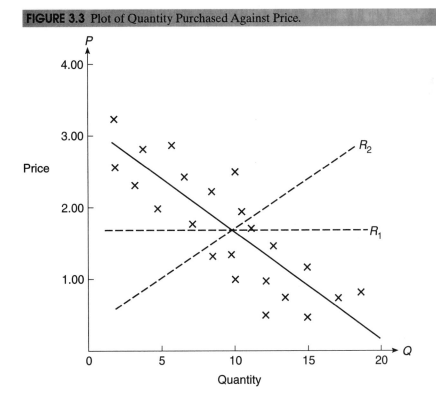

FIGURE 3.3 Plot of Quantity Purchased Against Price.

The second criterion is to minimize the sum of the squared deviations of the actual data points from the line that is fitted. Even though the sum of the deviations equals 0, the sum of the squared deviations must be positive (any number multiplied by itself is either 0 or positive). Hence, one can choose among the many lines that have sums of 0 deviations by picking the one line with the minimum or least sum of the squared deviations. Such analyses are called ordinary least squares, or OLS analyses.

The resulting equation would have the following form:

$$q = a + bp + \epsilon \tag{3.8}$$

where p and q refer to price and quantity, and a and b are the parameters to be estimated. Parameter a is sometimes referred to as the constant, or the intercept. It might refer to the demand for q in the unlikely event that the price of aspirin were zero. Parameter b refers to the slope of the line and shows the direction and magnitude of the impact of a change in p on the quantity demanded. Because we expect a higher level of p to decrease the amount of aspirin purchased, we expect b to be negative.

The last parameter is the *error term*, ϵ. No regression analysis will fit the data exactly. Errors are likely and may reflect several causes. We may have omitted a variable, such as age (children should not take aspirin), the possibility of drug interaction (if one is taking certain other drugs, it may not be advisable to take aspirin), or health status (pregnant women should not take aspirin). We may have measured one or more of the explanatory variables or the dependent variable (the amount of aspirin) inaccurately. All of these may stand in the way of our predicting the amount demanded exactly. In advanced econometric work, the characterization of the term ϵ is crucial for assuring that the estimated parameters are accurate. In our exposition here, however, we will assume that ϵ obeys the rules to allow us to make appropriate inferences with OLS analyses. We will examine some exceptions later in the chapter.

A DEMAND REGRESSION

Suppose we estimate the following regression from a survey of 100 consumers:

$$Q = 20 - 6.1P \qquad R^2 = 0.10 \tag{3.9}$$
$$(2.5)$$

This equation indicates that a one-dollar increase in the price of a bottle of 100 aspirins leads to the purchase of 6.1 fewer bottles in a given year. The standard error of estimate for the coefficient of price, P, is 2.5. This term is similar to the standard error of the estimated mean in the example of men's and women's cholesterol levels earlier in the chapter. As before, the smaller the standard error is relative to the estimated value of b, the better the estimate is.

In this regression, the standard error is relatively small compared to the absolute value of the coefficient, 6.1; hence, the coefficient is significantly different from zero. The expression R^2 is used to measure the fraction of the variation of the quantity of aspirin explained by the price alone. An R^2 of 0.10 implies that 10 percent of the variation was explained.

It is useful to examine this simple regression in detail, because it has many features that occur in more complex analyses. Consider the following hypothesis:

H_0: Price doesn't matter; that is, $b = 0$

against the alternative hypothesis, which is:

H_1: Price is significantly related to quantity demanded; that is, $b < 0$.

The test of the hypothesis is similar to a difference of means test. In particular, we are testing the difference between −6.1(estimated with standard error 2.5) and 0. Remember that because demand is downward sloping, the coefficient will be negative. The *t*-statistic here is 2.44; that is, the value of the coefficient, 6.1, divided by the standard error of 2.5. The value of 2.44 suggests that we can be more than 95 percent sure that the price has an effect on quantity of aspirin demanded. This term is statistically significant in its difference from 0.

If 10 percent of the variation of the quantity of aspirin demand is explained, then 90 percent is unexplained. In part, this occurs because the regression does not include some variables that are likely to be important. These include the consumers' incomes, the prices of other pain-relieving drugs, and some taste variables. For example, given the well-documented concerns about the use of aspirin for young children, families with young children may purchase less aspirin than others. When variables indicating the numbers or ages of children are included in the regression, the equation may explain things better.

This example illustrates *cross-sectional* analysis, which provides snapshots of a slice of the population at one period in time. Because we do not follow the people in the sample over time, we may not be aware of continuing health problems, changes in wealth or income, or systematic differences in ability that cannot be measured and which in the cross-sectional model will be treated as "random noise." As a result, cross-sectional regressions often explain less variance than panel data, which follow households over time, or time-series data, which calculate aggregates over time.

ESTIMATING ELASTICITIES

Regressions also are used to estimate elasticities. Recall that the definition of the price elasticity of demand (E_p) is the percentage change in quantity demanded, elicited by a 1 percent change in price. This is written as:

$$E_p = \frac{\Delta Q/Q}{\Delta P/P}, \text{ or } E_p = \frac{\Delta Q}{\Delta P}\left(\frac{P}{Q}\right)$$

The term ΔP stands for a one-unit change in the price, while the term ΔQ represents the resulting change in the quantity demanded. It follows that $\Delta Q/Q$ is a measure of the percentage change in quantity, whereas $\Delta P/P$ is a measure of the percentage change in price. In rearranging terms at the right, the term $\Delta Q/\Delta P$ represents the ratio of changes and thus is the reciprocal of the slope of the demand curve. With a linear function as in this case, this is the coefficient of price; that is, −6.1.

In calculating an elasticity from the coefficients estimated in a regression, a different elasticity may be calculated for each different starting price that is assumed. Therefore, it is also necessary to have reference values for P and Q, and the mean (or average) values are often used. Suppose that the mean price for a box of 100 aspirins is $2.50. Then the predicted quantity demanded would be:

$$Q = 20 - 6.1 \cdot 2.5 = 4.75 \text{ boxes} \tag{3.10}$$

Hence, calculated at the mean,

$$E_p = -6.1 \cdot (2.5/4.75), \text{ or } -3.21$$

This says that a 1 percent increase in the price of aspirin would lead to a 3.21 percent decrease in quantity demanded. Does this make sense? A demand elasticity of this size suggests the availability of numerous alternatives, or that considerable competition exists in an industry with many substitutes. Such a characterization might serve the market for cold remedies well.

Multiple Regression Analysis

Students of economics are aware that real-world relationships are seldom two-dimensional, as useful as this situation would be in drawing graphs. As noted, demand for aspirin is probably related to income, Y; the prices of other pain relievers, P_o, such as acetaminophen (e.g., Tylenol), ibuprofen (e.g., Advil), or generic substitutes; and maybe some family characteristics, G. Indeed, the omission of important variables may lead to particular behavior in the error term, ϵ.

One could graph quantity of aspirin independently against any of these other variables, just as was done with price. Graphing quantity against income, for example, would likely yield, as noted in Figure 3.4, an upward-sloping curve.[6] Graphing quantity of aspirin demanded against the price of acetaminophen probably also would produce an upward-sloping curve. Because acetaminophen is presumably a substitute for aspirin, an increase in the price of acetaminophen is likely to result in an increase in the demand for aspirin.

If each of these relationships could be graphed, assuming that nothing else were changing (i.e., if the only variables were the price of acetaminophen and the amount of aspirin purchased), then simple regression would work fine. Fortunately, the mathematics necessary to estimate the appropriate relationship can accommodate more than two dimensions. It is easy to write the following multiple regression:

$$Q = a + bP + cP_o + dY + eG + \epsilon \tag{3.11}$$

Although the econometrician is fitting a surface through five dimensions now rather than two dimensions, he or she is using exactly the same least squares criteria as before. The interpretation of the coefficients is similar to before but is done with more confidence. With the simple regression, relating Q only to P, the econometrician would not know whether income, Y, or the price of alternative medications, P_o, was varying. Including them in this regression allows the econometrician to "hold constant" these other variables and reduce the error. As a result, elasticities can now be calculated under the condition that "all else is equal."

The R^2 measure of variation explained earlier also is available here. R^2 will always rise with more variables. (If you add variables, you can't explain less of the variation!) Several methods can be used to interpret R^2, and some statisticians wish to maximize R^2; that is, to explain as much variation as possible.[7] While this may be desir-

[6]If, however, aspirin is a "poor-man's substitute" for a trip to the physician, an increase in income may lead to more visits to the physician and to less aspirin purchased.

[7]Often, R^2 is adjusted for the number of explanatory variables and the number of observations, and is termed as the adjusted R^2 or \overline{R}^2. Its relation to R^2 is:

$$1 - \overline{R}^2 = [(n-1)/(n-k-1)](1-R^2)$$

where n is the number of observations and k is the number of explanatory variables. Adding more variables, k will always raise R^2, but will not necessarily raise \overline{R}^2.

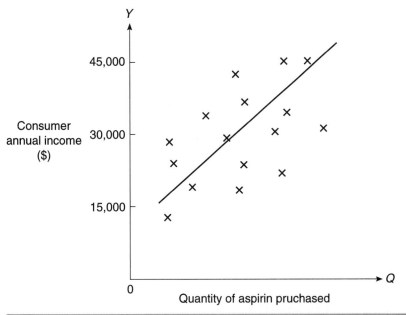

FIGURE 3.4 Relation of Demand for Aspirin to Consumer Income.

able, most econometricians are at least as interested in the values of the parameters that are estimated.

INTERPRETING REGRESSION COEFFICIENTS

Now consider a regression estimated in the following form:

$$Q = -5.0 - 4.1P + 3.2P_o + 0.25Y - 2.6G, R^2 = 0.25$$
$$(2.0) \quad (2.5) \quad (0.20) \quad (1.1)$$

(3.12)

where the standard errors of the coefficients are in parentheses below the regression. This regression says that, holding P_o, Y, and G constant, a one-dollar increase in the price of aspirin, P, implies a decrease in quantity of aspirin demanded of 4.1 boxes. Similarly, a one-dollar increase in the price of acetaminophen, P_o, implies an increase of 3.2 boxes in the quantity of aspirin demanded. It may be convenient to measure income in thousands of dollars; hence, an increase in income from \$20,000 (20) to \$21,000 (21) is a one-unit increase, implying an increase in aspirin demanded of 0.25 boxes per year. If G represents the number of children below the age of 5, then it indicates that households with more young children purchase less aspirin.

In this regression, the values of the coefficients of P and G are at least twice as large as their standard errors. This is usually fairly good evidence that the relationships are statistically significant. The coefficients of the price of acetaminophen, P_o, and income, Y, while in the expected directions are not statistically significant at the 95 percent confidence level. That is, although these coefficients differ from zero, the probability is less than 95 percent that the true values are different from zero. Also, as was done with the simple regression, predicted values of the dependent variable as well as values of the

elasticities can be computed. As before, hypotheses can be tested. Most often, again, econometricians are interested in whether coefficients are positive or negative and whether they differ significantly from zero.

DUMMY VARIABLES

In health care research, econometricians often are interested in whether particular groups of patients or subjects differ from others. These groups can be indicated by using binary, or *dummy,* variables. For example, an econometrician may wish to indicate whether a household is white (WHITE $= 1$), or not (WHITE $= 0$), or whether it is headed by a woman (FEMALE $= 1$) or not (FEMALE $= 0$).

Figure 3.5 shows how the estimated coefficients of these two variables can be treated. The northwest box indicates an observation for which both FEMALE and WHITE equal 0. If FEMALE $= 1$, then the coefficient b_f for both lower boxes indicates whether the household purchases more or less aspirin (and whether this is significant). This is a *row effect.* If WHITE $= 1$, then the coefficient b_w indicates whether white households purchase more or less aspirin (and whether that is significant). This is a *column effect.* If the household is both white and female-headed, then the combined effect is $(b_f + b_w)$.[8]

The Identification Problem

Up to this point, all of the exposition has concerned the estimation of a single equation. The examples have concerned an econometrician looking at the individual-demand equation for aspirin. Suppose, now, that the econometrician wishes to measure the demand for aspirin from data that represent market outcomes. The market outcome—that is, the amount of aspirin actually consumed—will depend on the interaction of both sup-

White (b_w)

	0 = No	1 = Yes
0 = No	0	b_w
1 = Yes	b_f	$b_f + b_w$

Female (b_f)

FIGURE 3.5 Interpreting the Effects of Dummy Variables.

[8]In fact, if one felt that white females may have particular attitudes or preferences for aspirin, one could estimate a coefficient that addresses the interaction of the two effects (1 if white and female, 0 otherwise). This would be coefficient b_{fw}. Here, then, the impact of being white and female would be $(b_f + b_w + b_{fw})$.

ply and demand. Thus, the econometrician would like simultaneously to measure market demand and market supply for aspirin.

Suppose, assuming that each state represents a market, the econometrician gets data on the reported price of aspirin, as well as on the quantity sold in the 50 states. He or she then sets up the demand regression such that

$$Q = A + BP + \epsilon \tag{3.13}$$

Previously, when dealing with data on individual consumers, the econometrician knew that he or she was dealing with a demand function, because, at least with respect to aspirin, individuals take the price as fixed and do not produce aspirin. Hence, the econometrician was estimating demand.

Yet in a market setting, the quantity consumed in equilibrium represents simultaneously both the quantity supplied and the quantity demanded. If the econometrician graphs the data, as in Figure 3.6, from the market for aspirin in the 50 states the set of points will reflect the intersection of 50 pairs of demand and supply curves. Will the pattern found and estimated by the computer reflect the supply curve, the demand curve, or a messy mixture of both?

This problem is known in econometrics as the *identification problem,* because the data at hand are not sufficient to identify whether the price and quantity data indicate a demand function, a supply function, or some combination of the two. If the econometrician does not realize that this problem exists and estimates the regression above, it is likely that the parameter B will not reflect either the underlying demand or supply curves exactly.

FIGURE 3.6 The Identification Problem of Supply and Demand.

The econometrician's task is to identify the true equations. If, somehow, the econometrician can find a variable that affects only the supply curve, then by shifting the supply curve, he or she will trace (or identify) the equilibria on a demand curve. Conversely, if somehow the econometrician can find a variable that affects only the demand curve, then similarly he or she will trace (or identify) the equilibria on a supply curve. The complete correct procedure is beyond the scope of this book. The discussion, however, shows that particular care is necessary, especially when dealing with cross-sectional economic aggregates. We will see examples of the identification problem in later parts of the book.

Discrete Choice Analysis

The exposition in this chapter has moved from variables that are characterized in categories to those that are continuous. It was argued that many economic outcomes are measured with continuous variables; hence, ordinary least squares (OLS) regression methods are appropriate.

However, classes of economic problems exist that do not meet these criteria. For example, someone needing treatment may choose to go to one doctor over another. A patient, together with a physician, chooses treatment A rather than treatment B. One chooses among a small number of insurance plans. These analyses are known as discrete choice analyses, referring to the fact that there are small numbers of possibilities, or discrete choices, rather than a continuous set of possibilities.

Suppose we wish to predict the factors that make people in a certain small town choose Dr. Stevens as their physician rather than Dr. Adams. Let variable Y equal 0 if patients choose Dr. Adams, and 1 if they choose Dr. Stevens. The underlying relationship between the independent variables and the dependent zero–one variable is often understood as probabilistic. We say that given certain prices, consumer incomes, and the like, "the probability that this patient will choose Dr. Stevens is _____." The probability in such choice problems often follows a pattern that can be graphed as an S-shaped curve, as noted for example in Figure 3.7.

Although the econometrician sees only values of 0 or 1 for Y, it is convenient to assume that there is an underlying response variable Y^*:

$$Y^* = bX + \epsilon \tag{3.14}$$

where variable ϵ reflects random or unknown terms. Each person may have some threshold value of Y^*, related to common parameters b, and to the person's error term. If Y^* is greater (less) than the threshold, then he or she chooses to go to Dr. Stevens (Adams).

Some of the independent variables that might push the individual over the threshold between Dr. Stevens and Dr. Adams would be the prices charged by each doctor, the distance from each doctor's office, the length of time that the person has lived in the town (old-timers may prefer Dr. Stevens), and so on. The interpretation of positive and negative coefficients in the resulting estimated equation and the testing of hypotheses are similar to that under ordinary least squares regression.

Two popular discrete choice analyses are the *probit* and the *logit models*. They differ by the mathematical form of the distribution that the error term is assumed to take, but they both provide the S-shaped curve. Maddala (1983) is a standard reference for these analyses.

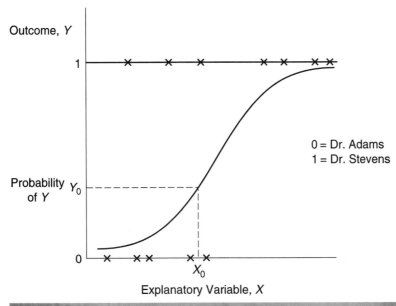

FIGURE 3.7 Discrete Choice Analysis of Physician Choice.

Statistical Inference in the Sciences and Social Sciences

The natural sciences attempt, if not always successfully, to control experimentally for all of the other possible sorts of variation. By contrast, econometricians are seldom so fortunate. Occasionally, experimental economic studies are done, but such projects are expensive. One such study was the multimillion-dollar Health Insurance Experiment of the late 1970s and early 1980s, funded by the Federal government. We discuss parts of that study in several later sections of the book.[9] Even with the careful planning that went into the experimental design, this study was not immune to major analytical concerns.

Other fields have similar problems. A 1988 report from the Panel of the Institute of Mathematical Statistics referred to analytical problems in chemistry:

> The data are frequently complex with a large number of dimensions, may sometimes have a time element, and can be further complicated because of missing values. In some instances, standard multivariate or time series methods may suffice for analysis, but, more commonly, novel developments are required, for example, to handle the problem of multivariate calibration (p. II-1)

Econometricians most often have to use natural experiments and must seek ways of accounting for the other variations. Because many policies, such as the provision of public health services or the regulation of the prescription drug industry, depend on

[9]There are excellent reviews by Manning and his collaborators (1987), and Newhouse et al. (1993).

accurate measurement of economic phenomena, it is essential that the measurements be accomplished carefully and scientifically.

Conclusions

This chapter has provided a "taste" of the statistical methods necessary to address questions that occur in health economics and to clarify the analyses where statistical material is presented later in the text. In order to understand the text, it is important to be able to formulate questions in terms of hypotheses, read statistical test results to determine if the result is significant, understand statistical significance, and interpret reported regression results.

The emphasis on problems to watch for in statistical analysis is not meant to generate undue skepticism over the statistical data to be reported. We do not wish to promote thinking that states, "Lies, damn lies, and statistics." On the contrary, the discussion is meant to help distinguish the better studies where confidence can best be placed. Statistics applied to health economics may provide important information even though individual statistical analyses may be flawed by the use of improper techniques. A lab dish may be dirty, but one does not conclude that it is impossible to prove anything through laboratory experimentation.

Summary

1. Economists usually must collect information from people doing day-to-day activities and use statistical methods to control for the confounding differences among the people that they are analyzing. The more successful they are in controlling for such differences, the more reliable the analysis will be.
2. Statistical methods suggest formulating economic assertions as hypotheses, and collecting data to determine whether the hypotheses are correct.
3. Hypotheses that are designed to test for equality among two or more items are called simple hypotheses. Hypotheses that are used to test whether two or more items are greater (or less) than each other are called composite hypotheses.
4. Several steps are necessary to test hypotheses appropriately. The econometrician must:
 • state the hypotheses clearly,
 • choose a sample that is suitable to the task of testing,
 • calculate the appropriate measures of central tendency and dispersion, and
 • draw the appropriate inferences.
5. Regression analysis allows the econometrician to fit a straight line through a set of data points. In ordinary least squares regression, the sum of the squared deviations of the actual data points from the line is minimized.
6. R^2 measures the proportion of the total variation explained by the regression model. While it may be desirable to maximize R^2, most econometricians are at least as interested in the values of the values of the parameters that are estimated.
7. Identification is the problem of estimating the underlying functions (structural relations) within the context of a joint (simultaneous) relationship, such as demand and supply.
8. Important skills in statistical analysis include:

- understanding statistical significance,
- interpreting reported statistical results, and
- detecting problems in reported statistical findings.

Discussion Questions

1. List at least three ways in which natural experiments differ from laboratory experiments.
2. What is the difference between a simple hypothesis and a composite hypothesis? Why might economists choose one over another?
3. In considering the difference in cholesterol levels between men and women, what is the null hypothesis? What is the alternative hypothesis? Is the alternative hypothesis simple or composite?
4. Suppose that we wish to compare the health status of two groups of people. What variable might we use to measure the status? What variables might we wish to control in order to draw the appropriate inferences?
5. If someone reports that the mean weight for fourth-grade boys is 50 pounds and for fourth-grade girls is 48 pounds, what must you know to test hypotheses using the difference of means?
6. If we are trying to relate output to labor inputs and capital inputs using regression analysis, would we expect the coefficients of the regressions to be positive or negative? Why?
7. What are *dummy variables?* How are they useful in identifying differences among groups?
8. Suppose that you used regression methods to estimate the demand curve for physician visits and found a positive relationship; that is, you found that the higher the price is, the more visits are demanded. What problem has likely arisen? Explain the problem in words. Why might it make statistical inference difficult?
9. What is *discrete choice analysis?* How does the variable to be explained differ, in this case, from ordinary least squares analysis?
10. Rich people consume more health care services than poor people. Explain two ways one might test this hypothesis.

Exercises

(For students with access to spreadsheet computer programs such as Excel, Lotus 123, Quattro, or others) Consider the following data for a cross section of individuals in the population, in which

$Q =$ Quantity (in 100s) purchased in a year
$P =$ Average price of aspirin in that year
$Y =$ Annual income
$A =$ Age of buyer

Now consider questions 1 to 4:
1. If we divide the population into two groups, up to age 35 and over age 35, which group purchases more aspirin?
2. If we divide the population into three groups—up to age 30, over 30 and up to 45, and over 45—do the purchases vary by age?

Obs	Q	P	Y	A
1	1	1.5	20	25
2	2	1.5	40	20
3	4	1	12	25
4	2	1	10	30
5	2	1	8	30
6	3	2	30	35
7	3.5	1.5	30	40
8	4	2	20	40
9	7	1	20	45
10	1	3	15	40
11	2	2	18	30
12	3	2	20	32
13	3.5	2	15	36
14	4	2	10	30
15	2	3	25	20
16	1	4	15	25
17	8	2	15	55
18	9	1	40	50
19	1	4	10	45
20	10	1.5	30	55
21	6	1.5	35	60
22	2	1	30	40
23	3	1	25	40
24	3	2	20	35
25	3	2	15	35
26	4	3	20	35
27	1	4	20	25
28	1	4	25	30
29	2	5	28	30
30	3	1	30	32

3. What is the relationship in a regression analysis between Q and P? Between Q and Y? Between Q and A?

4. Calculate the multiple regression that relates Q with P, Y, and A. Which variables are statistically significant? What is the elasticity of Q with respect to P, to Y, and/or to A?

5. In Equation (3.12), suppose income, Y, is 20, the price of aspirin, P, is $2, the price of acetaminophen, P_o, is $3, and there are no children. Calculate the elasticities of demand for aspirin with respect to Y, P, and P_o.

6. Consider demand curves for aspirin, estimated for two different sets of consumers:
 (a) $Q = 20 - 5P + 0.2Y$
 (b) $Q = 30 - 5P + 0.2Y$
 If $Y = 20 and $P = 1, calculate the price and income elasticities for group (a) and group (b). Whose elasticities will be higher? Why?

7. Given the regression estimate of the demand equation of

$$Q_x = 1{,}000 - 3.3P_x + 0.001Y$$

where Y is income, what is the change in demand if price rises by $1 holding income constant? What is the percentage change in demand if price rises by $1 from an ini-

tial price of $P_x = \$200$ given $Y = \$10,000$? What is the effect on demand of a $1 increase in income holding price constant?

8. Given the estimate demand equation of

$$Q_x = 1,000 - 3.3P_x + 0.2P_z + 0.001Y$$
$$(3.5) \quad (2.1) \quad (0.5)$$

with t values in parentheses, where P_z is the price of another good Z, and Y is income, is good Z a substitute or a complement? Can we say confidently whether good X is a normal good or an inferior good?

Cost–Benefit Analysis and Other Tools of Economic Evaluation

In health economics, as in other areas of economics involving public policy, we must frequently evaluate policy alternatives systematically. Just as the rational individual wants to choose efficiently among attainable possibilities, governments similarly face budget constraints. Legislators and policy makers must choose among alternatives such as spending more on preventive care versus giving additional support for acute care facilities versus investing additional sums in medical research. Even in cases of regulatory action, where government expenditures may be relatively small, rational decision makers recognize society's resource limitations and want to evaluate the effects of the regulatory actions on resource use.

Cost–benefit analysis (CBA) provides a sound method for evaluating proposed public projects and for comparing alternatives. CBA promotes the efficient use of society's scarce resources.

Early forms of CBA were introduced a century ago by the U.S. Army Corps of Engineers to evaluate flood control and other water systems. With the large public works projects during the Depression of the 1930s, the need to justify expensive programs became

increasingly apparent. In 1950, a congressional subcommittee recommended procedures for measuring and discounting for using the benefit/cost ratio when selecting projects to fund. The federal government continued to improve and standardize methods for program evaluation, and since 1981, all new federal regulations must undergo a CBA.

The introduction of Medicare and Medicaid in 1965 and the rapidly growing health care spending led economists to focus more on CBA. However, the limitations of CBA as a practical tool became obvious. CBA involves the enumeration of benefits and costs in monetary terms. For health interventions, this often requires placing a dollar value on additional years of life or improvements in health.

The challenges of placing a value on health led to the development of new tools. Health analysts now use the general term *economic evaluation* to represent the entire collection of tools that help decision makers compare the costs and consequences of alternative programs. Each of these tools takes a societal perspective rather than the narrower focus of the individual or firm. For example, a health maintenance organization or hospital may use similar decision-making tools when deciding whether to buy a new PET scanner. Decisions taken from a narrower firm perspective may or may not improve resource allocation for society. As a result, a broader view is needed.

Cost-effectiveness analysis (CEA) and cost–utility analysis (CUA) have emerged as the principal alternatives to CBA. *Cost-effectiveness analysis* involves a nonmonetary valuation of the health outcomes of alternative interventions. The outcomes, such as years of life gained or the number of patients diagnosed through a cancer-screening program, are measured in their natural units.[1] The cost-effectiveness ratio describes the cost of an additional unit of the outcome measure. Alternatives can be compared meaningfully when the same outcome measure is used. The ones with the lowest ratios represent the most efficient interventions.

Cost–utility analysis is a special form of CEA that introduces a measure of benefits to reflect individuals' preferences for the health outcomes resulting from a program. CUA represents a major advance because it can be used to compare programs with multiple outcomes, as well as different types of outcomes. The primary goals of this chapter are to develop and illustrate the basic principles of CBA and to show how cost-effectiveness and cost–utility analyses address some of the limitations of CBA.[2]

Cost–Benefit Analysis: Basic Principles

The fundamental rationale behind CBA reflects the need to determine an efficient allocation of resources when an underlying market is not readily available. In standard economic analysis, individuals and firms consume goods to the point at which marginal

[1] *Cost-minimization analysis* is a special case of CEA in which it is assumed that the consequences of all the alternatives are equal; hence, the task is to find the least-cost alternative. In light of the strong assumption needed to justify this approach and the absence of compelling conceptual issues, we will not pursue cost-minimization here. Similarly, we will not pursue another common technique, *cost-of-illness analysis,* that consists mainly of an examination of the costs and consequences of interventions. Although this approach can produce valuable information and often serves as a prelude to further evaluation, it offers no meaningful way to compare alternatives.

[2] Excellent collections of articles providing comprehensive analyses of many of the issues raised in this chapter are found in Gold et al. (1996) and Drummond et al. (1997). C. Goodman (1998) provides a concise summary of the literature as well as a practical guide to the evaluation process.

The Cost of Saving Lives

The need to encourage rational social choice has been forcefully made by Harvard University's Center for Risk Analysis. After reviewing publicly available studies of life-saving interventions, the Center found enough data to compute the cost per life–year saved for 587 interventions representing an unprecedented range of both health and nonhealth programs. Estimates for selective interventions include:

Intervention	*Cost per Life–Year ($1993)*
Medical	
Childhood immunizations	less than 0
Prenatal care for pregnant women	less than 0
Influenza vaccine for all citizens	140
Mammography for women age 50	810
Annual mammography for women ages 40–49	95,000
Intensive care for ill patients undergoing major vascular operations	850,000
Nonmedical	
Random motor vehicle inspection	1,500
Water chlorination	4,200
Pneumonia vaccination	12,000
Construction safety rules	38,000
Home radon control	141,000
Ban of asbestos in roof coatings	5.2 million
Strengthening of buildings in earthquake-prone areas	18 million

Source: Reprinted from *Risk Analysis,* Tengs, Tammy O. et al. "Five-hundred life-saving Interventions and their cost-effectiveness," *Risk Analysis* 15 (1995): 369–384, with permission from Plenum Publishing, and the author.

Resource savings are subtracted from costs. Thus, some programs, such as childhood immunizations and prenatal care, have negative net costs because the costs of the programs are more than offset by the subsequent savings from lower health care costs.

It is clear from such extraordinarily large variations in the cost per life–year that reallocations within and across the two categories of interventions can produce considerable savings in dollars, lives, or both. The estimates also demonstrate the clear need for an ongoing effort of this kind to help policy makers select programs that best use society's limited resources.

benefits equal marginal costs. Because the marginal benefits exceed marginal costs until the last unit, it follows that the total benefits exceed the total costs, and any additional cost–benefit analysis is unnecessary.

This scenario does not hold in several circumstances. Decisions to build bridges, parks, or athletic stadiums are not easily analyzed with standard supply-and-demand analyses. In the health care sector, public health decisions with regard to pollution control or water treatment, and private decisions including screening for disease or appropriate treatment modalities, do not provide comfortable market indicators regarding their desirability.

The rationale for a formal CBA rests on the premise that a project or policy will improve social welfare if the benefits associated with the project or policy exceed the costs. The benefits and costs include not only direct benefits and costs to individuals and organizations but also any indirect benefits or costs through externalities or third-party effects. Thus, CBA requires evaluation of social benefits and social costs.

APPLYING ANALYSIS AT THE MARGIN

To clarify these terms and the underlying efficiency concept, consider the example of pollution abatement. Pollution is a classic problem involving externalities—an indirect (third-party) effect of a market activity of either the buyers or the sellers that falls upon someone outside of the market relationship. Also, the third party is neither compensated nor required to pay for the external cost or benefit received. Thus, the market price of the transaction does not reflect the external costs and benefits.

For example, factories that discharge contaminants into the air or water create external costs by damaging the environment and adversely affecting third parties (residents downwind or downstream) who are not involved in the consumption or production of the good. In the absence of successful litigation or other agreements, the third parties are not compensated for the damages they suffer, so the prices of the goods produced do not reflect the external effects. Conversely, pollution abatement by a firm that needs clean water for its production process creates external benefits to others (e.g., boaters and home owners) who are not directly involved in the firm's decisions. They typically do not pay for the benefits they receive.

Figure 4.1 illustrates the principle for efficient use of resources when the marginal social benefits (MSB) and marginal social costs (MSC) of reducing discharges into the environment for a hypothetical effluent are known. The MSB curve represents the sum of all marginal benefits, both private and third party. For many pollutants, these marginal benefits will include the benefits of improved health. For example, the incidence of cancer and respiratory disease has been linked to various forms of air pollution. The benefits of reduced morbidity and mortality will be included. Other benefits to be considered include the slower deterioration rates of property, improvements in the yields and quality of agricultural production, and the recreational and aesthetic enjoyment resulting from a cleaner environment.

In Figure 4.1, the MSB is negatively sloped to reflect the likelihood that incremental reductions in discharges result in a diminishing marginal benefit. The MSC curve, which shows the marginal cost of reducing discharges and includes external costs where applicable, is positively sloped to reflect the increasing amount of resources often needed for incremental reductions in discharge levels. After some level of abatement, it is likely to be steep. That is, the marginal cost will be high.

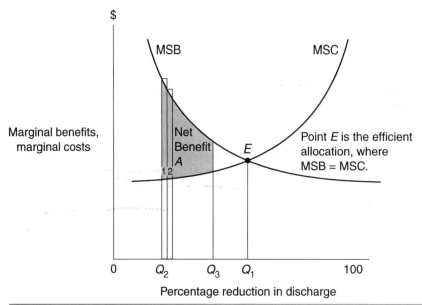

FIGURE 4.1 Efficient Use of Resources Where Marginal Benefits Equal Marginal Costs.

THE SOCIAL OPTIMUM

The social optimum is at point E, where MSB $=$ MSC, and Q_1 is the desired level of abatement. If the current standards for discharge result in a level of abatement shown by Q_2, the gap between MSB and MSC indicates an inefficiency and the desirability of further reducing discharge levels. The gains in welfare by moving toward Q_1 are similar to those described in the partial equilibrium of monopoly analysis discussed in other chapters. In monopoly, a gap is created between price, an indicator of marginal benefits to buyers, and the marginal cost of production. The level of production is inefficiently low.

Despite its apparent simplicity, the approach described through Figure 4.1 is sufficient to reveal the foremost problem facing public decision makers. The information underlying the MSB and MSC curves, and thus the optimum level, is unknown. CBA represents an attempt to get at some of that information and thus help in decision making. To illustrate, suppose the current level of discharge at Q_2 can be observed and that a project or legislation requiring Q_3 is proposed. If MSB and MSC are the true but unknown relationships, an accurate estimate of the project benefits will determine a value that corresponds to the area under the MSB curve between Q_2 and Q_3, and similarly for costs by the area under the MSC curve. The study will reveal a net benefit equal to area A in Figure 4.1.

Before such an estimation process can proceed, significant practical and conceptual problems must be resolved. First, all the relevant benefits and costs must be identified and measured in pecuniary terms.[3] In light of the task, it is often impractical and some-

[3]For those unfamiliar with these relationships, consider a one-unit increase in Q. The social benefit associated with that increase is given by the marginal benefit that can be approximated by the rectangle labeled as 1. Another one-unit increase will increase social benefits by rectangle 2, and so on until level Q_3 is reached. By making the units arbitrarily small, the total social benefits associated with the project will be represented by the area lying under MSB between Q_2 and Q_3. Similarly, the total cost of the project will be given by the area under MSC between Q_2 and Q_3.

times impossible to evaluate marginal increases in the scope of a project. This occurs when the project cannot be broken down into small parts even conceptually in order to evaluate the incremental costs or benefits of each part. Thus, discrete changes such as the one from Q_2 to Q_3 in Figure 4.1 are usually considered.

Second, many projects involve outlays and benefits that accrue over long periods of time. These benefits and costs must be estimated and discounted to present values. Closely related to the long life of a project is the considerable uncertainty in the estimates of benefits and costs.

Third, even where total benefits exceed total cost, not everyone's benefit will exceed cost. Winners and losers are bound to be associated with any project, and consideration will have to be given to equity, as well as to efficiency.

Choice becomes even more difficult when, in principle, many alternatives exist for achieving the social optimum. In the pollution abatement example considered previously, a variety of instruments are available to help reduce discharge rates. These include regulatory methods and incentive approaches through the use of taxes and subsidies or the auctioning of pollution rights. The differences in the distributional effects of these alternatives could be substantial.

DISCOUNTING

Before we examine criteria used in cost–benefit analysis, we review the concept of discounting. Discounting is used in many applications involving comparisons of different streams of returns and/or costs over a number of periods. For example, an analyst might be asked to compare Investment A, which provides $20 at the end of Year 1 and $20 at the end of Year 2, with Investment B, which provides $12 at the end of Year 1 and $29 at the end of Year 2. Although Investment B returns $41 over the two years compared to $40 for Investment A, most of the return on Investment B comes later, at the end of Year 2. It is often necessary to compare the investments with a criterion that considers the timing of the returns. The analytical tool used for such comparisons is usually referred to as *discounting*.

Suppose George is offered the opportunity to buy a bond that will return $1 one year from now. How much will he be willing to pay now? George always has the option to keep his money and earn interest rate r. He will buy the bond if he can pay a price far enough below the $1 return next year, such that that price, multiplied by one plus the interest rate, equals $1. Algebraically, if the rate of interest is r and the unknown amount is x_1, then:

$$x_1(1 + r) = 1$$

The value for x_1, then, can be solved as:

$$x_1 = \frac{1}{(1 + r)}$$

If the rate of interest is 5 percent (or 0.05), then x_1, the discounted value of $1, one year hence equals $1/1.05$, or 95.24 cents.

Similarly, the discounted value of $1 *two* years hence is:

$$x_2(1 + r)^2 = 1$$

leading to:

$$x_2 = \frac{1}{(1 + r)^2}$$

If, again, the interest rate is 5 percent, then x_2 equals $1/1.05^2$, or 90.70 cents.

Returning to the preceding example, we can calculate that the present discounted value (the sum of x_1 and x_2), or PDV, for Investment A will equal $37.19, or $20/1.05 + 20/(1.05)^2$. The PDV of Investment B is $37.73. Thus, George will prefer Investment B.

In summation notation, the present discounted value of a stream of returns, R, and costs, C, over time is given by

$$\text{PDV} = \sum_{t=1}^{n} \frac{(R_t - C_t)}{(1 + r)^t}$$

It is easy to demonstrate that the relative amounts of the PDVs of Investments A and B may depend on the interest rate chosen for the analysis. If an interest rate of 15 percent were used instead in the preceding example, the PDV for Investment A would be $32.51, compared to $32.36, for Investment B. Intuitively, the higher interest rate gives less weight to the larger, but later, return in Investment B.

COST–BENEFIT CRITERIA

To examine many of the issues we have raised, we begin with a formal statement of the net benefits (NB) of a proposed project:

$$\text{NB} = \sum_{t=1}^{T} \frac{(R_t - C_t)}{(1 + r)^t} \tag{4.1}$$

where B_t and C_t represent the social benefits and costs in year t, r is the discount rate, and T is the life of the project in years. Thus, net benefits represent the sum of a future stream of discounted values. Projects that have positive net benefits improve efficiency and are candidates for adoption.[4]

It is not uncommon to find the cost–benefit criterion expressed as a ratio of discounted benefits to costs. Here,

$$B/C = \sum_{t=1}^{T} \frac{B_t}{(1 + r)^t} \bigg/ \sum_{t=1}^{T} \frac{C_t}{(1 + r)^t} \tag{4.2}$$

Ratios greater than one indicate that the present value of social benefits exceeds the present value of social costs and that the project has a positive net benefit. In comparing projects, however, the benefit–cost ratio can be misleading because it does not reflect the scale of a project. Thus, even though a small-scale project could have a high benefit–cost ratio, it may be less attractive than another mutually exclusive, larger-scale project that has a lower benefit–cost ratio but a much higher level of net benefits.

[4]Those who have studied business investment criteria will see the similarity between equation (4.1) and the net present value criterion that replaces social benefits with revenues in equation (4.1). Projects that have a positive net present value raise the total profits of the firm and are candidates for selection.

The benefit–cost ratio also can be misleading in applications involving averted costs. These are costs that will not be borne in future periods because of the project. Such applications are common in health care in that the primary goal of many proposals (e.g., increased emphasis on preventive care) is to improve health and reduce subsequent costs of medical treatment. These averted costs can be viewed either as reductions in costs or as benefits. The method chosen to handle averted costs has no effect on net benefits but can play havoc with the benefit–cost ratio.

Consider the following example in which total benefits excluding averted costs are 10, total costs are 6, and averted costs are 2. The net benefits are 6, calculated either as:

$$NB = (\text{Total Benefits} + \text{Averted Costs}) - \text{Total Costs}$$
$$= (10 + 2) - 6$$

or:

$$NB = \text{Total Benefits} - (\text{Total Costs} - \text{Averted Costs})$$
$$= 10 - (6 - 2)$$

However, in the first case, the benefit–cost ratio is $12/6 = 2.0$, while in the second, the benefit–cost ratio is $10/4 = 2.5$. This example shows that care must be given in comparing analyses with differing benefit–cost ratios.

WHICH BENEFITS AND COSTS?

The task of identifying relevant benefits and costs, as well as delineating between them, is not a trivial one. We have already described how external benefits and costs need to be included. When a large number of third parties are involved, the challenge of preparing accurate estimates could be formidable. However, apart from practical considerations, it is important to sort out some conceptual issues that are often distorted in deliberations over the merits of a project. Perhaps the greatest source of confusion is found in the common practice of counting some costs as benefits and double counting some benefits.

To illustrate the former flaw, those who support the use of government funds to subsidize or build a major sports stadium will invariably and incorrectly argue that jobs will be created. Even where new jobs on balance are created, the wages paid to workers during the construction phase as well as during the operations phase are costs, not benefits.

The benefits are measured by the value that the public places on the activities held in the stadium. However, the jobs that may be created by multiplier effects originating from the initial expenditures should not be counted as benefits. Multiplier effects can result from the respending of income. Often, though, these effects are overestimated by a failure to recognize the diversion of expenditures from other activities. Finally, even if net unemployment is reduced by the project, the opportunity costs of the previously unemployed resources cannot be ignored. Thus, the general practice is to exclude employment effects except in areas of chronic unemployment.[5]

[5]This view is based on the idea that the opportunity cost of labor in areas with chronic unemployment is zero so that the jobs created do represent a benefit. However, those hired for the project will not necessarily have been unemployed previously, and an opportunity cost is always associated with the funds used for the project. Thus, it would be unwise to ignore or minimize the labor opportunity costs even where unemployment rates are high.

As for double counting, the value of land and commercial enterprises (e.g., parking lots, restaurants) situated close to the stadium may increase. It would be incorrect to include this added value, as well as the additional business generated at those sites. The higher property values incorporate the capitalized value of the additional business. Thus, the same benefit would be counted twice.

A more direct application of double counting in health care involves the value of life and productivity. More specifically, some studies may try to estimate a value for the increased length of life or improvement in the quality of life. These estimates are often closely related to the additional incomes that can be earned by the individuals who are treated. If the study also includes the additional productivity from the reduced morbidity and mortality, double counting occurs. The two concepts are different sides of the same benefit.

The Valuation of Benefits and Costs

As difficult as it can be to determine clearly the relevant benefits and costs, their valuation is perhaps a greater challenge. A prime reason for this difficulty lies in the absence of markets and corresponding prices for the goods and services resulting from the proposed project. This is particularly true for projects that involve public goods (e.g., national defense) and others that are intended to improve the quality of life, or where the benefits are intangible. In some cases, ingenious methods have been proposed to overcome the problem. For example, environmental improvements would be expected to raise property values or to reduce the compensation necessary to attract workers to the area that is being cleaned up. These are magnitudes that often can be estimated.

ASSIGNING MONETARY VALUES

However, even where private markets exist, the task of assigning monetary values is not always simple. Market prices and factor costs will not represent marginal social benefits and marginal social costs in cases of monopoly (monopsony) power and where third-party effects are significant. For example, the MSB of a commodity that generates substantial external benefits will exceed its price. Here, the use of market prices will underestimate the MSB unless the third-party effects also are evaluated properly. As an alternative, consider the case where some of the inputs for a project are provided by monopoly sellers. From the standard monopoly model, it follows that the prices paid for such goods and services exceed the marginal cost of producing those goods or services. It is the marginal costs that represent the opportunity costs of the resources needed for the project. These opportunity costs are the relevant costs for CBA.

One final observation can be made with respect to the valuation of social projects. Suppose that Figure 4.2 represents the demand for flu inoculations, and that there are no external costs or benefits. If each vaccination is priced at $1 and 10,000 people choose to get inoculated, total spending and therefore revenues will be equal to $10,000, as shown by rectangle A. This rectangle, however, does not represent total benefits.

There is a justification also for including the *consumer surplus*. This is the amount consumers are willing to pay for a commodity over and above the amount they have to pay. The consumer surplus is measured by area B under the demand curve and above the price line. The social benefits consist of the sum of A and B, which is the area under

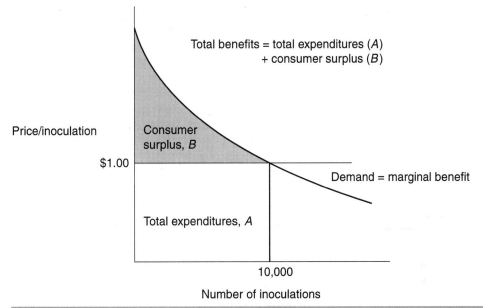

FIGURE 4.2 Total Expenditures and Consumer Surplus.

the demand curve, and this value should be compared to the total cost of the project. Thus, apart from revealing the inadequacy of using projected revenues as a measure of total benefits, the correct concept points to the even more difficult task of estimating consumer demand to derive a measure of consumer surplus.

THE LIFE OF THE PROJECT AND THE DISCOUNT RATE

Social projects involving capital expenditures, such as public hospitals and bridges, tend to have a long life. This does not affect the validity of CBA, but it does create difficulties. Clearly, benefits and cost have to be calculated far into the future. Thus, all the caveats described in the previous section apply for each year of the project's life.

Second, in some cases the selection of current projects may affect the kind and feasibility of future projects. For example, regulations that require firms to adopt a particular technology to control pollution may preclude the adoption of new, more efficient technologies that are subsequently available. Third, because future values have to be discounted, multiperiod analysis calls for a determination of the correct discount rate.

In the riskless, perfectly competitive, perfect information world of neoclassical economics, there is a single interest rate equal to the rate of return on private investment. This rate is also equal to the rate earned by savers. It reflects the rate at which they are willing to give up current consumption for future consumption (known as time preference). The appropriate discount rate for both private and public investment decisions would be this single interest rate.

In the real world of private investment decisions, the relevant rate is the rate at which the financial community is willing to supply funds for the project—that is, the rate

the borrower pays for the funds.[6] The rate typically will vary with the life of the project, as well as its riskiness in terms of the probability of default (i.e., a longer life and more risk require higher rates). How do these considerations of the borrowing rate and risk apply to social projects?

Though there remains ongoing controversy over this matter, it is widely accepted that the appropriate social discount rate is determined by the opportunities that are forgone in the private sector as a result of the social project.[7] The forgone opportunities reflect reduced private investment and consumption. Two crucial questions are whether the rate at which governments are able to borrow is the appropriate rate and whether adjustments to the rate are needed to account for the riskiness of the social project.

WHAT IS THE APPROPRIATE DISCOUNT RATE?

Aside from rates paid by financial intermediaries, the cost of borrowing to the U.S. Treasury is the lowest interest rate for borrowers because there is no practical possibility of default. This risk-free rate certainly does not account for the riskiness of the project itself as measured by the degree to which benefits and costs are projected to vary around expected levels. Further, the risk-free rate certainly does not necessarily correspond to the opportunity cost of the private sector investment or consumption that is displaced by the government spending. The opportunity cost of displaced investment will be considerably higher, as reflected by pretax returns, as well as by the risk premiums found in the private sector.

For example, assume a risk-free rate of 5 percent, a risk premium of 1 percent on the one kind of risky corporate investment available, and a 50 percent corporate tax rate. Corporate investment must earn $2 \times (5 + 1)$ or 12 percent in order to provide investors with an after-tax rate of return of 6 percent.[8] The opportunity cost of displaced consumption also will be 12 percent because consumers forgo current consumption through a net return of 6 percent as well as a tax collection of 6 percent that could be used for the provision of social goods.

In actual practice, a variety of private activities with different opportunity costs will be displaced by the social project. Unless these displaced activities and their returns are included, the decision maker receives little guidance. Nevertheless, agencies of the federal government have recognized that the appropriate discount rate will exceed the government's borrowing rate.

Should this rate also reflect the riskiness of the social project? Stiglitz (1988) argues that it would be inappropriate to adjust the discount rate to account for higher risk because, for example, projects with high but uncertain costs in the latter stages are made relatively more attractive when a higher discount rate is used. Conversely, projects with high but uncertain benefits in later years are made relatively unattractive compared to projects with higher near-term benefits. These results arise because higher discount

[6]Where one's own funds are used, the appropriate rate is the opportunity cost (i.e., rate of return on the next-best alternative). Because the financing of individual projects cannot be separated in many organizations, the financial literature also emphasizes the weighted average cost of debt and equity capital.
[7]Baumol (1968) is often credited with providing the clearest rationale for this view.
[8]This reasoning follows the exposition found in Sassone and Schaffer (1978). The authors also describe the alternative arguments in favor of adopting social discount rates that are lower than opportunity costs.

rates disproportionately reduce the present values of sums to be received well into the future as compared to discounting at lower rates.[9]

Stiglitz proposes introducing certainty equivalents to eliminate the biases that result from including a risk-adjustment factor in the discount rate. Under the certainty equivalent method, the uncertain net benefit in any period, often represented by a probability distribution of outcomes, is replaced by its equivalent, in the sense that the decision makers are indifferent between the former and a value to be received with certainty. The more risky the project, the lower will be the certainty equivalent to someone who is risk averse. The cost–benefit criterion represented by equation (4.1) is then applied using the certainty equivalents for each period.

OTHER CONSIDERATIONS

Though cost–benefit analysis is intended primarily to improve efficiency, as some of these examples have shown, changes in the distribution of income often result from a project. In cases of narrowly focused projects, the tendency is to have a relatively small number of large gainers and perhaps many small losers. To the extent that society is concerned about equity, the distribution of the gainers and losers by income group should be a consideration. At the practical level, after projects are ranked according to their net benefits, decision makers could invoke informal judgments as to the relative effects on the distribution of income and then adjust their rankings. More formally, Stiglitz proposes distributional weights through which the net benefits or losses of lower-income groups are given more weight than other groups. Of course, the method still will be subjective in that the weights themselves will necessarily reflect the judgments of the decision makers.

A second concern deals with the treatment of inflation. Conceptually, macroeconomic inflation is not a problem. Because estimates of the inflation rate often turn out to be incorrect, it is best to measure both benefits and cost in current or real terms and then discount at the real (inflation-free) discount rate. If an inflation factor is introduced, then the discount rate should be increased by that inflation rate to get the nominal rate.[10] It is important, though, that the discount rate reflect that inflation factor and not some other rate.

Apart from the treatment of the overall inflation rate in the economy, it is important to determine whether the relative prices (real prices and costs) for the goods related to the project will change. For example, the real cost of health care services has increased markedly in the last 30 years. Projections of real price changes can be problematic, but they must be made.

Cost–Benefit Analysis in Health Care

The usefulness of CBA to evaluate health care programs can be especially troublesome because of the need, in many instances, to place values on human life, increased longevity, and improvements in health status. In addition, a major benefit of a proposed

[9]Compare the present values of $1 million to be received in 20 years at 5 percent and at 10 percent. An actual example of what happens to the net benefits as the discount rate changes in a project with a long life is found in Hanke and Walker (1974).

[10]There is actually a divergence between the two methods. A correct statement of the relationship between real (r) and nominal (n) rates is $(1+n) = (1+r)(1+f)$ where f is the expected inflation rate. If the cross-product term rf is ignored, as it is previously, the two methods will be equal.

program can be the averted hospital, physician, and other health care costs. With wide variations in treatment costs for some conditions, these costs can be difficult to estimate, especially for those conditions requiring long-term care and where rapid changes in medical technology are taking place.

VALUING HUMAN LIFE

One of the most difficult but often unavoidable tasks in health care CBA is to place a value on human life. Two approaches are widely used. The first, known as the human capital approach, estimates the present value of an individual's future earnings. This approach has been especially favored in legal applications that require estimates of damages. It also measures the loss of national output from mortality and morbidity or the production gains from saving and extending life.[11] On the other hand, the human capital approach is flawed as a welfare measure in that it does not directly measure an individual's willingness to pay to avoid death, injury, or illness. It is this willingness to pay—the second major method—that corresponds to the welfare losses or gains used by economists in efficiency criteria.

Though measuring willingness to pay may look like a formidable if not impossible task, various ingenious approaches have been developed. These include estimates of wage differentials among occupations that vary by likelihood of death and injury, because individuals must be compensated (bribed) for undertaking more risky work. The objective is to measure the additional compensation for the expected decrease in mortality and increased probabilities of injury and morbidity. Similar applications are found through estimates of willingness to pay for safety, as with automobile air bags and antilock brakes.[12] Table 4.1 illustrates the wide range of estimates that one investigator has found from various applications of the willingness-to-pay approach. The wide range calls for explanations. Do households underestimate or overestimate risks for some activities? Are there inadequacies in the underlying data and methods? Until such questions are answered, the valuation of benefits will remain problematic and will limit the role of CBA.[13]

Apart from the need for future research that will further refine these estimates, recent literature also focuses on the relationship between human capital, willingness to pay, and other approaches.[14] Will systematic relationships exist between the measures? Though no definitive answers have been found, it is believed that value of life, as measured by willingness to pay, exceeds the discounted value of future earnings because the latter ignores the value of nonmarket activities.

COST–BENEFIT ANALYSES OF DISEASE-SCREENING PROGRAMS

Notwithstanding the shortcomings of CBA, one can find exemplary studies in the literature. To illustrate such a study,[15] as well as to highlight methods that have been used to

[11]Blomquist's (1981) review of several studies found a range of $330,000 to $2.5 million in 1979 dollars.

[12]There is a distinction between willingness to avoid risks and the bribe needed to incr risks. The former is constrained by a person's income, and thus willingness to pay can be highly income dependent. No such constraint exists with a bribe in that the needed bribe can exceed a person's income.

[13]Cropper and colleagues (1992) determined that the EPA weighed benefits and costs in decisions to ban pesticide use. However, they estimated that the implicit value placed on a life was $35 million for applicators of a pesticide but only $60,000 for consumers who expose themselves through pesticide residues on food.

[14]See, for example, Linnerooth (1979), Blomquist (1981), and Berger et al. (1987)

[15]See also Weisbrod (1971) for an early, but classic, cost–benefit study involving research on poliomyelitis.

TABLE 4.1 How Much Is One Life Worth?

Range of implied values of a human life extrapolated from what people pay for various products, services, or regulations that can change the risk of death.

Basis for Calculation	Value of Life ($1990)
Labor Market Studies	
Leigh (1987)	$10.4
Moore & Viscusi (1987)	$2.5–$7.3
Kniesner & Leeth (1991)	$7.6
Gegax, Gerking, & Schultz (1991)	$1.6
Outside of Labor Market Studies	
Fire fatality risks	
Garbacz (1989)	$2.0
Automobile accident risks	
Atkinson and Halvorsen (1990)	$4.0
Cigarette Smoking	
Ippolito and Ippolito (1984)	$0.7
Air pollution	
Portney (1981)	$0.8

Viscusi (1993), various tables.

value benefits (including intangibles), we examine a CBA of various screening tests used to detect gonorrhea in asymptomatic women. The study was published by Goddeeris and Bronken (GB) in 1985. Screening for various forms of cancer, sexually transmitted diseases, and other conditions is commonly endorsed or proposed. The GB example provides a framework that is helpful to a consideration of the broader issue of screening programs.

Screening will result in four possibilities: true positive, true negative, false positive, and false negative. By considering the probabilities that individuals with positives (including false positives) return for treatment and that some may have adverse reactions, the GB study developed an expression for the expected net benefit per individual screened. The costs include screening costs, time costs, treatment costs including those for adverse reactions, and subsequent treatment costs that are averted.

The benefits consist of three components: the improvement in treatment quality resulting from early detection, the value of reassurance from negative test results, and the external benefit that earlier detection has in limiting the spread of the disease.[16] For the first component, GB distinguishes among benefits representing future medical costs that are averted, greater productivity, and other subjective benefits.

With regard to future medical costs, the study concentrated on pelvic inflammatory disease, the main complication avoided by early detection. The authors estimated that this condition is prevented in 15 percent of the true positive cases. For this condition, lost productivity was determined to be two weeks for those treated on an outpatient

[16]The study did not attempt to estimate the third-party effects. All monetary values are measured in 1983 dollars.

basis and six weeks for those who are hospitalized. A consensus method involving a panel of physicians and social workers was used to provide a simple majority consensus estimate of the benefit of pain and suffering per case ($15,000) and the benefits of avoiding other possible conditions ($350) such as infertility. Consensus methods also were used to place values on reassurance ($10), mild adverse reaction ($15), and a false positive case ($4,500).

Table 4.2 shows the per-case net benefits of three alternatives for the estimated values of the parameters. These consist of the modified Thayer-Martin (TM) test; the Gonozyme immunoassay; and a slower, but less expensive, Gonozyme immunoassay. Only the TM test, the most common test, produced positive net benefits per patient screened at the baseline parameter values. In general, the results were not sensitive to other estimates of the parameters. Thus, the authors concluded that TM is both worthwhile and superior to the alternatives considered (although many more alternatives were not considered).

The analysis in Table 4.2 reflects a larger policy debate with respect to disease screening. The major categories of positive benefits from screening programs accrue from the treatment of disease for people who were unaware that they had a disease. This is directly related to the *prevalence* of the disease. The major costs of the screening program are related to the unneeded treatments that accrue to patients who are incorrectly judged to have a disease, reflected by the *false positive* rate.

Russell (1994) looks at three major screening initiatives: (1) the Pap smear for cervical cancer (for women); (2) screening tests for prostate cancer (for men); and (3) high blood cholesterol. She notes that in many cases, the probability of a false positive result from the screen (yielding major costs) is greater than the probability of disease prevalence (treatment of which provides major benefits). Thus, cost–benefit analysis of screening programs in which false positive rates are high may indicate net economic losses due to the unnecessary treatment, even though the diseases that they address may be life-threatening.

TABLE 4.2 Net Benefits of Gonorrhea Screening

	Screening Alternative		
	TM	**Gonozyme Fast**	**Gonozyme Slow**
Dollar values			
S (screening cost)	10	20	13
T (treatment cost)	28.5	21	28.5
R (reassurance)	10	10	10
B (benefit from early treatment)	2,869	2,869	2,869
A (adverse reaction cost)	15	15	15
F (false positive cost)	4,500	4,500	4,500
Net benefits V	18.6	−124.7	−118.7

Source: Reprinted from *Medical Care,* Goddeeris, John H., and Thomas P. Bronken, "Benefit–Cost Analysis of Screening." *Medical Care* 23 (1985) 1242–1255, with permission from Lippincott Williams & Wilkins.

Cost-Effectiveness Analysis

Given the difficulties of placing monetary values on life and health, as well as valuing other intangible costs and benefits, cost-effectiveness analysis (CEA) was offered as a more practical approach to decision making than CBA. CEA compares the costs of achieving a particular nonmonetary objective, such as lives saved. In cost-effectiveness analysis, one assumes that the objective is desirable even though the benefits cannot be evaluated in monetary terms (so that, strictly speaking, none of the alternative projects may actually yield positive net benefits were it feasible to compute the net benefits). Though the valuation of benefits is not considered, all of the problems in determining costs remain.

ADVANTAGES OF CEA

The task under CEA is conceptually similar to the production decision of the firm, which is to produce a given level of output from among alternative production methods at the lowest possible cost. Also, as in the firm-production decision, the objective must be quantifiable and similar across projects. Otherwise, a clear relationship between costs and output cannot be determined, and programs cannot be compared and evaluated because their outputs are not similar.

Cost-effectiveness analysis has been applied widely by the Department of Defense to determine, for example, the most cost-efficient means of achieving a particular level of military preparedness. Objectives can be quantified, say, in terms of ability to deploy forces, and the most efficient means of achieving the objectives is estimated. Note that CBA is not feasible in such cases because the benefits of the military capability cannot readily be evaluated in monetary terms. To take another example, many communities are currently interested in recycling to the point where mandatory recycling is becoming more widespread. Assuming that a community has decided on the goal of reducing garbage, cost-effectiveness analysis can be used to compare recycling with incineration and other waste-management strategies.

Finally, CEA can be a useful first step toward undertaking a cost–benefit study. If the analysts run into significant problems in undertaking a CEA, it is unlikely that a CBA will be feasible. Conversely, good progress in developing a CEA can often determine whether it is possible to take the next step and extend the CEA into a cost–benefit study.

AN APPLICATION: THE SIXTH STOOL GUAIAC TEST

We earlier described the problems of valuing human life and other benefits. CEA completely sidesteps this issue. Nevertheless, CEA can provide extremely helpful evidence for improving medical practice through the evaluation of treatment techniques that have a homogeneous measure of output, such as saving a human life or detecting an illness. The lengthy debate over the sixth stool guaiac test for colonic cancer illustrates both the strengths and weaknesses of CEA.

In 1975, Neuhauser and Lewicki studied a protocol recommended for screening cancer of the colon. The protocol consisted of six sequential stool tests for occult blood.

TABLE 4.3 Cancer Detection and Screening Costs with Sequential Guaiac Tests

| No. of Tests | Cancer Detection | | | Screening Costs ($) | | | |
	No. of Cases	Incremental Gain	Total[a]	Incremental	Marginal[b]	Average[c]
1	65.9469	65.9469	77,511	77,511	1,175	1,175
2	71.4424	5.4956	107,690	30,179	5,492	1,507
3	71.9004	0.4580	130,199	22,509	49,150	1,810
4	71.9385	0.0382	148,116	17,917	469,534	2,059
5	71.9417	0.0032	163,141	15,024	4,724,695	2,268
6	71.9420	0.0003	176,331	13,190	47,107,214	2,451

[a]Calculated by addition of cost of guaiac stool testing on 10,000 people and cost of barium-enema examination on all of those with positive tests.
[b]Calculated by division of incremental cost by incremental gain for cancer detected, subject to rounding errors.
[c]Calculated by division of total cost by number of true positive results detected.
Source: Copyright © 1975 Massachusetts Medical Society. All rights reserved.

These are called guaiac tests. A barium-enema procedure is administered if any of the tests are positive. From other sources, the authors assumed that 72 persons out of a population of 10,000 who are screened have colonic cancer and that the probability of detection is 91.66 from any single test, with a false positive rate of 36.51 percent.

The authors calculated that the second test will detect 99.3 percent of the cancer cases $(91.67 + 91.67 (100 - 91.67))$. Using similar computations, Table 4.3 shows the number of cases detected in a population of 10,000, the incremental gain in detection, and the associated total and incremental costs for each test. The total and incremental screening costs assume values of $4 for the initial guaiac test, $1 for each additional test, and $100 for a barium-enema procedure. The last two columns in the table show the marginal and average cost per case detected. These figures are determined by dividing the incremental and total screening costs by the incremental gain in cases detected and the number of cases detected, respectively.

The results are startling. The average cost per case detected is small and increases relatively slowly to $2,451 after six tests. Based on average costs, the recommended protocol seems more than reasonable. However, the point of the article is to focus on marginal costs as a basis for decisions. The marginal cost rises rapidly and exceeds $47 million for the sixth test. Even though no monetary value is placed on the benefits of detection (this is not a cost–benefit study), by almost any reasonable standard, the sixth test is not worthwhile.

This investigation has been regarded by some as a model of CEA and the application of marginal analysis. Perhaps, as a result of its standing, it has been the object of justifiable criticism. Among other oversights, subsequent articles point out that the assumed true positive and false positive values are based on limited information and have been improperly calculated.[17] Even small changes in these rates could have large impacts on the marginal cost of detection, although marginal costs still may run to the thousands of dollars.

[17]See Brown and Burrows (1990) and Gastonis (1990).

Cost-Utility Analysis and QALYs

Cost–utility analysis represents a special case of CEA that uses preferences for health to rank alternative interventions. CUA is additionally appealing because, unlike CEA, it addresses interventions that have multiple outcomes such as additional years of life and better health over those years. CUA makes these improvements while maintaining its foundation in welfare theory (Garber and Phelps, 1997; Ried 1998).

Of various indicators, including healthy-years equivalents, quality of adjusted life years (QALYs) has emerged as the principal outcome measure for CUA. The QALY is a weighting system that assigns values ranging from 1 (perfect health) to 0 (death) to represent quality of life for each year. The details of QALY construction can be found elsewhere (Gold, et al. 1996; Torrance 1997), but the process begins with a health status index. A health status index sums indicators of physical, cognitive, and other functions into an overall score. To determine the weights for QALYs, various methods have been devised to elicit individuals' preferences for different states of health.

Wagstaff (1991) provides a useful discussion of resource allocation under QALYs. Consider two types of individuals—some like Alex (type A) and some like Betty (type B). In Figure 4.3, in the absence of treatment, both Alex and Betty enjoy the same number of QALYs, $A_1 = B_1$, at point M. Additional societal resources could be used to improve their health to point R on the health frontier. The location and shape of the health frontier, the bowed-out curve in Figure 4.3, depend on the resources available, the capacity of Alex and Betty to benefit from health care, and the costs to society of that health care. The frontier's bowed-out shape assumes that health care is subject to the law of increasing opportunity costs. Any point on the frontier, including R, represents a feasible result from a given increment of societal resources.

Society's health may be defined as the sum of QALYs, or $A^* + B^*$. This graph has several points of interest. As drawn, the frontier in Figure 4.3 implies that Betty can be treated at lower cost than Alex. Alternatively, the same resources will provide more QALYs to Betty than to Alex; that is, B_{max} is greater than A_{max}. The sum of A^* and B^* is greatest at point R. This is determined as the point where a line with a slope of -1.0 is tangent to the frontier. We can verify this by realizing that going southeast (northwest) from R, along the frontier, an additional 1 QALY for Alex (Betty) reduces Betty's (Alex's) QALYs by *more than* 1, thus reducing the sum.

Thus, if QALYs count equally (e.g., it does not matter whether the extra years go to the old or young or the rich or poor), point R represents the most cost-efficient point for society. The QALYs per dollar are minimized at R even though this allocation provides Betty (who may be rich) more QALYs than Alex (who may be poor). An allocation in which Betty and Alex have equal QALYs (but where relatively more resources are provided to Alex) is determined at point Q. This point is defined by the intersection of the health frontier with a 45-degree line, which by definition provides equal QALYs to both.

Although proposals to distribute QALYs equally, regardless of the cost of providing them to different persons, would be considered extreme, society may decide that some deviation from point R is appropriate. In principle, a social welfare function giving more weight to the poor or more seriously disabled could be adopted. A solution in which Alex is given more weight is shown at point N, the tangency between the health frontier and social indifference curve, U. In practice, the inherent difficulty of determining the weights limits this approach.

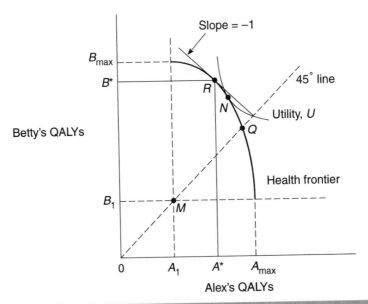

FIGURE 4.3 Evaluation of Health Alternatives Using QALYs.

Other equity and distribution issues also are important. When QALYs count equally, research may show that two alternatives produce the same cost per QALY although one provides small health benefits to many and the other provides large benefits to a few. We would undoubtedly expect decision makers to be informed of the distributional differences among alternatives and to take these differences into account.

The methods chosen to measure QALYs also can have equity and distribution implications. Analysts often use patient preferences to calculate QALYs rather than those of a representative community population. Because a representative population will reflect only the proportion of those with illnesses, some argue that the use of community preferences discriminates against people with severe disabilities. For example, an intervention that improves the ability of stroke patients to function will likely receive higher QALYs from stroke patients than from the general public.

Despite such compelling examples, there is increasing agreement that cost–utility analysis should incorporate the community's preferences. CUA is intended to help with decisions bearing on society's use of resources. As such, all health outcomes and all costs must be considered. A societal perspective provides the most consistent framework for meeting this objective.

Conclusions

Cost–benefit analysis is a methodology intended to improve the efficient use of resources allocated through the public sector. The efficiency concept is a social welfare concept in that the value of the social project to users and third parties is compared with the opportunity costs of providing the project.

The high level of government involvement in the health economy suggests an extensive role for CBA through a wide variety of applications. These would include

screening programs, evaluating alternative treatment procedures and new technology, and medical research. Cost–benefit analysis also can be applied to regulatory measures, such as those affecting the costs and length of time of new drug product development.

Despite its potential, CBA applications in health care still are less prevalent than one would expect. Difficulties in evaluating benefits, especially the value of life and improved quality of life, place limits on CBA and its usefulness to decision makers. As a result, cost-effectiveness analysis and cost–utility analysis have emerged as the principal tools for program evaluation.[18]

In 1993, the U.S. Public Health Service convened a panel of experts to help resolve controversies, standardize methods for cost-effectiveness studies, and develop consensus-based recommendations.[19] The panel recommended that these evaluative studies should take a societal perspective and that analysts should try to measure consequences through QALYs. Most importantly, the panel cautioned against decisions based solely on cost-effectiveness measures. Equity (see chapter 19) and other considerations also should be examined.

Summary

1. Unlike private decisions made in the marketplace, (social) cost–benefit analysis (CBA) involves evaluation of social benefits and social costs in public project analysis. Often, markets do not exist to evaluate the benefits and costs of such projects.
2. CBA rests on the principle that society's welfare will be improved whenever the benefits of a project exceed its costs.
3. CBA represents an example of marginal analysis. The social optimum is achieved when marginal social benefit is equal to marginal social cost.
4. Though in principle CBA appears simple, it can be difficult to apply. The difficulties include identifying all the relevant costs and benefits, including third-party effects, assigning monetary values, and making projections over many years for projects with long lives.
5. The monetary values of future net benefits must be discounted. The choice of the appropriate discount rate remains controversial.
6. Health care projects often involve the need to value human life. The human capital approach and the willingness-to-pay approach have been the most widely applied methods.
7. Cost-effectiveness analysis can be used when it is difficult to place a monetary value on the benefits of a project. CEA is used to compare the costs under alternative projects of achieving some desired and quantifiable nonmonetary objective, such as the cost of detecting a case of cancer or the cost of a year of life saved.
8. Cost–utility analysis (CUA) is a special case of CEA in which the objective is measured in Quality Adjusted Life Years (QALYs) or some other indicator that takes into account individuals' preferences for health.

[18]Comprehensive bibliographies of CBA and CEA studies are found in Elixhauser (1993) and Elixhauser et al. (1998).
[19]Details are found in Gold et al. (1996) and a series of articles in the *Journal of the American Medical Association*. See Russell et al. (1996), Weinstein et al. (1996), and Siegel et al. (1996).

Discussion Questions

1. In what ways is social cost–benefit analysis similar to a consumer's decision about allocating his or her resources or to a firm's investment decision? In what ways is it different?
2. Why do third-party effects have to be considered in the social decision?
3. Why are jobs that are created as a result of a social project not normally considered as a benefit?
4. Some suggest that a dollar value cannot be placed on life; that is, life is priceless. Explain the dilemma to social decision making that is created by this view.
5. Why is the discount rate controversial? That is, as long as one discounts all projects that are considered at the same discount rate, is there a need to worry whether the rate is too high or too low?
6. What are some possible reasons to explain the kinds of EPA decisions described in footnote 13, under which a $35 million value is being placed on the life of applicators of a pesticide but a value of only $60,000 is placed on consumers?
7. How are QALYs similar to economic benefits? How do they differ?
8. Distinguish between cost–benefit analysis and cost-effectiveness analysis.
9. Cost–benefit analysis often is presented in terms of willingness to pay for a project. How is willingness to pay related to consumer demand?
10. Consider the information provided in the feature "The Cost of Saving Lives." If a society has a fixed budget that it can devote to all interventions, formulate a general principle or rule to save the greatest number of years of life for a given budget. Assume that the incremental cost per life-year saved for any intervention increases with the amount spent on that intervention.

Exercises

1. Using Figure 4.1, explain why a pollution abatement program that reduces discharge beyond Q_1 is inefficient.
2. Consider the following two projects. Both have costs of $5,000 in Year 1. Project 1 provides benefits of $2,000 in each of the first 4 years only. The second provides benefits of $2,000 for each of Years 6 to 10 only. Compute the net benefits using a discount rate of 6 percent. Repeat using a discount rate of 12 percent. What can you conclude from this exercise?
3. Consider the following table of costs and benefits from a governmental policy to clean the water in a local area.

Level of Abatement	Total Costs	Total Benefits
0%	$ 0	$ 0
10	10	80
20	22	150
30	40	200
40	70	240
50	105	280
60	150	320
70	210	350
80	280	375
90	350	385
100	420	390

 a. What level of abatement is most efficient by general economic criteria?

 b. Would a 70 percent level of abatement pass a benefit–cost test? Is it efficient?

 c. How would you respond to those who argue for 100 percent abatement?

4. Consider a project that costs $10,000 today. It will provide benefits of $4,000 at the end of Year 1, $3,500 at the end of Year 2, and $3,500 at the end of Year 3. If the discount rate is 6 percent, will this project be approved using cost–benefit analysis? Would your answer change if the discount rate is 5 percent? Four percent?

5. Consider a hypothetical three-stage screening test for a cancer with the following rates of detection and costs:

	Number of Cases	
Stage	*Detected*	*Total Costs*
1	100	$200,000
2	105	260,000
3	106	300,000

 a. Calculate the average cost per cancer detected in the three stages.

 b. Calculate the marginal cost per cancer detected in the three stages.

 c. Suppose that the marginal benefit per treated case is $10,000 per person. What would be the optimal screening, given the costs?

CHAPTER 5

The Production of Health

- ■ The Production Function of Health
- ■ On the Historical Role of Medicine and Health Care
- ■ The Production of Health in the Modern Day
- ■ On the Role of Schooling
- ■ Conclusions

The production of health is a central concern to the health economist and to public policy. Consider that the role of health care in society, including medical care provided by physicians, is ultimately a production question. What is the contribution of health care to the health status of the population? Second, what is the best way to produce and distribute health care?

The Production Function of Health

A production function summarizes the relationship between inputs and outputs. The study of the production of health function thus requires that we inquire about the relationship between health care inputs and health. The answers that economists and medical historians offer to this question are surprising to many people. First, the contribution of practitioner-provided health care to the historical downward trends in population mortality rates was probably negligible at least until well into the twentieth century. Second, while the total contribution of health care probably is substantial in the modern day, its marginal contribution is small.

This distinction between total and marginal contributions is crucial to understanding these issues. To illustrate this distinction, consider Figure 5.1A, which exhibits a theoretical health status production function for the population. Set aside the difficulties of measuring health status in populations, and assume that an adequate health status (HS) measure has been agreed on. Health status is shown here to be an increasing function of health care. Also, to avoid a perspective that is too narrowly focused on health

care, we specify further that health status depends at least upon the population's biological endowment, environment, and lifestyle.[1] Thus, HS = f(Health Care, Lifestyle, Environment, Human Biology). Improvements in any of these latter three factors will shift the curve upward.

A production function specifies the relationship of flows of inputs and flows of outputs over a specified time period, so the inputs and output in Figure 5.1A are measured over an implied period of time, such as a year. In practice, we might use the number of healthy days experienced by the population per capita or the reciprocal of a reverse indicator, such as mortality rates or disability days, to indicate health status.

To simplify the depiction of the production of health process, we have reduced all health care inputs into one scale called Health Care. In reality, health care consists of many different health care inputs. Many of them include types of medical care provided by doctors of medicine or osteopathy, but many also are provided by other professionals in the health care field. Conceptually, the health care measure, HC, may be thought of as an aggregate of all these types of health care, the aggregation being based on dollar values.

The marginal contribution of health care is its marginal product, meaning the increment to health caused by one extra unit of Health Care, holding all other inputs constant. Increasing Health Care from zero to 1 unit in Figure 5.1A improves health status by ΔHS_1, the first unit's marginal product. Numerically, this first unit of Health Care has increased the health status index from 32 to 43; thus, $\Delta HS_1 = 11$ Health Status units. The next unit of medical care delivers a marginal product of $\Delta HS_2 = 7$, and so on. That these marginal products are diminishing in size illustrates the law of diminishing marginal returns. If society is employing a total of n units of Health Care, then the total contribution of Health Care is the sum of the marginal products of each of the n units. This total contribution as shown, AB, may be substantial. However, the marginal product of the nth unit of medical care is ΔHS_n, and it is small. In fact, we are nearly on the "flat of the curve." Marginal product is graphed on Figure 5.1B.

We have drawn the health production function as a rising curve that flattens out at higher levels of health care but never bends downward. Would the health production function eventually bend downward? Is it possible to get too much health care so that the health of the population is harmed? This is a logical possibility under at least two scenarios. Iatrogenic (meaning provider-caused) disease is an inevitable byproduct of many medical interventions; for example, each surgery has its risks. If the rate of iatrogenic disease does not fall while diminishing returns sets in, it is possible for the balance of help and harm from health care to be a net harm.

Medical scientists, such as Cochrane (1972), have pressed the case that much medical care as often practiced has only weak scientific basis, making iatrogenesis a real probability. Intellectuals (Illich, 1976; Dubos, 1960) writing for the public audience have warned of a medical "nemesis" taking away our abilities to face the natural hardships of life by "medicalizing" these problems. Illich argued that this medicalization would lead to less personal effort to preserve health and less personal determination to per-

[1]This categorization of groups of inputs is not the only reasonable one, but it illustrates the main issues and it has an excellent history. It was developed by the Canadian government for its pioneering work begun three decades ago (Lalonde, 1974).

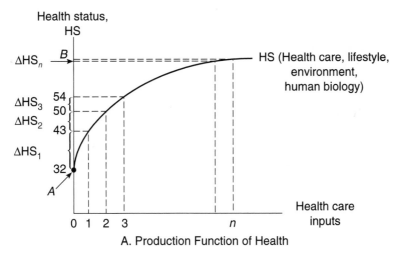

A. Production Function of Health

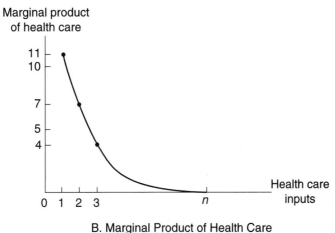

B. Marginal Product of Health Care

FIGURE 5.1 Production of Health.

severe; the result becomes a decline in the health of the population, and thus a negative marginal product for medical care.[2]

Return to the distinction between total product and marginal product. Often, it is the marginals that are relevant to policy propositions, not the totals. For example, no one seriously recommends that society eliminate all health care spending. However, it is reasonable to ask whether society would be better off if it could reduce health care expenditures by $1 billion and invest those funds in another productive use, such as

[2]The medicalization argument was reinforced by Thomas McKeown's (1976) research showing that medical care warranted little credit for the historical declines in mortality rates in England and Wales. The works by McKeown and by Cochrane remain the reference points for the continuing debate within medicine and the social sciences over the role of medicine (Alvarez-Dardet, 1993; Farmer and Nardell, 1998; Frenk, 1998).

housing, education, transportation, defense, or other consumption. We could even reasonably ask if health itself could be improved by transferring the marginal $1 billion to environmental or lifestyle improvements.

Many of our government programs are designed to encourage health care use in certain population groups, such as the poor and elderly. Many programs, such as tax preferences for health insurance, benefit people who are neither poor nor elderly and encourage their consumption of health care. The theoretical issues raised here necessitate that we question the wisdom of each of our programs.

The theoretical questions can be investigated with data of several kinds either directly or indirectly relevant to the production-of-health issue. It is useful to begin with the historical role of medicine, which indirectly bears on the issue of health production. After providing an overview of these efforts, largely the work of medical historians, we then turn to econometric studies of the modern-day production function.

On the Historical Role of Medicine and Health Care

Among many medical historians, it is agreed that practitioner-provided medical interventions played only a small, perhaps negligible, role in the historical decline in population mortality rates in countries where data are available. Effective medicine is a fairly recent phenomenon, and the delivery of effective medical interventions on a scale sufficient to affect population health indicators most likely appeared only well into the twentieth century. Though the magnitudes of other causes of mortality declines are still disputed, it is clear that a larger role, perhaps the most significant one, might be attributed to public health measures and the spread of knowledge of the sources of disease. However, at least one provocative scholar in this field attributes the lion's share of the credit to improvements in environment, particularly to the greatly increased supply of foodstuffs that became available due to the agricultural and industrial revolutions.

THE RISING POPULATION AND THE ROLE OF MEDICINE

The notion that medicine played a relatively minor historical role is certainly not new, and it has been asserted by researchers of various ideologies. This point of view is associated with the work of Thomas McKeown (1976) who focused on the dramatic rise in population in England and Wales from 1750 to modern day.

The pattern over time of world population growth, including population growth in England and Wales, is one that has posed a significant research question to many scholars including McKeown. World population is hard to estimate for the distant past, but recent research by the United Nations (1996) and others make some things clear: something extraordinary has happened during the last 300 years. At the time of Christ, the population probably reached a record of roughly 300 million people. For a thousand years thereafter, until the era of Viking ships, little or no change occurred. By the Age of Enlightenment, starting just before 1700, the population may have risen to 600 million. Then things began to change. Within a single century, the world population passed 1 billion people. The next 5 billion arrived within a mere 200 years. What had happened?

Returning to the history of England and Wales, the large rise in their populations in the period roughly following 1750 is to a large degree a story of the population's health. Population increase comes from three sources: increased birthrates, reduced mortality, or increased net in-migration. Migration was probably not an important

source of population increase in England and Wales; when accurate birthrate and deathrate data became available from 1841, these data alone proved able to account for the population change. Likewise, fertility probably did not account for the change because recorded birthrates declined during the period since data became available. Declines in birthrates are a common finding in countries undergoing industrialization or modernization. In contrast, recorded mortality rates did decline substantially.

To assess the role of medicine, McKeown began by investigating which diseases contributed to the decline in death rates. Mortality data are often limited prior to the mid-1800s, but from available records he produced an emerging picture. Table 5.1 shows death rates by disease category for three different time periods. The table shows that airborne infectious diseases account for the largest single portion of mortality reduction, and waterborne infectious diseases also make up a substantial portion of known causes. Regarding the airborne diseases, other data suggest that the main airborne diseases showing a decline in mortality include tuberculosis, bronchitis, pneumonia, and influenza.

WHAT CAUSED THE MORTALITY RATE DECLINES?

Many presume that the declines in the mortality rates were due to improvements in medical science provided to the public through medical practice. Nevertheless, counterarguments to this proposition bring this presumption into question. In most cases, an effective specific medical intervention was not available until late in the period, well after the greater part of the mortality decline had occurred.

For example, the argument can be illustrated for the cases of respiratory tuberculosis and a group of three upper respiratory diseases—bronchitis, pneumonia, and influenza. Mortality rates for these diseases fell to relatively low levels prior to the availability of effective medical interventions, whose availability occurred respectively

TABLE 5.1 Death Rates* (per million) in 1848–1854, 1901, and 1971

	1848–1854	1901	1971	*Percentage of Reduction (1848–1854 to 1971) Attributable to Each Category*	*For Each Category, Percentage of Reduction (1848–1854 to 1971) That Occurred Before 1901*
I. Conditions attributable to microorganisms:					
1. Airborne diseases	7,259	5,122	619	39%	32%
2. Water- and foodborne diseases	3,562	1,931	35	21	46
3. Other conditions	2,144	1,415	60	12	35
Total	12,965	8,468	714	72	37
II. Conditions not attributable to microorganisms	8,891	8,490	4,070	28	8
All diseases	21,856	16,958	5,384	100	29

*Standardized to the age/sex distribution of the 1901 population.

Source: Reprinted from McKeown, Thomas, *The Modern Rise of Population,* New York: Academic Press, 1976. (p. 54) with permission from Academic Press.

after 1930, and for some cases well into the 1950s and 1960s. The picture is shared by waterborne diseases. About 95 percent of the mortality declines in cholera, diarrhea, and dysentery occurred prior to the 1930s when intravenous therapies became available. Likewise, typhoid and typhus mortality already had fallen to low levels by the beginning of the twentieth century.

The pattern McKeown found for England and Wales also can be illustrated for the United States. McKinlay and McKinlay (1977) provided data for the United States from 1900 to 1973. Figure 5.2 shows these patterns for several infectious diseases. In most cases, as is shown, the availability of the effective medical intervention occurs well after the majority of the mortality declines.

One of the most important changes in mortality in the twentieth century was the decline in infant mortality. Does this type of mortality follow the same pattern? A highly readable account of the modern historical pattern of infant mortality is offered in Victor Fuchs's *Who Shall Live?* (1974). Fuchs noted that infant mortality rates in New York City improved markedly from 1900 to 1930 and that this decline was due significantly to declines in deaths from "pneumonia–diarrhea" complex. Fuchs concluded as follows:

> It is important to realize that medical care played almost no role in this decline. While we do not know the precise causes, it is believed that rising living standards, the spread of literacy and education, and a substantial fall in the birth rate all played a part . . . (p. 32).

In the 1930s, antimicrobial drugs were introduced. During the period 1935 to 1950, the fall in infant death rates accelerated. Fuchs proposed that during this period "both

FIGURE 5.2 Fall in the Standardized Death Rate per 1,000 Population for Four Common Infectious Diseases, in Relation to Specific Medical Measures, for the United States.

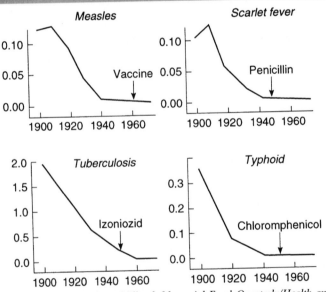

Source: Reprinted from *Milbank Memorial Fund Quarterly/Health and Society*, McKinlay, John B., and Sonja M. McKinlay, "The Questionable Contribution of Medical Measures to the Decline of Mortality in the United States in the Twentieth Century," *Milbank Memorial Fund Quarterly/Health and Society* 55 (1977): 405–428, with the permission of Blackwell Publishers.

Tuberculosis and the Magic Mountain

Thanks to the efforts of writers such as Nobelist Thomas Mann, the tuberculosis (TB) sanitarium of 100 years ago has found a permanent place in literature. Mann's novel, *The Magic Mountain,* describes with a mastery of medical detail, often admired by physicians, a sanitarium retreat in the Alps, its colorful clients, and their experiences with the deadly disease. Mann's incomparable development of characters and dialog bring a reality to the society unique to this sanitarium, representing one he had visited. Hans Castorp, a young German engineer, is smitten with Clavdia Chauchat, a young woman at the "good" Russian table. The Italian Settembrini's intellectual arguments with Naptha can only result in a duel. We grieve when Hans's cousin Joachim, a good, simple military man, succumbs to TB and his body is sledded down the mountain. Hans survives to return to the lands below.

Though effective chemical interventions were not available until after 1940, doctors did treat TB prior to 1940, notably with the widespread use of sanatoriums, such as the one in *The Magic Mountain.* Declines in TB mortality during the period studied by McKeown represented perhaps the single most important example of declines in the mortality rate. Can we credit the sanitorium for this progress? This is unlikely because it is unlikely that sanatorium capacity or the capacity of sanatorium dispensaries were ever large enough to affect the pattern of mortality in populations, (Smith, 1988). In the modern era, with effective drug therapies, tuberculosis still ranks at or near the top of the world's killer diseases. The persistence of pockets of TB often is blamed on local economic conditions and on problems with patient compliance (Farmer and Nardell, 1998).

medical advances and rising living standards contributed to the reduction in infant deaths" (p. 32). Declines in infant deaths flattened somewhat beginning about 1950 but resumed a stronger decline about 1965.

Returning to McKeown's work, if specific effective curative medicines were not largely responsible for mortality declines, is it nevertheless possible that other tools in the physician's black bag were effective? The problem is that there probably were few effective tools in the physician's metaphorical black bag until well into the twentieth century.

ON THE ROLE OF PUBLIC HEALTH AND NUTRITION

If medicine cannot be credited with the large declines in population mortality rates after 1750, what then can be credited? Other alternative candidate causes seem together sufficient to explain the decline: reduction in exposure to infection and improvement in the human host's ability to resist infection. Of these two, reduction in exposure was the primary method through which public health measures could be effective. The role of public health measures is of interest in itself.

The magnitudes of the effects of these alternative causes, including the role of public health, are open to dispute—a dispute whose settlement lies largely outside of an account of health economics. For the present purpose, however, an overview of the issues may suffice.

Available evidence is sufficient to establish that public health contributed significantly to mortality declines, though some historians dispute the proposition that public health was the major contributor. McKeown disputed the preeminence of public health. His argument is that while surely public health was effective for many diseases, its effects were noted primarily through the limitation of exposure to waterborne and foodborne disease organisms, and it cannot account for the large decline in airborne infectious disease mortality.

Public health measures include, among other things, immunization of populations, quarantines, standards for sanitary water supplies and sewage systems, and standards for the sanitary handling and treatment of foodstuffs. During the historical period of study, the most important public health influences appear to be on the waterborne and the foodborne diseases. Here, public health measures appear to have helped notably to improve the quality of water supplies.

However, public health measures came into widespread use late in the period of population mortality declines. For example, among foods carrying pathogens, milk was perhaps most important because it became more widely available in the eighteenth century, and it was a carrier of microorganisms for such diseases as dysentery, typhoid, streptococcal sore throat, and infantile gastroenteritis. It was not until the late nineteenth century that commercial pasteurization was developed, and it was widely used only in the twentieth century.

Control of water purity and sewage systems came into play in the latter part of the nineteenth century, and these changes surely had a positive effect. McKeown argued:

> From the evidence it is clear that the death rate from water- and food-borne diseases declined continuously from the second half of the nineteenth century. . . .
> There is no doubt that [this decline] was due to reduced exposure brought about by improvements in hygiene . . . and their decline coincided with advances in hygiene, particularly, in the nineteenth century, purification of water and sewage disposal (p. 121).

In acknowledging a significant role for public health, the remaining dispute is over its relative importance in comparison to other health-enhancing improvements. McKeown argued that the public health contribution was less important than improvement in population nutrition. He emphasized the lateness of the arrival of widespread public health practices and the limitations of public health measures in improving mortality experience from airborne diseases.

Nevertheless, some studies emphasize the importance of public health. Notably, Woods and Hinde (1987) demonstrated that improvements in mortality in England and Wales during the study period narrowed the gap between urban and rural areas. Dietary differences between urban and rural populations were probably less important than adverse environmental conditions for which public health efforts were effective. They corroborate the conclusions that medical care, however, had no bearing on mortality.

McKeown's argument in favor of nutrition has credibility for many scholars. The introduction of two American foods—corn and potatoes—may alone have made a significant contribution. Agriculture experienced large advances, including new crops, crop rotation, seed production, winter feeding, and improvements in farm implements.

The connection between improved nutrition and infectious diseases is fairly clear.[3] Infectious disease creates a relationship between host and agent of disease. While control of the agent is directly helpful in reducing disease incidence, the condition of the host helps determine its resistance to disease. A person who is better housed, better rested, and—with emphasis here—better fed will be more resistant and less likely to die subsequent to exposure.

What do we know of the role of nutrition in fact versus theory? Do the improvements in health result from better nutrition, as McKeown hypothesized? Some scholars dispute the claim for nutrition, and contradictions can be found. For example, wealthy aristocrats in England, people who could afford as much food as desired, suffered about the same death rates as the working class until well into the eighteenth century. Even after this time, they had substantially worse mortality than average Americans, including farmers.

The puzzle and its potential importance intrigued the noted economic historian Robert Fogel (1986): "The decline in mortality rates since 1700 is one of the greatest events in human history" (p. 105). His work suggests that about 40 percent of the historical decline in mortality rates was due to improved nutrition, a figure he noted is " . . . neither inconsequential nor everything." The biggest rewards went to the infants, he argued, and neither a high caloric diet nor the ability to afford one were necessarily improvements in nutrition. The healthy American farmers probably had better protein in their diets than the English of either social class.

WHAT LESSONS ARE LEARNED FROM THE MEDICAL HISTORIAN?

The study of historical declines in mortality rates is thus one of controversy over the relative importance of public health measures versus nutrition and other environmental factors. The consensus is fairly clear over the minor role of medical practice. What conclusions for modern health policy can be drawn?

First, we cannot conclude that medical research is unimportant in history or in the present day. Medical research contributes not only through improvements to medical practice, but also through its influence on health-enhancing practices.

Typhoid provides a good example. As we have seen, mortality from typhoid declined substantially well before the arrival by 1950 of chloramphenicol. Medical research, however, contributed to our understanding of the cause and transmission of typhoid and generated public health measures such as filtering public water supplies, chlorination of water supplies, and establishment of drinking water standards. All of these factors occurred historically in time to have a major effect on mortality.[4] Selma Mushkin's (1979) estimates on the contribution of medical research to mortality experience tend to confirm this idea. She estimates that medical research accounts for almost one-third of the cost savings to society from reduction in sickness or death rates in the United States from 1900 to 1975. The period 1900 to 1930 accounts for half the

[3]We may presume that a similar argument holds for improvements in housing conditions.
[4]The ideas in this paragraph owe to the discussion in Schneyer, Landefeld, and Sandifer (1981). Vehorn, Landefeld, and Wagner (1982) estimated the contribution of medical research to mortality reductions in the United States over the period 1930 to 1978. From 23 percent to 48 percent of the mortality improvements were attributed to medical research, which they concluded is a cost-beneficial investment.

value of medical research effects, even though it came largely before the specific effective medical practice interventions.

Second, the question of whether a given medical intervention works with afflicted patients requires a different numerator and a different denominator. For example, if we wish to assess the effectiveness of a given treatment for a particular form of cancer, the numerator more plausibly should be the mortality, not in the general population, but of patients who have cancer. Likewise, the denominator would more plausibly be the number of afflicted patients, not the general population.[5]

Finally, the argument regarding the role of medicine is after all a historical one. Successful medical intervention came late in the period, but it did come. Today, the arguments must be different. For example, we might be called on to advise a developing country on the best strategy for investment in health care relative to investment in industry or education.

If the inferences from history are sometimes overdrawn or even invalid, what, then, have we learned from history that we can apply to modern policy? Perhaps the best result of this overview is a healthy skepticism toward the effectiveness of any given medical practice, and more importantly, to its significance and benefits to the population. It is in this spirit that the U.S. government has increasingly come to fund outcomes studies. Outcomes studies are intended to address the effectiveness and appropriateness of specific medical practices on patient outcomes. The studies attempt to reduce the prevalent uncertainties in medical practice, and they offer important inquiries into the wisdom of using the marginal billion dollars on medical care delivery, particularly in terms of costs and benefits to the population as a whole.

The Production of Health in the Modern Day

The investigation of the modern health production function requires that we apply econometric techniques. An understanding of the strengths and limitations of these contributions requires attention to the underlying conceptual issues.

PRELIMINARY ISSUES

Two conceptual issues bear on our interpretation of the results. These two issues can be posed as questions faced by every researcher: (1) how to measure health, the dependent variable in these studies, and (2) how to eliminate biases in the estimates.

How to Measure Health

Consider first the measurement of health. We desire a measure of population health status that has at least two characteristics: It must capture the aspects of health status that are meaningful to us, and it must be measurable with adequate precision. It is difficult to attain both of these goals. We are most confident of the accuracy of mortality rate data; however, mortality rates do not adequately capture several meaningful aspects of health status, such as reduction in pain and suffering and other improvements in the quality of life. The approach of past research in this field is understandable. Mortality data have necessarily been emphasized because of their accuracy, as well as because of their importance in the public mind. However, other indicators of health status,

[5]The ideas in this paragraph owe to work by Pernick (1991).

such as morbidity (illness) rates and disability days, also have been used. In discussing the empirical literature, we begin with the mortality studies and then consider studies of morbidity.

How to Eliminate Biases?

Second, consider the difficulties of eliminating biases in the estimation process. Conceptually, the statistical estimates should be based on combinations of all health care inputs used and the resulting outputs. Such data, along with appropriate econometric techniques, would permit the estimation of the production function directly—the goal of much of this research. Unfortunately, available data often have permitted only a more indirect approach. Researchers often have used data on the availability of some health care inputs in the population, not on the amounts of all inputs actually used.

It is safe to say that empirical work in this area has been developing and improving over time, and this progress includes a more recent emphasis on more direct and unbiased estimation of the production function. The problems that can introduce bias into other estimates can be illustrated with an example. Suppose we have measures for the availability of one health care input, say physicians per capita, but lack data on some other input measure such as the amount of exercise that local people generally get. Unfortunately for the econometrician, these two input variables may be related. More physicians may be demanded in areas where people do fewer health-promoting activities on their own. Unaware of this correlation, or simply lacking the needed data, the econometrician might underestimate the productivity of physicians. One way in which this literature has been progressing is in having greater success in eliminating such biases. This is noteworthy, for example, in the studies of neonate mortality, which we will report shortly.[6]

THE CONTRIBUTION OF HEALTH CARE TO POPULATION HEALTH: THE MODERN ERA

Health economists inevitably use different study designs and data sources to estimate the marginal product of health care. The resulting numbers need to be converted to a common basis, and for this we use the elasticity of health with respect to expenditure on health care inputs: (% change in health)/(% increase in health care expenditures).

Table 5.2 reports the elasticities from several studies of the production of health published from 1969 to 1998. Each study applies econometric methods to analyze survey data; these range from statewide data (Auster et al., 1969) to data on county groups (Hadley, 1982, 1988) to data on individuals (Sickles and Yazbeck, 1998). The first three studies apply mortality rates as an inverse measure of health, while the most recent applies measures of activity and mobility (the more active and the more mobile individuals are assumed to be, the healthier.

The several studies offer advantages because of their differences. The older one suggested that lifestyle and environment expenditures could provide more marginal

[6]The issue of bias discussed here involves the problem of omitted variables and the distinction between reduced-form equation studies, which suggest incorrect inferences about input productivity, and structural equation studies, which correctly estimate the productivity of inputs. For a discussion of the distinction between reduced-form and structural function approaches, see Grossman and Joyce (1990). Atkinson and Crocker (1992) explain "omitted variable bias," such as the omitted "physical exercise" variable in our example, and warn of the potentially more serious problem of "mismeasures" in the study variables.

TABLE 5.2 Measuring the Contribution of Health Care to Population Health

Study Cited	Date of Study	Health Care Elasticity[1]	Significant?
Auster et al.	1969	0.08 to 0.12	Usually not
Hadley	1982	0.12 to 0.17	Yes
Hadley	1988	0.20 to 1.00	Yes
Sickles & Yazbeck	1998	0.03 to 0.05	Yes

[1]This is the elasticity of health with respect to health care expenditure.

benefits per dollar of cost than health care; among the particulars, efforts to improve schooling or reduce cigarette smoking offered appealing trade-offs with health care spending. The Hadley studies applied newer data at a more refined level of aggregation; they helped to establish that health care spending does make a statistically significant marginal contribution to health and argued that health care is still beneficial at the margin. The latest study follows its subjects through time and takes an approach better designed to avoid biases.

A picture emerges that health care *is* a statistically significant contributor to health on the margin, but that its marginal effect on health is small. Health care matters, but we are nearly "on the flat of the curve." To illustrate the issue, suppose that 0.10 were the true production elasticity of health care, and let the U.S. Congress reallocate $110 billion from other programs to health care expenditure. In 1997, the United States was spending $1 trillion on health care. This $110 billion transfer would have increased health care expenditure by 10 percent. We would extrapolate the improvement in health to be $10 \times 0.10 = 1$ percent. If "health" were defined as *average life expectancy,* a 1 percent gain would mean an increased *average life expectancy* of $76 \times 0.01 = 0.76$ years, provided this increased expenditure were maintained indefinitely. Spread over the population (for a life span), however, the 0.76 years of life could prove fairly cheap, even making the extra investment cost beneficial.

Hadley's data help remind us of the old truism that "averages often conceal important facts." His data show that health care affects different subpopulations differently. Table 5.3 reports the health care production elasticity for Medicare (65 or over) populations, and it splits the data into subpopulations. Reading across the row labeled "Medicare Expenses," higher elasticities for females (as opposed to males of the same race) and higher elasticities for blacks (as opposed to whites of the same gender) suggest that presently blacks and females benefit from health care relatively more at the margin. Hadley (1988) confirmed the pattern that the health of blacks responds more strongly to health care at the margin.

The point of focusing on the experience of population subgroups is reinforced by neonate mortality studies.[7] A neonate is an infant one month old or younger. Thus, the neonate mortality rate is deaths to neonates per 1,000 live births. What can be done to reduce these deaths? The early studies observed for counties in the United States and identified several factors that seemed to cause higher neonate mortality rates. Table 5.4 displays the production of neonate mortality study by Corman, Joyce, and Grossman (1987).

[7]Corman and Grossman (1985) and Corman, Joyce, and Grossman (1987) are the starting points for these paragraphs.

TABLE 5.3 The Production Elasticity of Health Care, Education, Income, and Cigarette Consumption, Medicare Populations, 1970 Country Group Data

Independent Variable	White Males 65+	Black Males 65+	White Females 65+	Black Females 65+
Medicare Expenses	0.123^2	0.163^2	0.141^2	0.173^2
Education	0.128^2	0.060	0.025^2	0.106
Income	0.020	0.012	NS	0.011
Cigarette Sales	-0.053^2	-0.134	-0.110^1	0.045^1

Medicare Expenses = Medicare expenditures per Medicare enrollee; Education = average number of highest education year attained; Income = total family income and other unearned income; Cigarette Sales = cigarette sales per capita.

NS = coefficient is not significant and rounds to zero.

[1]Significant at the 5 percent level.

[2]Significant at the 1 percent level.

Source: Reprinted from Hadley, Jack, *More Medical Care, Better Health?* Washington, D.C.: Urban Institute, 1982, pp. 61–2.

The table presents their estimates of the contribution of each measured factor to the reported mortality rate decline. Use of medical services—both for neonatal intensive care and for prenatal care—is included. The WIC program is a shortened name for the governmental program designed to provide improved nutrition for women, infants, and children; it is a means-tested program, meaning that it is directed to the poor. The BCHS variable is the authors' measure combining various Bureau of Community Health Services projects, including maternal and infant care, as well as community health centers.

TABLE 5.4 Contribution of Selected Factors to Reductions in Neonate Mortality Rates, 1964–1977

Factor	Whites Total Effect	Blacks Total Effect
Organized family planning	0.084	0.526
WIC	0.425	1.330
BCHS	0.002	0.030
Neonatal intensive care	0.140	0.534
Abortion	0.824	2.109
Prenatal care	0.434	1.949
Total explained reduction	1.9	6.5
Total reduction	7.5	11.5
Percentage explained	25.3	56.5

Note: Figures record estimates of the reduction in deaths per 1,000 live births predicted to have been caused by various factors.

Source: Reprinted from *Journal of Human Resources,* Corman, Hope, Theodore J. Joyce, and Michael Grossman, "Birth Outcome Production Function in the United States," *Journal of Human Resources* 22 (1987): 339–360 with permission from The University of Wisconsin Press.

The data recorded in Table 5.4 indicate that of the total reduction in neonate mortality for whites during the period, 1.9 deaths per 1,000 live births or 25.3 percent, can be explained by the observed factors, whereas for blacks a greater amount, 6.5 or 56.5 percent, can be explained. The table is read, for example, as follows: During the period studied, the WIC program resulted in a reduction of white neonate mortality rates of 0.425 deaths per 1,000 live births, while for blacks WIC reduced neonate mortality by 1.330 deaths per 1,000 live births.

The effectiveness of prenatal care (WIC is also partly a prenatal program) is illustrated by these data. The contribution of expensive, neonatal intensive care is "shown-up" by prenatal care and WIC, especially in the column for blacks. The effectiveness of prenatal care programs is a repeated finding in health economic research, and it was corroborated in a study of a New Jersey Medicaid program, which was designed to enrich prenatal care (Reichman and Florio, 1996). Liu (1998) argues further that studies tend to understate the importance of prenatal care.[8]

MORBIDITY STUDIES

Up to this point, the production of health might be better termed a production of mortality rates. Research has focused on mortality for good reasons: These data are more widely available, they are measured accurately, and they are meaningful in themselves. However, they do not tell the whole story. Anderson and Morrison (1989) put it perhaps more forcefully than many:

> The authors of the 1970s raised the question: Do personal health services reduce mortality rates? And they answered with a resounding "No!" . . . The health policy analysts of this decade have revealed an increased sophistication by asking: Is it appropriate to measure the effectiveness of personal health services by gross measures of mortality? And they have answered that question with an equally resounding "No!" (p. 148).

We would argue somewhat to the contrary that personal health services *do* reduce mortality in populations significantly, and while the marginal contribution is small, it nevertheless is probably cost beneficial on the margin for some population subgroups. Second, data on mortality rates such as we have examined *are* meaningful; that is, they tell an important part of the story. However, the point is well taken that mortality rates tell *only* part of the story, and for many people who use health care, it may not be the most important part. Other measures of health also should be examined. These include morbidity data and other indicators of health. Work also is being done on developing a measure of the quality of life, and quality of life may become the subject of production studies.

How Does Health Care Affect Other Measures of Health?

When Newhouse and Friedlander (1980) began to look at the production of health, they already recognized the need for studies to examine measures of population health besides the mortality rates:

[8]Similarly, Currie and Gruber (1996) showed general Medicaid eligibility to improve birth outcomes in a study across states in the United States. (This is distinguished from particular Medicaid spending directed to prenatal care.) These authors, however, raised issues about the cost-effectiveness of improvements in Medicaid eligibility.

FEATURE

The Length of Life Is Fixed

For medical researcher James Fries, recent data reveal what he terms a "compression of morbidity." People don't live much longer on average than they did 30 years ago, but their illnesses and diseases are becoming ever more compressed toward the last few years of life. To Fries, the human life span appears to have a maximum. Medical treatment, improved lifestyles, and cleaner environments eliminate some premature deaths, but they primarily postpone morbidity and have little effect on life span (Fries, 1980, 1989). "Therefore survival curves have assumed an ever more rectangular form" (1980, p. 130).

This theory may distress some of those generations raised on post World War II optimism and for whom everything seemed possible eventually, even immortality. While Fries recognizes the possible anguish for some, he argues that for others "exhilaration may come from recognition that the goal of a vigorous long life may be an attainable one" (1980, p. 135). Like the beautiful, one-horse carriage that was the "Deacon's Masterpiece" by Oliver Wendell Holmes, the human body will live "strong and sound" until its last day, when it crumbles as from an earthquake shock:

"You see, of course, if you're not a dunce,
How it went to pieces all at once,-
All at once, and nothing first,-
Just as bubbles do when they burst.

End of the wonderful one-hoss shay.
Logic is logic. That's all I say."

Professor Fries cannot be taken so literally, however, as his theory depicts the maximum life span more accurately as the gradual compression of the distribution of the human age at death to a narrower range, say 85 to 87 years, which is what Fries finds to be the maximum. Figure 5.3 illustrates this idea.

FIGURE 5.3 Mortality According to Age, in the Absence of Premature Death.

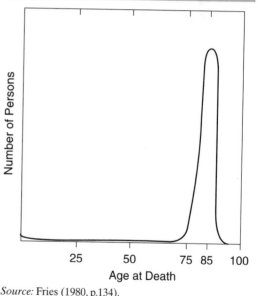

Source: Fries (1980, p.134).

If, as many believe, most diseases that are currently treated are either selflimiting or irreversible, the possibilities for additional medical services to reduce mortality are small. In this case, . . . the observed effect of medical care will be both small and hard to detect. By contrast, there may be some diseases, such as hypertension or periodontal disease, where additional medical-care resources can make a difference (p. 201).

They examined six physiological measures taken on individuals evaluated in the Health Examination Survey between October 1959 and December 1962. The measures included blood pressure, cholesterol, electrocardiogram abnormalities, abnormal chest X rays,

varicose veins, and periodontal disease. The authors found that the availability of health care was rarely significantly related to these physiological measures. Even in the few exceptions, the effect of health care was small. In contrast, better educated individuals often had better health, though the effect of income was small, if significant. Better-educated people tended to have much better gums—that is, better periodontal indicators—whereas the availability of dentists per capita did not seem to matter. The authors concluded that "the results are consistent with the view that what the individual does (or does not) do for himself affects health more than do additional medical resources" (p. 200).

The Rand Health Insurance Experiment (RHIE) provided the best opportunity to verify those early results. Led by Joseph Newhouse, the RHIE was one of the largest, randomly controlled economic experiments ever conducted. It was designed to test the effect of alternative health insurance policies on the demand for health care and on the health status of a large and closely watched group of people from all walks of life.

Our interest in this chapter is derived from a big side effect of that experiment. It was discovered that the greater the portion of their health care bill that individuals are required to pay, the less health care they choose to purchase. While this should not have been surprising, what did surprise most health economists was how great the difference was; the fully insured purchased roughly 40 percent more health care than those who had to pay their own bills. This provides a great opportunity for us to ask: "Were the people with 40 percent more health care also 40 percent more healthy?" It is a serendipitous, but perfectly valid, way to test the real contribution of health care to people's health within the context of a scientifically controlled experiment.

Fortunately, RHIE analysts kept careful and voluminous records on each subject, including a dozen or more measurements under each category of physical health, mental health, social health, and general health index. They also examined their subjects' dental health, persistence of symptoms, health habits, and disability days. The results are easy to summarize. For dozens of items, virtually no differences were found between the groups studied.

A simple example from the RHIE illustrates the point well. Table 5.5 provides detail on Work Loss Days per employed person per year—a measure of health status and morbidity that some economic researchers like to use because it ties directly to both

TABLE 5.5	**Work Loss Days Per Employed Person Per Year, by Plan**			
Plan	*Mean*	*Standard Error of Mean*	*95% Confidence Interval*	*Number of Persons*
Free	5.47	0.42	4.65–6.29	1,136
Intermediate (25%, 50%)	4.82	0.37	4.09–5.55	983
Individual Deductible	4.54	0.36	3.83–5.25	787
Family Deductible (95%)	4.82	0.53	3.78–5.86	600

Source: Reprinted by permission of the publisher from *Free for All?: Lessons from the RAND Health Insurance Experiment* by Joseph P. Newhouse, Cambridge, MA: Harvard University Press, Copyright © 1993 by the RAND Corporation.

health and productivity. This table separates the Rand subjects into four groups, which differ by type of health insurance policy. Some subjects pay nothing out-of-pocket for their health care/health insurance package; some foot 25 percent to 50 percent of their bill themselves; others also have to pay all of their health care bills up to a certain amount called a deductible. The subject's out-of-pocket cost thus ranges from zero (free) to about 95 percent of the bill. Newhouse et al. (1993) summarizes: "Our results show that the 40 percent increase in services on the free-care plan had little or no effect on health status for the average adult."

The effects on children showed a somewhat similar pattern. Valdez et al. (1985) examined data for 1,844 children in the Rand study—children who differed primarily by the type of insurance plan their families obtained. Children under the cost-sharing plans consumed up to one-third less care. However, the reduction in care was not significantly related to health status measures. It appears clear that while free provision of health care to children might be justified on equity grounds, it may not be justified on the basis of benefits to health (Newhouse et al., 1993).

ON THE IMPORTANCE OF LIFESTYLE AND ENVIRONMENT

The importance of lifestyle and environment for a population's health is illustrated by Barbara Wolfe (1986). She investigated the trends in health status in several industrialized countries, and looked at trends in medical expenditures and lifestyle factors such as cigarette and alcohol consumption. Previous international studies indicated little or no significant effect of medical expenditures, but by controlling for lifestyle she demonstrated a positive relationship between health care and health in several countries. Later work (Hitiris and Posnett, 1992) corroborated this finding: Nations that have better health care in comparison with other nations have healthier citizens. However, what about lifestyle and environment, whose importance was revealed indirectly? Didn't we always know that much of our health depends on the wisdom of our own choices?

The role of lifestyle was best illustrated by Victor Fuchs in his book *Who Shall Live?* (1974). He compared death rates in Nevada and Utah with average for 1959 to 1961 and 1966 to 1968. These two states are contiguous, and they share "about the same levels of income and medical care and are alike in many other respects" (p. 52). Nevertheless, average death rates in Nevada are much in excess of those in Utah. Table 5.6 shows the results of Fuchs's work. Fuchs argued that the explanation for these substantial differences surely lies in lifestyle:

> Utah is inhabited primarily by Mormons, whose influence is strong throughout the state. Devout Mormons do not use tobacco or alcohol and in general lead stable, quiet lives. Nevada, on the other hand, is a state with high rates of cigarette and alcohol consumption and very high indexes of marital and geographical instability (p. 53).

Inasmuch as Fuchs's illustration lends support to his point regardless of the time period, it may not appear necessary to see how Utah is doing today. However, it is hard not to be curious. The age-adjusted death rate per 100,000 resident population is a good, rough tool to measure average health. In the period 1994 to 1996, with its low age-adjusted death rates, Utah was a national leader in health (the death rate equals 412.9), second only to Hawaii (389.4), while Nevada's rate was much higher (555.2). Before concluding that a simple life and plenty of sun are the tickets to good health in and of

TABLE 5.6	Excess of Death Rates in Nevada Compared with Utah, Average for 1959-1961 and 1966-1968.	
Age Group	*Males (%)*	*Females (%)*
<1	42	35
1–19	16	26
20–39	44	42
40–49	54	69
50–59	38	28
60–69	26	17
70–79	20	6

Source: Reprinted from Fuchs, Victor R., *Who Shall Live? Health, Economics, and Social Choice,* Expanded Edition, Singapore: World Scientific Publishing Company, 1995. p. 52, with permission from the author and World Scientific Publishing.

themselves, consider that many of the top ten healthful states, while they may be sunny, are known to be chilly: Minnesota (419.8), North Dakota (425.4), Iowa (436.9), Idaho (437.5), and Colorado (436.6). Yet Fuchs's point rings true; what we do for ourselves often matters the most for our health.

CIGARETTES AND HEALTH

One thing many of us have chosen to do is to quit smoking (or to avoid becoming addicted to cigarette smoking in the first place). Americans know that heart disease and cancer are the two leading killers, but most of us do not realize how substantial a part is played by smoking-related deaths. Letting the category "malignant neoplasms of the respiratory system" (the category for lung cancer) be our guide, we find that the 1996 death rate[9] (39.3) is twice as high as that for any of the following: pulmonary disease (21.0), prostate cancer (14.9), pneumonia and influenza (12.8), diabetes melitus (13.6), HIV (18.1), or motor vehicle-related injuries (13.2). We already have seen the negative health production elasticity of cigarettes, which makes clear that cigarette smoking affects the average health of the community and is statistically significant at that level.

MATERNAL BEHAVIOR AND NEWBORN HEALTH

Women have long been warned to avoid cigarettes and alcohol while pregnant. Are such lifestyle factors important enough to be included as factors in the production of newborn health? The answer is yes. In the production of newborn birth weight (an important guide to infant health outcomes), maternal cigarette smoking has a significant negative effect (Rosenzweig and Schultz, 1983; Rosenzweig and Wolpin, 1995).

Maternal behavior also can have strong and tragic consequences in the case of drug use. Health economists Joyce, Racine, and Mocan (1992) found that the alarming increase in low birth weight births in New York City, particularly among blacks, was due

[9]These death rates are age-adjusted deaths per 100,000 resident population, based on data from the National Vital Statistics System.

in large part to an epidemic of illicit substance abuse by pregnant women. The explosion of cocaine use had horrible consequences for these babies. More recent work (Kaestner, Joyce, and Wehbeh, 1996) cautions that the ever-present problem of getting honest and accurate self-reports of drug use will cause the researcher to overstate somewhat the harm done to newborn health. The issue, however, is only one of degree; maternal drug use causes significant harm to newborns.

ENVIRONMENTAL POLLUTION

It is well known that pollution causes ill health and death in individuals and that the elderly and people with respiratory diseases are more susceptible. The degree to which reductions in pollution will improve the health of populations is somewhat less clearly defined. That pollution effects on health are sizable and statistically significant can be shown in both industrialized and lesser-developed countries (Cropper et al., 1997; Schwartz and Dockery, 1992). Based on levels of total suspended particulates (TSP) in New Delhi between 1991 and 1994, the average pollution level was determined to be five times the limit recommended by the World Health Organization (WHO). Variations in deaths in New Delhi responded statistically to the variations in pollution; if these estimates prove true, then a reduction of pollution levels of about one third would reduce deaths by more than 2 percent. A similar study in Philadelphia suggests that reducing the pollution level there by the same 100 micrograms per cubic meter would reduce deaths by more than 6 percent in the general population and nearly 10 percent for the elderly. This is because with our generally better health status in the United States, more people live long enough to become part of the population groups most sensitive to respiratory problems stemming from factors such as pollution.

We know that good health during the years when an individual is forming a career can be a big boost to that person's income later in life (James Smith, 1998). We also know that being rich does not necessarily cause one to choose to live and eat wisely. Even programs designed to raise the income of poor families, such as the (pre-welfare reform) Aid to Families with Dependent Children in the United States, did not always correlate with good health habits among the recipients (Currie and Cole, 1993; Currie and Gruber, 1996). A better case can be made that the *distribution of income* matters significantly for the health of nations in cross-country comparisons (Waldmann, 1992). We reemphasize that public programs for prenatal care demonstrate their positive effects easily (Reichman and Florio, 1996).

On the Role of Schooling

What of education? Inasmuch as our education includes everything we read and study privately as well as formally, a portion of education is impossible to measure accurately, and health economists focus instead on schooling. Health status *is* significantly correlated with schooling as we have seen.[10] If the marginal product of health care is truly small ("we are on the flat of the curve"), then perhaps we should reduce public health

[10]In addition to Auster et al.'s findings across states, Hadley (1982) found education a significant contributor to population health at the small area level of analysis. Education also contributes significantly in studies within developing countries (Pitt, 1997).

expenditures on health care at the margin and transfer the expenditures to education. However, the wisdom of such a policy depends on which of the two theories is correct.

TWO DIFFERENT THEORIES ABOUT THE ROLE OF SCHOOLING

The ideas and work of two health economists serve to develop and contrast the two theories. First, Michael Grossman's (1972a, 1972b) theory of demand entails a central role for education. Under Grossman, better-educated persons tend to be economically more efficient producers of health status. Better-educated people understand the technology or have the know-how needed to stay healthy. They also know better how to use medical and other market inputs and their own time to produce health. Under this view, the marginal transfer of resources makes good sense.

Other health economists have put forward hypotheses under which schooling and health status are correlated only because they are both related to one or more other factors. The problem can be seen as the familiar self-selection problem. Do people who self-select to choose higher levels of education have an unobserved characteristic that also makes them likely to be healthier?

Victor Fuchs (1982) has suggested a theory that serves as a prime example and involves certain microeconomic aspects of time discounting. Chapter 4 on cost-benefit analysis explained why decision makers must discount future benefits and costs of a social investment to make them comparable in terms of present values. It also showed that a decision maker with a high rate of discount will tend to prefer projects with immediate payoffs versus long-term projects. Now consider individuals facing a possible investment in education. Because education requires current costs to gain distant payoffs, individuals with relatively low discount rates will be the more likely to invest in education. Similarly, health investments require substantial current outlays to gain distant payoffs; for example, the payoffs may be extended years toward the end of life. It follows that individuals with low time discount rates, or long *time horizons,* will tend to invest in both education and health. This will cause health status to be correlated with education, but further increments to education will *not* cause improvements in health status.[11]

EMPIRICAL STUDIES ON THE ROLE OF SCHOOLING IN HEALTH

Health economists investigated the reasons why schooling is associated with better health. Berger and Leigh (1989) examined data on thousands of individuals in two samples. One, the Health and Nutrition Examination Survey, used blood pressure as a measure of health status. The other, the National Longitudinal Survey of Young Men, used measures of functional limitations and disability.

The authors' statistical methods permitted a useful test. They first observed the individual's choice of schooling using standard techniques. They found that years of schooling for an individual is related to several demographic characteristics such as age, race, ethnic background, family characteristics, and IQ. They also developed a measure of the effect of unobserved factors, which include factors such as personal time preference. They then posed the question: Do such unobserved self-selection factors affect

[11]Fuchs (1982) proposed as well the alternative related hypothesis that schooling tends to effect a change in people's time preferences. Both of the Fuchs hypotheses and the Grossman hypothesis would imply the observed positive correlation between schooling and health.

health status or does schooling directly improve health status? Their results are consistent for both samples and for all measures of health status. Schooling directly improves health status measures, but no significant effect results from unobservables such as time preference. This result is consistent with the view that schooling improves one's ability to produce health.

The issue of schooling and health is also of crucial importance to health in developing countries. Studies of families in Nicaragua by Jere Behrman and Barbara Wolfe are relevant. Behrman and Wolfe (1989) posed the question: "Does more schooling make women better nourished and healthier?" They took steps to control for the influence of other factors that affect both schooling and health. In particular, they controlled for the women's childhood background factors. They concluded that "the estimated positive health impact of the woman's schooling is largely representing schooling per se rather than unobserved fixed endowments so that . . . the woman's schooling does seem to make the woman healthier" (p. 660).

If a woman's schooling makes her a more efficient producer of health, then we also should expect that it will improve her children's health. Standard estimates of the effect of a woman's schooling on her children's health indeed show this effect. However, other work by Wolfe and Behrman (1987) casts serious doubt. The two authors collected data for sisters in Nicaragua. This allowed them to compare the health status of the children of the more educated of the sisters using econometric techniques. Because the sisters had essentially the same childhood background, these data and methods allowed them to control for unobserved elements in childhood background. Their results were clear: Once childhood background is controlled for, a mother's education has no significant effect on her children's health status.

Thus, not all pieces of evidence fit the same pattern, and this will be a continued area of health economics research in this decade. We must recognize as well that the major evidence we have examined addresses schooling per se, not necessarily schooling in health production. Introspection will serve quickly to show that most of one's schooling from elementary school through college or graduate school deals with knowledge and intellectual skills most often not related to personal hygiene. Even a negative result on the effect of schooling is consistent with a policy of increased investment in specific education devoted to health information—that is, to health production technology.

Conclusions

In this chapter, we have investigated many topics related directly or indirectly to the production of health. The health production function exhibits the law of diminishing marginal returns. While the total contribution of health care is substantial, the marginal product is small in the United States.

Historically, much of the decline in mortality rates occurred prior to the introduction of specific, effective medical interventions. Thus, historically both the marginal and the total contributions of health care, at least as provided by the health practitioner, were probably small until well into the twentieth century.

The small, modern-day marginal product of health care is statistically significant. However, in the major, controlled health insurance experiment, the better insured exhibited little or no health gain from the extra health care they consumed. Health care benefits people differentially and is generally more productive on the margin for

women and blacks. Similarly, certain categories of health care have greater marginal effects on the population than others; prenatal care programs are examples of the more productive categories.

Whether schooling or health care is the better investment toward improving health depends on which alternative theory is correct: Does schooling improve one's own health production skill, or do some individuals select for both schooling and health because of other factors? The production of health will continue to stimulate both theoretical and empirical research.

Summary

1. The production function for health exhibits diminishing marginal returns. In developed countries, the total product of health care is probably substantial at the same time that the marginal product is relatively small.
2. The historical declines in mortality rates in representative industrial countries were substantially responsible for the large growth of populations.
3. The historical declines in population mortality rates were not due to medical interventions because effective medical interventions became available to populations largely after the mortality had declined. Instead, public health, improved environment, and improved nutrition probably played substantial roles.
4. The marginal product of health care in the United States is small. Recent studies find elasticities in a narrow range around 0.10.
5. The Rand Health Insurance Experiment found that increased use of health care has little effect on the illness rates of the study population.
6. Lifestyle and environment are major and statistically significant determinants of population health status.
7. Health care contributes more substantially to health for subgroups of the population, including infants and also certain ethnic minority groups.
8. Education, as measured by years of schooling, is positively related to population health; however, the reason for this relationship is subject to debate. One theory proposes that schooling improves the efficiency by which one produces one's own health. Other theories suggest that both schooling and health are linked to other unobserved variables.

Discussion Questions

1. Assume that health production is subject to diminishing returns and that each unit of health care employed entails a constant rate of iatrogenic (medically caused) disease. Would the production of health function eventually bend downward? Explain.
2. What evidence is there to suggest that the United States is on the "flat of the curve" in health production? Is a typical developing country likely to be on the flat of its health production function? Discuss the differences.
3. Which of the following are important in explaining the modern rise in population in England and Wales: birthrates, death rates, and net migration rates? Describe the evidence.
4. "Medical interventions were not important in the historical declines in mortality rates, but that does not imply that medical research was unimportant." Explain this viewpoint.

5. What role did public health play in the historical decline in mortality rates?

6. Suppose you were hired as an adviser to a developing country and you were versed in the theory of production, the historical role of medicine, and the modern-day health production function studies. Their government seeks advice on the wisdom of a relative emphasis on health and health investment versus other forms of economic investment. What would be your advice?

7. Someone says the following: "Lifestyle may be the most important determinant of health status, but changing lifestyles may not be the least costly way to improve population health status." Explain the circumstances under which this opinion could be true. Is it likely to be true in reality? What does the evidence on lifestyle suggest about government policies to improve the public's overall health?

8. Summarize the two theories on how schooling is correlated with health status. Wolfe and Behrman investigated the health status of the children of pairs of sisters in Nicaragua. The sisters, who shared a common environment as children, often had different levels of schooling. Which of the two theories does the Wolfe and Behrman evidence support?

9. Research shows that the returns for prenatal health care are high, whereas it may cost hundreds of thousands of dollars to keep some acutely ill, elderly person alive. What does this suggest about the appropriate allocation of resources among members of society?

Exercises

1. Graph the production of health function $HS = 10HC^{0.5}E^{0.3}LS^{0.4}HB^{0.2}$ in a graph with axes HS and HC assuming $E = 10$, $LS = 5$, and $HB = 7$. Graph the marginal product of health inputs. Is it increasing or decreasing? Show how the curve changes when E is increased to 15.

2. Which factors in Table 5.4 were important in explaining improvements in black neonate mortality rates? White neonate mortality rates? Speculate on why some of these factors may have been more important for blacks.

3. What are the differences between mortality and morbidity? Would you expect the two variables to be related to each other? If so, how?

4. We know that correlations never explain; it is our theories that provide explanations. Reexamine Table 5.4 and draft theories to explain why WIC has a larger contribution than Organized Family Planning. Why do the contributions differ between blacks and whites on WIC, abortion, and prenatal care?

Demand for
Health Capital

The previous chapter considered the production of health in the aggregate by looking at the impacts of various factors on health for society as a whole. In this chapter, we show how individuals allocate their resources to produce health. Economists' understanding of this decision has been deepened by the important work of Michael Grossman. His model has enabled us to understand thoroughly the role of several variables such as age, education, health status, and income in the production of health through the demand for health capital.

The Demand for Health

THE CONSUMER AS HEALTH PRODUCER

Grossman (1972a, 1972b) used the theory of human capital to explain the demand for health and health care. His work has become a standard beginning point for much subsequent work. According to human capital theory, individuals invest in themselves through education, training, and health to increase their earnings. Grossman shows the

way in which many important aspects of health demand differ from the traditional approach to demand:

1. It is not medical care per se that the consumer wants, but rather health. Medical-care demand is a derived demand for an input to produce health. People want health; they demand inputs to produce it.
2. The consumer does not merely purchase health passively from the market. Instead, the consumer *produces* it, spending time on health-improving efforts in addition to purchasing medical inputs.
3. Health lasts for more than one period. It does not depreciate instantly, and thus can be treated like the capital good that it is.
4. Perhaps most importantly, health can be treated both as a consumption good and an investment good. As a consumption good, health is desired because it makes people feel better. As an investment good, health also is desired because it increases the number of healthy days available to work, and thus to earn income.

Consider the consumer, Ed Kramer as a producer, or a firm that buys market inputs (e.g., medical care, food, clothing), and combines them with his own time to produce the services that increase his utility. The consumer not only increments his stock of health, but using market inputs and personal time produces the other pleasures of life.

These pleasures are meant to include virtually all other things that the consumer does. Included are time watching television, reading, playing with and teaching one's children, preparing meals, baking bread, or watching the sun set. We do not mean that they are all simply pleasures. Instead, they are intended to represent a composite of other things we do with our leisure time, both for pleasure and out of a sense of duty to family and community. We shall call this composite *home good B*.

TIME SPENT PRODUCING HEALTH

An increment to capital stock such as health is called an investment. Each period Ed produces an investment in health, I. Health investment, I, is produced by time spent improving health, T_H, and market health inputs (providers' services, drugs, exercise), M. Likewise, home good B is produced with time, T_B, and market-purchased goods, X.[1] Thus, Ed is using money to buy health care inputs, M, or home good inputs, X. He is using leisure time either for health care (T_H) or for producing the home good (T_B).

Using functional notation:

$$I = I(M, T_H; E) \tag{6.1}$$
$$B = B(X, T_B; E) \tag{6.2}$$

These functions indicate that increased amounts of M and T_H increase I, and that increased amounts of X and T_B increase B. The variable E in these functions is included to suggest that productivity in producing I or B may vary from person to person. Grossman proposed that this technical efficiency level would be related to the individual's education level, E. That is, educated people may produce one good or the other more efficiently.

[1] If, for example, we considered good B as baking bread, the market goods might include flour; yeast; kitchen appliances; and gas, water, and/or electricity.

In this model, Ed Kramer's ultimate resource is his own time. Treat each period of analysis as being a year in length, and assume that Ed has 365 days available in the year. To buy market goods such as medical care, M, or other goods, X, he must trade some of this time for income; that is, he must work at a job. Call his time devoted to work T_W. Because our focus is on the health aspects of living, we realize that some of his time during each year will be taken over by ill health, or T_L. Thus, we have accounted for his total time in the following manner:

$$\text{Total time} = T = 365 \text{ days} = T_H \text{ (time spent improving health)}$$
$$+ T_B \text{ (time spent in producing home goods)}$$
$$+ T_L \text{ (time lost due to illness)} \qquad \textbf{(6.3)}$$
$$+ T_W \text{ (time devoted to work)}$$

Recall that his leisure time is spent either improving his health or producing home goods.

Labor–Leisure Trade-Offs

The potential uses of Ed's time are illustrated by the labor–leisure trade-off. Our variation on this analysis also helps illustrate the investment aspects to health demand.

TRADING LEISURE FOR WAGES

In Figure 6.1, the x-axis represents Ed's work and leisure time. Suppose that he considers his time spent creating health investment to be "health-improvement time" and that he calls T_B his leisure. In reality, he may do some health-improving activities at work, may obtain some enjoyment or satisfaction from healthful time, and so on, but assume here that these categories are exclusive. Assume further that the number of days lost to ill health and the number of days spent on health-enhancing activity are fixed (we relax this assumption later). Variables T_{L0} and T_{H0} refer to time lost and time spent on healthy activities, respectively. The maximum amount of time that he has available to use for either work, T_W, or leisure, T_B, is thus $365 - T_{H0} - T_{L0}$, so:

$$\text{Time Available for Work or Leisure} = 365 - T_{H0} - T_{L0} = T_W + T_B \qquad \textbf{(6.4)}$$

Thus, leisure time, T_B, is measured toward the right while time spent at work, T_W, is measured toward the left. For example, if Ed chooses leisure time, OA, then he has simultaneously chosen the amount of time at work indicated by AS. These are indicated in Figure 6.1.

Recall that Ed's total amount of time available for either work or leisure is given by point S. If he were to choose point S for the period, he would be choosing to spend all this available time in leisure; that is, in the pursuit of the pleasures of life (albeit without the wage income to produce them). The y-axis represents income, which can be obtained through work. This income can be used to purchase either market health goods or other market goods. Thus, if he chooses point S, he will be able to purchase no market goods because he has no earned income.[2]

[2]We ignore here income that is earned through nonwork efforts—for example, through returns to financial investments.

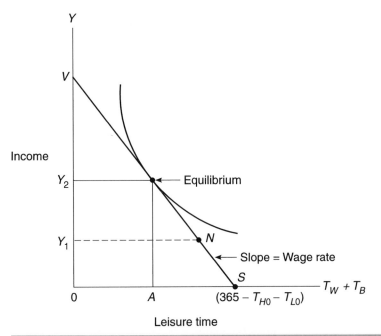

FIGURE 6.1 Labor–Leisure Trade-Off.

If, beginning at S, Ed gives up one day of leisure by spending that day at work, to point N, he will generate income equal to OY_1. OY_1 thus represents his daily wage. In economic terms, this quantity represents income divided by days worked—that is, the daily wage. Thus, the slope of the line VS depicting the labor–leisure trade-off reflects the wage rate.

PREFERENCES BETWEEN LEISURE AND INCOME

The consumer has preferences regarding income and leisure, just as he or she had among other goods in chapter 2. As before, Ed would like more income and more leisure, so the indifference curve map is shaped normally. In Figure 6.1, in equilibrium, Ed's trade-off of leisure and income is the same as the market trade-off, which is the wage rate. Here, he takes amount OA of leisure and trades amount AS of leisure for income, OY_2.

In Figure 6.2, Ed has made a different choice with respect to time spent investing in health status. To illustrate, suppose that time spent on health-producing activities, T_H, is increased from T_{H0} to T_{H1}. Correspondingly, suppose that the number of days lost to ill health has been reduced from T_{L0} to T_{L1}. What effect will this have on the horizontal intercept, which is the total time remaining for work or leisure? On the one hand, time spent producing health reduces time available for other activities. On the other hand, time spent on health investment increases health stock and in turn reduces time lost to illness.

If the net effect is a gain in available time, then this illustrates the pure investment aspect of health demand. The health investments "pay off" in terms that not only add to potential leisure but that also increase the potential income, shifting the income–leisure

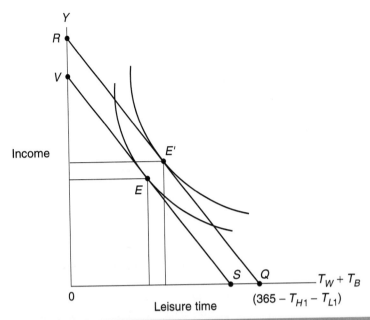

FIGURE 6.2 Increased Amount of Healthy Time Due to Investment.

curve outward from *VS* to *RQ*. The expenditure of time (and medical care, too) for health-producing activities may *later* improve Ed's available hours (because he is sick less) of productive activity.

As a result of his investment, Ed can increase his utility, moving from point *E* to point *E'*. Not only does investment in health lead to his feeling better, but it also leads to more future income and may lead to more leisure, as well.

The improvement in health status also might increase Ed's productivity at work, perhaps resulting in a higher wage and thus a steeper income–leisure curve. In any case, it is clear that Ed might wish to engage in activities to improve his health, even if the only value of health is its effect on his ability to earn future income.

The Investment/Consumption Aspects of Health

The Grossman model describes how the consumer simultaneously makes choices over many periods or years. It is also instructive, on occasion, to represent a whole life span as a single period. This can show the dual nature of health as both an investment good *and* a consumption good.

PRODUCTION OF HEALTHY DAYS

Health is a productive good that produces healthy days. This production function relationship is illustrated in Figure 6.3. The horizontal axis measures health stock in a given period. The greater one's stock of health, the greater the number of healthy days, up to a natural maximum of 365 days. The bowed shape of the curve illustrates the law of diminishing marginal returns (additional resources have decreasing marginal impacts on

FIGURE 6.3 Relationship of Healthy Days to Health Stock.

the output). Note also the concept of a health stock minimum shown as H_{min}. At this point, production of healthy days drops to zero, indicating death.

PRODUCTION OF HEALTH AND HOME GOODS

Consider the possibilities for producing health, H, and home good, B, given the total amount of time available. Figure 6.4 shows this production possibilities trade-off. Note that the curve differs from the usual production possibilities curve in several respects. First, from point A to point C, increments to health increase the amounts of both home good, B, and health, H, attainable. It is necessary to increase health beyond H_{min} in order to obtain income and leisure time from which to produce B.

Moving along the production possibilities curve, Ed Kramer is shifting his uses of available time and is distributing his purchases of market goods. Thus, the move from E to C indicates that he has made more time available for health and that this move has reaped the side benefit (increased leisure time) of increasing the availability of market goods and time used to increase production of bread.

U_1 = Ed derives utility from bread only

U_2 = Ed derives utility from both health and bread

FIGURE 6.4 Allocation of Resources between Health and Bread.

Suppose that Ed gets no psychic benefit at all from health; that is, health is desired solely for its effect on the ability to produce income and the leisure time to produce the home good bread, B. This would imply that his indifference curves between H and B would be vertical lines. (Ed places no intrinsic value on H, so he would not trade any B to get additional health.) In such a case, he would maximize his utility by producing as much B as possible. The utility-maximizing choice would be at point C, a point of tangency between indifference curve U_1 and the production possibilities curve. He produces amount B_0 of the home good, and H_0 of health.

Now assume instead that Ed achieves utility not only from producing B, but also directly from health itself (he likes feeling better). In this case, his indifference curves, U_2, have the more familiar shape in Figure 6.4, sloping downward from left to right. It is more realistic to say that he values health both as a consumption good, as is shown in Figure 6.4, *and* as an investment in productive capacity. The former suggests that he enjoys feeling healthy; the latter, that feeling healthy makes him more productive, thus allowing him to earn more. In general, by including Ed's "feeling healthy" in this consumption feature of the model, he will choose a higher health stock than under the pure investment model. Health stock, H_1, exceeds H_0 in Figure 6.4. This is achieved by Ed's taking less home good, or $B_1 < B_0$.

Investment over Time

Choices are made for the many periods over one's life cycle, rather than just for one representative period. As a beginning point for each analysis, we feature the pure investment version of the model (point C in Figure 6.4). We then discuss the analytical changes when consumers, in addition, value health intrinsically (point D in Figure 6.4).

Because health is a capital good, it is necessary to understand the cost of capital as well as the capital good demand process. A health clinic, for example, purchases thousands of dollars of X-ray equipment. The return to the X-ray equipment is in the future earnings that ownership of the equipment can provide.

Suppose that an X-ray machine costs $100,000, and that its price does not change over time. Suppose that the annual income attributable to the use of the X-ray machine is $20,000. Is purchasing the machine a good investment? Consider the alternative: Instead of purchasing the X-ray machine, the clinic could have put the $100,000 in a savings account, at 5 percent interest, yielding the following:

$$100,000 \times 1.05 = 105,000 \text{ at the end of Year 1}$$
$$105,000 \times 1.05 = 110,250 \text{ at the end of Year 2}$$
$$110,250 \times 1.05 = 115,763 \text{ at the end of Year 3}$$
$$115,763 \times 1.05 = 121,551 \text{ at the end of Year 4}$$
$$121,551 \times 1.05 = 127,628 \text{ at the end of Year 5}$$

For the investment in an X-ray machine to be desirable by these criteria, it should provide at least $27,628 in incremental revenue over the five years.

The problem is more complicated, however, because most capital goods depreciate over time. Suppose that the clinic knows that the X-ray machine will wear out (or depreciate), so that it will be worth only half its original value in five years. The clinic must earn enough not only to cover the opportunity cost from the bank, but also to maintain

the value of the machine. For the investment to be worthwhile, then, it must not only earn the competitive 5 percent return each year, it also must provide enough return to cover depreciation of the machine. This suggests that the cost of holding this capital good for any one year, as well as over time, will equal the opportunity cost of the capital (interest foregone) plus the depreciation (deterioration of value).

The Demand for Health Capital

Conventional economic analysis provides a powerful conceptual apparatus by which to analyze the demand for a capital good. The cost of capital, in terms of foregone resources (for health capital, both time and money), is a *supply* concept. The other needed tool is the concept of the marginal efficiency of investment, the MEI, a *demand* concept that relates the return to investment to the amount of resources invested.

MARGINAL EFFICIENCY OF INVESTMENT (MEI)
AND RATE OF RETURN

The MEI can be described in terms of the X-ray machine example. A busy clinic may wish to own more than one X-ray machine. But how many? The clinic management may logically consider them in sequence. The first machine purchased (if they were to buy only one) would yield a return as we have discussed. Suppose that return each year were $20,000.

We also can calculate the rate of return, which would be $20,000/$100,000 or 20 percent per year. The management would buy this machine if the incremental revenue brought in covered its opportunity cost of capital and the depreciation. In terms of rates, management would choose to own the first X-ray machine as long as the rate of return, 20 percent, were greater than the interest rate (the opportunity cost of capital) plus the depreciation rate.

If management considered owning two machines, it would discover that the rate of return on the second X-ray machine probably would be less than the first. To understand this, consider that a clinic buying only one X-ray machine would assign it to the highest-priority uses, those with the highest rate of return. If the clinic were to add a second X-ray machine, then logically it could be assigned only to lesser-priority uses (and might be idle on occasion). Thus, the second machine would have a lower rate of return than the first. The clinic would then purchase the second machine only if its rate of return were still higher than interest plus depreciation.

THE DECREASING MEI

Other machines probably could be added at successively lower rates of return. In Figure 6.5, the marginal efficiency of investment curve, MEI, describes the pattern of rates of return, declining as the amount of investment (measured on the horizontal axis) increases. In Figure 6.5, the cost of capital (that is, the interest rate, r, plus the depreciation rate, δ_0) is shown as the horizontal line labeled $(r + \delta_0)$. The optimum amount of capital demanded is thus H_0, which represents the amount of capital at which the marginal efficiency of investment just equals the cost of capital. This equilibrium occurs at point A.

Like the marginal efficiency of investment curve in this example, the MEI curve for investments in health also would be downward sloping. This occurs because the

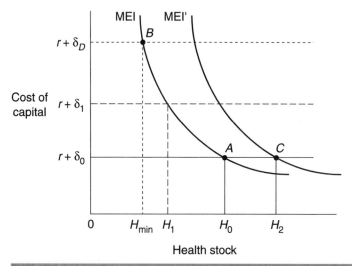

FIGURE 6.5 Optimal Health Stock.

production function for healthy days (see Figure 6.3) exhibits diminishing marginal returns. The cost of capital for health would similarly reflect the interest rate plus the rate of depreciation in health. Understand that a person's health, like any capital good, also will depreciate over time. Thus, the optimal demand for health is likewise given at the intersection of the MEI curve and the cost of capital curve $(r + \delta_0)$.

Changes in Equilibrium: Age, Wage, Education, and Uncertainty

The model depicted in Figure 6.5 provides a useful way to investigate several important model implications. Return to Ed Kramer. How does his investment in health change in response to changes in age, wage, and education? Consider age first.

AGE

One may ask in this context how the consumer's optimal stock of health varies over a lifetime. In this model, the person's death itself is endogenous. Endogenous means that this variable is determined within the model, not external to it. Ed chooses his optimal life span, a life span that is not infinite. By this model, all of us, at some time, will optimally allow our health stock to dissipate to H_{min}. This feature depends in a critical way on how the depreciation rate varies with age.

The rate at which Ed's health stock depreciates may increase during some periods of life and decline during others. Eventually, as he ages, the depreciation rate is likely to increase. In other words, the health of older people is likely to deteriorate faster than the health of younger people.

Consider then the effect of aging on Ed's optimal health stock. Return to Figure 6.5. We assume that the wage and other features determining the MEI are not substantially altered by this aging. However, by hypothesis, the depreciation rate, δ, increases with

age from δ_0 to δ_1 and ultimately to δ_D. These assumptions imply that the optimal health stock decreases with age.

This situation is shown in Figure 6.5 by the fact that the optimal health at the younger age, H_0, is greater than H_1, the optimal stock at the older age. Higher depreciation rates increase the cost of holding health capital stock. We adjust to this by holding a greater amount of health in periods when health is less costly. In old age, health depreciation rates are extremely high, δ_D, and optimal health stock falls to H_{\min} at point B.

This conclusion is consistent with the observation that elderly people purchase a greater amount of medical care, even as their health deteriorates. Grossman explains the phenomenon:

> Gross investment's life cycle profile would not, in general, simply mirror that of health capital. . . . This follows because a rise in the rate of depreciation not only reduces the amount of health capital demanded by consumers but also reduces the amount of capital supplied to them by a given amount of gross investment (p. 238).

Other features of the model suggest that people generally will increase their gross investment (the amount of dollars spent) in health as they age. This suggests in turn that the elderly would demand more medical care than the young, as we frequently note to be the case.

Thus, the pure investment model generates the prediction that optimal health will decline as the person ages. Will this prediction change when we more realistically assume that an individual also will value health for consumption reasons (good health makes one feel better)? The issue turns on whether older persons get more or less direct utility from the enjoyment of healthy days. If people increase their valuation of healthy days as they age, this offsets the predicted health stock decline somewhat. However, we have no theoretical reasons, intuition, or empirical evidence to suppose that this is true.

WAGE RATE

Figure 6.5 illustrates the effect of a change in the wage rate on Ed's optimal level of investment. Increased wage rates increase the returns obtained from healthy days (8 hours' work will bring in $128 rather than $120 if the wage rate rises to $16 from $15). Thus, higher wages imply a higher MEI curve, or MEI'.[3]

Assume now that the original MEI curve describes the lower-wage case and yields optimal health stock, H_0. MEI', above MEI, shows the marginal efficiency of investment for someone with higher wages. At new equilibrium point C, the higher wage will imply a higher optimal level of health stock, H_2, in this pure investment model. The rewards of being healthy are greater for higher-wage workers, so increased wages will tend to increase their optimal capital stock.

The model illustrates an additional rich implication of the wage factor. Consider that when Ed retires, his wage effectively drops to zero. The pure investment version implies that he would change his optimal health stock to H_{\min} upon retirement. Once

[3]This result is not unambiguous. Although the increased wage rate potentially increases the return to investment, it also represents an increased opportunity cost of time in producing health investment. Hence, the MEI curve may shift downward, and it is possible that the equilibrium demand for health investment will fall.

he retires, he would make no further investment in health, but instead would allow health to depreciate until death.

How would our analysis be amended by considering the consumption aspects of health—that is, that good health makes one feel good? First, the retired person would presumably continue to obtain utility directly from healthy days. Thus, optimal health stock would not necessarily drop to H_{min} directly upon the person's retirement, but it would do so only when depreciation rates became sufficiently severe.

Second, if retirees and those who are still working obtain utility directly from healthy days, then the only significant change upon retirement would be the pure investment aspects. Therefore, even when we include the consumption aspects of health, we would expect people to reduce their health stock upon retirement.

EDUCATION

Education is of special interest in the demand for health. Recall that education is seen as a factor that improves the efficiency with which one can produce investments to health and the home good. The effect of education is illustrated in Figure 6.5. Here the MEI curve illustrates the marginal efficiency of investment for the consumer with a low level of education (measured, for example, by years of schooling), while the MEI′ curve illustrates the same person with a higher level of education. This model indicates that because education raises the marginal product of the direct inputs, it reduces the quantity of these inputs required to produce a given amount of gross investment.

It follows that a given investment in health can be generated at less cost for an educated person, and thus he or she experiences a higher rate of return to a given stock of health. The result, as shown, is that the more educated person will choose a higher optimal health stock, H_2, than the less educated person who will choose H_0.

This explains the widely observed correlation between health status and education. Educated people, *ceteris paribus,* tend to be significantly healthier. However, this explains only the correlation of health status and education from the supply side in that it considers only the increased efficiency with which we produce health. One also might wish to explain education from the demand side.

Educated people are likely to recognize the benefits of improved health. They may enjoy eating nutritious food or doing physical exercise. They may recognize the dangers of smoking and the long-term problems of overexposure to the sun. They may enjoy feeling and looking good. As such, all else equal, they would have a greater taste for health relative to other goods.

The demand for health due to education is difficult to separate from the supply effect of education, which implies more productivity in producing health. Clearly, however, both exist and are important.

UNCERTAINTY

The Grossman model starts with the assumption of perfect certainty as to future outcomes as do most economic models. However, outcomes are not always certain.[4] What impact does uncertainty have on the optimal level of health investment and health

[4]The role of physician uncertainty with regard to treatment outcomes is central to the study of small area variations, which is discussed further in chapter 10.

capital? In a given year, Ed Kramer has to choose how much to invest in health care. Alternatively, he may choose to consume his resources, or he may choose to invest in a nonhealth financial asset, which by assumption is less risky than health investment. Following Chung (1996), two effects can occur.

Suppose that Ed's earnings depend on his health. If he were to fall ill next year, his ability to work and his earnings (the return on his next year's health capital) would fall, and Ed is concerned about that risk. An additional dollar of investment in health capital this year will help insure against that loss by increasing his health capital stock, and hence his earnings and consumption next year. This first effect, the improvement of future earnings, will thus lead Ed to increase his investment in health capital to reduce his risk.

However, Figure 6.5 shows that the marginal efficiency of investment is downward sloping. This second effect means that unless changes occur in productivity, increased health investment has a lower return. Therefore, if the increased investment this year has no impact on Ed's ability to earn income next year (Ed gets headaches, but he still can work full days for a full day's pay), then increased risk will affect health investment negatively by lowering the return on the health investment.

We do not live in an either/or world, so if the first effect is larger than the second, increased risk will lead to more investment in health capital. If the second is larger than the first, Ed either will choose current consumption rather than health investment or alternatively will invest in a financial asset that, by assumption, is less risky than health investment.

Empirical Analyses Using Grossman's Model

In the last several years, many researchers have examined health production using Grossman's model. The resulting literature examines the separable impacts of age and education. It also looks at the various time components of health investment within families. Finally, the analytical methods and insights from the Grossman model permit researchers to examine the impacts of health status on the demand for health and health care.

Sickles and Yazbeck (1998) developed and estimated a structural model of health production that looks at the demand for leisure and the demand for consumption for elderly males. Measuring health production is a difficult problem. The authors use a Quality of Well-Being (QWB) scale, developed by Kaplan and Anderson (1988), based on mobility, physical activity, social activity, and physical symptoms and problems.

They find that both health care and leisure consumption tend to improve health. A 1 percent increase in health-related consumption improves health by from 0.03 percent to 0.05 percent. Depending on the technique used, the impact of a 1 percent increase in leisure increases health by 0.25 percent to 0.65 percent.

Strauss et al. (1993) examine the depreciation of health capital by using indicators of adult health for men and women in Malaysia, Jamaica, Bangladesh, and the United States. They find that activity limitation increases with age; in Grossman's terms, this implies that health decreases. Furthermore, this activity limitation tends to occur more frequently for women than for men. They also find that increased education leads to improved health, but that the impact of education decreases for older people.

Mwabu, Ainsworth, and Nyamete (1993) examine the impacts of both market goods and time prices on the production of health care in Kenya. Higher relative prices lead

Rational Addiction—An Adaptation of the Demand for Health

Economists Gary Becker and Kevin Murphy (1988) provide an interesting perspective on addictive behavior and describe conditions under which a rational person would choose to consume an addictive good or service. Their work is interesting because of its economic content and because it challenges our common moral concepts and attitudes toward addiction. It also offers similarities and contrasts with Grossman's model of the demand for health.

Becker and Murphy argue that addictive behavior (as any current or former smoker would agree) must provide some pleasure or people would not pursue it. One necessary condition for a good to be addictive, in their model, is that past consumption of the good increases the marginal utility of current consumption of the good. Becker and Murphy conceive of past consumption as contributing to "consumption capital" regarding the good in question. For example, smoking cigarettes presently may entail a learning experience in the sense that future consumption of an additional cigarette becomes more enjoyable. This important feature of their model is also general in that it applies to many goods and services and does not necessarily separate those goods that society has made taboo or bad. For example, listening to Mozart presently also may entail a learning experience. Mozart symphonies may become more enjoyable in the future as this learning experience continues.

A characteristic of many addictions, however, is that they *are* harmful. Harmful, in the Becker and Murphy context, means that the capital good—that is, the consumption capital—has harmful effects similar to a reduction in health status in the Grossman model. Smoking cigarettes, for example, may reduce healthy days, and may reduce income. Such harmful effects are part of what Becker and Murphy call the "full price" of the addictive good.

In the model, a good is potentially addictive to the consumer if a certain pattern appears over time. It occurs when the effects of present consumption of the good tend to increase future marginal utility more than they increase future full price. This pattern is called "adjacent complementarity."

For example, the potential cigarette smoker would choose to start smoking, even knowing that it is addictive, if smoking tends to increase future enjoyment from smoking more than it increases future harmful effects from smoking. The interesting aspect is that this dynamic model explains why a rational person may choose to ingest a harmful substance, knowing fully its harmful effects.

A permanent increase in the tax on cigarettes may reduce consumption by a considerable extent, even though smokers are addicted. Estimates of the price elasticity of cigarettes are usually thought to be between 0.2 and 0.7 in absolute value, with some estimates higher (toward 1.0). This evidence suggests that addictive consumption patterns for cigarettes do respond rationally to economic stimuli. How the individual values the present relative to the future determines how reactive he or she will be to the imposition of such a tax.

Current researchers are making use of such models to study the implications of many public health policies regarding addictive behavior. Chaloupka (1991) and Cameron (1997), among others, apply rational addiction models to the impacts of cigarette prices and taxes. Chaloupka, looking at the United States, finds support for the models. Cameron, examining Greek smokers does not. Generally speaking, however, most studies that are based on appropriate data do provide support for the rational addiction model.

consumers to shift among (from more expensive to less expensive) health care providers, and the higher relative prices also move some consumers to treat themselves or to use traditional healers. The authors also find that women are more responsive to time and monetary costs of medical care than are men, but that they use medical care more frequently.[5]

Kenkel (1994) investigates health investment through demands for preventive care. He estimates the determinants of women's purchases of medical screening services, designed for the early detection of breast and cervical cancer. Annual use of these screening tests decreases with age, a result consistent with women rationally reducing care as the payoff period shortens over the life cycle and as the depreciation rate rises. Furthermore, increased schooling tends to increase the use of the screening services, implying more efficiency in producing health.

Grossman's model also suggests ways in which health status can impact demand for health. Wedig (1988) finds that those who are less healthy have reduced demand elasticities to seek care. However, health care declines have no measurable impact on the elasticity of demand at mean levels of health care consumption.

Mullahy and Sindelar (1993) examine the relationships among alcoholism, income, and working. Poor health may reduce income either by reducing productivity, which results in lower wages, or by reducing labor market participation (whether and/or how much one is working). Alcoholism is an illness that reduces people's health capital. Mullahy and Sindelar find the labor market participation effects are more powerful than the wage (productivity) effects in reducing earnings, and hence reducing the return to health. By these criteria, successful alcoholism treatment would appear to have significantly positive economic returns.

Grossman's model has guided cross-disciplinary work to examine other health and family issues, as well. Mauldon (1990) looks at the impact of marital disruption on children's health. Among several models, she finds the most support for a health investment model in which marital disruption reduces family resources including family income, parental time, and health care, thus reducing children's health.

In short, Grossman's model has yielded considerable insight into the determinants of health and into the allocation of resources (both time and money) into health-creating activities. It has crossed fields of economics, including labor and development economics, and has provided fruitful results in cross-disciplinary demographic and sociological research, as well.

An Integrated Framework for the Grossman Model*

Earlier in the chapter, we saw four separate decisions for the Grossman model. In maximizing utility subject to both time and money constraints in a given period, the consumer must do the following:

1. Allocate time between work and leisure.
2. Allocate leisure time between health and nonhealth activities.
3. Purchase health (medical) and nonhealth resources.
4. Produce health capital that may help in future years.

[5]These articles come from a conference on families that emphasized Third World countries. Many of the articles were published in the *Journal of Human Resources.* For more discussion, see Schultz (1993).
*For more advanced students.

Although an integrated framework is complicated, it can be presented with some modest changes. The first three decisions are treated explicitly in this analysis. The investment in health capital is considered indirectly by adjusting the model from year to year.[6]

THE LABOR–LEISURE TRADE-OFF

Consider Figure 6.6. Quadrant II indicates the labor–leisure trade-off with respect to the allocation of time to wage-earning activities. The *x*-axis going west from the origin reflects Ed's entire time constraint, *L*; the *y*-axis going north indicates the amount of income, *G*, possible from the labor–leisure choice. The budget constraint indicates the trade-off (a steeper line indicates higher wages) between labor and leisure in the market.

Assuming that no days are lost to illness, T_L, at equilibrium point A', Ed has chosen how many days to work ($365 - T^*$), and how much income, G^*, to earn for spending on the medical (for health production) and home good inputs. Although the market work–leisure decision is made simultaneously with the others, it is useful to treat the process in a two-stage sequence. First, Ed decides how much income and leisure to take in a given year; then, he decides how to divide each of them.

Quadrant II also indicates how health is produced. Ed's resource constraints can be modeled as an Edgeworth Box. The box width indicates the amount of leisure remaining after the allocation of time between work and leisure. The box height indicates the dollars, G^*, of income that he earned. Amount G^* is divided between medical inputs, *M*, and home inputs, $B = (G^* - M)$. The amount of money he spends on medical inputs, M^*, is measured downward from G^*; the remainder, B^*, is spent on home inputs.[7]

The isoquants in the Edgeworth Box are mapped in opposite directions (with health investment $= 0$ in the northwest corner and home good production $= 0$ in the southeast corner). The contract curve indicates that any change in Ed's allocation of time and market inputs to the production of one of the two goods must decrease the production of the other good.[8]

Moving to Quadrant I, we can show that the analyses depend on the relative intensities (market inputs per day) of the two production processes. We begin by assuming that health investment uses more market inputs per day (it is less time intensive) than the home good. Economic theory has shown that differential intensities with either constant or decreasing returns to scale provide a production possibilities curve (*PPC*) that is bowed outward from the *y*-axis.

[6]This model is a simplified version of a presentation by Goodman, Stano, and Tilford (1999). For our presentation, we will assume that the relative market prices of health market inputs and home inputs, as well as wage rates, are constant.

[7]Our treatment of the Edgeworth Box, following Bator (1957), considers an endowment of wage income and leisure time. In this presentation, we normalize the prices of home inputs and medical inputs each to 1 so that quantities reflect expenditures.

[8]Although all of these variables are determined simultaneously, this aspect can be considered as follows. Given optimal G^*, Ed maximizes utility with respect to health investment, *I*, and home good, *C*, allocating *M* and T_h such that:

$$\max U\,[C\,(G^* - M, T^* - T_h), I\,(M, T_h)].$$

The optimum with respect to the marginal products of the production functions is the tangency of *I* and *C* isoquants.

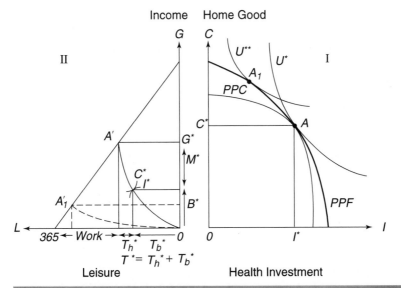

FIGURE 6.6 Two-Quadrant Representation of the Grossman Model.

Health is resource intensive. Production technologies and preferences jointly determine the amount of leisure, amount of work, and purchases of medical inputs and home inputs.

Ed recognizes that time and market goods are complements for some health investment activities and substitutes for others. Niacin tablets, which reduce cholesterol levels, substitute for time-consuming exercise. In contrast, cholesterol tests require time-consuming visits to a clinic. However, in a two-dimensional framework, it is essential only that the factor intensity of health investment differs from the factor intensity of home production (otherwise, no distinction is made between the two goods).

OPTIMAL LEVELS OF HEALTH INVESTMENT AND THE HOME GOOD

Assume that Ed has chosen a large amount of leisure at A'_1, and thus has little earned income as shown by the horizontal Edgeworth Box (dashed lines) in Quadrant II. Because health investment I is assumed to be market intensive, Ed would be able to produce only a small amount of it, although he would be able to produce considerable amounts of home good C (as shown at A_1 in Quadrant I). It is likely that more I (and less C) would increase utility so that Ed will move northeast up the income–leisure trade-off in Quadrant II. Each point on the leisure-income line provides a box in Quadrant II and a corresponding PPC in Quadrant I. We show, in Quadrant I, only the PPC corresponding to the box determined by A and the production possibilities frontier PPF (*i.e.,* the outer portion (or envelope) of all of the $PPCs$ from Quadrant II). Ed chooses optimal levels of I^* and C^* at point A.

Quadrant II indicates how Ed produces I^* and C^*. From the derivation given, Point A (Quadrant I) implies a unique Edgeworth Box in Quadrant II with dimensions G^* and T^*. Moving down the y-axis from G^* shows the amount of medical inputs, M^*, to be combined with leisure, T_h^*, to produce health investment, I^*. The remainder

of time, $T_b^* = T^* - T_h^*$, and the remainder of expenditures, $B^* = G^* - M^*$, are combined to produce home good C^*.

This analysis shows that the optimal amounts of health investment and home goods depend on production and on preferences. Suppose that Ed had preference function U^{**}, valuing the home good relative to health investment. Point A would not be efficient. Ed could choose more leisure (and less income), producing less investment, with the resulting equilibria at points A_1 and A_1', respectively.

The construction of Ed's production trade-offs occurs without any reference to his utility function. Ed may be able to produce health investment efficiently yet not "value" it much, or vice versa. This implies that the demands for leisure and medical inputs depend jointly on the ability to produce and the utility derived from consumption.

Although this presentation does not explicitly address the intertemporal investment aspects of Grossman's model, it can be used to consider them. Health investments are reflected through successive snapshots of this model. Earlier, we ignored sick time. Suppose, however, that Ed typically has been unable to work (i.e., unable to produce either market goods or home goods) 10 days per year due to illness. Relabeling the x-axis in days, this implies an x-intercept at 355 days rather than 365 days. Thus, an increase in health capital may yield an outward parallel shift in the opportunity locus of Quadrant II.

Ed can calculate the investment level, I_h, that would maintain the health capital stock at a constant level over time, but I_h may not be the same as the optimal investment I^* in the given period. If $I^* > I_h$, net health capital rises; if $I^* < I_h$, it falls. The wage rate, or slope of the trade-off, also may be related to the level of health capital. If $I^* > I_h$, increased productivity might be modeled as an increased wage rate.

CHANGES IN EQUILIBRIUM

This section shows how the equilibrium changes with an increase in income. It then indicates the importance of the relative factor intensities of home and health investment production.

Figure 6.7 shows the impact of an increase in nonwage income, such as interest or dividends. The initial equilibrium point A in Quadrant I has (home good/health investment) ratio $(C/I)_0$, produced with (market input/leisure) ratio $(G/T)_0$, noted in Quadrant II. The initial Quadrant II input levels are marked as point a'. The increase in nonwage income shifts the budget line in Quadrant II and the production possibilities frontier to PPF_2 in Quadrant I.

If the new equilibrium has the same Quadrant II (G/T) ratio, the optimal (C/I) ratio remains the same in Quadrant I (where $(C/I)_0$ intersects PPF_2) due to the constant returns to scale assumption. With the *given* utility function, however, increased production of health investment at the expense of the home good provides a Pareto superior improvement. With market-intensive health investment, this implies taking a greater percentage of the increased income in market goods than in leisure at point A_1' in Quadrant II and equilibrium point A_1 in Quadrant I. The new equilibrium input levels are indicated at point a_1'.

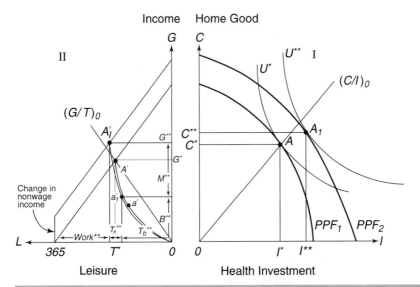

FIGURE 6.7 Income Effects in a Two-Quadrant Representation.

Change in nonwage income, such as interest or dividends.

With Ed's stronger preference toward (market-intensive) health investment, the increased income translates into a high income elasticity for medical inputs and for health investment. If Ed had a stronger preference for the (time-intensive) home good, he would take the increased (wage + nonwage) income in more leisure time. In that case, the increased nonwage income would translate into a modest (if any) increase in total income and a lower income elasticity for health investment. The income elasticity is thus determined jointly by the production technology (Quadrant II) and the taste for health investment relative to the home good.

OBSERVATIONS

This type of analysis can provide a framework for examining the influences of many economic factors including changes in incomes and wages and alternative insurance arrangements (including managed care). Observed differences between the income elasticities for medical goods and health investment can be resolved through relative resource intensities in production of health and nonhealth goods.

Factor intensity plays a key role in several applications. Contrast low and high wage earners, for example. Both are endowed with 365 days per year. Therefore, if health investment is relatively time intensive, the investment opportunities in health capital may be similar for those in either group (although the low wage earners would have much less of the home good). However, if health investment is relatively market intensive, high wage earners, who have more opportunities to purchase market goods than do low wage earners, will be able to combine more market goods with their leisure time. In this case, factor intensity may exacerbate wage rate inequality into further inequality in health investment.

Conclusions

This chapter has addressed the demand for health and medical services from an individual perspective. It has treated health as a good that is produced like all others, using market inputs as well as an individual's time. People benefit from health in four important ways:

1. They feel better when well.
2. They lose less time to illness, and hence can work more.
3. They are more productive when they work and can earn more for each hour they work.
4. They may live longer.

By analyzing the demand for health in this way, we recognize that the demands for health care inputs—from physicians' services, to drugs, to therapy—are demands that are derived from the demand for health itself. Consumers, jointly with providers, allocate resources among health care inputs based on the demand for health. We address the specific demand for health inputs in chapter 8.

Summary

1. It is not medical care per se that consumers want, but rather health itself. Medical care demand is a derived demand for an input that is used to produce health.
2. Consumers do not merely purchase health passively from the market, but instead produce it, spending time on health-improving efforts in addition to purchasing medical inputs.
3. Health lasts for more than one period. It does not depreciate instantly, and thus can be treated as a capital good.
4. Demand for health has pure consumption aspects; health is desired because it makes people feel better.
5. Demand for health also has pure investment aspects; health is desired because it increases the number of healthy days available to work and thus earn income.
6. Consumers prefer more income and more leisure, so indifference curves between income and leisure are negatively sloped. The slope of the line depicting the labor–leisure trade-off is the wage rate.
7. Because health is a capital good, the cost of holding health for any one year, as well as over time, will equal the opportunity cost of the capital (interest foregone) plus the depreciation (deterioration of value).
8. The MEI curve for investments in health are downward sloping. This occurs because the production function for healthy days exhibits diminishing marginal returns. Thus, the optimal demand for health is likewise given at the intersection of the MEI curve and the cost of capital curve $(r + \delta)$.
9. The pure investment model generates the prediction that optimal health will decline as the person ages if the depreciation rate of health increases as a person ages.
10. The rewards of being healthy are generally greater for higher-wage workers, so those with increasing wages will generally tend to increase their optimal health stock.
11. Health can be generated at less cost for more highly educated people, resulting in a higher optimal health stock than for less educated people.

Discussion Questions

1. Why do we treat leisure and earnings as ordinary utility-increasing goods?
2. Describe the aspects of health that make it a consumption good. Describe those that make it an investment good.
3. Give examples of how health is produced from market and nonmarket goods.
4. Why is the depreciation of a capital good a cost to society? In what ways does a person's health depreciate?
5. Why might older people's health care expenditures increase in the Grossman model even though their desired health stock may be lower?
6. List at least three factors that might increase an individual's marginal efficiency of investment in health capital.
7. Suppose that Amanda Robertson goes on to medical school and becomes a physician. Would you expect Amanda's expenditures on medical goods for her own health to be higher or lower than a nonphysician? Why?
8. From your experience, do you think the typical person becomes less healthy upon or shortly after retirement? What does the Grossman model predict?
9. People who earn a higher salary can afford more of all goods, including health care. However, according to Grossman, they will choose a higher desired health stock. Why is this so under the model?

Exercises

1. Draw an isoquant between medical inputs and other inputs in the production of a given amount of health investment. What does the isoquant mean? How would the isoquant look if substitution were limited? If a high degree of substitution were possible?
2. Suppose that no amount of other goods can compensate for a loss in health. How would the individual's indifference curves look? Is this a reasonable assumption in terms of what we actually see taking place?
3. Suppose that a person gets promoted to a job that causes two changes to occur simultaneously: the person earns a higher wage, and a safer environment causes his or her health to depreciate less rapidly. How would these two changes together affect the person's desired health capital?
4. Suppose that John Smith could work 365 days per year and could earn $200 per day for each day he worked. Draw his budget line with respect to his labor–leisure choice.
5. Suppose that John Smith chooses to work 200 days per year. Draw the appropriate indifference curve, and note his equilibrium wage income and labor–leisure choices.
6. Suppose, in exercise 5, that John's wage rises from $200 to $210 per day. Show how his equilibrium level of income and labor–leisure will change.
7. Suppose that John is ill 10 days per year. Draw the impact of this illness on the equilibrium defined in exercise 5. How will it change his equilibrium allocation of earnings and labor–leisure?
8. a. Depict Sara's optimal stock of health capital at age 18, with a high school diploma and a wage of $6 per hour.
 b. Suppose that she invests in a college education, expecting to get a better and higher-wage job. Show how her optimal stock of health capital changes by

the age of 30 due to the increased wage. Then, show how her education would affect her optimal health stock if education also made her a more efficient producer of health.

c. Suppose that after age 30 her wage stays the same. As she ages, show what happens to her optimal stock of health capital, assuming that the depreciation rate of health increases with age.

Demand and Supply of Health Insurance

- Risk and Insurance

- The Demand for Insurance

- The Supply of Insurance

- The Case of Moral Hazard

- Health Insurance and the Efficient Allocation of Resources

- Conclusions

Health insurance is of paramount concern in the discussion of the health economy. Most Americans, and indeed citizens of other countries, do not pay directly for their health care. Rather, an insurance company or other program indirectly pays for much of the care, with the consumer paying directly only a portion of the bill. The patient's portion is sometimes called coinsurance. Insurance coverage is provided through the payment of premiums (in privately financed systems) or taxes (when insurance is provided publicly). The premiums are often, although not always, purchased through the consumer's participation in the labor force.

Health care expenses are uncertain. Many illnesses occur rarely and seemingly at random. When they do, they may cost a great deal, and they can be financially troublesome, if not ruinous, to households. Costs could be so high that without financial help treatment might not be available.

Because insurance is so important to the demand and supply of health care, as well as the government's role in allocating health resources, we introduce several fundamental factors relating to the demand and supply of insurance. This provides a set of tools for addressing issues such as the demand for and supply of health care, the role of information in health care markets, and the variation of health care among various markets. We return to insurance issues in chapter 11, which will look at the operation of insurance markets.

WHAT IS INSURANCE?

For a clear picture of what insurance is, consider the demand for insurance without all of the detailed trappings (deductibles, premiums, coinsurance, etc.) that accompany

141

modern insurance plans. Consider a club with 100 members. The members are about the same age, and they have about the same lifestyles. It seems that about once a year one of the 100 members gets sick and incurs health care costs of $2,000. The incidence of illness seems to be random, not necessarily striking men, women, the old, or the young in any systematic fashion. The club members, worried about potential losses due to illness, decide to collect $20 from each member and put the $2,000 in the bank for safe keeping and to earn a little interest. If a member becomes ill, the fund is used to pay for the treatment. This, in a nutshell, is insurance. The members have paid $20 to avoid the risk or uncertainty, however small, of having to pay $2,000. The "firm" collects the money, tries to maintain and/or increase its value through investment, and pays claims when asked.

In general, insurance reduces the variability of the insureds' incomes by pooling a large number of people and operating on the principle of the law of large numbers; that is, although outlays for a health event may be highly variable for any given person in the insurance pool, the average outlays for the group can be predicted fairly well. The law of large numbers shows that for a given probability of illness, the distribution of the average rate of illness in the group will collapse around the probability of illness as the group size gets larger and larger.

This chapter considers the theory and practice of health care insurance. It is necessary to quantify the idea of risk, as well as attitudes toward risk. With those ideas, it is then possible to consider the structure of insurance policies and how markets evolve to provide them.

INSURANCE VERSUS SOCIAL INSURANCE

It is useful at this point to distinguish between insurance, as provided through the pooling of risk, and government programs (often referred to as social insurance) such as Social Security, Medicare, and Medicaid in the United States. The former is provided through markets in which buyers are protecting themselves against rare events whose probabilities can be estimated statistically. The government programs are insurance programs with the government as insurer, and are distinguished by two features:

1. Premiums (the amounts paid by purchasers) are heavily, and often completely (as in the case of Medicaid), subsidized.
2. Participation is constrained according to government-set eligibility rules.

In addition, government insurance programs often transfer income from one segment of society to another. Given the importance of such social insurance programs, we address an entire chapter (chapter 22) to them later in the text.

INSURANCE TERMINOLOGY

It is helpful to consider some terms that are used in the discussion of insurance. Although much of the analysis that we will consider is in the standard economic language of prices and quantities, the insurance industry has developed a set of definitions that should be understood. These include:

Premium Coverage When people buy insurance policies, they typically pay a given premium for a given amount of coverage should the event occur.

Coinsurance and Copayment Many insurance policies, particularly in the health insurance industry, require that when events occur, the insured person share the loss

through copayments. This percentage paid *by the insured person* is the *coinsurance rate.* With a 20 percent coinsurance rate, an insured person, for example, would be liable (out of his or her own pocket) for a $10 *copayment* out of a $50 charge. The insurance company would pay the remainder, or 80 percent. Thus, coinsurance refers to the percentage paid by the insured; copayment refers to the amount paid by the insured (such as a fixed payment for a prescription).

Deductible With many policies, some amount of the cost of health care is paid by the insured person in the form of a deductible, irrespective of coinsurance. In a sense, the insurance does not apply until the consumer pays the deductible. Deductibles may be applied toward individual claims, or, often in the case of health insurance, they may be applied only to a certain amount of total charges in any given year.

Coinsurance and *deductibles* often are used together. For example, an insurance policy may require that John pay the first $100 of his medical expenses out-of-pocket each year. It may then require that he pay 20 percent of each additional dollar in charges. This policy would then be said to have a deductible of $100 and a coinsurance rate of 20 percent.

Many feel that deductibles and coinsurance are simply ways that insurance companies gouge consumers to make extra money. Economists, in contrast, have found that deductibles and coinsurance may be used to design policies that lead to desirable economic consequences. The requirement that some copayment be paid makes consumers more alert to differences in the true costs of the treatment they are purchasing. The charging of deductibles discourages frivolous claims or visits, and also makes insured people more aware of the results of their actions. Both may serve to avoid claims and to reduce costs.

Risk and Insurance

To this point in the book, we have assumed in our models that all decisions occur under conditions of certainty; that is, consumers know what the prices, incomes, and tastes are and will be. Clearly, however, many decisions are made in which the outcome is risky or uncertain.[1]

We begin by considering the insurance coverage of an event that occurs with the known probability, p, leading to a predictable loss and/or payment. This assumption will be used to characterize individuals' choices under uncertainty. We will then extend the general characterization to health insurance, which differs because the payment may be affected by the insurance. We address this difference once the basic points regarding risk are developed.

EXPECTED VALUE

Suppose that Clyde asks John to play a game in which a coin will be flipped. If it comes up heads, John will win one dollar; if it comes up tails, he will win nothing. How much would John be willing to pay in order to play this game? Analysts rely on the concept of *expected value* for the answer. With an honest coin, the probability of heads is

[1]Sometimes economists distinguish between *risk* and *uncertainty*. Risk refers to a situation in which we can list all outcomes and assign probabilities to them. Uncertainty refers to situations in which we may neither be able to list the outcomes nor assign the probabilities. Except where we make explicit distinctions, we will simplify our exposition by using the two terms interchangeably.

one-half (0.5), as is the probability of tails. The expected value, sometimes called the expected return, is:

$$E = \text{(probability of heads)} \times \text{(return if heads, i.e., \$1)}$$
$$+ \text{(probability of tails)} \times \text{(return if tails, i.e., \$0)}$$

(7.1)

The expected value is 50 cents; that is, $(\frac{1}{2} \times 1) + (\frac{1}{2} \times 0)$. If he uses the decision criterion that he will play the game if the expected return exceeds the expected cost, John will play (pass) if it costs him less (more) than 50 cents.[2]

The special case where the price of the gamble is exactly 50 cents and is equal to the expected return is analogous to a situation in insurance in which the expected benefits paid out by the insurance company are equal to the premiums taken in by the company. This equality of expected benefit payments and premiums is called an *actuarially fair* insurance policy. In reality, insurance companies will have additional administration and transaction costs that they also will have to cover to break even, but the definition of an actuarially fair policy provides a benchmark in talking about insurance.

MARGINAL UTILITY OF WEALTH AND RISK AVERSION

The foregoing example implies that John is indifferent to risk. That is, for him the incremental pleasure of winning 50 cents (one dollar less the amount he paid to play) is exactly balanced by the incremental displeasure of losing 50 cents. Suppose, however, the sizes of the bets were changed so that the coin flip would now yield $100, or nothing, and that John was now asked to bet $50 to play. He may now refuse an actuarially fair bet—$50—on the grounds that he cannot afford to risk the $50 loss if the coin lands tails. This suggests that the disutility of losing money is larger than is the utility of winning a similar amount. This would be true, for example, if he felt that the utility of an extra dollar of wealth were worth more when he is relatively poorer than the utility of an extra dollar of wealth is worth when he is relatively richer. The utility from an extra dollar is called the marginal utility of wealth.[3]

It is important to incorporate the individual's utility of wealth function into the analysis. In chapter 2, we assumed that consumers can only rank bundles but could not (and need not) compare magnitudes of satisfaction. To understand the utility model of risk behavior, however, we must further assume that consumers can rank alternatives *and* compare their magnitudes.

Consider the top panel of Figure 7.1. Suppose that John's wealth is $ 10,000. That amount of wealth gives him a utility level $U_1 = 140$ and allows him to buy some basic necessities of life. This can be denoted as point A.

Suppose his wealth rises to $20,000. Will his utility double? While it is hard to know for certain what will happen, it is likely that the next $10,000 will not bring him the incremental utility that the first $10,000 brought. Thus, U_2 is likely to be less than twice U_1. Suppose, for example, that $U_2 = 200$. This is denoted as point B.

[2]More generally, with n outcomes, expected value E is written as follows:

$$E = p_1 R_1 + p_2 R_2 + \ldots + p_n R_n$$

where p_i is the probability of outcome i (i.e., p_1 or p_2 through p_n) and R_i is the return if outcome i occurs. The sum of the probabilities, p_i, equals 1.
[3]Wealth refers to the sum (or stock) of the consumer's net assets in money terms. It is related to income, which is the flow of additional funds in any given period. It may be sensible to refer to one or the other for certain discussions, but the substance of the insurance analysis refers to both.

FIGURE 7.1 Top: Total Utility of Wealth and the Impact of Insurance. Bottom: Marginal Utility of Wealth.

Do all of the points on the utility function between U_1 and U_2 lie on a straight line? If they do, this is equivalent to saying that the utility from the 10,001st dollar is equal to the 19,999th dollar, and hence the marginal utility is constant. This also is unlikely. Because the marginal utility of earlier dollars is likely to be larger than that of later dollars, the utility curve is likely to be bowed out, or concave, to the *x*-axis.

The marginal utility of wealth is the amount by which utility increases when wealth goes up by one dollar. This rise in utility, divided by the one-dollar increase in wealth, is thus the slope of the utility function. The bowed shape of the utility function shows a slope that is getting smaller or flatter as wealth rises; thus, the marginal utility of wealth is diminishing. This is graphed in the bottom panel of Figure 7.1 as points A_1, F_1, and B_1. When the marginal utility of wealth is decreasing, the consumer is said to be risk averse.

Suppose that John's wealth increases to $20,000. He understands, however, that if he becomes ill, which may occur with probability 0.05, his expenses will cause his wealth to decline to $10,000. If this occurs, he can calculate his *expected utility, E*:

$$E = 0.95 \times (\text{utility of } \$20{,}000) + 0.05 \times (\text{utility of } \$10{,}000)$$
$$= 0.95 \times (200) + 0.05 \times (140) \tag{7.2}$$
$$= 190 + 7 = 197.$$

Thus, the expected utility is 197 or point C because of the risk of illness. Geometrically, this is the line segment between points A and B, evaluated at wealth level \$19,500. It must be compared to the utility of 199 (point D), corresponding to the utility that he would receive if he were certain to have \$19,500. Point D is sometimes referred to as the *certainty equivalent*. Clearly, the uncertainty leads to a loss of 2 units of utility, (i.e., $199 - 197$).

PURCHASING INSURANCE

Suppose that John is able to buy an insurance policy costing \$500/year, such that his wealth would be guaranteed to be \$20,000 irrespective of his health. Is it a good buy? We see that at net wealth of \$19,500, which equals his initial wealth minus the insurance premium, his certainty utility is, in fact, 199. John is better off at point D than at point C, as shown by the fact that point D gives the higher utility. Thus, if insuring to get a *certain* wealth rather than facing the risky prospect makes John better off, he will insure.

We can, in fact, use Figure 7.1 to calculate the maximum amount that John would be willing to pay for the insurance by moving southwest down the utility function to the level of $U = 197$ and reading the level of wealth (off the x-axis) to which it corresponds, or point F. The maximum amount he can spend on insurance and still be better off than were he to go without insurance is his wealth (here, \$20,000) minus the amount (e.g., \$17,000) that provides the same level of utility as point C (which represents his expected utility when not insuring). So, John would be willing to pay \$3,000 for insurance and still be as well off as if he had remained uninsured. This amount (distance FC) reflects John's aversion to risk. The difference between amount FE and the actual premium, CE (or \$500), reflects his consumer surplus from having to pay only \$500, rather than \$3,000, to reduce his risk. This analysis illustrates several facts:

1. Insurance can be sold only in circumstances where there is diminishing marginal utility of wealth or income—that is, when the consumer is risk averse. By examining Figure 7.1, we can see that if marginal utility were constant, a requirement that the individuals pay an actuarially fair premium for insurance would leave them no better off than if they were uninsured.

2. Expected utility is an average measure; the individual either wins or loses the bet. If exposed to risk, John will have wealth, and hence utility, of either \$20,000 (with utility of 200), or \$10,000 (with utility of 140), with a risky expected wealth of \$19,500. Insurance will *guarantee* his wealth to be \$19,500. If he does not fall ill, his wealth will be \$20,000 less the \$500 insurance premium; if he falls ill, his wealth will be \$10,000 plus the \$10,000 payment for the loss of health, minus the \$500 premium—again \$19,500.

3. If insurance companies charge more than the actuarially fair premium, people will have less expected wealth from insuring than from not insuring. Even though people will have less wealth as a result of the purchase of insurance, the increased well-being comes from the elimination of risk.

The Demand for Insurance

Given that risk-averse people will purchase insurance, how much will they purchase? The next two sections present a model introduced by Mark Pauly (1968) to consider the fundamental demand and supply decisions regarding insurance.

HOW MUCH INSURANCE?

We have discussed why John would choose to buy insurance. Now consider how much insurance he would choose. Recall that John's expected utility involves his wealth when ill, with a probability of 0.05, or when healthy, with a probability of 0.95. If ill, his wealth will fall from $20,000 to $10,000.

We address John's optimal purchase by using the concepts of marginal benefits and marginal costs. Consider first a policy that provides insurance covering losses up to $500. Although it would hardly seem worth buying a $500 insurance policy when John loses $10,000 if he is ill, it is a useful place to start.

Suppose that John must pay a 10 percent premium ($50) for his insurance or $1 for every $10 of coverage that he purchases. Consider the following worksheet describing his wealth if he gets sick.

The familiar economic context for the maximization of total net benefits provides the framework for understanding the consumer's choice regarding health insurance. We benefit from health insurance only in the case when we are ill receive the insurance benefit payments. We still pay the insurance premiums when ill, but we gain financially net of those premiums. When well, only the premium applies to us, it is thus a net cost. In turn, the marginal benefits when well will decline as additional insurance coverage is purchased; this is understood by applying the law of diminishing marginal utility. In contrast, the marginal costs when well will rise as additional insurance in purchased. The consumer's solution is to purchase so that the marginal benefits equal the marginal costs.

Insurance Worksheet—$500 coverage		
	Original wealth	$20,000
less	Loss	$10,000
	Remainder	$10,000
plus	Insurance	500
	Sum	$10,500
less	Premium	50
or	**New** wealth	$10,450

If he stays well, his wealth is $20,000 less the $50 premium, or $19,950. His marginal benefit from the $500 from insurance is the expected marginal utility that the additional $450 brings him. His marginal cost is the expected marginal utility that the $50 premium costs him. If John is averse to risk, the marginal benefit (point A) of this insurance policy exceeds its marginal cost (point A'). We plot these points in Figure 7.2.

Should John buy $1,000 of insurance coverage rather than $500? To determine the answer, we must compare the marginal benefits of this next $500 increment to the marginal costs. Because John is slightly wealthier than before, if ill (starting at $10,450 rather than $10,000) the marginal utility from an additional $450 of wealth (calculated as before) will be slightly smaller than before. Hence, the marginal benefits from the second $500 increment will be slightly smaller than for the first $500 increment. His marginal benefit curve, MB_1, is downward sloping, with his new marginal benefit at point B.

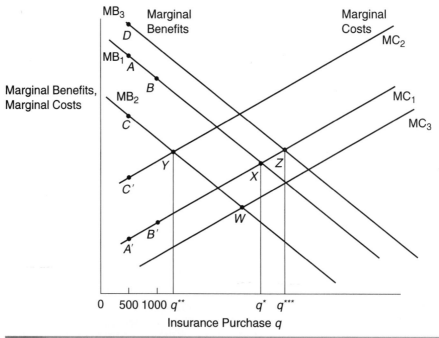

FIGURE 7.2 The Optimal Amount of Insurance.

Similarly, because he is a little less wealthy than before if well, an additional $50 in premiums will cost a little more in foregone (marginal) utility than the first increment at point B'. Thus, his marginal cost curve, MC_1, is upward sloping.

By reiterating this process, we can see that John will adjust the amount of insurance, q, that he purchases to the point at which the marginal benefits equal the marginal cost. The quantity, q^*, at which they are equal (point X) is John's optimum insurance purchase.

CHANGES IN PREMIUMS

How will the insurance decision change if premiums change? Consider first the impact of a higher premium, say 15 percent rather than the 10 percent used earlier. With the 15 percent premium ($75), John faces the following calculation regarding a policy that provides $500 worth of coverage:

	Insurance Worksheet—Increased Premium Rate	
	Original wealth	$20,000
less	Loss	$10,000
	Remainder	$10,000
plus	Insurance	500
	Sum	$10,500
less	New Premium	75
or	**New** wealth	$10,425

If he stays well, his wealth is $20,000 less the $75 premium, or $19,925. John's marginal benefit from the $500 from insurance is now $425 rather than the previous value of $450, so point C lies on curve MB_2 below the previous marginal benefit curve, MB_1. We can fill in additional points on this curve, which reflects the higher premium.

Similarly, John's marginal cost is the expected marginal utility that the (new) $75 premium costs him. This exceeds the previous cost in terms of foregone utility, so point C' lies on curve MC_2 above the previous marginal cost curve, MC_1. Again, we can fill in additional points on this curve and find the intersection of MB_2 and MC_2 at point Y. The resulting analysis suggests that consumers react rationally to increased premiums by reducing their optimum coverage from q^* to q^{**}.

CHANGES IN EXPECTED LOSS

How will the insurance decision be affected by changes in expected losses? Returning to the original example with a premium of 10 percent, suppose that instead of $10,000, John expected to lose $15,000 if ill. Consider, again, the first $500 of insurance coverage. His wealth, if he stays healthy, is $19,950 so nothing changes with respect to marginal cost. John remains on curve MC_1 at point A'. The marginal benefit calculation, however, does change:

	Insurance Worksheet—Increased Expected Loss	
	Original wealth	$20,000
less	*New Loss*	*$15,000*
	Remainder	$ 5,000
plus	Insurance	500
	Sum	$ 5,500
less	Premium	50
or	**New** wealth	$ 5,450

As before, the insurance gives him a net benefit of $450. However, this net benefit increments a wealth of $5,000 rather than $10,000. If we assume that an additional dollar gives more *marginal* benefit from a base of $5,000 than from a base of $10,000, then the marginal benefit curve shifts upward because of the increased expected loss. This provides point D on curve MB_3 in Figure 7.2. It follows that in equilibrium, an increase in the expected loss will increase the amount of insurance purchased at point Z, or q^{***}.

CHANGES IN WEALTH

Finally, consider the impact of changes in an individual's initial wealth. Suppose John was starting with a wealth of $25,000 instead of $20,000. Again, assume a premium rate of 10 percent.

Insurance Worksheet—Increased Wealth

	Increased wealth	*$25,000*
less	Loss	$10,000
	Remainder	$15,000
plus	Insurance	500
	Sum	$15,500
less	Premium	50
or	**New** wealth	$15,450

At the higher level of wealth, the same insurance policy provides a smaller increment in utility, so the marginal benefit curve shifts down from MB_1 to MB_2. However (for the same expected loss), the $50 premium costs less in foregone marginal utility relative to the increased wealth, leading to a downward shift from MC_1 to MC_3. As a result, the new equilibrium value of q at point W may be higher or lower than the original value of q^* (as drawn in Figure 7.2, it is lower). If, however, increased wealth is accompanied by increased losses, then the marginal return curve may shift down less; in such cases, the amount of insurance may increase, because increased expected losses would make increased insurance more desirable.

The Supply of Insurance

In the last example, we assumed a 10 percent premium rate. Ultimately, to determine the amount of coverage an individual *will* buy, we must know how insurers determine the premium. To do this, we develop a model of the insurance market, beginning again with the club that insures its members against illness. The officers of the club do not know, nor necessarily care, who will file a claim.[4] All that is necessary for the club to function as an insurer is that revenues cover costs. In practice, insurance companies will incur administrative and other expenses that also must be covered by premiums.

COMPETITION AND NORMAL PROFITS

Let's return to John's insurance problem from the previous section. John is buying insurance in a competitive market, and under perfect competition, all firms earn zero excess, or normal long-run profits. Recall that John faced a potential illness with a probability of 0.05 (one in 20). He sought to buy insurance in blocks of $500, and at the outset, the insurer was charging him $50 for each block of coverage, or an insurance premium of 0.10 ($50 as a fraction of $500). Assume also that it costs the insurer $5 to process each insurance application. The insurer's profits per policy are:

$$\text{Profits} = \text{Total revenue} - \text{Total costs}$$

[4]It is, in fact, crucial for insurers to recognize whether they are getting a nonrepresentative slice of the risk distribution. This is sometimes referred to as *adverse selection,* and it can lead to financial losses for the insurer. It will be discussed later in the chapter and in chapter 9.

The firm's revenues are $50 per policy. What are its costs? For 95 percent of the policies, the costs are $5, because the insured does not get sick, and hence need not collect insurance. The only costs are the $5 processing costs per policy. The costs for the other 5 percent of the policies are $505, which consist of the $500 payment to those who are ill plus the processing costs of $5.

Thus, the profits per policy are:

$$\text{Profits} = \$50 - (\text{Probability of illness} \times \text{costs if ill}) - \tag{7.3}$$
$$(\text{Probability of no illness} \times \text{costs if no illness})$$
$$\text{Profits} = \$50 - (0.05 \times \$505) - (0.95 \times \$5)$$
$$\text{Profits (premium} = 10\%) = \$50 \text{ (revenues)} - \$30 \text{ (costs)} = \$20$$

These are positive profits, and they imply that another firm (also incurring costs of $5 to process each policy) might enter the market and charge a premium of, say, 8 percent. The cost side of the equation would remain the same but the revenues, which equal the premium fraction multiplied by the amount of insurance, would fall to $40. Hence, profits fall to:

$$\text{Profits (premium} = 8\%) = \$40 - \$25.25 - 4.75 = \$10$$

which is still positive. It is easy to see that entry will continue into this industry until the premium has fallen to $0.06 per dollar of insurance, or 6 percent, which would provide revenues of $30, offset by the $30 in costs, to give zero profits.

A little algebra can verify that the premiums must be tied directly to the probability of the claim. Quite simply, for the firm, the revenue per policy is αq, where α is the premium, in fractional terms. The cost per policy in terms of pay-out is the probability of pay-out, p, multiplied by the amount, q, plus a processing cost, t. So:

$$\text{Profit} = \alpha q - (pq + t) = \alpha q - pq - t \tag{7.4}$$

With perfect competition, profits $= 0$, so:

$$0 = \alpha q - pq - t$$

We can solve for the competitive premium α as:

$$\alpha = p + (t/q) \tag{7.5}$$

This expression shows that the competitive value of α equals the probability of illness, p, plus the processing (sometimes called *loading*) costs as a percentage of policy value, q, or t/q. If loading costs are 10 percent of the policy value, q, then $(t/q) = 0.10$. Hence, in equilibrium $\alpha = (0.05 + 0.10) = 0.15$. The premium for each dollar of insurance, q, is $0.15. If insurers charge less, they will not have enough money to pay claims. If they charge more, the business will have excess profits and other firms will bid down rates in perfectly competitive markets.

Previously, in the discussion on the bearing of risk, we considered insurance policies that would compensate the individual against the loss based solely on the probability of the event occurring. Such rates are referred to as actuarially fair rates. The actuarially fair rates correspond to the rates in which the loading costs, t, approach 0 as a percentage of insurance coverage, hence:[5]

$$\alpha = p + (t/q) = p + 0 = p \tag{7.6}$$

[5]If loading costs, t, are relatively constant per policy, then t/q is likely to approach 0 as q becomes large.

Knowing that premium α equals p under perfect competition (with no loading costs), we can now solve for the optimal coverage against any expected loss. It can be shown that to maximize utility, John will add coverage up to the point where his expected wealth will be the same whether he is ill or well. In the earliest example, the particular illness occurred with a probability of 0.05 and incurred a loss of $10,000. In a competitive insurance market (ignoring loading costs), John's wealth, if well, will be:

$$\text{Wealth (well)} = \$20,000 - \text{cost of insurance, or:}$$
$$\$20,000 - (\text{premium } \alpha) \times (\text{coverage } q)$$

His wealth, if ill, will be:

$$\text{Wealth (ill)} = \$20,000 - \text{loss} + \text{insurance payment} - \text{insurance premium}$$
$$\$20,000 - \$10,000 \text{ loss} + (\text{coverage } q) - (\text{insurance premium } \alpha q)$$

Equating the two, yields:

$$\text{Wealth (well)} = \$20,000 - \alpha q = \$20,000 - \$10,000 + q - \alpha q = \text{Wealth (ill)}$$
$$(7.7)$$

Subtracting $\$20,000 - \alpha q$ from both sides, and rearranging terms yields:

$$q^{opt} = \$10,000$$

John's optimal level of coverage for a loss of $10,000 in the absence of transactions costs is $10,000. The realistic case is that of positive transactions costs, t; in fact loading charges are often substantial. When the realistic case obtains, John's best choice is to insure for less than the full health expense. This standard result from the mathematics of health insurance is often constrasted with the propensity of consumer to seek full coverage.

The Case of Moral Hazard

To this point, we have discussed the theory of risk, as well as the demand and supply of insurance when the events and the losses are random. The insurance policies discussed thus far represent indemnity policies, in which the insurer's liability is determined by a fixed, predetermined amount for a covered event. Indeed the term *indemnity* comes from the Latin *indemnis,* meaning "unhurt." Insurance renders the insured party unhurt by the random event.

In the previous section, we determined that the optimal insurance policy covers all of the loss when there is no transaction cost, and less than the full loss in the more realistic case when transactions costs are positive. We now address the effects of the price system on the provision of insurance.

Thus far, we have assumed that the amount of the loss was fixed—that it did not change merely because people bought insurance. However, in many cases, buying insurance lowers the price per unit of service at the time that the services are purchased. If people purchase more service due to insurance, then many of the insurance propositions just presented must be modified.

DEMAND FOR CARE AND MORAL HAZARD

Suppose John faces the probability $1 - p = 0.5$ that he will not be sick during a given time period and so will demand no medical care. He also faces probability, p, also equal

"Viatical" Life Insurance Deals Get Tougher

Thus far, we have shown that an insurance market will function if the insurers and the insured can predict the probability that the adverse event will occur. Insurers who underestimate the probability or the timing of an event may lose money.

Laura Casteneda writes about recent problems in the "viatical" insurance market. The term *viatical* comes from ancient Rome, where travelers embarking on a difficult journey prepared a package of supplies and money called a viaticum. With viatical settlements, insurance holders immediately receive lump sums of between 60 percent to 90 percent of the face value of the policy, depending on how long they're expected to live. The shorter the time until the expected death, the larger the percentage that is paid to the insured.

For a number of years, viatical brokers have provided settlements to people with AIDS. With an almost certain probability of death, often in a short time, brokers could calculate the probabilities of death and provide funds to ailing patients such that the patients could have cash assets during the last few years of their lives.

The success of a potent combination of drugs called protease inhibitors has extended the lives of many AIDS patients. Although the inhibitors are good news for the AIDS pa-

tients, they are bad for business for many viatical companies. Suppose a broker paid an AIDS patient 80 percent of the face value of a $100,000 policy, based on the expectation that the patient would live for two more years. The economic cost to the broker would be the $80,000 payment plus the interest rate that represents the opportunity cost of carrying the debt. Suppose, however, that the improved treatment enables patients to live for three to four years rather than for two years. What had seemed to be a good "buy" for the broker might become a money-losing proposition.

Casteneda writes that some viatical companies were still buying life insurance policies from AIDS patients but that these companies have had to change the criteria they previously used to make offers to AIDS patients because it is becoming harder to predict when they will die. "Through 1995, we had a sense that AIDS equaled death," said Dr. Mervyn F. Silverman, vice president of a Minneapolis-based viatical brokerage company. "We weren't sure how short the term would be from diagnosis until death. But it was fairly well-assumed it would be the eventuality, and in a matter of two to three years . . . With protease inhibitors, our whole way of thinking has changed."

Source: San Francisco Chronicle, March 10, 1997, p. E2.

to 0.5, that he will contract an illness that requires medical care. In Figure 7.3, panel A, we assume that the demand for medical services is perfectly inelastic; that is, unresponsive to the price of the services. We saw earlier (ignoring the transactions costs) that John would be willing to pay insurance for coverage expenditures P_1Q_1, which represents his expenditures should he need care. An actuarially fair insurance policy would then charge John $0.5P_1Q_1$, and he would purchase the policy because it insured him against the risk of illness.

Suppose, instead, that due to his income, his tastes for care, how ill he is—in short, all of the factors that shape demand—John's demand curve is responsive to price; that is, the quantity demanded varies inversely with price. This is noted in Figure 7.3, panel B.

FIGURE 7.3 Demand for Care and Moral Hazard.

If he purchases insurance that pays his entire loss, then this insurance makes treatment (ignoring time costs) free. Because the marginal price to John is zero, he would demand Q_2 units of care for a total cost of care of P_1Q_2, shown as rectangle $0P_1CQ_2$, which is obviously larger than rectangle $0P_1BQ_1$.[6]

This response to economic stimuli leads to one of two possibilities that was not a problem earlier:

1. If the insurance company charges the premium $0.5P_1Q_1$ for the insurance, the company will lose money. This occurs because the expected payments would be $0.5P_1Q_2$, which is larger.

2. If the insurance company charges the appropriate premium, $0.5P_1Q_2$, for the insurance, John may not buy insurance. This amount may exceed the medical expenses that he would have spent on average had he chosen to self-insure. While John may be willing to pay more than $0.5P_1Q_1$ to avoid the risk, he may not be willing to pay as much as $0.5P_1Q_2$.

This rational response to economic incentives brought about by the elasticity of demand to the price of care is often termed *moral hazard*. Moral hazard refers to the increased usage of services when the pooling of risks leads to decreased marginal costs for the services.[7] Our analysis gives a simple measure of the costs of moral hazard—the excess of premiums over John's expected outlays had he not purchased insurance.[8]

Thus, John's insurance premium has two components. The first is the premium for protection against risk, assuming that no moral hazard exists. The second is the extra re-

[6]Recall that even when the out-of-pocket price is zero, time costs generally keep the full price from being zero.
[7]Moral hazard also may refer to the disincentives created by insurance to reduce the probability of a loss.
[8]One would have to net out the transactions costs of servicing the insurance in this example, because they do not reflect increased use of services.

source cost due to moral hazard. As before, John chooses insurance coverage q^* by weighing marginal costs against marginal returns, whereas before the returns are the utility gains when John is ill. The twist here is that the costs now have two dimensions—the pure premium and the moral hazard. For some categories of care, the second may be important.

This analysis helps predict the types of insurance likely to be provided. It is clear that the optimal level of insurance is likely to increase relative to the expected loss as the degree of moral hazard decreases. Suppose we use demand price elasticity as an indicator of the potential for moral hazard. Theory then suggests the following:

1. Deeper (more complete) coverage for more inelastic services.
2. Development of insurance first for those services that are most inelastic, and only later for more elastic services.

Data on current insurance coverage by area of service support the first hypothesis, and historical data support the second.

EFFECTS OF COINSURANCE AND DEDUCTIBLES

This analysis also provides insight into the impacts of deductible provisions and coinsurance in insurance policies. Returning to Figure 7.3, Panel B, suppose that Q_1 reflects $500 of expenses (rectangle OP_1BQ_1) and that Q_2 is three times Q_1 (rectangle OP_1CQ_2), which reflects $1,500 of expenses. If the insurance contains a deductible, John will compare the position he would attain if he covered the deductible and received level Q_2 free with the position he would attain if he paid the market price for all the medical care he consumed.

Assume again that the probability of illness, p, equals 0.5. Consider first a policy containing a deductible, which requires John to pay the risk premium plus the first $500 of his medical care (rectangle OP_1BQ_1), after which all additional care is free. John will buy this policy because it protects him from risk and allows him to purchase Q_2 units of medical care for $500. His gain is the area under the demand curve, Q_1BQ_2.

Suppose now that the insurance company raises the deductible from $500 to $700. Will John continue to buy the insurance? Recall that without insurance, John would have purchased amount Q_1 of health services; the $700 deductible yields amount Q_3. When ill, John is paying more for the amount $(Q_3 - Q_1)$ of incremental health care than he believes the incremental care value to be. The incremental costs are rectangle Q_1BDQ_3; the incremental benefits are the area under his demand curve (trapezoid Q_1BFQ_3). The difference is triangle BDF, and this represents a welfare loss to John.

However, after paying the deductible, he can get as much additional health care as he wants at zero cost, and he will buy quantity Q_2. This yields welfare gain triangle Q_3FQ_2 (incremental benefits less zero incremental costs). If Q_3FQ_2 (his welfare gain) is larger than BDF (his welfare loss), he buys the insurance, even with the $700 deductible. If BDF is larger than Q_3FQ_2, the loss exceeds the gain, and John is better off self-insuring and spending P_1Q_1 (in this example, $500) with probability 0.5.

Hence, the deductible has two possible impacts. A relatively small deductible will have no effect on the individual's usage. A large deductible makes it more likely that the individual will self-insure and consume the amount of care he or she would have purchased with no insurance.

A wide range of coinsurance coverages has been developed. Many analysts have considered how they may be formulated to lead to more economically efficient outcomes. We turn to that analysis next.

Health Insurance and the Efficient Allocation of Resources

This section examines the impact of health insurance on the demand for health care. Economists often are concerned about the efficient allocation of resources, which occurs when the incremental cost of bringing the resources to market (marginal cost) equals the valuation in the market to those who are buying the resource (marginal benefit). If the marginal benefit is greater (less) than the marginal cost, one could improve the welfare of society by allocating more (fewer) resources to the sector, or individual, and less (more) resources to other sectors.

Consider Figure 7.4, which shows the marginal cost of care and the demand for care by a consumer under alternative conditions of insurance. If this consumer is not insured, then the optimal choice of health care is Q_0 units. The price (including travel time, parking, and the cost of bringing the service to market) reflects the cost to society of bringing the entire package to the market. Based on the consumer's (and the physician's) preferences, the marginal benefit, as described through the demand curve, equals the marginal cost. In economic terminology, this is an efficient allocation.

THE IMPACT OF COINSURANCE

Consider now what happens when John pays only a fraction of the bill, say, at a 20 percent coinsurance rate. The demand curve rotates outward and a new equilibrium is reached with the new quantity demanded, Q_1. The cost of bringing services to market has remained the same, P_0. Services valued at $P_0 Q_1$ rather than $P_0 Q_0$ are now being provided. The incremental amount spent is $P_0 \times (Q_1 - Q_0)$, or the rectangle $A B Q_1 Q_0$.

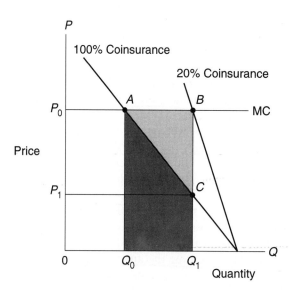

FIGURE 7.4 Health Care Demand with Insurance.

The incremental benefit can be measured by the area under John's original demand curve, ACQ_1Q_0. The remaining triangle ABC represents the loss in well-being that occurs because John is purchasing more health care than is optimal. It is a loss in well-being because the incremental resource cost, ACQ_1Q_0, exceeds the incremental benefits, ACQ_1Q_0, by triangle ABC.

What exactly does this mean? It means that John is led by insurance to act as if he were not aware of the true resource costs of the care he consumes. It also means that the insurance implicitly subsidizes insured types of care (often in organized health care settings) relative to other types of health care (e.g., good nutrition, exercise, uninsured types of care) that may be just as effective. It also subsidizes insured types of care relative to nonhealth goods. Although the degree of this distortion depends on the exact specification of the policy (that is, deductibles, maximum payments, rates of coinsurance), it is apparent that insurance can distort the allocation of resources among health care and other goods.

An interesting example of the moral hazard impacts of insurance comes through interactions between primary and secondary insurance coverages. One example of this type of interaction concerns so-called "Medigap" plans, which provide additional coverage to the elderly above the amount paid by Medicare. Another example involves insured employees who have secondary coverage through their spouse's insurance. Moral hazard problems in these cases may be magnified.

John's employer, General National, provides health insurance to all of its workers, with policies that pay 60 percent of all medical expenditures. Many of General National's workers also are covered under their spouse's insurance plans, but General's plan is considered the primary insurer for these dually covered workers. The secondary policies cover 60 percent of the expenses left uncovered by General's plan.

Figure 7.5 shows a demand curve for visits for the typical General National family if they had no insurance. The family would purchase 12 visits of care per year, at a price of $50, spending $600. If General National is the primary insurer, the out-of-pocket price to its insured will fall by 60 percent to $20 per visit. As drawn, the lower "out-of-pocket" price to patients increases quantity demanded to 24 visits. General National will pay $720, or 60 percent of the $1,200 total cost; its employees will pay $480.

Consider, however, the impact of secondary insurance. By paying 60 percent of the remainder, the secondary insurers reduce the out-of-pocket cost to the employees by another 60 percent, from $20 per visit to $8 per visit. Not surprisingly, the quantity of visits demanded increases again, this time from 24 to 29 visits. The secondary insurers pay $12 per visit, or $348 for the 29 visits. Moreover, the primary insurer, General National, faces increased claims due to demand induced by the coverage of the secondary insurers. General's liability increases from 60 percent of the original $1,200 in expenditures to 60 percent of $1,450 in expenditures—the higher level resulting from the secondary coverage.

A combination of coverages, while providing additional employee benefits, exacerbates the moral hazard problem brought on in general by health insurance. The inefficiencies and welfare losses that occur when decisions of one firm increase the health care costs facing another pose a difficult problem for policy makers.

Losses may be even more significant in the market context as described by Figure 7.6. Clearly, as before, more services are used than are optimal. This has elements of both a redistribution of resources (from consumers and insurers to providers) and a

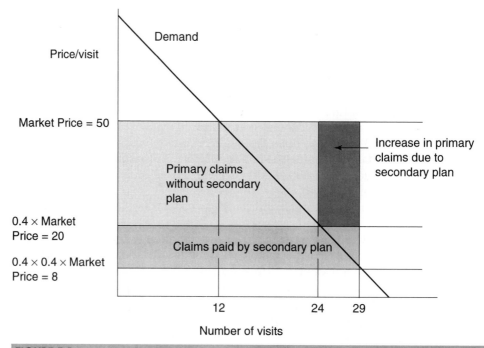

FIGURE 7.5 Impacts of Secondary Insurance on Primary Coverage and Utilization.

deadweight loss (referring to a loss that comes from the misallocation of resources between types of goods). At the original price, P_0, and quantity, Q_0, producers were being paid the marginal cost to bring the products to market. Moving from Q_0 to Q_1 leads to an increase in total expenditures from P_0Q_0 (rectangle OP_0JQ_0) to P_1Q_1 (rectangle OP_1FQ_1).

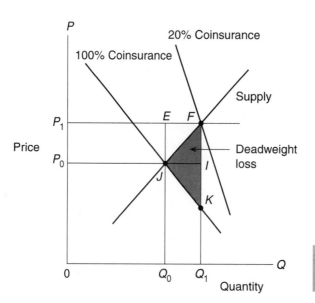

FIGURE 7.6 The Effect of Insurance Cost Sharing with Upward Sloping Supply.

The deadweight loss comes from a misallocation of resources among goods (i.e., more health care is provided than "should" be, according to consumer preferences). Incremental benefits induced by the establishment of a coinsurance regime (i.e., the area under the original demand curve) are measured by the trapezoid Q_0JKQ_1. Similarly, the additional resource costs of bringing the treatment level $(Q_1 - Q_0)$ to society is trapezoid Q_0JFQ_1. The deadweight loss to society from the overproduction of health services due to insurance can thus be summarized as the difference in areas between the two trapezoids, or triangle FKJ.

THE DEMAND FOR INSURANCE AND THE PRICE OF CARE

It is easy to show following Martin Feldstein (1973) that the demand for insurance and the moral hazard brought on by insurance may interact to increase health care prices even more than either one alone. Insurance is related to the expected loss; in health care, this is related in part to the price of care. Increased price of care is related to an increased demand for insurance, as noted in the upward sloping I curve in Figure 7.7.

The second impact is that of insurance on the price of care. More generous insurance and the induced demand in the market due to moral hazard lead consumers to purchase more health care. Curve P_1 shows that if the supply curve for health care is horizontal, then increased insurance will not increase the price of care above PC_1. The equilibrium is at point A, with health care price PC_1 and insurance quantity Q_1.

FIGURE 7.7 The Interaction of Insurance and Price of Care.

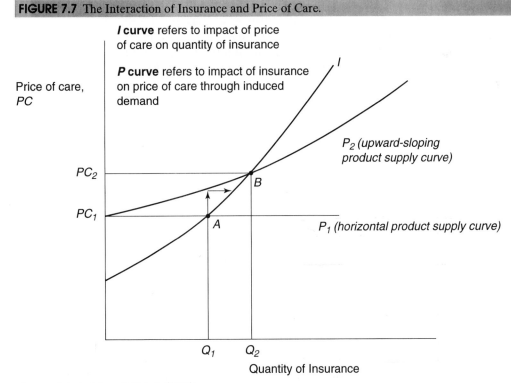

Source: Adapted from Feldstein (1973).

If, however, the product supply curve is less than perfectly elastic (the product supply curve rises), more generous insurance causes market price to rise. This impact is traced as curve PC_2. We see here that the increased product price (the vertical arrow) due to the moral hazard brought on by insurance leads to an increased demand for insurance (the horizontal arrow), which again feeds back on price of care and so on. The moral hazard together with the upward-sloping product supply curve leads to a new equilibrium, B, with higher price of care, PC_2, and higher quantity of insurance, Q_2. The combination of factors leads to a higher price of health care and a higher demand for insurance than would have occurred were there no insurance.

THE WELFARE LOSS OF EXCESS HEALTH INSURANCE

From the preceding discussion, one would ask why society would support policies that seem only to result in misallocations of resources. In fact, the foregoing analyses concentrate only on the costs. It is important to emphasize that people buy insurance, willingly taking on additional costs to themselves, to protect against the risk of (possibly substantial) losses.[9] This protection provides major benefits through the protection against risk; these benefits offset the losses discussed here.

Many researchers have attempted to calculate the welfare losses of excess health insurance. One of the earliest and most prominent of the researchers was Martin Feldstein (1973). In principle, Feldstein's method is straightforward, although the statistical challenges are substantial. The researcher measures the cost of the excess insurance by measuring the demand for health care and the coinsurance rate, and calculating the size of the loss polygons in Figure 7.6.

Measuring the benefits also is straightforward conceptually. In Figure 7.1, the horizontal difference between John's expected utility and his actual utility represented the dollar amount that he would have been willing to pay for insurance over and above the amount that he was charged. Provision of insurance to John at the actuarially fair rate provides a utility gain to John through the reduction of uncertainty that can in principle be measured in money terms. Adding these gains across individuals provides a measure of net benefits to be compared to the costs of the excess insurance.

In plain terms, insurance policies lead to increased costs to society because they lead to increased expenditures on health services. These increased expenditures may occur in several ways:

- increased quantity of services purchased due to decreases in out-of-pocket costs for services that are being purchased already;
- increased prices for the services that are being purchased already;
- increased quantities purchased and prices paid for services that would not be purchased unless they were covered by insurance;
- increased quality in the services purchased, including expensive, technology-intensive services that again might not be purchased unless covered by insurance.

Any procedures that raise the coinsurance rate will tend to reduce the costs of excess insurance, but also will reduce the benefits from decreased risk bearing. Feldstein

[9]One might ask about people whose employers pay the whole insurance bill. Most economists believe that employees choose the insurance in lieu of a compensating take-home wage. Hence, even in this case, the employee has "paid" for the insurance. We discuss this further in chapter 11.

found that the average coinsurance rate was about one-third, or 0.33; that is, people paid 33 cents of every dollar of costs out of their pockets. Raising the coinsurance to 0.50 or to 0.67 would cut the amount of insurance purchased, reducing the excess insurance, but also increasing the amount of risk borne by the clients.

The welfare gains from changed coinsurance, then, are:

$$\text{Welfare gains} = \text{Change in benefits} - \text{change in costs} \qquad \textbf{(7.8)}$$

Feldstein's analysis considers the welfare gains from increasing the average coinsurance rate from 0.33 to 0.67. He discovers that the costs fall much more than do the benefits as coinsurance rates rise. He estimates the welfare gains to be approximately $27.8 billion per year (in $1984) under the "most likely" parameter values.

Feldman and Dowd (1991) update Feldstein's 1960's estimates by using 1980's parameters from the Rand Health Insurance Experiment (as discussed in chapter 5) regarding both price elasticity of the demand curve and attitudes toward risk. They calculate that the lower bound for losses was approximately $33 billion per year (in $1984) and that the upper bound may be as high as $109 billion, depending on the exact parameters used. Although the exact values of these benefits depend crucially on the econometric estimates, the order of magnitude of these losses suggests an important role for the restructuring of insurance in the reduction of excess health care expenditures.

Conclusions

This chapter has concentrated on the unique role of insurance in the health care economy. No other good in people's day-to-day budgets is so explicitly tied to the arrangements for insurance as is health care. Such arrangements have an impact not only on expenditures for serious illnesses and injuries, but also on plans for more routine expenditures such as children's well-care visits (for infants and toddlers) and for eye and dental care.

We have characterized risk and have shown why individuals will pay to insure against it. The result, under most insurance arrangements, is the purchase of more services than might otherwise have been desired by consumers and/or their health care providers. Considerable health care policy debate focuses on how insurance policies can be structured in order to reduce purchases and minimize insurance costs without compromising the health of the insured.

Summary

1. Many illnesses occur rarely and seemingly at random, but when they do, they entail substantial costs.
2. Insurance reduces variability of the insureds' assets by pooling a large number of units and operating on the principle of the law of large numbers. Although outlays for a health event may be highly variable for any given unit in the pool, average outlays for the group are fairly predictable.
3. One should distinguish between insurance, as is provided through the pooling of risk, and government programs such as Social Security, Medicare, and Medicaid, which also redistribute wealth.
4. Insurance can be sold only in circumstances where there is diminishing marginal utility of wealth or income (i.e., when the consumer is risk averse). With constant

marginal utility, requiring that individuals pay actuarially fair premiums would leave them no better off than if they were uninsured.

5. Expected utility is an average measure; the individual either wins or loses the bet.

6. If insurance companies charge more than the actuarially fair premium, people will have less expected wealth through insuring than through not insuring. Even though people will be less wealthy by purchasing insurance, the increased well-being comes from the elimination of risk.

7. In theory, the optimal amount of insurance in the absence of loading costs is to fully insure against the expected loss. With loading costs, the optimal coverage is less than the expected loss.

8. Moral hazard refers to the increased usage of services when the pooling of risks leads to decreased marginal price for the services. This suggests:
 • more complete coverage for price inelastic services, and
 • earlier development of insurance for services that are most inelastic.

9. Insurance policies lead to increased costs to society because they lead to increased expenditures on health services. They provide increased benefits through the reduction of risks.

10. Losses due to excess insurance are estimated at between $33 and $109 billion ($1984) per year. This suggests the importance of restructuring insurance to reduce excess health care expenditures.

Discussion Questions

1. Discuss the difference between cardinal and ordinal utility. Why is cardinal utility necessary for the analysis of risk and insurance?

2. What does the term *moral hazard* mean? Give examples.

3. The deductible feature of an insurance policy can affect the impact of moral hazard. Explain this in the context either of probability of treatment and/or amount of treatment demanded.

4. Describe the benefits to society from purchasing insurance. Describe the costs. Define and discuss the welfare gains from changes in insurance coverage.

5. If only risk-averse people will buy health insurance, why do many people who buy health insurance also buy lottery tickets (an activity more consistent with risk taking)? Speculate on the differences and similarities.

6. Because health insurance tends inevitably to cause moral hazard, will the population necessarily be overinsured (in the sense that a reduction in insurance would improve welfare)? Are there beneficial factors that balance against the costs of welfare loss?

Exercises

1. Suppose that Nathan's employer provides a health insurance policy that pays 75 percent of each dollar over the first $50 spent. If Nathan incurs $500 in expenses, how much will he pay out-of-pocket? What percentage of his expenses will this be?

2. Suppose that rather than flipping a coin, one rolls a die. If the value is 1, 2, 3, or 4, the player wins a dollar. If it is 5 or 6, the player loses a dollar. Calculate the expected return.

3. What would the marginal utility of wealth curve in Figure 7.1 look like if points A, F, D, and B lay on a straight line? If A, F, D, and B were on a curve that was bowed inward toward the x-axis?

4. We have discussed the role of utility functions in the purchase of insurance.
 a. Suppose Edward's utility function can be written as:

 $$U = 10Y \text{ where } U \text{ is utility and } Y \text{ is income/month.}$$

 What is his marginal utility if income is $1,000 per month? $2,000 per month? Is Edward likely to insure against loss of income? Why?
 b. Suppose instead that Edward's utility function can be written as $U = 10Y^{0.5}$. What is his marginal utility if income is $1,000/month? $2,000/month? Is Edward likely to buy insurance against loss of income? Why?

5. Suppose, if ill, that Fred's demand for health services is summarized by the demand curve $Q = 50 - 2P$, where P is the price of services. How many services does he buy at a price of $20?

 Suppose that Fred's probability of illness is 0.3. What is the actuarially fair price of health insurance for Fred with a zero coinsurance rate?

6. In Exercise 5, if the insurance company pays Fred's entire loss, what will Fred's expenses be? How much will the company pay? Will it continue to offer him insurance at the actuarially fair rate? Why?

7. Suppose that the market demand for medical care is summarized by the demand function:

 $$Q_d = 100 - 2p$$

 and the market supply is summarized by the supply function:

 $$Q_s = 20 + 2p$$

 a. Calculate the equilibrium quantity and price, assuming no health insurance is available.
 b. Suppose that health insurance is made available that provides for a 50 percent coinsurance rate. Calculate the new equilibrium price and quantity. (Hint: How does the demand curve shift?)
 c. Calculate the deadweight loss due to this insurance.

CHAPTER 8

Consumer Choice and Demand

- Applying the Standard Budget Constraint Model
- Two Additional Demand Shifters—Time and Coinsurance
- Issues in Measuring Health Care Demand
- Empirical Measurements of Demand Elasticities
- Impacts of Insurance on Aggregate Expenditures
- Conclusions

We have described health capital investment as a choice made by the consumer who values health but who also values the home good, which is the entertainments and enjoyments made possible by using income and time. These ultimate goods, health capital and the home good, are produced by the consumer by allocating a portion of time to each, as well as a portion of income to those marketed goods, such as medical care, M, and various other goods, OG, that are used in the production process.

Figure 8.1 helps illustrate this transformation from one model (see chapter 6) to the other—the conventional analysis of choice over marketable goods—which is the focus of this chapter. Adapted from our earlier work in this text, the production possibilities frontier in the figure illustrates the consumer's trade-off between health investment and the home good. Choosing these optimal quantities, I^* and B^*, the consumer also is implicitly choosing an allocation of time available for these production tasks, to work that provides income, and to leisure. The final step in understanding this process is to see how that income will be used to buy those marketable goods, such as medical care, that will in turn help the consumer produce health investment and the home good. The consumer faces a trade-off in the marketplace between use of income to purchase medical care versus use of the money to purchase other goods; this trade-off is the budget constraint of standard consumer theory and is the focus of this chapter.

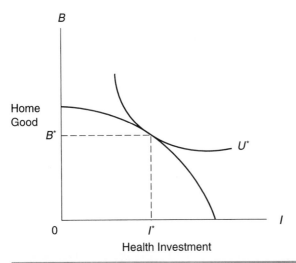

FIGURE 8.1 Demand for Health Capital Determines the Optimal Amounts of the Home Good, *B** and Health Capital Investment, *I**.

Applying the Standard Budget Constraint Model

As with the demand for health capital model, standard indifference curve analysis of consumer choice under a budget constraint describes the consumer with fairly strong assumptions. We assume that the consumer is rational and perfectly informed, that there is no uncertainty about the future, and that important decisions are made as if the future were known with certainty. Although we will later relax some of these assumptions, this standard model produces many reliable predictions on consumer behavior related to health.

Many might object to this approach at the start, believing that we have few choices when we need health care; sometimes little rationality seems possible, at least for the urgently ill. If you are lying on the pavement and the ambulance arrives, do you ask for a list of prices and providers?

Nevertheless, a theory of rational choice over health care and other goods is defensible on several grounds. First, many health care options leave room for some thoughtful consideration or at least some planning. Second, the physician serves as an agent for patient-consumers and can make rational choices on their behalf even in urgent situations.[1] Finally, the ultimate test of any theory is whether it predicts well, and we will show empirically that people, as consumers of health care, do respond to economic incentives.

In economic theory, the logic of consumer choice is straightforward. The logic is that the consumer can choose any affordable combination or bundle of goods, and from among these affordable bundles, he or she will choose the one preferred. The depiction of this choice thus requires two elements:

- The consumer's preferences—described by a set of indifference curves.
- The consumer's budget constraint—described by the straight budget line.

[1]Problems may occur in describing a relationship where the provider, acting as an agent for the patient, helps to determine the amount of care. This is known as *supplier-induced demand,* and is explained in chapter 10.

To make the graphical depiction possible, it is essential to abstract from the many goods available in the real world and assume instead that only two goods are available. The results we get for this two-good world tend to continue to hold when the model is extended to many goods. Let one of these two goods represent a composite of other goods, and call this good Other Goods, or OG. Assume that the health care good is physician office visits consumed during a year, or VISITS. The consumer's name is Ellen Anderson.

THE CONSUMER'S EQUILIBRIUM

Figure 8.2 depicts these elements of the choice problem. The indifference curves labeled U_1, U_2, and U_3 represent some of Ellen's indifference curves (not all are depicted), and together the indifference curves describe her preferences. The indifference curve U_1, for example, represents all points—that is, bundles of OG and VISITS—that provide this consumer with the utility level U_1. Utility is an index of preferences that can most easily be understood as a measure of satisfaction.[2] Because OG and VISITS are both goods to the consumer, it follows that indifference curve U_2 is preferred to U_1 and so on; that is, "higher" indifference curves are preferred.

Let Ellen's budget be Y dollars for the period. If the price of other goods, OG, is P_{OG} and the price of VISITS is P_V, then the sum of her expenditures, $P_{OG} \times OG$ plus $P_V \times VISITS$, cannot exceed her income, Y. To spend all her income means to be on the budget line, which is given by the equation:

$$Y = P_{OG} \times OG + P_V \times VISITS$$

Point M represents the amount of other goods consumed if no visits occur. Point N represents the amount of visits if no other goods are purchased. The budget line is shown as line MN in Figure 8.2, and its slope will be given by $-P_V/P_{OG}$, which is the negative of the ratio of prices.

The consumer equilibrium is shown as point E in Figure 8.2, a point of tangency between the highest indifference curve attainable, U_2, and the budget line. In contrast, all points on indifference curve U_3 are unattainable, and points on U_1 are not chosen because the consumer can afford points she prefers to these. The equilibrium point E is a point of tangency, meaning that the slope of the indifference curve equals the slope of the budget line at this point.

The slope of the indifference curve is called the marginal rate of substitution or MRS. It tells the rate at which Ellen is *willing* to trade other goods for physician visits. Recall that the slope of the budget line is the negative of the ratio of prices. This is the rate at which she is *able* to trade other goods for physician visits at current market prices. An equilibrium is thus reached only if the rate at which she is willing to trade the two goods, the MRS, is equal to the rate at which she is able to trade the two goods, $-P_V/P_{OG}$. This will have the result that in equilibrium, a dollar's worth of OG will yield the same extra utility as a dollar's worth of VISITS.

[2] Utility, as discussed in chapter 2, is an index of preferences in which higher numbers are assigned to "higher," or preferred, indifference curves. Utility need not correspond to a physically measurable level of satisfaction, although it may be easier to imagine it as such a measure. In this chapter, calling utility *satisfaction* will not lead to errors in the logic of choice.

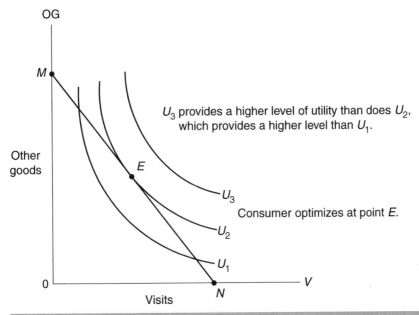

FIGURE 8.2 Consumer Equilibrium Analysis.

DEMAND SHIFTERS

Ellen's response to price changes can be determined by examining the new equilibria that would occur as the price of V varies. Figure 8.3 shows the effects of changes in prices at constant income Y, dropping from the highest price, P_V^1, to a lower price, P_V^2, to the lowest price, P_V^3.

At the highest price, P_V^1, income Y buys V_1 visits at equilibrium point E_1. At the lower price, P_V^2, Ellen chooses equilibrium point E_2 (with V_2 visits), and at the lowest price, P_V^3, Ellen chooses equilibrium point E_3 (with V_3 visits). The number of visits, V, increases because visits have become less expensive relative to other goods.

Figure 8.4 plots a demand curve relating the price of visits to equilibrium quantity demanded. The data come from Figure 8.3. Point E_1 from Figure 8.3 corresponds to point A in Figure 8.4, and similarly points E_2 and E_3 correspond to points B and C. The demand curve summarizes Ellen's response to price changes, holding income and preferences constant.

The responsiveness of the consumer's demand to price is measured by the *price elasticity*. Price elasticity, E_p, is the ratio of the percentage change in quantity demanded to the percentage change in price. Algebraically, it is:

$$\text{Elasticity} = E_p = (\Delta Q/Q)/(\Delta P/P) \tag{8.1}$$

Here the numerator is the change in quantity divided by the quantity level; that is, the numerator is the percentage change in quantity. Because the demand curve is downward sloping, the percentage change in quantity (the numerator) will always be negative in response to a rise in price. Likewise, the denominator is the percentage change

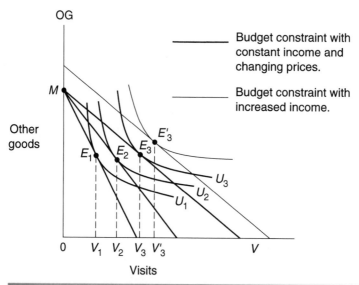

FIGURE 8.3 Change in Number of Visits as Visit Price and/or Income Changes.

Number of visits increases from V_1 to V_2 to V_3 as the price of visits decreases from $P_V{}^1$ to $P_V{}^2$ to $P_V{}^3$. Number of visits increases from V_3 to V'_3 as income rises.

in price. The higher the elasticity is in absolute value (the farther away from 0), the more responsive the consumer is to price. Note that (8.1) also can be written as:

$$E_p = \frac{\Delta Q}{\Delta P}\left(\frac{P}{Q}\right)$$

FIGURE 8.4 Demand Curve Derived from Figure 8.2.

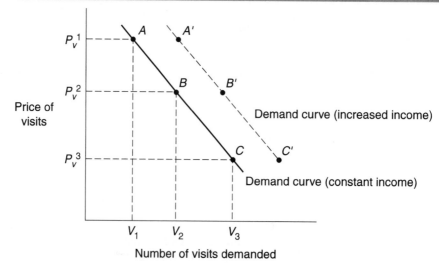

A similar analysis develops the consumer's response to changes in income. Returning to Figure 8.3, recall that point E_3 is determined by income, preferences, and price, $P_V{}^3$. Suppose that Ellen's income now increases. Because the relative prices are not changed by the income increase, the slope of the budget line is not changed, but Ellen can now buy more of both visits and other goods. Her new equilibrium point is E_3'. This is translated in Figure 8.4 to point C'. We can similarly draw points A' and B' on Figure 8.4 to indicate the impacts of an income change and prices, $P_V{}^1$ (new point A') and $P_V{}^2$ (new point B').

The responsiveness of demand to changes in income is measured by the *income elasticity*. Income elasticity, E_Y, is the percentage change in quantity demanded divided by the percentage change in income:

$$\text{Income elasticity} = E_Y = (\Delta Q/Q)/(\Delta Y/Y), \text{ or}$$

$$E_Y = \frac{\Delta Q}{\Delta Y}\left(\frac{Y}{Q}\right) \tag{8.2}$$

Finally, although two-dimensional indifference curves are not well suited to the handling of larger numbers of substitute and complement goods, the effects of changes in the prices of other goods can be analyzed. One would expect that increases in the prices of substitutes to physician visits (hospital outpatient services, visits to other providers) would increase the demand for office visits; that is, an increase in the price of a substitute will shift the demand curve to the right in Figure 8.4. Increases in the prices of complements (diagnostic services) would reduce demand for office visits.

HEALTH STATUS AND DEMAND

Figure 8.5 illustrates how differences in patient health status can be handled. Suppose that Ellen is viewed in two different time periods in which her situation is the same in all economic respects except her health status. In Period 1 (equilibrium point E), she is fairly healthy. In Period 2, her overall health status is lower because she is ill. The change in health status will affect Ellen's preferences (often referred to as tastes) over VISITS and OG as reflected by *different* sets of indifference curves and changed levels of physician care, here point E'.

Note that although Ellen consumes more visits in Figure 8.5 when she is ill, in both cases she has the same marginal rate of substitution, or MRS, of visits for other goods at the equilibrium. Indeed, as long as the prices of the two goods do not change, all consumers in equilibrium will adjust to the prices until all consumers have the same MRS.

The analysis thus far suggests that price, income level, tastes, health status, and other circumstances influence the consumption of physician services. Other considerations, however, cannot be overlooked. Two such considerations are the roles of insurance and of time.

Two Additional Demand Shifters— Time and Coinsurance

Two demand-shifting variables "look" like changes in the price: time price and coinsurance. First, Ellen's time price, the value of the time she must give up for a physician visit, can represent a significant portion of her full price. Second, insurance causes Ellen's effective price, the price paid "out of pocket," to be reduced below the market price.

OG

Other goods

FIGURE 8.5 Changed Preferences Due to Illness.

THE ROLE OF TIME

Recall from chapter 6 that time is an important element in the demand for health. The consumption of health care services requires considerable time for some services and procedures. Economic observation suggests that people value their time. Many turn down additional work, even at increased wages. Still others decline to drive across town to save $5 or $10 on an item, even though the cost of driving is far less than the $5 or $10. These choices probably occurred because the additional time spent wasn't worth it to the consumer.

Given the opportunity cost of time, a focus on the money costs of health care ignores a substantial portion of the economic costs. The discrepancy between the total economic costs and the money costs will be especially large for low-priced services, for services where patient copayments are small, and for patients with high opportunity costs of time.

As an example of time cost effects, suppose that Ellen must go to the doctor for a 10-minute visit. It will take her 15 minutes to travel each way (30 minutes in all), 20 minutes to wait in the office, and 10 minutes with the doctor. Suppose further that the money cost of the visit is $25, and that she values her time at $10 per hour. Traveling and parking cost $5 total. The full price of each visit is then $40:

- 1 hour of time valued at $10.
- 1 visit priced at $25.
- Travel and parking costs at $5.

Figure 8.6 illustrates that Ellen demands six visits when her full price is $40. A money price increase of $5 causes the new full price to be $45, at which she demands

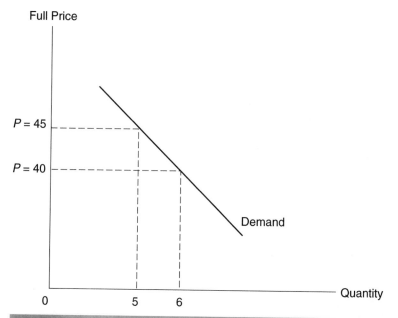

FIGURE 8.6 Demand and Time Price for Physician Visits.

five visits. Restating the price elasticity formula from Equation 8.1, we find that the elasticity with respect to the full price is:[3]

$$E_P = (\Delta Q/Q)/(\Delta P/P) = -(1/5.5)/(5/42.5) = -1.545$$

Here P represents the full price; that is, $P = P_M + P_T$. The full price is the sum of money price and time price. In contrast, the money price elasticity in this case is:

$$E_{PM} = -(1/5.5)/(5/27.5) = -1.000$$

In general, the money price elasticity is smaller than the full price elasticity by the same proportion as the money price is smaller than the full price. To make sense of this, try comparing the ratio:

$$P_M/(P_M + P_T) = 27.5/42.5 = 0.647$$

to the ratio:

$$E_{PM}/E_P = -1.000/1.545 = -0.647$$

How might this apply? Assuming that the poor have a lower opportunity cost of time than the well to do, one would predict that they would more likely tolerate or endure long waiting times in clinics or physician offices. At the same time, even those poor

[3]Note the conversion to absolute values for convenience, and note that the arc elasticity formula, appropriate in this case, requires that we average the beginning and ending values for both P and Q.

whose physician's fees are subsidized (e.g., by Medicaid) must pay their time price. Wishing to increase physician visits among the poor, we might choose to reduce the time price by building local clinics and expanding outreach programs, a strategy that has been developed in many localities.

In practice, does time price affect demand? In a pioneering study on time price, Acton (1975, 1976) examines the effects of travel times, waiting times, and other variables on quantity demanded of outpatient visits and physician care. Table 8.1 reports his elasticity estimates. For example, outpatient care, T_{Out}, is the own-time price, and T_{Phys} refers to the other good (cross-time price). The own-time price elasticity for outpatient visits, −0.958, nearly reaches unity, and the own-time price elasticity for physician visits, though much smaller in absolute value at −0.252, also exhibits a significant role for time.

Subsequent work usually supports an important role for time. Coffey (1983) finds time price also relevant to the decision to seek care initially, as well as the quantity consumed, though her estimates are small (with the exception of public provider care). Mueller and Monheit (1988) find time-price elasticities for dental care to significantly affect the quantity of dental care consumed. Does time-price affect health care demand? Yes. It makes sense in theory, and it matters in practice.

THE ROLE OF COINSURANCE

Building on our study of insurance in chapter 7, we see coinsurance as a demand shifter that works by modifying the effective price. When a third party, such as an insurance company, pays a portion of one's hospital bill, the remaining portion paid by the consumer is called the coinsurance rate; let us call it r. Thus, more insurance means a lower r.

Effects of Reduced Coinsurance on the Individual Consumer

Suppose Ellen has no health insurance and thus pays all her health care bills out of pocket. Figure 8.7 shows Ellen's demand for health care as D_0. Because she is uninsured, the market price also is always Ellen's effective (out-of-pocket) price. At a market price of P_1, her quantity demanded is Q_1. A simple thought experiment reveals the issue. Suppose Ellen is given a health insurance policy at no charge[4] that pays 50 percent of each of her bills, giving her a coinsurance rate of $r = 0.5$. The market price, P_1, is no longer the effective price; the effective price becomes $0.5 \times P_1 = P_1'$. Using her demand curve, D_0, as our guide, we see her now demanding Q_1'. This develops a first principle—her quantity demanded under coinsurance can be found along the out-of-pocket demand curve, provided we identify and apply the effective price.

It is more useful to identify her demand curve with respect to the market price. Ellen acted as though her health care demand had shifted, and this "rotating shift" can

TABLE 8.1 Acton's Time Valuation Equations		
Dependent Variable	*Outpatient Visits*	*Physician Visits*
Elasticity with respect to T_{Out}	−0.958	0.640
Elasticity with respect to T_{Phys}	0.332	−0.252

[4]This leaves her income available for the rest of her budget items the same as it was before.

Market Price

FIGURE 8.7 The Effect of a Coinsurance Rate Less Than Unity on Health Care Demand.

be shown to be equivalent to the previous analysis. In Figure 8.7, let us reverse the question and ask: If Ellen demands Q_1' when she has 50 percent insurance coverage and faces an effective price of P_1', then what market price is she apparently willing to pay (part paid by her out of pocket and part paid by her through her insurance company)? The answer is P_1, and the resulting combination of quantity demanded and market price is Point E in Figure 8.7. By plotting such points (not forgetting the case where $P = P' = 0$), we trace the demand curve with respect to the market price, D_1. Ellen, by receiving the insurance, will act just like an uninsured Ellen whose health care demand curve had shifted and rotated to the right, hinged at Point B.

The exercise makes two theoretical facts clearer: insurance will increase Ellen's demand for health care, and insurance will make Ellen's demand for health care less elastic. At present, the "less elastic" prediction is informal because the curve is visibly steeper, but it can be proved more generally for this and other contexts. Suppose Ellen's coinsurance rate were zero, meaning she pays nothing for health care. Would her demand be even less elastic? Most health economists would predict that her demand curve would become vertical, hence perfectly inelastic.

Market Effects

The effect of a reduced coinsurance alone, for Ellen, is an increase in the quantity demanded. Ellen does not demand enough care to influence market prices. Individual consumers are price takers; their individual actions have no effect on the price, so they face essentially a horizontal supply curve.

Suppose, however, that the coinsurance rate is changed for many consumers in the market. For the market as a whole, the relevant supply curve may be upward sloping,

indicating that higher prices might be required to motivate producers to offer greater market quantities.

Figure 8.8 shows an equilibrium of price and quantity with an upward-sloping supply curve. The original market equilibrium price is P_0 and the equilibrium utilization is V_0. In this case, if coinsurance rates are generally reduced, the increased market demand will raise market quantity demanded to V_1 and the market price to P_1. Total health care expenditures will rise from $P_0 V_0$ to $P_1 V_1$. Many economists feel that such effects are major reasons for the increases in health care costs in the United States.

Issues in Measuring Health Care Demand

With the current concern about health care expenditures, reliable estimates of demand elasticity become essential. Recall that elasticity measures the responsiveness of demand to a change in a related variable. Price elasticity helps determine the effects of health insurance practices and policies. The effect of public policies to improve the accessibility of health care will depend on the money and the time price elasticities.

Prices, incomes, time prices, and coinsurance rates do matter. Increased prices and coinsurance rates reduce demand for services. Raising income increases the demand for services. "Economic" factors are not consumers' only considerations, but they matter.

In this section, we focus on variables of interest to science and public policy. We examine how health care demand responds to money price, insurance coverage, and time price. In addition, we examine the effects on market demand of income and other variables. Each study attempts to apply econometrics to estimate a demand function statistically; all variables relevant to demand are considered simultaneously. For ease in exposition, we consider the important variables separately.

Reviewing the difficulties faced by researchers and the differences between studies can be helpful to understanding the results. In effect, we ask the question: Why do

FIGURE 8.8 Market Impact of Coinsurance.

the reported elasticities vary so often from one study to another? In most cases, the differences arise because of the different choices the researcher made in the face of problems common to research in this field. We identify five issues.

INDIVIDUAL AND MARKET DEMAND FUNCTIONS

Our analysis so far has focused on the individual. It suggested the following type of demand function for physician visits, referred to as *V*:

$$V = f(P, r, t, P_0, Y, HS, AGE, ED...)$$

where *P* is price per visit, *r* is the patient's coinsurance rate, P_0 is the price of other goods, *Y* is a measure of income, *t* is a time price, HS is the patient's health status, and AGE and ED stand for variables such as age and education to reflect other need and taste factors. This functional notation shows that certain variables are likely to affect *V*, but it does not specify the relation exactly.[5]

Often, however, economists are interested in *market* demand functions. Care is needed to move from individual to market demand. Even the measure of utilization poses a challenge. For example, most studies will use the number of visits per person (rather than the total quantity of visits) as the dependent variable. They then attempt to control for the size of the market by considering total population. This leads to serious problems in the interpretation of results.

MEASUREMENT AND DEFINITIONS

Unlike the carpenter's simpler problem of measuring the length of a wall, there are alternative definitions of health care quantities to be measured, as well as many alternative measuring tools. Investigators often measure the *quantity* of services in dollar expenditures. One problem is that expenditures reflect a complex combination of price of care, quantities of care, and qualities of care.

Alternative measures include quantity of visits, patient days, or cases treated. Yet these do not necessarily measure the intensity of care. One person may spend five days in the hospital for "observation"; another may spend five days for brain surgery. Consequently, the literature contains a variety of measures and thus a variety of reported elasticities.

A related problem is to define the price of services. Because of the prevalence of health insurance, most patients do not pay the full price for their treatments. Moreover, the price they pay may be related to the size of the bill because of deductibles, coinsurance, or limits. A $50 treatment, for example, may cost $50 if it occurs before the deductible limit is reached, or $10 (assuming 20 percent coinsurance) if it occurs after the deductible limit has been reached. The statistical problems in this case are fairly complicated, but it should suffice here to note that the resulting price elasticities may vary.

[5]Econometricians often use the OLS method discussed in chapter 3. In this case, the regression is:

$$V = b_0 + b_1P + b_2r + b_3t + b_4P_0 + b_5Y + b_7AGE + b_8ED ... + E + \epsilon$$

with the variables defined as before, and ϵ is the error term.

DIFFERENCES IN THE STUDY POPULATIONS

Different researchers, naturally, use different samples or populations. Elasticities will differ between populations and even within populations at different points in time. For example, many health economists believe that income elasticities for health care have become smaller over the years in the United States, presumably because of the effects of programs like Medicare and Medicaid.

Furthermore, it is possible, in theory, for Californians to have a different price elasticity for physician services than Minnesotans. People in one state may be older (for example, Florida) or have better access to larger varieties of health providers. It is theoretically possible that people will exhibit a different price elasticity for dental care than for pediatric care. Thus, some variation in reported elasticities is inevitable even when one uses the "same" measures, definitions, and techniques.

DATA SOURCES

Populations differ between studies, and the sources of data may differ in ways that result in different elasticity estimates. For example, a common source of health care data is the insurance claim. Claims data, however, are limited to services covered by insurance and used by the insured. Furthermore, they often lack detail on individuals' characteristics, such as education and income. In contrast, health interview survey data often incorporate personal data, but their accuracy depends on the recall ability of the person being interviewed.

EXPERIMENTAL AND NONEXPERIMENTAL DATA

Much of health care demand research used nonexperimental data, and thus the researcher could not control the environment or assure that other extraneous variables were held constant. These data typically represent samples across individuals or markets—that is, a slice of experience. If the necessary assumptions hold, then available statistical techniques can provide valuable analytical insights.

A useful alternative involving the natural experiment is sometimes possible. A natural experiment, for example, may occur when a given Canadian province changes its health insurance plan. The change enables one to observe differences in health care utilization before and after. We presume that only the policy changes and all other things are held constant. Unfortunately, other demand-related factors often change also.

In a *controlled* experiment, subjects are randomly assigned to treatment and control groups to measure responses directly to changes in the levels of demand-related variables. Such experiments, however, are costly to perform and are not without their own difficulties. Fortunately, we have the benefit of a substantial, carefully executed controlled experiment on health insurance conducted by the Rand Corporation.

Empirical Measurements of Demand Elasticities

PRICE ELASTICITIES

The focus of health care demand studies is on price elasticity. Table 8.2 reports a selection of estimates by type of care.

The dependent variable in each case is the quantity demanded. In some cases, it is a market aggregate, such as admissions per capita; in other cases, the unit of observa-

TABLE 8.2 Price Elasticity Estimates from Selected Studies

Study	Dependent Variable	Price Elasticity
All Expenditures:		
Rosett and Huang (1973)	Expenditures for hospital and physician services	−0.35 to −1.5[a]
Manning et al. (1987)	All expenditures	−0.17 to −0.22
Physician Services:		
Fuchs and Kramer (1972)	Physician visits per capita	−0.15 to −0.20
Newhouse and Phelps (1976)	Physician office visits	−0.08
Cromwell and Mitchell (1986)	Surgical services	−0.14 to −0.18
Wedig (1988)		
Health perceived excellent/good	Physician visits	−0.35
Health perceived fair/poor	Physician visits	−0.16
Hospital Services:		
Feldstein (1971)	Hospital admissions per capita	−0.63
Newhouse and Phelps (1976)	Hospital length of stay	−0.06
Manning et al. (1987)	Hospital admissions	−0.14 to −0.17
Nursing Homes:		
Chiswick (1976)	Nursing home residents per elderly population	−0.69 to −2.40
Lamberton et al. (1986)	Nursing home patient days per capita elderly	−0.69 to −0.76

[a]Rosett and Huang report that price elasticity varies by level of coinsurance. Elasticities reported range from −0.35 for 20 percent coinsurance to −1.5 for 80 percent coinsurance. Wedig reported estimates based on the National Medical Care Utilization and Expenditure Survey (NMCUES) for 1980 and separated 5,322 observations on adults into subsamples by perceived health status.

tion is the individual consumer. Most reported elasticities are in the inelastic range (between 0.0 and −1.0), indicating that consumers, while responsive to price, are not responsive to a substantial degree. Suppose that the price elasticity for physician services was between −0.08 to −0.20 and physicians raised their prices by 10 percent. This would reduce consumption by 0.8 to 2.0 percent.

A further distinction among studies should be made. The price elasticities reported in Table 8.2 are each measures of the individual consumer's or the market's response to price changes. That is, they are not firm specific, but represent the demand for the health care good or service in general.

The demand for physician care in general will be less elastic than the demand for the services of a particular physician. For example, suppose a medical symptom is worrisome and the patient chooses to see a physician. The more worrisome the symptom, the less responsive he or she is likely to be to market price. Which physician to see is a completely different question. The consumer who knows the quality and price of each physician would choose the lower-priced physician among those of equal quality. The point is that there are few substitutes for physician care but there are many substitutes *among* individual physicians. Thus, firm (physician)-specific demand will be more price responsive than overall demand.

This point is illustrated in Table 8.3, which reports studies of firm-specific demand elasticities. As we observe, these elasticities tend to be considerably higher in absolute value than most of the elasticities reported previously in Table 8.2.

The firm-specific elasticities have further significance. They indicate the degree of competition in the market. Under perfect competition, firm-specific elasticities will tend to approach negative infinity. The reported physician care elasticities may be large

TABLE 8.3 Firm-Specific Price Elasticities

Study	Dependent Variable	Price Elasticity
Physician Services:		
Lee and Hadley (1981)	Physician price	−2.80 to −5.07
McCarthy (1985)	Physician visits	−3.07 to −3.26
Hospital Services:		
Feldman and Dowd (1986)	Hospital patient days	−0.74 to −0.80
	Hospital admissions	−1.1

enough that competition is a reasonable approximation. In contrast, the estimates for hospitals suggest considerable market power.

Firm-specific elasticities help to assess the degree of competition in the market, and the elasticities for physician or hospital care in general help to assess public policies, such as government policy on health insurance. Two findings are salient. Price elasticities are significant; that is, prices matter. Second, the market level elasticities are usually between 0 and −1.0, or inelastic. This means that price increases (decreases) will increase (decrease) expenditures.

INDIVIDUAL INCOME ELASTICITIES

Economic theory suggests that increased income causes increased purchases for most goods. Most goods thus have positive income elasticities and are referred to as *normal* goods. Those with negative elasticities are referred to as *inferior* goods. Table 8.4 reports estimated income elasticities for a selection of studies by type of health care. In most cases, the magnitudes are small. This indicates that while health care is generally a normal good, the response is relatively small; that is, inelastic.

Income elasticities also help define when goods are necessities or luxuries. We call goods "necessities" when the income elasticity is between 0 and +1. When income elasticities exceed +1, goods are called "luxuries." From the properties of elasticities, a

TABLE 8.4 Income Elasticities from Selected Studies

Study	Dependent Variable	Income Elasticity
All Expenditures:		
Silver (1970)	Expenditures	1.2
Rosett and Huang (1973)	Expenditures	0.25 to 0.45
Hospital Services:		
Newhouse and Phelps (1976)	Admissions	0.02 to 0.04
Dental Services:		
Silver (1970)	Expenditures	2.40 to 3.20
Andersen and Benham (1970)	Expenditures	0.61 to 0.83
Physician Services:		
Silver (1970)	Expenditures	0.85
Andersen and Benham (1970)	Expenditures	0.22 to 0.41
Fuchs and Kramer (1972)	Visits per capita	0.20 to 0.57
Newhouse and Phelps (1976)	Visits	0.01 to 0.04
Nursing Homes:		
Chiswick (1976)	Residents per elderly population	0.60 to 0.90

1 percent rise in income increases the budget share devoted to a luxury and decreases the budget share devoted to a necessity. From Table 8.4, the results are not surprising; people commonly perceive health care to be a necessity.[6]

INCOME ELASTICITIES ACROSS COUNTRIES

Given these findings, it may be surprising that studies of aggregate health expenditures across countries report substantially higher income elasticities. Often the magnitudes exceed unity. A good example of a cross-national study is one published by Newhouse in 1977. Newhouse regressed per-capita medical expenditures for 13 developed countries on a variable representing per-capita income. From the estimated coefficient of this equation, he then calculated the implied income elasticity for various levels of income. The elasticity estimates ranged from 1.15 to 1.31. He concluded that despite within-country results showing health care to be a necessity, health care in fact is a luxury good.

Parkin and colleagues (1987) point out several potential weaknesses in most existing cross-national studies.[7] Despite their objections, their improved results tend to support the finding that cross-national income elasticities are greater than 1.0. Gerdtham et al. (1992) also support the finding that cross-national income elasticities are greater than 1.0. More recent work, including more sophisticated efforts to measure properly general price levels, income levels, and health care prices (Goodman, 1999), finds even higher income elasticities. Is it an inconsistency that within-country health care income elasticities tend to be small, while cross-national estimates are greater than 1.0? Can health care be a necessity at the individual and market levels but a luxury at the country level?

A hypothetical example illustrates that income elasticity results at the national aggregate level do not necessarily apply to individual or market level. Suppose that two countries, one rich and one poor, each provided free health care to their citizens irrespective of income. Then within-country income elasticities might be small if not zero. Yet the richer country might provide greater quantities, higher technology, and better qualities of health care to each of its citizens. Thus, the cross-country income elasticities could be high.

Olsen (1993) warns us on two counts to avoid misunderstanding. First, although health care is a luxury at a cross-national level ("in the macrodata"), health may be a necessity because the production function of health may not be responsive to health care ("flat of the curve"). Second, in everyday usage, we tend to think of luxuries as wasteful or even extravagant, but an income elasticity greater than 1.0 may merely describe the health care a nation's people had wished their nation could afford.

INSURANCE ELASTICITIES

Consumer responses to changes in insurance are important because insurance coverage has grown dramatically in the past 30 to 40 years and because we frequently must con-

[6]Issues also arise regarding the appropriate definition of income, particularly with respect to short-term versus long-term (or permanent) income. Those interested should examine Goodman (1989).

[7]Three of these arguments are especially noteworthy. First, highly aggregated data such as national income or national health care expenditures do not necessarily imply individual behavior. Second, most studies use exchange rates to convert foreign country values to U.S. dollars, but exchange rates may not accurately reflect the purchasing power of the currency. Finally, the results are sensitive to the functional form (econometric method) used.

sider possible changes in social insurance. Among such changes is a possible national health insurance plan. While the issue of insurance effects must be treated separately from price effects, they are closely intertwined with the issue of price elasticities.

Consider a health insurance policy where the consumer pays a fixed percentage of the bill—that is, a fixed coinsurance rate, r. In such a case, the net price that the consumer pays, NP, would be a simple multiple of the market price, P:

$$\text{Net price} = rP$$

When the market price rises by 1 percent, so does the net price; that is:

$$(1.01)\text{NP} = r(1.01P)$$

Under such an insurance plan, the coinsurance elasticity would be the same as the price elasticity.

However, most health insurance plans are not so simple. In practice they have many features including deductibles and maximum dollar expenditure (MDE) limits in addition to the coinsurance rate. The result is that the effective coinsurance rate depends in part on the size of the bill. In practice, price and coinsurance elasticities will differ somewhat.

A further difficulty arises because most studies have been performed on nonexperimental data. One of the major concerns with nonexperimental data is that the groups compared are not always randomly selected. For example, suppose that a company allows its employees to enroll in a *high*-coverage plan or a *low*-coverage plan. Some people may choose to work for the company because it offers the high-coverage insurance plan. Others who expect to use large (low) amounts of services will naturally enroll in the high- (low-) coverage plan. Still others, if sufficient insurance is not available from the company, will purchase more generous insurance privately. If the demand analysis proceeds by comparing these groups, the results may misstate the true effect of coinsurance. This is because the major decision was made in deciding *which* group to join. The behavior is known in economics as *adverse selection*.

The Rand Corporation, funded by the United States Public Health Service, mounted an experiment beginning in 1974. Households at six sites across the nation were randomly assigned to groups that had different levels of cost sharing, ranging from free care to care with 95 percent coinsurance and including a maximum dollar expenditure limit. The families were paid a lump-sum payment to be sure that no family was made worse off by the experiment. Because the assignment was random, adverse selection could be minimized, and the random assignment of coinsurance also allowed researchers to investigate the effects of coinsurance on expenditures.

They observed family health care use and expense experience over a period that varied from three to five years for various experimental groups. This intensive and expensive experiment was immensely important to our understanding of the response of health care consumers to economic incentives. Table 8.5 summarizes some of the key results of the Rand Health Insurance Experiment.

We note that coinsurance has a considerable effect on the level of average medical expenditures. From an extreme of a 95 percent coinsurance to the opposite extreme of free care, or zero coinsurance, the average family's medical expenses increase by nearly 50 percent, from $679 to $982. Even hospitalization rates are responsive, increasing from 7.9 percent of those in the 95 percent coinsurance group to 10.3 percent in the free care

TABLE 8.5 A Summary of the Effects of Coinsurance on Mean Annual Use of Medical Services in the Rand Health Insurance Experiment

Plan	Likelihood of Any Use (%)	One or More Admissions (%)	Total Expenses (1991 $)
Free	86.8	10.3	982
	(0.8)	(0.5)	(50.7)
Family Pay			
25 Percent	78.8	8.4	831
	(1.4)	(0.6)	(69.2)
50 Percent	77.2	7.2	884
	(2.3)	(0.8)	(189.1)
95 Percent	67.7	7.9	679
	(1.8)	(0.6)	(58.7)
Individual Deductible	72.3	9.6	797
	(1.5)	(0.6)	(60.3)

Note: Standard errors shown in parentheses. Medical services exclude dental and outpatient psychotherapy.

Source: Reprinted by permission of the publisher from *Free for All?: Lessons from the RAND Health Insurance Experiment* by Joseph P. Newhouse, Cambridge, MA: Harvard University Press, Copyright © 1993 by the RAND Corporation.

group, representing an increase of about 30 percent. We must conclude from the Rand experimental data and analysis that both price and insurance do matter considerably.[8]

Newhouse and colleagues conclude:

All types of service—physician visits, hospital admission, prescriptions, dental visits, and mental health service use—fell with cost sharing. There were no striking differences among these services in how their use responded to plan. Another partial exception was demand for mental health services—which, the results indicate, would have been more responsive than other services to cost sharing had there been no cap on out-of-pocket expenditure (pages 338–339).

OTHER VARIABLES AFFECTING DEMAND

The studies we have reviewed often incorporate many other variables of interest in the demand function estimates, and considerable information relevant to policy issues has been obtained.

Ethnicity and Sex

Many studies of demand examine the influence of race, and it is frequently found that Blacks tend to consume less medical care than the other large, self-identified ethnic groups when other factors are held constant.[9] Although the majority of studies of ethnic differences in health care have focused on the experience of Blacks and Hispanics, other ethnic differences also have been noted, often when a given disease, for example Tay-Sachs disease, appears predominantly within one group—in this case, the Jews.

[8]The Rand researchers ignored those households with zero expenditures. Inclusion of such households may move the estimated price elasticity closer to zero.
[9]For Blacks, see Andersen and Benham (1970) and Newhouse and Phelps (1976). For females, see Newhouse and Phelps (1976), Silver (1970), and Scheffler (1984). Scheffler found that although females have an increased probability of entering a hospital, mean hospital expenditures thereafter tend to be somewhat lower.

Part of the differences may be of social origin; for example, Blacks and other ethnic groups may be reluctant to seek care or may be treated differently by white physicians. However, ethnic differences, more broadly understood, may help explain geographic patterns across the United States. For example, westerners tend to rely less on hospitals and physicians, while the more snowbound north central states rely more heavily on nursing home care for the elderly than other areas on a per-capita basis.

Females differ from males most clearly in their time pattern of medical care usage. During child-bearing years, women are relatively heavy users of health care, but women are more durable in the long run and they predominate in the numbers of old elderly. Thus they are predominant among physicians' older patients. Though a great deal of public attention and concern in the past decade has turned to the science of treating diseases prominent among women, death rates for cancers are often as high or higher among men as among women. For example, mortality rates from prostate are not much different than mortality rates from breast cancer. Myocardial infarction (heart attack) is a notorious killer of men, though women's rates have been increasing. Thus, researchers will continue to study the differences in medical demand between the sexes, and the many differences between ethnic and cultural groups. This includes not just differences among skin color groups but among the many subcultures and local cultures within these larger groups. These differences may offer the explanation for demand variations not accounted for by the usual demand variables and may yet help identify and explain many health demand questions that have remained unanswered.

Variations in sexual behavior have proved tremendously important in explaining variations in the pattern of infections with HIV and mortality due to AIDS. Homosexuals in the United States have long been the major group at risk and most prominent among deaths; intravenous drug users are second in numbers. Though much public effort was addressed to the prevention of a feared epidemic among heterosexuals, especially youth, the pattern has remained steady. In contrast, the world's attention is turned more toward Africa, where transmission of the disease is primarily heterosexual and the size of the epidemic forms a crisis for world public health efforts.

Urban vs. Rural

Studies sometimes find differences in health care usage due to rural status. If rural residents use less care, the reasons why are not necessarily clear. Rural dwellers may differ culturally, and some analysts argue that this factor is more important to one's perception of life than ethnicity is. Whether born to rural life or to have adopted it, it may become linked to tastes, health status, and relative reluctance to seek out a physician. The lesser health demand by westerners, already identified above, could be understood in this view as an artifact of the predominance of rural areas in the region. The contrasting argument is made that it is the greater travel distances required to obtain health care in rural areas rather than rural culture or tastes that account for the demand patterns. Thus, studies of geographical patterns of health care demand must take special care to measure the full price of physician or hospital care; that is, to include the travel time price.

Education

Education is strongly associated with better health. If you are reading this book as a college student, the odds are very good that you are healthier than your noncollege counterparts. As in the demand for health capital model, this may be because you are a

more efficient producer of health, you are less likely to smoke, and you are more likely to eat a healthful diet. Or, it may be that you are the sort of person with a long-term goal, and to meet that goal you have identified the need to take proper care of yourself. For the researcher sorting out such questions, the complexity of the issue is multiplied by confounding factors, especially income. Educated people tend to earn more income, a fact not lost on most college students. We then must determine: Does education improve one's health, or is it the income that affords a healthier life?

Age

Older people consume three to four times more health care than the younger population. Though the relationship is no surprise, Grossman's theory of this pattern makes the issue more intriguing to the research community. If we invest in our health each period and yet our health depreciates somewhat during each period, why do we necessarily buy greater quantities of health care as we get older? Very plausibly, as Grossman assumed, the depreciation rate gets larger as we age, thus greater inputs of our own time and health care are required to restore our health. This makes the correlation of health demand and age appear logical. Yet, our own goals for our health may decline as we age, which, at some point, may work in the opposite direction.[10]

Perhaps more interesting is the relationship of health status to the price elasticity of health care demand. Theory is not clear on this point, but it is plausible that sicker people will tend to be less sensitive to price.

Wedig (1988) finds that the price elasticity of the decision to seek health care tends to be lower in absolute value for those with poorer health status, regardless of which measure is used to record health status. However, no clear pattern over health status can be determined with respect to level of care—that is, the amount of health care consumed given that the consumer has chosen to seek health care.

Finally, uncertainty will affect health care demand. When a consumer, worried about a future health risk, seeks advice or preventive treatment, we call this a precautionary demand (Picone, Uribe and Wilson, 1998). The elderly patient, for example, may smooth his utility over time by spending now to avoid sharp drops in well-being and mobility in the future. Some empirical evidence suggests that older people have somewhat less tolerance for risk and that one's degree of risk tolerance influences one's decision whether to buy health insurance.

Impacts of Insurance on Aggregate Expenditures

Rand researchers, estimating coinsurance and income elasticities to be approximately 0.2, estimated the portion of the sevenfold post-World War II real increase in U.S. health expenditures due to the spread of health insurance.[11] The answer was "not much"—only 10 percent of the increase. All else being equal, the spread of health insurance would have increased health expenditures by 70 percentage points, rather than the 700 percent measured.

[10]See, for example, Andersen and Benham (1970), and Cromwell and Mitchell (1986).

[11]Rand researchers also attempted to measure the impacts of possibly excess insurance, or "welfare loss." We address this analysis in some detail in chapter 7.

Income tripled over the period. Given an income elasticity of 1.0, this would have increased expenditures by only 60 percentage points. The income elasticity estimate was, in fact, 0.2, according to Rand, indicating that only $0.6 = 3 \times (0.2)$, or 60 percentage points of the 700 percent increase could be explained by increased income. Adding 60 percent to the 70 percent attributed to insurance still yields only a 130-percentage-point increase, or less than one-fifth of the entire increase of 700 percent.

The Rand people attributed the remainder to increased costs brought on by technological change. Certainly, products such as kidney dialysis or organ transplant procedures have improved technology dramatically, and at increased costs. The extent to which every technological development is desired, or efficient, is still open to question.

Conclusions

This exploration of traditional consumer theory along with its empirical research on health care demand reveals that much has been learned. This is true particularly when we include the findings of the Rand experiment.

We must reemphasize the general findings. Price, coinsurance rate, time price, and income all matter. Lowering the price or lowering the waiting time increases demand. Providing income subsidies to users also increases the demand and hence the utilization. Economic incentives have meaningful effects, large and small.

Summary

1. The theory of rational choice over health care and other goods is useful because many health care options are not urgent, leaving room for thoughtful consideration or at least some planning.
2. In addition, physicians serve as the patient-consumer's agents and can make rational choices even in urgent situations.
3. Depiction of the consumer's choice requires knowing preferences, as described by a set of indifference curves, and resource constraints, described by the budget line indicating income and market prices.
4. Consumer equilibrium occurs only if the rate at which they are willing to trade, or MRS, equals the price ratio at which they are able to trade the two goods. In equilibrium, a dollar buys the same utility from all goods.
5. Price elasticity, E_p, is the ratio of the percent change in quantity demanded to the percent change in price. Income elasticity, E_Y, is the percent change in quantity demanded divided by the percent change in income.
6. The time spent acquiring services constitutes a substantial portion of the economic costs. The discrepancy between the total economic prices (including time) and the money prices will be especially large for low-priced services, services where patient copayments are small, and for patients with high opportunity time costs.
7. Insurance plays a major role in health services demand. Many health care purchases are at least partially covered by health insurance, so that a portion is paid for by someone other than the consumer.
8. The impact of coinsurance depends critically on the price elasticity of demand for health care. If consumers do not respond to price changes in the absence of insurance, changes in coinsurance will have no impact on quantity of services demanded.

9. Coinsurance makes the demand curve for health services less responsive (less elastic) with respect to the price.

10. Quantity of services is often measured by dollar expenditures. One problem is that expenditures reflect a combination of price of care, quantity of care, and quality of care. Alternatively, quantity may be measured in numbers of visits, patient days, or cases treated.

11. It is often difficult to define prices of services since insured patients usually do not pay the full price. Moreover, the net price paid by consumers is influenced by deductibles, coinsurance, or other limits.

12. Most reported price elasticities indicate that consumers respond to price changes. However, these elasticities (between 0.0 and −1.0) are not large compared to many other goods and services.

13. In most cases, income elasticities are low. While health care is a normal good, since its demand increases with income, the response is relatively small. However at aggregate levels, across countries income elasticities often exceed +1.0.

14. Coinsurance has a considerable effect on the level of average medical expenditures. Both price and insurance matter.

15. Income and insurance changes since World War II may explain approximately 130 percentage points of the 700 percent increase in U.S. health expenditures, through increased demand for services. Researchers attribute the remainder to increased costs brought on by technological change.

Discussion Questions

1. Discuss the various types of waiting time whose costs may affect demand for health care.

2. Define price elasticity of demand. How does an increase in the coinsurance rate affect the consumer's price elasticity?

3. Why are firm-specific demand price elasticities higher than elasticities for demand in general? Why does a high elasticity indicate a very competitive market?

4. For the following pairs of services, which of the two services would you expect to be more income elastic? More price elastic?
 a. Surgical services versus allergist services.
 b. Heart surgery versus cosmetic surgery.

5. It has been discovered that countries with higher per capita incomes spend more than proportionally as much on health care. What does this imply about the cross-national income elasticities? Why might this occur, even though individual income elasticities seem to be quite low?

6. The frequencies of health care visits are often used to measure service demand. Many, however, criticize the use of this variable. What are some pros and cons of the use of visits?

7. We often speak of how price rations goods. What are other rationing measures in clinics in which free care is provided?

8. Explain or show why the impact of changes in coinsurance rates on demand depends on the elasticity of demand. What sorts of health care goods or services will be responsive to changes in coinsurance rates? What sorts will tend to be relatively less responsive?

9. A profit-maximizing firm finding that its demand is inelastic will necessarily find it profitable to increase its price; therefore, its equilibrium price elasticity will necessarily be greater than 1.0 in absolute value. Are the market- and firm-specific elasticity data reported here consistent with this theory?

10. The consumer's indifference curves in Figure 8.1 indicate substitutability between visits and other goods. What will the indifference curves look like if the consumer perceives no substitutability? What will happen to the elasticity of demand in this case?

Exercises

1. Suppose that Martha's income is $20,000 per year. She can spend it on health care visits, which cost $40 per visit, or on groceries (standing for all other goods), which cost $50 per bag of groceries. Draw Martha's budget constraint. Using indifference curves, show Martha's optimum, if she buys 300 bags of groceries per year.

2. Suppose that Martha's income rises to $21,000 per year, and that she increases her consumption of health care visits by five visits. Using the graphs for Exercise 1, draw the new equilibrium. What is her income elasticity of demand for health care visits?

3. Consider the following information on Alfred's demand for visits per year to his health clinic, if his health insurance does not cover (100 percent coinsurance) clinic visits.

P	Q
5	9
10	9
15	9
20	8
25	7
30	6
35	5
40	4

Alfred has been paying $30 per visit. How many visits does he make per year? Draw his demand curve.

What happens to his demand curve if the insurance company institutes a 40 percent coinsurance feature (Alfred pays 40 percent of the price of each visit). What is his new equilibrium demand?

4. Suppose that a consumer makes V_0 physician visits each year at a price of P_0. If the price elasticity is −0.4, what will happen to the number of visits, if the price rises by 10 percent? What will happen to total physician expenditures? Why?

5. If the price elasticity of demand is −0.5 and the income elasticity is +0.3, then what will be the effect of a simultaneous 10 percent increase in price, and 10 percent increase in income on health expenditures?

6. Draw a diagram for hospital care that reflects the income-elasticity estimates found empirically. As income increases, what happens to the proportion of income spent on hospital care?

7. Would the opportunity cost of waiting time be higher for higher-income people or lower-income people? Given your answer, for which income group would money price tend to be a smaller portion of the full price?

C H A P T E R

Asymmetric Information and Agency

- ■ Overview of Information Issues

- ■ Asymmetric Information

- ■ Application of the Lemons Principle: Health Insurance

- ■ The Agency Relationship

- ■ Consumer Information, Prices, and Quality

- ■ Conclusions

The traditional theory of demand, as we have seen, begins with the assumption that individuals are fully informed about prices, quantities, and the relationships of medical care and other inputs to their levels of health. We examined decision making within a model that assumed perfect information. Depending upon the purpose of the model, such an assumption may be justified even if it is not realistic. However, a more complete understanding of the health economy requires particular insight into the effects of various informational problems in health care markets.[1]

Though imperfect information has long been regarded as prevalent throughout the health economy, until recently, insight into its specific effects has been lacking. The economics of information has emerged as a distinct specialty, and needed tools to study informational problems have been developed. Health economics has been greatly enhanced by the study of asymmetric information and agency relationships. The former

[1]The emergence of health economics as a distinct field is often traced to Kenneth J. Arrow's (1963) seminal article, "Uncertainty and the Welfare Economics of Medical Care." Arrow emphasized the role of imperfect information and uncertainty, especially the features of health care markets due to the "imperfect marketability of information."

encompasses situations where buyers and sellers have different levels of information; the latter concerns situations where, for lack of information, buyers or sellers rely on other parties to help make decisions.

Overview of Information Issues

The markets for many health care services and for insurance in particular are marked by significant degrees of asymmetric information and agency relationships. For example, adverse selection, a phenomenon in which insurance attracts patients who are likely to use services at a higher-than-average rate, results from asymmetric information. It seems plausible, and most analysts agree, that a potential beneficiaries have better information than the insurer about their health status and expected demand for health care. As a result, premiums for higher-risk patients will be underpriced, encouraging such patients to overinsure while the opposite holds for lower-risk patients. This phenomenon, which will be discussed further, reduces the efficiency of health insurance markets while redistributing income from the healthy to poorer risks.

Information and agency problems account for many other important characteristics of health care markets. The possible preference for health care delivery by nonprofit hospitals and nursing homes (chapter 18) has been attributed to patients' lack of information and inability to discern quality. For some patients, a nonprofit status might be taken as reassurance of higher quality because decisions are made independent of a profit motive. Lack of quality information also is thought to be an important motive for licensure and other regulatory measures (chapters 16 and 20).

The present chapter has three goals. First, we introduce information asymmetry, describe its relative prevalence, and determine its consequences, especially for insurance markets. It will quickly become clear, however, that adverse selection in insurance is only one consequence of asymmetric information.

Asymmetric information, as when a patient is less well informed about appropriate treatments than the attending physician, typically leads to an agency relationship between the patient and provider. The second goal of this chapter is to describe the agency relationship and examine some of the problems arising in health care markets from imperfect agency. The special and controversial case of supplier-induced demand (SID) is revealed as an asymmetric information/agency problem in the following chapter.

Our final goal is to examine the effects of imperfect consumer information on the price and quality of health care services. Despite informational disadvantages for consumers, they often influence markets in predictable ways. Here and throughout the chapter, we identify arrangements that commonly evolve to reduce the disadvantages for the less well-informed parties. Thus, the ultimate consequences of asymmetric information and imperfect agency on the efficient functioning of markets are often not as severe as one would assume initially.

Asymmetric Information

Basic microeconomic theory usually includes an assumption that the market being analyzed exhibits perfect information. Under conditions of perfect information, all decision makers, meaning all consumers and producers, have complete information on all prices,

as well as the quality of any good or service available in the market. Consumers also will be as well informed about the product as the seller.

Obviously, information is never perfect in the real world. However, theories in many disciplines are necessarily developed with concepts that are rarely or never actually obtained in practice. Examples from other sciences include the idea of a perfect vacuum, frictionless motion, or the idea of a geometric point that has no dimensions. In economics, perfect information is often a useful starting point because the properties and predictions of the standard models relying on this assumption are so well understood. The researcher's task is then to assess whether the actual functioning of a given market is close enough to the predicted behavior that the application of the model is useful, even though all of the assumptions of the model are not fully satisfied.

On the other hand, cases do arise where imperfect information does seem to matter. During the past three decades, economists have developed new insights into the effects of imperfect and asymmetric information. This section examines some of that work, including contributions by health economists to the specific problems of the health sector.

ON THE EXTENT OF INFORMATION PROBLEMS IN THE HEALTH SECTOR

Before investigating several contributions to the economic theory of information, we begin by asking how prevalent information problems are in the health sector. It is obvious not only that imperfect information is prevalent in health care markets, but also that there is asymmetry of information. Levels of information will differ among participants in many transactions, such as between physicians and patients. Often, the patient is poorly informed compared to the provider about his or her condition, the treatment available, expected outcomes, and prices charged by other providers. Furthermore, it is our presumption that information problems exist in the health sector that are prominent enough to require the special analysis of the economics of information.

Although we can agree that information problems arise in health care markets, we must avoid the temptation to overgeneralize or to draw the point too far. To say that information problems exist in the health sector does not mean that these problems are necessarily worse than in any other market. For example, markets for insurance, other professional services, automobile and appliance repairs, and many other goods and services also exhibit asymmetries. We should not necessarily conclude that information asymmetries in health care markets make it impossible for corrective institutions, practices, or products to evolve; nor does it necessarily preclude the possibility of competition.

Pauly (1978) notes that half or more of physician visits customarily are made for services such as general checkups or chronic care for which the patient has some if not considerable experience. From data on the portion of medical expenditures attributable to ambulatory physician care, we can estimate that if half of this care is reasonably well informed, then about 8 percent of total medical care is informed. Reasoning in this manner about all sorts of medical care and products, Pauly concluded that plausibly "one-fourth or more of total personal health-care expenditures might be regarded as 'reasonably informed'" (p. 16). By adding nursing home services and chronic conditions, Pauly (1988a) subsequently argued that this ratio is about one third.

The second branch of this argument notes that the information gap in several medical care issues is shared by the provider. As we will emphasize when describing the "small area variations" literature in chapter 10, the physician often is uncertain if not uninformed about the outcomes of many medical procedures. In such cases, information asymmetry does not necessarily arise even though it may well be correct that the patient is ill informed.

Finally, economic analysts of information asymmetry problems have been able to show that markets may perform well in the face of some degree of information asymmetry provided a sufficient portion of the consumers are reasonably well informed.[2] For example, perhaps a majority of consumers who use personal computers are relatively poorly informed about their technical aspects and relative qualities and prices. However, a significant minority of consumers tends to be highly informed. In markets like this, it is possible that the informed minority is sufficient to provide the economic discipline it takes to make the market perform well so that the rest of us will tend to find reliably that the higher-priced computers also tend to be of higher quality.

We conclude this section by summarizing its main point. Certainly information gaps and asymmetries exist in the health sector. They are perhaps more serious for health care than for other goods that are important in household budgets. This makes it useful for the student of health economics to investigate the theory of information asymmetries and its application to health care. However, it may be unwise to overgeneralize to the point of asserting that information gaps preclude the possibility of having a high degree of competition. In particular, mechanisms to deal with information gaps should not be overlooked. These mechanisms include licensure, certification, accreditation, threat of malpractice suits, the physician–patient relationship, ethical constraints, and having some informed consumers.

Will a state of relative consumer ignorance preclude high levels of competition? Will health care markets be characterized by a high degree of price dispersion and the provision of unnecessary care or care that is not in the patient's best interests? Can some of the characteristics of health care markets and the evolution of their institutional arrangements be related to asymmetric information? The following sections address these and other questions by beginning with the pioneering work on asymmetric information.

ASYMMETRIC INFORMATION IN THE USED-CAR MARKET: THE LEMONS PRINCIPLE

Akerlof (1970) is often credited with introducing the idea of asymmetric information through an analysis of the used-car market. Though seemingly unrelated to health care, his classic article is worth studying for two reasons. First, it tells us much about adverse selection and the potential unraveling of health insurance markets. Adverse selection is one of the keys in our understanding of some major contemporary issues such as the uninsured and the performance of health maintenance organizations or other delivery systems. Second, Akerlof's example leads right into the issue of agency.

In Akerlof's example, used cars available for sale vary in quality all the way from cars that are still in mint condition to some that are complete lemons. Information asym-

[2]See Salop (1976) and Grossman and Stiglitz (1976).

metry arises if, as is often plausible, the sellers know better the true quality of their cars than do the potential buyers. Akerlof devised an example that showed that cases may arise where such information asymmetry causes the market for used cars to perform poorly or even to disappear entirely.

To illustrate the nature of the used-car example, consider a somewhat simpler example, but one that retains the essential features. In particular, suppose nine used cars are to be sold (potentially) that vary in quality from 0, meaning a lemon, to a high of 2, meaning a mint-condition used car. In fact, suppose that the nine cars have respectively quality levels (Q) given by the cardinally measured index values of $0, \frac{1}{4}, \frac{1}{2}, \frac{3}{4}, 1, 1\frac{1}{4}, 1\frac{1}{2}, 1\frac{3}{4}$, and 2. Under a cardinal index, a car with a value of 1 has twice the quality of a car with an index of $\frac{1}{2}$. The distribution of these cars is shown in Figure 9.1, where the horizontal axis shows the quality level and the vertical axis shows the uniform probability, $\frac{1}{9}$ in this case, of randomly picking a car of each given quality.

Suppose further that the owner of a car knows its quality level exactly but that the nonowners (potential buyers) know only the distribution of quality. It is known that the owners have a reserve value on their cars, so that Reserve Value to the seller = $1,000 \times Q$. That is, the owners would sell their car only if they could get at least $1,000 for every unit of quality that the car has. On the other hand, the nonowners are more eager for used cars and value them so that the Value to Nonowners = $1,500 \times Q$. To make this experiment a complete market, suppose that an auctioneer is hired to call out market prices; sales take place when the auctioneer finds a price that successfully equates quantity demanded with quantity supplied.

Does a Market Exist?

Consider what would happen here under asymmetric information. Suppose the auctioneer calls out an initial trial price of $2,000 per car. At this price, all owners know it is worthwhile to sell their cars, so all nine cars will be supplied. However, nonowners, knowing only the distribution of quality but not the quality of each individual car, will make a best guess that a given car is of average quality; that is $Q = 1$. They would not buy any cars at a price of $2,000, because they are willing to pay only $1,500 per unit of quality. They guess that all cars have a quality of 1, for a product of $1,500 \times 1 = \$1,500$, which is less than the $2,000 asked. They would be willing to buy cars only if the price were less than or equal to $1,500.

FIGURE 9.1 The Availability of Products of Different Quality (Uniform Probability of Picking Each Car).

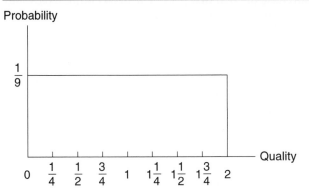

So the auctioneer, perhaps trying to accommodate the potential buyers, tries a lower price, say $1,500. Unfortunately, at this price, the owners of the two best cars will withdraw from the market. Why? The owner of the car with 2 units of quality is receiving only $1,500/2, or $750 per unit of quality; the owner of the car with $1\frac{3}{4}$ units will act the same way. The withdrawal of the two best cars causes the average quality of the seven remaining cars to fall. With nine cars, the average of the distribution was $Q = 1$. Now at a price of $1,500 per car, the best car offered will have a quality level of $\frac{3}{2}$, and the average quality will now be $\frac{3}{4}$. Potential buyers would now be willing to pay only $1,500 per unit quality \times ($\frac{3}{4}$ unit of quality per average car) or $1,125 for any car. Just as the previous price of $2,000 per car was too high, the new price of $1,500 is too high for buyers.

Will an equilibrium price ever be found? Surprisingly, in this example, an equilibrium, one that satisfies both buyers and sellers, will not be found. The reader can discern this by trying several successively lower prices. In the end, the cars will not be sold even though nonowners value the cars considerably more than their current owners. Akerlof saw the problem this way: When potential buyers know only the average quality of used cars, then market prices will tend to be lower than the true value of the top-quality cars. Owners of the top-quality cars will tend to withhold their cars from sale. In a sense, the good cars are driven out of the market by the lemons. Under what has become known as the Lemons Principle, the bad drives out the good until, in some cases such as this one, no market is left.

Imperfect Versus Asymmetric Information

To see that the problem is asymmetric rather than imperfect information for both buyers and sellers, consider what would have occurred if information had been symmetric. Suppose, in particular, that both owners and nonowners were uncertain of the quality, that they knew only the average quality of used cars on the market. Again, let the auctioneer start with a trial price of $2,000 per car. All owners, at their best guess, may presume that their car is of average quality, and that the average will again be $Q = 1$. Thus, at a price of $2,000 per car, all nine cars would be offered for sale. However, the nonowners would be willing to pay, at most, $1,500 based on their guess that a given car is of average quality (that is, $1,500 per unit of quality, multiplied by expected quality of $Q = 1$). Again, suppose the auctioneer tries to accommodate the potential buyers by offering a lower trial price, say $1,500. If the owners have imperfect information rather than better information, they will guess that their cars are of average quality, and thus worth (to them) $1,000 per unit of quality, multiplied by average quality of 1. So the owners are willing to supply nine cars at a market price of $1,500, and the buyers are willing to purchase them at that price. The market thus exists, and clears (supply equals demand) if the information is symmetric—in this case equally bad on both sides.

This example is extreme in several respects. The assumption of an auctioneer, the assumption that there is only one price for the used cars, the implicit assumption that the parties are not influenced by risk, and even the assumption that the quality of the cars is exogenously given could each be modified to add more realism. Since the lemons example was published, several analysts have worked on models that modify these assumptions. In some cases, this changes the result significantly. However, Akerlof's main point remains illuminating. Phlips (1988) notes:

> Obviously, the example is extreme. It is meant to make the point that the presence of unidentifiable lemons makes it difficult to sell cars of better quality at a good price. . . . The more general phenomenon of asymmetric information

coupled with a reduction of average quality of the goods and services traded in the market has received the name "adverse selection" (p. 70).

Application of the Lemons Principle: Health Insurance

Adverse selection is a problem for markets involving health insurance, as well as for analysts studying the relative merits of alternative health care provider arrangements. The application of the Lemons Principle to the problem of health insurance can be seen directly with the help of the previous example, which is a mirror image of the insurance problem. In Figure 9.2, let the horizontal axis measure the expected health expenditure levels of a population of n potentially insured people, instead of measuring the quality of used cars. Assume that they have the same demographic characteristics and that their expected health expenditure levels for the insured period range from a low of $0 up to an expenditure level of M. The vertical axis represents the probability with a uniform distribution (so that the probability of any level of spending is $1/n$). The insurer must at least break even, which means that the premium (or price) received from each insured must cover the insured population's average expenditure and other expenses (including marketing and overhead).

Information asymmetry is likely to occur here because the potential insureds know more about their expected health expenditures in the coming period than does the insurance company. To illustrate, assume a potential insured knows his or her future expenditure exactly but that the insurance company knows only the distribution of expenditures for all insured persons.

Again, use the device of the auctioneer to illustrate the point. Suppose this time that the auctioneer attempts a first trial price of $0! All potential beneficiaries would certainly demand coverage at this price. Just as certainly, the insurance company, expecting an average expenditure of $ $(\frac{1}{2})M$, would require a premium of at least $ $(\frac{1}{2})M$.

Following Akerlof's analysis, suppose the auctioneer tries a higher price, say $ $(\frac{1}{2})M$, hoping that this will clear the market. In this case, all potential beneficiaries who expect an expenditure level below $ $(\frac{1}{2})M$ will choose to self-insure, that is, leave the insurance market altogether, because this premium is higher than their privately known levels of health expenditure. When these healthier people leave the market, the average expected

FIGURE 9.2 Uniform Probability of Expenditure (Expected Health Expenditure Levels).

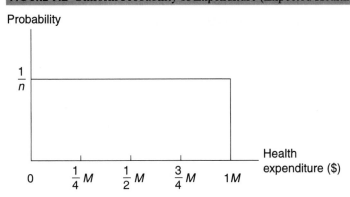

expenditure level of the remaining insured persons, those with expected expenditures from $ $(\frac{1}{2})M$ to M, rises to $ $(\frac{3}{4})M$. Thus, the higher health risks tend to drive out the lower health risk people, and a functioning market may even fail to appear at all for some otherwise-insurable health care risks.

Observe again that it is the asymmetry of information rather than the problem of incomplete information that leads to this result. If patients were no better at predicting their health expenditures in our example than the insurer, adverse selection would not take place. That is, all potential beneficiaries would have expected expenditures of $ $(\frac{1}{2})M$ and would be willing to purchase insurance at the premium of $ $(\frac{1}{2})M$.

INEFFICIENCIES OF ADVERSE SELECTION

This example illustrates the effects of adverse selection. Analysts of the health insurance industry recognize that even in its less extreme forms, adverse selection will appear. Even if functioning health insurance markets do evolve in the presence of information asymmetry of this kind, the resulting adverse selection tends to result in economic inefficiencies.

What are the inefficiencies? Unlike the example, few people can know exactly their future level of expenditures. Risk is the main reason for insurance. However, if the lower risks are grouped with higher risks and all pay the same premium, the lower risks face an unfavorable rate and will tend to underinsure. They sustain a welfare loss by not being able to purchase insurance at rates appropriate to their risk. Conversely, the higher risks will face a favorable premium and therefore overinsure; that is, they will insure against risks that they would not otherwise insure against. This, too, is inefficient.[3]

If information asymmetry threatens to lead to inefficiency and even to the elimination of functioning markets in some cases, we would expect consumers and providers to resort to other economic devices and institutions to help overcome the problem. To illustrate, reconsider the used-car example. While the lemons problem in used-car markets is real, many economic devices have evolved to help counter it. For example, a buyer may hire a mechanic to examine the car of interest, the seller may offer a warranty, and agencies or consumer unions may arise to provide quality information. Similar features have evolved in health care markets. In health insurance markets, beneficiaries often are not covered for preexisting conditions. Premiums for individual policies may be based on other information that insurers use to predict expenditures. They may consider factors such as age, employment status, and occupation.

EXPERIENCE RATING AND ADVERSE SELECTION

Group insurance can be a more useful mechanism to reduce adverse selection. Most employees and their families in the United States are insured through employer group plans rather than through individual policies. Group plans enable insurers to implement experience rating, a practice where premiums are based on the past experience of the group, or other risk-rating systems to project expenditures. Because employees usually

[3]Adverse selection is not merely a theoretical prediction. It appears in the markets for supplemental Medicare insurance (Wolfe and Goddeeris, 1991) and individual (nongroup) insurance (Browne and Doerpinghaus, 1993). In addition to inefficiency, income is redistributed from consumers who are lower risks to those who are higher risks.

have limited choices both within and among plans, they cannot fully capitalize on their information advantage. Van de Ven and Van Vliet (1995) show that adverse selection can be reduced substantially if insurers use just a few risk factors to determine premiums.

Although experience rating can reduce adverse selection, it has come under increasing attack with the rapid growth of managed care plans such as health maintenance organizations (HMOs). HMOs, described more fully in chapter 12, are organizations that receive a predetermined premium to provide the contracted health care for its enrollees. In contrast to traditional insurance where providers are independent of insurers, HMOs integrate insurance with the provision of health care.

HMOs and similar entities have been promoted heavily on the belief that they have a powerful self-interest in eliminating the inappropriate care that might be recommended by agents in traditional fee-for-service systems. However, the intense competition to enroll healthy populations in managed care plans, known as "cream skimming" or "cherry picking," has led to concerns that insurers are more interested in finding favorable groups than providing quality care. Experience rating also redistributes income toward healthy populations, and the perceived inequity of such redistributions has become a public issue.

To deal with these concerns, several states have introduced some degree of mandated community rating, a practice in which an insurer charges all groups within an area the same premium. In a less rigid form, upper and lower limits on premiums are established through rate bands. The effects of these changes have not yet been determined, but Goldman et al. (1997) predict some serious redistributional consequences of the community rating schemes considered for California. In particular, because health care spending in wealthy, urban areas is relatively high, their model predicts large regional transfers of income from poorer, rural communities to those areas.

The Agency Relationship

An agency relationship is formed whenever a *principal* (for example, a patient) delegates decision-making authority to another party, the *agent*. In the physician–patient relationship, the patient (principal) delegates authority to the physician (agent), who in many cases also will be the provider of the recommended services. The motive behind this delegation of authority is that the principals recognize that they are relatively uninformed about the most appropriate decisions to be made and that the deficiency is best resolved by having an informed agent. Thus, asymmetric information and agency are closely related phenomena.

AGENCY AND HEALTH CARE

What would the perfect agent do? Following Culyer (1989), the perfect agent physician chooses as the patients themselves would choose if only the patients possessed the information that the physician does.[4] This is in line with the medical code of ethics to the extent that the patient's own interest focuses on his or her health. When any conflict arises, the perfect agent focuses on the patient's preferences, not his or her own.

[4]See also Clark and Olsen (1994) for a model and analysis that makes use of the assumption of perfect agency.

The problem for the principal is to determine and ensure that the agent is acting in the principal's best interests. Unfortunately, a divergence of interests may arise, and it may be difficult to introduce arrangements or contracts that eliminate conflicts of interest.

As an example, Dranove and White (1987) ask why physicians are not reimbursed on the basis of improvements in patient health. More simply, why are they not reimbursed only if the patient is cured? It would appear that such a contract would be a naturally arising device that would merge the interests of both principal and patient. The authors suggest that the unavailability of such contracts in health care lies in the problem of asymmetric information, although in this case it is the physician who may lack information about the patient's well-being.

To illustrate, take patients with low back pain. Regardless of their improvement, the patients have a financial incentive to understate the extent of their improvement. The provider also has an incentive to overstate the difficulty in treating the patients and in improving their health in order to increase the payment (which, let us assume, is based on the difficulty of the case). Further, it is these information problems and not other special characteristics of health care delivery that preclude payment based on the degree of improvement of the patients' conditions.

Dranove and White further apply agency theory to explain other features in the organization of health care delivery. A feature we commonly find is that patients often establish a long-term relationship with a physician and pay that physician on a fee-for-service basis. As discussed earlier, such an arrangement would appear prone to lead to conflict between patient and provider. It is thus natural to ask the following questions: Why does this particular physician–patient arrangement arise and why is it so common?

Dranove and White explain this phenomenon with an argument based on information theory. They argue that a continuous relationship between patient and physician provides the patient with increasing information with which to monitor the physician. This information places constraints on the extent to which the provider is able to deviate from an agency responsibility. Monitoring also encourages the physician to make appropriate referrals to other providers when he or she is unable to provide the services alone.

We also can add to their argument by further pointing out that a continuous relationship reduces the cost of transferring information about medical history, circumstances, and preferences from patient to provider. These advantages of the usual physician–patient relationship would be eroded if patients and providers were to switch to limited-period contracts under which providers are reimbursed on a different basis.

Consumer Information, Prices, and Quality

A further objective of this chapter is to examine the effects of imperfect information on the price and quality of medical services. Would relatively poor consumer information reduce the competitiveness of markets? Does increasing physician availability increase competition and lower prices as traditional economics suggests? What happens to quality? How do consumers obtain and use information? Although research on these issues is still limited, several studies provide helpful insight.

Contingency Fees and Medical Malpractice

Guarantees of satisfaction are common in the market for many consumers' goods. Most large retailers will accept returns without question if the customer is not satisfied. However, guarantees also have found their way into some services, such as for car tune-ups and even hair styling. One of the most interesting and controversial examples of a service guarantee is the contingency fee system in tort cases, particularly for malpractice suits. Under the contingency fee system, the plaintiff (party that sues) pays only if he or she wins damages (at a rate that is usually at the legal maximum, about one-third of the award in many states). Contingency fees are possible because, unlike with many medical services, the outcome is clear.

Opponents of this system charge that it leads to unnecessary litigation and frivolous suits. Supporters, by contrast, claim that it provides access to the courts to those with more limited financial means. They also suggest that the client and attorney share the common goal of maximizing the award. Although at first glance this appears to be an obvious proposition, there remain significant problems of agency and asymmetric information under the contingency fee system.

An inherent conflict arises because the rational client would want an attorney to spend more and more time on the case, so long as each additional hour would yield some positive benefit. In Figure 9.3, the marginal benefit curve, $(\frac{2}{3})$MB, represents the benefit of each additional hour (in terms of additional monetary gain) to a client who keeps $\frac{2}{3}$ of the court-awarded damages or settlement and pays an attorney the remaining $\frac{1}{3}$ as a contingency fee. Thus, the fully informed client wants an attorney to spend a total time of OB hours on the case, the point at which $(\frac{2}{3})$MB becomes zero. The attorney, on the other hand, wants to maximize his or her own income net of costs. The attorney's marginal benefit curve is given as $(\frac{1}{3})$MB and the marginal cost is represented by MC. The attorney maximizes net income at OA hours where $(\frac{1}{3})$MB equals MC. He or she has a different utility function and will recognize that there is an opportunity cost to the time spent. Thus, the attorney will prefer to spend less time on the case than would be desired by a fully informed client. The extent to which attorneys deviate from client responsibilities is not known. Nevertheless, some critics of contingency fees have recognized this conflict and have thus charged that the system promotes early settlement of cases that would be further pursued if attorneys acted solely in the best interests of their clients.

CONSUMER INFORMATION AND PRICES

One of the most novel approaches to issues of consumer information and competition was introduced by Satterthwaite (1979) and Pauly and Satterthwaite (1981). The authors identify primary medical care as a reputation good—that is, a good for which consumers rely on the information provided by friends, neighbors, and others to select from the various services available in the market. Each firm offering physician services provides a service that is differentiated from others, that is, the firms do not offer identical services. As such, the market can be characterized as monopolistically competitive.

FIGURE 9.3 Attorney Hours and the Marginal Gains to Attorney Versus Client.

Reputation Goods

Under these conditions, the authors show that an increase in the number of providers can increase prices. The reasoning behind this surprising prediction is logical. Recall that a typical consumer relies on other consumers for information regarding their experiences with physicians. Thus, when physicians become numerous, the average number of friends who see any provider diminishes; this, in turn, diminishes the average level of information available. The consumer's responsiveness to prices and other practice characteristics depends on his or her knowledge of—that is, information about—the available alternatives. Thus, this reduced information reduces the price responsiveness (i.e., the elasticity) of the firm demand curves, causing the equilibrium prices to rise. The economic idea is that reduced information tends to give each firm some additional monopoly power.

That reduced information enhances monopoly power and reduces the elasticity of the firm demand curves is consistent with standard theory. That such a situation may arise as the number of sellers increases is an unconventional idea. It is understandable if the results run counter to one's intuition. The authors have, however, provided empirical support for their theory, and the interested reader is referred to their work for further study of the issue.

The Role of Informed Buyers

The degree to which imperfect price information contributes to monopoly power should not be overemphasized. Recall that it is not necessary for every buyer of a commodity to have perfect price information to elicit relatively competitive pricing conditions. Realistically, most consumers lack complete price information about many of the goods and services they buy (that is, they don't know what alternative sellers are charging). Yet, despite variations in the prices of individual items among, for example, grocery stores, the average charges for a set of items across similar types of stores are likely to be similar and close to competitive pricing. A growing body of literature shows that

it is sufficient to have enough buyers who are sensitive to price differentials to exert discipline over the marketplace. This is likely to hold especially where the damaging threat exists of having any systematic differentials publicized by consumer organizations or the low-priced merchants themselves.

The thrust of these arguments is to suggest that while imperfect price information is likely to produce higher prices, this phenomenon may be substantially limited. In health care markets, where many services are fully or partially covered by insurance, there are added considerations. While a patient may become less sensitive to price levels and price differentials in the choice of providers, third-party payers, such as insurers, have assumed a monitoring function. Through selective contracting and other fee agreements, the actual reimbursement is often lower than the provider's charges.

Price Dispersion

The distinction between the effective transaction price and a provider's charge also obscures evidence of dispersion of fees as distinct from the average level of fees. Under conditions of imperfect consumer information, Nobel Laureate George Stigler (1961) argued that variation in prices will increase.

Building on Stigler's insight, Gaynor and Polachek (1994) have developed measures of the degree of both buyer and provider ignorance by using frontier regression methods. These authors separated price dispersion into measures of incomplete buyer information, incomplete seller information, and random noise. They found that both patients and physicians exhibited incomplete information with the measure of ignorance being one and a half times larger for patients than for physicians.

In addition, Juba (1979) found that the variations in physician fees appear to be larger than those found in other relatively competitive markets. It is not clear, though, that variations in effective transactions pricing resulting from insurance agreements lie outside of competitive norms.

CONSUMER INFORMATION AND QUALITY

Because quality is not easily monitored, the search for information regarding it can be costly to the consumer. At the same time, the consequences of poor quality care can be severe. Thus, as previous discussion suggested, despite asymmetric information, patients rely on a variety of countervailing arrangements that are intended to reduce their search costs. These include licensure and certification, the threat of malpractice suits, codes of ethics, and quality assurance schemes that are either mandated or voluntary. The public's demand for regulation and licensure, the role of accreditation such as that offered by the Joint Commission on Accreditation of Healthcare Organizations (JCAHO), and other arrangements are taken up in later chapters.

At this point, we pursue the consumer's direct role through the Dranove and White argument that the physician–patient relationship enables patients to monitor providers and to encourage physicians to make appropriate referrals. To the extent that many specialists rely on referred patients, it would seem that these specialists have incentives to maintain quality. Are they also rewarded with higher prices when they provide higher-quality services? Theory suggests that if consumers have the ability to distinguish between quality, then the demand for higher-quality providers and thus price should be greater than for lower-quality providers. Haas-Wilson (1990) examined this proposition using data from the psychotherapy services market. She investigated whether

the prevalence of referrals from informed sources affects the price of social workers' psychotherapy services. Informed sources include other health providers and other professionals such as school counselors and clergy.

Regression analysis of a sample of social workers' fees indicated that fees are positively and significantly affected by the percentage of clients who were obtained through informed referrals. The evidence thus shows that patients rely on informed sources (agents) for information and that higher quality, as measured by informed referrals, is rewarded by higher fees. Although more research is needed on other services, this work indicates that asymmetric information does not necessarily lead to market failure.

OTHER QUALITY INDICATORS

Luft and colleagues (1990) examined the influence of quality indicators and other variables on the choice of hospitals for patients with seven surgical and five medical conditions. Various quality indicators—such as teaching status, transfer and referral patterns, medical school affiliation, and various indexes of outcomes—were examined. The authors found that medical school affiliation increased the probability of selection for seven of the twelve conditions studied and that poorer-than-expected outcomes index measures were associated with a lower probability of selection.

Studies such as the previous one raise interesting questions about quality indicators and patients' perceptions of quality. The medical literature has been strongly influenced by the structure, process, and outcome distinctions established by Donabedian (1966) to represent quality. Owing to its relative ease of measurement, the focus is often on structural indicators, which refer to the availability of resources such as personnel per bed.

However, an extensive marketing literature focuses on expressive quality as manifested through caring and communication skills. The marketing discipline also has stressed the credence properties of health care services.[5] These are dimensions of quality that cannot be evaluated, even after experience, and that are thought to be especially relevant to high-skill services. Considerable interest centers on the extent to which price, advertising, and other sources of information serve as signals for credence properties.

Finally, despite licensure requirements and other schemes to promote quality, the media has disseminated claims by those within the profession that approximately 10 percent of physicians are incompetent or seriously impaired by drug and alcohol addiction. Consider also reports that some medical doctors are not actually medical doctors but have falsified credentials, work under the assumed names of deceased physicians, or practice without licenses. Though the extent of these problems of incompetence, impairment, and fraud are not known with any accuracy, their acknowledged existence raises troubling questions about patients' perceptions of quality and their ability to monitor quality. The role of licensing boards and other organizations is similarly called into question.

Conclusions

There is little doubt that information gaps, asymmetric information, and agency problems are prevalent in provider–patient transactions. However, for some health care ser-

[5]See Bopp (1990) and Lynch and Schuler (1990). Health economists also are beginning to examine the attributes of the physician–patient relationship. Vick and Scott (1998) found that the most important attribute is "being able to talk to the doctor."

FEATURE

Health Plan Report Cards

The National Committee for Quality Assurance (NCQA), a private accreditation body for HMOs, issues report cards based on about 50 standardized measures of a plan's performance (such as childhood immunization rates, breast cancer screening, and asthma inpatient admission rates). *Newsweek, U.S. News & World Report,* and various consumer groups also regularly rate HMOs.

A key assumption behind these efforts is that information about quality will, like price information, help discipline providers through patient choices. Low-quality HMOs will not survive or at least they will not be able to change high-quality prices.

Initial evidence on the intended effects of plan performance ratings questions the report card strategy. Through a consumer survey, Tumlinson et al. (1997) found that independent plan ratings are relatively unimportant to their choices. Only 17 percent of respondents indicated that such ratings are essential, compared with 72 percent for specific plan benefits and 62 percent for out-of-pocket costs. Chernew and Scanlon (1998), employing multivariate statistical methods on consumer choice of plans, confirm that "employees do not appear to respond strongly to plan performance measures, even when the labeling and dissemination were intended to facilitate their use" (p. 19).

vices, the problems are not necessarily great or larger than those for other goods. Patients are likely to be relatively poorly informed about treatment for conditions that they have not previously experienced and about care involving newer technologies. The informational asymmetries and reliance on provider-agents are likely to be most pronounced in these situations.

Although there is a potential lack of competition, even wide information gaps do not necessarily lead to market failure. Leaving aside the role of licensure and regulation, arrangements have evolved to enable patients or their insurers to monitor the quality and prices of providers. Furthermore, higher-quality producers are rewarded by greater demand and higher prices. Evidence suggests that the variation in physician fees is greater than what is found in more competitive markets. Price dispersion data indicate some ignorance on both parts, physician and patient, with the patient being the lesser informed. Nevertheless, because of the use of referrals, accreditation, and other arrangements, the provider's ability to raise prices above those charged by others and to sell low-quality services at high-quality prices is significantly constrained.

Summary

1. Health care markets tend to be characterized by both imperfect information and asymmetric information. Asymmetric information describes a situation in which those on one side of a transaction have better information than those on the other side.
2. Often, providers are relatively well-informed (e.g., about the patient's illness and possible treatments). In other cases, buyers are relatively well-informed (e.g., the purchaser of insurance knows more about his or her health status and pertinent habits than the insurer does).

3. The extent of consumer information problems should not be exaggerated. Consumers are reasonably well-informed on about one-fourth to one-third of their health care spending.

4. One possible consequence of asymmetric information is that a market will not exist. Even if it exists, a general reduction may occur in the quality of goods available (the "Lemons Principle").

5. The Lemons Principle appears as the problem of adverse selection in health insurance and other health care markets.

6. Adverse selection results from asymmetric information, not equally imperfect information. Adverse selection in insurance results in inefficiencies through higher-risk consumers overinsuring, relative to the amounts they would purchase at actuarially fair rates, and lower risks correspondingly underinsuring.

7. An agency relationship tends to be formed when a party (principal) delegates decision making to another party (agent). The problem for the principal is to develop a contract or relationship to ensure that the agent is acting in the principal's best interests.

8. Various agency relationships have evolved to mitigate the problems associated with asymmetric information between patient and provider. These include the continuous physician–patient relationship and the health maintenance organization.

9. Other constraints, such as licensure and accreditation, codes of ethics, and the threat of litigation, limit the ability of providers to deviate from their agency responsibilities.

10. Many health care services are reputation goods. In markets for reputation goods, an increase in the number of providers can lead to an increase in monopoly power and higher prices.

11. The existence of informed buyers helps exert discipline over the market by limiting price increases and price differentials among sellers.

12. Higher quality tends to be rewarded with higher prices. Patients also respond to quality indicators in selecting a hospital. However, they rely relatively little on objective plan ratings in their selection of HMOs.

Discussion Questions

1. The market for higher education is another example a high degree of information asymmetry is likely. What mechanisms have evolved to help students in their choice of schools and classes within schools? Do you have confidence that higher-priced institutions provide higher-quality education?

2. The situation in which an individual is interviewing for a job also exhibits information asymmetry. Explain why. How does the relatively poorly informed party deal with this?

3. The use of professional and independent buyer-agents to help individuals purchase automobiles or houses is becoming a more common phenomenon. Given the conflict of interest facing the physician-agent, why do we not see greater use of a buyer-agent who is retained by the patient?

4. The used-car market has publications that provide information on the quality and prices of used cars. Are similar avenues of information available to health consumers? What kind of information do they provide? Is it more or less effective than

the information available on used cars? How would you, as a patient, find information about a provider's quality or prices? How would you assess the confidence you have in that information?

5. What is a reputation good? What are examples of reputation goods outside the health care sector? Show what Pauly and Satterthwaite predict will happen to the demand curve for health services as a result of an increase in the number of providers.

6. Stigler argued that the variation in fees increases as buyer information decreases. Suppose you observe that each seller in a market is charging the identical price. What potentially conflicting inferences can you draw?

7. Why don't physicians guarantee their work as do many auto repair shops?

Exercises

1. Suppose that in the Akerlof example, there are only eight cars ranging in quality from $\frac{1}{4}$ to 2 (i.e., there is no complete lemon). Hence, the mean quality level is 1.125. Determine whether the market disappears completely and, if not, how many cars will be sold.

2. Using Figure 9.3, explain how the two MB curves shift if the attorney receives $\frac{1}{6}$ of the expected gain. What will happen to the number of hours the attorney would prefer to spend on the case? What will the client prefer?

3. Give three examples of asymmetric information in which the health consumer has information that is unavailable to the health provider. Give three concrete examples in which the health provider has information that is unavailable to the health consumer.

4. In the Akerlof example, the individuals are treated as indifferent to risk. What would you expect to see in these markets if individuals wanted to avoid risk? What if there were some "risk lovers?"

10

Imperfect Information: Supplier-Induced Demand and Small Area Variations

■ Supplier-Induced Demand (SID)

■ Models of SID

■ The Identification Problem

■ Evaluation of SID

■ Small Area Variations (SAV)

■ The Physician Practice Style Hypothesis

■ SAV and the Social Cost of Inappropriate Utilization

■ Evaluation of SAV

In chapter 9, we examined various applications of asymmetric information and im-
perfect agency. In particular, we saw that problems of information asymmetry affect
the health insurance industry with serious consequences. This chapter describes two
problems of information that have generated even more academic and policy interest.
The phenomenon of supplier-induced demand (SID) occurs when physicians abuse the
agency relationship with their patients in order to generate demand for personal gain; this
is made possible because physicians are more fully informed than patients. The phenom-
enon of small area variations (SAV), the frequently wide variations in per-capita rates of
surgery, physician visits, and hospitalization among otherwise-similar market areas, may
arise even when the physician acts as a perfect agent. In this case, it is imperfect informa-
tion on treatment outcomes that creates a distinctive problem leading to welfare losses.

SID and SAV have become major policy issues, and this chapter is devoted to both problems. The two parts are best read together to understand the similarities and the distinctions. However, the bodies of literature have developed separately and are presented here so that they can be studied separately. Because no single hypothesis has generated more interest and controversy among health economists than supplier-induced demand, we begin with this issue.

Supplier-Induced Demand (SID)

The idea behind SID is that health care providers have and use their superior knowledge to influence demand for self-interests; that is, they take advantage of the "information gap." The conditions for SID also are made possible through the physician's dual role as advisor to the patient and the provider of services. For many, these propositions have intuitive appeal and seem consistent with anecdotal evidence. Nevertheless, as we will see, it is difficult to develop and test formal models of SID.

In a world where physicians and patients were equally well informed or where physicians always act as well-meaning agents who are concerned only with patient welfare, SID would not occur. However, it is commonly argued that providers sometimes abuse their influence to generate demand—actions that can subvert the market's normal function.

On this point, Uwe Reinhardt (1989) went so far as to declare:

> The issue of physician-induced demand obviously goes straight to the heart of probably *the* major controversy in contemporary health policy, namely, the question whether adequate control over resource allocation to and within health care is best achieved through the demand side . . . or through regulatory controls on the supply side (p. 339).

Reinhardt questions whether health care markets can function according to the standard demand–supply model. In the standard model, consumers are sovereign and the volume and kinds of goods and services produced respond to independent consumer demands. If, however, consumers' demands are strongly influenced by providers, market forces may not restrain prices, limit the consumption of care, and allocate resources to their best uses. If SID is a major problem, Reinhardt argues that regulation should be a policy option.

A COMMON REPRESENTATION OF SID

The origins of SID can be traced to Shain and Roemer (1959) and Roemer (1961) who found positive correlations between short-term general hospital beds per 1,000 population and hospital days per 1,000 population. The relationships held across states as well as across upstate New York counties. The apparent phenomenon was interpreted as "a bed built is a bed filled," and this observation became known as Roemer's Law or the Roemer Effect.[1]

[1]Roemer (1961) also reported on a natural experiment where a sudden increase in hospital beds in one county, with no changes in other factors, led to a sharp increase in utilization rates. The terms *Say's Law* or *Parkinson's Law* for hospital beds as well as the availability effect have been used to describe the Roemer Effect.

The principle of Roemer's Law was thought by some to apply as well to physician services, and the general term identified as *supplier-induced demand (SID)* seemed a natural extension of the same basic idea. The underlying notion can be understood as an agency problem in that the reliance of the patient on a physician gives the physician a degree of discretionary influence.

Not all health economists, however, accept the SID proposition; they are divided into two camps. Those who believe that SID is an important phenomenon are labeled as the "broads" (Bs); those who challenge the phenomenon are called the "narrows" (Ns).

Figure 10.1 illustrates a commonly used model to explain SID, as well as to distinguish between the Ns and the Bs. Here, D_1 and S_1 represent the initial demand and short-run supply of physician services with an equilibrium at Q_1. Suppose the supply of physicians increases to S_2, *ceteris paribus*. The Ns would use standard analysis to predict that the price will fall from P_1 to P_3 and that the quantity demanded will increase from Q_1 to Q_3. Total spending will increase or decrease depending on the elasticity of demand. For services with an inelastic demand, such as physician care, total spending will decrease. Also, because more physicians are dividing up a smaller pie, the typical physician's share of patients and earnings also will diminish.

According to the Bs, however, an increase in supply leads directly to an increase in demand through the SID effect. Physicians are motivated by what otherwise would be a loss of patients and earnings to use their discretionary influence to shift demand. That is, demand will not remain independent and stable at D_1 but will be shifted out. Where it increases to a level such as D_2, the equilibrium price declines to P_2 with equilibrium quantity Q_2. However, if the increased demand is sufficiently large, such as shown by the shift to D'_2, the equilibrium price may even rise above the initial level to P'_2 with equilibrium quantity Q'_2.

Thus, as shown through Figure 10.1, the new equilibrium fee may be lower or higher under this view of SID. The case where the fee becomes higher came to be called the Reinhardt fee test of inducement. Under this test, evidence that fee increases follow increases in supply is interpreted as unequivocal support of the SID proposition.[2]

Much of the early empirical support for SID, however, came not from evidence regarding fees but from studies showing correlations (either simple or through multiple regression analysis) between physician availability and utilization rates. Although this evidence is consistent with SID, it also is consistent with standard analysis, as can be seen in Figure 10.1. Note that the equilibrium quantity of health care is larger after the supply curve shifts outward, regardless of whether or not the demand curve also shifts outward. Unless the study carefully distinguishes between shifts in demand versus a movement along a demand curve, the evidence of positive correlations does not support one theory over another.

Furthermore, even evidence that determines that demand has shifted somewhat following increases in supply is consistent with traditional economic arguments. An explanation of a demand shift is plausible under standard theory when the opportunity cost of patient travel times is a significant component of total cost. When increases in physician availability reduce travel times or waiting times, one would predict that the demand will increase. Furthermore, if increases in availability also lead to improvements in the quality of care, this too will shift the demand curve.

[2]Recall though from chapter 9 that the Pauly/Satterthwaite consumer information model offers an alternative explanation of higher fees.

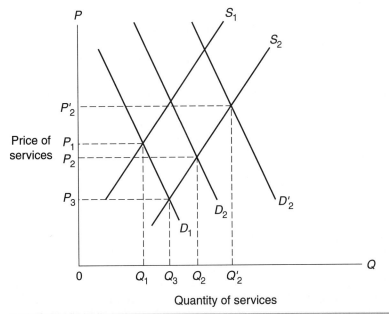

FIGURE 10.1 Increase in Supply Leading to Increases in Demand.

Models of SID

The representation of SID in the familiar context of a competitive market raises important questions that must be answered by a better working model. What is the motive to induce demand? Why would providers induce demand to a certain degree at one time and to a lesser degree at another? Why do providers not simply induce fully all the time? What is the mechanism through which they induce demand? How does inducement change in the face of increased supply? To answer questions like these, economists have developed several models of SID.

Price Rigidities and SID

One approach that can provide a logical explanation of demand inducement within the context of a competitive market model is to argue that prices tend to be rigid; that is, price does not adjust quickly to changes in demand or supply. To elaborate, suppose that prices in Figure 10.1 do not drop from their initial equilibrium at P_1 as supply increases. With the new supply curve, S_2, there is now an excess supply at P_1 if physicians continue to provide the original quantity of services. An excess supply means that at least some physicians are not on their supply curves providing the quantities they would like to sell at the existing price, and thus they would clearly have a motive for inducing additional quantities if that is possible.

The ability to induce demand depends on the agency responsibility that gives physicians opportunities for inducement. However, the motive to use this power and the extent to which it is used depend on the relative gains from the additional earnings versus the costs of the additional inducement activities. Aside from direct costs, time

costs are incurred because it may take time to persuade patients to consume more care. There is also a potential loss of patients who detect that the physician is not acting in their best interests.

Thus, while the demand may ultimately be shifted to the right, there is no way of theoretically determining just how far to the right. It depends upon the relationship between the incremental earnings and incremental inducement costs. If the incremental costs of inducement are relatively large because of serious damage to a physician's reputation, then we would expect little or no inducement. If it is easy to persuade patients to consume more services and professional and ethical constraints are minimal, then the demand shift can be substantial. We suggest though that demand will never be shifted to a level such as D'_2 where there would be an excess demand at the price P_1. Given the costs of inducement activity, providers have no reason to shift demand to the point where the quantity demanded exceeds the quantity providers are willing to supply at P_1.[3]

THE TARGET-INCOME MODEL OF SID

The target-income model often is used to explain the rapid increases in physician fees experienced in the 1960s and 1970s. These increases occurred despite rapid increases in physician availability. Under the target income hypothesis, instead of leading to lower fees and incomes, increases in physician availability led to higher fees in order for earnings to be maintained. Consumer ignorance provides physicians with discretionary influence to manipulate demand when, for example, fees are controlled. Physicians also have an untapped degree of monopoly price power that could be used to raise fees and incomes to some target level.

Evidence of physician behavior under fee controls, especially under the Economic Stabilization Program introduced in the early 1970s, has been cited to support the target-income hypothesis. The imposition of fee controls that limited the annual increases to 2.5 percent is often offered as a natural test of inducement.

Under conditions of price controls, several investigators found that utilization tended to increase—evidence consistent with the target-income model. Similar support comes from studies of Medicare utilization in Colorado.[4] In 1977, Colorado restructured its Medicare reimbursement rates by virtually freezing rates for urban physicians while providing large increases for nonurban physicians. Rice (1983) found that the relative decrease in fees for urban physicians led to increased surgical and ancillary services, as well as to more intensive medical and surgical care (measured by the number of standardized units per service).

Despite strong initial interest in target-income pricing, extreme versions of this approach have been largely discredited within the academic community. Significant prob-

[3]Some previous work on price rigidities in the physician services market found evidence of SID (Stano et al., 1985; Cromwell and Mitchell, 1986). Despite these contributions, however, price rigidities and disequilibrium models have not received wide attention in literature so that the corresponding picture remains incomplete. Further, the support has been weakened by empirical evidence for the hospital services markets that is consistent with a standard demand–supply model rather than with various disequilibrium models that incorporate inducement (Hay and Anderson, 1988).

[4]See Rice and Labelle (1989) for a review of this work. McGuire and Pauly (1991), however, distinguish between inducement effects following fee changes and income effects on physician behavior.

lems arise in explaining how the target income is established and why physicians do not consistently exploit their monopoly power by always pricing at profit-maximizing levels.[5] Note also that the target-income concept is similar to often-heard claims that large corporate firms have unexploited monopoly power to be able always to pass on tax increases or increases in other costs in order to maintain profit margins. Such claims, which would otherwise require these firms to price below profit-maximizing levels, are largely unsupported by empirical evidence. Furthermore, if physicians had the ability to target price, it would be reasonable to predict that physicians would have little concern about increases in costs, such as increases in malpractice insurance premiums, because they could always pass the increased costs on to consumers in the form of higher prices. Such, however, is not the case.

THE DISUTILITY OF DISCRETION MODEL

To understand the SID literature as a progression of ideas, we should reconsider one of the problems identified with the target-income approach. In particular, we will direct our attention to the problem of accounting for the chosen target. Why are physicians satisfied with a given target income? How can we explain the equilibrium inducement level and income level within the model itself?

A major innovation in this regard was introduced by Evans (1974). Evans represented the physician as a utility-maximizing provider whose utility function is expressed as follows:

$$U = U(Y, W, D)$$

where Y is net income, W is hours of work, and D represents the discretionary influence used to augment demand. The physician has monopoly power so that he or she faces a negatively sloped demand curve that shifts inward as the number of physicians increases. A key feature of the model is the assumed increasing marginal disutility of augmenting demand. According to Evans, physicians prefer not to induce demand and find greater incremental displeasure with greater inducement. This displeasure must be counterbalanced by the gains to income that inducement provides. When competition tends to reduce income, the physician may increase inducement to help offset this.

By placing limits on the extent to which demand will be increased, this feature addresses a weakness of earlier SID models that had no apparent brakes on physicians' abilities and willingness to increase demand. In the Evans framework, a physician will augment demand to the point where the marginal utility of the additional income equals the marginal disutility of the added work plus the marginal disutility of the discretionary influence.

Graphical Representation of the Evans Model

Several essential ideas of the Evans model can be made clearer with the aid of a graph. To do this, let us suppress the variable W, the work effort of the physician. Work effort was important to Evans's empirical tests, and thus we refer the interested reader

[5]Rizzo and Zeckhauser (1998) draw on economic theory to resurrect the possible importance of income targets to physician behavior. See also Rizzo and Blumenthal (1996).

to the original article. In this simplified model, let the physician's utility depend solely on income, Y, and discretionary demand, D.

In Figure 10.2, the indifference curves represent the physician's preferences. The indifference curves slope upward because one of the two "goods," that is D, is really a "bad." Can you see why they must slope upward? In order to remain on the same indifference curve, the physician must be compensated for engaging in a higher level of D. As is the usual case, however, higher curves are preferred.

To make the example straightforward and the measure of discretion concrete, let discretionary demand, D, be measured in units representing the number of induced units of service. If these induced units are sold at a constant profit rate of π, and if the maximum profit level with zero inducement is πQ_0, then the physician's total profit (income) can be described by $Y = \pi Q_0 + \pi D$. This equation is a linear equation with an intercept of πQ_0 and a slope of π. This linear equation represents the attainable combinations of Y and D available to the physician, and thus it represents the physician's income possibilities.

Figure 10.2 can now be used to describe a disutility of discretion equilibrium. In the figure, the physician seeks to reach the highest indifference curve attainable, and this outcome occurs at the point of tangency shown as point A. Furthermore, the figure illustrates the physician's response to increased competition. Let increased competition be represented as a reduction in the average profit rate the physician receives from providing units of service. A lower profit rate, π', results in a budget constraint with a flatter slope and a lower intercept. The new equilibrium occurs at point B. In this example, increased competition has led the physician to choose a higher degree of inducement (i.e., $D_B > D_A$).

FIGURE 10.2 Discretionary Influence and Income at Two Different Profit Rates.

Discretionary influence

Limitations of the Model

This simplified version accounts for inducement and income endogenously, one of the benefits of Evans's original model. The figure also illustrates a drawback of the original model—the fact that the model is ambiguous in its predictions of the effects of increased physician availability on the level of D. To see this, experiment with Figure 10.2 by drawing other indifference curves representing physicians with different preferences. You will find that a physician might alternatively reduce the inducement level, D, when the budget constraint rotates downward. That is, tangency can be achieved at point B' with a lower level of D on the indifference curve represented by the dotted curve. Economists summarize this ambiguity by saying that the comparative static properties of the model are not determinate. Using a different utility function, Ellis and McGuire (1986) note that imperfect agency may, in some circumstances, lead to an undersupply of care.

Another concern with the approach stems from the fact that physician producers are firms. In conventional economic theory of the firm, economists have found that the profit-maximization model often yields strong results. An alternative SID approach would determine whether a profit-maximization model yields stronger predictions in the context of SID.

A PROFIT-MAXIMIZING MODEL

Before describing such a framework, begin with the standard profit-maximizing conditions for a firm with a negatively sloped demand curve. This is shown in Figure 10.3 (at the intersection of the marginal revenue curve with the marginal cost curve) to produce the equilibrium price–quantity combination, P_1, Q_1. One of the key distinctions between monopoly and competition is that, at the monopoly equilibrium, price exceeds marginal cost. In competition, to the contrary, price equals marginal cost.

The gap between price and marginal cost in imperfect competition, much like the price rigidities case for price takers, creates an incentive to enhance demand. Why? If the seller can sell more at a price that is higher than marginal cost, profitability increases. Of course, alternatively, if there had been perfect information and perfect agency, the seller could not thus improve its position.

The Parallel Between Inducement and Advertising

On the other hand, with imperfect information and the ability to induce increases in demand, sellers often can improve their profits by inducing customers to buy more output. This idea is similar to theories of more typical commodities where sellers have an incentive to introduce advertising and product promotion in order to increase demand. However, these activities also raise costs so they should be undertaken only to the point where their marginal revenues equal marginal costs. The new equilibrium is illustrated in Figure 10.3 by the price–quantity combination P_2, Q_2.

As noted, the decision to induce, under this theory, has elements that are similar to standard advertising/product promotion decisions. The physician expects revenues to increase, but costs in the form of reputation loss and time costs also have to be recognized. Following Stano's (1987) representation of SID within this context, several observations follow from the advertising analogy.[6] First, the incentive to advertise will be linked to the gap

[6]Although it appears that the utility approach introduced earlier has been abandoned, in order to simplify the analysis, the various costs associated with foregone leisure and imperfect agency can be incorporated into the cost function.

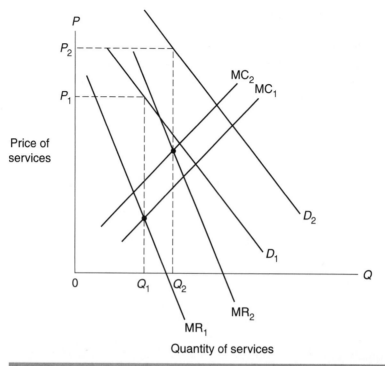

FIGURE 10.3 The Effects of Inducement on Marginal Revenue and Marginal Cost.

between marginal revenue and marginal cost. A small gap, which arises under a relatively elastic demand, reduces incentives. If the typical physician has a high degree of monopoly power, the gap will be large. Empirical evidence indicates that while the overall elasticity of demand for physician care is low, the elasticity of demand facing individual providers is considerably higher.[7] That is, the market for physician services is monopolistically competitive. Further, with suggestions that the market has become more competitive,[8] the foregoing approach predicts that the incentive to induce demand is likely to be diminishing.

A second important consideration follows in that the optimal level will depend on the relative costs and gains of manipulating consumer demand. Previous discussion of agency suggested that consumers are not as ignorant as is often assumed. Ethical and professional considerations restrict physician activities, and, notably, various contracts between principal and agent have evolved to limit physicians' informational advantages. These include the monitoring feature of the traditional physician–patient relationship, as well as other arrangements introduced by third-party payers and managed care contracts. The effects of the various constraints on physician behavior are to raise costs of imperfect agency and thereby reduce the extent of SID.

Finally, if we draw the advertising analogy closely, we also can expand somewhat our concept of physician inducement. That is, we can recognize some forms of inducement by physicians that are no more or less harmful to the patient than are some forms

[7]See Langwell and Nelson (1986) for a review of the evidence.
[8]See P. Feldstein (1986) and Newhouse (1988).

of advertising to the general consumer. Certainly, if inducement takes the form of a physician providing misinformation, recommending procedures or risks not suitable for the patient, or recommending excessive levels of care, then inducement is correctly characterized as a problem of imperfect agency. This is understandably the form of SID that is worrisome to policy analysts. However, just as advertising may sometimes work its demand-enhancing effects through its informational function, so sometimes may physician inducement take the form of providing enhanced information to the patient.

The Identification Problem*

Despite extensive literature on the subject, the difficulties of developing and testing theoretically consistent models of SID have limited the applicability of much of the empirical work. The problem is that in much of the empirical work, the SID effect cannot be econometrically identified. The identification problem in econometrics was explained in chapter 3, and reference to that chapter may be helpful.

THE IDENTIFICATION PROBLEM: AN ALGEBRAIC EXAMPLE

The problem will be illustrated next with the help of an algebraic example. For those readers who wish to forego the algebraic derivations, we summarize as follows. Begin with demand and supply curves such as those illustrated in Figure 10.1. The identification problem is exemplified by the following fact: If we construct an algebraic model *with no SID*, the resulting equation that is commonly estimated by researchers will look much the same as the equation derived from an algebraic model *with SID*. This fact is suggestive of the problem faced by the econometrician in that SID often cannot be distinguished from no SID by the statistical evidence.

To confirm this point, following Folland and Stano (1990), we begin with an algebraic demand–supply model without SID as represented by the following linear equations:

$$QD = a_0 + a_1 P + a_2 Y + u_1 \tag{10.1}$$

and

$$QS = b_0 + b_1 P + b_2 X + b_3 \text{MD} + u_2 \tag{10.2}$$

where QD and QS represent quantities demanded and supplied and P represents price. Exogenous demand variables such as income and education are represented in the demand equation by Y, and while exogenous variables in the supply equation, such as the price of inputs, are represented by X. The variable MD represents the availability of physicians. From these two equations plus the condition that the quantity supplied, QS, equals the quantity demanded, QD, we can solve for the equilibrium quantity:

$$Q = c_0 + c_1 X + c_2 Y + c_3 \text{MD} + v \tag{10.3}$$

The coefficients in equation (10.3) are complicated combinations of those in equations (10.1) and (10.2), as will be discovered when one performs the algebra (see exercise 5). When the econometrician estimates the parameter c_3 and discovers it to be greater than zero, he or she can conclude correctly that increased physician availability (that is, increased MD), has a positive effect on equilibrium utilization. However, this cannot be taken as evidence of SID; recall that by assumption we started with a model with *no SID*.

*For more advanced students.

For SID to exist would mean that physician availability affects demand directly; that is, it would mean that MD appears directly in the demand equation. To illustrate, suppose that SID does exist. In that case, a model of demand with SID would be as follows:

$$Q = a_0 + a_1 P + a_2 Y + a_3 MD + u_1 \qquad \textbf{(10.4)}$$

Here the availability of physicians (that is, the variable MD) appears directly in the demand equation as a demand shift variable. Upon solving algebraically equations (10.4) and (10.2), the resulting equation with SID looks just like equation (10.3) without SID.

Furthermore, the econometrician usually will not be able to use the resulting estimates to determine whether or not SID exists. As Auster and Oaxaca (1981) have shown, this identification problem is not resolved easily, even when more sophisticated estimation methods are used. This finding has been reinforced through an innovative approach involving the demand for childbirths. Dranove and Wehner (1994) show that a statistical method (two-stage least squares) often used to estimate the inducement effect produces "evidence" of inducement for childbirths even though one would not expect to find inducement here. The apparent anomaly arises because that method does not deal properly with identification issues.

Dranove and Wehner tested this issue in an unusual and revealing way by beginning with the "assumption" that obstetricians per capita (OBGYN) have the power to induce demand for childbirths and asked "suppose we test this hypothesis using the typical approach in the SID literature—the two-stage least squares technique." This technique, like other regression techniques, requires that the equations be correctly identified.

Applying U.S. county data, the researchers first showed that OBGYN and childbirths per capita were positively correlated (0.33, $p < 0.01$), a result to be expected through the ordinary long run operations of supply and demand. They then applied the two-stage procedure, as it is typically used in the SID literature, to measure the "pure SID" effect, an effect that is logically impossible to occur in the experimental circumstances. Their estimated SID elasticity for obstetricians per capita was 8 percent, seeming to ludicrously imply that an influx of obstetricians per capita of one standard deviation (a standard deviation was 0.064 obstetricians per 1,000 population) would induce an additional 7 percent in childbirths per capita! As a result, we conclude that much of the reported evidence of SID is unreliable. An account of the evidence must appeal to studies that have in some way successfully avoided the identification problem.

THE EVIDENCE ON SID

One way of overcoming the identification problem is through the study of the effects of fee rigidities or price controls. These studies, some of which were reviewed earlier, generally indicate that the volume of services increases after controls are imposed; that is, some SID effect is found. The magnitude of the effect, however, tends to be modest.

Another way of overcoming the identification problem is to circumvent it. In this regard, Hay and Leahy (1982) formulated a simple proposition. If imperfect agency leads to a higher volume of services provided, we ought to see those with more complete information consuming fewer services. The authors, in fact, found that after controlling for other socioeconomic factors including health status, medical professionals and their families are at least as likely to visit physicians as others who are presumably less well informed.

The contributions by Rossiter and Wilensky (1983, 1984) are also noteworthy. These authors distinguished between patient-initiated visits, presumably not subject to physician control, and what may be subsequent physician-initiated visits. The authors attempt to identify the extent of SID by focusing on the relationship between the physician-initiated component and variables representing physician self-interests. In particular, if SID exists, increases in physician availability would be expected to increase physician-initiated services, *ceteris paribus,* but would not affect patient-initiated visits. The authors found exactly this pattern; however, the estimated SID effect elasticity, although it was statistically significant, was small—less than 0.1. This means that a 10 percent increase in physician availability produces an inducement effect of less than 1 percent. In the context of Dranove and Wehner's findings, even these magnitudes are suspect.

In a similar study of Medicare beneficiaries, Escarce (1992) found that greater availability of surgeons increased initial contacts with surgeons but had little effect on the intensity of subsequent services. The higher utilization resulting from an increased supply of surgeons is thus associated with patients' preferences for access to care or referrals rather than to SID.

Elsewhere, Grytten and colleagues (1995) also distinguished between patient and primary physician-initiated visits under the fixed-fee schedules of Norway's public health care system. The investigators did not find any evidence of either SID or rationing of physician-initiated visits, though there was some indication of inducement for laboratory tests. More recently, Sørenson and Grytten (1999) studied the effects of increased competition in Norway. Increases in the number of physicians in an area, as expected, reduced the number of patients seen by a typical physician. However, contrary to the SID hypothesis, Norwegian physicians did not compensate for their falling incomes by increasing services for patients who remained.

OTHER LIMITATIONS ON SID

Two other contributions provide theoretical grounds to suppose that there are inherent limits on the physician's ability to influence demand. Rochaix (1989) recognized that a patient is not fully dependent on any physician and in fact forms prior expectations about his or her own condition. If the physician's suggestions deviate sufficiently from those expectations, the patient may not consent to the proposed care, but rather seek another opinion. This ex ante monitoring constrains physicians' behavior. The author demonstrates that it takes only a small number of informed patients to constrain physicians to act as "better agents."

Similarly, Dranove (1988) proposed that patients form expectations about the severity of their conditions. In the inducement decision, a physician is concerned about the loss of business were he or she to develop a reputation as overly aggressive. Among various factors, Dranove showed that improvements in patients' diagnostic skills reduce the gains from inducement.

Evaluation of SID

Our partial review of the SID literature has selected from a wide range of contributions and ideas. The whole of the SID literature shows that the intuitively simple idea of physicians inducing demand actually has many, often interesting complexities. Pauly (1988b) and Phelps (1986) have even suggested that the complexities inherent in

the SID-imperfect information controversy mean that the issue may never be settled completely.

Elements of competition, agency relationships, and consumer search place substantial limits on the ability and willingness of physicians to generate increases in demand. Research contributions that lend support to SID are often unable to overcome theoretical or statistical problems that cloud their interpretation. Often reports of SID confound the normal workings of markets with the perception of extraordinary workings. SID must first be separated from cases where the supply of physicians increases but no shift of demand occurs. This problem in econometric analysis is the "identification problem" to which two stage least squares analysis is typically addressed. Two-stage analysis is itself prone to errors and misinterpretation. The best two stage analyses, in any case, suggest a very small SID effect, if any. Other approaches also tend to minimize our estimates of SID.

Therefore, it seems safe to suggest that health care markets often can be studied using models that postulate stable demand functions even though there may be some degree of SID. In other words, consumers are not nearly as helpless as many might imagine in that they take steps to protect their self-interests when those interests are threatened. It follows that it would be reckless to argue market failure, at least on the basis of SID, and to dismiss policy analysis based on standard models as ineffective.

Small Area Variations (SAV)

Our work on asymmetric information and agency relationships emphasized the effects of a patient's information disadvantage, as well as the physician's dual role as provider and agent. We have not yet, however, considered the likelihood that physicians themselves are not perfectly informed about the outcomes and relative effectiveness of alternative treatments. For conditions with alternative treatments, it is easy to imagine physicians having different levels of information or disagreements about the most appropriate care. Are the wide geographic variations in the per-capita utilization rates for many medical and surgical procedures related to this information problem, and what is the significance of these variations?

The study of medical decision making and small area variations (SAV) developed in medical research. Economists became increasingly interested in SAV once they recognized its policy implications, as well as the potential role of information in explaining this phenomenon. Whereas SID occurs in theory due to the information gap between physicians and patients, differences in treatment patterns across small areas may occur because of physicians' uncertainty and ignorance over the best medical practice. Thus, even if physicians acted as perfect agents, the consequences resulting from their own information gaps must be examined.

Much of the modern interest in SAV stems from the pioneering work of John Wennberg and colleagues (1973, 1977, 1982), who studied New England hospital markets. Their evidence of wide variations across small service markets has been corroborated by many others. Nevertheless, the sources for these variations, as well as their importance to public policy, remain controversial. Why do women in one New England town undergo hysterectomies at more than twice the rate of another, apparently simi-

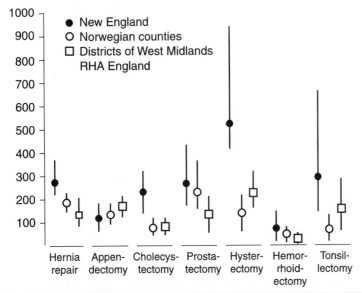

FIGURE 10.4 Mean and Range of Age- and Sex-Standardized Rates for Common Surgical Procedures—New England, Norway and the West Midlands of England.

McPherson et al. (1982, Figure 1) Copyright © 1975 Massachusetts Medical Society.

lar, New England town? As Figure 10.4 shows, the phenomenon is not limited to New England or even to small areas

Figure 10.4 illustrates some early findings for seven common surgical procedures in regions of New England, the United Kingdom, and Norway. The use rates, which have been corrected for age and gender differences across populations, vary widely for some procedures, as shown by the ranges in Figure 10.4. Wide intercountry differences also exist in the mean rates.

Despite many possible sources of the variations, most of the controversy has focused on the role of physician practice style and the question of whether the observed variations are evidence of unnecessary or inappropriate care. The resolution of this controversy is clearly crucial for policy. As we will show, if the variations can be reduced through scientific research on patient outcomes, substantial welfare gains for society can be achieved.

The Physician Practice Style Hypothesis

SAV analysis often focuses on service utilization rates in small, contiguous hospital markets with populations that are relatively homogeneous. This method helps rule out differences in population characteristics (e.g., health status, education, and income) as the sources for the observed variations. Because initial studies of this type suggested that

population characteristics do not account for much of the observed variations, some researchers proposed that SAV is caused in part by supplier-induced demand. This explanation further links SID and SAV. Others posit a distinct source of the variations through the "practice style hypothesis."

Wennberg (1984) argued that much of the observed variation is closely related to the degree of physician uncertainty with respect to diagnosis and treatment. When there is little consensus about the effect and value of a medical procedure, a wide range of physician practice styles is considered to be within the bounds of accepted practice. The physician's habits, beliefs, and patterns of practice are seen as his or her "style." Some analysts have further suggested that physicians within a given market tend to "follow the pack" and eventually share a common set of beliefs. These beliefs, and therefore practice styles and utilization rates, often will differ across markets.

MODELING PRACTICE STYLE

To develop and test a rigorous model of practice style is a more difficult challenge than simply to postulate this hypothesis. One approach introduced by Folland and Stano (1989) modeled differences in practice style through differences in physicians' beliefs about the true production function of alternative procedures to treat a particular condition. Within the language of health economics, the practice styles of physicians relfect their imperfect information about the technology of producing health (i.e., the production function). Figure 10.5 shows three different production functions for a patient with uterine leiomyoma (fibroids)—a condition often leading to hysterectomy, which is a high variation surgical procedure. In reality, there is a true production function but it is not known by the physician. The physician must conjecture or estimate what the effects of each treatment step will be.

FIGURE 10.5 Different Physician Beliefs About the Relationship between Medical Care and Health Status.

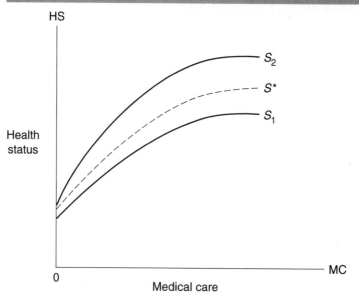

Suppose that the horizontal axis, MC, measures the medical care labor and capital combinations that are used to treat the patient. Moving along the horizontal axis represents a progression of care from simple office visits and surveillance to surgery. Differences in practice style are shown by differences in beliefs about the true production function. Physician 2 with the production function S_2 is much more optimistic about the effects of medical care on the patient's outcome or health status (HS) than Physician 1 with production function S_1. In principle, both physicians could be "misinformed," and the true production function might be one such as S^*.

Which physician is more likely to recommend more services including hysterectomy? Under the practice style hypothesis, those like Physician 2 who most strongly believe in the effectiveness of hysterectomy will be more likely to recommend surgery. Differences in practice styles, therefore, provide a possible accounting for interarea differences in utilization rates. If physicians of type 1 and 2 are not distributed similarly across markets, then the hysterectomy rates will vary. Of course, wide variations in practice styles within markets can be consistent with little variation in average practice styles across markets, and therefore in the predicted per-capita rates of utilization. This possibility marks one of the deficiencies of studying the practice style phenomenon through population-based utilization data.

The production function approach to practice style also helps to show that a seemingly high surgery rate in a market does not automatically represent unnecessary care, particularly where there is ambiguity or incomplete scientific information about the true production function. Furthermore, as medical science uncovers better information about the true production function (assume it is S^*), efforts to disseminate this information will help reduce unnecessary surgery among Physician 2 types, but it also will promote hysterectomies among those who were previously overly pessimistic about their effectiveness.

Finally, our approach indicates why it can be difficult to distinguish SID from SAV. Areas with a high proportion of providers like Physician 2 will have high surgery rates, tempting some observers to conclude that SID is prevalent, whereas the true source is practice style. It also can be true that physicians in those high utilization areas are merely acting as good agents by supporting their patient beliefs and preferences for surgery. Here the variations are due to patient preferences rather than SID or SAV.

TESTING THE PRACTICE STYLE HYPOTHESIS

How well does the practice style hypothesis hold up empirically? The basic problem with even well-defined theoretical concepts of practice style is that the empirical researcher has no apparent objective measure of practice style. In the absence of an operational measure, evidence for the hypothesis will necessarily be indirect. Such indirect evidence is available, and it comes from several sources.

Education, Feedback, and Surveillance

Some studies show that education, feedback, and surveillance programs directed at physicians can alter their behavior and thus presumably their practice styles.[9] One study found that an informational program significantly affected the tonsillectomy rates in 13

[9]Those discussed here are Wennberg et al. (1977), Dyck et al. (1977), and Nyman et al. (1990).

New England areas. Another similarly found that the rate of unjustified hysterectomies dropped by two-thirds subsequent to a review program introduced in the Canadian province of Saskatchewan. But even though intuitive reasoning suggests that monitoring should change behavior, the effects are not always large. For example, reviews to identify inappropriate claims submitted by physicians under Medicare only marginally reduce the rates at which inappropriate claims are submitted.

Comparing Utilization Rates in Homogeneous Areas

A second empirical approach to investigate the practice style hypothesis is illustrated through an early but influential study by Wennberg and Fowler (1977). The authors extensively studied utilization rates and population characteristics for six areas in Vermont. After finding that morbidity and many other socioeconomic variables were not statistically significant, they concluded that the differences in use rates probably are due largely to practice style differences across areas.

Though practice style differences can contribute to differences in utilization across areas, the inference that interarea differences in utilization rates, even in apparently similar areas, are due largely to differences in practice style is incorrect. Green and Becker (1994) performed a SAV analysis in which they compared two demographically similar towns in Michigan where acute cardiac ischemia (ACI) discharge rates differed by a factor of three. Large differences in admission were due more to differences in the proportions of patients with ACI who went to their hospital emergency department rather than to differences in physician decision making. Area variation does not necessarily mean variation in practice style.

Multiple Regression Approaches

It is generally desirable to examine interarea utilization through statistical techniques that control for the other factors simultaneously. The inclusion of many or conceivably all relevant measurable variables in the analysis suggests another indirect approach to the practice style issue. As more variables are added to the analysis, one learns better how much of the observed variation can be explained by standard socioeconomic variables without resorting to the hypothesis of practice style. In cases where the variations are largely explained by such variables, the potential role of practical style is small and much of the mystery of the variations phenomenon is eliminated. In contrast, an inability to explain the variations in terms of the usual variables leaves open the possibility that practice style and other unknown factors are responsible for much of the variation. Practice style is then essentially the residual when other impacts have been explained.

Multiple regression studies using standard socioeconomic variables explain substantial amounts of the interarea variations, especially when they focus on aggregated utilization rates (commonly representing a weighted average of many procedures) in larger geographic areas.[10] Multiple regression analysis at the small area level for individual procedures, as opposed to aggregates over large numbers of procedures, has generally been less successful in explaining the variations. Nevertheless, Phelps and Parente

[10]See Folland and Stano (1990). Folland and Stano (1989) also show the conditions under which the residual variation from multiple regression can be taken as an upper bound for the contribution of practice style. They showed that practice style is relatively unimportant for large aggregated sets of commodities.

(1990) found that standard demand and supply variables typically account for between 40 percent and 75 percent of the variation in their study of 134 separate diagnostic categories. Elsewhere, Escarce (1993) found that 43 percent of the variation in cataract surgery rates for the Medicare population is explained by socioeconomic variables. This still leaves a potential 57 percent that may be due to practice style. However, after purging the surgery rates of any possible practice style influence, Escarce found that the variation in cataract surgery rates was reduced by only a small amount.

These contributions indicate that practice style could be important for some procedures, but the contribution of other variables should not be overlooked. As Escarce demonstrates, it also would be wrong to attribute all or most of the unexplained variation in utilization rates to practice style. For many procedures, conventional economic and demographic influences may well dominate the as-yet-undetermined effects of practice style.[11]

SAV and the Social Cost of Inappropriate Utilization

The most important and controversial issue in the SAV literature is the proposition that substantial variation in utilization rates across market areas is an indication of inappropriate care. It is tempting to reach these conclusions (even though our previous discussion warns against this) and to extrapolate savings under the assumption that high-use areas experience the rates found in lower-use areas. For example, Wennberg and colleagues compared utilization rates in Boston and New Haven.[12] The authors argued that the cities are demographically similar, but because Boston has much higher utilization rates, substantial reductions on health care spending in Boston are possible.

The potential savings from improving the quality of care and reducing excessive utilization in particular has led to a national focus on research into patient outcomes. Indicative of this priority, the U.S. Congress in late 1989 created the Agency for Health Care Policy and Research. The agency's primary missions are "to determine what works and to develop practice guidelines and standards to assess and assure quality of care."

The concept of consumers' surplus shows how welfare losses due to variations in utilization rates can be measured (Phelps, 1995). The basics are illustrated in Figure 10.6, where the true marginal benefit curve for medical care involving a procedure X is given by the curve MB^*. This curve reflects the benefits as perceived by the patient if he or she were to have full and complete scientific knowledge. We emphasize that the marginal benefit curve is not objectively determined by medical science but reflects patient valuations over the health and other consequences of the procedure. The efficient, fully informed rate of use is thus R_2, the rate at which MB^* crosses the marginal cost curve, MC.

With underutilization, such as at R_1, a gain in consumers' surplus could be achieved by increasing use of medical care up to R_2. The gain in consumer surplus is shown by triangle A, measured under the marginal benefit curve and above the marginal cost curve. This area represents the inefficiency or welfare loss to society from underutilization. In

[11]This result is illustrated by Coyte and colleagues (1997), who found that more than 90 percent of the variation in knee replacement (KR) rates in a large Canadian province was explained by demographic and regional variables. Surprisingly, the reported prevalence of arthritis and rheumatism was not a statistically significant determinant. The authors recognize that the remaining variation could be accounted for by many factors including "clinical perceptions of the appropriate rate of KR."

[12]Wennberg, Freeman, and Culp (1987); Wennberg et al. (1989); Fisher et al. (1994).

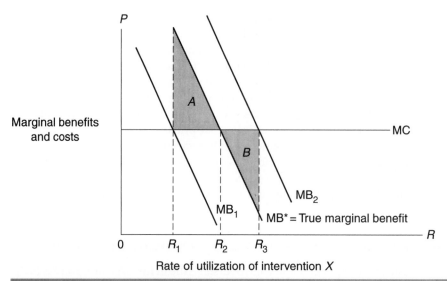

FIGURE 10.6 The Inefficiency of Misinformation about the Marginal Benefit of Health Care.

a similar fashion, one can measure the welfare loss of inefficiently excessive utilization at rate R_3 by triangle B.

Despite the simple and direct application of consumers' surplus concepts to the welfare losses of practice variations, it has proved difficult to generate reliable estimates of these costs. Phelps and Parente (1990) and Phelps and Mooney (1992) approached the problem by using regression analysis to estimate true marginal benefit curves.[13] However, the approach has drawn criticism in several respects. Regression always predicts the dependent variable imperfectly, leaving a residual. How much of the residual is due to inappropriate use and how much to legitimate omitted factors, such as patient preferences, can never be known with certainty.

Furthermore, Dranove (1995) has pointed out that patients also make errors ex ante when estimating the true value that medical care will deliver ex post. This additional "noise" disturbs our estimates further. Most economists studying the issue probably would agree that while we are sure that inappropriate use occurs commonly and is often costly, we do not yet have confident estimates of the total costs of inappropriate care.

Regardless of the empirical challenges, many leading scholars in the medical community now recognize the importance of using an economic concept of benefits, as opposed to benefit measures determined strictly by medical science, and they are urging physicians to involve patients in treatment decisions. Differences between economists and medical researchers over SAV, practice style, and appropriate care thus apear to be narrowing. In particular, the consensus is growing in the health services literature that cost-effectiveness analysis and other forms of program evaluation (chapter 4) are the best means to identify and rank treatments through their effects on social welfare.

[13]After eliminating legitimate sources of variation, and by assuming that the average rate across markets is the correct rate, Phelps and Mooney (1992) estimated that the total welfare loss from the top 25 procedures exceeded $6 billion in 1987.

Clinical Decision Making and Patient Preferences

David Eddy is a pioneer in studying the role of information, medical science, and preferences in clinical decision making. Eddy (1990) breaks the treatment decision into two main components—evaluating the outcome of alternatives and then comparing and choosing from among the options.[14] The first component is largely a scientific one determined primarily through clinical studies of patient outcomes. However, for many patient conditions, even a fully informed physician will face the problem of inadequate scientific information.

The second component, comparing the alternatives, involves judgment and patient preferences. Eddy emphasizes that "it is the patient's preferences that should determine the decision" (p. 442).

A failure to make appropriate decisions can arise from failures in both stages. Clearly, a physician's inadequacies in education and training, as well as deliberate attempts to misrepresent outcomes (e.g., to engage in SID), will distort information needed at the second step. Similarly, if patients misrepresent or physicians misinterpret their preferences, or if inadequate information is communicated to patients, the second step will be flawed.

The medical community is increasingly being alerted to the role of the patient through the development of new information technology to improve the decision-making process. For example, Wennberg and colleagues have developed an interactive videodisc that helps patients with prostate cancer choose from among several treatment options. To help with the decision, patients answer questions designed to measure their attitude toward risk and their ability to tolerate discomfort.

Evaluation of SAV

Many medical and surgical procedures have wide variations in use rates. Some of the variation involves little or no welfare loss, and health economists caution against the notion of a scientifically correct use rate for all areas. Efficient rates will vary to the extent they reflect the confluence of patient preferences and other economic factors with scientific information.

Nevertheless, physician uncertainty and practice style may lead to unwanted or unnecessary variations in care. The degree to which they contribute to the variations is not completely understood. Despite the emphasis on practice style, some SAV researchers believe that SID and the availability of hospital resources are also important. Others have found less obvious sources including some associated with purely statistical phenomena and inadequacies in data-gathering methods.[15]

[14]Eisenberg's (1986) work on physician decision making and practice patterns is also a major contribution and valuable reference.

[15]For example, Diehr and colleagues (1990) have demonstrated that, due to random variation, the observed variation across small areas can be high even when the underlying rates across the areas are the same. Legnini et al. (1991) showed that information about new technologies contributes to increasing variation, as well as increasing use of these technologies. Schwartz et al. (1994) found that variations in hospitalization rates using more than one year of data are substantially reduced.

Regardless of the relative contribution of practice style to interarea variations, it is likely that uncertainties in the clinical benefits of many procedures create substantial welfare losses through overuse, underuse, and misuse. The growing recognition of informational inadequacies as major barriers to better care has led to massive private and public efforts to determine "what works." More formally referred to as evidence-based medicine, this search involves the systematic collection and evaluation of clinical data. With its strong emphasis on cost-effectiveness analysis, many scholars are optimistic about the role of evidence-based medicine in helping health plans improve the quality and efficiency of their care.

Summary

1. Supplier-induced demand (SID) refers to the phenomenon of physicians deviating from their agency responsibilities to provide care for their self-interests rather than their patients' interests.
2. SID represents one of the major intellectual and policy controversies in health economics. Its origins can be traced to Roemer's Law, which predicts that a "bed built is a bed filled."
3. SID is typically represented graphically by increases in demand following increases in supply, although there are theoretical flaws with this representation.
4. The target-income hypothesis is a related idea that suggests that physicians use their discretionary advantage to achieve a target level of income.
5. Evans theorized that the utility of the gain in income has to be balanced by the disutility of inducement and the disutility of the work in providing care. This idea establishes theoretical limits on the level of inducement.
6. The disequilibrium approach to SID resulting from price rigidities establishes a gap between demand and supply and a motive to induce increases in demand.
7. Another approach develops the analogy between inducement and advertising. It predicts that inducement will diminish as competition reduces the gap between a physician's marginal revenue and marginal cost.
8. The identification problem, which refers to the difficulty of determining the extent of SID, has plagued much of the empirical literature on the subject.
9. The empirical work that has overcome or sidestepped the identification problem has found evidence of SID. However, the magnitudes tend to be much smaller than was believed originally by supporters of the hypothesis.
10. Although conventional economic analysis oversimplifies the physician services market, the standard competitive and monopoly models provide useful insight into the effects of changes in demand and physician availability on prices and quantities.
11. The small area variations (SAV) phenomenon refers to the wide interarea variations in the per-capita use rates found for many medical and surgical procedures. Such variations have been found in the United States and many other countries.
12. The practice style hypothesis, which refers to physician uncertainty in diagnosis and treatment, has been proposed as the major explanatory factor for the variation.
13. Practice style can be modeled through differences among physicians in their beliefs about the marginal benefits of alternative treatments.
14. Most of the evidence for the practice style hypothesis is indirect, coming from studies showing the following:

- changes in practice patterns following physician education and monitoring;
- wide variations in utilization rates across small, homogeneous areas;
- high, unexplained residuals in multiple regression analyses of interarea utilization rates.

15. The SAV phenomenon is often interpreted to suggest that considerable amounts of unnecessary care are being provided and that major savings are possible through elimination of that care.
16. Substantial problems remain, however, in identifying inappropriate care and properly accounting for the role of patient preferences.

Discussion Questions

1. Suppose that insurers monitored all health care payments to determine whether the services were appropriate. Would you expect to see more or less tendency toward SID?
2. Figure 10.2 shows how increased competition can lead to a higher degree of inducement at point *B*. This suggests that providers try to induce more usage to compensate for lower profit margins. Suppose, however, that the physician ends up at point *B'*, where there is less inducement. What types of preferences would lead to reduced inducement in response to less profits?
3. How is the possibility of SID related to the price elasticity of demand for services? Does increased demand elasticity increase or decrease the possibility of SID?
4. If prices are relatively rigid so that they do not adjust rapidly to changes in supply, explain how SID can be manifested.
5. What are some criticisms of the target-income approach to SID? In the target-income model, what determines the physician's target income? Would target incomes differ between physicians in practice? Would some physicians choose instead to be income maximizers?
6. What forces limit a provider's ability and willingness to engage in SID? In the profit-maximizing model of SID, what are the costs to the physician of inducement? Give examples of inducement costs.
7. Assume that SID is prevalent and that few forces limit or check this phenomenon. What are some of the implications for policy?
8. In what ways is inducement similar to advertising? In what ways is it different?
9. How do the medical care consumption patterns of physicians and their families differ from those of nonphysicians? If physicians may be considered well informed, what does this suggest about the SID hypothesis? Does it matter for this point that physicians tend to have larger-than-average incomes? Discuss.
10. What is the SAV phenomenon? What are some economic forces that can help explain SAV? What are some demographic and other considerations? How might physician uncertainty lead to SAV? What evidence supports the practice style hypothesis?
11. What possible criticisms can you propose for the idea that areas with high utilization rates for a procedure indicate the provision of unnecessary care?
12. Suppose you observed that there are no interarea variations in the use rates for some procedures. Can this be taken as evidence that good health care is being provided? If not, what other kinds of information would be useful?

13. If one cause of SAV is lack of information about various procedures, would you expect SAV to have increased, decreased, or stayed the same over time? Why?

14. As new technologies become available more rapidly for given procedures, would you expect an increased or decreased amount of small area variation?

15. Suppose large variations occur in average use rates per person within small areas, as well as between small areas. Does this necessarily mean that the practice style hypothesis is incorrect? Suppose there are zero or small variations in average use rates between small areas. Does this necessarily mean that the practice style hypothesis is incorrect? Discuss.

Exercises

1. Roemer's Law states that "a bed built is a bed filled." Use demand and supply analysis to show how Roemer's Law may be an example of the false cause fallacy where cause and effect have been reversed. *Hint!* Assume an increase in demand for hospital beds under conditions where beds can be supplied at a constant unit cost.

2. Explain why the standard demand–supply framework in which prices adjust immediately to a new equilibrium is inconsistent with SID.

3. Explain why the indifference curves in Figure 10.2 are positively sloped.

4. If the use of discretionary influence were not a "bad," what would the indifference curves in Figure 10.2 look like? Where would the equilibrium solution along the physician's income locus be found?

5. Set QD in equation (10.1) equal to QS in equation (10.2) and solve for P, showing that it is a linear function of the remaining variables.
 Substitute your solution for P back into either (10.1) or (10.2) and solve for $Q = QD$ (or QS) to find equation (10.3). Alternatively, solve for P in each of the equations by putting P on the left-hand side. These are known as the inverse demand-and-supply equations. Then eliminate P by setting the two equations equal to another and solve for Q.

6. Consider the evidence that fee controls or price ceilings tend to be followed by utilization increases. Why doesn't this evidence necessarily support either the target income pricing or SID hypotheses? *Hint:* Consider a physician with some degree of monopoly power and, for simplicity, constant marginal cost. Examine the profit-maximizing price and quantity combinations before and after a price ceiling is introduced to determine what will happen to utilization and spending.

7. In comparing SAV across diseases and diagnoses, would more complicated diseases suggest greater or lesser variation?

8. Using Figure 10.6, what are the welfare gains to consumers in going from R_1 to R_2? What are the costs of the increased consumption? Show that the net gain corresponds to the area represented as A.

9. Consider the approximation of the welfare loss due to interarea deviations from the correct rate of care. All else equal, which procedures would yield the largest welfare losses—those with low price elasticities or those with high price elasticities? Why is this the case?

CHAPTER

The Organization of Health Insurance Markets

- Loading Costs and the Behavior of Insurance Firms

- Employer Provision of Health Insurance and the Tax System

- Who Pays for Health Insurance?

- Employer-Based Health Insurance and Job Mobility

- The Market for Insurance

- The Uninsured—An Analytical Framework

- Conclusions

Chapter 7 introduced the concept of insurance with a primary focus on health insurance. Insurance is an arrangement that allows risk-averse individuals to reduce or eliminate the risks they face. Consumers buy insurance to replace the uncertainty of a large loss or major expenditure with the more certain prospect of regular premiums. Profit-seeking firms supply insurance. In an idealized insurance market, the premium as a percentage of the loss resulting from an event will approach the probability of the event's occurring.

We concentrated fundamentally on the impact of insurance on individuals. In this chapter, we focus on the insurance market and the behaviors of firms within that market. Within the context of the employer-provided health insurance that is so common in the United States, we establish who pays for health insurance. We continue with an examination of employer-provided insurance and job mobility. We then look at the traditional community-rated health insurance (where individuals or groups all pay the same premium) and show how that market has changed. An analysis of the uninsured concludes the chapter.

Loading Costs and the Behavior of Insurance Firms

Consumers can improve their well-being by sacrificing a (relatively) small, certain premium to insure against the probability of a considerably larger loss. It is important now to demonstrate how the policies will be offered to specific groups and why, in fact, some groups will find it difficult to get insurance at all.

We have referred to the model of a competitive industry, in which the firms will compete to where profits become zero, or normal. If profits are higher (lower), firms will enter (leave) the market. Only when profits have become zero, or normal, will entry and exit cease. In this model, the insurance carriers would collect money during the year and pay some of it out. In good years (for the carriers), carriers would pay out less than collected; in bad years, they would pay out more. The good (and bad) years should be random. If firms have systematically good (bad) years, it suggests excess profits (losses), and the probability of entry into (exit from) the industry by other firms.

We also have previously shown how moral hazard can lead firms to offer certain types of coverage and not others. In particular, firms would shy away from covering conditions that are accompanied by price elastic demands for services.

IMPACTS OF LOADING COSTS

Firms have additional costs of doing business, often referred to as *loading costs*. These costs are largely related to the numbers and types of customers and claims that they process. As a result, even in perfect competition, these costs must be passed on to consumers or the firms will not be able to cover all costs and will be forced to leave the market. The incidence of these costs suggests that firms will shy away from covering events that are almost certain to occur, or those that seldom occur.

Consider again, as in chapter 7, consumers who behave as though they have a utility of wealth function exhibiting diminishing marginal utility of wealth. Consider Figure 11.1, in which we see that the amount this consumer would be willing to pay over the actuarially fair amount is shown by the horizontal distance between the expected utility line and the (curved) utility function, measured in dollars. For example, at point F, this horizontal distance is FG. Clearly, the horizontal distance between the expected utility line and the utility function is zero if the event never occurs (i.e., if we are at point A). It increases up to some point as we move in a southwest direction, with increased probability of illness, and then decreases, as the illness becomes more certain, toward point B. This means that the extra premium people are willing to pay to avoid risk is smallest either for rare events or for almost certain events.

Because insurance is taken against risk, as probability of the uncertain event approaches either 0 or 1, insurance is less desirable. Near point A, the expected loss—that is, the probability of the event—multiplied by the loss if the event occurs, is not big enough for the consumer to bother to insure. Near point B—because the event is almost certain—the consumer might as well put away the money himself or herself, and avoid the trouble of dealing with the insurer. For example, most people do not seek insurance against losses due to common colds.

Figure 11.1 addresses this issue graphically. The top portion of Figure 11.1 shows the utility function as we have just discussed. Moving southwest from the initial wealth (point A), we see that the gain from insurance increases initially, then eventually falls back to zero when the probability of illness becomes 1. Below this graph, we plot the

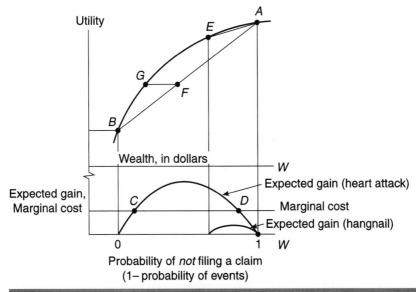

FIGURE 11.1 Impacts of Loading Costs on Availability of Insurance.

probability of the event on the *x*-axis and the expected gain on the *y*-axis. The lower *x*-axis is best understood as the probability of *not* filing a claim, which decreases from 1 (under point *A* where the event never occurs) to 0 (under point *B* where the event always occurs). Thus, at $p = 0$ (at *A* where there is no loss) or at $p = 1$ (at *B* where a loss is certain), the expected gain from insurance is 0. Because the marginal benefits are positive in between, the marginal benefit curve has a hump in the middle.

INSURANCE FOR HEART ATTACKS AND HANGNAILS

Comparing types of losses, at any value of *p*, the larger the expected loss, the larger the gain from the insurance. This is easily seen by comparing the distances between the expected utility line and the utility curve for a small loss (line segment *EA*) and for a large loss (line segment *BA*). The former shows a small distance; the latter, a larger one. Hence, if the consumer has equal probabilities of a hangnail (small loss) and a heart attack (large loss), the expected gain from insurance for major (heart attack) coverage will be larger than for minor (hangnail) coverage.

Given the marginal benefits, consider the firms' decisions in providing insurance. Clearly, if the event is almost certain to happen, the costs of administering the policy may exceed the benefits. In other words, the costs of administering claims are positive. For simplicity, we have drawn these costs as constant marginal costs—a horizontal line.[1]

From probability 0 to point *C*, it will not pay to insure claims because the marginal costs exceed the expected marginal benefits. Between points *C* and *D*, expected marginal benefits exceed marginal costs. To the right of point *D*, again the marginal costs

[1] All else equal, the higher the probability of claims is, the more administration there is (forms filled out, or verification, for example). Hence, the marginal cost of processing the claims may rise the more claims there are, or the more complicated the claims become.

exceed the expected marginal benefits, and no insurance will be provided. As the diagram is drawn, no firm could afford to offer hangnail coverage.

LOADING COSTS AND THE UNINSURED

The analysis provides one avenue for addressing the problem of the uninsured. Health insurance in the United States is largely available through participation in the labor market. Those who do not participate in the labor market, and indeed those who are employed by small businesses, who are self-employed, or who are sporadically employed, may find it difficult to get insurance.

Although many explanations have been proposed, it is apparent that the costs of processing information and claims of people who are outside larger organizations (either companies or unions) may be higher. This would result in an increase in the marginal costs relative to the marginal benefits and would reduce or eliminate the range of services that may be offered.

The analysis also helps address the impacts of entry and exit in the insurance market. More efficient processing and information handling presumably will lower the premiums that must be paid by customers in the market. If we again address Figure 11.1, we recognize that improved information handling and processing not only would lead to lowered prices, but also would permit firms to offer services (based on probability of occurrence) that had not previously been offered.

Consider points *C* or *D*, where the expected marginal benefit was previously just equal to (or possibly just below) the marginal cost. The ability of a firm to lower costs would allow that firm to offer insurance for types of events that previously were uncovered. Conversely, increased costs, either due to market forces or often due to mandated types of coverage, would force firms to cut back coverage on events for which the limited amount of consumer surplus would not allow the firms to pass the increased costs on to the customers.

Employer Provision of Health Insurance and the Tax System

Unlike most other types of insurance, for the largest segment of the American population, health insurance is provided through the workplace. The reason this began was almost an accident. During World War II, because of the booming economy and coupled with wartime shortages in consumer goods, not much was available to buy, and wage and price controls were imposed as anti-inflationary devices. Predictably, compensation needed to be changed in order to attract workers.[2] *Fringe benefits,* which were not legally considered as part of the wage package, were used to provide some flexibility in worker compensation, and hence to improve the allocation of workers among sectors of the economy. One of these fringe benefits was health insurance.

Who Pays for Health Insurance?

It is important to relate health insurance benefits to the wage rate that workers are paid. The simplest way is to examine the supply and demand for labor in the absence of in-

[2]Wage controls in a full-employment economy would prevent companies from raiding each other for workers; price controls would prevent consumers from bidding up the prices of scarce goods.

surance, and then institute health insurance and see what happens. The analysis follows Lee (1996).

Consider a labor market with a typically downward sloping demand for labor, D, and a typically upward sloping supply of labor, S, as noted in Figure 11.2. The demand for labor is related to the marginal productivity of workers. Employers will hire workers as long as the value of their output (marginal revenue product) is greater than or equal to the wage that employers must pay them. The supply of workers is related to the wage in this industry relative to the wage in other industries. Workers will choose to work in this industry as long as the wage they can earn exceeds their opportunities in other jobs. In Figure 11.2, at equilibrium point b, the equilibrium wage is W_1 and the equilibrium quantity of labor demanded and supplied is L_1.

Now suppose that workers in the market negotiate a health insurance benefit worth z/hour at that margin, and it costs employers exactly z/hour to provide. What happens? Employers who before were willing to pay W_1 per hour for workers will now pay W_1 less z. Other points on the demand curve will shift downward in a similar manner, so the demand curve will shift downward by exactly z to D'.

What will happen to the supply curve? Because the workers were willing to supply various amounts of labor at various wage rates according to the supply curve before, now that they are receiving a benefit worth z, they will offer their labor for z less. Hence, the supply curve will shift downward by exactly z to S'.[3]

What is the result? The net wage remains the same, but the money wage falls by z. The equilibrium wage has fallen to W_2 at point b', or by exactly the amount of the benefit. Workers have taken their benefits in lower money wages, and the same number of workers, L_1, is employed at the same net wage.

By assuming that the marginal benefit was worth exactly what it cost to provide, the previous example ignored the moral hazard involved in health insurance. Recall from chapter 7 that for many types of health care, fractional coinsurance leads consumers to consume health care past the point at which marginal benefits equal marginal costs. This provides benefits that, on average, may be worth less to the workers than what they cost to provide.

Suppose, for example, that workers negotiate subsidized coverage for prescription drugs. This benefit might induce workers to purchase drugs beyond the point at which marginal benefits equal marginal costs. If the average benefit is worth z'/hour, or less to the workers than the z/hour that it costs to provide, then the new supply of labor curve, S'', will have fallen by less than the demand for labor (still D', reflecting what it costs to provide the benefit).

Our new equilibrium at c' yields wage W_3, which is higher than W_2. The net wage $(W_3 + z)$ at point c is higher than the original equilibrium wage W_1 (without insurance). Not surprisingly, employers react to the higher net wage by reducing employment in the industry from L_1 to L_2.

SPOUSAL COVERAGE—WHO PAYS?

An analysis derived from Mark Pauly (1997) helps to examine the issue of spousal insurance coverage. What happens if the husband has family insurance coverage where

[3]The workers, of course, would like to continue to earn W_1 *plus* the health benefits, but if they were satisfied with W_1 in the absence of health benefits, they should be just as satisfied to earn W_1 less z if they value the benefits at z/hour.

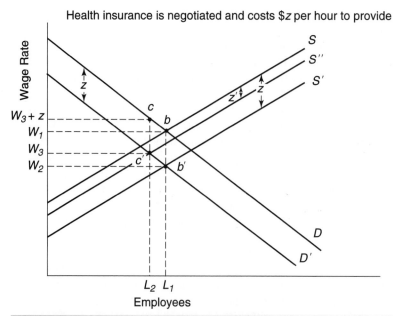

FIGURE 11.2 Interaction of Health Insurance and Employee Wages.

Who Pays for Health Insurance?

Students sometimes have trouble accepting the premise that health insurance constitutes part of the wage package and that a higher level of health insurance often is attained at the expense of lower wages. Economists have no doubt about the validity of this phenomenon, illustrated by an August 1998 story by *New York Times* writer Robert Pear.

Pear reports more than 41 million Americans (at any time during 1998) were without health insurance. Particularly problematic is the instance of small businesses that argue that premiums are too high, their profits are too uncertain for them to commit to insurance, and health benefits are not always a high priority for their workers.

Sal Z. Valiani operates four dry-cleaning shops in Austin, Texas. In the article, Mr. Valiani notes that he offered health insurance long ago and even paid half the cost. However, employees repeatedly asked him not to deduct their share of the premiums from their wages.

"It's one or the other, a pay raise or health benefits," said Mr. Valiani, who noted that in the eyes of many employees, higher wages are considered more important.

This article implies that workers recognize the trade-off between higher wages and health benefits, and that they recognize that higher health benefits mean lower wages.

Source: Pear, Robert, "Policy Changes Fail to Fill Gaps in Health Coverage," *New York Times,* August 9, 1998, A1, A18.

he works and the wife chooses not to take coverage where she works? Who pays in this case?

Following Pauly, suppose that employees in a town can work in either Alpha or Beta types of firms. Alpha firms employ only married men; half of the spouses do not work, and half of the spouses work in the Beta sector. Half of the Beta firms' employees are spouses of the men in the Alpha sector and half are single people. At the outset, no health insurance is provided and the "pure" wage (W_1 from Figure 11.2) for each employee in both the Alpha and Beta sectors is $50,000 per year. Assume that whatever health insurance is implemented, all employees of each firm are given the same take-home pay regardless of insurance cost.

Suppose now that the Alpha firms offer to buy family coverage for their employees worth $4,000 per year. The Beta firms offer to pay $2,000 per year per person for their employees, as long as those who elect coverage pay an additional $10 per month, or $120 per year. In this situation, all Alpha workers will choose family coverage; it is a better buy because one is covering the employee, his spouse, and his children for $4,000. As a result, money wages for Alpha workers fall by $4,000 to $46,000. In the Beta sector, wages per worker will fall by $1,000 to $49,000 (because half of the workers use coverage that costs $2,000 per person). Who pays?

- Two-worker families covered through Alpha firms pay $5,000 for $4,000 in coverage. This occurs because wages have fallen by $4,000 in the Alpha sector (where the men work) and by $1,000 where their spouses work.
- Single-worker families covered through Alpha firms pay $4,000 for $4,000 in coverage, again because wages have fallen by $4,000 in the Alpha sector.
- Single-worker families covered through Beta firms pay $1,120 (reduced wages of $1,000 + $120 from the monthly payments) for $2,120 ($2,000 + $120 from the monthly payments) in coverage.

Are the Beta firms better off because they don't pay for the health care for half of their employees? No, because they are still paying a net wage of $50,000 for the labor services that they use. Are the Alpha firms worse off because they are paying benefits for people who don't work for them? No, they too are still paying a net wage of $50,000 for the labor services that they use. Single workers benefit, because they receive $1,000 *more* in coverage than they are paying for—a transfer from married households, which receive $1,000 *less* in coverage than they are paying for.

HOW THE TAX SYSTEM INFLUENCES DEMAND
FOR HEALTH INSURANCE

One of the most important factors in the increased demand for health insurance in the post–World War II era has been the tax treatment of health insurance. Suppose John earns $1,000 per week and would like to buy health insurance. Ignoring state and local taxes, assume that he is in the 28 percent marginal tax bracket, so his take-home income is $720 per week. Suppose further that health insurance would cost him $50 per week. His net take-home pay would then be $670 per week.

Suppose, instead, that John's employer purchases insurance for him, also at a price of $50 per week. This fringe benefit is exempt from income taxation, as it has been since World War II. Although John's total compensation is still $1,000 per week, he is taxed

only on the wage portion, or $950. His take-home pay will now be 72 percent of $950, or $684 per week. His $14 improvement in well-being occurs because he does not pay $14 in tax on the $50 insurance benefit.

Clearly, with increased marginal tax rates, consumers have incentives to increase employer health expenditures.[4] In the 1950s, federal marginal rates went as high as 91 percent, and even today many people pay marginal rates well over 30 percent.

The allocative problem within the economy is that certain goods, in particular health expenditures, have been chosen for special treatment. Consider Figure 11.3. This figure shows an entire wage package consisting of the sum of wages, W, and insurance, I. Intercept M on the y-axis shows the amount of wages if no insurance is in the package. Similarly, intercept N on the x-axis shows the amount of insurance, if the employee wanted his or her entire compensation as insurance benefits. If no special tax treatment is given, then the line has a 45° relationship to both the x- and y-axes, a slope of -1.0. In other words, a dollar of insurance trades for a dollar in wages.

The subsidy of health insurance through the government policies lowers the price of a dollar of insurance relative to a dollar of wage remuneration. This causes the budget constraint line to rotate to N', leading to the purchase of more insurance, relative to wages, than otherwise. The subsidy rotates the budget line outward so that now one dollar of wages actually buys more than one dollar of insurance. Figure 11.3 shows that without special tax treatment, John is consuming package A of I_0 and W_0. Thus, the tax system leads John to choose combination B with more insurance at the expense of less wages.[5]

OTHER IMPACTS OF EMPLOYER PROVISION OF HEALTH INSURANCE

Employer provision of health insurance has other impacts, as well. Because the employer is a large, single buyer of coverage, the purchase of insurance through the employer provides scale economies of dealing with insurance providers that single purchasers could never enjoy. This tends to lower the effective price of coverage to the employees.

In addition, group purchase by employers addresses the problem of adverse selection in the provision of insurance. Recall that in chapter 7, we considered a club whose members participated in an insurance arrangement. The arrangement worked well because the contract provided a necessary service to the members. In particular, the probability of a claim was a random event that could be calculated, and that was independent of the actions of the members.

Central to this result is the proposition that the probability of usage is independent of the insurance plan. Suppose that the consumer "knows" that the probability of a claim is not the 5 percent that was assumed by the insurance company, but rather 10 percent. If able to convince an insurer that he or she indeed belonged to the less risky

[4]Employers also would benefit from this arrangement because their levels of Social Security taxes would fall. Currently, both employees and employers pay 6.20 percent for the Social Security portion and 1.45 percent for the Medicare portion. Because insurance is an expense to the employer rather than a factor payment, it is exempt from Social Security taxes.

[5]Not only will John buy more insurance, but the tax subsidy may encourage him to insure for the kinds of low- or high-probability events (e.g., routine dental care) that would otherwise be left uninsured. In terms of Figure 11.1, when the net cost of insurance is lowered, the range of probabilities over which the individual insures, as represented by distances such as CD, will increase.

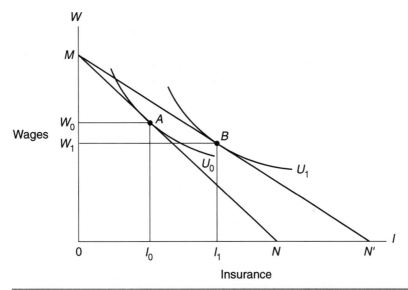

FIGURE 11.3 Impacts of Preferential Tax Treatment for Employee Insurance.

(5 percent) category, the consumer would be able to buy insurance at much less cost than the actuarially fair premium. This consumer would get a bargain; the insurer would lose money. The inability to identify probabilities, and hence their impacts on the insurance market, is often referred to as *adverse selection*.

As an example, consider an insurance plan that offers major hospitalization coverage. Consider also the fact that many heavy smokers may recognize their higher probabilities of lip, throat, or lung cancer and heart disease. If they can prevent the insurer from finding out about their smoking, then they can purchase insurance at much less than the appropriate premium, given their prior conditions.

It can be argued that the purchase of insurance by employers minimizes adverse selection by providing a more appropriate pool for the fixing of insurance rates. This is because most groups contain a broad mix of risks, by virtue of having been formed for some purpose other than insurance.

Employer-Based Health Insurance and Job Mobility

Because most private health insurance is obtained through employment and is typically not portable to different employers, researchers have sought to determine the extent to which health insurance may inhibit worker mobility. In particular, employees may fear losing coverage for preexisting conditions, which are generally defined as any medical problem that has been treated or diagnosed within the past six months to two years. This *job lock* may have several economic effects:

- The inability of workers to change jobs could lead to less productive workers staying at jobs for insurance reasons only; this would lead to decreased economic output because they would not be replaced by more productive workers.

- Even if all workers are equally productive, some workers may stay in jobs for fear of losing the health insurance benefits to the exclusion of those who would otherwise fill the jobs.
- Those who do change jobs may be denied coverage, face higher premiums, or only be able to obtain insurance subject to a waiver that excludes coverage of their health condition.

Both Cooper and Monheit (1993) and Madrian (1994) address the issue. We look more closely at Madrian's presentation.

Madrian uses a simple matrix of the probability of job mobility to consider the impact of job lock. She notes that because job lock is caused by the potential loss of health insurance coverage with changing jobs, one would not expect those with coverage through both their own employment and an outside job to face job lock:

	Employer-Provided Health Insurance	
	No	*Yes*
No Other Health Insurance	*a*	*b*
Other Health Insurance	*c*	*d*

A simple test for the magnitude of job lock is whether those workers with employer-provided health insurance and other coverage are more likely to change jobs than those without alternative coverage, or:

$$(\text{cell } d) - (\text{cell } b) > 0$$

However, if a man is in cell d, it may be due to the insurance provided by his wife, who may be providing income as well; all else equal, the additional income could lead to increased mobility. Hence, Madrian derives a second test: whether having other health insurance increases mobility more for those who have employment-based insurance than for those who do not, or:

$$d - b > c - a$$

which can be rewritten as:

$$(d - b) - (c - a) > 0$$

This test is referred to as *difference-in-difference,* referring to the difference between $(d - b)$ and $(c - a)$.

Madrian's most general model looks at the probability of turnover of married men. The data come from the 1987 National Medical Expenditure Survey (NMES), which collected detailed information for 1987 about health insurance and medical care utilization, with several questions about employment, for approximately 14,000 households. She estimates a probit model where the dependent variable is whether the married man changed jobs (1 if he did; 0 if he did not) during the 15-month survey period. Recall that the coefficients of a probit model determine the probabilities of job change.

The easiest way to present the results is to insert predicted job turnover probabilities into Madrian's matrix (Table 11.1). The *raw estimate* indicates that job lock is responsible for a 26 percent reduction in mobility, calculated as $(0.115 - 0.085)/0.115$. The difference-in-difference estimates, attempting to account for any independent effect of other health insurance on mobility, give an alternative estimate of 31.1 percent.[6]

These results are consistent with anecdotal evidence of job lock as an unintended consequence of the system of employment-related coverage in the United States. It could be addressed through changes that are broadly consistent with prudent insurance practices. These include elimination of preexisting condition clauses and the development of health insurance pooling mechanisms in local labor markets that might promote continuity of coverage across employers. Job lock also must be considered as a consequence of mandated approaches to health insurance benefits, both at state and national levels.

The Market for Insurance

Although we have discussed the provision of insurance in theory, we now consider some institutional features of the market for health insurance. Such a discussion must address the roles of the Blue Cross insurers, which were originally nonprofit firms, and the commercial insurers, which were typically for-profit. With increased competition in the health care sector, many distinctions have blurred. Nonetheless, to understand the current insurance market, it is helpful to consider how it has developed over time.

THE MARKET FOR PRIVATE INSURANCE

The number of people privately insured in the United States has burgeoned since the pre–World War II period. From a base of 12 million insured in 1940, the number increased by a factor of more than six by 1950 (to 76.6 million), and doubled again (to 158.8 million) by 1970. Table 11.2 provides a summary of insurance coverage.

TABLE 11.1	Predicted Job Turnover Probabilities under the Possibility of Job Lock		
		Employer-Provided Health Insurance	
		No	*Yes*
No Other Health Insurance		0.256	0.085
Other Health Insurance		0.244	0.115
Estimates of job lock			
$(d - b)$		26.1% (13.8%)	
$(d - b) - (c - a)$		31.1% (17.7%)	

Standard errors are in parentheses.
Source: Madrian (1994) Copyright © 1994 MIT Press Journals. All rights reserved

[6]Cooper and Monheit, using slightly different methods to analyze the NMES database, calculate a 25 percent decline in the likelihood of job change when comparing those who are insured to those who are uninsured.

TABLE 11.2 Number of Persons with Private Insurance by Type of Insurer (Millions)

End of Year	Total Insurance Companies			Individual Family	Blue Cross/ Blue Shield	Self-Insured and HMOs
	All Insurers	Total Persons	Group			
1940	12.0	3.7	2.5	1.2	6.0	2.3
1945	32.0	10.5	7.8	2.7	18.9	2.7
1950	76.6	37.0	22.3	17.3	38.8	4.4
1955	101.4	53.5	38.6	19.9	50.7	6.5
1960	122.5	69.2	54.4	22.2	58.1	6.0
1965	138.7	77.6	65.4	24.4	63.3	7.0
1970	158.8	89.7	80.5	26.7	85.1	8.1
1975	178.2	99.5	87.2	30.1	86.4	13.1
1980	187.4	105.5	97.4	33.8	86.7	33.2
1985	181.3	100.4	99.5	21.2	78.7	55.1
1990	181.7	83.1	88.7	10.2	70.9	86.2
1991	181.0	78.0	83.3	9.9	68.1	93.5
1992	180.7	76.6	82.1	8.5	67.5	97.9
1993	180.9	74.7	80.9	7.4	65.9	105.7
1994	182.2	75.8	82.4	7.0	65.2	112.9
1995	185.3	76.6	82.3	7.0	65.6	120.1

Note: Data for 1987 and 1988 reflect revised HIAA survey form. Data for 1989 and 1990 reflect a change in methodology.
Note: Data split is available for years 1990 through 1994.
Sources: Health Insurance Association of America; Group Health Association of America, Inc.; Blue Cross/Blue Shield Association. HIAA (1998) Table 2.10.

Table 11.2 also divides the insurance coverage among private insurance companies, Blue Cross and Blue Shield plans, and other plans, which include self-insured and HMO plans. Well into the 1970s, most of the coverage was provided either by insurance companies (usually in group settings) or by Blue Cross and Blue Shield plans. Since the late 1970s, use of other plans has increased, with declines in both the shares and the absolute numbers of those covered by both the insurance companies and the "Blues." This would suggest the movement toward self-insurance by large firms, as well as toward various arrangements through HMOs, Preferred Provider Organizations (PPOs), Point of Service (POS) providers, and other forms of managed care.

INSURANCE PRACTICES

At least two organizational and practice issues characterize the health insurance industry and link it to the emerging issues of managed health care, which will be considered in more depth in chapter 12. The first issue is a conflict between insurers and the insured (most often represented by the health care providers) regarding the amounts of claims, and indeed whether the claims should be paid at all. From the earliest instances of health insurance, providers, most particularly physicians, have argued that their judgments must not be questioned on cost grounds. Insurers, in contrast, have felt that they could increase their profits and reduce premiums by judiciously questioning treatments and costs.

One might ask why providers ever would consent to having someone second-guess their decisions. Goldberg and Greenberg (1977) traced the growth of health insurance

in Oregon in the 1930s. At that time, physicians shared in the Great Depression with the larger population, and they saw acceptance of health insurance, even with its accompanying oversight, as a way of increasing earnings.[7] Although insurance was attractive when times were difficult, considerable opposition arose from physicians' groups, such as the Oregon State Medical Society. They threatened to expel physicians who participated in the plans and to establish their own plans. The plans established by the physicians tended to be less strict in their cost reviews.

Blue Cross and Blue Shield plans were started by medical providers, with Blue Cross providing hospital payment and Blue Shield providing physician payment. The Blues typically offered more complete and more comprehensive coverage, and they paid participating providers directly. They also were usually generous in the payment of hospital care. The development and success of large hospitals in the post–World War II United States was at least in part supported by the generosity of Blue Cross and Blue Shield reimbursement of hospital stays on per-diem bases. The fiscal distress facing many large hospitals in the 1990s may be traced to the changes in financing that have accompanied the demise of Blue Cross and Blue Shield leadership in the provision of health insurance, in part related to the strictures placed by Diagnosis-Related-Group (DRG) controls. DRGs were introduced through Medicare to provide prospective fixed payments for specific diagnoses. These payments induced cost-containment measures that often resulted in reduced hospital stays.

The second organizational pattern that has characterized the industry is the change in the "rating" of clients. Insurers must pool their clienteles to determine risk premiums based on their experiences with the groups. Blue Cross plans began with a method called *community rating.* All subscribers in a given location, irrespective of age or health experience, were charged the same premium. This contrasts with experience rating, or risk rating, in which the insurer charges group premiums (to a company or to a fraternal or service organization) based on its experience with the group.

Community rating provides a fundamental information problem. Low-risk clients are overcharged, and their premiums are transferred to higher-risk clients in the same pool. Advocates of community rating argue that this allows high-risk and low-income clients to buy insurance that would otherwise have been unavailable.

If an insurer can identify groups with low risk, however, it may offer members of these groups lower-cost insurance, or "pick off" these segments of the market. Alternatively, many large firms choose alternative carriers who, again, will charge lower premiums than the community-rated Blue plans. The large firms may in fact choose to self-insure. This "cream skimming" practice may leave the plans that continue to community rate their clienteles with risk pools that are so risky they require almost prohibitively high premiums. Clearly, the extent to which community rating can survive is related to the amount of competition in the health insurance market.

THE PAST 10 YEARS

The shift toward managed health care through HMOs and PPOs in the past 10 years has induced a change in philosophy among Blue Cross and Blue Shield insurance plans.

[7]Wolinsky (1988) argues from a sociological perspective that similar pressures forced the acceptance of DRGs and their controlled payments by hospitals.

The typical Blue Cross and Blue Shield system (69 in all across the United States) was facing stiff competition from smaller organizations that were peeling off supposedly more desirable clients from the community-rated system. As noted, this would suggest higher costs for those who remained in the system.

One explicit response to the changing marketplace was the approval in 1994 of a change in organizational status. Blue Cross plans now can become for-profit firms or establish for-profit subsidiaries. An important example of this occurred in California, where Blue Cross sought to go nonprofit. By California law, if such a conversion occurs, the value that has been created in the process must be earmarked for charitable purposes.

Why change? One fundamental reason involves the ability to raise capital. Nonprofit organizations must generate funds through their revenues, whereas for-profit firms may sell stock. With more competition in the marketplace and renewed emphases on lowering premiums and costs of care, the option to sell stock became more attractive.

In a wide-ranging 1995 interview, Blue Cross of California Chief Executive Leonard Schaeffer offered three reasons for the changes in the Blue Cross system:

1. Most Blues plans are big, and thus have not reacted quickly to marketplace changes.
2. The Blues were successful for a long period of time, and traditional operations got "embedded." This led to a resistance to change.
3. The national association was made up of an "unwieldy" national association with 69 independent plans.

Schaeffer envisioned that there will be "30, perhaps even 20" associations, organized on a regional basis.

It should be pointed out that not all nonprofit carriers are changing, and the interview with Mr. Schaeffer engendered an exchange of letters from David Lawrence of the Kaiser Foundation, indicating that Kaiser Permanente, the large managed care provider in California, would not be converting. How the marketplace will change in the next several years is a matter of conjecture, but it is safe to say that the traditional environment defined by the Blues has changed for good.[8]

The Uninsured—An Analytical Framework

Given the high costs of health care and the inevitability of at least some expenses, it has become crucial for individuals to have access to health insurance. In the United States, health insurance availability has been linked to the workplace. Yet surveys have shown that more than 40 million Americans have no health insurance at any moment in time, and that a large fraction of these people are employed.

Table 11.3 shows that not all people get health insurance through the workplace, and that the problem is particularly severe for small firms and for certain age groups. In 1995, of the 231.9 million nonelderly Americans (the elderly are covered through Medicare), 40.3 million, or 17.4 percent, were uninsured. The problem was particularly severe for individuals and families getting coverage through small employers. Of those working in firms with 10 or fewer employees and their families, nearly 6.4 million

[8]For the original interview with Leonard Schaeffer and the exchange of letters following, see Iglehart (1995), Lawrence (1996), and Schaeffer (1996).

TABLE 11.3 Health Insurance Status, Nonelderly Americans, by Work Status and Firm Size, 1995							
	Total Population	*Total Private*	*Employer Coverage*	*Other Private*	*Total Public*	*Medicaid*	*Uninsured*
Total	231.9	163.9	147.9	16.0	38.4	29.0	40.3
Percentage[1]		70.7	63.8	6.9	16.6	12.5	17.4
Self-Employed	21.9	15.9	11.1	4.8	1.6	1.1	5.1
Percentage		72.6	50.7	21.9	7.3	5.0	23.3
Private	143.8	109.0	101.8	72.0	16.1	13.0	24.2
Percentage		75.8	70.8	50.1	11.2	9.0	16.8
Fewer Than 10 Employees	20.4	11.4	9.3	2.1	3.2	2.8	6.4
Percentage		55.9	45.6	10.3	15.7	13.7	31.4
10 to 24 Employees	15.3	10.1	9.1	1.0	2.1	1.7	3.8
Percentage		66.0	59.5	6.5	13.7	11.1	24.8
25 to 99 Employees	22.5	16.5	15.4	1.1	2.6	2.2	4.3
Percentage		73.3	68.4	4.9	11.6	9.8	19.1
100 to 499 Employees	23.5	18.7	17.8	0.9	2.2	1.8	3.4
Percentage		79.6	75.7	3.8	9.4	7.7	14.5
500 to 999 Employees	9.3	7.7	7.3	0.4	0.9	0.8	1.1
Percentage		82.8	78.5	4.3	9.7	8.6	11.8
1,000 or More Employees	52.8	44.6	42.9	1.6	5.0	3.8	5.3
Percentage		84.5	81.3	3.0	9.5	7.2	10.0
Nonworkers	37.3	14.4	11.5	2.9	16.4	13.4	8.7
Percentage		38.6	30.8	7.8	44.0	35.9	23.3

[1]Percentages do not add to 100 because persons with both private insurance and Medicaid appear in both columns.

Source: HIAA (1998) Table 2.7.

people (or 31.4 percent of the 20.4 million people included in this category) were un-insured. Contrast this to workers in firms with 1,000 or more employees. A total of 52.8 million workers and families are in this category, with 5.3 million (or 10.0 percent) uninsured.

Under any circumstance, it is important to examine the reasons that some individuals lack insurance. As noted, insurers must be able to lower the loading factors, which are the costs of determining probabilities of claims and processing claims. The ability to insure through the workplace gives the opportunity to improve the experience rating. In principle, private insurers can insure those outside the workplace, and many do, particularly with relation to affinity groups such as organizations and clubs, or in terms of insuring the elderly. If high costs lead to onerous payments, then the problem may be poverty rather than high prices. This would suggest the need for governmental subsidies in a social insurance scheme.

It also is interesting to examine insurance coverage by age of the population. In Table 11.4, researchers examined the percentages of the uninsured by age and found considerably higher, and growing (over time), percentages of uninsured persons in age categories 18 to 24 and 25 to 34. These higher rates might be explained in part by intermittent spells of unemployment that may cost workers insurance coverage, or by part-time jobs that come without insurance. Moreover, even if employed, many did not have insurance. Approximately half of the poor full-time workers were uninsured in 1996 and 1997 (Bennefield, 1997, 1998).

TABLE 11.4	Percentage of Population under Age 65 Not Covered by Insurance			
Age Category	*1984*	*1989*	*1993*	*1996*
Under 6	14.9	15.1	12.7	11.9
Ages 6–17	13.4	14.5	14.9	14.1
Ages 18–24	25.0	27.1	31.1	29.6
Ages 25–34	16.2	18.3	22.5	22.5
Ages 35–44	11.2	12.3	15.1	15.2
Ages 45–54	10.5	11.0	12.7	12.5
Ages 55–64	8.7	10.0	11.1	11.6

Source: U.S. Department of Health and Human Services, *Health United States* (1998) Table 133.

THE WORKING UNINSURED

Consider now the working uninsured. Employees' remuneration may be considered as *net wage, w_n,* an hourly sum that equals the sum of money wage, w, plus insurance, i_0:

$$w_n = w + i_0 \tag{11.1}$$

Figure 11.4 shows the equilibrium employment point A for the profit-maximizing firm, where the value of the marginal product equals the net wage, w_n, that must be paid for benefit level i_0. At this equilibrium, L_0 workers are employed.

The literature suggests that many businesses, especially small businesses, may have limited experience ratings; as a result, their loading costs may be high, as much as 10 percent to 40 percent higher than those paid by large firms. If the loading costs are high, then the small firms may be able to afford to pay only small, or zero, i. To compete

FIGURE 11.4 Impact of Mandated Benefits on Employment.

Net wage rate

A is the initial equilibrium at which the value of the marginal product equals the wage rate.

Wage rate = Supply of labor

Numbers of workers

with other firms, they must match the w_n; hence, it may be necessary that their w be larger than the wage level for other firms.

McLaughlin and Zellers (1994) summarize three major types of barriers to small business provision of health benefits. The first, affordability, is a price-related barrier and is well summarized in Figure 11.4, leading to increased net wage, w_n. Particularly in low-wage industries, a combination of low profit margins, low wages, and high premiums may make it difficult to provide health benefits.

There are two other broad categories of nonprice-related barriers to the offering of health benefits. Insurance *redlining* or preexisting-condition clauses may exclude specific individuals, or companies that employ them, from insurance coverage. McLaughlin and Zellers note that redlined industries typically employ older workers (over age 55), have high employee turnover, seasonal workforces, or workforces paid by commission or on the basis of other contractual terms. Lawyers' offices may be redlined because of fears of litigation, and physicians' offices because of fears of high utilization of health care services.

A particular confluence of such factors occurs in the case of beauty shops, who have great difficulty buying group insurance for their employees (McLaughlin, 1993). Compared with the general population, three large groups of beauty shop employees are costly to insure:

1. Workers who work only intermittently. Evidence shows that some workers enter the labor force when they need health care. Such adverse selection of the insured pool may lead to high costs for insurers.
2. Young women of child-bearing age who are likely to have children. This again leads to high insurance costs.
3. An apparently large homosexual workforce, whose members are at higher risk of exposure to AIDS, also may raise costs substantially.

In short, many nonprice barriers are placed before certain groups, including preexisting-condition clauses, long delays in processing applications, and, if the would-be client is persistent, extraordinarily high premiums, which make enrollment prohibitively expensive. As a result, many small businesses simply cannot obtain insurance.

A third barrier to the provision of coverage may be termed *attitudes.* Many firms are uninterested in offering insurance. Sometimes a large number of their employees can *piggyback* on health plans of spouses' or partners' employers. In such cases, employees prefer to be compensated in higher wages rather than in benefits.

Feldman and colleagues (1998) analyze a 1993 survey of Minnesota small employers. One of the problems with this type of research is that the costs of premiums are available for those firms that do buy insurance, but they are not for those that do not. (Consider asking people who did not buy cars how much they didn't spend!) The researchers carefully assigned insurance premiums to those who did not buy, and found that a \$1 decrease in the price of individual insurance increased the probability of coverage from 0.610 to 0.6274. This seemingly small change implies that a 1 percent decrease in insurance premium leads to a substantial 3.91 percentage point increase in small firm demand for insurance (an elasticity of -3.91).

The authors suggest that voluntary efforts to increase small business insurance offers can be successful if the price reductions are "widely publicized and permanent" and if low-priced policies are available with few restrictions as to who must pay for them (the

employer and/or the employee). They also suggest that purchasing pools through which small employers can reduce health insurance administrative costs, special small-employer policies that are exempt from state-mandated benefits, and the elimination of "antimanaged care" law also may reduce costs (and thus premiums) for small firm health insurance.

THE IMPACTS OF MANDATED COVERAGE

Many groups have advocated that the federal government or individual states mandate some, more, or particular types of coverage. Returning to Figure 11.4, if such coverage is provided through employer insurance, the mandates would raise the amount of i, as well as its costs. Firm responses to the increased marginal costs may result in two adverse impacts. The first is for the company to stop offering insurance entirely because it is too expensive.[9] Thus, rather than having modest health coverage with the benefits of whatever experience rating may exist within the workplace, there may be no coverage at all. The firm then may have to raise the wage to keep employees, who would then have to buy their own insurance. This may allow for employee choice, but it also denies the employee workplace-related experience rating.

The second adverse impact also may be understood by examining Figure 11.4. The equilibrium of value of marginal product and net wage at point A represents a labor force of the appropriate size to maximize profits for the producer. To the extent that mandated coverage reflects increased worker benefits—that is, to the extent that i_1 exceeds i_0—it must either increase gross wage, w_n, or decrease base wage, w. If gross wage, w_n, rises, marginal workers now cost more than they are worth in terms of marginal productivity, and if firms are acting to maximize profits, some workers may be let go, leading to the new equilibrium point B. By this analysis, the result of mandated coverage, similar to the result of a binding minimum wage, is likely to be some additional unemployment amount $(L_0 - L_1)$, which, of course, means sharply curtailed insurance benefits.[10] How much the employment falls is related to the elasticity (or responsiveness) of the labor demand curve to the increased gross wage.

Alternatively, if base wage, w, falls to maintain gross wage, w_n, in the face of increased benefits, the workers have less money to spend on other goods; insurance has effectively crowded out other expenditures. Furthermore, the firm may lose workers to other firms that are willing to pay the increased w_n as a result of the mandated coverage.

Mandated insurance benefits have become most popular at the state level. Jensen and Morrisey (1999) find that states mandate providers, benefits, and coverage extension. Coverage mandates as of 1996 included chiropractors (41 states), optometrists (37 states), and dentists (34 states). Benefit mandates included mammography screening (46 states), alcoholism treatment (43 states), and maternity length of stay (34 states). Thirty-eight states mandated continuation of coverage to employees, and 34 states mandated coverage for handicapped dependents.

The authors found that smaller firms were affected disproportionately by mandates in part because they were less likely than larger firms to be able to avoid the costs of

[9]Alternatively, *play or pay* proposals might require firms to provide a minimal level of insurance or to pay into an insurance pool that would insure the uninsured.

[10]Although a minimum wage may be in place, if employers must pay more due to local market conditions, then an increase in the minimum wage may have no impact on employment. Similarly, if employers are already offering more than the mandated coverage, broadening the mandates may have little or no impact.

mandates by self-insuring. This implied that because health insurance would be more expensive for smaller firms (because they must include the mandated benefit), they would be less likely to offer coverage to employees.

One response to this problem would be a total overhaul of the insurance system to separate it from the workplace. Although alternative systems exist in other countries, it is unlikely that they would be politically feasible in the United States. Governmental solutions within the current system (with workplace-provision of insurance) would be to subsidize at least a minimal standard of insurance for all who are working full-time. Purchase of insurance for nonworkers is more problematic and must be treated as an equity-based transfer program.

Conclusions

Chapter 7 introduced readers to the concept of insurance and to the specific issue of health insurance for individuals. In this chapter, we focus on the insurance market and the behaviors of firms within that market. We establish that in a market setting, insurance constitutes an important part of the wage package, and to the extent that it is valuable to the workforce, higher insurance is reflected in lower money wages. This market result occurs irrespective of who contractually pays for the insurance.

We show how many of the trappings of the U.S. health care system are related to the employer base of the health insurance. The system of tax deductibility pushes employees to ask for higher proportions of untaxed insurance relative to taxed wage benefits. The linkage of insurance to the workplace also tends to lock employees into certain jobs, constraining mobility.

We continue with a brief discussion of the evolution of the health insurance industry. This industry was formerly defined by the Blues (Blue Cross and Blue Shield) with their nonprofit status, community rating, and predilection for hospital care. The erosion of all three of these facets of health insurance in the late 1980s and 1990s has led to profound changes in the provision of health insurance and the delivery of care.

The chapter also includes several implications about the uninsured. These are often people who are not working, and hence are uninsured. There are others whose health, employment, or lifestyle statuses may not permit commercial insurers to provide insurance profitably. Government mandates to employers that they insure everyone, if they insure anyone, often cause employers to drop insurance plans entirely, thus leaving larger numbers at risk. A safety net for those who are difficult to insure requires a social contract that only the government can provide.

We discussed the changes in industry structure in the current chapter. We now turn to issues of managed care.

Summary

1. In theory, individual health insurance trades off a guaranteed reduction in wealth (the insurance premium) for a reduction in uncertainty due to ill health through the pooling of risk. The organization and cost conditions in some health insurance *markets,* however, suggest that some contingencies may not be insurable.
2. The economies of scale in processing information suggest that smaller firms or unions may see marginal insurance costs relative to marginal benefits levels. These higher costs may reduce or eliminate the range of services that they offer.

3. If health insurance is valued by the workers in an industry, then competitive pressures mean that increased health benefits are offset by reduced money wages.

4. Subsidizing health insurance through government tax policies lowers the price of a dollar of insurance premium relative to a dollar of wage remuneration. This leads employees to purchase more health insurance relative to wages than would otherwise occur.

5. Employer-provided health insurance may inhibit worker mobility between firms, thus locking employees into jobs. Researchers find this job lock to be responsible for 25 percent to 31 percent reductions in employee mobility.

6. Much of the American health insurance environment has been defined by Blue Cross and Blue Shield plans, which as nonprofit firms were typically exempted from profits taxes, property taxes, and federal and state corporate taxes. Early on, many analysts felt that such tax treatments gave the Blues considerable competitive advantages. However, in the past decade, the Blues have been subjected to considerable competition.

7. Many groups have advocated that the federal government or individual states mandate either more coverage or various types of coverage. In reaction:
 - Companies may stop offering insurance entirely because it is too expensive.
 - Marginal workers may now cost more than they are worth, and some of them will be let go.

Discussion Questions

1. Suppose each person's health expenditures can be predicted with certainty by both the insured and the insurer. What are the implications for insurance markets? Explain the prevalence of insurance for highly predictable events such as routine dental services.

2. In 1986, the U.S. federal income tax system changed marginal tax rates so that the top marginal rate fell from 50 percent to 33 percent. Given the way that fringe benefits are negotiated, what would you expect to happen to the demand for health insurance as a fringe benefit? Why?

3. Suppose that a company pays its workers $12 per hour and provides an additional $2 per hour worth of fringe benefits, including a basic health insurance policy. Discuss the firm's reaction to a state mandate that requires it to expand the items covered in the health care policy. What is likely to happen to the number of people employed?

4. Blue Cross plans typically have practiced community rating. If other insurance firms are seeking healthier patients at reduced rates, what impact will this have on Blue Cross net revenues? Why?

5. It often is advocated that health insurers be prevented from denying insurance to those with preexisting conditions, such as cancer or AIDS, at "reasonable" rates. Analyze the impacts of such regulations on insurance markets.

6. What is the meaning of *job lock?* Would you expect job lock to increase or decrease if employer-based health insurance were to be replaced by government-provided health insurance?

7. Suppose a household does not carry health insurance. Can we conclude that this reflects failure of insurance markets? Why or why not?

Exercises

1. Using Figure 11.1, illustrate the probability that someone will obtain insurance for treatment for:
 - a hangnail
 - a broken arm
 - a "bad hair" day
 - viral meningitis
2. Using Figure 11.2:
 - calculate an initial labor market equilibrium (wages and employment) determined by the demand and supply of labor.
 - indicate the wage and employment impacts of a health insurance policy that costs $2 per hour to workers and is worth exactly $1.50 per hour to the workers.
3. Using Figure 11.2, consider an insurance policy that provides free "purple aspirin" to all workers. This benefit provides no conceivable advantage (workers don't care whether their aspirin is purple or white) but comes with cost z. Show the new labor market equilibrium indicating the wage and employment impacts.
4. Using Figure 11.2, indicate the wage and employment impacts of a health insurance policy that costs $2 per hour to the workers and is worth exactly $3 per hour to the workers. Why do your answers to exercises 2, 3, and 4 differ?
5. Consider two workers, Ralph and Steve. Both of them work for the same employer, and each earns $15 per hour. Ralph is taxed at the 15 percent marginal rate. However, Steve is married, and due to his wife's income, he is taxed at the 28 percent marginal rate. Using Figure 11.3, indicate which one would be expected to seek more health insurance and why.
6. Suppose that Charlie's Pizzeria in Kalamazoo, Michigan, employs 10 employees at a wage level of $8 per person. All other costs (ovens, rent, advertising, return to capital) total $40 per hour, and the pizzeria sells 12 pizzas per hour at a cost of $10 per pizza. Suppose that the State of Michigan mandates health coverage that can only be covered at a cost of $1 per hour, if it is offered at all. Charlie determines that if he offers insurance, he could maintain his production by letting one worker go and running his ovens a little hotter, leading to hourly costs of $45 per hour.
 a. What are Charlie's original profits?
 b. What is Charlie's elasticity of demand for labor? How is this calculated?
 c. What will happen to Charlie's profits in the short run if he chooses to pay for mandated insurance?
 d. What will Charlie's long-run decision be? Why?

CHAPTER 12

Managed Care

- What Is the Organizational Structure?

- What Are the Economic Characteristics?

- The Emergence of Managed Care Plans

- Development and Growth of Managed Care—Why Has It Taken So Long?

- Modeling Managed Care

- Are Managed Care Costs Lower?

- Quality of Care

- Growth in Spending

- Competitive Effects

- Conclusions

Insurance coverage generally will lead to overconsumption of health care by the insured. The insured considers only the out-of-pocket cost of care and not the true full cost at the point of service. Overconsumption here means that the insured purchases health care beyond the point where the marginal benefit equals marginal cost. For insurance to be a net benefit to society, the costs of this overconsumption must be overcome by the benefits in the sense that risk has been reduced. Even with the risk-reduction benefits, however, it is clear that improved insurance coverage leads to increased costs to society.

A simple analogy may help us address the dilemma. Suppose that rather than health care insurance, employers provided food and clothing (F&C) insurance for their workers. A "fee-for-service" F&C plan would allow the consumers to purchase their food and clothing at any merchant they chose, and would reimburse the consumers subject to coinsurance rates and deductibles. A consumer facing a 20 percent coinsurance rate could purchase a pound of filet mignon for $15 per pound and have the insurer pay $12 per pound, or 80 percent of the price. Another consumer could purchase designer athletic shoes for $150 and have the insurer pay $120, again 80 percent of the price. Consumers would likely buy more filet mignon or athletic shoes than if they had to pay the

full amount themselves. The market effect of such plans would likely cause consumers and their insurers to worry about F&C cost inflation.

Suppose that in response to the perceived high costs of food and clothing, a group of consumers and their employers organized and offered a "managed F&C" plan. In this plan, members (consumers and the employers) would pay a fixed amount per person per month into the plan for food and clothing, presumably less than they were paying (together) under the fee-for-service plan. In return for this reduced cost plan, the consumers would be limited to shopping at a single shopping center with whom plan managers had negotiatied lower prices for food and clothing. Moreover, the plan managers could limit the types of goods purchased (no filet mignon) and might attempt to curb total consumer expenditures. It is likely that at least some consumers would find such a plan attractive due to its lower costs.

Analysis of this "managed care" F&C arrangement raises a host of questions. For individual consumers, one might ask:

- Are they getting the same quality of goods as before?
- Are they being denied goods that they "should" be getting?
- Are their expenditures reduced?
- Are they less well fed, less healthy, or less well dressed than before?

At the market level, one might ask:

- Have aggregate F&C expenditures decreased or has their growth rate decreased?
- Do the managed plans meet consumer preferences?
- Can the merchants earn sufficient returns to stay in business?
- Is there competition in the managed care F&C market, and do the managed care F&C plans influence the fee-for-service F&C plans in terms of the prices or selection of goods?

With this in mind, we turn to the issue of managed health care. One might argue that physician practice must be managed in order to address high health care costs. This suggests that networks of providers, including HMOs, PPOs, and individual practice associations (IPAs), are widely seen as means to restore competition to the health care sector and as means to control expanding heath care costs. We devote this chapter to managed care with particular attention to the distinctive combination of insurance and care exemplified by HMOs and similar organizations. Unless distinguishing the individual types of institutions, we will refer to them as managed care. The prominent form, the HMO, receives special attention in this chapter for its size and for the fact that much of the scholarly and policy research has focused on HMOs.

HMOs appear to overcome the information problems inherent in fee-for-service (FFS) health care markets that may be exacerbated by ordinary insurance coverage. Under FFS, the provider provides health care and advises the consumer on how much is needed. At first glance, it appears that the consumer's imperfect information about health care, when combined with FFS remuneration, may create the incentives for substantial overconsumption. The organizational form of HMOs appears to eliminate the overconsumption incentives and replace them with cost-control incentives and even possibly incentives toward *underconsumption*.

We begin this chapter by describing managed care and its cost-cutting potential. We then turn to HMOs as a form of health care organization in which the functions of insurance and the provision of care are combined. We describe the HMO and its organizational relatives, and we assess the theory and evidence on the effects of HMOs. We then turn to the market effects of managed care on providers, insurers, and the adoption of new health care technology.

What Is the Organizational Structure?

It is instructive to provide a general description of managed care, leading to a more specific discussion of HMOs, while recognizing that the concept of managed care is undergoing constant changes.[1] Most generally, analysts speak of an *organized delivery system* as a network of organizations (for example, hospitals, physicians, clinics, and hospices) that provides or arranges to provide a coordinated continuum (from well care to emergency surgery) of services to a defined population. This system is willing to be held clinically and fiscally accountable for the outcomes and the health status of the population served. It is tied together by its clinical (treatment) and fiscal (financial) accountability for the defined population. Most often, the organized delivery system is defined by its association with an insurance product.

Shortell and his colleagues view the key feature of managed care as the provision of care to a defined number of enrollees at a capitated (fixed) rate per member per month. As a result, cost centers such as hospitals, physician groups, clinics, and nursing homes must be managed under a fixed budget. Under traditional fee-for-service, because cost centers generate revenue, more volume means more profit. Under managed care, more volume means less profit.

Managed care creates incentives for keeping people well by emphasizing prevention and health promotion practices, and when people become sick, by treating them at the most cost-effective (least cost per unit care) location in the continuum of care. Clearly, incentives are given to underuse services, which may be harmful to patients. Through a more centralized management of services, the goal is to provide additional quality-enhancing features for a given price, or to provide a given set of quality attributes or outcomes for a lower price. The primary provider has a paramount role as the gatekeeper to limit further and more expensive services.

Figure 12.1 shows an integrated delivery system for an enrolled population with a predetermined set of benefits. An economic analysis of this model shows the importance of integrating the information among the various services. Information systems are the hub of the wheel; Shortell and his colleagues note that the "embryonic" development of most clinical information systems is a fundamental barrier to the success of managed care systems. Large health centers have budgeted tens of millions of dollars per year to integrate systems that often were developed separately and almost never "talk to each other."

A second feature of these systems is a studied de-emphasis of the acute care hospital model. Hospitals provide expensive care, and moving toward cost-effective mod-

[1]This discussion draws heavily from the work of Shortell, Gillies, and Anderson (1994).

FIGURE 12.1 Model of Integrated Service Delivery.

Source: Shortell, Stephen M., Robin R. Gillies, and David A. Anderson. "The New World of Managed Care: Creating Organized Delivery Systems." Health Affairs 13 (Winter 1994) 46–64. Copyright © 1994 The People to People Health Foundation, Inc., All Rights Reserved.

els necessarily moves away from hospital care. As noted earlier, primary care physicians are the gatekeepers of managed care systems, directing patients to appropriate (i.e., cost-effective) treatment settings. If they are induced to "feed" patients into the hospital instead, this will lead to increased costs.

It is apparent that managed care seeks a vertical integration of what had previously been a generally unintegrated system of health care treatment. Through coordination of care and improved information, such integration has the potential to address the health care costs in a manner that would appear to address criteria of economic efficiency. Yet the integration is costly, and the quality of the resulting care may not match all consumer preferences. A prime example of managed care on which there has been considerable research is the HMO. We begin with a description of HMOs and continue with their history and the rationale for a government policy that has promoted their development.

What Are the Economic Characteristics?

We have seen that managed care features an integrated health care delivery structure involving the integration of insurers, payment mechanisms, and a host of providers, including physicians and hospitals. What distinguishes managed care from the fee-for-service care that also might plausibly attempt to integrate the various health care system parts?

Analysts identify three particular mechanisms by which health insurance plans seek to contain costs and/or improve quality of care:

- *Selective contracting,* in which payers negotiate prices and contract selectively with local providers such as physicians and hospitals.
- *Steering* of enrollees to the selected providers.
- *Utilization review* of the appropriateness of provider practices. This utilization review may be prospective (in advance), concurrent (at the same time), or retrospective (looking back).

Of the three, most analysts find selective contracting to be most important. Dranove, Simon, and White (1998) point out that contracts may be awarded on the basis of the providers' willingness to accept particular payment plans, and monitoring of treatment styles and quality of care. Morrisey (1998) notes that under selective contracting (unlike fee-for-service care), some providers get contracts and some do not. Service price becomes important in managed care system negotiations with providers.

The selective contracting and the steering distinguish managed care from the more standard fee-for-service care. Although the press concentrates on utilization reviews attributed to managed care, Morrisey points out that indemnity plans that include pre-hospital admission certification would be managed care plans under this definition. In short, almost everyone now reviews utilization; as such, utilization review, in itself, is not helpful in discussing managed care.

How, then, might we distinguish between the care that would be expected from managed care organizations (MCOs) and FFS? Cutler, McClellan, and Newhouse (1998) provide a useful conceptual model that asks how much a patient would have to be compensated to move from FFS to MCO coverage. The compensation presumably would be related to the patient's difference in utility (satisfaction) between FFS and MCO coverage. If an MCO and an FFS plan were identical, the compensation would be zero; if the MCO leads to less (more) utility, compensation must be positive (negative) to make the client indifferent.

Three differences can be identified between MCOs and FFS that might affect compensation:

1. *Difference in health.* If the MCO provides reduced health (relative to FFS) due to reduced treatment, then the compensation must be positive, providing compensation to those who choose the MCO. This positive compensation might be offset if the MCO is better at managing the overall care process or at providing "well-care."
2. *Cost savings.* If, holding health constant, the MCO provides savings due either to less treatment or cheaper treatment, then the compensation must be negative, because the MCO is saving money for its clients.

3. *Financial risk from different out-of-pocket payments.* Clients may prefer an MCO if it insures them from having to make large out-of-pocket payments. If so, the compensation will be negative, because payment variability is reduced. The size of the compensation would depend on the MCO's cost-sharing provisions, as well as reimbursement for out-of-plan use.

This framework suggests that one must measure the differences between managed care and fee-for-service along several dimensions: health, price of care, and quality of care. It also suggests that patients who value health less (or other things more) may choose less health and/or health care by choosing an MCO, or possibly even no insurance, rather than FFS care.

It does not necessarily tell us which mechanism provides the appropriate level of care when marginal benefits equal marginal costs. Recall that under FFS, with fractional coinsurance, clients may overuse services. Under MCO, they may use fewer services and possibly not enough service, but it is not clear whether they will use the efficient amount.

With this framework established, we can look at the emergence of managed care plans and what the market for managed care will look like. We also can look at the differences in health, price, or quality of care, recognizing that consumers and employers, acting on their behalf, will evaluate all of these dimensions in spending their health insurance dollars.

The Emergence of Managed Care Plans

Managed care describes a variety of arrangements with the following common features. First, much, if not all, of the patient's care is provided through a specific network of hospitals, physicians, and other health care providers. Second, considerable centralized oversight of resource use occurs within the network, often referred to as utilization review. Here, we provide a brief overview of the types of managed care plans and the extent to which physicians and hospitals are now contracting with insurers under capitation arrangements.

EMPLOYER-SPONSORED MANAGED CARE

Managed care now accounts for about three-quarters of all employer-sponsored health insurance, with traditional fee-for-service plans making up the rest. Managed care plans for patients with employer-sponsored coverage come in three types:

Health maintenance organizations (HMOs) provide relatively comprehensive health care, entail few out-of-pocket expenses, but generally require that all care be delivered through the plan's network, and that the primary care physician authorize any services provided. Each subscriber is assigned a primary care physician upon joining the HMO. If health care services are provided but not authorized by the primary care physician, then the HMO does not cover the services. The subscriber is personally liable for payment of the nonauthorized services.

HMOs that directly employ physicians in their network are called *staff model* plans. In the simplest characterization, the network physicians are simply paid a salary by the HMO, although some HMOs do base payments on factors such as patient load. Alternatively, plans that set up their network by contracting with physicians in geographically

spread out, independent, either solo or small group practices are called *independent practice associations* (IPAs). Both types assign primary care physicians as gatekeepers for covered services. IPAs are more common than staff model HMOs and constitute the fastest-growing type of HMO.

Preferred Provider Organizations (PPOs) give subscribers two distinct tiers of coverage. When subscribers use the PPO's preferred provider network, the required cost sharing (e.g., deductible and coinsurance) is lower than when they use non-network providers. Although a network is formed, PPOs have no physician gatekeepers. Rather, patients simply must pay more out of pocket if they choose to go outside the network. In this way, PPOs create financial incentives for subscribers to use network providers rather than go outside the network for care.

PPO contracts with physicians and hospitals generally address the prices providers will charge the PPO. In return for promising to charge a lower-than-average price, selected providers become part of the PPO's preferred network. No guarantee is given that the provider will see patients under the plan, but if the network is not too large and the PPO's cost-sharing provisions for subscribers are network-favorable, then the provider may enjoy a large increase in patient care business by joining the network. Prompt payment for services may be another advantage.

Providers often agree to submit themselves to some form of utilization review under the contract. Most PPOs (88 percent) require preadmission certification for a hospital stay and concurrent utilization review for such stays (83 percent). About half (47 percent) require a mandatory second opinion for a recommendation of surgery.

Point-of-service (POS) plans are a hybrid of HMOs and PPOs. Like PPOs, POS plans offer two tiers of insurance benefits. Coverage is greater (out-of-pocket costs are lower) when members use network providers and less generous (out-of-pocket costs are higher) when they use non-network providers. Like HMOs, however, POS plans assign each member a physician gatekeeper, who must authorize in-network care in order for the care to be covered on in-network terms. Most POS plans do not require authorization for a member to use out-of-network services, but such care is covered on less-generous terms. As recently as 1993, POS plans were relatively rare, but by 1995 they had increased their market share to 20 percent of the group coverage market nationwide. Some POS plans have been developed by HMOs; others have been developed by existing PPOs.

Table 12.1 categorizes the organizational structures. The matrix rows indicate whether an organized provider network is formed. The columns indicate whether a gatekeeper is part of the arrangement. Basically, the gatekeeper and the provider network provide two particular forms of health system control. HMOS provide both, while FFS plans provide neither.

MEDICAID MANAGED CARE PLANS

In the last few years, many states have adopted managed care models for the Medicaid coverage they provide to families with dependent children and pregnant women who meet their low-income criteria for Medicaid eligibility. They believe that managed care may help contain program costs, which are a major part of most states' budgets. As of 1996, 13.3 million Medicaid beneficiaries nationwide were enrolled in some form of managed care. This represents a sharp increase from the 2.7 million in 1991.

TABLE 12.1 Different Health System Organizational Structures

		Gatekeeper	
		No	*Yes*
Provider Network	*No*	Fee for Service (**FFS**)	Point of Service (**POS**)
	Yes	Preferred Provider Organization (**PPO**)	Health Maintenance Organization (**HMO**)

As with employer plans, Medicaid managed care plans vary considerably. In some areas, states have contracted directly with HMOs that already exist in their local markets. In others, states have created their own loosely structured provider networks, which contract with selected providers for discounted services and use physician gatekeeping to control utilization. Some Medicaid programs, such as Michigan's, use a combination of the two approaches.

MANAGED CARE CONTRACTS WITH PHYSICIANS

Managed care contracts with physicians vary considerably. Most HMO and POS plans pay their network physicians on a capitation basis. Under capitation, the plan pays the physician's practice a fixed fee, generally an actuarial per-member–per-month (PMPM) dollar amount, in return for the treatments provided to members of the insurance plan. Physicians also may be responsible for the costs of referrals, laboratory tests, and hospital services. Thus, HMOs and POS plans shift the costs of care, as well as the risk associated with those costs, directly onto physician practices. In so doing, these contracts put physician earnings at risk. If care provided under such arrangements turns out to cost less than the fixed-dollar plan payment, the practice makes a profit. Likewise, if care turns out to cost more than the payment, the practice must take a loss.

In contrast, PPO contracts with physicians rarely involve capitation. Instead, they specify the discounted fees for various services that the plan will pay in exchange for the privilege of being in that plan's network. If a physician joins the PPO's network and happens to provide services to one of that plan's subscribers, the practice must accept the prenegotiated fees as payment in full. "Balance billing" of the patient (for the remainder of a higher bill) is not allowed.

Plan utilization review procedures are commonly covered in managed care contracts, whether they are HMOs, PPOs, or POS plans. Physicians must follow particular care-review procedures. Most managed care contracts also require a certain degree of physician record keeping on their enrollees (e.g., plan specific) patient encounter forms may have to be filed with the insurer each time care is provided).

Medicaid managed care contracts with physicians parallel those of private managed care plans, although specific service packages are determined heavily by the state's policies. In states that have set up their own Medicaid provider networks, the state contracts directly with individual gatekeeper physicians, agreeing to pay them a small fixed fee (e.g., $3 per month) for each Medicaid enrollee under their jurisdiction. In return for this payment, the physician serves as the gatekeeper for Medicaid-covered services.

Based on a 1995 nationwide survey (Simon and Emmons, 1997), primary care physicians exhibit the highest prevalence of capitation contracts, because they serve

more often as gatekeepers in HMO and POS plans. Primary care physicians include general family practitioners (50 percent), general internists (48 percent), and pediatricians (64 percent).

Some physicians limit the risk associated with capitation by obtaining stop-loss provisions in their contracts or by purchasing reinsurance against large losses. A stop-loss provision limits the physician's liability per enrollee under the plan to, for example, $25,000 per year for any single enrollee. With stop-loss protection, once the cost of services provided to any one patient reaches a certain threshold (e.g., $25,000 over 12 months), the insurer would cover all additional expenses. Reinsurance works the same way, although the coverage need not be part of the explicit contract with the insurer; it may be purchased separately from a reinsurance company. Reinsurance for physician practices may specify either a stop-loss threshold per patient or a stop-loss for all patients (collectively) with that insurer. The reinsurer would pay all or most of any additional expenses once incurred expenses reach the specified threshold.

MANAGED CARE CONTRACTS WITH HOSPITALS

A key feature of the managed care sector is the fact that HMO and PPO plans contract with only a subset of the providers (physicians and hospitals) in the areas that they serve, allowing plans to promote price competition among hospitals that might otherwise lose plan business. This reflects a substantial managed care sector change in the past 20 years.[2]

As recently as the early 1980s, less than 20 percent of the insured population was enrolled in managed care plans, with most in Kaiser-model HMOs (after Kaiser-Permanente HMO system) where the HMO owned the hospitals that its members used. In the 1980s, many states passed "selective contracting" laws, which provided insurers with greater flexibility to develop alternative health plans and to test different design features. These laws led to growth in PPOs and allowed more flexibility than the "closed-system" HMOs such as Kaiser.

In 1998, 51 percent of large hospitals (400 beds or more) reported at least 20 percent of their patients being covered by HMOs, with expectations that the figure would be at 74 percent by the year 2000. The same survey indicated that more than half of the hospitals (53 percent) had 10 or more managed care contracts, with 46 percent of the large hospitals (500 beds or more) having 30 or more contracts.[3]

The probability and characteristics of contracts between individual managed care organizations and hospitals appear to depend on three sets of factors:

1. Plan characteristics including whether it was a PPO or an HMO (and possibly what type of HMO), plan size, whether the plan serves several localities, and how old the plan is.
2. Hospital characteristics including size, ownership (including for-profit versus non-profit status), location (city versus suburb), teaching status, and cost structure (reflecting prices).
3. Market characteristics, generally measured at the metropolitan area level, including the penetration and rate of growth of managed care plans.

[2]This section draws heavily on work by Zwanziger and Meirowitz (1998).
[3]For more detailed results, see Deloitte and Touche (1999).

Research has found equivocal results, most often on the important issue of hospital costs, which are used to reflect prices to the plans. Early studies found that before managed care plans became popular, more competitive markets had higher hospital costs. This occurred because under cost-reimbursement, fee-for-service systems, hospitals could (and did) compete on the basis of services and quality rather than price. More recent research has suggested that competition in hospital markets can lead to lower costs when the insurance market includes sufficient managed care penetration.

Zwanziger and Meirowitz (1998) examine the determinants of plan contracts with hospitals in a study that looks at the three categories above. Looking at HMOs and PPOs in 13 large, metropolitan statistical areas (MSAs), they report:

- Managed care plans prefer to contract with nonprofit hospitals, preferring even public hospitals to for-profit ones.
- Plans are more likely to contract with large hospitals compared with medium-sized hospitals, and with medium-sized hospitals compared with small ones.
- Hospital cost factors (reflecting hospital prices) do not significantly affect contracts.

It is useful to elaborate on a couple of the findings. The authors suggest that for-profit hospitals may be less willing to agree to managed care plan concessions than are nonprofit hospitals. Alternatively, plan choice may reflect consumer demand, and consumers might prefer nonprofit hospitals, using the nonprofit status to indicate a higher quality of care.[4]

The insignificant role of costs, reflecting prices, indicates a need for further analysis. The authors believe that the price of services ought to matter in the decision to affiliate, particularly when one has controlled for other factors. They conclude that their cost terms may not reflect the prices, as they believed they would. Alternatively, it is possible that managed care plans may use costs as quality proxies, or alternatively that low costs are correlated with perceived lower quality by the public.

Development and Growth of Managed Care— Why Has It Taken So Long?

If managed care has so many apparently appealing characteristics, why has it taken so long to become a force in the marketplace? A variety of institutional, economic, and political forces has influenced the pattern of their significant growth. HMO enrollment jumped from approximately 3 million consumers in 1970 to about 67 million consumers in 1997.

The story of the development and growth of managed care in the United States requires an account of the strenuous historical opposition from organized medicine. Early on, organized medicine fiercely opposed alternatives to free patient choice and particularly alternatives to FFS. Kessel (1958) described the historic political actions of organized medicine and proposed the thesis that FFS enabled physicians to charge some patients a higher fee than others for essentially the same service, a pattern known as price discrimination.

[4]Feldman and colleagues (1990) found similar results.

THE ECONOMICS OF PRICE DISCRIMINATION

The ability to charge different prices to different consumers allows a seller to increase profits. Consider a market such as depicted in Figure 12.2, in which services can be provided at constant costs; that is, marginal cost, MC, equals average cost, AC. If providers are perfect competitors, then each is a price taker, and each will charge a price, P^*, equal to marginal cost, MC.

Suppose, however, that providers have some monopoly power such that they face the downward-sloping demand curves shown in Figure 12.2. Suppose also that the providers can distinguish between two groups of consumers. Group H (Panel A) places a high value on health care, whereas Group L (Panel B) gives health care a lower value. If providers can charge different consumers different amounts, above the average cost of providing services, they can earn additional profits.

With some monopoly power, the provider faces a marginal revenue curve that lies below the demand curve (recall why this is the case). To maximize profits, he or she will provide services to the level where marginal revenue, MR_H, equals marginal costs, or Q_H, charging price, P_H. This earns excess profits, π_H, by reducing the quantity sold from the competitive, Q^* (at price P^*) to the monopoly, Q_H (at price P_H).

However, a group of buyers (Group L) still would be willing to pay more than it costs (MC) to provide the services. These buyers generate marginal revenue, MR_L, and the provider can provide quantity Q_L to them at price P_L. If health care were like other goods that could be resold, then Group L could purchase health care at price P_L and resell it at price P_H, negating the providers' attempt to practice price discrimination. However, one cannot purchase treatment for a broken arm and then sell it to someone else. Hence, the markets may remain separate with differing prices. In this case, otherwise similar individuals are charged different prices based on their valuations of the service.

Such price discrimination is difficult or impossible under the contracts that characterize prepayment-based organizations. First, providers will find it difficult to determine how much individual consumers value their services. Second, the prepayment-based organization may be able to shop among providers, thus limiting the providers' monopoly power.

FIGURE 12.2 Profits for a Monopolist Who Can Discriminate Between Markets.

It also is essential to examine the impacts of managed care at the individual consumer level. Recall that consumers may have the choice between fee-for-service and managed care options in employment-based insurance coverage. An analysis of consumer choice can provide insights into the cost impacts of managed care programs, and provide predictions as to changes in usage and in expenditures.

Figure 12.3 starts with consumer demand, D_f, under fee-for-service insurance. Assuming that the price is constant at P_f, total expenditures, P_fQ_f, are represented by the larger rectangle. These total expenditures also would represent the expected insurance component of the individual's wage package.

A managed care option by constraining choice of provider as well as various coverages is viable only if it reduces expenditures. By exerting market power over suppliers, by reducing inpatient care, and by limiting length of stay, HMO managers may lower prices from P_f to P_m.

Demand also may be reduced. Care managers have incentives to minimize supplier-induced demand, thus shifting demand from D_f to D_m. Furthermore, a managed care option may appeal to consumers who are younger, healthier, or less concerned about risk—in short, those who would choose to demand less health care. The resulting expenditures are shown by the smaller rectangle representing total expenditures, P_mQ_m.

It follows that managed care trades some constraint of consumer choices in return for lower per-unit prices for care. As drawn in Figure 12.3, both decreased price per unit of care and decreased quantity of care contribute to decreased expenditures. Note, however, that a natural response to decreased prices is to increase quantity demanded. Total consumer expenditures will fall as long as the price decreases are not fully offset by increased quantity demanded.

BARRIERS TO MANAGED CARE BY ORGANIZED MEDICINE

Organized medicine also has posed barriers to managed care development. Organized medical groups opposed physicians' participation in plans and organizations that were

FIGURE 12.3 Treatment and Expenditures under Managed Care.

not controlled by physicians and/or that were not offering a free choice of physician. Such restrictions were challenged successfully by the Federal Trade Commission in the 1970s.

FEDERAL POLICY AND THE GROWTH OF MANAGED CARE

The HMO Act of 1973 represented a turning point in federal policy in promoting the development of alternative delivery systems as a cornerstone of a cost-containment strategy. The act enabled HMOs to become federally qualified if they provided enrollees with comprehensive benefits and met various other requirements. Loan guarantees and grants for startup costs were made available, but the main advantage accruing to a federally qualified HMO was that it could require firms in its area with 25 or more employees to offer the HMO as an option. Other regulatory barriers subsequently were reduced.

Despite these changes, numbers of HMOs and HMO enrollees did not accelerate until the 1980s. When incentives to enroll Medicare and Medicaid recipients were improved, the entry of for-profit HMOS led to growth from 235 in 1980 to 623 in 1986. Growth slowed in the late 1980s and some consolidation occurred in the number of HMOS, but the upward trend in enrollment resumed in the 1990s. From 1990 to 1997, the number of plans rose from 572 to 651, and total enrollment increased from 36 million to 67 million persons.

It also is useful to consider the growth experience of preferred provider organizations (PPOs). Offering more flexibility in choosing providers, they have grown rapidly in recent years. In 1995, 2,687 PPOs were operating, covering 117 million eligible employees.

Although percentage enrollments are highest in the Northeast and the West (California alone accounted for more than 20 percent of national HMO enrollment), HMOs and PPOs have increased their market penetration in other areas recently. The most recent figures regarding the industry structure (1997) indicate that mixed and IPA models dominate HMO membership. Table 12.2 provides additional information on the characteristics of HMOs and their enrollees.

TABLE 12.2	Number of HMOs and HMO Enrollment by Selected Characteristics—1997			
	Plans		**Enrollments**	
Characteristics	*Number*	*Percent*	*Number*	*Percent*
All Plans	*651*	*100.0*	*66.8[1]*	*100.0*
Model Type				
IPA	284	43.6	26.7	40.0
Group	98	15.1	11.0	16.5
Mixed	258	39.6	29.0	43.4
Geographic Region	*Number*	*Percent*	*Percent of Regional Population*	
Total	*651*	*100.0*		
NE	110	16.9	32.4	
MW	184	28.3	19.5	
South	236	36.3	17.9	
West	121	18.6	36.4	

[1]Includes 10.3 million Medicare and Medicaid HMO members. They are not included in the other data.

Source: U.S. Department of Health & Human Services, *Health United States 1998,* Table 135.

At the firm levels, changes have been substantial. Jensen and colleagues (1997) sampled employers in 1993 and 1995 to determine their usage of various types of health plans. Even in two years, the move from conventional coverage to managed care was substantial. Nowhere was it more substantial than for the smallest firms (between one and 24 employees). In 1993, 78.3 percent of the workers in this category were insured in conventional FFS plans. By 1995, the percentage had fallen to 30.5.

Why did the small firms switch? First, their conventional plans before the switch had tended to be worse than average in terms of the deductible to be met before claims could be covered. Second, most of the plans had experienced higher-than-average premium increases between the years 1992 and 1993, thus providing an incentive to turn to a new type of coverage.

Modeling Managed Care

The changed incentives from managed care have caused many to predict success in constraining utilization and cost of care. The underlying logic behind this proposition is intuitive. When providers agree to handle all of patients' health care needs for fixed, prearranged fees, the providers accept and bear a substantial part of the financial risk. By bearing the risk of delivering services at a fixed premium, managed care plans have strong incentives to reduce excessive care. The fixed premiums also would seem to provide incentives to offer forms of preventive care that are cost-effective from the care managers' perspectives. Such preventive care could decrease the need for more subsequent (expensive) curative care.

Will managed care plans provide enough care or the right types of care? The following analyses, derived by Goodman and Stano (2000), treat managed care plans as "staff model" HMOs (where physicians are HMO employees).

MODELING INDIVIDUAL HMOS

Individual HMOs wish to determine the number of consumers to serve and the level of service to provide. One might compare them to urban suburbs, which set the qualities of public schools and the sizes of the police forces, for example, by the preferences of their residents and by the costs of providing them. Just as suburbs provide a menu of public services, HMOs provide a menu of both palliative and curative care in inpatient and outpatient settings. To keep things simple, however, we will assume that HMOs provide only one type of service (visits), and are differentiated in quality by how many visits each offers.[5]

We assume that HMO treatment costs are related to member health status, which is a function of care received at the HMO and elsewhere, as well as other factors including diet, environment, and lifestyle. People's long-term health relates in part to short-term decisions about how much care to provide. This follows directly from the long-term nature of human capital, most particularly health capital. Thus, because patients live for many years, treatment decisions at one HMO may affect treatment costs

[5]Wildasin (1986, Section 4) presents the public finance literature. Goldstein and Pauly (1976) examine workers' choices among employers, each of which offers a single health insurance plan.

at other HMOs. Moreover, HMOs have the dual incentives of keeping people healthy and attracting healthy people.

An HMO's total annual costs are higher if it provides more services per enrollee or if it has more members. Having healthier members lowers HMO costs. Assume that health care works—that health is related positively to the level of services by all providers. Because at any time in the future these individuals may be members of a given HMO, average health status of the population is related to the level of treatment of the whole population by all providers. This will affect the costs for these providers in that better health will lower costs.

HOW MUCH CARE?

The previous section indicated that profit-maximizing HMOs might not recognize the system-wide impact of health services on consumers' health. Although an individual HMO seeks to maintain the health of its own clientele, it does not recognize that its decisions may affect the costs of other HMOs. We call this an externality because it is a benefit that affects others but is not considered by any individual firm.

Suppose instead that an HMO has clinics at a number of locations throughout several states, referred to as HMO_1, HMO_2, and so on. Although HMO_1, for example, may not account for this possibility, the HMO entrepreneur, to maximize profits, must consider the impacts of health services on the health of others elsewhere.

This is easily shown in Figure 12.4. Without the externality, HMO_1 optimizes at point A, providing quality level x_1^{mkt}. Level x_1^{mkt} is economically *inefficient*, however, because it does not account for the fact that improved treatment at HMO_1 lowers costs throughout the system.

The optimal quality level of x_1 is at point B, or x_1^{opt}. This occurs by recognizing the downward shift in the marginal cost curve by a factor that reflects the effect of the health externality on the costs facing HMO_2, HMO_3 and so on, as well as HMO_1.

FIGURE 12.4 Externality Model of HMO with Random Disenrollment.

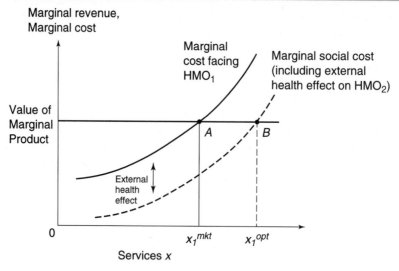

Marginal revenue,
Marginal cost

Marginal
cost facing
HMO_1

Marginal social cost
(including external
health effect on HMO_2)

Value of
Marginal
Product

A *B*

External
health
effect

0

x_1^{mkt} x_1^{opt}

Services x

Level x_1^{mkt} indicates an inefficiently small level of HMO services, and by implication a substitution of non-HMO and/or nonhealth care inputs (such as the patient's own time) for the HMO care.

While the potential loss of patients may influence treatment decisions of fee-for-service providers as well as HMOs, the capitation method of payment to HMOs makes the disenrollment problem particularly important. Fee-for-service providers are paid for each unit of care. Aside from uncollectible bills, they do not risk losses on services provided currently or in the future.

In contrast, by integrating insurance with the provision of health care, the HMO receives a fixed payment per enrollee to cover costs in the current period, and over time, for those who remain enrolled. Thus, unlike fee-for-service care, where payment in every period is likely to cover costs, the HMO must consider the timing of expenditures and the financial losses of overspending on patients who may disenroll. One way for an HMO to self-insure against long-term losses attributable to disenrollment is to economize on care for those currently enrolled.

WHAT TYPES OF CARE?

In this section, we consider the long-term consequences of potential movement among HMOs on decisions among treatment practices. If an HMO receives constant revenue per patient each period, its goal is to minimize costs. Patients stay in the HMO for two periods, which might be considered as early and late in their lives. The HMO may offer:

- High-tech, possibly capital-intensive procedures leading to high Period 1 costs and zero Period 2 costs.
- Low-tech, less capital-intensive procedures, leading to low costs in both periods.

Because the revenues are the same with either high-tech or low-tech care, the HMO's problem is to minimize costs, using the cheaper (over time) of the two procedures.

Suppose that increased competition through increased choice raises disenrollment rates. With higher disenrollment rates, low-tech continuing care becomes the more financially viable option, even if the present discounted values are equal and even if high-tech treatment is more economically efficient in producing health. Here, HMOs self-insure against future disenrollment by reducing current costs through (low-cost) continuing care rather than high-tech treatment.

In evaluating how much and what types of care are offered by HMOs, we see that the HMO faces an economic externality because it cannot capture fully the gains of its treatment over time. As a result, it will offer less care and lower-tech care than FFS plans. As noted, if the HMO were to merge with others forming a larger network, the larger firm might internalize this positive externality, because the network owners could expect that clients who leave one HMO might join another HMO within the network. The receiving HMO would then take advantage of the now-healthier clients who had benefited from their earlier treatment.

FRAMEWORK FOR PREDICTION

Clearly, this model simplifies the situation, because many forms of managed care exist providing a myriad of services. It provides a framework, however, for addressing possible HMO cost savings relative to FFS plans. FFS plans encourage overutilization to

the point where marginal private benefits can be far less than marginal costs. HMOs are widely believed to discourage this deadweight loss and other forms of overutilization, such as supplier-induced demand. To evaluate utilization, however, one must control for the health of the client population, which might be impacted by HMO "cream skimming" of the healthier clientele.

This simple model provides predictions that are consistent with the rising conflict between HMOs and their members. The popular press prints stories about inadequate levels of services and the unavailability of expensive, high-tech treatment options. Many states, as well as the federal government, are considering legislation aimed at regulating HMO practices.

WHERE MANAGED CARE DIFFERS FROM FFS—
DUMPING, CREAMING, AND SKIMPING

We recognize that one of the key differences between HMOs and FFS plans involves the form of payment. Hospitals and other FFS providers are paid for each treatment in order to cover costs. HMOs are paid fixed rates per person irrespective of the amount of treatment used. These differences have led to discussions within the medical and policy communities regarding three purported practices.

Dumping Refusing to treat less-healthy patients who might use services in excess of their premiums.

Creaming Seeking to attract more-healthy patients who will use services costing less than their premiums.

Skimping Providing less than the optimal quantity of services for any given condition in a given time period.

Because the HMO's costs are related to the average health of its clientele, practices such as dumping (unhealthy patients) and creaming (healthy patients) may occur. If the HMO can identify patients who are sicker than some arbitrary level, it can improve the average health of its clientele and hence lower its costs. As noted in Ellis (1998), the patient and the public at large may not notice this decision. The HMO may honestly say that it is not equipped for this kind of case and that the patient would be better served elsewhere. This behavior contrasts with cost-based FFS care. Inasmuch as every penny spent on even the most severe case theoretically is paid back to the hospital, the cost-based hospital will not dump anyone.

Creaming is the practice of seeking out or emphasizing low-severity patients. The HMO benefits from creaming, because all patients of sufficiently low-case severity require few hospital services, so that premium, P, exceeds patient costs. Some patients believe that their malady is so mild that the hospital care is hardly worth the trip; these patients correspond in practice to the young, vigorous, and healthy people that HMOs prefer to have in their service populations. The FFS provider also creams because its reimbursement covers costs for each of its patients.

Skimping involves cutting back on services to the point that patients' welfare is reduced. FFS providers will not skimp because each nursing hour, electronic instrument, and surgery that they employ will be reimbursed. In contrast, skimping provides the opportunity for the HMO to increase profits. Because the HMO has been paid premium P in advance, reducing the amount of services will lower costs and *may* raise profits. The

uncertainty regarding profits occurs because reducing the benefits for a given severity of illness may cause the HMO to lose some patients to FFS plans or to other HMOs.

EQUILIBRIUM AND ADVERSE SELECTION IN A MARKET WITH HMOS

Providers may have incentives for seeking patients, but patients also may select themselves into particular types of care. Recent work by Cutler and Reber (1998) demonstrates the potential adverse selection of sicker consumers toward FFS care and healthier patients toward HMOs. This work also explains how HMO penetration can respond strongly to small changes in relative pricing.

Suppose Jeff has just graduated from college and landed a job with Sante Fe Futons, Inc. The firm offers its employees a choice of membership in one of two health plans—an HMO that charges a flat, prearranged price, P_H, or a deluxe care FFS plan with deductible, D, and coinsurance rate, r. Letting the severity of illness, s, be measured by the expenditures required to treat at the FFS level, Jeff calculates the extra cost of FFS to be:

$$E = \text{FFS cost} - \text{HMO cost} = [\text{Deductibles} + \text{FFS copay}] - \text{HMO Price}$$
$$E = [D + rs] - P_H \qquad \textbf{(12.1)}$$

Is it worth it to use FFS, or should Jeff use HMO care instead?

To evaluate Jeff's decision, we must find market values for the parameters in equation (12.1), and then compare them to the value received. Under perfect competition, both FFS and HMO providers earn zero profits. For the FFS providers, profit for the average patient is written as:

$$\pi_F = D + r\bar{s}_F - \bar{s}_F = 0$$

indicating that the firm collects patient deductibles, D, and patient copayments, $r\bar{s}_F$, and spends \bar{s}_F for treatment. Rearranging terms, this means that the market deductible is:

$$D = (1 - r)\bar{s}_F$$

For the HMO parameters, we again assume that in the long run, competition will drive profits to zero. Hence, premium, P_H, must cover average payments for condition s_H, or $\alpha\bar{s}_H$:

$$\pi_H = P_H - \alpha\bar{s}_H = 0$$

Parameter α reflects Cutler and Reber's assumption that HMOs achieve efficiencies in providing care, as well as restricting the amount of hospital care provided, reducing the cost of care. With no cost reductions, α would equal 1; Cutler and Reber assert that the real-world value of α is approximately 0.9.

Substituting these terms into (12.1) provides the following expression for Jeff:

$$E = [(1 - r)\bar{s}_F - \alpha\bar{s}_H] + rs \qquad \textbf{(12.1')}$$

Assuming that the market-determined term in brackets is positive (a reasonable assumption), we show E as the upward-sloping line in Figure 12.5.

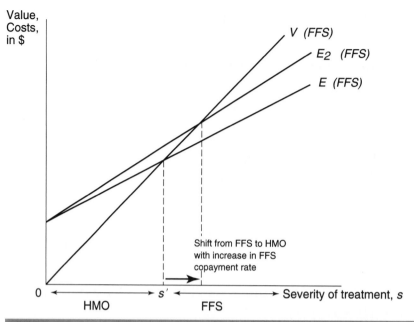

FIGURE 12.5 Selection into HMO and FFS Settings.

How much does Jeff value health care? Let's assume that he values each unit of s equally. Then, he values $100 worth of care at $100, $200 worth of care at $200, and so on. In other words, we can draw a 45° line for his valuation, V, of FFS care. Jeff will choose the plan that provides value, V, that exceeds the extra costs, E.

Let's start at expected level of care, $s = 0$. Jeff is young, healthy, and doesn't expect to use much service. If he were to join the FFS plan, however, he would have to pay the average FFS client expenditure, which is more than the average HMO fee, plus his share, r, of the services that he uses. Because the FFS costs are higher than the value that he puts on them (the E curve is above the V curve), Jeff chooses to join the HMO. If Jeff has a chronic condition requiring ongoing treatment, he recognizes that each unit of on-going treatment is subsidized by the FFS plan at rate $(1 - r)$. With increasing treatment, FFS becomes a more attractive option as V exceeds E.

At severity level s', Jeff would be indifferent between the HMO and FFS plans be-cause the extra value of FFS was just equal to and just canceled by the extra cost. If all consumers were similar to Jeff in everything except their health, consumers with ex-pected severity less than s' would join the HMO, while those expecting severity greater than s' would choose FFS.

Suppose the FFS plan increased its coinsurance rate, r. Then the FFS plan becomes less attractive; this can be seen by rotating the E line counterclockwise to E_2. Consumers who were previously indifferent between HMOs and FFS plans will shift to the HMOs. The younger and healthier HMO patrons are now joined by some of the (not as young and not as healthy) former FFS patrons. Hence, the healthiest among the former FFS patrons become the sickest HMO members. As a result, the average severity in both plans increases.

Are Managed Care Costs Lower?

Several reasons have been provided for predicting that HMOs will spend less per member. Policymakers have considerable interest in whether this theoretical proposition is true. From early on, it has been reported that total costs—that is, the sum of premiums and out-of-pocket expenses—were from 10 percent to 40 percent lower for HMOs. The cost differences were attributed largely to lower hospitalization rates, not to lower ambulatory care-use rates.

AN INTRODUCTION TO THE DATA

An understanding of how these comparisons were made will help to make clear the research issues involved. In one study reported in 1978, Luft examined 26 pairs of patient groups. Each pair included an HMO group and a comparison FFS group. This pairing was done to control for population differences. The research question regarding these 26 pairs was whether HMOs tended to have different ambulatory care-use rates than FFS. In general, Luft found that HMO members in most cases had similar numbers of visits per period; however, IPA members had consistently higher rates.

Using a similar pairing procedure, Luft further investigated possible differences in hospital-use rates. He studied 51 pairs of HMO and non-HMO patient groups. HMO members tended to have lower utilization as measured by hospital days per capita, the product of admissions times length of stay. Contrary to the usual predictions, there were no clear differences in lengths of stay. The lower hospital-use rate was explained by a lower admission rate. The lower admission is consistent with theoretical predictions.

In a 1981 review, Luft reached the same general conclusion. HMO enrollees, especially prepaid group practice members, have lower hospitalization rates. Knowledge that HMOs have lower hospital use rates, however, still leaves many questions to answer. For example, no clear evidence showed that these lower rates were attributable to reductions in the less important, discretionary procedures. Furthermore, the evidence at hand could not dismiss the possibilities that biased self-selection of HMO membership or even underutilization in HMOs were responsible for the observed differences.

Reduction in use rates is only one way to reduce costs; cutting costs of producing services is another. Evidence on the service costs is even more limited. Are HMOs more efficient in production? Luft's 1978 study found that in examining eight types of discretionary procedures, contrary to expectations, there was no general pattern of differences in production costs favoring HMOs (except for lower rates of tonsillectomy in HMOs).

Arnould and colleagues (1984) examined both use and cost questions in a setting that helps to isolate the effect of the HMO from possible extraneous differences. They examined use rates and treatment costs for four surgical procedures—appendectomy, hysterectomy (surgical removal of the uterus), cholecystectomy (surgical excision of the gallbladder) and herniorrhaphy (hernia repair). Multiple regression was used to control for patient characteristics, and the data indicated whether any patient had already decided on surgery. HMO and other patients were treated at the same sites and by the same groups of physicians, which minimized the confounding problem of provider differences that plagued other comparison studies.

Arnould and colleagues confirmed Luft's conclusion that length of stay is not significantly different between the HMO and the FFS patients. They also found that the use of surgeon visits, as well as lab charges, per patient were lower for the HMO users

(significantly lower for hysterectomy and appendectomy), although total hospital charges were significantly lower for the HMO patients only in the case of appendectomies. Thus, although differences occur in costs of elements of hospital care, no strong case can be made to conclude that HMOs produce hospital care more cheaply overall.

Miller and Luft (1994) update the analysis of cost differentials in a literature review through the 1980s and early 1990s. Compared with FFS, HMO plans generally had from 1 percent to 20 percent shorter hospital lengths of stay. HMOs recently have exhibited slightly higher rates of physician office visits than comparable FFS plans. HMO plans used an average of 22 percent fewer procedures, tests, or treatments that were expensive and/or had less costly alternative interventions for conditions including childbirth, heart disease, colon and colorectal cancer, and cardiovascular disease.

Miller and Luft provide the following evidence regarding bottom lines with respect to costs:

1. Inpatient services account for a higher percentage of total expenditures than do outpatient services.
2. HMO plans used fewer services that are expensive and/or have less costly alternatives.
3. HMOs provided more comprehensive coverage than did indemnity plans.

These facts imply that HMOs provide care at lower cost than do indemnity (FFS) plans.

THE PROBLEM OF SELECTION BIAS

The lower overall costs for HMOs have been confirmed in many studies, and it is clear that HMO members tend to use less hospital care. What is less clear is whether HMOs encourage more efficient practice patterns or whether their savings result from favorable selection of enrollees. On the one hand, HMOs offer comprehensive benefits and so they may attract and retain sicker members. On the other hand, HMOs may attract disproportionately younger members and families who tend to be healthier and for whom the costs of care tend to be relatively lower.[6]

Two studies illustrate the potential importance of selection bias. One, by Strumwasser and colleagues (1989), examined a large firm that offered employees the option of retaining Blue Cross or switching either to an HMO or PPO. In the case examined, those employees who switched to the HMO or PPO plans were younger and had much lower utilization rates. In the year prior to switching, employees who later chose to switch to the HMO had incurred only 16 percent of the average expenditures of those who later chose to retain their traditional Blue Cross and Blue Shield coverage.

In a similarly relevant study, Lewis (1984) compared populations that leave an HMO with those that choose to continue. It was found that those who remained enrolled in the HMO used more services than those who left. Though the two studies suggest somewhat different implications, both emphasize the need to control for possible selection bias.

[6]Luft (1981) reviews the extensive literature that compares the characteristics of HMO members versus other populations, including data on their relative health status and their attitudes toward health care.

THE RAND STUDY—A RANDOMIZED EXPERIMENT

Several studies investigate the problem of selection bias in studying differences in costs between HMOs and FFS populations. In the Rand Health Insurance Experiment, patients were assigned randomly to different plans in a controlled experiment, thus apparently eliminating selection bias. Would HMO costs still be lower under such circumstances?

The Rand study compared HMO and FFS patients in the Puget Sound area where 1,580 individuals were assigned randomly to either an FFS physician of their choice or to the Group Health Cooperative (GHC) of Puget Sound—an HMO in Seattle, Washington.[7] The 431 FFS individuals were in one of four groups:

1. free care
2. 25 percent of their expenses up to a maximum out-of-pocket liability of $1,000 per family
3. 95 percent of their expenses up to a maximum out-of-pocket liability of $1,000 per family
4. 95 percent coinsurance on outpatient services, up to a limit of $150 per person ($450 per family)

In addition to the experimental GHC group of 1,149 persons, a control group consisted of a random sample of 733 GHC members who had previously been enrolled for at least 1 year.

Total expenditures per person were $439 for the experimental group, including out-of-plan use, compared to $609 for the free care (group 1) FFS group.[8] As seen from Table 12.3, ambulatory utilization, as indicated in the columns labeled "Face-to-Face Visits" and "Preventive Visits," was about the same. Thus, the 39 percent increased spending for FFS members (or 28 percent reduction for GHC) was due largely to a much higher admission rate and increased hospital days per person. The study could not pinpoint the reasons for GHC's lower hospital use.

To put the potential cost savings into better perspective, note that the use rates for the experimental HMO patients did not differ materially from the last two categories of FFS, the categories on "95 percent" coinsurance (group 3) and "Individual deductible" (group 4). Thus, for some population groups, a shift to HMOs would not lead to savings, although the cost savings for other population groups might conceivably be important.

Quality of Care

Do managed care organizations offer quality of care that is comparable to care under FFS? Given the growth of managed care enrollments and the historical public policy encouragement of managed care growth, this question merits substantial interest. Managed care provides incentives to reduce the costs of care. Does it also provide incentives to cut corners by reducing the *quality* of care?

[7]See Manning et al. (1984).
[8]Out-of-plan use can be substantial. Mott (1986) described numerous ways in which out-of-plan use by HMO members may be unrecorded.

TABLE 12.3 Annual Rates of Admission and Face-to-Face Visits

Plan	Admission Rate	Hospital Days	Face-to-Face Visits	Preventive Visits
	Per 100 Persons		Per Person	
GHC experimental	8.4	49	4.3	0.55
	(0.67)	(9.6)	(0.14)	(0.02)
GHC control	8.3	38	4.7	0.60
	(1.01)	(9.0)	(0.17)	(0.02)
Fee for service				
Free	13.8	83	4.2	0.41
	(1.51)	(26)	(0.25)	(0.03)
25%	10.0	87	3.5	0.32
	(1.43)	(28)	(0.35)	(0.03)
95%	10.5	46	2.9	0.29
	(1.68)	(9.9)	(0.34)	(0.04)
Individual deductible	8.8	28	3.3	0.27
	(1.20)	(5.1)	(0.33)	(0.03)

(Standard errors in parentheses.)

Source: Manning et al. (1984). Copyright © 1984 Massachusetts Medical Society. All rights reserved.

The answer is by no means obvious. Cutting quality would likely lower costs in the short term, but it might increase the longer-term costs if patients required additional services later. Furthermore, if information about quality were available to consumers, lowering quality would tend to erode demand. Despite the importance of quality-of-care issues to health care analysis in general and to analysis of managed care in particular, quality issues are among the most difficult to resolve.[9]

A good place to begin is by defining and measuring quality. Quality, in common usage, may range from consumer perceptions of the provider–patient relationship to the outcome effects of health care on health status. Most important for public policy are those aspects of quality that affect health status outcomes.

Quality may refer to three stages of health care (Donabedian, 1980):

- *Structure.* the quality and appropriateness of the available inputs and their organization.
- *Process.* the quality of the delivery of care.
- *Outcome.* measures ultimate quality of care but most difficult to measure scientifically.

In a nutshell, little evidence can be found that MCO quality of care is inferior to FFS care.

1. Regarding structure, Luft (1981) reports that HMOs tend to provide specialists as readily or more readily than FFS plans and are more likely to have board-certified specialists.

[9]The following discussion uses reviews by Luft (1981); Wyszewianski, Wheeler, and Donabedian (1982); and updated reviews by Miller and Luft (1994, 1997).

2. Process assessment provides an even wider mix of evidence, although often some of the more established HMOs show well on measures such as completeness of physical exams, appropriateness of referrals, and appropriateness of drug prescribing. Little reason is found to conclude either in favor or against managed care organizations regarding process.
3. Regarding outcome, Quick et al. (1981) found better infant mortality rates for prepaid group practice versus the general population. More general measures, such as disability days, also have sometimes favored HMOs.
4. Overall consumer satisfaction is comparable between managed care and fee-for-service settings. Other surveys show that relatively few members who voluntarily disenroll from HMOs cite dissatisfaction with the care they receive as the reason for their decision.

Miller and Luft (1994, 1997) summarize more recent material on quality of care and customer satisfaction. Compared with FFS plans, managed care plan enrollees recently have received more preventive tests, procedures, and examinations (such as cancer screening; pelvic, rectal, and general physical examinations). Outcomes on a wide range of conditions (including congestive heart failure, colorectal cancer, diabetes, and hypertension) have been better or equivalent to those using FFS plans. HMO enrollees were less satisfied with quality of care and physician–patient interactions but more satisfied with costs.

Miller and Luft (1997) note that HMO plans and providers cut hospitalization and use of more costly tests and procedures, often with little visible effect on quality of care "given the high prices of the indemnity insurance/fee-for-service system." However, they note that simply carrying out the same clinical processes but with fewer resources can negatively affect quality of care in some cases, such as Medicare home health care.

In summary, quality comparisons between managed care and FFS settings remain difficult to make, but it is hard to conclude that managed care is either better or worse. This assessment of the literature is itself important, however, because managed care quality has been questioned consistently. It is surely unwarranted to conclude from the literature that HMOs provide consistently inferior care.

Growth in Spending

The consensus is strong that managed care reduces utilization, especially of hospital care. A different but related question is whether managed care organizations also have lower growth rates in spending. If they do, a continued shift toward managed care will result not only in reductions in spending levels, but also in the long-term rate of increase.

It is important to provide a framework for discussing the relationship among FFS, managed care organizations (MCO), and total costs, particularly because terminology can be confusing. Suppose we are concerned about costs per person for treating a particular illness over three periods. Let us assume that people use either FFS or MCO and that the population is fixed. We can calculate the total treatment costs as:

$$\text{Total Treatment Costs} = (\text{Number in FFS}) \times (\text{FFS Costs/FFS Enrollee}) \\ + (\text{Number in MCO}) \times (\text{MCO Costs/MCO Enrollee})$$

(12.2)

Dividing both sides by the total population, we get:

$$\text{Treatment Costs/Person} = (\text{Fraction in FFS}) \times (\text{FFS Costs/FFS Enrollee}) \\ + (\text{Fraction in MCO}) \times (\text{MCO Costs/MCO Enrollee})$$

$$(12.3)$$

Suppose, in Period 1, that FFS treatment costs $200, MCO treatment costs $100, and that 60 percent use FFS and that 40 percent use MCO care. The treatment costs per person will be:

$$\text{Treatment Costs/Person} = (0.6) \times 200 + (0.4) \times 100 = 120 + 40 = 160$$

This is noted in column 1 of Table 12.4 as Period 1.

Obviously, if FFS and MCO costs were to stay constant and patients were to switch from FFS to MCO, costs per person would fall. As noted in Table 12.4, if a 10 percentage-point movement occurs from FFS to MCO, treatment costs per person would fall, because one in 10 people would be substituting a (MCO) treatment that is half the price of the other (FFS treatment). As calculated in Table 12.4, the total costs per person would fall by $10, or 6.25 percent.

What is less obvious is that unless the population shift from FFS to managed care continues, cost reduction and cost containment may be difficult. Suppose that in Period 3 the percentage in FFS remains at 50 percent but the costs of both FFS and MCO increase by 10 percent. The total cost per person accordingly rises by 10 percent from $150 to $165. If total costs per enrollee in each sector were to continue to rise by 10 percent and no change occurred in the MCO market share, the total costs per person on aggregate also would rise by 10 percent. This occurs irrespective of the fact that a larger proportion of the population (Period 3) is now being treated in managed care settings than was being treated in Period 1.

This analysis provides important insights into the impacts of managed care plans on health care costs and health care cost increases. To the extent that large shifts of insureds into managed care have led to lower-cost treatments, there may have been one-time cost decreases relative to what they would have been. However, if managed care and FFS plans face the same cost inflation for the services that they offer apart from the one-time decreases, overall cost inflation is unlikely to abate.

Evidence from Luft (1981) and Newhouse and colleagues (1985) leads us to conclude that the growth rate of spending in HMOs is roughly the same as the growth rate under FFS. Policy makers may rely on shifts into managed care to reduce health care costs and health care growth rates. However, if the shifts do not continue, costs will continue to inflate, albeit from lower bases.

TABLE 12.4 Managed Care and Cost Containment—An Example

	Period 1	Period 2	Percent Increase	Period 3	Percent Increase
Fraction of Population in MCO	0.4	0.5		0.5	
FFS Costs Per Enrollee	200	200	0.00	220	10.00
MCO Costs Per Enrollee	100	100	0.00	110	10.00
Total Costs Per Person	*160*	*150*	*−6.25*	*165*	*10.00*

Competitive Effects

Up to this point, we have concentrated on the *direct* effects of managed care and managed care organizations. We have asked what managed care organizations look like, whether they provide less costly care, and whether they provide different quality care. In this section, we address the *indirect* effects of managed care through the market mechanism. By indirect, we mean that existing health providers must respond to competition from the managed care sector.

After discussing some of the theoretical concerns, we will evaluate the impact of competition in three ways. We will look at the impact of managed care on hospital markets, on insurance markets, and finally on the adoption of technological change.

THEORETICAL ISSUES

The spread of alternative delivery systems can elicit substantially greater competition in other sectors only if competition is absent at the start. Otherwise, both providers and insurers would be operating at, or close to, their minimum costs of production. Although there is bound to be disagreement on the extent of the degree of market imperfections, most would agree that the insurance and provider markets are less than highly competitive.

Consider the consequences of having a larger number of products and competitors to an existing monopolistic seller. In Figure 12.6, D_1 is the current market demand and P_1 is the monopoly profit-maximizing price for each firm. The entry of other firms will have the following effects on each individual firm:

- shift the demand curve to the left to D_2
- shift the marginal revenue curve to the left to MR_2
- increase the elasticity of demand at any price because there are now more competitors

FIGURE 12.6 Impact of Entry of Alternative Providers into a Monopolistic Market.

With the same costs facing each firm, the new profit-maximizing price (where marginal revenue equals marginal cost) for each is reduced to P_2. If the decrease in firm demand is sufficiently large, it is possible that an individual firm will no longer be able to earn a competitive return at Q_2. This would occur if the demand curve shifts (due to the entry of competitors) so that it is everywhere below the firm's average cost curve.

The existing firm also may respond in other ways. It may attempt to reduce its administrative costs. More importantly, it may try to court customers by attempting to market plans that limit utilization of services, and hence the costs of the services, through various devices. These include utilization review and the adoption of health care plans with increased cost sharing. Of course, it could establish its own HMOs and PPOs, further increasing competition. It also could improve the quality of its service. Further, it may embrace forms of emerging nonprice competition, such as advertising and marketing.

Is this theoretical scenario applicable? Many items are likely to be affected by the spread of HMOs and PPOs. These include the provider and health insurance markets, the phenomenon of biased selection, the roles of employers, and the rate of innovation and diffusion of technology.[10] To focus our discussion, we will limit it to three areas: (1) the impact of HMOs/PPOs on hospital markets; (2) their impact on insurance markets; and (3) the impact on the adoption of technological change.

HMO COMPETITION IN HOSPITAL MARKETS

A first step in looking at the impacts of managed care penetration is to examine the determinants of the penetration itself. What is it about particular markets that lend themselves to high levels of HMO activity? Dranove, Simon, and White (1998) use a supply-demand framework to address this question.

What are the demand characteristics? The authors view employers as the primary health insurance shoppers. Serving as agents for their employees, they seek the best deals.

What are the supply characteristics? The authors seek to identify market features that would reduce costs of payers to contract with providers. They expect that the supply of managed care will be higher in markets where the managed care organizations can negotiate with and monitor the providers more cheaply. They also expect that excess hospital capacity may make hospitals more amenable to negotiation.

Regarding demand, higher managed care penetration accompanies more educated and more urbanized populations. Regarding supply, higher managed care penetration is related to lower percentages of physicians in solo practice, hospital market concentrations, and hospital occupancy. In short, managed care comes in where large numbers of half-filled hospitals are found. The authors express concern that the low rate of managed care penetration in more concentrated markets may imply anticompetitive behaviors, meriting antitrust consideraions.

Much of the research investigating the actual impacts of managed care penetration in hospital markets has been conducted in Minneapolis/St. Paul, an area with a high HMO market share. Investigators have addressed the degree of competitive bidding for HMO contracts, whether HMOs can get discounts, and whether HMOs tend to rely on low-price hospitals.

[10]Many of these issues are reviewed in Frank and Welch (1985).

Feldman and colleagues (1990) find that HMOs generally did not extract major discounts. In fact, price did not seem to be the major HMO consideration in the selection of hospitals with whom to affiliate. Rather, it was hospital location and the range of services that the hospital offered. There was no indication as to whether HMOs tend to affiliate with lower-priced hospitals.

To update and extend the evidence, the authors studied data from hospital markets in four cities. They explored and included various quality indicators. HMOs were distinguished solely on the basis of whether they followed IPA or staff–network models.

From statistical analysis, the authors found that hospital affiliation is not affected by prices. However, the estimated price elasticities of demand for hospital admissions were large in absolute value, indicating that consumer demand at a given hospital is responsive to price. Thus, although hospital affiliation is not affected by price, the elasticities show that use of services, especially by staff–network plans, is responsive to price. It also was found that these plans are able to concentrate patients at lower-priced hospitals more effectively than IPAs.

McLaughlin (1988) provides a different and more ominous interpretation of market responses to HMOs. She argues that the "providers are responding not with classical cost-containing price competition but, instead, with cost-increasing rivalry, characterized by increased expenditures to promote actual or perceived product differentiation" (p. 207). Therefore, although the increased presence of HMOs and PPOs has either indicated or projected greater hospital competition, it is still premature to draw definitive conclusions.

HMO COMPETITION IN INSURANCE MARKETS

Commensurate with the spread of HMOs, PPOs, and various forms of managed care, the health insurance industry is changing rapidly. Many have noted that health insurers were previously lethargic in introducing innovative insurance products and in their cost-containment efforts. In addition, we consider the historic opposition by organized medicine, tax advantages and provider control of the Blues, and the constraints imposed by state regulation and antitrust laws, all of which previously inhibited change in the insurance market.[11]

From 1977, when the insurance market was divided about equally between the Blues and commercial insurers, Frech and Ginsburg (1988) identified the dramatic changes that occurred. The growth of HMOs and PPOs has been accompanied by substantial increases in patient cost sharing, increased utilization review, and self-insurance by many large firms.

Under self-insurance, a Blue Cross and Blue Shield or another organization will act only as a third party in processing claims. More competition is introduced because self-insured firms have more control over their health plans and more direct interest in cost-containment measures.

Baker and Corts (1995, 1996) identify two conflicting effects of increased HMO activity on conventional insurance premiums:

Market discipline HMO competition may limit insurers' ability to exercise market power, thus driving down prices, a standard competitive argument.

[11]See, for example, Frech and Ginsburg (1988) and Havighurst (1988).

Market segmentation HMOs may skim the healthiest patients from the pool, thus driving insurers' costs and prices up.

Their model suggests that if increased HMO penetration does lower the premium levels, the market discipline effect becomes relatively less important, so at higher levels of penetration, the market segmentation effect may raise premiums. Their empirical work verifies this hypothesis: Across metropolitan areas, market penetration up to 14 percent decreases premiums, but market penetration beyond that point raises them. Wickizer and Feldstein (1995) find comparable market discipline effects, although they do not investigate market segmentation effects.

Joesch, Wickizer, and Feldstein (1998) investigated nonprice impacts of HMO market competition. They found that increased HMO penetration reduced insurers' likelihood of increasing insurance deductibles, or "stop-loss" levels (the levels limiting losses to those insured). Moreover, groups located in markets with higher HMO enrollments were more likely to adopt utilization management or PPO options.

MANAGED CARE AND TECHNOLOGICAL CHANGE

The impact of managed care on technological change is potentially significant in controlling health care costs, as well. Increased incomes and changed coinsurance rates are insufficient to explain the increases in health care costs over the past 50 years. Most analysts attribute a major role to the advances in high-cost technologies that were fed by payment mechanisms that were at best indifferent to controlling costs. To the extent that managed care plans explicitly seek cost containment, one would expect careful monitoring of attention directed toward high-cost technologies.

Baker and Spetz (1999) compile an index using 18 technologies available in 1983, including cardiac catheterization and neonatal intensive care units. They then aggregated hospitals within metropolitan statistical areas (MSAs) and compared MSAs on the basis of degree of HMO market shares. Fundamentally, they found that HMO market shares did not matter. Although modest variations were found, no substantive differences were seen in technology at given points in time or in the dispersion of technologies over time.

These nonresults are important. Managed care plans, through their emphases on cost containment, would seem to be important vehicles for reining in the usage of high-cost–high-technology procedures and facilities, but research has not (yet) proved this. To the extent that medical facilities and medical practice styles change slowly, it may be too early to see changes induced by the recent market penetration of managed care plans. Or, it may be that the public demands high (and costly) technology, irrespective of who provides it.

Conclusions

This chapter has considered HMOs and other managed care health delivery systems, in which the functions of insuring patients and providing their care are combined. We begin by describing managed care and providing the rationale for a government policy that promotes it.

Our discussion has emphasized that HMOs and other care managers have incentives to curtail costs because they serve as both insurers and providers. Thus, the incen-

FEATURE

Drive-Through Deliveries—Managed Care and Mandates

Certainly one of the heated issues regarding managed care involves the movement toward one-night hospital stays for mothers expecting normal (or non-Cesarean deliveries) childbirth. Fueled by stories in the popular press of instances where children died shortly after the mother's release, there has been an enormous public outcry to require managed care plans to provide at least a second night of hospital care. What are the economics of the analysis? Jensen and Goodman (1999) examine them.

As recently as 1980, almost 70 percent of the mothers experiencing vaginal delivery had hospital stays of 3 days or more.[12] Inpatient care is expensive, costing several hundred dollars per day. Yet, as long as hospitals were reimbursed for what they charged, no incentive was provided to send the new mother home earlier. Such practices almost certainly failed the comparison of marginal benefits to marginal costs. Almost certainly, the marginal benefits to the woman of being in the hospital for a third day did not measure up to the costs of keeping her there.

This became apparent to care managers. Pressure to reduce the stay has been considerable, and by 1995, the average length of stay for a mother with a vaginal delivery was 1.7 days, with 46.8 percent of all mothers staying one day or less. For the vast majority, home care (starting the second day) along with appropriate outpatient follow-up has become the alternative. Home care carries its own costs, requiring the woman's time and probably assistance from family, friends, or hired caregivers. Nonetheless, it generally provides an appropriate level of care at a far lower cost than the inpatient care that it replaces.

Although the economics would seem to be transparent, debate over the policy has been considerable. Medical care is not exact and mistakes are made. The key phrase is "normal" childbirth. Opponents of managed care have seized on cases where a baby who was sent home the second day after birth developed an ailment and needed to return to the hospital or, worse still, died. Keeping the baby an extra day, they say, would prevent these problems.

Legislation has been passed to require that insurers guarantee at least 2 nights of hospital stay to all mothers with normal deliveries. For example, the state of Maryland's 1996 Early Discharge of Mothers and Babies Bill guaranteed that mothers and babies have coverage in the hospital for 48 hours for a normal vaginal delivery and 96 hours for a normal Cesarean delivery.

This is expensive insurance against potential ills. The incremental cost of a hospital stay must be compared with the prevalence of newborn infant problems and the cost of treating them. With approximately 4 million children born each year in the United States, an incremental day of stay at a cost of $500 per day implies additional costs of more than $2 billion per year. Improved care while in the hospital, as well as improved newborn screening methods while in the hospital, could provide similar benefits and far lower costs, freeing up extra resources for the rest of society. To its credit, the Maryland law recognizes such substitutions, indicating that if the mother, in consultation with her physician, requests to leave early, she receives one home visit within 24 hours of discharge and a second home visit if ordered by her provider.

[12]For these and other figures, see Gillum, Graves, and Wood, (1998) Table R.

tives for additional, less essential procedures are reduced, and we can show that systemwide, even less care may be given than would be economically efficient. One key finding is that managed care organizations tend to reduce hospitalization—one of the most expensive of the health care services. While other findings are mixed, little evidence suggests that the quality of the care provided in HMOs is inferior to FFS care.

The penetration of managed care organizations into the health care marketplace would seem to represent a tug-of-war between traditional providers who are fighting an erosion in their market power, and the sellers of somewhat less costly, although also less personalized, product. This competition suggests important roles for both types of service well into the future.

Summary

1. Managed care seeks to integrate what previously had been an unintegrated system of health care treatment. Such integration has the potential to reduce health care costs, but the integration is costly and may limit choice of provider.

2. In HMOs, PPOs, and other MCOs, the functions of insurance and the provision of care are combined. In return for a prepaid premium, MCOs agree to provide enrollees with comprehensive health care over a given period of time.

3. By agreeing to handle all of a patient's health care needs for a fixed, prearranged fee, a provider is bearing a substantial part of the financial risk. By bearing such a risk, the managed care organization has a strong incentive to develop strategies for reducing excessive care and minimizing other inefficiencies.

4. HMOs control utilization and costs by imposing physician gatekeepers and requiring treatment within defined provider networks. PPO plans maintain the provider networks but do not require physician gatekeepers. Point of Service (POS) plans maintain the physician gatekeeper role but do not require treatment within defined provider networks.

5. A theoretical model of the structure of the managed care market shows that different size providers may be offering different levels (or qualities) of care. Due to the impact of potential disenrollment that is not faced in the fee-for-service sector, one might expect inefficiently low levels of care in the managed care sector.

6. If providers can charge different consumers different amounts, the providers can earn additional profits. Price discrimination is difficult or impossible under the contracts characterizing prepayment-based organizations because:
 • providers will find it difficult to determine how much individual consumers value the services.
 • prepayment-based organizations may be able to shop among providers, thus limiting the providers' monopoly power.

7. Managed care organizations typically provide comprehensive sets of ambulatory and inpatient services, including routine office visits and preventive care, generally without coinsurance or a deductible. Paperwork is reduced and uncertainty over coverage is minimal. These features make membership attractive to consumers, especially to some who are concerned about out-of-pocket costs.

8. In contrast to FFS arrangements, the managed care enrollee's choice of providers and access to hospitals (aside from emergency care) are limited. Also, direct ac-

cess to specialists may require referral from the patient's gatekeeper—the primary care physician.

9. The consensus is strong that managed care reduces utilization, especially of hospital care, but there is little evidence that the quality of care is inferior to that in an FFS system.

10. Managed care organizations generally do not extract major discounts from hospitals. Hospital location and the range of services that hospitals offer, rather than price, seem to be the major considerations in the selection of hospitals with which to affiliate.

11. In addition to individual cost-related impacts of managed care organizations, there are also competitive impacts. Although market penetration does not always lead to lower hospital prices, it does appear to reduce insurance premiums.

12. Managed care plans, through their emphasis on cost containment, would seem to provide important opportunities for reining in the usage of high-cost–high-technology procedures and facilities. Research findings to date have not supported this hypothesis.

Discussion Questions

1. We speak of the millions of dollars that managed care plans must spend on information systems. Why do we not speak of such expenditures under fee-for-service plans?

2. What are the organizational differences among HMO, PPO, POS, and FFS plans?

3. Why would price discrimination in the provision of health care services be more prevalent than price discrimination in the purchase of food?

4. Why is selection bias such an important issue in measuring HMO performance?

5. Discuss ways that managed care organizations may be able to reduce costs of care to their clientele.

6. Why do some critics argue that managed care organizations provide lower-quality care than FFS plans? Evaluate this possibility from a societal perspective.

7. After a large increase in membership, HMO enrollments flattened in the late 1980s and many HMOs suffered financial difficulties. How might this be explained according to what is known about the supply and demand for HMOs?

8. If everyone chose to join an HMO, would average HMO expenditures per case tend to rise or fall? Would national health expenditures tend to rise or fall?

9. What features of managed care organizations tend to inhibit or discourage people from joining? What features tend to attract people? Discuss the advantages and disadvantages of managed care enrollment.

10. Why is the growth of managed care plans a relatively recent phenomenon? Describe governmental policies and practices that have encouraged managed care organizations and inhibited them.

11. If traditional FFS leads to demand inducement, what constrains the HMO from underproviding care?

12. Explain how the availability of alternative delivery systems is expected to produce competitive effects throughout the health economy.

13. Discuss the ways that managed care organizations can influence the adoption of new technologies.

Exercises

1. Consider an HMO with a demand curve of the following form: $Q = 100 - 2P$. Suppose that its marginal and average costs were $20. If the firm maximizes profits, determine its price, output, and profits.

2. In exercise 1, if the firm must act as a perfect competitor, in the long run what will happen to equilibrium price and equilibrium output?

3. In Figure 12.2, a health provider can provide all of the care necessary at a constant cost of $30 per visit. In a more affluent area, M, the demand curve is $P_M = 100 - 2Q_M$. In the less affluent area, L, the demand is $P_L = 60 - 3Q_L$.
 a. What will the equilibrium price be in area M? In area L?
 b. What will the equilibrium quantity be in both areas?
 c. How do the equilibrium quantities compare to the competitive quantities?

4. Consistent with Figure 12.3, assume that the FFS price was $100 per visit and the average patient made eight visits per year. A competing managed care organization came in and charged $80 per visit, providing seven visits per year.
 a. Calculate the change in total expenditures.
 b. Graph the FFS and the managed care market equilibria as was done in Figure 12.3. What do our findings suggest about demand for managed care compared to demand for FFS care?

5. Consider the discussion on adverse selection into HMOs and FFS care, as noted through Equation (12.1) and Figure 12.5. Suppose that on average, FFS clients bought $2,000 in services ($\bar{s}_F = 2,000$) and HMO clients bought $1,500 in services ($\bar{s}_H = 1,500$), with an efficiency factor α of 0.9. The FFS plan charges a 10 percent coinsurance rate.
 a. Set up this problem graphically, labeling the E and V curves.
 b. If a client expects to spend $250 on care, will he or she choose an HMO or an FFS plan? Why?
 c. At which value of s would the client expect to be indifferent between an HMO and an FFS plan? Why?
 d. How would your answer to parts (b) and (c) change if the HMO adopted a 20 percent coinsurance rate?

6. Assume that in Figure 12.6, so many providers entered the health care market that individual demand curves fell below the average cost curves. Draw the new equilibrium. What would happen to short-run profits in the health care market?

7. Exercise 6 discusses a short-run equilibrium in the health care market. With entry and exit into and from the market, graph and discuss the long-run equilibrium.

8. In Table 12.4, the market penetration for managed care rises from 40 percent to 50 percent between Periods 1 and 2 and stays at 50 percent. Suppose, instead, that it fell from 40 percent to 30 percent and stayed at 30 percent.
 a. What would happen to total costs and to rates of cost increase?
 b. How do your results compare to the discussion regarding Table 12.4. Why?

13

The Production and Cost of Health Care

- ■ Substitution between Health Care Inputs

- ■ The Cost Function and Economies of Scale and Scope

- ■ Empirical Cost Function Studies

- ■ The Survival Analysis Approach

- ■ Technical and Allocative Inefficiency

- ■ Conclusion

Recognizing that health is the ultimate output in the health sector, we understandably find that much policy interest is directed toward the production and cost of the intermediate output, health care. Despite exceptions, politicians seeking to cut health costs do not seek cuts in "necessary" health care—only that which is "purely wasteful." Yet, health care, even when needed, inevitably "costs too much."

This chapter and the next one address production, cost, technology, and efficiency of health care. We investigate the question of what degree of flexibility the manager or the public policy maker can find in the production process in order to make improvements. Must physicians always be used for certain tasks, or can nurses and other less expensive inputs be substituted? Can managers vary the mix of types of nurses employed? These first three questions reduce to a single question: To what degree can health care inputs be substituted?

The second issue concerns the efficient size of the health care firm. Economists find that economies of scale and scope exist in many industries. Often in theory, society would be better off if firms were to choose the size at which their per-unit costs were at a minimum. In theory, the perfectly competitive industry achieves this in the long run without outside interference. Health care firms are generally not perfectly competitive, however, and we must question whether health firms in reality are producing at the optimal size.

The final issue of the chapter, the technical and allocative efficiency of health care firms, currently absorbs the research interest of many health economists. These types of

efficiency and the inefficiency they define articulate in economic terms the central research issue of the American consumer's complaint: "I am paying an arm and a leg for my family's health expenses. Am I really getting my money's worth?" Technical efficiency issues investigate how health care output achieves its potential given the health care inputs used; allocative efficiency issues investigate whether the chosen combination of health care inputs is the cost-efficient one, given the relative input costs. Those who doubt the real significance of such technical sounding economic issues, we are quickly reminded of managerial and public policy questions that will someday be answered in large part by future research results: licensure of nurses to perform medical care, continued tax exemption of nonprofit hospitals, the bottom line on national health insurance, and the value of competition in the health sector.

Substitution between Health Care Inputs

Economists often note that there is more than one way to skin a cat; different techniques are available to produce goods and services. A single technique is a particular recipe for production, meaning a particular combination of inputs. To have numerous techniques available means that one has the advantage of choosing a relatively capital-intensive (labor-intensive) technique during times when capital (labor) is relatively cheap. It also may mean the ability to use cheaper forms of labor in substitution for some more expensive forms.

While we find in many industries that producers use numerous alternative techniques, it is common to hear health practitioners argue that there is basically only one correct way of treating a given illness. The belief that only one technique is possible or wise is what Victor Fuchs has called the monotechnic view.

Such a rigid view of the production process means that cost-saving substitutions are difficult if not impossible without reducing either output or quality. A more flexible production process permits cost-saving improvements that may be beneficial to consumers. Economists perform an important service when challenging the monotechnic view and demonstrating, where it is true in the real world, the available flexibility.

THE CONCEPT OF SUBSTITUTION

Flexibility in production means the ability to substitute one input, such as capital, for another input, such as labor, while maintaining the level and quality of output. Substitution does not mean that the two inputs are equivalent, but rather that output can be produced using more than one technique.

Figure 13.1 illustrates a case where no input substitution is possible and a case where an infinite number of techniques are available. In Figure 13.1, panels A and B depict examples of the two cases illustrating the issue.

In panel A, the isoquant shows the possible combinations of nurse hours and physician hours required to treat one patient case in a hospital; the isoquant is labeled $Q = 1$. Given this case, only one sensible production technique combines the two inputs. Physicians and nurses must be combined in the ratio given by $0P/0N$, the ratio of inputs used at the corner point M. Notice that $0P/0N$ is also the slope of line segment $0M$.

What does this mean? In panel A, $0P$ physician hours are required to produce one case, and the addition of nursing hours beyond $0N$ will not add to output unless physician hours also are increased. This imagines that patient care requires certain profes-

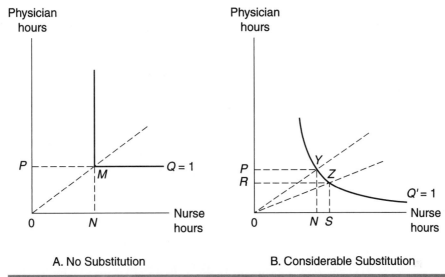

FIGURE 13.1 Degree of Substitution between Physicians and Nurses.

sional physician tasks that only a physician is trained and competent to perform. To use nurses to perform these tasks would result in less care or at least lower-quality care.

The figure shows that if $0N$ nursing hours are required to treat one case, the addition of physician hours will not replace these minimum required nursing hours. The fact that the isoquant is flat when moving to the right from M means that adding nurses beyond the required combination produces no more output (i.e., they would be wasted). Likewise, the fact that the isoquant is vertical when moving upward from M means that additional physician hours beyond the required ratio combination are simply wasted resources.

How would an isoquant look if substitution were possible? Panel B illustrates such a case. A unit isoquant is depicted, but a smooth downward sloping convex curve illustrates that many different combinations of inputs could be chosen without necessarily being wasteful. In fact, an infinite number of possible techniques are implied by the graph. For example, one case can be treated with the $(0P, 0N)$ combination of inputs or equivalently with the $(0R, 0S)$ combination. Each point on the isoquant represents a different technique. The slope of any isoquant, such as the isoquant labeled $Q' = 1$ is called the marginal rate of technical substitution (see chapter 2), and it represents the rate at which nurse and physician hours can be exchanged while still maintaining output.

It should be emphasized that even though substitution is available in panel B, nurses and physicians are not equivalent. It is not even true of the graph that a fixed number of nurses always can replace a physician. Moving along the curve from point Y to point Z, the rate of substitution changes; that is, the slope becomes flatter, indicating a diminishing marginal rate of technical substitution. To replace one hour of physician time at point Y requires some number of nursing hours; however, at point Z, where fewer physician hours are being used, it requires a much greater number of nursing hours. That is, as physician time is more scarce relative to nursing hours, it becomes more difficult to replace. This retains the idea that while substitution is possible, it is difficult,

expensive, or unsafe to have nurses do certain physician tasks, and vice versa. The curve may even become flat at some point, indicating that a minimum of required physician time has been reached.

WHAT DEGREE OF SUBSTITUTION IS POSSIBLE?

The graphs in Figure 13.1 merely define terms; they do not tell us which of the two cases, or possibly a modified one, is true of the real world. From the 1970s on, economists addressed the question of whether and to what degree physician extenders were able to substitute for physicians. *Physician extender* is an umbrella term referring to specially trained physician assistants or nurse practitioners who are utilized to perform certain tasks, including some that formerly were performed by the physician.

The estimates obtained at that time were equivalent to the measurement of a few points along an isoquant, such as the ones depicted previously. This work suggested that physician extenders were able to substitute for physicians to a substantial degree. Depending on the number of physician hours employed (recall that the rate of substitution may depend on the particular starting point on the isoquant), one physician extender could "replace" from 25 percent to more than 50 percent of a physician's services.

Inasmuch as physician extenders represent a substantially lower cost of training, this degree of substitutability could mean a substantial savings in cost. Reports at the time suggested, in fact, that physicians were not employing sufficient numbers of assistants even in the sense that it would have been more profitable to the physician owners of the practice to employ more extenders. There is controversy over this question, and the issue is worth further investigation. We take up this further investigation, however, in chapter 16 on physicians. The point at present is that physician extenders can substitute for physician labor inputs to an important degree, depending on the level of physician inputs.

Elasticity of Substitution

A second focus of production studies has been the hospital. One study of hospital production is worth detailed examination because it provides evidence of substitution among various categories of hospital inputs. It also illustrates a second and more convenient way to report on the possible degree of substitution between inputs. A convenient way to summarize the possibilities for substitution between any two inputs is the elasticity of substitution (E_S), a measure of the responsiveness of a cost-minimizing firm to changes in relative input prices. It is defined as the ratio of the percentage change in the factor input ratio to the percentage change in relative factor prices:

$$E_S = \frac{\text{Percentage change in factor input ratio}}{\text{Percentage change in factor price ratio}}$$

What does this elasticity mean? Consider that if a firm were a cost minimizer, then it would not be indifferent to changes in input prices. As long as it were possible to substitute between inputs, it would tend to respond to input price changes by shifting away from the now costlier input to the now relatively cheaper input. For example, suppose that a hospital is currently at combination Y in panel B of Figure 13.1 using $0P$ physician hours and $0N$ nursing hours to treat one case. Suppose also that physicians are paid $200,000 per year and nurses are paid $40,000 per year. Suppose, finally, that the hospital employs 100 physicians and 100 nurses. As a result of a 10 percent increase in the rela-

tive wage rate of physicians (from $200,000 to $220,000), the cost-minimizing hospital moves to combination Z, which substitutes NS nursing hours for PR physician hours. The relative physician input ratio decreases from the one shown by the slope of the line segment $0Y$ to the one shown by the slope of $0Z$.

Assume that the decrease in the slopes (i.e., relative factor inputs) is 6 percent. The elasticity of substitution is one way of measuring the degree of substitution. Here E_S has a value of 0.6, indicating that every 1 percent change in relative factor prices leads to a 0.6 percent change in the relative use of those factor inputs. Whereas the ratio of physicians to nurses was previously 1.00, a 10 percent increase in relative physician wages (from 5 to 5.5 times nurses' wages) would change the input ratio to 0.94 (a 6 percent decrease). This would represent the replacement of one physician ($220,000) with five nurses ($200,000), hence lowering costs by $20,000.[1] We will report E_S as positive numbers even though it is understood that firms respond to an increase in the relative price of one input by decreasing the relative use of that input.

The minimum value of E_S is zero. A firm with isoquants represented by the one shown in Panel A of Figure 13.1 will have an elasticity of substitution equal to zero because it always will use the same input combination to produce a given level of output regardless of relative factor prices. Higher values of E_S indicate more substitutability for any 1 percent change in the factor price ratio.

Estimates for Hospital Care

Following work showing that physicians greatly affect the productivity of all hospital inputs (Pauly, 1980; Bays, 1980), Jensen and Morrisey (1986) took care to incorporate physician inputs into their analysis of the elasticity of substitution between inputs to U.S. hospitals, both teaching and nonteaching. Their estimates of the production function for hospital care provided the needed information to discover the isoquants and the various elasticities of substitution. They found the patterns of input use in the typical hospital by observing the variations in input use across a cross section of hospitals.

Table 13.1 presents the estimated values for the elasticities of substitution between the indicated pairs of inputs. The numbers have, for example, the following literal interpretation. A 1 percent rise in the price of medical staff relative to nurses would result in a 0.547 percent drop in the ratio of medical staff to nurses.

How are we to judge the estimated degree of substitutability? The elasticities reported are sufficiently larger than zero to show that some significant substitutability exists between several categories of hospital inputs. In fact, the authors conclude that "all inputs in both teaching and nonteaching hospitals are substitutes for each other."

The smallest values for substitution reported here are between beds and categories of labor. *Beds* is a convenient measure of the various and often complex capital inputs used by a hospital. The data suggest that even in hospital care production, for which labor is often thought to be the critical input, capital can be substituted for labor.

The reader must take warning that the gains of economists in even seemingly straightforward empirical work are often modest. Others (Custer and Willke, 1991; Lehner and Burgess, 1995) have shown that the results are sensitive to the particular definition of the physician's input. Our range of confidence is still wide, meaning that the available estimates cannot yet confidently narrow down the true values. Although most

[1] The new ratio is 99 physicians to 105 nurses or 0.94.

TABLE 13.1 Substitution Elasticities for Teaching and Nonteaching Hospitals Evaluated at the Mean

Input Pair	Nonteaching Case-Mix Adjusted Admissions	Teaching Case-Mix Adjusted Admissions
1. Medical Staff with Nurses	0.547	0.159
2. Medical Staff with Beds	0.175	0.155
3. Nurses with Beds	0.124	0.211
4. Nurses with Residents	—	2.127
5. Medical Staff with Residents	—	0.292

Source: Jensen and Morrisey (1986). Copyright © 1986 MIT Press Journals. All rights reserved.

health economists probably would agree that substitution possibilities exist among many health care inputs and that the monotechnic view is incorrect, it is premature to claim this as proven by these data.

The Cost Function and Economies of Scale and Scope

The production function, its isoquants, and the elasticities of substitution are important because they have consequences for costs. In this section, we will show what a cost function is and how it is derived in order to explain the meaning of the technical terms *economies of scale* and *scope*.

DERIVING THE COST FUNCTION

While the production function describes the relationship between inputs and outputs, the cost function describes the relationship between outputs and costs. Production and cost functions are closely related, and under certain circumstances the two functions can be derived from one another. This close relationship can be illustrated with the aid of Figure 13.2, panels A and B.

Panel A depicts several isoquants, collectively illustrating the production function for a hypothetical physician practice. Of the infinite number of different isoquants that exist in principle, we have chosen to show three. The first or lowest isoquant shown, for example, depicts the many different points or combinations of capital and labor that are capable of producing 100 physician office visits. The higher isoquants produce more as shown, 150 and 200 visits, respectively.

Use your imagination to see Figure 13.2, panel A as if there were no straight, slanted lines (AB and so on); as we will see shortly, the lines you have "removed" identify the cost consequences of the firm's input choices. Without them, the graph would characterize a health care firm that knows only half of the story; it knows the output consequences of its input choices. Do health care firms exist that would simply stop at this point—firms that would ignore costs entirely and say perhaps: "We are here to help people get well regardless of what it costs; economics is not an appropriate consideration."

In reality, health care firms must meet their creditors or close their doors; they must at least break even. However, economists have for some time taken two related and more realistic questions seriously:

A. Production Isoquants

B. Derived Cost Function

FIGURE 13.2 Production Function for a Hypothetical Physician Practice.

1. Do nonprofit health care firms minimize costs?
2. Among health care firms that desire to minimize costs, how well do they achieve the desired goal?

Question 2 is empirical and is addressed later in the chapter; question 1 illuminates the theory that follows (Ellis, 1993).

Were a hospital run by people intent to deliver maximum output to the community, that hospital must minimize its costs. A simple thought experiment provides the

intuition. If the hospital board discovered that it could treat 1,000 patients with proper care and still permit a waste of resources worth $20,000, then some board member could sensibly suggest: "Eliminate the waste and we could treat even more patients." However, a contrasting case illustrates the knottier problem. Suppose the hospital board favored some inputs intrinsically over others; for example, suppose they did everything possible to enlist physicians with national reputations for research—this might enhance the hospital's prestige but not necessarily its efficiency. They may not even intend to minimize the cost of either the patient day or the case treated.

Given that many such hospitals exist, we propose the standard case for hospitals and other health care firms to entail the goal of cost minimization. To consider this case, reconsider Figure 13.2, including those straight lines, as well as the isoquants.

Cost Minimization

These isoquants show the many achievable combinations of inputs and outputs; they do not in themselves describe the cheapest choice of inputs to produce any given output choice. To understand how the firm can minimize its costs of producing a given level of output, we also need to introduce a second tool—the isocost curve. The downward-sloping straight lines in the upper panel of Figure 13.2, lines such as AB and DE, depict isocost curves.

An isocost curve illustrates all combinations of capital and labor that cost the same amount. A given level of total cost, TC, can buy many possible combinations of capital and labor, K and L, whose costs add up to $TC = rK + wL$ where r is the rental price of capital and w is the wage rate of labor. The rental price of capital here means the cost to the firm of using the capital for one period, regardless of whether it actually rents the capital or owns it. This particular isocost equation can be transformed algebraically so that K appears on the left-hand side and all other terms appear on the right, yielding the equivalent equation, $K = TC/r - (w/r)L$, which is an isocost function.

The firm that wishes to produce a given output level, say 100 visits, will minimize its costs by choosing the lowest isocost curve that is tangent to the 100-visit isoquant. In the figure, least-cost production of 100 visits occurs at input combination ($L = 20$, $K = 25$) at point C on isocost curve AB. Given knowledge of the input prices, we can calculate the output cost. For example, let $r = \$1,200$ and $w = \$1,000$; then, least-cost production of 100 visits will cost $50,000. Alternatively, if the firm wishes to produce 150 visits, the least-cost production would occur at point F, which entails 30 units of labor and 40 units of capital for a total cost of $78,000. In this fashion, the combination of the production function represented by the isoquants and the cost requirements represented by the isocost curves, together with the assumption of cost minimization, generates a set of outcomes, or points C, F, and G. The set of all possible points of tangency is called the expansion path.

The expansion path supplies the information that associates a given level of output with its minimum cost. When these cost and output data are recorded in a graph, as in panel B, the result is the firm's total cost function. This cost function has a lazy S-shape that is thought to be typical of many firms in practice. It also goes through the origin, indicating that if the firm produces nothing, it will incur no costs, meaning that the firm illustrated has no fixed costs. A period of time long enough for the firm to alter or avoid any of its commitments to input suppliers is called *the long run*. The implication is that the cost function shown is depicting the firm in the long run.

This cost function is a frontier in that it represents the minimum possible cost of producing a given output. Actual firms may operate somewhat inefficiently, and we will observe cost levels above the frontier. It is a contradiction in terms to say that one could observe a cost level below the cost frontier. An important efficiency issue is to determine whether health care firms are operating on or above their cost frontier, and we will return to this efficiency issue later. At present, we address a different sort of efficiency issue—the issue of whether a firm is operating at an economical *point* on the frontier from the point of view of society as a whole. In the terms we have introduced, we will address the issues of economies of scale and scope.

ECONOMIES OF SCALE AND SCOPE

To simplify the exposition, we separate the issues of economies of scale and scope, treating scale economies first.

Economies of Scale

Consider a physician firm such as the one depicted in Figure 13.2. The long-run total cost function as shown in panel B can be transformed to express information about economies of scale. The average costs for this firm can be calculated by dividing the given cost level by the corresponding number of physician visits. The resulting long-run average cost (LRAC) function is shown in Figure 13.3. A firm is said to experience economies of scale when its long-run average cost curve is declining as output increases. Thus, the firm depicted exhibits economies of scale in, for example, the region AB. Conversely, the firm experiences diseconomies of scale if and only if the long-run average cost curve is increasing as output increases, such as occurs, for example, in the region BC.

What output level would a firm organized for profit choose in this case? It is tempting to suppose it would choose output Q_B, at which its average costs are lowest (AC_B), but this is not necessarily the case. A firm is not in the business of minimizing its

FIGURE 13.3 The Long-Run Average Cost Function.

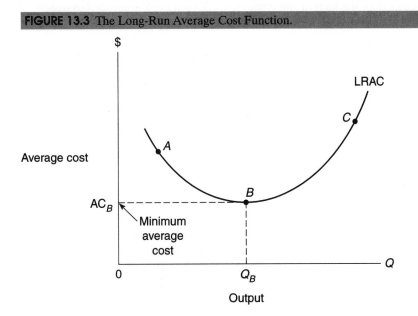

Output

average costs and would do so only if, coincidentally, the output that minimized average costs also maximized profits.

Economies of Scope

A related concept is economies of scope. By definition, economies of scope are possible only for a multiproduct firm; inasmuch as many health care firms are multiproduct in nature, the concept is highly relevant to health care. Economies of scope occur whenever it is possible to produce two or more outputs of different goods jointly more cheaply than they can be produced separately. As an illustration, consider the provision of pediatric hospital care (for children) and geriatric hospital care (for the elderly).

Suppose there were two hospitals in town—one that provided only pediatric care and one that provided only geriatric care. Would the total cost of pediatric plus geriatric care be lower if one single hospital provided both? It may be cheaper to combine the two hospitals and achieve scale economies, but that is not the point at present. Conceivably, as well, it could be cheaper to combine them because the inputs needed for both types of care interact well together: Perhaps things learned in pediatrics have applications in geriatrics; perhaps the two together could support each other so that the result would be lower total costs. If so, we would say that by producing the two different outputs jointly, we achieve economies of scope.

The concept of economies of scope is illustrated by equation (13.1). Here a cost function is depicted in mathematical notation. Two different outputs are shown, Q_1 and Q_2. For example, Q_1 may represent pediatric care and Q_2 may represent geriatric care. The example in equation (13.1) concerns the attempt to produce output levels $Q_1 = 100$ and $Q_2 = 150$ either jointly or separately. Economies of scope exist if the cost of producing the two outputs jointly, that is,

$$TC(Q_1 = 100, Q_2 = 150)$$

is less than the sum of the costs of producing each quantity separately, that is,

$$TC(Q_1 = 100, Q_2 = 0) + TC(Q_1 = 0, Q_2 = 150)$$

That is, economies of scope occur in this example if the following inequality holds:

$$TC(Q_1 = 100, Q_2 = 150) < TC(Q_1 = 100, Q_2 = 0) \quad \textbf{(13.1)}$$
$$+ TC(Q_1 = 0, Q_2 = 150)$$

WHY WOULD ECONOMIES OF SCALE AND SCOPE BE IMPORTANT?

The concepts of economies of scale and scope are of considerable interest. We will illustrate their significance using the idea of economies of scale, but similar arguments can be used to show the importance of economies of scope.

Recall that a profit-maximizing firm has no intrinsic interest in producing at that level of output at which average costs are at a minimum. It would do so if that output also coincidentally were profit maximizing, but this generally is not the case. From the consumer's point of view, it would be best for each firm to produce so that average costs were minimized, as long as these cost savings were passed on to the public. One of the reasons that the theory of perfect competition is so intriguing to economists is that com-

petition forces the firm in the long run to operate so that it minimizes average costs. Though the competitive firm has no intrinsic interest in doing this, it is guided by competition, as if by an invisible hand, to serve society's interests in keeping costs low.

Relevance to Health Care Firms

Most health care firms, such as hospitals and physician practices, do not operate in perfectly competitive markets. Therefore, the forces of perfect competition will not necessarily force them to operate at the most efficient scale of operation. There may conceivably be too few of them or too many. If there are too many, existing hospitals could in principle be operating below the efficient scale of output; likewise, small hospitals may in theory be forgoing the opportunities available through greater economies of scale.

Areawide health planning, promoted by various government programs since the 1940s, encouraged the reduction of "excess beds." These programs also promoted the "rationalization" of geographic patterns of critical and expensive diagnostic equipment, such as CAT scanners. These programs, expressly aimed at reducing the growth in health expenditures, make more sense to economic thinking if the health care were unnecessary or if the rationalization were expected to improve the use of economies of scale.

Present-day hospital mergers also raise questions about economies of scale: "To what degree are hospital mergers justified by the existence of economies of scale?" Sinjay and Campbell (1995) ask. They offer theory and evidence to support their belief that mergers can be motivated by the desire for scale economies. In theory, this could be true. For example, suppose two neighboring hospitals are both so large that they are operating at outputs achieving well above minimum average costs. Resistance by physicians and nurses within each hospital makes the needed trimming impossible. Let Mercy Hospital merge with St. Boniface and the combined management might gain the muscle to make the needed reductions.

We question whether the case has been made, however. The motivations for mergers can be highly individualized, and the reasons offered may differ from the true economic factors. At this point, understanding of the economic issues involved in hospital mergers remains cloudy.

The gain to society from exploiting economies of scale also illustrates the natural monopoly. The essential idea can be seen from a simple example. Figure 13.4 shows a health care unit (for example, of a hospital) that provides the diagnostic services of a CAT scanner. If many such firms are in the market area, then perhaps no single CAT scanner is operating at an output level at which it achieves lowest, long-run average cost. Because of its competition, the hospital unit depicted operates at point D, where average costs are OF. Were society to have fewer CAT scanners, the remaining ones could operate at a higher capacity, say at point B, with lower average costs of OG.

These arguments depend on the empirical result that economies of scale are available to society. The average cost curve in Figure 13.4 records only the costs incurred by the hospital unit. From society's broader perspective, the costs incurred by the patients and their visiting families and friends also are relevant. To see the point more clearly, draw the CAT scan example to its extreme. Suppose the minimal average cost occurs when one scanner serves a rural region of 400 miles in radius. Would residents of this region be better off building only one centrally located scanner? Or would the necessarily huge travel costs make such a plan a foolish extreme?

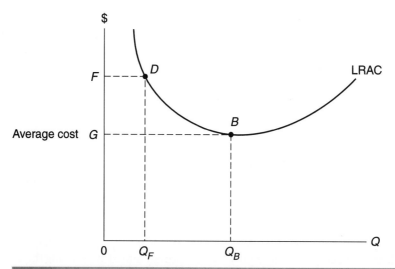

FIGURE 13.4 Gains from Exploiting Scale Economies.

Empirical Cost Function Studies

Once the theoretical ideas are understood, the fundamental questions become empirical. Are there, in fact, economies of scale and scope available to be exploited in real-world health care firms? At what level of output and for what combinations of outputs are these economies achieved?

DIFFERENCES AMONG HOSPITAL COST STUDIES

Two themes occur often and represent differences in approach. We will describe long-run versus short-run studies, and behavioral versus structural cost functions.

Long-Run Versus Short-Run Studies

Economies of scale, as we have seen, are defined by the shape of the long-run average cost curve. The difference between the long run and the short run is well defined. The long run is a period of time sufficiently long for the hospital to end any fixed commitments and to make any cost-saving adjustments that are possible. The short run is a period of time during which the hospital still has some fixed commitments; that is, some inputs that cannot be varied. An example is the number of beds set up for service.

While the distinction is clear in theory, it is difficult to determine which case is represented by the data. Are hospitals that are being observed in cross section (at a given point in time) all achieving long-run cost minimization? Have they all adjusted their levels of capital, equipment, and other fixed commitments to their desired long-run levels? These assumptions seem doubtful, particularly during times when our health system is in flux.

Conversely, are the hospitals observed in cross section using capital and equipment levels that were determined as if without reference to the current state of their markets? This, too, seems an extreme view. Perhaps neither view is exactly correct, and it is understandable that various analysts have taken one or the other approach to the study of existing data.

Structural Versus Behavioral Cost Functions

Frequently, one distinguishes between structural and behavioral cost functions. By structural cost function, we mean a cost function that is derived in a consistent manner from economic theory, just as we have derived it in the previous section. That is, the production isoquants and the isocost curves are used to derive the cost-minimizing level of costs for each possible level of output.

A behavioral cost function[2] is one derived from analysis of the patterns in costs in actual data across hospitals. Variables are included that distinguish real-world differences between hospitals. The variables matter for costs but often do not have a clear role in the theory of cost functions. Sometimes behavioral cost functions omit variables, like input prices, that are difficult to measure in the real world but that are theoretically important.[3]

DIFFICULTIES FACED BY ALL HOSPITAL COST STUDIES

The difficulty of measuring the heterogeneous hospital output trips up nearly all hospital cost studies. The problem has two aspects. First, hospitals differ by type of cases they treat; this is the *case-mix* problem. Medicare's Diagnosis Related Group (DRG) payment system identifies 495 groups of cases; the hospital is a multiproduct firm to an unusual degree. Studies have responded to this problem widely, some with virtual neglect of the problem, others with the use of multiproduct cost functions including many adjustments for case mix and related variables. Although it is clear that the multiproduct approach is superior, even these methods rarely incorporate more than four or five hospital output categories given inherent limitations. Even the question of whether sufficiently refined hospital cost estimates are achievable in principle has not gained a consensus among health economists.

A related output measurement problem is how to treat quality. Unobserved or incorrectly measured variations in quality between hospitals may be mistaken in research for economies or diseconomies of scale. Research to more adequately measure quality is ongoing, and much of our understanding of hospital costs may need to be amended when better-quality measures are incorporated into cost studies.

The case-mix issue is illustrated in Figure 13.5, and the quality issue, though not illustrated explicitly in the figure, is similar. The figure illustrates a case where the true, long-run average cost function is flat, exhibiting neither economies nor diseconomies of scale. The three cost curves shown represent three hospitals, each with a distinct case-mix. In order of ascending costs, these are Hospital 1, which treats uncomplicated medical cases; Hospital 2, which treats more complicated surgical cases; and Hospital 3, which treats the most highly complex level or *tertiary* cases.

Suppose that points *C*, *D*, and *E* represent the data observations available to the researcher for each hospital type for a given statistical study. The researcher may mistake the unobserved case-mix differences for diseconomies of scale; that is, the researcher may mistakenly believe that the long-run average cost curve is rising as shown by the connecting line. This case is illustrative only, because the underlying patterns of

[2]The term *behavioral cost function* is often attributed to Evans (1971).
[3]Cowing, Holtmann, and Powers (1983) have argued that omitting input prices is equivalent to assuming no substitution possibilities between inputs, which is an incorrect assumption.

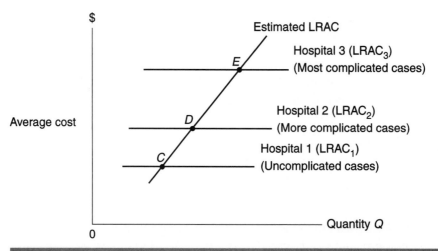

FIGURE 13.5 The Case-Mix Issue.

case mix, quality, and size of output if unknown or not adequately controlled for could yield errors in either direction.

Alternative approaches to treating the case-mix problem have been investigated extensively.[4] These studies show that case-mix differences between hospitals are materially important when estimating scale economies; thus, they cannot be overlooked.

The researcher may groan just as much over the lack of sound measures of hospital input prices. The cost of capital or the starting registered nurses' wage may seem like simple data to collect (a matter of contacting an executive in the finance office"), but they are sometimes difficult to define adequately. Unfortunately, it has been shown that errors in measurement of hospital input prices have substantial consequences for the results.

Finally, a common difficulty faced by most cost-function studies of hospitals is that the data omit physicians' input prices entirely. The independence of the physician from hospital control and accounting and the physician practice of billing the patient separately become problems for the researcher. Physician costs are properly part of production costs, and their omission results in biased estimates.

Bays (1980) found that including versus excluding physician costs in a study of California hospitals caused his data to switch between economies and diseconomies of scale. Also in 1980, Pauly's *Doctor's and Their Workshops* established empirically what was known through common sense: that physicians affect the productivities of all inputs and are basic to cost. Despite our basic common sense, data limits have meant the publication of several hospital cost studies lacking physician data.

[4]An example of an investigation of the importance of case mix is the study by Hornbrook and Monheit (1985). From data for 380 hospitals, they found that larger-scale hospitals in their sample tended to admit case mixes with relatively shorter lengths of stay. This study is one confirmation of the fact that the case-mix problem is materially important to the issue of estimating economies of scale.

THE EVIDENCE ON HOSPITAL ECONOMIES OF SCALE AND SCOPE

Given the several differences between hospital cost studies and the imposing problems that they face, it is not surprising that results vary across the studies. The earliest studies in hospital economics yielded a bewildering array of results. Several found evidence of economies of scale with an optimum output level varying from 150 beds to as high as 900 beds.[5] Others reported either no economies of scale or weak economies at best.

By the early 1980s, a consensus seemed to emerge that hospitals achieve economies of scale up to a size of about 250 beds. The work of Bays and others working in that decade brought more sophistication to hospital cost estimation, and the consensus quickly evaporated. A sample of studies from then to the present provides a perspective.

A BALANCE BETWEEN THE STRUCTURAL AND THE BEHAVIORAL

In the early 1980s, attention focused on estimating structural cost functions.[6] Conrad and Strauss (1983) applied a structural approach and the multiproduct approach, finding "constant returns to scale" in their sample of North Carolina hospitals. Cowing and Holtman (1983) also chose the structural approach but argued that the hospital data were short-run (not long-run) equilibrium data. They found economies of scale though only mixed evidence of economies of scope.[7]

Some research argues that the push toward structural cost functions sacrifices too much real-world validity for the sake of theoretical consistency. The solution proposed by Grannemann, Brown, and Pauly (1986) was to "strike a balance between the two extremes." The result was a more extensive treatment of the case-mix issue than appears in structural approaches, and in much previous work for that matter. Even so, the authors suggested that they had not fully captured case-mix effects.

They found that hospitals with larger inpatient volumes have higher average costs, suggesting diseconomies. However, the authors argued that the observed differences in average costs cannot be accounted for solely by scale; instead, they are probably the result of unobserved case-mix effects. Emergency departments exhibit fairly strong economies of scale though.

DOES LONG RUN VERSUS SHORT RUN MATTER?

Vita (1990) drew the distinction between long-run and short-run costs and took a structural approach, generating estimates of long-run scale phenomena from short-run data.

[5]For examples of differing early hospital cost function studies, see Cohen (1967); Carr and Feldstein (1967); M. S. Feldstein (1967); Ingbar and Taylor (1968); and Lave and Lave (1970).

[6]In 1983, a widely cited review of hospital cost studies (Cowing, Holtmann, and Powers) called upon the profession to make several improvements in the way hospital cost function analysis was done. High priority was given, among other things, to the use of more general and theoretically correct approaches.

[7]Dunn et al. (1995) introduce a different concept of economies of scope in examining selected multiple surgeries, defined as the performance of more than one procedure on the same day (e.g., excision of breast mass followed by modified radical mastectomy). Such multiple surgeries, which are becoming increasingly common, have important fee and third-party reimbursement aspects. The authors found that doing two procedures in one surgery reduces total work by 22 percent compared to separate surgeries.

He found that his sample of nearly 300 California hospitals tended toward diseconomies of scale. Diseconomies were less pronounced for "hospitals operating at low levels of output . . . but are more severe for larger hospitals" (p. 19). Furthermore, applying his methods to the previously cited study of Cowing and Holtmann, he found that their short-run evidence, when translated to the long run, also was consistent with slight diseconomies of scale. Unfortunately, the Vita study was somewhat less vigorous in addressing the case-mix problem than were Grannemann, Brown, and Pauly.

As part of a larger study, Fournier and Mitchell (1992) examined 179 short-term general care hospitals in Florida. Controlling for case mix, competition, ownership, and other variables, the investigators determined that hospitals were not operating in long-run equilibrium but were employing too much capital and equipment.

How does "too much capital to be consistent with the long run" come to be measured, and why is it inconsistent with long-run equilibrium? The logic follows from the mathematics of profit maximization. In the short run, your capital is fixed. If you could magically change this capital, you probably could improve your profits. By contrast, the long run is defined as so long a time as to enable you, quite unmagically, to vary your capital and thus achieve the higher profits. Although we are all stuck with the short-run reality, the econometrician is able to assess what might have been if capital had been variable.

Summarizing These Cost Studies

What can we conclude from this discussion of cost function analysis? Recall that at the end of the 1970s, a consensus seemed to emerge that hospitals exhibited economies of scale with a moderate ideal size of about 250 beds. Instead of polishing this consensus and affirming it, the succeeding work brought it into question. The articles we just reviewed do not support a conclusion in favor of scale economies. They even suggest diseconomies. We are left with a caution, as well that this result may itself be an artifact of unobserved heterogeneity of output, the case-mix problem.

If a consensus is emerging, it is the recognition of important issues in cost function analysis. The value of more sophisticated attention to problems is clearer. However, we may wonder whether some problems—such as the successful treatment of heterogenous output, quality,[8] and incorporation of physician costs and inputs—are even tractable. It is frustrating in social science not to have clear answers, but it is progress to see the problem more clearly.

The Survival Analysis Approach

The difficulties of hospital cost function research led to interest in an alternative, survival analysis. Bays (1980) argued that "the analytical strength of the survivor technique is its simplicity: those size categories which grow relative to the rest of the industry are presumed to have some advantage over other sizes" (p. 362). Given the predominance of nonprofits, the role of physicians, and the regulatory environment of American

[8]A study of nursing homes highlights the quality issue. When quality was ignored, Gertler and Waldman (1992) found scale economies. On the other hand, a quality-adjusted model showed scale economies only for low-quality nursing homes. Average-quality homes had constant costs, while high-quality homes were associated with diseconomies of scale. Carey and Burgess (1999) study the importance and adequacy in hospital cost studies; this work is cautionary over the objectives of devising sound measures.

hospitals, survival analysis applies less forcefully to hospitals than to many other industries. However, the data on relative growth of hospital size categories suggest phenomena at work that are at least similar in effect to the advantages of scale.

SURVIVAL ANALYSIS APPLIED TO HOSPITALS

Bays studied the changing size distribution of U.S. hospitals over the period 1971 to 1977. Table 13.2 reports a selection of his findings and illustrates the approach. Market shares are reported for each year. In addition, he tested the null hypothesis that the market share for a given size category has remained constant over these years. The test statistics calculated suggest that we can confidently reject the null hypothesis of constant market shares over time for four of the hospital size categories.

The only two size categories that have declined in market share in the sample are the categories 0–99 beds and 500+ beds. Combining both statistical significance and the material size of change, only the category 0–99 shows much of a decline. Within the context of the assumptions of survivor analysis, this small hospital category seems to show evidence of being uneconomical, perhaps in the sense of diseconomies of scale.

The complete story of hospital size category change is more complex than what has been illustrated here. Along with these reported results, Bays also found that the pattern of growth varied from nonprofit to for-profit hospitals and that the pattern varied across geographical regions.[9]

SURVIVAL ANALYSIS APPLIED TO PHYSICIAN GROUP PRACTICE

Although most attention to scale phenomena has concerned hospitals, a significant amount of literature and concern also has developed for economies of scale in physician group practices. The physician services industry, being typically a for-profit monopolistically competitive industry, is more approachable through survival analysis.

TABLE 13.2 Market Shares by Bed Size Categories: 1971–1977

	Year			*Statistical Significance?*
Size Category	*1971*	*1974*	*1977*	
0–99 beds	54.9	50.9	46.7	Yes
100–199 beds	26.2	28.9	30.8	Yes
200–299 beds	11.5	13.1	14.5	Yes
300–349 beds	3.1	3.2	3.5	No
350–399 beds	1.8	1.5	2.0	No
400–449 beds	0.9	1.2	1.2	Yes
450–499 beds	0.4	0.5	0.5	No
500+ beds	1.1	0.7	0.9	No
Total number	*3,274*	*3,282*	*3,215*	

Source: Bays (1986). Reprinted with the permission of Taylor & Frances Ltd. http://www.journals.tandf.co.uk/journals

[9]A sophisticated survivor analysis by Frech and Mobley (1995), which controls for quality and type of services rendered by hospitals, supports the existence of scale economies for sizes up to 370 beds.

By the early 1970s, a substantial body of literature on group practice economies had developed with somewhat mixed results. A variety of methods had been used. Some evaluated correlations of physician income with practice size. Others examined cost functions as was commonly done in the hospital literature. Still others examined productivity measures by size of practice. A useful alternative applied by Frech and Ginsburg (1974) seemed to account for the differences in previous studies and to provide some resolution of their differences.

Let us reconsider the underlying model of survival analysis and its application to physician group practice. We will assume that a physician manager or group of managers will tend to select a scale of practice that is most profitable to them. Under certain conditions, perhaps conditions that are close enough to being met in the physician care markets, the cost-efficient scale of practice will prove most profitable. If so, it follows that physician group practices will tend to gravitate in size toward this optimum:

> Over time, the size distribution of medical practices will tend toward an optimum where all sizes are equally efficient *at the margin.* Until this optimum is reached, those sizes that are growing most rapidly can be identified as most efficient at the margin (Frech and Ginsburg 1974, p. 26).

The authors applied this technique to changes in market share of physician practices between 1965 and 1969. Table 13.3 shows the ratio of market share in 1969 to market share in 1965 for physician practices of various sizes. As can be seen in the table, the market share of solo practitioners declined during the period, suggesting possibly that this form of practice was operating at a less efficient scale. The market share for all sizes of groups increased during the period. Note, however, that growth was slower in the group sizes of 7 to 25 physicians. Thus, the data suggest that this lower-middle range of groups was less able to capture certain scale advantages. In contrast, both relatively larger and relatively smaller groups were growing faster and thus appeared to be more

TABLE 13.3 Ratio of Market Share in 1969 to Market Share in 1965

Market Group Size Number of Physicians	All in Office-Based Practice	Multispecialty	Fee for Service	Prepaid Practice
1–2	0.92	—	—	—
3	1.41	1.50	1.37	3.60
4	1.34	1.49	1.29	5.64
5	1.41	1.31	1.38	1.94
6	1.59	1.47	1.44	3.65
7	1.06	0.79	1.05	1.70
8–15	1.24	1.19	1.29	0.89
16–25	1.08	1.09	1.10	0.93
26–49	2.37	2.44	2.45	2.95
50–99	2.10	2.12	1.44	7.21
100+	1.62	1.62	1.68	1.58

Source: Reprinted from *Journal of Business,* Frech, H. E. III, and Paul B. Ginsburg, "Optimal Scale in Medical Practice: A Survivor Analysis." *Journal of Business* (1974): 23–36, with permission from The University of Chicago Press.

TABLE 13.4	Distribution of Physicians in Practices of Different Sizes. Market Share in Percent				
	Size of Practice				
	1–2	*3–7*	*8–25*	*26–99*	*100+*
1965	84.69	8.37	4.30	1.33	1.31
1969	78.25	11.53	5.09	3.00	2.12
1975	68.67	13.31	8.53	5.08	4.42
1980	67.45	13.14	7.78	4.66	6.97

Source: Reprinted from *Journal of Health Economics.* Marder, William D. and Stephen Zuckerman, "Competition and Medical Groups A Survivor Analysis." *Journal of Health Economics* 4 (1985) 167–176, with permission from Elsevier Science.

efficient in scale. This result tended to incorporate previous results in a single coherent pattern. Frech and Ginsburg accounted for their results by arguing that

> Standard industrial organization literature suggests that costs per unit of output increase after a point due to problems of coordination and control. However, the typical manner in which firms attempt to counteract these tendencies—hiring managers and varying labor remuneration—may not be available to the smaller medical groups (p. 33).

These results were more or less confirmed and were extended to new time periods by a later study. Table 13.4 shows the market share of physician practices of various size categories. It is notable that the size category 1–2 has declined substantially in market share, probably mostly indicating a decline in solo practice. All other size categories, however, have grown since 1965.

Confirming the earlier results, we see a decline in solo and dual practice for the period 1965–1969, and growth in market share, which occurred for all group practice sizes, was relatively smaller for the 8–25 size category. These later data, however, show a change in the growth pattern for the last interval studied. In this period, growth shifted more strongly to the very large groups.

Technical and Allocative Inefficiency

Inefficiency can be measured in two other ways, each also of great concern to health care firms and policy makers. Economists refer to these as technical and allocative inefficiency.

TECHNICAL INEFFICIENCY

Technical inefficiency is illustrated in Figure 13.6, panels A and B. Panel A depicts a production process with one input, while panel B depicts a production process using two inputs, capital and labor.

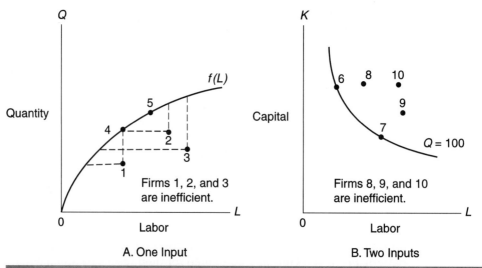

FIGURE 13.6 Technical Efficiency and Inefficiency at the Firm Level.

Technical inefficiency implies that the producer is not achieving a maximum amount of output from a given input combination. It is as if workers or machines were misused, not working at full capacity, or not cooperating well.

In both panels, each firm's actual experience is shown as a point indicated by a firm number. A technically inefficient firm is indicated by a firm that falls off its frontier. In panel A, the production frontier is shown as the production function labeled $f(L)$. Firms 4 and 5 are shown to be on the frontier; that is, they are currently technically efficient. In contrast, Firms 1, 2, and 3 are off the frontier and thus are currently technically inefficient. In panel A, the inefficiencies of the firms are measured as relative distances from the frontier. The distance measured may be the output distance, when inefficiency is measured vertically; for given inputs, what portion of feasible output does the firm achieve? Alternatively, it may be input reduction distance when inefficiency is measured horizontally; for the given output, what portion of the actual firm input combination is wasted? Generally, these alternative approaches to inefficiency measurement will yield different results.

In panel B, an isoquant for 100 cases treated is shown. This isoquant represents frontier practice for producing 100 cases. Suppose that the actual current output of all firms depicted in panel B is known to be 100 cases. Firms 6 and 7 in the panel are on the isoquant for 100 cases and thus are currently representing frontier practice and are technically efficient. Firms 8, 9, and 10 are off the isoquant, indicating that they have employed more input quantities than technically efficient production requires. As was the case in panel A, both output and input distance functions can be used as measures of inefficiency.

ALLOCATIVE INEFFICIENCY

Technical efficiency applies conceptually to production within a given firm. By contrast, allocative efficiency requires the efficient allocation of inputs between firms and between outputs. Essentially, it requires that each type of capital and labor be put to its most

rewarding use in society. Economic theorists have shown that allocative efficiency in production will result if each firm buys or hires inputs in competitive markets and if each firm minimizes production costs. Assuming competitive input markets—and thus fixed input prices common to all firms—permits us to describe allocative efficiency at the firm level. Here, allocative efficiency requires that each firm respond optimally to input prices; correspondingly, allocative *inefficiency* implies choosing an inappropriate combination of inputs in the sense that input prices have not been appropriately considered.

To illustrate, consider Figure 13.7. In this figure, the isoquant for 100 cases is illustrated as the curve labeled $Q = 100$. Assume that the firm being examined is currently producing its desired level of output and that the desired level happens to be 100 cases. Two isocost curves also are depicted, one indicating a cost level of $50,000 and the other a cost level of $42,000. Suppose that the firm in question were observed operating at point A. Because this firm is treating 100 cases using an input combination on the 100 cases isoquant, we can say this firm is technically efficient. However, it is not allocatively efficient.

To confirm this idea, consider that the firm in question alternatively could have produced 100 cases at point B. Inasmuch as point B lies on a lower and thus less costly isocost curve, the firm at B would incur less cost, and in this instance costs are reduced from $50,000 to $42,000 by moving from point A to point B. Point B entails a tangency of the desired isoquant with the lowest feasible isocost curve. Tangency in turn entails that the slope of the isoquant will equal the slope of the isocost curve. This condition implies the equality of the ratio of input prices to the ratio of marginal products for the inputs. This is the firm's appropriate response to input prices; that is, it is the key condition for allocative efficiency.

Though the conditions for efficiency of both types are well defined, several different empirical techniques have appeared to address them. These techniques can be grouped into two categories: *nonfrontier* and *frontier* studies. In the nonfrontier studies, actual outputs or cost experiences for two or more groups of firms are compared while

FIGURE 13.7 Technical and Allocative Efficiency.

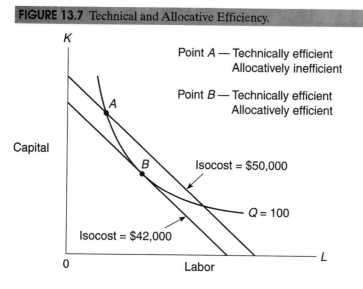

attempting to control for the effect of extraneous variables. In frontier studies, actual outputs or costs of firms compared to the best possible experience. Presently, we emphasize frontier because these studies can stand alone and because they are conceptually closer to the definitions of technical and allocative efficiency.

Two types of empirical frontier analysis have been developed. One, data envelopment analysis (DEA) was developed earlier and has been used the most often in hospital studies. The other, the stochastic frontier method, was developed in 1977, and applications in health care proliferated beginning in the late 1980s.

THE DATA ENVELOPMENT METHOD

DEA is illustrated in Figure 13.8. The frontier production, initially unknown to the researcher, is revealed more and more accurately as more firms are observed. A few such firms are represented by the points labeled 1 through 10. The data envelopment method finds the frontier isoquant for a selected level of output (for example, $Q = 100$) by forming an envelope of the data. Researchers use linear programming to construct this efficient outer shell of the data points. Techniques also are available to reject certain data points on statistical grounds that they are outliers from common practice. Given the estimated frontier, technical inefficiency then is measured as a relative distance from the frontier, as already described.[10]

The DEA method attracts researchers and research readers because it imposes no assumptions about the parameters of the underlying distribution of inefficiency. It lets the data speak for themselves: it is nonparametric. Its cousin, stochastic frontier analysis (SFA), contrasts with DEA because researchers must make guesses in advance about the statistical distribution of the inefficiencies. On the other hand, people who prefer the SFA tend to show concern about a potential weakness of the DEA, which assumes that all firms lying distant from the frontier are inefficient. Suppose that during a given year, the Huron, South Dakota, hospital nurses are organized and go on strike. Further suppose that the hospital is measured to have substantial inefficiency; the hospital is operating at a substantial distance off the frontier for similar hospitals. Was the hospital really inefficient or only apparently so? Should the researcher charge all the shortfall in output to management error? Or should management be granted a "handicap" frontier reflecting its special difficulties?

Many health economists recognize pluses and minuses to both approaches and treat them as complementary tools (Kooreman, 1994). Meanwhile, the work of theoreticians in econometrics moved the approaches toward each other. Work with panel data—gathered when a sample of hospitals are followed for many periods—suggests how the SFA method can be used without imposing such strong assumptions (Sickles and Schmidt, 1984; Lee and Schmidt, 1993). Work with measuring "distance" now makes possible a stochastic interpretation of DEA, though the technique uses a parametric function. The empirical researchers, of course, ask whether the technique makes a difference in the real world. We look at two empirical questions as examples of DEA and SFA:

1. How efficient are U.S. hospitals on average?
2. Are for-profit hospitals more or less efficient than nonprofits?

[10]The DEA approach is due originally to Farrell (1957) and further developed by Fare and Lovell (1978). See also Boles (1966) and Charnes et al. (1978).

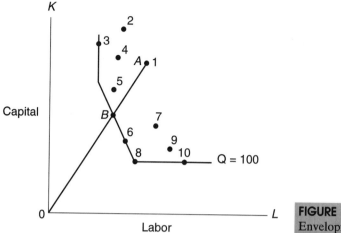

FIGURE 13.8 The Data Envelopment Method.

Valdmanis (1990) applied the DEA technique to two groups of hospitals in 1982, one representing 33 nonprofits and the other 8 public hospitals in Michigan. Her measures indicated that the nonprofits achieved on average 86.6 percent of technically efficient use of inputs, while the public hospitals performed better, achieving 98.5 percent or near frontier efficiency.

Though an early study (Register and Bruning, 1987) reported somewhat higher inefficiency levels, the typical range of roughly 5 percent to 20 percent inefficiency levels in U.S. hospitals includes the most recent results as well as the low inefficiencies reported recently from Norway (Magnusson, 1996).

The efficiency differences among for-profit and public hospitals in the Valdmanis study favored the public hospitals, though some might consider the difference small; the pattern also was noted again a few years later (Ozcan et al., 1992). More recent DEA studies show even smaller differences, causing two to describe the pattern plainly (Burgess and Wilson, 1996a, 1996b, 1998): "We find no evidence that differences in ownership structure affect technical efficiency after controlling for other factors" (1998, p. 100).

THE STOCHASTIC FRONTIER METHOD

Stochastic frontier analysis treats each firm uniquely by assuming it to be affected by a potential shock to its ability to produce care. Consider a hospital that is managed with perfect technical and allocative efficiency. Suppose this hospital discovers that its long-time major supplier has gone bankrupt. It takes months before comparable prices, qualities, and reliability are restored with new suppliers. Regardless of management's response to these events, the hospital's cost and output data for the year will be out of sync with similar hospitals having standard experiences. This will be true even if the management is "perfect," a model for other managers.

If each firm is potentially shocked during the period in ways that affect its production and cost performance, the firm's best possible practice, its frontier, will be randomly shifted. When the frontier function is thus partly random, the result is called a stochastic process—hence, the stochastic frontier name for the approach.

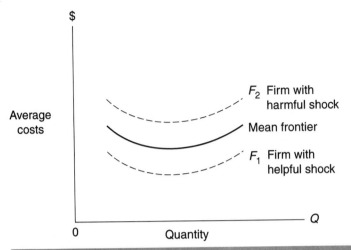

FIGURE 13.9 The Stochastic Frontier Method.

Techniques due originally to Aigner, Lovell, and Schmidt (1977) make it possible, under somewhat strenuous preconditions, to estimate the individual firm's expected frontier and the firm's inefficiency. The stochastic frontier concept is illustrated in Figure 13.9, an example that focuses on average costs. The mean average cost frontier is the dark curve. The individual firm's frontier is shifted by random shocks whose distribution must be assumed by the researcher from among known, parametric distributions. Thus, each hospital has a unique frontier and inefficiency distance from its frontier.[11]

Stochastic Frontier Studies Despite differences from DEA in approach and some differences in study design and data, stochastic frontier studies generate mean inefficiency estimates similar to DEA. The 10 percent to 20 percent mean inefficiencies suggested by an early study (Hofler and Folland, 1991) were corroborated by those published soon after by Zuckerman, Hadley, and Iezzoni (1994). These same lines of research find small and usually insignificant differences in efficiency among hospitals grouped by ownership types—nonprofits and for-profits are not much different—and this particular result appears robust to common variations in study design (Folland and Hofler, 1999). Both DEA and stochastic frontier methods have wider application, even though we chose the hospital as the prime example up to this point.[12]

Conclusions

The chapter has the following main purposes: to explain the ideas and language of production and cost studies, and to report some key results. We began with the concept of substitution among inputs. Substitution describes the possibility of producing a given

[11]Methods by which to calculate the individual firm data were published by Jondrow et al. (1982).
[12]Psychiatric hospitals (Mark, 1996), nursing homes (Kooreman, 1996; Vitaliano and Toren, 1994), group homes (van Lear and Fowler, 1997), physician clinics (Gaynor and Pauly, 1990) and physicians working in hospitals (Chilingerian, 1995) also have been studied.

health care output with more than one, and perhaps many, alternative techniques. The degree of substitutability that is possible reflects the degree of flexibility available, which in turn provides a means to lower costs by choosing less expensive techniques from among those available.

The results of the study of substitution in health care contrast to the opposing view that health care can be produced in only one possible way—the monotechnic view. To the contrary, the data suggest that substitution is possible and may occur to a considerable extent among some health care inputs. This is reported for substitution between health care capital and labor, but also among various labor inputs including nurses, physicians, and residents.

Economies of scale and scope in the production of health care were examined over the short and sometimes frustrating history of hospital cost studies. The seeming consensus of past years suggesting slight economies of scale in hospitals has not been supported by more recent studies. It is more reflective of an increasing sophistication in the literature to say that no clear consensus has yet emerged.

Survivor analysis asks whether certain size categories of hospitals and physician group practices have better survival capability, perhaps evidencing underlying economies of scale. Results vary for hospitals and physician practices, but the clearest trends in both instances appear to be declines in the market share of the smallest-size categories.

Finally, we explored the distinction between technical and allocative inefficiency. The former represents a situation in which a firm is not getting as much output as can be expected with its inputs, whereas the latter represents a situation in which a firm is not using the best combination of inputs relative to its costs. We have examined the two principal methods—data envelopment and stochastic frontier—used to estimate inefficiencies.

Throughout this chapter, we have set aside certain production and cost issues for later discussion. These remaining issues, which have the themes of technology and technological change, are taken up in the next chapter.

Summary

1. Frequently, health care goods and services can be produced in different ways in the sense that they use different combinations of factor inputs.
2. Isoquants are used to represent the alternatives and to illustrate the possibilities for substitution. The marginal technical rate of substitution represents the amount of one factor that needs to be given up for a unit increase in another factor while maintaining the level and quality of output.
3. The elasticity of substitution is another way economists measure substitution. It represents the percentage change in the ratio of factor inputs resulting from a 1 percent change in relative factor prices.
4. Empirically, some substitution has been found not only among different kinds of medical staff but even between hospital beds and medical staff.
5. The principles of cost minimization, as represented by the locus of tangencies between the firm's isoquants and isocost curves, are used to derive the cost curves (total and average).
6. Economies of scale refer to a declining long-run average cost. Economies of scope represent situations where the cost of producing goods jointly is less than the sum of the costs of separate production. Both concepts are relevant to policies intended to promote efficient size and scope of hospitals.

7. Some important issues must be considered in estimating hospital cost functions to determine economies of scale and scope. These include the handling of case-mix and quality differences and determining whether firms have made long-run adjustments.

8. Early empirical work on hospitals found evidence of economies of scale and an optimum size of about 250 beds. Several recent contributions suggest no economies or perhaps even some diseconomies of scale.

9. Survival analysis is an alternative to estimating cost functions. Inferences on optimum size are made from changes in the size distribution of firms over time.

10. Survival analysis for hospitals suggests diseconomies of scale for small hospitals but no strong evidence for other size categories. For the physician firm, the decline in the market share of solo practitioners suggests diseconomies for this form of practice. Rapid growth of relatively small and relatively large groups suggests scale advantages for those forms.

11. Technical inefficiency occurs when a firm fails to achieve the maximum potential output from a given set of inputs. It can be measured as a relative distance from the frontier production function surface or correspondingly as a distance from the isoquants of the frontier production function.

12. Allocative inefficiency arises in the case of competitive input markets when a firm fails to purchase inputs, given their prices, in a manner that minimizes costs.

13. Efficiency can be measured by recently developed frontier methods of two types. The data envelopment method estimates the frontier by statistically forming an envelope of data points representing production data. The stochastic frontier method estimates simultaneously a randomly shifting frontier and the firm's distance from that frontier.

Discussion Questions

1. Explain whether there is any difference in trying to maximize output for a given cost or to minimize the cost of producing a given level of output.

2. Distinguish between the concepts of economies of scale and economies of scope.

3. What is the relevance of economies of scale and scope to (A) health care providers and (B) policy makers and health care planners?

4. What are cross-sectional data? Why do economists find it so critical to control for case mix in studying health care cost functions? What are the analytical dangers if they do not?

5. Describe the technique of survival analysis and how it is used to make inferences about optimal scale and scope.

6. Are nurses and physicians likely to be perfect substitutes in the production of health care? For what tasks can they easily substitute for each other? For what tasks is this difficult?

7. How do legal restrictions on practice for nurses and physicians tend to affect the observed elasticities of substitution? Would they tend to be higher if legal restrictions were removed? Would quality of care be affected?

8. Given the cost function and economies of scale and scope information reviewed in this chapter, does a policy encouraging large, centralized hospitals seem wise? Will market forces tend to reward centralization of hospital services?

9. Speculate on what types of services are more appropriate to large, regional hospitals, and what types of services are more appropriate to small, local hospitals.

10. Economists define the elasticity of substitution as the percentage change in the capital–labor ratio elicited by a 1 percent change in the factor–price (wages/capital costs, for example) ratio. Would you expect the elasticity of substitution to be positive or negative? What would be the elasticity of substitution of a set of right-angled isoquants? Why?
11. Contrast technical and allocative efficiency. How can technical and allocative inefficiency in health care firms affect patient welfare?
12. If the available data envelopment estimates of hospital inefficiency by Valdmanis are correct, can significant cost savings to the consumer be achieved through improved efficiency? What if the Register and Bruning estimates are correct?
13. What does *stochastic* mean in stochastic frontier efficiency estimation? Give several real-life examples of events that could shift the production frontier.

Exercises

1. Draw an isoquant that shows relatively little substitution between two factor inputs and one that shows relatively large substitution. Let the vertical axis represent capital and let the horizontal axis represent labor.
2. Draw isocost curves that are tangent to your isoquants in exercise 1 and that have the same slope. Mark the points of tangency and note the capital–labor ratio. Draw new, flatter isocost curves that are tangent, again each having the same new slope. Mark the points of tangency and note the capital–labor ratio. In which case is the change in the capital–labor ratio greater? Which will have a higher elasticity of substitution?
3. Determine the elasticity of substitution in the case of the isoquant in panel A of Figure 13.1.
4. Explain why the isocost curves in panel A of Figure 13.2 have the same slope. What will happen to the slope if the price of capital decreases?
5. Suppose a firm has the following production technology for Goods 1 and 2.

Good 1		Good 2		Both		
Q_1	Cost	Q_2	Cost	Q_1	Q_2	Cost
10	50	10	60	10	10	100
20	100	20	100	20	20	180
30	150	30	130	30	30	250

a. Does Good 1 indicate economies of scale? Why?
b. Does Good 2 indicate economies of scale? Why?
c. Do the two goods indicate economies of scope? Why?
6. If any firm's price of labor and capital each double, what will happen to the expansion path (i.e., locus of tangencies between the isoquants and isocost curves)? What will happen to the firm's average cost curve?
7. Reproduce Figure 13.6, panel B, and draw in a family of isocost curves, choosing the common slope as you wish. As you have drawn these curves, show the point of least-cost production of 100 units of output. Are firms 8, 9, and 10 more costly

producers than this? Are the technically efficient firms 6 and 7 either least-cost producers?

8. Figure 13.6, panel A, illustrates technical inefficiency for firms with a one-input production function; it was explained that inefficiency could be measured by output distance or, alternatively, input reduction distance. Sketch and explain the comparable measures for the two-input production function case shown in panel B.

14

Technology

- Technological Change and Costs
- Insurance and the Bias Toward Cost-Increasing Technological Change
- On the Diffusion of New Health Care Technologies
- Conclusions

The rapid pace of technological change in the health care industry raises economic questions about the effects these changes will have. Technological change may reduce costs when it improves the productivity of health care resources, or it may increase costs when it improves the quality of care or introduces new and costlier products. Because it often raises costs in the health sector, technological change is hypothesized to be the major contributor to health sector inflation. Deep and widespread insurance coverage in the health sector may induce technological innovations of the type that increase costs. The effects on costs and the improvements to quality of care will depend on the diffusion of these new technologies to providers. Thus, patterns of diffusion have become a critical subject of study. We investigate these issues in the present chapter.

Technological Change and Costs

The production function, which embodies the technology available to the firm, shifts as technology changes. This shift has consequences for costs, quality, and the availability of new products.

TECHNOLOGICAL CHANGE: COST INCREASING OR DECREASING?

Technological change necessarily entails an improvement either by providing less costly production methods for standard "old" products, or alternatively by providing new or improved products. In either case, cost experience is improved in the sense that it will be less expensive to produce a given output, holding quality constant. However, the mix of products and services sold may change in directions that raise the average cost of a patient day, a case treated, or a physician visit. Consequently, the total health care expenditure per capita may rise.

Cost-Reducing and Cost-Increasing Shifts in the Isoquants

These concepts are illustrated in Figure 14.1. In panel A, we hold quality of care constant and illustrate the isoquants representing 100 cases before and after a technological change. The technological improvement in panel A shifts the isoquant inward. The firm chooses an efficient combination of inputs at point E and after the change at point E'. This change results in the attainment of a lower isocost curve for treating the 100 cases.

Panel B illustrates the introduction of a new technology that makes it possible to treat 100 cases with better health status outcomes, thus providing a higher quality of care. Improvements entailing new products or, as shown in panel B, an improved quality of care are beneficial to the consumer, but they may be more costly. This is illustrated by a shift outward of the 100-case isoquant, resulting in production on a higher and costlier isocost curve. The typical patient treated will pay more for care. In some cases where patients are heavily insured, we may question whether the change is worth it to patients when they pay increased insurance premiums, or to society as a whole.[1]

MEASURING HEALTH CARE PRICE INCREASES WHEN TECHNOLOGICAL CHANGE OCCURS

How do you measure the cost of a treatment when the treatment changes radically over a mere one or two decades? For example, heart attack treatment (myocardial infarction) changed substantially from 1975 to 1995. Some new effective inputs proved ex-

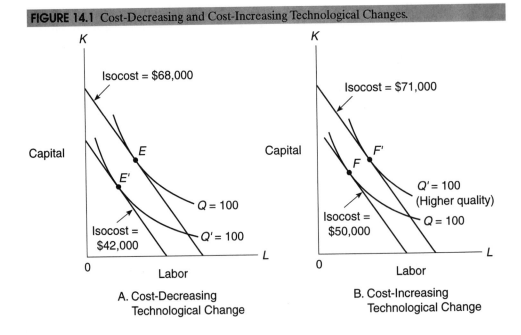

FIGURE 14.1 Cost-Decreasing and Cost-Increasing Technological Changes.

A. Cost-Decreasing Technological Change

B. Cost-Increasing Technological Change

[1] A model by Chetty (1998) shows how it is possible for technical change to increase costs when quality is held constant. When production involves benefits as well as harmful side effects and when the outcomes involve an element of chance, then the socially optimal rate of service may increase after a technological improvement in diagnostics.

tremely inexpensive; many people still are unaware that common aspirin has been shown to be effective at reducing mortality from cardiac diseases. Some materials did not exist in 1975, such as the intraortic balloon pump. Treatment practices changed; for example, the average length of hospital stay is now shorter. More important to the patient, the treatments are now more effective and have improved the length and quality of life for heart attack victims.

From the standpoint of our economic analysis, the essential facts are that overall treatment effectiveness improved (that is, the *quality* of treatment improved), in some cases *less* expensive inputs replaced more costly inputs, and several improved or newly designed inputs were added. Many of these were *more* costly than inputs they replaced. To understand fully whether heart attack treatment in 1995 was genuinely more expensive per episode than in 1975, we hold constant within the analysis the quality of the treatment. Quality constant increases in the price of care are commonly referred to as inflation, though more precisely the term *inflation* refers to quality constant increases in the general level of prices. Consumers are familiar with the Consumer Price Index (CPI) reported by the newspapers, which is a measure of how much general price have risen. A subset of this index focuses on medical care.

The official Medical Care Price Index, a component of the familiar Consumer Price Index, until recently took a disaggregated approach to the problem of measuring medical care price increases. Hospital price increases were disaggregated into selected components of hospital care. Room charge per day, nursing, and lab and other service centers were singled out; their price changes were sampled regularly; and the results were combined into a hospital price index. Though useful, the disaggregated approach was subject to distortions. For example, when the room charge component was given substantial weight and when room charges soared beyond other hospital services, the index tended to exaggerate hospital price increases in general. Worse yet, the rapid decline in the average length of patient stays in the United States provided another risk of exaggerating hospital price increases: patients paid much more per day, but they stayed many fewer days.[2]

Recognizing these and other inherent problems for measuring inflation while undergoing technological change, Anne Scitovsky (1985) proposed that health economists select

> a number of specific illnesses that can be regarded as representative of illness in the population . . . obtaining detailed data on the number of and charges for specific services used in the treatment of these conditions . . . and comparing average charges for the episode of illness in the later years with average charges of treatment in the earlier years in the later year's prices (p. 1,346).

Gathering data on clinic care in Palo Alto, California, she applied this approach to myocardial infarction (heart attack) and several other diseases. Her data covered three decades, beginning in 1951, and they showed a mixed pattern. The cost of treatment for earache in children declined, but the treatment cost for appendicitis rose. Often, the trend for a specific treatment depended on the decade: heart attack treatment costs inflated sharply from 1964 to 1971 but declined somewhat from 1971 to 1981.

[2]Nevertheless, these data were some of the main data available and were the compelling force behind political and regulatory measures to control hospital costs. The DRG legislation installed in 1983 was partly a reflection of concern about inflation as measured by the Medical CPI.

Scitovsky's episode approach and the Medical CPI's disaggregate approach omit measures of quality defined as a measure of the effect of the treatment on the patient's health. Most health economists would prefer that quality be defined in terms of the quality of the health care system's ultimate output—the patient's health. Cutler et al. (1999) recommend and develop an approach of this kind, and conveniently, they select for study one of the diseases studied by Scitovsky—myocardial infarction.

If a heart attack victim treated today stays alive longer and lives more fully than a patient treated 20 years ago, we must adjust inflation estimates downward, recording more properly the price of a life year saved. Cutler and his colleagues developed two myocardial infarction treatment price indexes, which adjust in this way for patient gains in either life years or quality-adjusted life years (QALYs). They evaluated life year gains in dollar terms to make this adjustment. Allowing for errors, particularly in valuing life years, these authors provide a range of price inflation estimates.

Their research makes clear that

1. the evaluation of quality is necessary for sound measures of inflation, especially when technological change occurs.
2. the substantial quality improvement in the treatment of heart attack probably requires that previous estimates of inflation in health care be reduced.

Let us examine whether and to what degree these ideas are corroborated by the data in this case. Table 14.1 indicates that technological change has improved the quality of heart attack treatment and that this quality adjustment can turn what superficially appears to be a case of price inflation into proof that the case is really one of price deflation. Reporting their research provides best estimates and not certainties, as is true of all statistical research, Cutler and colleagues offered a range of possible values; these suggest that the true decline in the heart attack treatment price might be much larger than these figures.

Technological Change, Inflation, and Health Insurance

The heart attack example makes clear that quality improvements can be substantial and matter considerably to the patient. This helps explain why consumers pay increasingly large amounts of money for care. How much, then, of health care inflation can be attributed to technological change and how much to increased use of and prices of the inputs?

Technological change in the aggregate is always hard to measure and usually is residual—the part left over when everything else is explained. What, then, is left over when we have accounted for other factors? The task of answering this question requires an understanding of these other factors and the role they play. Begin with insurance. As we have seen, increased coverage shifts (increases) demand. Increased demand raises price levels, a mode we call demand pull inflation. However, health insurance also can induce innovations, which may be cost decreasing as well as cost increasing; furthermore, as Weisbrod has explained (1991), a two-way relationship exists between insurance and innovation as new health products also may stimulate the demand for insurance.

Following Newhouse's (1992, 1993) exposition, we begin by identifying all logical contributors to health care inflation and make estimates of their contribution. The residual then is a candidate for interpretation as the effect of technological change. Newhouse identifies five factors that potentially make a significant contribution to health

TABLE 14.1	Comparing the Unadjusted Approach with a Quality-Adjusted Measure of Price Increases of Treatment for Myocardial Infarction (1983–1994)

Index	Average Annual Price Changes
Unadjusted Indexes	
Official Medical Care CPI	3.4%
• Hospital component	6.2
• Room	6.0
• Other inpatient services	5.7
Heart attack unadjusted episode approach[a]	2.8
Quality-Adjusted Indexes	
Quality (extra years of life)	−1.5
Quality (extra QALYs)[b]	−1.7

[a]Experts recognize that several alternatives are applied when selecting for analysis the market basket of goods and services whose inflation is to be measured. The table reports a fixed-basket method; the patient is assumed to purchase essentially the same combination of medical goods in each year studied. Chain indexes allow for the representative market basket to change over time, and it therefore adds realism. But, how frequently should the basket be recalibrated? When a 5-year recalculation of the basket is used, the average annual percentage change becomes 2.1 percent; with an annual recalculation, it becomes 0.7 percent.

[b]QALYs are quality-adjusted life years. This quality of treatment is the same as the previous one except for the additional consideration of the degree to which the patient is able to lead a full, active life in the years after treatment.

Source: Adopted from Cutler, et al. (1999).

care inflation: aging, increased insurance, increased income, supplier-induced demand, and factor productivity problems in the service sector.

The proportion of the population over age 65 increased from 8 percent in 1950 to 12 percent in 1987. Newhouse estimates the effect of this change by applying as weights the average expenditure of persons in each age group. He finds the effect to be only a 15 percent increase in expenditures. This explains only a tiny fraction of inflation; during the period, average expenditure per person increased by a factor of five.

Newhouse (1988) shows that inflation due to insurance-induced demand increases can account for only a minority portion of the rise in expenditures. Evidence on the role of insurance from the Rand Health Insurance Experiment is useful because it isolates the role of insurance from that of technological change. By randomized assignment of insurance provisions to patients with access to essentially the same service facilities, the Rand study effectively held technology constant as it experimentally varied insurance coverage.

Applying the Rand estimates to the problem, one would expect the shift in average coinsurance rates from about 66 percent in 1950 to 28 percent in 1984 to have increased expenditures on the order of 50 percent to 100 percent, which is considerably less than

the increase experienced. "Thus, it seems reasonable that the change in insurance (technology held constant) can only account for a small portion—perhaps a tenth—of the postwar increase in medical care expenditures" (Newhouse 1988, p. 274).

Income increased substantially during roughly this period. Looking at a slightly longer period, Newhouse (1992) finds per-capita income rising by 180 percent from 1940 to 1990. With typical estimates of the income elasticity (0.2 to 0.4), this implies an inflationary impact of 35 percent to 70 percent, which is much lower than the 780 percent increase observed.

The effect of increased numbers of physicians on the demand for health care also is unlikely to have accounted for a substantial effect on costs for this period. Health care expenditures have been inflating in real terms at about 4 percent per year since 1940. The increase in physicians came most strongly in the 1970 to 1990 period, yet the rate of inflation did not change. Recent estimates of the extent of supplier-induced demand also suggest a modest role.

It also has been argued that inflation is an endemic problem of service industries, which include the health care industries (Baumol, 1993). The problem comes when service sector jobs, which are labor intensive, cannot be done more productively over time. How can you speed up a haircut, for example, without harming quality? As productivity and wages rise in other sectors, health, according to this theory, experiences the wage increases without the productivity increases. Hence, inflation ensues. A counterargument notes the many cases in health care in which a substantial change occurred in diagnostics and in treatment. Compare a haircut from 1940 with one given today; then compare the 1940 treatment for a heart attack with current methods. Clearly, the lack of productivity growth does not apply to the health sector, at least not across the board.

Newhouse also notes that health maintenance organizations have experienced rates of expenditure growth similar to fee-for-service care. HMOs have economic incentives to cut production costs. The fact that HMOs have experienced similar inflation rates to other parts of the health sector suggests that this inflation is not a result of growing inefficiency in the health care sector.

How much of the inflation in health care expenditures can these alternative hypotheses explain? Newhouse argues that it is difficult to measure largely because of the difficulty in measuring health sector productivity growth. However, his own view "is that they account for well under half—perhaps under a quarter—of the 50-year increase in medical care expenditure. Thus, we are left with trying to explain a large residual" (Newhouse, 1992, p. 11). Technological change appears to play a leading role in health care inflation.

Insurance and the Bias Toward Cost-Increasing Technological Change

If insurance is not the main contributor to inflation through its direct effect on demand, it may nevertheless be the major player through inducement of cost-increasing technological innovations.

THE COST-INCREASING BIAS HYPOTHESIS

The intuitive argument is that because increased health insurance reduces the out-of-pocket portion of the bill, the patient may be willing to spend considerably more

when insured. The consumer may realize that premiums will tend to rise if all patients act likewise but will make use of the best, new, expensive technology to the maximum extent affordable, beyond the point where the marginal benefits equal the full marginal costs. Consequently, the payoff to owning a patent to new, costly health care technology becomes greater.

Process innovations (improvements to existing treatment processes that make them less costly) and product innovations (improvements through the introduction of new products, which could make the treatment more costly even when lowering the cost of improvements to the patient's well-being) may be affected differently. Insurance can encourage new products and can be biased toward increasing cost.

THE GODDEERIS MODEL

The elements of the relationship between insurance and innovation can be made more explicit (Goddeeris, 1984a). Figure 14.2 shows the theoretical relationship of improvements in health, Δh, to changes in health expenditures, Δm. As shown, this relationship is labeled $\Delta h(\Delta m)$. Health care innovations may be either cost increasing (entailing positive values of Δm) or cost reducing (entailing negative values of Δm). It is hypothesized that innovations that tend toward cost-increasing change (higher values of Δm) also yield greater improvements in health status (higher values of Δh). Thus, health improvements, Δh, are an increasing function of cost change, Δm. Here the function Δh (Δm) also is hypothesized to be concave as shown.

Consider a model in which a health services provider is also a potential innovator, and in which a consumer maximizes utility. Let this consumer be insured so that he or she pays only a fraction, z, of the provider's bill out of pocket. Suppose that the market for this service is initially in equilibrium and that the provider considers undertaking the

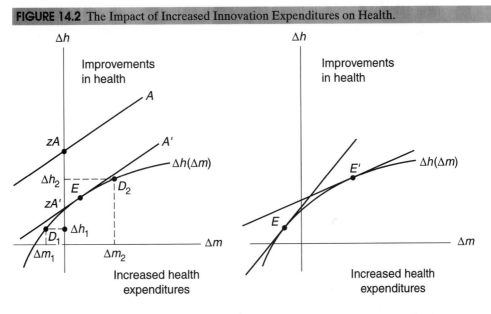

FIGURE 14.2 The Impact of Increased Innovation Expenditures on Health.

A. Equilibrium

B. Comparative Statics

development of an innovation in treatment technology. Potential innovations may have consequences for the equilibrium health of the consumer and for the costs of treatment. The possibilities are summarized by the function we have just described, $\Delta h\,(\Delta m)$. For example, an innovation may be available that raises health by Δh_1 and reduces treatment costs by Δm_1; this example case results in the outcome indicated by point D_1 in panel A. An alternative innovation may result in a rise in treatment costs, say by Δm_2, but substantially increase health, say by Δh_2, the outcome of which is shown by point D_2 in panel A. We shall assume that the innovations tend always to improve equilibrium health status.

By investing in a given innovation, the provider seeks to increase profits. We presume the provider will select innovations of the type that tend to give the highest potential profits. We can understand which innovations will provide the highest potential profits by the aid of the isoprofit curves. The provider's extra profit obtained through the innovation equals extra revenue minus the extra costs, Δm. The provider can charge the patient only as much and at least as much as the improvement in health is worth to the patient. Assume that the patient values each additional unit of health at a constant rate, and further let the changes in health be measured in units representing $1 of worth to the consumer. Thus, the consumer is willing to pay at most $1 for each unit of increase in health status. However, the provider can charge a full price per unit of health increase greater than $1 because the insured consumer pays only a fraction of the bill out of pocket, the coinsurance rate, z. Thus, the innovator–provider can charge $\Delta h/z$ for the innovation. The provider profits from the innovation are, thus:

$$\text{Extra profits} = \Delta h/z - \Delta m \qquad \textbf{(14.1)}$$

In Figure 14.2A, we represent these profit data by the isoprofit lines. An isoprofit line is defined as a collection of points $(\Delta m, \Delta h)$ that yields a given profit level. The isoprofit equation for profit level A is thus:

$$A = \Delta h/z - \Delta m$$

If we algebraically rearrange terms, the isoprofit equation can be written treating the dependent variable, Δh, as a function of the remaining terms. That is, the isoprofit equation is written equivalently as:

$$\Delta h = z(A + \Delta m) = zA + z\Delta m$$

This is a linear equation with intercept zA and slope z.

Two isoprofit lines are shown in panel A. The isoprofit line for an extra profit level of A dollars is so labeled in the graph. Its intercept is found by setting Δm equal to zero in the function $\Delta h = zA + z\Delta m$; thus, the intercept is zA. Similarly, the A' isoprofit line has an intercept of zA'. Because $zA > zA'$, it follows that $A > A'$. In general, higher isoprofit lines yield higher extra profit levels.

In panel A, the isoprofit line A is unattainable given the function $\Delta h\,(\Delta m)$ shown. In contrast, isoprofit line A' is just attainable. The equilibrium choice will be a point of tangency between the $\Delta h\,(\Delta m)$ function and the highest isoprofit curve attainable. Under the circumstances shown in panel A, the equilibrium will be at point E.

COMPARATIVE STATIC ANALYSIS

Comparative static analysis allows us to investigate the role of insurance and its effect on the incentives for innovation. Increased insurance coverage in this model is

represented by a fall in the coinsurance rate, z. The slope of the isoprofit lines is z; thus, when z becomes smaller, the isoprofit lines become flatter. In panel B, the innovator finds his or her optimal choice to have changed when the isoprofit curves became flatter. Assume that the innovator's optimal choice initially is point E, a point of tangency. When the insurance coverage increases, z falls, implying that the highest extra profit will be attained at a new point of tangency. This new equilibrium is shown as point E' in panel B.

Note that the equilibrium under greater insurance coverage entails a higher level of Δm than for the initial equilibrium. Thus, the presence of higher insurance coverage has induced the innovator to switch from an emphasis on cost-reducing innovations such as at point E, to cost-increasing innovations such as at point E', which now will have a higher profit.

EVIDENCE ON THE RELATIONSHIP OF INSURANCE, TECHNOLOGICAL CHANGE, AND INFLATION

Newhouse (1978b, 1988) set out the basic empirical models designed to test the underlying hypotheses and measure the contribution of health insurance to health care inflation. First, the conventional view emphasized the role of insurance as a demand shifter; this is measured by the variable "change in insurance." Second, the level of health insurance (indicated by the average coinsurance rate) was hypothesized to induce innovations, thus causing inflation indirectly through cost-increasing technological change. By 1988, Newhouse had found, though somewhat tentatively, evidence that supported the induced-innovation hypothesis, leaving uncertain whether any role at all existed for the conventional demand-shifting avenue.

Investigating a larger data series and providing more testing of underlying econometric issues, Peden and Freeland (1999) helped resolve the remaining questions. They studied coinsurance *level,* the level of noncommercial research spending and the annual change in average coinsurance from 1963 to 1993, during which time real per-capita health spending grew by 373 percent. About half of this expenditure increase was due to the level of coinsurance, giving support to the induced-innovation hypothesis. In contrast, their data offered little support for the demand-shifting effect of reduced coinsurance. Personal income growth over the period contributed more than 20 percent of the inflation, which was more than previously thought.

DOES TECHNOLOGICAL CHANGE IN HEALTH CARE MAKE THE AVERAGE PATIENT BETTER OFF?

A troubling aspect of the relationship of insurance coverage to innovation was pointed out by Goddeeris (1984b). Health insurance coverage, which reduces the fraction of the bill paid by the patient out of pocket, may induce many patients to use new health technologies that are not worth their full cost. The average patient pays the full cost of new technologies through a rise in insurance premiums in addition to out-of-pocket costs. Goddeeris showed that the average patient may be worse off after the new technology is introduced than before it was invented; however, this issue of potential welfare gains or losses from innovation is complex to pursue.

One problem is that the current insurance system tends to provide the consumer with incentives such that what is good for an individual is bad for society. The patient may understand fully that if everyone used the new, expensive health technology, then

costs would rise substantially for all. However, the individual may receive significant personal benefits and correctly ascertain that his or her personal contribution to higher premiums is small.

A second problem is that alternative insurance schemes with better incentive structures may never arise. Goddeeris shows that if insurance plans paid a flat lump sum per given diagnosis instead of a fraction of the charges, then the problem of "harmful" innovations would not arise. However, the transactions costs of providing such insurance policies probably are insurmountable.

Although this analysis does not prove that the recent pattern of technological change in health care has harmed patient welfare in net, it explains the possibility. It also shows that the possibility for harmful patterns of innovation is consistent with the existing incentive structure of insurance coverage.

On the Diffusion of New Health Care Technologies

It takes time for a new product innovation to be widely adopted by providers. As always, some firms adopt rapidly, some slowly, and some not at all.

WHO ADOPTS AND WHY?

Students of the adoption process of health technologies, such as José Escarce (1996), identify several general ideas. Adoptions follow two principles: the profit principle and information channels. The first posits that physicians, for example, will be more likely to adopt a new surgical technique if it is expected to increase their revenue stream by enhancing prestige or by improving the well-being of their patients. The second, a compatible principle deriving originally from sociology, emphasizes the role of friends, colleagues, journals, and conferences at informing and encouraging the adoption decision.

While profit measurements are familiar and need no reintroduction, Escarce emphasized the "information externalities" inherent in adoption by the first physician to adopt. The externality is the uncompensated, beneficial effect on a third person caused by the actions of a market, in this case, the actions of the first adopter. By choosing the technology, the physician communicates to friends and colleagues the expectation that the new product will benefit his or her patients and practice. The adopter paves the way for new infrastructure, new seminars, and library materials that reduce the cost of adoption for colleagues. The process tends to build on itself, perhaps at an increasing rate, until all the main body of potential adopters have acted, only then slowing the increase in total adopters until the community's maximum potential is reached.

The data are consistent with this process; in many industries, adoption occurs slowly at first, then at an increasing rate that continues at a decreasing rate asymptotically approaching its limit. Compare this description in words with Figure 14.3 which illustrates the classic pattern of diffusion as a logistic curve. A new data set is tested empirically by estimating the logistic function where P is the proportion of individuals or firms adopting, the maximum potential proportion of adopters is K, with parameters a and b to be estimated:

$$P_t = K/(1 + e^{-(a+bt)}) \tag{14.2}$$

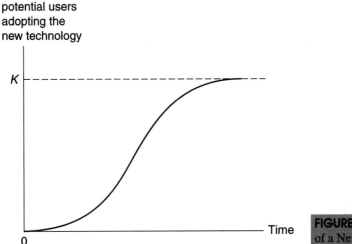

Proportion of
potential users
adopting the
new technology

K

Time

0

FIGURE 14.3 The Diffusion
of a New Technology.

Escarce's data fit this time pattern quite well. He studied a new surgical proce-
dure, laparoscopic cholecystectomy, introduced in 1989; it is a technique to remove dis-
eased gall bladders, a technique that proved attractive to patients because it was
minimally invasive. He found the diffusion curve to fit the logistic pattern common to
diffusion studies.

He then examined the differences between those who adopted and those who did
not. *Ceteris paribus,* adopting surgeons more likely to be younger, male, board-certified,
U.S. medical school graduates, and urban-located. That younger individuals are more
likely adopters is a common finding; in one study, older physicians proved less likely to
adopt even though their expected gains in profit were much higher than for their
younger counterparts (Rizzo and Zeckhauser, 1992). Finally, Escarce's data showed lit-
tle difference between managed care and fee-for-service; there was no clear winner in
the race between these two to adopt the newest technology.

OTHER FACTORS THAT MAY AFFECT ADOPTION RATES

The economic theory of innovation sheds some additional light on these issues.[3] As we
have described the firm will tend to adopt an innovation when the present value of fu-
ture profits due to the innovation is positive. Waiting too long may provide competitors
with an advantageous share of the market, which may be permanently sustained. How-
ever, waiting has benefits in that one may take advantage of future advances and learn
from the experience of others. Waiting thus may reduce risks, so more risk-averse firms
may choose to wait somewhat longer. Small firms, which are less able to diversify, may
tend to be more risk averse,[4] partially explaining the slower rate of adoption among
small hospitals.

[3]See Kamien and Schwartz (1982) and Scherer (1984).
[4]See Sloan et al. (1986).

A study done in Norway investigates the profit principle further (Klausen et al., 1992). The authors show that new dry chemical laboratory equipment was adopted sooner by physicians whose (later shown) profitability from the equipment was higher. The equipment allowed physicians to conduct tests on patient blood chemistry in their offices and be reimbursed for each analysis by the state. Alternatively, the physician could send the test to a central laboratory and be reimbursed by the state. The reimbursement rates and rules differed, and physicians would find one or the other approach more profitable depending on their practice characteristics. The profitability variable in this study was the strongest statistically, and this serves to support the conventional economic theory. However, physicians also tended to adopt "too late" in the sense that marginal revenues from adoption were much higher than marginal costs. This latter point suggests that information issues probably play a role in adoption.

Regulation may work to slow adoption. Prospective payment methods of financing patient care in hospitals mean that payers or government agencies set limits on the rates of payment. Medicare's Diagnosis Related Group (DRG) payment system, adopted in 1983, is a prospective system, and many states experimented with prospective systems prior to Medicare. The effect of a prospective payment system (PPS) on the diffusion of new health care technologies may be anticipated on theoretical grounds. A severe PPS program, one that sets relatively low payment rates, will tend to lower the profitability of new technologies. This issue has been pursued empirically by several analysts. An early study reports on the diffusion of five new hospital care technologies in six states, some of which are subject to PPS. The data suggest that the New York program tended to retard significantly the diffusion of three cost-increasing technologies and tended to enhance diffusion of one of two cost-reducing technologies for the larger hospitals. The results for the other PPS states studied were less strong, but "taken broadly, these results are consistent with the incentive structures inherent in each program" (Romeo, Wagner, and Lee, 1984, p. 20). Sloan and colleagues (1986) found that mandatory rate-setting programs retard diffusion of technology in *some* cases, particularly in the instances of coronary bypass surgery, morbid obesity surgery, and intraocular lens implants. However, the degree of slowing tended to be small. A recent contribution by Teplensky et al. (1995) concludes that restrictive rate-setting programs tend to retard significantly the adoption of new technology.

DIFFUSION OF TECHNOLOGY AND MANAGED CARE

Managed care arrived with hopes that it would control health care expenditure increases by removing the financial incentives for physicians to overprescribe, overtreat, and overhospitalize their patients. The same flattening of incentives—no extra money for extra treatment—potentially dampens the physician's interest in cost-increasing technological change. As we have seen throughout this chapter, the flattening of financial incentive must be expected to slow innovation and the adoption of innovative technologies. Although we address the ultimate effect of managed care on health care inflation elsewhere in this text, it is appropriate here to ask: "Does a higher penetration of managed care into the health system tend to slow the growth in availability of new technologies?"

The recent studies are somewhat mixed, but the weight of evidence is to the null hypothesis. Hill and Wolfe (1997) examine Wisconsin, where political initiatives provide

an opportunity to investigate the effect of the growth of a managed care-like system. The authors reported time trends of availabilities of selected technologies suggest retardation of several but continued growth or advancement of several others. Friedman and Steiner (1999) investigate a single high-tech service, intensive care units; they find no difference in admission rates under managed care versus fee-for-service care in two states studied, although some reduction occurred in ICU length of stay in one state. We look to a recent and broader time series study by Baker and Spetz (1999), which looks to the same question with their own aggregated index of more than 30 health care technologies analyzing more than 200 metropolitan statistical areas over the decade ending in 1993. Provided this wider look, including graphs showing little apparent difference in technology growth rates in high-penetration (managed care) areas versus the low-penetration areas, the conclusion appears clear. The authors concluded: "(H)igh managed care areas did not have slower technology growth rates than low market share areas in the late 1980s and early 1990s, even when new technologies are incorporated into the indices" (p. 20).

Conclusions

We developed several issues. The first showed that technological change can increase or decrease costs. Scitovsky found that technology has been cost increasing in several eras; a thorough index of heart attack prices showed a reduction.

We then turned to the broader issue of whether insurance coverage tends to cause technological change to be biased toward cost-increasing changes. Finally, we investigated the diffusion of technology and found that it plausibly follows a logistical function pattern. We investigated the causes for early or late adoption. Finally the influence of managed care on adoption proved to be negligible.

Summary

1. Technological change in health care may reduce costs if it improves production technology of existing products, or increase costs if it emphasizes new products and higher-quality versions of old products.
2. Evidence from heart attack pricing shows the importance of measuring price changes against the growth in quality of the ultimate product, health itself.
3. Technological change is a major suspected cause of the substantial inflation in health care since 1950. Other sources of inflation, such as increased insurance coverage, cannot explain the larger portion of inflation. Technological change is assumed to account for the unexplained residual.
4. The Goddeeris model shows how technological change can be influenced by insurance coverage. Greater insurance coverage increases the relative profitability of cost-increasing technological innovations versus cost-reducing ones.
5. In turn, the proliferation of health care innovations may induce changes in the prevalent forms of insurance coverage so as to expand insurance coverage.
6. New health care technologies are adopted gradually in an industry, and the pattern of adoption fits the logistic curve. Adoption patterns are influenced by regulation, age of the adopter, profitability and channels of communication.

Discussion Questions

1. Which of the following types of technological change in health care are likely to be cost increasing: (A) threats of malpractice suits cause physicians to order more diagnostic tests on average for a given set of patient symptoms; (B) a new computer-assisted scanning device that enables physicians to take much more detailed pictures of the brain; (C) the introduction of penicillin earlier in this century; (D) greater emphasis on preventive care? Discuss.

2. How can the net effect of technological change in the health care sector hypothetically harm average patient welfare? Discuss.

3. As technologies diffuse, why do some firms adopt them before others? What types of technologies would you expect to be adopted most quickly? Most slowly? What factors can slow the rate of diffusion of new medical technologies?

4. How do economists define technological change with respect to quantity of goods produced? With respect to quality of goods produced?

Exercises

1. Is it possible theoretically for a newly adopted technology to increase the cost of health, assuming that health is fully meaured as attempted by Cutler et al. to assess heart attack inflation?

2. In Escarces's account of diffusion, do improved "channels of information" matter regardless of the information content? Does all information increase the adoption rate? If not, what information does?

3. In the Goddeeris model in Figure 14.2, how would the equilibrium change in expenditure, Δm, be affected if there were a vertical parallel shift in the $\Delta h(\Delta m)$ curve, say caused by increased support of medical technological research? Show graphically the alternative possibility if support for research tended to emphasize cost-reducing innovations.

4. Technological change often is distinguished by whether it is labor saving, capital saving, or neutral. These are determined by the relative capital–labor ratios. For example, if the capital–labor ratio diminishes, the technological change is capital saving. Use isoquants as in panel A of Figure 14.1 to illustrate the three possibilities.

5. Use demand-and-supply analysis to show the effects of increased insurance on demand and costs, and the indirect effect of insurance on costs through the induced effect on technological change.

CHAPTER

Labor Markets and Professional Training

- The Importance of Labor in the Health Care Sector

- The Demand for and Supply of Health Care Labor

- The Human Capital Theory of Investment in Education

- Factor Productivity and Substitution among Factors

- Health Manpower Availability

- Manpower Planning and the Meaning of Shortages

- Conclusions

Commensurate with its high component of GDP and the labor-intensive nature of its output, the health care economy employs a large number of workers. We use the term *labor* here in the general economic sense of an input in production that is distinct from capital and that is provided by human beings. Like other goods and services, the production of health services requires both labor and capital. Labor with various levels and types of skills, from hospital custodial personnel to brain surgeons, is needed in the production of health care.

While many health sector workers are relatively unskilled, the health sector also requires large numbers of highly trained professionals. Most physician specialists have years of postgraduate education past their medical school education. Labor issues in health economics thus range from general supply and demand, to labor theory and human capital theory, to specialized topics regarding professionals. Issues include health manpower planning, medical school resources, physician location decisions, and shortages of professionals.[1] This chapter addresses general labor issues. Chapter 16 concentrates on issues pertaining to the training, location, and practice decisions of physicians.

[1] Although regrettably sexist, the term *manpower* has evolved as the standard term for planning health care labor needs.

323

The Importance of Labor in the Health Care Sector

To emphasize the importance of labor to the health sector, and the importance of health sector labor to the economy, we refer to Table 1.3a in chapter 1. The table shows the magnitude and variety of health care occupations. In 1998, 11.5 million people, nearly 9 percent of the U.S. labor force, were employed at health services sites.

These data do not include millions of other workers in the health economy. Those not shown include workers in the pharmaceutical and health insurance industries, as well as those in industries providing supplies, capital goods, and services for people providing direct patient care. Workers in some other health-related occupations such as pharmacists employed in drugstores also are not shown.

Many of these numbers have been increasing as health care spending has increased. Between 1970 and 1996, the number of active physicians rose from 291,000 to 701,000, or more than 140 percent; the number of registered nurses increased from 750,000 to 2,162,000, or nearly 190 percent. The per-capita ratios are shown in Table 1.3b. In other cases, the growth rates are more modest, but growth is the common finding. Thus, the labor component in the health sector is large, important, and growing.

The Demand for and Supply of Health Care Labor

How labor is used—and how it is combined with other factors of production—helps determine both the amount of health care provided and the wages and salaries of the providers. The productivity and training of health care providers are important to the working of labor markets and to the demands and supplies of labor.

We begin by describing the factors that determine demand for labor. Demand for a factor of production, either labor or capital, is a derived demand. We demand health care providers because we demand health care, and in turn we demand health care because we demand health.

PRODUCTION FUNCTIONS AND ISOQUANTS

Recall that we use the production function to describe the relationship of factors of production (the inputs) to the resulting ultimate goods produced (the outputs). The production function shows the maximum sustainable output that can be obtained from the possible combinations of inputs such as labor, materials, buildings, and equipment with existing technology and know-how.

Economists often simplify the production relationship as follows:

$$Q = f(L, K) \tag{15.1}$$

where Q represents output and L and K represent the quantities of labor and capital inputs. Many features of a production function can be illustrated graphically through isoquants. Recall that an isoquant represents all combinations of inputs (e.g., labor and capital) that result in a given level of output. Figure 15.1 (panels A and B) describes isoquants for two different situations.

In panel A, the isoquant shows a technology in which labor and capital are fairly good substitutes for each other; to be more exact, labor and capital can be combined in many different proportions to produce output. The budget line, *AB*, reflects the trade-

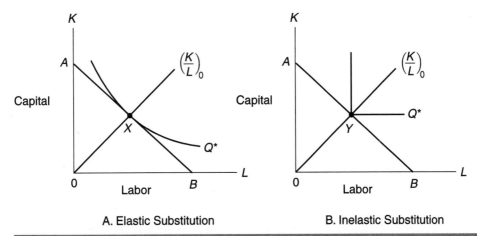

A. Elastic Substitution B. Inelastic Substitution

FIGURE 15.1 Production with Varying Rates of Substitution.

off of the costs of capital and labor, and point X is the location at which the costs of producing Q^* units of output are minimized.

With the given set of factor prices (wages and payments to capital) the equilibrium capital–labor ratio $(K/L)_0$ is the slope of a ray from the origin through point X. Due to the curvature of the isoquant (reflecting the elasticity of substitution of production), a change in relative prices leads to a change in the capital–labor ratio. Here labor and capital are good substitutes as we move along a given isoquant. Lower prices of labor (i.e., a flatter budget line) will lead to a relatively large substitution of labor for capital, and vice versa.

In contrast, panel B shows a technology in which labor and capital are not good substitutes; as they drawn, they must be used in fixed proportions to one another. Although point Y represents the same (K/L) ratio as point X, changes in the factor prices will not change the capital–labor ratio. Specialized surgeries, for example, may require specific ratios of labor to capital with little substitution available. The degree to which substitution among inputs is possible, either between health care labor and capital, or among different types of health care labor, is a key issue in manpower planning and in determining the efficiency of production exhibited by health care firms. The demand for any type of health care labor depends in part on these substitution possibilities.

The demand for a factor of production also depends on the price of the output. Consider an example. Suppose you were working as a skilled worker in a bicycle manufacturing plant, and suppose that bicycle riding was becoming more popular. The increase in demand would result, at least temporarily, in a higher price for bicycles. More bicycle workers would be demanded as a consequence.

MARGINAL PRODUCTIVITY OF LABOR

Finally, consider that the demand for a factor, and consequently the wage paid to the factor, will depend at least in part on the factor's productivity. This is one explanation as to why college-educated workers earn more money than others. If college-educated workers are more productive than others, then the demand for them will be greater.

Although this is only one theory that explains earnings advantages of college graduates, it illustrates the premise that more productive laborers are in greater demand.

Reconsider the idea of marginal product—the increase in output when an input is increased by one unit. Suppose that labor in equation (15.1) represents the number of laboratory technicians employed. If we add one lab technician to the production process, holding constant the available lab equipment and materials (i.e., K), we probably would increase lab output. This increase is the marginal product of lab technicians.

Although additional lab technicians in the production process are likely to add to output, they likely will add incrementally less output. As we increase an input, holding all others constant, output will tend to increase but at a decreasing rate. This illustrates the law of diminishing returns.

The number of lab technicians that one should hire depends also on the price of output. Suppose that lab tests sell for $50 per unit. Suppose also that an additional technician would increase output by four tests per day. If these tests sell for $50 each, the technician is bringing in an additional $200 in revenue. The extra revenue generated is called the marginal revenue product (MRP).

Would it pay to hire this extra technician? Clearly, the answer depends on the wage per day. If technicians earn $100 per day, the technician nets the hospital a $100 gain ($200 marginal revenue product less $100 wage), and it thus pays to hire another one. It always pays to hire laborers whose marginal revenue products exceed their wage.

Would it pay to hire still another technician if he or she has a marginal product of three tests per day? Because output (the tests) sells for $50 each, this next technician is netting the hospital $50 because the marginal revenue product, $150 in this case, exceeds the wage, $100. It will pay the firm to continue to hire more workers up until the point where the marginal revenue product equals the wage.

Figure 15.2 represents the marginal revenue product curve for lab technicians. The curve is downward sloping, illustrating the law of diminishing returns. Assuming competitive markets, the MRP curve in Figure 15.2 is found by multiplying the marginal product curve (not shown) by the price of output. The optimal number of lab technicians depends on the wage rate. At wage W_1, the optimal input demand at point A is L_1; in contrast, at a higher wage, W_2, the firm would demand fewer technicians, L_2, at point B.

This analysis shows that the demand for labor is precisely the marginal revenue product of labor curve. It is closely related to the production function for the laboratory test and is related directly to the price of the output laboratory tests. If the price of the lab tests rises, then the marginal revenue product $P \times MP_L$ rises, and more labor is demanded. If better machines are made available, then the technicians might become even more productive, also raising the demand for their services.

FACTOR SUBSTITUTION AND LABOR DEMAND

At this point, recall the meaning and importance of the substitutability of one input for another. Suppose, for example, a new machine is invented that allows lab technicians to perform certain functions that were formerly done by radiologists. This makes technicians better substitutes for radiologists. As a result, the demand for technicians will tend to increase. Furthermore, this change also will tend to shift the demand for radiologists and probably make it more elastic—that is, flatter and more responsive to the wage rate. As a result, if the firm finds it can substitute more easily between inputs, it will tend to

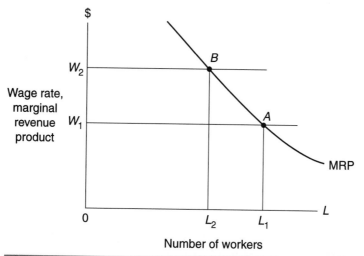

FIGURE 15.2 Firm Hiring Decision at Different Wage Levels.

become more resistant to input price changes, replacing increasingly expensive inputs with cheaper substitutes.

In recent decades, firms and policy makers have become especially interested in substitution possibilities because of the impetus to turn to physician extenders in efforts to control health care costs. To the extent that nonphysician providers can substitute for physicians, they allow firms to hire lower-cost workers, hence cutting costs and possibly increasing the amount of the service provided. We address this issue in more detail later in the chapter.

The market demand for various occupations is determined by the combined labor demands of all firms. The market demand is determined by horizontally summing the demands of the individual firms. The market demand for laboratory technicians is illustrated in Figure 15.3 by the downward sloping curve labeled D_1. Under competitive conditions, the determination of a labor market equilibrium, and consequently of the equilibrium wage, depends on the interaction of both demand and supply.

THE SUPPLY OF LABOR

The supply of labor tends to slope upward, implying that the higher the wage rate is in a given market, the more workers will be forthcoming. First, those workers currently employed may choose to work more hours if higher wages are offered. Second, similar workers may be attracted into the market from elsewhere. The labor supply curve for lab technicians is shown in Figure 15.3 as S.

The equilibrium market wage, W_1, for technicians, along with the market clearing number of technicians, L_1, is determined by the intersection of the supply and demand curves. Consider that the market equilibrium wage will tend to rise in response to any demand-increasing event. These include increases in the firms' desires to substitute lab technicians for other laborers, increased productivity of the technicians, and increases in the price of the lab outputs. Here demand increases to D_2, with resulting increases in equilibrium wage to W_2 and number employed to L_2.

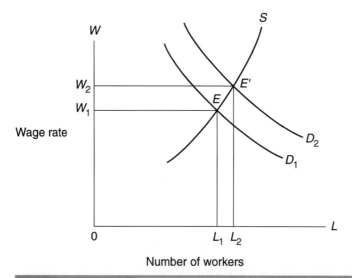

FIGURE 15.3 Market Demand and Supply for Laboratory Technicians.

Similarly, the market wage will tend to fall in response to events that increase the labor supply. These include increased graduations of trained technicians or influxes of technicians into the market from other professions or other locations.

The Human Capital Theory of Investment in Education

A major concern of manpower planning specialists is the availability of new graduates. To have an appropriate number of graduates at any given time requires that an appropriate number of applicants entered school years before. Thus, the number of graduates depends on the individual decision of the potential health professional to go to school and get the required education.

PROFESSIONAL TRAINING AS AN INVESTMENT

Consider the issues behind choosing whether or not to go to medical school. Suppose that Janet Miller, who has just graduated with a B.S. degree in biology, has an academic record that would qualify her to become a physician. She has a choice of going to work for a pharmaceutical company or going to medical school.

Her decision to become a physician is essentially an investment decision. In chapter 6, we introduced the theory of investment that suggested that people will at least in part base their investment decisions on the potential net returns from the investment.[2] Because investment decisions usually deliver their payoffs over time, we must consider the entire stream of costs and benefits that Janet will incur over the life of the investment.

What are the costs of an investment in medical school to Janet? Two categories of costs exist:

[2]This, of course, is a simplification. Physicians are likely to get utility out of doing good for other people. To the extent that this is the case, then part of the investment in medical school does in fact provide utility.

- The opportunity costs of forgone earnings because Janet cannot work while going to school.
- The out-of-pocket costs for the medical education.

Medical education takes a considerable amount of time: four years of medical school plus several years of residency. During at least part of this time, Janet will earn less than she would have earned had she gone directly to work with her B.S. degree. These forgone earnings are a cost like any other. In addition, medical school is costly in itself.

Also consider her potential earnings stream. By investing in a medical education, Janet can expect to have an earnings advantage—in most countries a substantial one—over a worker who has a B.S. degree. As we have noted, this advantage comes only after many years, but then it likely continues throughout her working life.

Notice that the largest costs come in the early years, while the largest payoffs come in later years. Thus, Janet needs to consider the value of a given dollar today in comparison to her valuation today of a given dollar that she will receive only many years from now. Most people will tend to give less value or importance to dollars paid in the distant future.[3]

DISCOUNTING AND THE INTERNAL RATE OF RETURN

Discounting future values is done by dividing future dollars by a discount factor that equals $(1 + r)^t$ where r is the discount rate and t represents the year, starting with $t = 1$ to represent the first year. Suppose that the costs Janet incurs through time are C_t, where t refers to each period of time. Recall that her costs in the early years, C_1, C_2, C_3, and so on, will be fairly high because of medical school costs and forgone earnings, but the costs in later years, such as C_{12}, C_{13}, C_{14}, and so on, will be small. Similarly, the monetary and psychic returns that she earns, R_t, will be small in early years and then larger in later years. If Janet were to discount future values at 4 percent, then the present discounted value (PDV) of the investment would be:

$$\text{PDV} = \frac{R_1 - C_1}{(1 + 0.04)^1} + \frac{R_2 - C_2}{(1 + 0.04)^2} + \frac{R_3 - C_3}{(1 + 0.04)^3} + \cdots + \frac{R_n - C_n}{(1 + 0.04)^n}$$

$$= \sum_{t=1}^{t=n} \frac{R_t - C_t}{(1 + 0.04)^t} \tag{15.2}$$

If the present value is positive, this is a good investment. However, consider the fact that the present value will depend critically on the rate at which she discounts the future. If she cares little about the distant future, she will choose a high discount rate. In the present example, if she chooses a rate higher than 4 percent, the present value calculated for this investment will tend to become smaller.

We also might ask what her rate of gain is, so that we can compare the rate of gain or rate of return to that of her other investment opportunities. A common choice among economists is to calculate the internal rate of return. This is equivalent to that discount rate that would yield a net present value of zero. The internal rate of return is defined as i, such that:

$$\text{PDV} = \sum_{t=1}^{t=n} \frac{R_t - C_t}{(1 + i)^t} = 0 \tag{15.3}$$

[3]We present fundamental aspects of discounting in chapter 4.

Higher internal rates of return imply better returns on investment. Among investment opportunities, Janet will tend to choose the one with the highest internal rate of return. If this rate of return is sufficiently high, she will go to medical school because in time, the increased skills will allow her to earn more than she invested, and also will make her wealthier in the long term than she would have been otherwise.

AN EXAMPLE

Table 15.1 demonstrates this issue by example. Suppose that Janet could begin her work for a pharmaceutical company at a salary of $30,000 and could increase her earnings by 3 percent each year over 40 years, after which she would retire (in this analysis, we assume no inflation so that all of the figures are in "real" dollars). Column (b) shows Janet's salary from Years 1 through 40.[4] This is a *cost* of her education because she is giving up job earnings to go to medical school. The second cost in this admittedly simplified example is medical school tuition, which we assume starts at $20,000 and rises by $2,000 each year from Year 1 to Year 4. Total costs are noted in column (d), which adds columns (b) and (c).

What is the return to this investment in human capital? Returns to the education involve the salary that is earned because of the training. In this example, salary begins in Year 5 at $20,000 and increases by $3,000 per year each year to Year 8. In Year 9, Janet begins practice at a salary of $50,000 per year, which will increase at a rate of 5 percent each year through Year 40, at which point it will be $226,902. Column (f) shows the net return each year, which equals the gross return (column e) less the total cost (column d). Over the eight years of medical school, the net return (total returns less total costs) is −$260,770. Continuing down column (f), we discover that the net return per year once Janet begins practice rises from $11,997 in Year 9 to $131,891 in Year 40.

Is this a good investment? If r is small or 0, this implies the ability to lend or borrow at 0 percent interest. As a result, the big future returns have a big present value. The denominators of the terms referring to future returns stay close to 1, and PDV becomes large. As noted in Table 15.1, if the rate of interest were 0 percent, the net present value (total or the returns less the costs) of the investment would be $1,508,905. It would be a good investment indeed.

What if it cost 10 percent to borrow money? The denominators of the terms referring to future returns would get large (evaluate 1.10^{40} for yourself to see), discounting the future improvements in income severely. Calculating the net present value at an interest rate of 10 percent would lead to a net present value of −$56,337. Janet would be better off working in the pharmaceutical industry.

As it turns out, net present value equals 0 at a discount rate of 8.2 percent. If Janet can borrow money at a rate of less than 8.2 percent, it will pay by our investment criteria for her to invest in being a physician.

Clearly, the higher the wage level is for health providers (in this case physicians), the higher the rate of return will be for training in medical education. As a result, higher wages should lead to an increased supply of health care providers. This analysis implies the upward-sloping supply of labor curve, as we have assumed.

[4]One might argue that Janet took her biology degree as an investment to get into medical school. If this is the case, then this portion of her education also should be treated as a capital investment.

TABLE 15.1 Net Present Value of a Medical School Education (in dollars)

(a) Year	(b) Job Earnings	(c) Medical Tuition	(d) Total Costs (b) + (c)	(e) Returns	(f) Net Returns 0%	(g) Net Returns 10%	(h) Net Returns 8.2%
1	30,000	20,000	50,000	0	−50,000	−45,455	−46,210
2	30,900	22,000	52,900	0	−52,900	−43,719	−45,184
3	31,827	24,000	55,827	0	−55,827	−41,944	−44,070
4	32,782	26,000	58,782	0	−58,782	−40,149	−42,885
5	33,765	0	33,765	20,000	−13,765	−8,547	−9,281
6	34,778	0	34,778	23,000	−11,778	−6,648	−7,339
7	35,822	0	35,822	26,000	−9,822	−5,040	−5,657
8	36,896	0	36,896	29,000	−7,896	−3,684	−4,203
End of Formal Training							
9	38,003	0	38,003	50,000	11,997	5,088	5,901
10	39,143	0	39,143	52,500	13,357	5,150	6,072
11	40,317	0	40,317	55,125	14,808	5,190	6,222
.
.
25	60,984	0	60,984	109,144	48,160	4,445	6,712
26	62,813	0	62,813	114,601	51,788	4,345	6,670
.
.
39	92,244	0	92,244	216,097	123,854	3,010	5,725
40	95,011	0	95,011	226,902	131,891	2,914	5,634
Total	2,262,037	92,000	2,354,037	3,862,942	1,508,905	-56,337	0

CREATION OF HUMAN CAPITAL

Because Janet is investing in capital stock of knowledge for herself, economists term such an investment as the creation of *human capital*. Human capital investment consists not only of paid schooling but also of:

- explicit on-the-job training programs.
- improved skills from actually doing the work, which economists call *learning by doing*.

Surgeons are taught procedures with the slogan "see one, do one, teach one." The formation of human capital in all fields varies from job to job, depending on the combination of these factors. Here we emphasize the types of human capital formation achieved through education. We realize, however, that substantive differences exist among types of education.

Information regarding the rate of return to a medical education also is useful to the policy analyst. Suppose we were to discover that the average rate of return to medical education is high and rising. This information might suggest that physicians are becoming increasingly scarce, thus suggesting a shortage. Numerous studies have attempted to estimate the rate of return to a medical education.

Factor Productivity and Substitution among Factors

The supply of health services, and consequently health care prices, clearly depends on the number of workers. However, a critical determinant of supply is the productivity of labor inputs. Productivity improvements increase output: Alternatively, the same output can be produced with fewer inputs. In a macroeconomic sense, general improvements in productivity represent a major source of economic growth and rising standards of living. At a microeconomic level, productivity gains in an industry can lead to lower prices for the goods and services produced in that industry and possibly to higher rates of remuneration for workers.

The productivity of a factor of production can be measured as the average product of the factor—that is, the ratio of total output (Q) to the amount of a particular labor input (L):

$$\text{Average product of labor} = Q/L \qquad (15.4)$$

This definition corresponds to the concept of average product used in microeconomics and is distinguished from marginal product, which is defined as the change in output associated with a one-unit increase in the input, holding all others constant.

Despite the simplicity of the concept of average product, difficult problems are involved in measuring it. Output may be heterogeneous, consisting of many different outputs. In such cases, one often uses the dollar value of output for the numerator, Q. Similarly, many different kinds of labor are used in the production process. In such cases, a weighted sum of related inputs often is used in the denominator term, L.

MEASUREMENT OF PHYSICIAN PRODUCTIVITY

The classic study of physician productivity was undertaken by Reinhardt (1972). He examined general practitioners in private practice for three measures of output: total patient visits, office visits, and patient billings. In addition to physician time, he considered the use of various auxiliary personnel. Reinhardt estimated the marginal product of physician time—the increment to output resulting when one extra hour of physician time is added to the production process.

Reinhardt found that the physician's marginal product tends to increase up until the point where the physician is working a total of about 25 hours per week; the marginal product eventually declines to zero at about 110 hours per week. He found that starting from a base of 60 hours per week, a 1.0 percent increase of physician input would result in an increase of 0.8 percent in the number of patient visits produced.

In addition to studying the physician's productivity, Reinhardt examined the substitution possibilities between physician and other labor inputs. Consider physician aides. He found that the aides' marginal products were highest when approximately one aide was present per physician. Reinhardt found that physicians could improve productivity of their practices and increase profits if they doubled the number of aides from two aides per physician (the average he found) to four aides per physician.

THE EFFICIENT UTILIZATION OF PHYSICIAN ASSISTANTS—
SUBSTITUTION AMONG INPUTS

The possibility that physicians were underutilizing aides was a provocative one. In 1988, Brown reexamined this issue and refined Reinhardt's work. Brown's estimates of the marginal products of physician time and other inputs, calculated at mean values of the

variables, are shown in Table 15.2. The marginal products of auxiliary workers are shown in the columns labeled *MP* for data from physician offices of various categories: These include all physicians, solo physicians, and group practice physicians.

The columns labeled are of special interest. By dividing *MP* by the wage rate of each input to get the marginal product per dollar spent on each factor, we can draw inferences about whether physicians are underutilizing or overutilizing various categories of workers. The marginal product per dollar is the relevant measure when determining which input to increase. To increase profits, one should hire the extra input that has the greatest *MP/W*. If this marginal product per dollar is not equal for each category of worker, the firm can save money by trading lesser-producing workers per dollar (low *MP/W*) for higher-producing ones (high *MP/W*).

Brown concluded from these data that physicians were underutilizing nursing inputs. Consider, for example, the data for practical nurses in all physicians' offices. These practical nurses have a higher marginal product per dollar, 0.129, than do physicians, 0.114; thus, the offices would become more profitable if one substituted practical nurses for physicians.

In addition, Brown found that physicians in group practices were on average 22 percent more productive than those in solo practices. He suggested that this figure, much higher than the 5 percent estimated by Reinhardt, resulted from advantages that group practices have in employing physician assistants. From Table 15.2, we can see that the marginal product of physician assistants (PAs) for solo practices was estimated to be negative; in contrast, PAs are productive on the margin in group practices. Even so, group practices are underutilizing PAs.

Other more recent work provides considerable evidence on the extent of the substitutability between physician time and other labor inputs. Escarce and Pauly (1998) found that each hour of time for an office-based internist substitutes for $60 in nonphysician costs or vice versa. Elsewhere, the growth of managed care organizations has heightened interest in physician assistants (PAs) and nurse practitioners (NPs) to improve productivity and lower costs. Jacobson and colleagues (1998/99) report that PAs/NPs can perform 50 to 90 percent of the tasks of primary care physicians without

TABLE 15.2 **Marginal Products and Efficiency of Input Use**						
	All Physicians		*Solo Physicians*		*Group Physicians*	
Input	*MP*	*MP/W*	*MP*	*MP/W*	*MP*	*MP/W*
Physician	2.967	0.114	2.686	0.102	2.793	0.110
Secretary	0.192	0.043	0.253	0.058	0.105	0.023
Registered Nurse	0.585	0.104	0.628	0.109	0.625	0.114
Practical Nurse	0.542	0.129	0.533	0.132	0.485	0.109
Technician	0.320	0.067	0.321	0.059	0.278	0.057
Physician Assistant	0.231	0.040	−0.014	−0.003	1.082	0.192

MP = Marginal product
MP/W = Marginal product per dollar wages spent on input

Source: Reprinted from *Journal of Human Resources,* Brown, Douglas M., "Do Physicians Underutilize Aides?". *Journal of Human Resources* 23 (1988): 342–55 with permission from The University of Wisconsin Press.

compromising quality when they work collaboratively with physicians. They also found that PAs/NPs have greater scope of practice and autonomy as the proportion of managed care patients in a health care organization increases. Despite legal impediments and other limits on the use of PAs/NPs, the delivery of primary care is likely to rely increasingly on these skilled physician substitutes as organizations try to move toward their optimal input mix.

Health Manpower Availability

A recurrent policy concern in twentieth-century America has been the availability of various critical categories of health manpower. The issue usually hangs on whether we have or will have enough of these people; that is, whether there will be shortages or surpluses. Before addressing such questions, we first examine the data, asking how many health care laborers of various kinds there are, and how these numbers have been changing.

Table 1.3b presented data on a selection of health manpower groups. In each category, the total number of professionals has increased, often substantially, since 1970. The population of ordinary citizens (the potential consumers) also increased during the period. Except for podiatrists and dentists, however, Table 1.3b made clear that the number of professionals has been increasing more rapidly, so the number of professionals per 100,000 population also has increased. In fact, the rate of increase for physicians and registered nurses per capita has been sharp.

AVAILABILITY OF PHYSICIANS

In the following sections, we will use the example of physicians to explore manpower planning and nurses to examine concepts of shortages. Because medical physicians have a substantial degree of control over input use in the U.S. health care system, we will consider this critical group in some detail. An important consideration in manpower availability analysis is the availability of personnel to provide needed or demanded patient care. Many federal physicians (approximately 20,000, or 3 percent of the total) provide services only to the portion of the population eligible, such as veterans. Furthermore, many physicians are in nonpatient care employment. Because the portion providing office-based patient care to the public has not changed much over recent decades, the rapid increase in physicians per capita also has meant a greater number of patient care physicians per capita.

Of the 644,000 active, nonfederal medical doctors (M.D.s) in the United States in 1996, about 581,000 provided direct patient care (Table 15.3). Of those, about three-fourths were office based and the rest were hospital based, including residents. As we noted previously, the pattern of the portion of physicians available for patient care has not been changing rapidly.[5]

[5]Doctors of Osteopathy (D.O.s) numbered 37,000 in 1996. Although it is often useful to combine osteopaths with M.D.s when considering physician supply and access to physician care, there have been major differences in the historical development and organization of the two groups. Thus, unless otherwise indicated, our discussion will focus specifically on M.D.s.

TABLE 15.3 Physicians by Type of Practice: 1980–1996

Type of Practice	Number in 1,000s			Percent		
	1980	*1990*	*1996*	*1980*	*1990*	*1996*
All Physicians	487	646	775	100	100	100
M.D.s	468	615	738	95	95	95
Active Nonfederal	418	540	644	86	84	83
Patient Care	362	488	581	74	76	75
Other	56	52	63	11	8	8
Federal	18	21	20	4	3	3
Inactive/Unknown Address	32	55	74	7	9	10
Doctors of Osteopathy	19	31	37	4	5	5

Source: U.S. Department of Commerce, *Statistical Abstract of the United States* (1998).

Physicians do not form a homogeneous group. Instead, they form a large number of specialties. About 50 percent of office-based physicians practice in primary care and 20 percent are in general surgery or the surgical specialties. The remainder have other specialties. Concerns about specialization as well as about uneven distributions between rural and urban areas have long been heard in the United States.

PHYSICIAN SPECIALTIES AND LICENSURE

Physicians must be licensed by a state in order to practice in that state. Requirements for licensure include graduation from an accredited medical school, passing a licensure examination, and completing one to two years of internship or residency in an accredited graduate medical education program. Many graduates, nevertheless, complete three- to four-year residency programs. Many physicians also become board-certified specialists. The requirements typically include advanced residency training for periods of three to six years, practice in the specialty, and passing of the board examination.

Like the decision to become a physician in the first place, the decision to seek board certification plausibly will respond to economic incentives. Wilensky and Rossiter (1983) suggest that board certification tends to increase the typical physician's annual income by nearly $13,000 on average but varies from specialty to specialty. Against these substantial future income gains, the physician considering whether or not to seek board certification would have to weigh the opportunity costs, as in any human capital investment decision.

Manpower Planning and the Meaning of Shortages

In one sense, planning, or looking ahead and preparing for the future, speaks for itself. What is more at issue, at least in America, is whether someone else, such as a government body, must, should, or can plan effectively on behalf of society as a whole.

THE ROLE OF HEALTH MANPOWER PLANNING

In the case of health manpower, the long time lags between entering a professional school and becoming a practicing professional suggest the need for forethought and invite the question of whether market forces alone will suffice. Thus, health manpower

planning, at least in the further sense of investigating whether or not market forces are adequate, also seems eminently sensible.

What market forces exist that would tend to ensure that a sufficient number of health professionals will complete their training when they are needed? The market relies on certain information signals to achieve this spontaneous coordination.

Recall the human capital investment decision of the potential health professional. The individual must investigate whether the stream of costs and benefits over time of this particular career provides a sufficient rate of return, meaning a sufficient reward. In doing this analysis, the individual inherently must guess at the salary levels that can be attained as a professional. A physician's future salaries, for example, will depend on the supply and demand of physicians in the future. If physicians are in "short supply"—one sense in which we would say they are needed—then physician salaries will tend to be high, thus sending the right signal to potential physicians.

Will these information signals and the thousands of individual decisions suffice to provide adequately for future needs? They seem to work for other forms of professional education, such as for law schools. One way in which they may do poorly is in a case where the information available to potential professionals is weak or otherwise faulty. One role for manpower planning is to provide potential professionals with better information.

Often, however, we act through our government agencies to use other devices to ensure that adequate manpower is available. One common device is government subsidization of professional education, sometimes to the point where the government virtually controls access to education. In fact, the present level of subsidization for education of all kinds is so substantial that the argument comes full circle. One may well argue that if the government controls access to health manpower training already, then it must do health manpower planning.

Nevertheless, a less prominent government role is required to the extent that market forces—perhaps with the aid of increased information and existing government involvement—will lead to adequate availability of manpower in future years. We must ask, regardless of one's preferences for governmental involvement, what *is* an adequate quantity of health manpower?

NEED-BASED APPROACHES TO HEALTH MANPOWER PLANNING

The lay public may see different possible answers to the question of an adequate quantity of health manpower. Much of the confusion can be resolved through an analysis of the various reasons for the many determinations of manpower requirements, including necessarily the many definitions of health manpower shortages.

Two basic types of shortages are described in the literature: need shortages and economic shortages. Need shortages, for the present purpose, will be identified as determinations of manpower shortages that use a nonmarket, or noneconomic, definition of shortage. In some cases, determinations of need shortages in the health literature inappropriately ignore economics and economic laws. In other cases, need determinations either implicitly or explicitly reject the market as the arbiter of how much health care people will get.

Shortages Based on Medical Grounds

One common method of determining health manpower requirements is to base these calculations on purely medical grounds. Health care professionals and providers

will recognize a far different standard of needed health manpower than will others, such as politicians, economists, or perhaps the public at large. The most important early work that employed a medical determination of health manpower needs was a study by Lee and Jones (1933). Their method calculated the number of physicians necessary to perform the needed number of medical procedures. The needed number of medical procedures, in turn, was based on the incidence of a morbidity (illness) in the population.

Consider, for example, condition A, which strikes 1 percent of the population in a given county. Suppose further that its treatment requires 6 hours of physician time and that 250,000 residents live in the county. How many physicians are needed if a physician works 2,000 hours per year? The answer is fairly easy to analyze:

- 250,000 persons \times (1 morbidity/100 persons) = 2,500 morbidities
- 2,500 morbidities \times (6 hours/morbidity) = 15,000 hours
- 15,000 hours \times (1 physician/2,000 hours) = 7.5 physicians

Whether this involves seven full-time physicians and one part-time physician or some larger number of providers who also do other things is not important for this discussion, although it will be important as a practical problem. For the present, it may be concluded that 7.5 full-time equivalent physicians are needed based on the Lee–Jones style of need determination.

Suppose that the county currently has 7.5 physicians and that the county's population is projected to rise from 250,000 to 400,000. Without any adjustment for the morbidity rate or for the technology of care, the need for physicians would be projected to rise to (400,000/250,000) \times 7.5, or 12.0 physicians. If the projected (actual) total is less than 12.0, then a projected (actual) shortage is said to exist.

This type of analysis entails some severe assumptions. Even if we supposed that there are only two factors of production, physicians (L) and some amount of capital or equipment (K), the Lee–Jones approach tends to ignore the possibilities for substitution among inputs. That is, the presumption that a constant number of physicians is necessary to give a certain amount of care implies the following assumptions:

1. No substitution is made of other inputs for physician inputs.
2. No projected technological changes occur in the production of health care services.
3. The question of how many medical procedures are appropriate given the illness data for a population has one single, unique answer.
4. Manpower provided to the public will be demanded by the public or otherwise paid for.
5. Medical doctors are the appropriate body of people to determine population needs.
6. Prices and costs of various inputs are ignored.

Are these implicit assumptions realistic, and is this planning scenario realistic? As we have shown here and elsewhere, substitutions are possible in the provision of health care. Thus, Assumption 1 can be challenged.

Assumption 2 also can be challenged, as new technologies are constantly changing the answer to the question of what the best combination is of the various inputs for producing health care. Both Assumptions 1 and 2 imply falsely that a fixed single technique produces health care. This is what Fuchs (1974) has criticized as the monotechnic approach.

It also is possible to substitute alternative medical techniques or procedures in treating a given illness; the best choice of technique will depend in part on the patient's value system. Furthermore, medically determined needs, even if they were to reflect a consensus of the medical profession, may not represent a consensus of the public, given the multiple public and private objectives involved in setting national as well as personal priorities. Also, even some people who are not usually cynical might question the wisdom of asking the physicians to determine how many physicians are needed. Finally, the medically determined needs approach suggests by omission that one can ignore costs in determining national priorities, a proposition that could be true only if there were no scarcity.[6]

Assessing Need-Based Approaches

Rejection of so many of the premises underlying the medically determined needs approach cannot easily be extended into a rejection of *all* need-based approaches. Need determinations need not be determined only medically. Consideration of the public's preferences can in principle be incorporated in setting health goals. We can recognize that health manpower need determinations must operate within the context of markets and must obey economic laws. After all, the expression by an informed group within the public at large might reasonably argue that many people in America are not getting the health care they need.

If we accept the health manpower need determination of any group of concerned citizens as being an expression of their informed opinions and their values, much of the mystery surrounding need determinations disappears. To treat health manpower need determinations as expressions of needs derived from legitimate health goals is not to trivialize them. To recognize that different groups will plausibly make different statements about how much health care the country needs is not to say we should ignore them all. The alarms sent by such groups, while perhaps not as objective as some scientific determination, may be important to society's well-being. However, a recognition that need determinations inherently reflect people's values explains the multiplicity of reported needs because people's values differ.

This account of need shortages—that is, accounts of health manpower requirements based at least partly on nonmarket criteria—inevitably leads to many questions. For example, is there a best way to determine these needs? Is there a fair way? Such questions lie in the realm of normative economics.

ECONOMIC DEFINITIONS OF SHORTAGES OF HEALTH PROFESSIONALS

Economic definitions of manpower shortages are usually different from those based solely on medical grounds. Economists often apply definitions based on considerations of how a given market for professionals deviates from an ideal, efficient market.

One can expect that economic definitions of shortages will be somewhat more objective, inasmuch as the concept of an efficient market can be defined objectively. Consequently, one might expect the development of a single, clear definition of an economic shortage of health manpower. Unfortunately, several economic definitions exist.

[6]See Pauly (1971) for further discussion on this issue.

Workforce Planning versus the Power of Markets

The rapid growth of managed care in the 1990s has led to the popular view that there are too many specialists and physicians overall, though probably not enough primary care physicians. HMOs and other managed care organizations are under intense pressure to control their costs by eliminating unnecessary care, by improving physician productivity, and by substituting cheaper inputs for more expensive inputs (e.g., primary care providers for specialists; nonphysician providers for physicians). These trends are expected to reduce the demand for physicians, especially specialists. Various projections of the "correct" supply of physicians have been based on HMO ratios.

Can we rely on the marketplace to make these and other adjustments? Support for planning and regulating the health care workforce is based in part on the idea of supplier-induced demand; that is, the demand–supply model just does not apply to physician markets. Reinhardt (1994b) summarizes the two main weaknesses of health care markets as follows:

First, . . . our medical schools and teaching hospitals can dictate the size and composition of the physician supply with virtual autonomy. Second, . . . once trained, physicians enjoy almost total discretion in dictating the volume and composition of the health care they render patients. Combined with considerable discretion in setting their own fees, the physicians' ability to control the volume of their services "demanded" by the patients allows physicians to extract from society very high "target incomes," virtually regardless of the local physician–population ratio (pp. 252–253).

On the other hand, some experts suggest that the aging population, new diseases, and new technologies requiring additional physician inputs invalidate existing projections of physician surpluses. The questionable historical record of regulation in the United States coupled with the public's distrust of government and its preference for market solutions are also powerful arguments for relying on market forces. Finally, Moore (1994) describes how markets are already working (e.g., through higher salaries and benefits for primary care physicians in HMOs) to meet the transition to managed care.

Excess Demand

Consider as a starting point the conventional economic definition of a shortage: the excess of the quantity demanded over the quantity supplied at market prices. Figure 15.4 depicts a shortage defined in this way: The health manpower shortage at the wage W_1 is equal to $L_{d1} - L_{s1}$. If the wage instead had been W_2, no shortage would exist. This is because at the higher wage, less labor services would have been demanded and more would have been supplied.[7]

[7]Lane and Gohmann (1995) provide a dramatic example of the difference between the economic approach to nursing shortages and a noneconomic need-based approach developed by the Office of Shortage Designations. The office identifies counties with shortages by using the ratio of full-time equivalent nurses in short-term general hospitals to the average daily number of patients. The economic model identified 423 counties (out of 1,880) as shortage areas, while the noneconomic approach designated 565 counties. Notably, the two models agreed on only 133 cases of shortage.

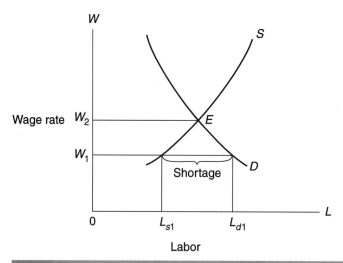

FIGURE 15.4 An Economic Shortage.

This definition, though valid, raises critical questions in the case of health manpower. The main question is why the wage does not rise to equilibrium, thus automatically eliminating the shortage. The usual case of persistent excess demand is associated with stickiness in wages or prices imposed by law or regulation. A common example is rent control, which is sometimes found in the market for rental housing.

What would cause wage stickiness in health manpower markets? It seems doubtful that health manpower wages are sticky in this sense, or that health manpower shortages in terms of excess demand are a serious policy problem. Some analysts have argued, in fact, that excess demand shortages are not serious concerns for most categories of professionals.

Relatively Rapid Increases in Wages: Dynamic Shortages

An unnecessary focus on excess demand also obscures the fact that economically meaningful shortages of professionals may well exist even when supply and demand are in short-term equilibrium. In particular, a shortage may occur when demand and supply conditions change over time. Suppose, for example, that demand for a category of health professionals expands over time, and that the supply of these professionals is slow to respond or even perhaps faces barriers in responding. The result may be a large rise in wages relative to the wage gains of other professionals.[8]

To illustrate, consider Figure 15.5, which depicts the demand for physicians at two points in time: an initial Period 1 and a subsequent Period 2. We compare the equilibrium (supply equal to demand) in Period 1 with that in Period 2. The wage increase from W_1 to W_2 may indicate a shortage, even though supply equals demand (at L_1 and L_2) in both periods. We would say a shortage exists if the relative wage of physicians has risen sharply relative to that of other professionals. The measure of shortage under this approach is the relative wage and the direction of its movement.

[8]See Blank and Stigler (1957) for further discussion.

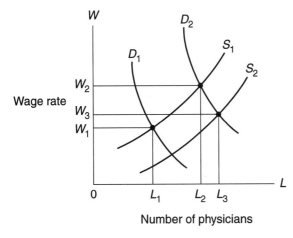

FIGURE 15.5 Change in Equilibrium Wage over Time Depending on Supply Adjustments.

Several variations on this general approach have been described. The pattern of wages over time may be more complex than the movement described from equilibrium at W_1 to an equilibrium at W_2. We might find, for example, that the initial market response to increased demand for the professionals would be to raise wages to W_2; only after these high wages had induced the expansion of supply to S_2 would we observe market wages adjusting to W_3 (and supply to L_3). Under this scenario, the professional's wage for a time falls, here from W_2 to W_3. Thus, a decline in relative wage during a given period may reflect a long-run adjustment offsetting a shortage and not necessarily an indication of excessive supply.

Relative Rates of Return

How should we measure the monetary gains from professional training?[9] Hansen (1964) provides a measurement approach that is both plausible and consistent with the theory we have developed. He proposes that the relevant measure of monetary gains to a given health professional group must take into account the various opportunity costs incurred by professionals in obtaining their training. As we have seen, a measure that attempts to accomplish this conceptual task is the internal rate of return.

Because the internal rate of return to education is the rate of discount that equates the present value of the stream of costs and benefits of education to zero, the higher the rate of return is, the greater the financial rewards are to investment in the human capital attained through education. Thus, to determine whether a given health professional group is in relatively short supply, we can compare the internal rate of return to that of other professionals and examine the pattern of these comparative data over time.

High, even excessive, rates of return may occur whenever the supply of labor fails to respond quickly to changes in demand. In some instances, the underlying reason for this slowness in response may be barriers to entry faced by potential health professionals. A barrier to entry exists, in this case, when a potential health professional faces higher entry costs than incumbents faced.

[9]Yett (1975) provides a detailed discussion of the problems of the alternative approaches to measurement.

This definition includes cases where potential entrants are completely barred from entry. Such barriers would occur if controls on slots in health professional schools limited entry. They also occur to some degree whenever entry to the profession is limited by licensure laws. The issue of licensure laws is of special interest here because it is common in the health professions. Because of this connection, we treat the empirical literature on rates of return to physician education in the discussion of licensure in chapter 16.

THE ROLE OF MONOPSONY POWER— SHORTAGES OF REGISTERED NURSES

Practitioners who describe health manpower availability often rely on reported percentages of unfilled, budgeted positions. One explanation of this measure (using Figure 15.4) is excess demand. Excess demand, however, is generally a temporary phenomenon; as long as prices are not rigid, price rises will tend to cure the problem. More plausibly, the analyst will focus on changes in the percentage of unfilled, budgeted positions, analogous to dynamic definitions of manpower shortages. First, however, we must address the problem of interpreting reported data for markets that are monopsonistic.

Monopsonistic Labor Markets

Under monopsony, a firm may report unfilled, budgeted positions, for example, for registered nurses, even when the firm is actually in equilibrium. A *monopsony* is a market that in theory has only one buyer; for example, a monopsony would be one hospital that hires virtually all registered nurses in the market. The paradox is that such a monopsony firm may announce that it wishes to hire more nurses even though it is unlikely to take the necessary steps to do so.

The paradox is explained by the monopsony firm's upward-sloping supply curve. Because it is a big employer, it has the power to influence nurses' wages and thus to induce more nurses to work by raising the average nurse wage level. The monopsony firm is willing to hire more nurses *at the current wage,* but it has no intention of paying a higher wage in order to hire more nurses.

These ideas can be illustrated with the help of Figure 15.6. Here we imagine that one hospital is the only demander of nurse labor in the market. The hospital's demand curve for nurse labor, labeled D, represents the marginal revenue product curve for nurses employed at that hospital.

What the monopsony element brings to the analysis is the fact that the supply curve for labor will no longer represent the marginal labor cost, MLC, to this hospital. Contrast what would have happened had this hospital been a competitive hirer. Competition would have meant that the hospital could have hired as many nurses as it wanted at any given wage. In a competitive market, N_d workers will be hired at wage W_1. In contrast, the monopsonist will hire fewer and at a lower wage.

Consider the monopsonist's marginal labor cost curve, MLC. When the monopsonist hospital seeks to add one nurse to its labor force, it must pay a higher wage than before in order to induce this marginal (extra) nurse to work. But it then must pay *all* of its employed nurses a higher wage. The problem arises entirely because the labor sup-

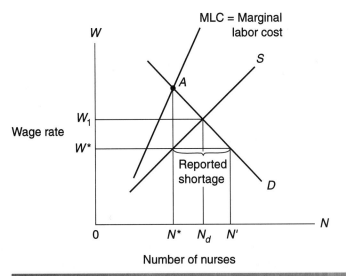

FIGURE 15.6 Nurse Shortage under Monopsony Conditions.

ply curve faced by this firm is rising as is typical under monopsony, instead of being flat as is typical under competition.

The extra (marginal) labor cost incurred for that one nurse is not just the wage it pays, it also includes the extra wages it must pay all its other nurses. As a result, the marginal labor cost curve, MLC, will lie above the labor supply curve, *S*.

Reported Shortages

Suppose now that the hospital acts to maximize its profits. It would find it profitable to hire an additional nurse as long as the extra revenue the new nurse brought in, the marginal revenue product, is greater than the extra cost of the nurse to the hospital, the marginal labor cost. Thus, as long as the demand curve (the marginal revenue product) lies above the marginal labor cost curve for a given level of nurse employment, it always will pay to hire more nurses. The hospital achieves its profit-maximizing complement of nurses where $D = \text{MLC}$, an employment level of N^* nurses in Figure 15.6. The equilibrium wage is found on the corresponding point of the labor supply curve; here it is W^*.

At this equilibrium wage, W^*, the hospital would desire to hire N' nurses. It may well budget for these nurses and effectively report a shortage of $(N' - N^*)$. The hospital acts as if it did not realize that if it wants more nurses to work, it must pay its nurses more. At any rate, a shortage in this case has a limited meaning; it only means additional nurses are desired *at the current wage level.*

This theoretical point suggests the hazards of interpreting data on unfilled budget positions. The existence of monopsony power in labor markets suggests that unfilled positions data may overstate the problems of nursing availability. The problem is somewhat mitigated by the fact that these data typically represent unfilled *budgeted* positions because a hospital is unlikely to budget for all the positions it theoretically

Are Nursing Markets Monopsonistic?

Do nursing labor markets, in fact, tend to be monopsonistic? The question has been approached by many empirical researchers, but there are generally two approaches. Some have examined the relationship between hospital market concentration measures and measures of nursing wages. If markets are more like monopsonies (having higher levels of market concentration), then the typical firm labor supply is more likely to be upward sloping (reflecting the monopsony power). Thus, nurse wages will tend to be depressed below their marginal revenue product. Studies of this type often have found a negative relationship as expected by the theory. Higher concentration levels were associated statistically with lower wages.[10]

A somewhat more direct measure of the theoretical constructs was reported by Sullivan (1989). Instead of estimating the association between concentration and wages, he developed estimates of the typical firm's labor supply curve. This is a more direct approach because the essential problem is that the monopsonist's labor supply curve is upward sloping.

Sullivan found that the typical hospital's labor supply appeared to be upward sloping to a degree that suggested considerable monopsony power. The Sullivan results support several previous studies that reported the existence of a significant degree of monopsony power in the nursing labor markets. Is this conclusion too strong? Hirsch and Schumacher (1995) correctly point out that an upward-sloping labor supply curve for nurses is a necessary but insufficient condition for monopsony effects. The authors examined RN wages relative to wages for females with a college degree across a large number of markets. Relative wages were not related positively to the number of hospitals per square mile as predicted by the monopsony model, and similar results were obtained from analyses of relative wages for other nursing personnel.

Is unionization a countervailing force to hospital monopsony power? The answer appears to be no. In another article, the same authors (1998) corroborate earlier research showing that the wage premium associated with unionization is lower in health care than elsewhere. Within health care occupations, the union effect is lower for more-skilled workers such as RNs than for lower-skilled workers such as nursing aides.

desires at the current wage. Furthermore, the analyst might in any case be interested in changes in the percentage of unfilled budgeted positions. If the number of unfilled positions were rising rapidly, it would suggest an increasingly relative scarcity of nurses.

Conclusions

In this chapter, we have discussed the training and utilization of labor in the health sector of the economy. We have shown how some fairly elementary tools of economic analysis can provide important insights into the demand and supply of labor in the health sector.

[10]See, for example, Hurd (1973), Link and Landon (1975), and Feldman and Scheffler (1982). However, Adamanche and Sloan (1982) found no evidence of association between wages and concentration.

Perhaps the most controversial aspect is the discussion of manpower planning, as it challenges some venerable traditions of health services research. The implications are not trivial. The training of health professionals is costly and time-consuming. Appropriate measures of the need, and of the productivity of the trained professionals and their substitutes, could save millions of dollars that might be used more productively elsewhere.

The training and location of physicians are two of the most important aspects of health sector manpower analysis, given their importance in the provision of health care. We turn to these issues in chapter 16.

Summary

1. In 1998, 11.5 million people, nearly 9 percent of the U.S. labor force, were employed at health services sites.
2. The demand for labor is precisely the marginal revenue product of labor curve. It is closely related to the production function and is directly related to the price of the output.
3. The supply of labor tends to slope upward, implying that the higher the wage rate is in a given market, the more laborers will be forthcoming. Workers currently employed may choose to work more hours if higher wages are offered; other workers may be attracted from elsewhere by the higher wages.
4. The higher the wage rate is for health providers such as physicians, the higher the rate of return is for medical education. As a result, higher wages should lead to an increased supply of health care providers.
5. Reinhardt found that the physician's marginal product tends to increase until the physician is working a total of about 25 hours per week; the marginal product eventually declines to zero at about 110 hours per week.
6. Reinhardt also found that physicians could improve productivity of their practices and increase profits by doubling the number of aides from the average of two aides per physician.
7. There are basically two types of shortages: need shortages and economic shortages. Need shortages use a nonmarket, or noneconomic, definition of *shortage.*
8. One definition of an economic shortage is the excess of quantity demanded over the quantity supplied at the market wage rate. Stickiness in wages helps explain why the wage does not rise to equilibrium, thus automatically eliminating the shortage.
9. Meaningful shortages of professionals may exist even when supply and demand are in short-term equilibrium. If demand for a category of health professional expands over time and supply is slow to respond, the result may be a rise in the wage that is large relative to wage gains of other professionals.
10. Under labor monopsony conditions, a firm may report unfilled, budgeted positions, for example, for registered nurses, even when the firm is in equilibrium. A monopsony firm may announce that it wishes to hire more nurses even though it is unlikely to take the necessary steps to do so.

Discussion Questions

1. Give examples of ways in which labor and capital can be substituted for each other in the production of health services.
2. What is the meaning of the term *internal rate of return?*

3. In the text, we considered only forgone income and tuition as costs to medical school. Enumerate other monetary and nonmonetary opportunity costs to medical school.

4. What is "learning by doing" for physicians and other health care professionals? How does this differ from formal education?

5. Why might demand for nurse labor by hospitals or other organized health providers be monopsonistic?

6. What is the marginal product of an input? Marginal revenue product? Why does the demand for a factor correspond to the marginal revenue product curve? What will determine whether the demand for a factor will be elastic or inelastic?

7. Why will a profit-maximizing physician firm want to equalize the marginal product per dollar spent across all inputs?

8. What are the key assumptions of the needs-based approach to manpower planning in the Lee–Jones study? Is there evidence to invalidate one or more of the assumptions?

9. What is meant by the term *barriers to entry?* What are some entry barriers for someone who wants to be an obstetrician? For someone who wants to be a nursing assistant?

10. If barriers to entry into a profession were absolute so that entry would not be possible, what would the supply curve look like? What would the supply curve look like if entry into an occupation were free and easy? Thus, what role do barriers to entry play in explaining relative rates of return to an occupation?

11. Define *monopsony* and *marginal labor cost*. Why is the marginal labor cost in the case of monopsony above the supply (average labor cost) curve? What is the nature of the inefficiency or misallocation associated with monopsony power? Is there any inefficiency when the supply curve facing the monopsonist is perfectly elastic?

Exercises

1. Consider the firm's demand for labor, such as in Figure 15.2. If the demand elasticity is −0.5, what will be the effect of increased wages on total labor earnings?

2. Using Figure 15.3, graph and analyze the impact of an increase in the price of lab tests on the labor market.

3. Consider the market for highly skilled laboratory technicians. Graph the impacts on market wages if limitations on immigration were lifted. Would more or fewer services be provided? What would happen to the price?

4. In this chapter, we discuss how physicians' marginal products rise up to 25 hours and then slowly fall to zero at 110 hours. Graph both marginal and total products from this statement.

5. In Table 15.1, Janet Miller's wage is assumed to rise by 5 percent per year once she graduates from medical school. What would happen to the net present value of her investment in medical education if her wage rose by 4 percent instead of 5 percent? What would happen to the internal rate of return to her investment?

16

The Training and Practice of Physicians

■ Medical Education Issues and the Question of Control

■ Licensure and Monopoly Rents

■ Physician Supply Decisions

■ Geographic Location of Physicians

■ Conclusions

From their authority in treatment decisions, physicians are the dominant providers in the health economy. Most other health care workers carry out their tasks under the direction of physicians. As a result, economists have concentrated on the training and practice of physicians even though they represent a minority of health workers providing patient care. We explore four aspects that provide particular insight, as well as the use of important economic analytical tools:

- **Medical Education** Physicians generally must attend four years of medical school, an additional three to four years of residency training, and often after that, engage in an additional amount of specialist training. They thus postpone their main earning years well past the age of 30. This training process clearly limits both short- and long-term responses to any changes in market conditions.
- **Licensure** Physicians must be licensed at the state level in order to practice medicine. We will address the motives for licensure laws, as well as the effects of entry restrictions on rates of return to medical education and the quality of care.
- **Supply Decisions** The private practicing physician makes two interrelated decisions: the supply of labor and, through use of nonphysician inputs in the production process, the supply of services to patients. We will examine the relationship between the two supply decisions and also consider the possibility and consequences of negatively sloped supply curves.

- **Geographic Location of Physicians** Many accounts have been given of towns losing their doctor, or not having one to begin with, while developers in major cities with large numbers of doctors may be building new clinics to accommodate still more doctors who wish to work there. We address the economic aspects of geographic location that may account for the patterns that have emerged over time.

Medical Education Issues and the Question of Control

Many professions require a considerable length of time for education and training, but the time period for formal training of physicians is among the longest. In addition, medical education poses the question of who has control. Does the medical profession itself exercise control over access to medical education in order to improve its own profitability? It is helpful to study medical schools and their funding, as well as information about the supply of potential medical students.

SOURCES OF MEDICAL SCHOOL REVENUES

Medical school education is subsidized heavily by government. This situation is an outcome of public concern for the adequacy of the supply of physician labor. The rapid growth in medical school enrollments did not arise by accident. Several actions by Congress, beginning with the Health Professions Educational Assistance Act in 1963, provided grants to medical schools and financial assistance to students. Some of this federal support hinged on enrollment increases. In 1971, however, federal support to medical schools was increased substantially and came in the form of capitation grants, which were grants that rewarded the medical schools for expanding their enrollments by giving money on a per-student basis, initially about $3,000 per year per student (Newhouse 1978a). With fears of physician surpluses emerging by the late 1970s, assistance under the Health Professions Educational Assistance Act was phased out and enrollments stabilized.

Nevertheless, medical education still is subsidized heavily. Table 16.1 shows the sources of revenue for U.S. medical schools during various years. Tuition represents a relatively small source of revenues; thus, the student pays only a small portion of the true costs of the investment in education. Note that governmental support comes both as support for operating revenues and through grants and contracts. Total government support for medical schools in the 1996 to 1997 school year was about 30 percent of total revenues.

CAPITAL MARKET IMPERFECTIONS JUSTIFY SUBSIDIES

The policy that students pay for a relatively small share of their training raises questions in light of the fact that physicians earn high incomes and receive relatively high rates of return on their investment. However, at least part of this subsidy can be understood as a policy that attempts to overcome imperfections in capital markets. The capital markets at issue are those markets where potential medical students would have to go to get the loans needed to pay for their education. The imperfections at issue are economic imperfections stemming from the difficulty to get these markets to lend up to the full value of the investment.

Even though it is clear that a medical education pays off handsomely, it is difficult for a potential lender to secure the loan adequately. The investment in education is an investment in human capital. Human capital cannot be bought and sold in the same way that physical capital can be.

TABLE 16.1 U.S. Medical School Revenues

	Academic Year		
	1960–1961	*1980–1981*	*1996–1997*
Number of schools reporting	87	119	125
	Percentage from Operating Revenues		
Federal/state/local appropriations	15.8	21.8	8.9
Other government support	4.4	6.9	---
Practice plans	3.0	15.6	34.2
Tuition and fees	6.4	5.4	3.9
Endowment and gifts	7.3	1.9	3.9
Parent university support	4.1	1.6	0.7
Reimbursement from hospitals		9.2	15.7
Miscellaneous	9.2	3.6	3.5
Total General Operating Revenues	50.2	65.9	71.0
	Percentage from Grants and Contracts		
Research	27.3	17.1	18.0
Teaching/training/other grants	22.7	17.0	11.0
Total grants and contracts	50.0	34.1	29.0
Total Revenues	*100.0*	*100.0*	*100.0*

Source: Jolin et al. (1991) for 1960–1961 and 1980–1981; Jones et al. (1998) for 1996–1997.

To make the point plain, one cannot repossess a human being. While the bank knows that the typical medical graduate easily can afford to repay the loan, it is difficult to guarantee this repayment in an individual case. Thus, potential medical students may not get the needed loans even though the investment is well worthwhile. From society's point of view, this problem may result in insufficient numbers of medical students.

Leffler and Lindsay (1981) conclude that with such capital market imperfections, reliance on private markets leads to an underinvestment in medical education. Thus, government support can be justified on economic grounds. These authors estimated that an optimal level of support would be about 36 percent of the costs of medical education, which is a substantial figure.

TEACHING HOSPITALS, MEDICAL SCHOOLS, AND JOINT PRODUCTION

Medical education is a good example of joint production. That is, medical schools produce at least three products jointly:

- Medical education.
- Patient care.
- Research.

To reimburse for patient care or to fund medical education appropriately, it is necessary to determine the pure costs and the joint costs of these activities. An example taken from Newhouse (1978a) illustrates these terms.

In Table 16.2, the total annual cost for a medical school that produces only education and patient care is shown to be $6 million. If the school produced only education

TABLE 16.2 Hypothetical Example of Joint Production at a Medical School	Millions of Dollars
Total cost of school	6
Cost if school produced only patient care	3
Cost if school produced only education	5
"Pure" cost of education[a]	3
"Pure" cost of patient care[a]	1
Joint costs[a]	2

[a]The pure cost of education is total cost (6) less the cost of producing only patient care (3). The pure cost of patient care is total cost (6) less the cost of producing only education (5). Joint costs are total costs (6) less all pure costs (3 + 1).

Source: Newhouse (1978a).

with only the minimum patient care needed to do this, its costs would be $5 million. If it produced only its present volume of patient care and no medical education, its costs would be $3 million.

Incrementally, the cost of patient care raises the school's budget from $5 million to $6 million. Thus, the *pure cost* of patient care is the extra $1 million. Reasoning in a similar fashion, adding education to the cost of patient care raises the budget from $3 million to $6 million. Thus, the pure cost of education is $3 million.

Notice that the difference between total cost of this hypothetical medical school and all the pure costs is $2 million. This $2 million is called the *joint cost*. It follows that if the school were reimbursed only for pure costs, it would run a deficit. Much of the controversy with respect to funding revolves around the problem of who will pay for the joint costs.

The issue of joint production has centered on the teaching hospital, which also jointly produces patient care and medical education through its provision of internship, residency, and medical research. In particular, with the substantial cost differences between teaching and nonteaching hospitals, third-party payers are concerned about whether they are unnecessarily subsidizing medical education. The conventional wisdom in the 1970s was that the cost of education and affiliation with a medical school was substantial.

An examination of the cost differences between teaching and nonteaching hospitals shows that nonphysician costs per day are 21 percent higher in teaching hospitals. However, sorting out the causes for cost differences and making appropriate statistical adjustments refine these data. After this is done, nonphysician costs, though still higher in teaching hospitals, show a difference that is typically less than 10 percent.[1]

FOREIGN MEDICAL SCHOOL GRADUATES (FMGs)

Physician supply in the United States is dependent to a significant degree on foreign medical school graduates (FMGs). Nearly one-fourth of all physicians are graduates of foreign medical schools. Furthermore, the relative reliance on foreign medical school

[1]See Sloan, Feldman, and Steinwald (1983) for more detail.

graduates has changed considerably. As a portion of the total number of active physicians, foreign medical school graduates increased from less than 14 percent of the total in 1963 to 23 percent in 1996.

The availability of physicians from other countries can have important policy and planning implications, especially now that the reliance on FMGs has grown. Politzer and colleagues (1989) have estimated that the growth in their numbers has exceeded the projections by the Department of Health and Human Services. The availability of foreign national FMGs can increase the responsiveness of physician supply in the United States to changes in the physician wage.

Rapid increases in physician wages send a market signal to potential physicians; this increases the estimated rate of return to an investment in medical education. It takes a long time, however, for new applicants among American college graduates to get to medical school, get trained, and get into practice. Thus, the supply of new American physicians will respond slowly to the wage signal. However, foreign national FMGs, already trained but currently practicing elsewhere, can respond more quickly. Therefore, the availability of foreign national FMGs makes total physician supply in the United States, in principle, more elastic.

These facts about FMGs can be used by policy makers during periods of shortages and rising fees. Immigration policy can be relaxed to admit more foreign national FMGs during periods of physician shortages, and vice versa during periods of perceived physician surpluses. This, in fact, is what happened during the 1960s, when preferential treatment was given to foreign national FMGs. Requirements subsequently were tightened by a 1976 act once shortages were no longer perceived.

In addition to immigration policy, the number of FMGs, including U.S. graduates of foreign medical schools, is influenced by certification and licensure requirements. All FMGs must take certification examinations required for admission into an approved graduate medical education program. The 1976 act also placed restrictions on the access of FMGs to graduate medical education.

A frequent concern about FMGs is quality of care. Arguments for tightening standards for FMGs usually are justified on the basis of claims that these graduates are inferior in quality to those of U.S. and Canadian medical schools. Such conclusions often are based on comparisons of examination performance and other measures of the credentials and personal attributes of FMGs and their U.S. counterparts.

Studies of the quality of care provided by FMGs, however, find little difference between the two groups. Some have argued that differences are more likely to arise, if they exist, in ambulatory care settings because of a much lower level of organizational control than in hospital settings. A study that examined more than 14,000 patient episodes by nearly 1,200 physicians in three specialty groups, however, found little difference in performance. FMGs, in fact, sometimes outperformed U.S. medical school graduates.[2]

THE CONTROL OF MEDICAL EDUCATION

In 1974, Victor Fuchs wrote that "most economists believe that part [of physicians' high incomes] represents a 'monopoly' return to physicians resulting from restrictions on entry to the profession and other barriers to competition" (p. 58). What Fuchs refers to is

[2]See Rhee et al. (1986).

the claim that physicians restrict entry to their profession in order to drive up prices for their services and thus themselves make larger incomes.

Do physicians control entry to their profession in order to earn above-normal returns on their investment? This question can be asked in two steps, taking first the issue of whether physicians do, in fact, earn above-normal returns. Historically, physicians often have earned above-normal returns. Distinguished economists found this to be the case using data from early in this century, and it was suggested that control of entry was the cause. More recent studies find high returns in at least some recent historical periods.[3]

How is it that physicians could control entry? Our present ideas and beliefs about the role of organized medicine in controlling entry owe much to the writing of Kessel (1958). Kessel argued that monopoly power was attained by organized medicine in several ways, two of the most important being licensure of physicians and control of access to medical education. The first, licensure, is explored later in this chapter. At present, consider Kessel's account of the control over medical education exerted by physicians primarily through the American Medical Association.

CONTROL OVER ENTRY

Early after the founding of the American Medical Association (AMA) in 1847, the organization campaigned state by state to get the medical profession controlled through licensure. Having largely achieved this goal by the turn of the century, the AMA turned its attention to the control of medical schools, which had proliferated in number. In 1906, the Council on Medical Education of the AMA inspected the 160 medical schools existing at that time, declaring only slightly more than half of them to be acceptable. The council sought support for this position through the Carnegie Foundation, which in 1910 issued the Flexner Report calling for substantial reductions in the number of medical schools and control on their quality. Kessel argued:

> If impact on public policy is the criterion of importance, the Flexner Report must be regarded as one of the most important reports ever written. It convinced legislators that only the graduates of first class medical schools ought to be permitted to practice medicine and led to the delegation to the AMA of the task of determining what was and what was not a first class medical school (p. 28).

Following this report, the number of medical schools fell to 85 by 1920 and to 69 by 1944. Kessel pointed out that giving the AMA charge over determining the supply of physicians was like "giving the American Iron and Steel Institute the power to determine the output of steel" (p. 29). The AMA also was able to gain control over the internship/residency process through its ability to certify hospitals for such training. It also maintained control over the process through which physicians become board certified. The picture is one of significant power and means to control entry.

The AMA also was able to exercise control over substitute providers (e.g., optometrists, podiatrists, chiropractors) by influencing licensure to limit their scope of practice and later to limit third-party reimbursement for their services. Starr (1982)

[3]See Burstein and Cromwell (1985). For earlier work, see Friedman and Kuznets (1945) and Leffler (1978).

wrote of a survey of 9,000 families conducted between 1928 and 1931, which found that nonphysician providers treated only 5.1 percent of all attended cases of illness. He concluded that "physicians had medical practice pretty much to themselves" (p. 127).

Kessel's argument is historical and written near mid-century, yet many analysts point to anomalies in recent medical school data as continuing evidence of control of entry by the medical profession. The large excess demand for medical school slots by qualified applicants to medical schools has been used to support the claims. Table 16.3 shows that historically large fractions of medical school applicants in the United States are rejected; that is, there appears to be a substantial excess demand for medical school slots. Is this evidence of monopolizing control by the medical profession? Kessel's view certainly suggests that it is.

ANOTHER VIEW—THE DONOR PREFERENCE HYPOTHESIS

This simple story of professional control can be challenged on several grounds. Hall and Lindsay (1980) argue that medical schools do not take larger proportions of applicants and medical school enrollments respond only partially to applicant demand because the administrators of medical schools are responding rationally to their economic incentives. As we have seen, medical school revenues come not so much from tuition paid by students but from "donors"—that is, sources such as government agencies, alumni, businesses, research organizations, and so on. For the most part, it is these donors who are the true demanders of the output of medical schools—trained physicians.

The donors, however, often are interested only in some of the many potential graduates—those with specific attributes in terms of personal characteristics and performance and professional goals. For example, medical schools discriminate among applicants by test scores, and they also discriminate among applicants by selecting younger ones, those with specific specialization interests, and those who indicate a willingness to return to shortage areas. These attributes reflect the preferences of the donors. In other words, to ensure that donations and financial support continue, medical schools establish a selection process to recruit the "appropriately qualified" students. Thus, the data on excess medical school applicants should not be viewed as true excess demand when we see that the true demander is the medical school donor.

In addition to providing an explanation for the apparent excess demand for medical school slots, Hall and Lindsay show that medical school enrollments rise in response to both applicant demand and the more important demand for trained physician graduates by the donors. These results tend to contradict the view that medical school enrollments are controlled by the AMA to maximize the returns to its members.

	Total	**Total Percent Accepted**	**Men Applied**	**Total Accepted**	**Percent Accepted**	**Women Applied**	**Total Accepted**	**Percent Accepted**
1968	21,118	47.8	19,021	N/A	N/A	2,097	N/A	N/A
1978	36,636	45.1	27,075	12,352	45.6	9,561	4,175	43.7
1988	26,721	64.0	16,457	10,785	65.5	10,264	6,323	61.6

TABLE 16.3 Excess Demand for Medical School Slots

Source: U.S. Department of Health and Human Services (March 1990, Tables VI-A-5 and VI-A-6).

Other evidence also supports this new view. If medical schools are artificially keeping their enrollments small to benefit organized medicine, then why don't these schools also raise their tuition charges to clear the market? The fact that tuition is only a small fraction of the true costs of education tends to support the Hall and Lindsay hypothesis.

In summary, we may say that organized medicine historically exerted considerable influence over the supply of trained physicians. Such influence is consistent with a view of the profession as one seeking above-normal returns by trying to control entry of new physicians. However, data in recent decades indicate that medical school enrollments are responsive to market forces. These data further suggest that continuing to view medical education as controlled by a monolithic or conspiratorial medical profession is somewhat implausible.

Licensure and Monopoly Rents

Licensure is not unique to the health care professions. However, licensure of physicians has received unparalleled attention. The first licensure requirements (though they had little effect and were minimally enforced) for prospective doctors were passed in New York City in 1760.[4] Subsequently, many states introduced licensing, often through state medical societies. After the 1820s, however, many of the same states modified or abolished licensure. It was not until after the founding of the AMA in 1847 and the last decades of the nineteenth century that stronger licensure laws were widely promulgated.

The primary controversies with respect to licensure are its role in limiting competition and the role of professional societies on state licensure boards. The conventional view held by many economists is that organized medicine has used control of licensure for self-interest by limiting entry (and by influencing the licensure requirements of potential competitor providers to the advantage of physicians). Some, however, have advanced a public interest argument for licensure—that is, as a result of information imperfections, the public demands quality controls. Licensure and certification help fill these information gaps.

Many economists believe that licensure and professional control over medical education ensure that physicians earn economic rents, which are payments to factors over and above those necessary to induce them to provide their services. These views have been heavily influenced by the early work of Friedman and Kuznets (1945) and Kessel (1958). Friedman and Kuznets examined the relative return of physicians and dentists. After adjusting for training differentials, they estimated that about half of the 33 percent excess earnings of physicians between 1928 and 1934 represented economic rents.

Much has changed in the health industry since the publication of these earlier articles. However, the broader issues of monopoly rents and motivation for licensure remain controversial. Despite other empirical estimates supporting the rent hypotheses, several critiques of these studies have appeared. Leffler (1978) argued that many earlier studies failed to take into account some important economic considerations that tend to reduce estimates of the return. These adjustments include the high number of hours worked by physicians, their expected mortality rates, and the progressive income tax structure.[5]

[4]Starr (1982, p. 44). Starr provides a fascinating history of licensure legislation in the United States.
[5]In addition to the adjustments suggested by Leffler, Headen (1990) separated the labor from entrepreneurial returns for self-employed physicians in family practice. He found that about 16 percent of the reported incomes are associated with their entrepreneurship.

Market Conditions and Choices Facing New Physicians

New physicians have to make many choices including specialization and geographic location. These choices help determine how, where, and to whom health care is delivered. We examine two issues relevant to these choices.

First, what are the physicians' opportunities? A survey conducted by Miller and colleagues (1996) of physician competition found that about two-thirds of new physicians seek professional positions. Most others pursue additional training, especially those in radiology, the surgical specialties, and internal medicine. However, some are unable to find full-time positions in their specialty (e.g., 11 percent in pathology), while others experience difficulty finding a position in their preferred geographic location (e.g., 25 percent of anesthesiologists versus 1 percent of family practitioners).

Managed care's increasing emphasis on primary care at the expense of hospital care is a possible explanation for these conditions. The incomes of primary physicians rose more rapidly (less rapidly for hospital-based specialists) in states with higher growth of managed care (Simon et al. 1998). The demand for physicians' services is clearly not immune from changing market forces. Serious concern has even been raised about possible "manpower surpluses" and how best to deal with these. The Health Care Financing Administration introduced one program in 1997 that pays 41 New York state teaching hospitals $400 million over a six-year period to reduce the number of residents they train.

Graduates who enter private office-based practice face additional hurdles. In many specialties, it is difficult to succeed financially without hospital admitting or staff privileges. These privileges, which enable physicians to admit and provide care for patients, are not granted automatically. Hospitals typically have committees, usually comprised of physicians who already have staff privileges, to review applications and make recommendations to its board.

Thus, a second important issue is the role and value of staff privileges. The conventional view of admitting privileges as a potential barrier to practice, and the intense legal activity relating to denial or suspension of such privileges, suggests possible anticompetitive effects of restrictions on privileges. Those with staff privileges have a financial interest in limiting competition to try to gain economic rents (i.e., higher-than-normal rates of return). The research on this subject is scant, but Rizzo and Goddeeris (1998) found that admitting privileges increase earnings of primary care physicians, but the gains are eliminated once the physician has privileges at three or four hospitals.

Here, too, market forces through increased managed care activity provide possible answers. With hospitals becoming increasingly dependent on managed care contracts and less on individual physicians for their patients, the influence and ability of staff physicians to pursue self-interests have diminished. A hospital will prefer staff physicians who provide quality care and who make careful use of its resources.

A subsequent study undertaken by Burstein and Cromwell (1985) compared the internal rates of return[6] of physicians to dentists and lawyers. The authors incorporate many adjustments into their estimates, including length of physician training, length of working life, and the earnings of medical residents. The rates of return were high

[6]The rate that equates the present value of the returns with the present value of outlays.

compared to lawyers; for example, 12.1 percent versus 7.2 percent in 1980, the last year included in the study. The returns were high also for specialization based on board-certification requirements. This was true despite the rapid growth in physician supplies and the constraints imposed by third-party payers to contain costs over the study period. The authors therefore concluded that "the conventional picture of medicine as a financially attractive profession is strongly confirmed" (p. 76).

This strong conclusion is further supported by a more recent and direct test of physician pricing. Seldon and colleagues (1998) examined physicians' price–cost margins, defined as $(P - MC)/P$ where P represents price and MC represents costs. Under highly competitive conditions and marginal-cost pricing (i.e., where P approaches MC), the price-cost margin is zero. If physicians have monopoly power and the ability to maintain price above marginal cost, the margin will be positive. The researchers estimated the margin at 23 percent overall (and from 13 percent to 54 percent across the nine regional markets in the study). These estimates indicate "nontrivial" levels of monopoly power that produced a welfare loss to the U.S. economy of about $8 billion in 1996 dollars.

PUBLIC INTEREST OR SELF-INTEREST

The specific issue of licensure is but a part of the broader issue of regulation reflecting the two competing theories: public interest versus self-interest motives.

Public Interest and Self-Interest Theories of Regulation

The *public interest* motive is based on theories of market failure such as information failure. According to the public interest view, the demand for regulatory measures such as licensure is due to the limited information patients have about quality and the relatively high costs of obtaining information. Drawing on Akerlof's lemons model introduced in Chapter 9, Leffler (1978) argued that asymmetric information will lower quality. Thus, a "state-enforced minimum quality standard is claimed to be an efficient response to costly quality information" (p. 173).

In contrast, the *self-interest* motives for licensure and other forms of regulation to reduce competition have long been accepted in economics but only relatively recently have been formalized.[7] In this theory, regulation is the result of special interests that provide financial and political support in return for favored legislation. Thus, a demand for political favors arises from the rent-seeking behavior of special interest groups. The effort and amount of resources expended by a special interest group are limited by the rents that would accrue from the favored legislation.

Evidence of Public Interests versus Self-Interests

Paul (1984) tested the public-interest versus self-interest theories using data on the initial decisions by states to license physicians and rejected the public interest theory. His findings show a strong negative association between the year of initial licensure and the per-capita number of AMA-associated physicians in a state.

Graddy (1991) also tested the competing hypotheses by estimating the probability (and type) of regulation by states of six health care professions. Variables representing the public interest view included the profession's educational requirements in years (to

[7]See Stigler (1971) and Peltzman (1976).

capture the complexity of the service) and professional liability insurance rates (to represent the potential risk to consumers in the absence of regulation). The legislative environment was represented by variables such as the strength of the majority party and the rates of turnover of legislators. Variables such as the size of the occupation and its proportion of members belonging to a professional association represented private interests.

The statistical approach was made possible through the fact that licensure practices for many professions vary substantially across states. The professions and type of regulation across the states are summarized in Table 16.4. Graddy found important roles for each of the categories of explanatory variables in determining the kinds of regulation. Her findings indicate a higher probability of a stricter form of regulation as the profession's educational requirements are higher—a finding consistent with a public interest motive. The overriding conclusion, though, is that no single dominant motive can be found for regulation. Legislators respond to organized interests, the public interest, and their own legislative environments.

LICENSURE AND QUALITY

The Graddy evidence supports, in part, a public demand for regulation. We also know that physician board certification, or even board eligibility, increases remuneration, meaning consumers are willing to pay more for those with additional training and credentials.[8]

However, does licensure actually improve the quality of care? Gaumer's (1984) review of the empirical evidence questions whether the goals of protecting the public and ensuring minimal standards of competency are being achieved. He found (1) that in spite of licensure, a substantial amount of deficient care is being rendered, (2) that quality of care would not be impaired if the scope of practice of secondary (nonphysician/dentist) providers were increased, (3) that the licensing process may "not accurately assess the practice competence of applicants" (p. 397), and (4) that fees and provider incomes are higher in states with more restrictive licensure requirements (supporting the self-interests motive for regulation).

TABLE 16.4 Number of States Regulating Occupations by Type of Regulation, 1984

Occupation	*Unregulated*	*Registration*	*Certification*	*Licensure*
Dietician	40	0	4	6
Occupational therapist	23	0	0	27
Psychologist	0	0	5	45
Social worker	17	5	3	25
Physician assistant	5	14	28	3
Nurse-midwife	8	0	17	25

Source: Reprinted from *Journal of Health Politics, Policy and Law,* Graddy, Elizabeth, "Interest Groups or the Public Interest— Why Do We Regulate Health Occupations?," *Journal of Health Politics, Policy and Law* 16 (1991): 25–49, with permission from Duke University..

[8]Wilensky and Rossiter (1983). Using an innovative approach, Fournier and McInnes (1997) examined the disciplinary actions of the Florida Medical Board. Supporting the public-interest and demand for quality hypothesis, physicians with high rates of malpractice were more likely to be disciplined. However, after controlling for quality and other factors, evidence shows that certified physicians (certification is used to represent special interests) are less likely to be disciplined.

More specifically, with respect to the quality of physician care, he cites studies indicating that 5 percent are "unfit to practice," 8 to 22 percent of obstetrics patients and 61 percent to 65 percent of well-care patients received deficient care, and that 7.5 percent of all cases in two hospitals indicated physician-inflicted injury (p. 395).

Brennan and colleagues (1991) provide additional evidence on the quality of medical care in hospitals. Licensure is just one of many regulatory requirements intended to ensure that standards are being met. From a large number of randomly selected admissions, the researchers found that nearly 4 percent produced "adverse events," defined as injuries caused by medical management. Nearly 14 percent of these injuries led to death. The authors concluded that "there is a substantial amount of injury to patients from medical management, and many injuries are the result of substandard care" (p. 370).

Though no one is suggesting that eliminating licensure and other requirements will reduce such negative outcomes, it is clear that regulation does not ensure quality care.[9] Will tighter regulation help? From his review, Gaumer concludes as follows:

> Research evidence does not inspire confidence that wide-ranging systems for regulating health professionals have served the public interest. Though researchers have not been able to observe the consequences of a totally unregulated environment, observation of *incremental* variations in regulatory practices generally supports the view that tighter controls do not lead to improvements in quality of service (p. 406).

As a result of the questionable effects of licensure on quality, changes in the health care environment, and the anticompetitive effects of restrictions on entry and restrictions on the scope of practice of potential competitors (e.g., podiatrists, nurse practitioners), the benefits of licensure are being reexamined. Svorny (1992) suggests that the benefits have been weakened by, among other things, the added liability that courts have placed on hospitals and HMOs for the negligent conduct of independent physicians and by the increased use of salaried physicians. In a stronger attack, Safriet (1994) concludes:

> Clearly these barriers serve no useful purpose, and in fact contribute to our health care problems by preventing the full deployment of competent and cost-effective providers who can meet the needs of a substantial number of consumers (p. 315).

Physician Supply Decisions

Among the earliest controversies in health economics were those dealing with the supply of physician services and the competitiveness of physician services markets. Is the supply curve for physician services necessarily positively sloped? Is the supply curve of physician time negatively sloped? Are the markets for physician care characterized by high levels of competition or by monopoly pricing including price discrimination? Because they provide rich and powerful applications of basic economic tools, we examine several of these controversies.

[9]Tamblyn et al. (1998) did find that physicians' clinical decisions are associated positively with higher licensing exam scores.

THE SUPPLY OF PHYSICIAN LABOR AND SERVICES

In a provocative article, Martin Feldstein (1970) raised the possibility that the short-run supply of physician services is negatively sloped. Estimates of his model indicated that physicians actually reduce their output (and, by implication, their own work time) as the price of services increases. Feldstein's contribution was important because it raised serious concerns about the stability and functioning of health care markets. Although those concerns have faded, his article remains important because it reminds us of the need to distinguish between a physician's own time and use of other inputs to produce output (services).

Before we examine the consequences of a negatively sloped output supply, we must determine the circumstances under which it can arise. A negatively sloped output supply curve means that physicians reduce services as their fees increase. From the standard theory of the firm, short-run supply curves are always positively sloped, reflecting the rising portion of a firm's marginal cost curve. What distinguishes physician services from "widgets" is the prominence of the physician's own time in providing care. Thus, we must examine two decisions to understand the effect of higher prices on the quantity of services. The two decisions involve the use of nonphysician inputs and the amount of physician time as the physician's effective wage rate increases.

Suppose the demand for physician services increases and fees increase. From analyses in chapter 15, we know that firms in general have incentives to add other inputs to the production process because the marginal revenue products of those inputs increase. Physician firms should be no different in this regard. As fees increase, physicians will use more nonphysician inputs as those inputs are now more valuable to them. If physicians also increase their own time or even hold it constant as fees increase, output would have to increase; that is, the physician's output supply curve will be positively sloped.

It logically follows that a necessary condition for a negatively sloped supply curve of output is that physicians reduce their own time. Can this happen? Intuitively, it seems possible. If one's wage increases, one may decide to work fewer hours and take more leisure time. Intuitively, also, it would seem that this response is more likely for those with high incomes such as physicians have.

In theory as well as in practice, individual labor supply curves can be negatively sloped. Many students will recognize that the impact of a change in wages on labor supply depends on income and substitution effects. A higher wage rate, by increasing the opportunity cost of leisure, reduces the amount of labor supplied. The income effect, assuming that leisure is a normal good, will increase work effort.

Figure 16.1 illustrates the net effects using the familiar income–leisure curve. Leisure hours per week, with a maximum of 168, are measured on the horizontal axis and income is measured on the vertical axis. The physician's income is determined by the number of hours worked multiplied by the net wage (wage after expenses) per hour. In Figure 16.1, the physician is initially maximizing utility at point A, with an income I_1 from working $(168 - H_1)$ hours and enjoying H_1 hours of leisure. A higher net wage rate resulting from higher fees rotates the physician's opportunity locus clockwise. Whether the physician works more or fewer hours depends on which effect—income or substitution—dominates.

When the individual's new equilibrium is at B, reflecting more hours of work and fewer hours of leisure, the substitution effect dominates the income effect. Alternatively,

Income

B

A to B means that substitution effect dominates. Wage increase leads to increase in work.
A to C means that income effect dominates. Wage increase leads to decrease in work.

C

I_1

A

Work

0 H_1 H_2 168 Leisure Hours

FIGURE 16.1 Income and Substitution Effects.

the individual's labor supply curve will be negatively sloped if the income effect dominates the substitution effect as shown by the movement from A to C. Here, the individual takes H_2 leisure hours, working less than before. When this response to higher wages is prevalent in an occupation, the market labor supply curve can be negatively sloped. Finally, if the negative physician labor effect on output offsets the positive effect of additional nonphysician inputs described above, the supply of physician output in the short run also can be negatively sloped as shown in Figure 16.2.[10]

Many unusual consequences result from a negatively sloped supply curve. With demand, D_1, and supply, S_1, in Figure 16.2, the equilibrium price, where quantity demanded equals quantity supplied, is P_1. At any other price, the excess demand or supply will force price back to P_1. The equilibrium is stable. Now suppose that demand increases to D_2. Ordinarily, one would expect both price and quantity to increase. The price does increase to P_2 but quantity decreases to Q_2. Again, though, the new equilibrium is stable.

On the other hand, consider Figure 16.3 where the initial demand, D_1, is more inelastic than the negatively sloped supply curve. The equilibrium price, P_1, is an unstable equilibrium. If for any reason price is not at P_1, it will be pushed further away from the equilibrium. Even more curious, an increase in demand from D_1 to D_2 reduces the equilibrium price to P_2. However, P_2 may never be reached because the excess demand will drive price away from P_2 rather than toward it.[11]

From casual observation, there is good reason to believe that the markets for physician services are stable and that the peculiar predictions associated with unstable

[10]In the long run, an increase in the number of physicians through entry will increase total market output even if individual providers reduce theirs so the long-run supply will be upward sloping and possibly very elastic.
[11]Other surprises are associated with an unstable situation. Price controls often are proposed as policies to contain fee increases or limit expenditures under public health insurance programs. A price ceiling set below P_1, with the initial demand and supply in Figure 16.3 creates an excess supply and downward pressure on fees. This result is completely contrary to conventional views on price ceilings.

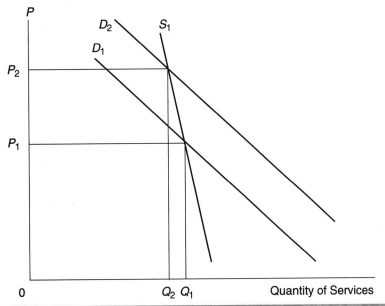

FIGURE 16.2 A Negatively Sloped Supply of Physician Services.

FIGURE 16.3 An Unstable Equilibrium.

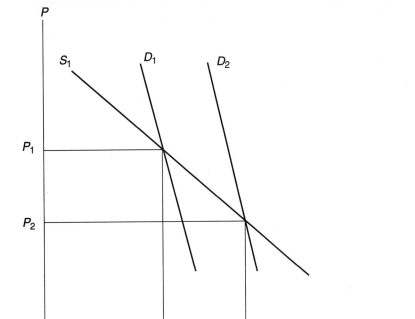

equilibria rarely, if ever, arise. Casual observation is supported by refinements of Feldstein's model indicating that physician output supply curves are positively sloped (though ones that approach a vertical shape cannot be ruled out).[12] Furthermore, a variety of analyses, including the effects of higher marginal tax rates, which reduce net remuneration, suggest substantial negative income effects of wage changes and that the supply curve for physicians in private practice may be negatively sloped. It is the addition of other inputs as prices increase that, despite declining physician hours, causes output to increase.[13]

PHYSICIAN PRICING, TRANSFER PRICING, AND PRICE DISCRIMINATION

As physician payment mechanisms have evolved with the growth of private and public insurance and the spread of managed care, physician decisions on pricing, accepting publicly insured patients, and entering into managed care contracts have become extremely complex. Many of these issues are taken up in other chapters, especially those on managed care and government regulation. Here we examine price discrimination, one aspect of physician pricing that received a great deal of attention in the early literature.

As a result of the market imperfections previously described in this and other chapters, there is widespread agreement that physicians in private practice have at least some degree of monopoly power. That is, physicians are not price takers and do not face horizontal demand curves. By raising prices, they will lose some but not all of their patients. With relatively low barriers to entry in regional markets for those who are already licensed physicians, it sometimes is useful to characterize physicians as monopolistic competitors with highly elastic demand curves. In many applications that do not directly involve entry and exit, however, it is easier and more useful to apply the monopoly profit-maximizing model to the physician firm. Under conditions of monopoly, the marginal revenue curve lies below the demand curve, because lowering the price to one customer requires lowering the price to all other customers. Hence, marginal revenue is less than price.

In a simple monopoly model, as described by Figure 16.4, the physician produces quantity, C, at which the marginal cost curve, MC, intersects marginal revenue curve, MR, or point F. At quantity C, the demand curve indicates that price A can be charged, and the total revenues equal $0ABC$. The physician's profits equal total revenues less total costs, which are indicated by the average costs and quantity C, or box $0CDE$. Hence, profits are equal to the remainder, or box $ABDE$.

Before we consider the possibility that a physician–firm will discriminate in pricing rather than sell at a single price such as A, we turn to an internal pricing problem that is commonly faced by large firms with divisions or subsidiaries that sell products or services to one another. The *transfer price* is the price that the selling unit charges the buying unit. Although it is not immediately obvious, the physician–firm also faces the transfer-pricing problem. It produces patient care with the owner's labor (which can also be sold in an external labor market) along with other inputs (e.g., nurses, physician assistants). The patient care is sold in a monopolized output market.

[12]See Brown, Feldstein, and Lapan (1974), Brown (1994), Thornton and Eakin (1997), and Thornton (1998).
[13]See Rizzo and Blumenthal (1994) and Showalter and Thurston (1997).

FIGURE 16.4 Profit Maximization and Price Discrimination by a Monopolistic Physician.

This transfer-pricing solution is straightforward when the external physician labor market is a competitive one. The competitive wage is the appropriate internal price. However, due to entry barriers facing new physicians, assume that the physician firm can hire physician labor or sell the owner's labor at a monopoly wage rate. Should the physician–firm use a competitive wage or the higher monopoly wage to calculate the profit-maximizing combination of inputs? This choice is important. Recall from chapter 15 that the marginal product of an input divided by its wage (MP/W) determines whether it is overutilized or underutilized. The selection of a wrong wage rate will give the firm a misleading signal on the cost-minimizing combinations of inputs. As a result, the profit-maximizing process described in Figure 16.4 will be based on incorrect cost information.

To find the correct cost curves and truly maximize profits, the firm should "buy" the owner's labor at its opportunity cost—in this case, the external monopoly wage. Why? Each hour that the physician provides to the firm could be sold at the external wage. Because the physician–owner forgoes that wage, it becomes the appropriate internal price.

An important feature of the pricing policies of the medical profession is the ability of the physician to discriminate among customers. In economic terms, discrimination means treating different customers differently. Consider a storekeeper who sells candy. He likes adults more than teenagers, so he charges the adults less for boxes of candy than he charges teenagers. Can this practice persist?

Certainly not over time. Teenagers who wish to have the candy simply will ask adults to buy the candy for them. Alternatively, adults who buy candy could resell the candy to teenagers for at least the price they paid. Competition among adults, in this example, would bid down the price of the candy to where the adults would be making normal, or zero, profits in selling the candy at the same price that it was sold to them.

Health services cannot be resold in this manner. Suppose a rich person needs knee surgery and the physician knows that the rich person could pay considerably more than a poor person for the surgery. The rich person cannot have a poor person buy knee surgery and resell it to him. This simple example suggests the considerable leeway that physicians have to charge different prices to different customers.

Returning to Figure 16.4, even after the physician has chosen to charge fee A for the service, there is still room for price discrimination. Suppose that one more customer, who was not willing to pay price A but instead is willing to pay $(A - 1)$, comes to the office. The marginal cost (MC) of providing patient care, although higher than at point F, is less than price $(A - 1)$. Thus the physician can increase profits by the amount of the shaded area. In principle, the physician can continue and attract yet additional patients by charging them even less than $(A - 1)$. As long as the price paid by those patients exceeds MC, the physician's profits will increase.

Price Discrimination by Physicians under a Charity Hypothesis

Traditionally, office-based physicians in the United States have been paid on a fee-for-service (FFS) basis. Although capitation and other payment methods have grown rapidly over the past two decades, physicians maintain fee schedules and generally expect to be paid for each unit of service provided.

When insurance was less prevalent, many physicians charged less to lower-income patients and even provided some free care. Price discrimination was widespread, but physicians explained this practice by stressing charitable motives; that is, earnings from those able to pay higher fees enabled physicians to provide care for those less able to pay.

Not surprisingly, many economists attributed this behavior to more selfish motives. Kessel's (1958) work was especially comprehensive and influential. He argued that price discrimination (and many other discriminatory practices of organized medicine, including "professional courtesy") were more consistent with profit motives. Price discrimination based on physician perceptions of patient income has become less common, and even Kessel's theory was challenged.

Ruffin and Leigh (1973) develop a competitive model of physician pricing that features, in contrast, a charitable motivation. They show that prices will vary with the patient's income in a model where physicians gain in marginal utility from serving the poor, after considering the compensating reduction in services for the rich. Thus, the pattern of price discrimination observed in the twentieth-century United States can be alternatively explained.

Furthermore, these authors argue that the charity model is more consistent with certain observed facts, two of which we note here. First, physician price discrimination existed prior to 1910, the approximate point at which organized medicine, according to Kessel, achieved sufficient power over hospital staffing privileges to maintain profit-motivated price discrimination. Second, price discrimination by income was observed in physician office care as well as in hospital care, where staff privileges are important and provide more power to organized medicine. On the force of Ruffin and Leigh's theory and discussion, it becomes clear that charitable motivations cannot be ruled out, and in fact, the hypothesis performs well.

Geographic Location of Physicians

Given the importance of access to highly trained health professionals, we discuss where providers, especially physicians, choose to practice. Public concern is considerable when rural residents must travel miles to see a physician at the same time that new facilities are constructed in already well-served urban areas. There is also public concern if inner-city residents must wait longer for clinic appointments than their suburban counterparts.

To address this dilemma, we consider two aspects of geographical distribution of people and activities:

- How health-related activities will cluster, given the technology of production.
- How physicians will respond to the clustering of activities in choosing where to practice.

LOCATION OF FACILITIES AND PROVIDERS

Consider a society in which all workers are self-sufficient in providing for their everyday needs. Physicians in this society are all trained as general practitioners, using their educations and small amounts of capital to treat others. In fact, at the limit in this model, each person has a small portion of physician training and cares for his or her own family. The geographic distribution of people in this society would be flat, as no place would be much different from anyplace else.[14]

Suppose now that many types of workers discover that it pays for them to specialize and that being geographically close to each other makes each more productive. These are components of increasing returns to scale, and this presents an economic explanation for the establishment of towns and cities. In the model, physicians as well as other workers discover that it pays for them to specialize, to be close to other physicians, and to share facilities; that is, the output of physicians increases by a larger proportion than the number. One might recognize this specialization in the construction of laboratories, clinics, and hospitals.

Moving a step further, it is easy to see that there may be some specialties such as major surgery that require large numbers of providers to work together and, because demand per customer is small, that require large market areas. As Starr (1982) has noted, the improvement in transportation in the early twentieth century fundamentally changed the way physicians and patients interacted. Physicians and hospitals could now expect patients to come to them. The more specialized the provider is, the farther patients can be expected to travel.

Because of the gains from agglomeration of activities, we note that large cities may have specialty clinics or hospitals that are not available in smaller cities. They also will have specialists and probably some general practitioners. The smaller cities will not have the major clinics but will have specialists who are not available in the towns. The towns may have general practitioners or no one at all. Thus, the distribution of resources

[14]Mills (1972, chapter 1) presents a classic and elegant discussion of this type of location theory. Mills and Hamilton (1994) discuss the implications in more detail.

within regions is not equal; it should therefore not be surprising to see more physicians and specialists in large cities than in small ones.

Other economic aspects of the specialization in the region can be described. The regional market area is defined by the patients' ability to travel to the location where care is needed. Because people in smaller towns must travel farther for care, the value of the land on which they live must compensate them for the increased travel. Land rents must be lower than in the larger cities. Because suburban and rural commuters must commute smaller distances to get to their jobs and to procure the goods and services that they need, wages may be less in these locations than they are closer to the larger cities in the region. The differences in wages and rents serve to equalize well-being among residents of small and large cities in the regional system.

IMPLICATIONS OF REGIONAL ANALYSIS

The size of a city, as well as the size of the surrounding region, is related in part to the incomes of the residents, because increased incomes imply the desire to buy more land, and more land (in the aggregate) can be acquired only by increasing the size of the city and the region. Thus, central cities, and especially suburban areas, must grow. This tendency has been bolstered by constant improvements in transportation, from horse carts to streetcars, to automobiles. These, once again, allow residents to disperse within an area.

Increases in income and decreases in transportation costs also explain dispersion of medical providers. As populations have grown, the shares of central cities' populations have fallen. As populations have decentralized, so have the providers who serve them.

This regional economic model is helpful in explaining why physicians may choose to locate in one part of a region rather than another. If all regions were the same, the story would end, because the explanation for location in one region would explain it in all regions. However, regions also may vary by climate, social values, or cultural amenities. Consider a specialist trying to decide whether to live in Detroit or San Francisco, and assume that the hospital facilities are identical. It is likely that the climate, recreational amenities, and possibly social values available in San Francisco would require would-be Detroit employers to make higher offers than would-be San Francisco employers.

Many economic models have tried to explain physician location by concentrating on differences among regions. The simplest model would argue that as long as income is higher in Ohio than in Mississippi, then physicians should migrate from Mississippi to Ohio. We have seen, however, that the income or earnings differences may be compensated by lower costs of living, different amenities, or different social values. Most studies have not addressed this issue well, and as a result a wide range of findings have, in sum, been inconclusive.

EMPIRICAL FINDINGS

The regional model has two types of implications. One is that migration will occur toward locations that are considered more desirable. The second implication is that location theory can predict existing patterns of physician location.

Many studies have tried to link location and migration of physicians to attributes of various regions. Ernst and Yett (1985) note that regression analyses of physicians' location patterns show that the patterns are not sensitive to physicians' net practice incomes, yet they are sensitive to proxies such as population size or per-capita income.

These findings are broadly consistent with the findings from location theory that more physicians will locate in population centers and that location will be correlated with the higher per-capita income that occurs there. A major problem with these types of studies is that the theoretically correct income measure, expected lifetime income, is difficult to model.

Similarly, patterns are sensitive to variables that proxy for "quality of life" in the specific area. Variables that are used for this include population size, educational attainment, or racial composition of the population. While there seems to be some consensus that these variables explain the stock of physicians in an area, they are much less successful in explaining the flow of physicians to the area.

The explanation, in part, is that if differences in prices and incomes are necessary to define a locational equilibrium, then we will not see migration as a response to these differences. It is apparent that more careful modeling of physician incentives is the answer.

One study explicitly integrates location theory into its analysis. The results are theoretically appealing and provocative with respect to location of physicians within regions.

LOCATION PATTERNS AND AVAILABILITY OF PHYSICIANS

Newhouse and colleagues (1982) seek to investigate physicians' location decisions. Framing their hypotheses in the location theory discussed previously, they provide strong tests of two hypotheses:

- Within a given specialty, larger towns have higher probabilities of having one or more specialists.
- As a specialty grows, its members disperse into smaller towns. As a result, smaller towns (which had fewer or no specialists) gain specialists at a higher rate than do large towns.

The researchers obtained data for all physicians from the American Medical Association for 1970 and 1979 for selected states, and they divided physicians into 17 specialty categories. They first investigated location of general plus family practitioners. In both 1970 and 1979, nearly all towns with populations of 5,000 or more included a general or family practitioner, and more than 85 percent of towns with populations between 2,500 and 5,000 also were represented. This compared, for example, to the distribution of neurosurgeons, which showed that only 28 (56) percent of the communities with populations between 30,000 and 50,000 people in 1970 (1979) had a neurosurgeon. These findings are consistent with the location theory, which suggests the appropriate market sizes for specialties.

Recall that location theory predicts that the more specialized practitioners would locate in the biggest market areas, the large cities. It would follow that as more were trained, competition would increase and some would diffuse into the smaller cities and towns. This would suggest that over time, larger percentage increases would occur in smaller towns than in larger ones. Consider Table 16.5, which reproduces summary results from the study.

In Table 16.5, the authors calculate the ratio of specialists per person in 1979 to specialists per person in 1970. If the hypothesis is to be supported, the ratio for smaller markets should be higher (where there is more infusion of physicians) than for larger markets. We see that in almost all cases, the hypothesis is indeed supported. Consider

TABLE 16.5 Ratio of Specialists Per Person in 1979 to Specialists Per Person in 1970

Size of Town (thousands)	2.5–5	5–10	10–20	20–30	30–50	50–200	200+
Specialty							
Internal medicine	1.79	1.56	1.64	1.54	1.62	1.68	1.65
General surgery	1.08	1.00	1.04	1.08	1.06	1.02	1.08
Obstetrics/Gynecology	1.50	1.27	1.23	1.42	1.25	1.21	1.22
Pediatrics	2.66	1.62	1.36	1.43	1.38	1.35	1.35
Psychiatry	—	1.29	1.30	1.56	1.42	1.34	1.50
Radiology	2.19[a]	1.50	1.34	1.38	1.44	1.39	1.56
Anesthesiology	1.01	1.01	1.40	1.46	1.44	1.28	1.42
Orthopedic surgery	—	3.46[a]	1.92	1.95	1.70	1.51	1.47
Ophthalmology	—	1.18	1.39	1.29	1.39	1.17	1.26
Pathology	—	2.06[a]	1.52	1.45	1.49	1.31	1.57
Dermatology	—	—	1.44	1.79	1.56	1.31	1.33
Neurosurgery	—	—	—	2.71[a]	2.57	1.44	1.28
Plastic surgery	—	—	—	—	2.47	2.19	1.69

[a]Only 5 percent to 10 percent of the towns in this population range had a specialist in 1970.

Source: Newhouse et al. (1982). Reprinted with the permission of the RAND Corporation, Santa Monica, California.

pediatrics, for example. The ratio in towns with populations of 2,500 to 5,000 was 2.66. It fell to 1.62 in the next group (5,000 to 10,000), and settled down to between 1.35 and 1.45 for the remaining categories. Most other specialties yield similar results.

GEOGRAPHIC LOCATION—SOME EQUITY CONSIDERATIONS

Two major groups of geographically defined consumers may be particularly influenced by physicians' location decisions. Consumers in sparsely populated rural areas are likely to have to travel longer distances at greater costs to obtain certain types of treatments. Consumers in disadvantaged (by socioeconomic income, race, or class criteria) urban neighborhoods may have to travel relatively far, at relatively high costs compared to other residents, because physicians have chosen to locate closer to their more affluent clientele.

One can conceive of incentives on both the supply and the demand sides to address this problem. On the supply side, initiatives to increase overall physician supply also might be expected to reduce maldistribution as market forces draw physicians to underserved areas.[15] (This was the U.S. policy until the mid-1970s when it became increasingly apparent that an overall shortage of physicians no longer existed.) As for more specific strategies targeting spatial inequalities, sponsors (either governmental or pri-

[15]Federal government policies and their effects on the geographic diffusion of physicians are analyzed by Foster and Gorr (1992). Elsewhere, Bolduc and colleagues (1996) develop a utility maximizing model of initial location decisions for physicians in the province of Quebec, Canada. Empirical estimates of the model produce expected effects for various geographic amenities, as well as relatively high price and income elasticities. A differential remunerations program that raises fees for those practicing in more remote and isolated regions therefore has a substantial impact on initial location decisions—16 percent more general practitioners in remote regions and 10 percent in isolated regions.

vate groups) may offer student loans that are "forgiven" if the recipient practices in a shortage area. Agencies may finance and/or subsidize clinics and/or practices that would not be economically viable otherwise. Ultimately, in some cases government may choose to employ providers at shortage locations. Many of these strategies have been adopted.

On the demand side, policy makers must recognize that lack of physicians and/or facilities stems from the inability of would-be patients to pay for services. This is a problem of poverty and insurance. As with other social insurance programs, this problem requires redistribution of resources from the more affluent to those in need.

If the disadvantaged were equally distributed throughout a city or a region, the uneven distribution of physicians would be less problematic. The geographic aspect of such shortages is related to the fact that many of the poor and needy live near each other, making it unprofitable for physicians to locate nearby. We already have considered supply possibilities regarding the location of physicians. Programs to provide income and to pool risks for health insurance may increase purchasing power for health care, and thus demand, such that more might be provided by physicians in a market setting.

Conclusions

This chapter has addressed several analytical issues in the training, pricing, and location of physicians. It is apparent that the long and arduous training procedures tend to reduce the responsiveness of physician supply to short-term changes in economic conditions. People can be trained to do simple procedures as nurses, assistants, or medics, and in many less-developed countries, simple examinations are administered by nonphysicians with limited training. The lore of World War II, for example, is replete with examples of medics who were trained to do emergency battlefield medical procedures. The barriers to entry to the physician profession would lead one to expect higher-than-normal rates of return to physician training, and this is borne out in empirical studies.

Our discussion of physician supply demonstrates the importance of distinguishing between the physician's own time and the physician's output of care. The theoretical possibility of a negatively sloped supply of output was described and used to illustrate several unusual predictions about the market for physician services. We also discussed price discrimination as a consequence of monopoly power. Given their monopoly power and the inability of patients to resell medical care, the ability to discriminate among patients by price has long been a factor in the pricing of physician services.

The location of physicians represents our final specialized discussion. We note that the agglomeration economies of cities can be appropriately applied to the health care sectors. There are cost-reduction benefits in being close to other providers. More specialized physicians have larger market areas and hence are located in larger urban areas.

Summary

1. Many professions require a considerable length of time spent in education and training. The time period for physicians is among the longest.
2. Medical education is heavily subsidized. Tuition is a relatively small source of revenues; thus, the student pays only a small portion of the true costs of the investment in education.
3. Medical education is a good example of joint production. Medical schools produce medical education, patient care, and research.

4. Immigration policy can be relaxed to admit more foreign medical school graduates (FMGs) during periods of perceived physician shortages, and vice versa during periods of surpluses. This happened during the 1960s, when preferential treatment was given to foreign national FMGs. Requirements subsequently were tightened in 1976 once shortages were no longer perceived.

5. Kessel argued that monopoly power was attained by organized medicine through licensure of physicians and control of access to medical education.

6. According to an alternative view of medical education, the donor–preference hypothesis, medical school revenues come not so much from tuition paid by students but from donors such as government agencies, alumni, businesses, and research organizations. For the most part, it is these donors who demand and control the output of medical schools: trained physicians.

7. Licensure is a prominent example of the controversy of self-interest versus public-interest views of regulation.

8. It is generally believed that licensure has given physicians economic rents. Licensure has not led to obvious improvements in quality, and calls are growing for reform of licensure laws.

9. It is important to distinguish between physician labor supply and the supply of physician services. Physician output depends on physician time and use of non-physician inputs.

10. In theory, physician labor supply and output supply both may be negatively sloped. The former is necessary but not a sufficient condition for the latter. A negatively sloped market output supply may lead to an unstable equilibrium and some unusual predictions.

11. Physicians have some degree of monopoly power and have engaged in price discrimination. Price discrimination is consistent with profit maximization and also a charitable motive.

12. In regional economic analysis, physicians discover that it pays to specialize, to be close to other physicians, and to share facilities. That is, the output of physicians increases by a larger proportion than the number of physicians. One might recognize this specialization as the construction of laboratories, clinics, and hospitals.

13. Location theory predicts that the more specialized practitioners would locate in the biggest market areas, the large cities. It would follow that as more were trained, competition would increase and some would diffuse into the smaller cities and towns. This hypothesis is borne out empirically.

Discussion Questions

1. It is argued that imperfect capital markets constitute one reason for subsidizing medical education. Discuss why the market for human capital differs from, say, the market for housing capital (that is, buying a house).

2. If there were no subsidy for medical education, would classes be larger or smaller? Would the return to medical education be larger or smaller? If physician education were not subsidized, would the economically warranted supply of physicians tend to emerge?

3. What are the social benefits and costs behind regulating the number of medical schools?

4. What is joint production? What does the term *joint production costs* mean? Given that medical schools engage in joint production of education, patient care, and research, what inferences can be drawn about the economies of scope in producing these three outputs?
5. In contrast to medical education, numerous night and part-time law schools have been established. Compare and contrast the various aspects of training that have led to these different educational systems.
6. What is an unstable equilibrium, and under what circumstances will it arise? Why does casual observation of the market for physician services suggest that these markets are not unstable?
7. What conditions are necessary for price discrimination? Why is a surgeon more likely to be able to price discriminate than an optician (seller of eyeglasses)?
8. Regional analysts refer to the gains from agglomeration of activities at central locations. Discuss such gains in the context of the provision of health services.
9. Suppose an analyst determines that the number of physicians in Cleveland is decreasing and the number in Atlanta is increasing, even though wages in Cleveland are higher than in Atlanta. How might the analyst explain this phenomenon?
10. The rate of return on investment in medical education exceeds that for other professions. What are arguments for and against government subsidies?

Exercises

1. Using supply-and-demand analysis, model the equilibrium level of physicians' incomes. What would be the impact on physicians' incomes of more stringent policies on the employment of foreign medical school graduates?
2. Suppose that a medical school provides three outputs—patient care, education, and research—and that the total cost of the school is $10 million per year. If the school produced only education, its costs would be $6 million. If the school produced only patient care, its costs would be $3 million. If it produced only research, the costs would be $2 million. Joint costs for each pair would be $1 million.
 a. What are the pure costs of education, patient care, and research?
 b. What are the joint costs?
3. Suppose that the licensure requirements for health care providers were eliminated. Use supply-and-demand analysis to predict what may happen to the price and quantity of health care services. Are there other considerations—in particular, mechanisms—that could evolve to replace licensure?
4. Draw an example of an unstable equilibrium. Show an increase in supply through a parallel shift in the supply curve. What happens to the equilibrium price? Will the price go to the new equilibrium?
5. Assume that a physician can earn $200 per hour. Draw the physician's income–leisure curve per day. Assume that a flat income tax rate of 20 percent is introduced. Draw the new locus and explain, using income and substitution effects, whether the physician will work more or less than before. Alternatively, assume (without the tax) that a physician earns $500 per day from investments in stocks and bonds. How do these earnings affect the curve, and do they unambiguously change the physician's work hours? Explain.

The Role of Nonprofit Firms

- ■ An Introduction to Nonprofits
- ■ Why Nonprofits Exist and Why They Are Prevalent in Health Care
- ■ Models of Nonprofit Hospital Behavior
- ■ The Relative Efficiency of Nonprofits versus For-Profits
- ■ Conclusions

Nonprofit firms account for less than 5 percent of the GDP, but they make up a significant portion of the health care sector. The 60 percent of community hospitals that are nonprofit provide nearly 70 percent of the beds and treat a similar proportion of the nation's hospital patients. Nonprofit firms also offer 30 percent of nursing home care and half of the inpatient specialty mental health and substance abuse treatment.

Inasmuch as nonprofits are prominent in health care, especially in the important hospital industry, they pose questions of considerable interest. Will the economic behavior of nonprofits be distinctly different from that of the more common for-profit firm or from government enterprise? A growing body of literature addresses such questions and adds to our understanding of nonprofit firms in general. Studies within health economics contribute to both the general theory of nonprofit firms and the understanding of vital issues of the health economy.

An Introduction to Nonprofits

What is the nonprofit firm? People commonly assume that nonprofits are firms organized to provide a charitable good or community service and that they obtain their revenues largely from donations. While it is true that several fit this category, the definition does not serve well conceptually, nor does it make an important economic distinction. On one hand, many profit-making firms provide important goods and services to the community, and many provide basic goods such as food and housing to the poor. On the other hand, many nonprofit firms serve the well-to-do, and many serve in competition

373

with for-profits. Many obtain the lion's share of their revenues from the sale of goods and services at prices similar to their for-profit competitors. Health care nonprofits obtain more than 90 percent of their revenues from "sales and receipts."

In economic language, the important distinction of the nonprofit is the *nondistribution constraint.* This means that the laws allow no one a legal claim on the nonprofit's residual. Residual means the difference between the revenues and its costs, or what an ordinary firm would call its profits. Because there is no residual claimant, it is possible that the nonprofit's objectives will differ from profit making. Two secondary distinctions between nonprofits and for-profits are also consequential. First, nonprofits are exempt from corporate income taxes and often from property and sales taxes. Second, donations to nonprofits receive favorable tax treatment. These three distinctions make the nonprofit a potentially different economic entity, but is it?[1]

Why Nonprofits Exist and Why They Are Prevalent in Health Care

In any economy like that of the United States, three types of firms can be found: private profit-making, government, and voluntary nonprofit enterprises. Why do each of these types of firms exist? It would be trivial to say that these firms exist because our laws say they can exist. However, society's economic institutions are not created at random; they must reflect some basic economic incentives and unmet needs that these firms and the laws establishing them were created to satisfy.

NONPROFITS AS PROVIDERS OF UNMET DEMANDS FOR PUBLIC GOODS

Burton Weisbrod (1975) has formulated a noteworthy account of the existence of nonprofits, and his analysis guides the following exposition. In the United States and other Western economies, a natural presumption favors for-profit competitive enterprises. Economists learn that a perfectly competitive industry under certain circumstances is economically efficient, and empirical data suggest that competition often fosters growth. Government enterprises under this account are needed only in cases where competitive markets fail. As this theory unfolds, nonprofits are needed, in turn, in cases where government enterprise also fails. We begin by reviewing the standard explanation of the role of government enterprise, and then we introduce Weisbrod's explanation in which the nonprofit firm satisfies demands for public goods unmet either by private markets or the government.

Under the standard economic explanation, government enterprise might possibly—though it need not necessarily—have a role in improving market efficiency in cases where competitive markets tend to fail. The most prominent cases of market failure involve public goods and externalities. Two examples will clarify these issues.

Market Failure: Externalities

Most consumer goods provide private benefits and little or no externalities. An externality is an uncompensated direct effect of the production or consumption of a good on persons other than the producers or consumers. Consider a good with no externality.

[1]For further discussion on the nature of nonprofit firms, see Weisbrod (1988).

When one enjoys a hamburger at a local fast-food restaurant, the pleasure is primarily private, and the benefit goes to the one who consumes. There is no effect on parties external to the market, to parties other than the producer or consumer. However, consider the case where one purchases a vaccination for influenza. This good entails a private benefit to be sure: The purchaser is less likely suffer from influenza. In addition, there is an external benefit to others because the purchaser will less likely be a carrier of the disease and is less likely to infect others.

Free markets will tend to underproduce goods for which there exist significant external benefits. For example, the purchaser of the vaccination will tend to consider primarily the private benefits and will ignore the external benefits to the community. The benefit to society is the sum of the private benefits and the external benefits to the community. Because demand will represent only the private benefits, it will understate society's benefits and give a false or inadequate signal to the market. The market then produces less than the amount that would maximize net social benefits. This is economically inefficient, and we call this situation a case of market failure.

Generally, economists recognize the existence of such externalities—both the beneficial and detrimental kinds—but they argue over their relative importance and the appropriate remedy. The existence of an externality of significant size raises the possibility of a role for government. This is only a possibility because the inefficiencies entailed in governmental activity may more than cancel the potential gains. If we recognize that markets may fail, we must recognize that governments too may fail to act efficiently. The mainstream approach, however, usually recognizes that in some cases governmental activity will improve the net benefits to society.

Market Failure: Public Goods

The vaccination is a private good with an external benefit. The external benefit of this good itself entails certain public good aspects. To understand this fully, let us first introduce the case of a pure public good. A public good in economics is defined as a good that is both nonexcludable and nonrival. *Nonexcludable* means that people cannot be economically excluded from consuming the good even if they refuse to pay for it. *Nonrival* means that one person can consume the good without depleting it for others. Our hamburger is an example of a private good, not a public good. The hamburger is excludable because McDonald's can easily refuse the hamburger to someone who refuses to pay. Likewise, the hamburger is a rival good, because the act of one person consuming the burger causes it to be depleted; it is eaten up.

Contrast the hamburger with a classic, though occasionally disputed, example of a pure public good: national defense. Imagine an antimissile system that effectively puts a defensive umbrella over a country. This defense system would be nonexcludable because any person living in the country would benefit even if he or she individually refused to pay for it. It would be impossible, let alone costly, to allow the nonpayer alone to be subject to an enemy missile strike. Likewise, the defense system is nonrival because the protection one individual receives (that is, consumes) arguably does not diminish the defense enjoyed by others in the country.

Public goods like this are often provided by government enterprise. Private enterprise may tend to provide too little of a public good or even none at all, if hypothetically it were given the responsibility. Remember that a public good like defense is nonexcludable. Therefore, if private enterprise were to attempt to provide defense, it

could well find many or most citizens choosing to be *free riders*. A free rider is a person who consumes the public good but refuses to pay. Private enterprise does not have the power to tax or otherwise force consumers to pay. It cannot resort to the standard means of private enterprise in inducing payment; that is, it cannot refuse or exclude service to nonpayers.

The Public Good–Private Good Aspect of Donations

Now consider an example of a public good that is conceptually more difficult: charitable donations. A charitable donation to the health of others in the community has the characteristics of both a public good and a private good. The need for both concepts becomes clear in Richard Steinberg's (1986, 1987) work, which argues that donations to public goods motivate the donor as both private and public goods. If you donate a parcel of wetland to a land conservancy, this dedicated land can be enjoyed by anyone in the public, including you, because one's enjoyment does not diminish the enjoyment of the same property for others. The dedicated land is a public good. At the same time, you can enjoy the act of giving, which some describe as providing you, the donor, a warm glow you get from doing (and perhaps from being known to have done) a good thing (Arrow, 1975; Andreoni, 1990).

Now consider a case where the government provides a public good. This case will enable one to understand Weisbrod's explanation of the kind of government failure that provides a rationale for the existence of nonprofits. In Figure 17.1, let the curves D_1 through D_5 represent the demand curves of five different voting individuals for a public good to be provided by the government. Let the demand curves represent the external benefits to these different groups of taxpayers. These demand curves thus represent the marginal benefits to the taxpayer donors.

To pay for this public good, assume that these five different taxpayers are to be equally taxed at a per-unit tax rate of MT, which is the marginal tax. Because the five individuals are being equally taxed, the marginal tax for each will be exactly one-fifth of the marginal cost to society. Thus, if the government were to provide output $0C$, then each of the five taxpayers would be charged $0C \times MT$, and the total tax receipts would exactly pay for the project. If the output were $0B$, then $0B \times MT$ would be collected from each individual, and so on.

What output level will government choose to provide if the outcome is left to the democratic political process? Economists find it convenient to imagine an elected manager whose continued term in office is determined by his or her ability to provide the "right" level. If level $0A$ is proposed, four of the five voters would prefer more (why?) and would vote against it. If level $0B$ is proposed, three of the five would prefer more and would vote against that level. In contrast, level $0D$ would provide too much public good for three of the five voters, and similarly for level $0E$. Only level $0C$ will gain a majority vote. This majority is made up of Voter 3, who is exactly satisfied because her marginal benefits equal the marginal tax, and Voters 4 and 5, who would like to see more but are satisfied with level $0C$. Suppose the manager proposed just a little more than $0C$. This is too much for Voter 3, who now votes against the manager in favor of someone else who would reduce the public good level back to $0C$.

Weisbrod's point is illustrated in this example. The government enterprise level chosen entails dissatisfied voters on the margin, whose demands are not exactly satisfied. The marginal tax rate is perfectly tailored only to Voter 3, the median person. For

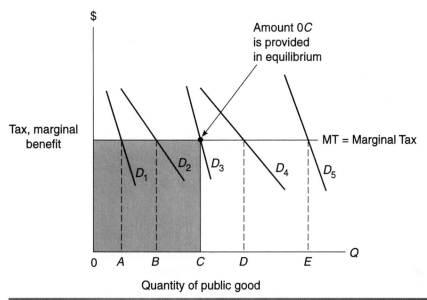

FIGURE 17.1 The Median Voter Model of Public Goods.

this person, the marginal benefit just equals the marginal tax rate at the provided output. It is theoretically possible to design a tax system so that for each person, the marginal tax is equal to his or her marginal benefit, however, it is difficult to accomplish this in practice. Without such a tax system, some voters will prefer less of the public good and some will prefer more of it. The government enterprise will have failed to satisfy the demands of those who would prefer more. Such unsatisfied voters will have the incentive to form a nonprofit enterprise and provide the good themselves.

It follows from Weisbrod's theory that nonprofits arise because private profit-motivated markets will tend to underproduce goods or services entailing beneficial externalities. In turn, government also may underprovide such goods and services in the eyes of a significant minority of voters. These citizens will tend to include those who perceive the external benefit to the community most keenly. Such citizens (here, Voters 4 and 5) become the founders of nonprofit corporations.

Weisbrod's analysis applies to health care when it is not a pure private good. The health care provided to the indigent is itself private because the indigent person could have been excluded had we wished. The care is also rival, as it is consumed by the recipient. Nevertheless, the health care provided to the indigent entails a beneficial externality to any charitably minded person. It is this external benefit that is a public good, and it is in this sense that health care is not a pure private good.

Relevance to Health Care Markets

Hospital services, nursing home services, and kidney dialysis services are probably not pure private goods. The Weisbrod analysis will be applicable in principle to any such services that provide external benefits to the community at large. Thus, nonprofit health care enterprises may arise where a sufficient minority of voters are dissatisfied with the quantity or quality of such services provided by the for-profit sector or government. The

theory provides a plausible account of the historical rise of nonprofit hospitals. Hospitals in the United States and in many countries began as charitable institutions, providing care primarily to the poor and relying heavily on donations.[2]

Furthermore, the theory encompasses a broader range of external benefits than are involved in the provision of indigent, uncompensated care. High-quality, prestigious hospitals may enhance a community's sense of pride and well-being. They may indirectly provide benefits to local businesses. Their excess capacity also provides insurance for the currently healthy citizens that a bed will be available should they need one.

However, the purely charitable aspects of hospital care have become less important. During this century, improvements in medical technology transformed hospitals into workshops for doctors—places for treating all patients, both rich and poor. By 1996, donations accounted for less than 3 percent of average hospital revenues, and only about 3 percent of patients relied on donations or welfare as their principle source of payment. Hospital finance departments wrote off unpaid patient bills, but these accounted for less than 1 percent of billings.[3] The demise of hospital donations has been attributed to the growth of hospital insurance coverage, especially since the advent of Medicare and Medicaid. The decline in donations is consistent with the Weisbrod theory: Individual demands have stayed fairly stable while increases in public sector provision or financing have occurred.

With the decline in cash donations, other forms of donations as well as other forms of nonprofit hospital advantages have become relatively more important. Donations of time and energy for board members and other individuals may, for example, now be relatively more important. To be sure, cash donations still play an important role in certain capital fund drives. But in the present day, the financial advantages enjoyed by nonprofit hospitals stem more importantly from the subsidization of nonprofits by the government through tax exemptions. Generally, nonprofits do not pay corporate, property, or sales taxes although for-profits do. The only tax advantage enjoyed by for-profits is the ability to write off losses during bad years.

NONPROFITS AS A RESPONSE TO CONTRACT FAILURE

A related theory of the role of nonprofit firms is complementary to Weisbrod's ideas. Hansmann (1980) theorizes that the nonprofit sector has a useful role in cases of a particular type of contract failure. The contract failure in point occurs when the quantity or quality of output is not easily observable by the purchaser. The asymmetry of information between the firm and the buyer of services becomes important (as noted in chapter 9) in explaining the nonprofit role.[4]

A classic example of the contract failure illustrates the problem. Suppose that you are motivated to contribute food and clothing to suffering people in Ethiopia. You can find a firm to deliver the care; however, it would be prohibitively costly to verify that the firm actually is delivering the desired goods to the designated population. You would hardly fly to Ethiopia just to check on this. Under these circumstances, you may prefer to employ a nonprofit firm.

[2] The history of hospitals and the relative importance of nonprofit versus for-profit status are further explored, for example, in Bays (1983), Frech (1990), and Temin (1988).
[3] See the U.S. Department of Commerce *Statistical Abstract of the United States, 1999.*
[4] The essential idea was developed further in a model by Easley and O'Hara (1983).

As a deliverer of the aid packages, a for-profit firm will be perceived to have a conflict of interest. Such a firm could increase its profits by reneging on its promise. Inasmuch as the nonprofit cannot distribute its residual, it would have less incentive to renege. In this case, the nonprofit, by better serving the donor's interests, also serves the market more efficiently.

Applications of Contract Failure to Nursing Home Care

Contract failure is not confined to the issues of donated goods and services, as it can exist even when the purchaser is close at hand. Contrast the management of hotels and nursing homes. Hotels are profit-seeking enterprises, which provide rooms and suites along with housekeeping services, dining, and recreation to travelers and residents. Nursing homes also provide rooms and suites, dining, and recreation along with housekeeping services and, of course, specialized nursing services largely for an older and often infirm population. In fact, many nursing homes began as hotels.

What is the difference? Hotel patrons are assumed to be utility-maximizing consumers who compare benefits and costs in deciding whether to stay at the hotel. Nursing home patients may not be able to assess the quality of the facility and the care they receive accurately, perhaps because of their health impairments. Relatives or friends may obtain only limited impressions upon visiting and may not be sophisticated assessors of the quality of long-term care. A for-profit home, in contrast to a for-profit hotel, may appear to have a conflict of interest in the eyes of some demanders.

Whether for-profit nursing homes in practice provide lower quality is a matter of dispute. The measurement of quality is itself an issue of dispute. Outcome measures, such as changes in patient health status, are best in principle, but reliable outcome measures are difficult to obtain. Analysts often are forced to rely on input data instead, but input data, such as the number of registered nurses per patient, although more readily available, can be misinterpreted easily.

For example, does a nursing home with more nurses per patient provide higher quality or is it simply less efficient? In practice, nursing homes with more personnel per patient do tend to have better patient outcomes, but it is difficult to sort out efficiency and quality. Gertler (1989) addressed these problems and found a higher quality level in nonprofit homes. However, continued review and study in the 1990s produced mixed results.[5]

Relevance of Contract Failure to Hospitals and Other Firms

If contract failure theory may apply to nursing home care, it does not appear to be appropriate for hospitals, a point noted by Hansmann (1980). Hospital patients are under the close supervision of the physician acting as the patient's agent. The physician has little incentive to misinform the patient by overstating the quality of care. More likely, the physician's incentives would cause him or her to encourage the patient to choose the highest quality available. Thus, the physician as agent of the patient may eliminate the potential contract failure.

Sloan (1988) further suggests that a double standard frequently is applied by those who favor the contract failure theory. The field of physician services, which are nearly all provided on a for-profit basis in the United States, seems ripe for the application of

[5]For further study, see Cohen and Spector (1996), Holtmann and Idson (1993), and Davis (1991).

contract theory. Consumers would find it just as hard to assess the quality of physician care as they would hospital care, so why do nonprofit firms not take over the physician care sector?

More recent research has supported the wisdom of contract theory. Hirth (1999), who develops models of health care markets that have contract and information problems, showed theoretically that nonprofits will tend toward the high end of the quality spectrum. He argues that nonprofits will induce higher quality efforts among the for-profits, in turn improving average quality overall.

The Role of Physicians in the Hospital Industry

The theories so far account for the presence of nonprofit institutions in general. Bays (1983) adds a special theory to account for the rise of nonprofit hospitals. His is called an *interest group theory*.

Bays begins with attention to the history of U.S. hospitals and their nature as institutions. He notes that in the nineteenth century, U.S. hospitals were charitable institutions where physicians largely donated their time. Notably, medical technology had not yet developed to the point where hospitals were important to the physician either technologically or economically. As rapid population growth and expansion of hospitals occurred in the early twentieth century, for-profit hospitals flourished, accounting for about half of existing hospitals in 1910 and reaching their zenith by 1930. These for-profit hospitals were generally small.

As medical technology advanced, hospitals became the workshops of doctors; holding admitting privileges at one or more hospitals was crucial to a physician's practice. Hospitals also grew rapidly in size. With greater interest in the operation of hospitals, physicians increasingly developed and used their influence as an interest group to exert some control over them. By controlling hospital admitting privileges, organized physicians gained a degree of market power including the ability to exercise discipline over physicians whose practices tended to erode the market power of the organized group. For example, the affiliation by some physicians with prepaid group practice was treated as "unprofessional conduct."

Under this theory, physicians prefer nonprofit hospitals because they have greater power within them. Power over decision making permits the physician to enhance personal income. Physicians can order hospital services complementary to their own services, ordering hospital services perhaps well past the extent that would be profitable to the hospital. This account, Bays points out, is consistent with the policy stand of the AMA in support of Hill–Burton, a federal act that provided construction aid and loan subsidies to nonprofit hospitals. Furthermore, the favored tax treatment and subsidies to nonprofit hospitals arise in part through physicians' political support—support that ultimately benefits the physician through the provision of lower-cost complementary hospital inputs.

How then can we account for public acquiescence in supporting the nonprofit mode? If the theory were correct, the subsidies (both tax relief and dollar subsidies) to nonprofit hospitals in effect tax the general public majority to support the narrower interests of the physician minority. To account for this anomaly, Bays appeals to interest group theory.

Under interest group theory, small groups may become more powerful than a majority when their interests are highly concentrated and their membership is homogeneous. It will be worthwhile in such case for physicians to support lobbying on behalf of measures that result in significant benefits to them, whereas the loss to the general public is diffused. While the individual consumer may benefit by challenging the status quo, the personal gains are small relative to the personal costs. The theoretical situation depicted by Bays, a situation that substantially and lopsidedly favors the physician at the expense of the general public, may nevertheless represent a regulatory equilibrium.

SUMMARY ON THE REASONS FOR THE PREVALENCE OF NONPROFITS

Several theories explain the existence of nonprofits. In some cases, these theories are complementary; in other cases, there are sharp contrasts. Weisbrod accounts for the existence of nonprofit firms in an economy with three sectors: for-profits, government, and nonprofits. In his view, nonprofits arise to provide for unmet demands for public goods, most notably in cases where there are significant external benefits to the provision of a good.

Hansmann's view is complementary to this account, emphasizing the special role for nonprofit firms in cases of contract failure (cases where it is difficult to observe the provision or quality of the good in question). These two theories provide insights into the prevalence of nonprofit firms in the provision of hospital care and nursing home care. Under either of these two accounts, the public deference to nonprofit firms (such as in allowing for special tax provisions favoring them) makes some sense.

In contrast, Bays offers an interest group theory of the preference of physicians for nonprofit hospitals. In his account, physicians prefer nonprofits and use their influence to further the role of nonprofits at least partly, if not primarily, out of interest for personal gain. Under Bays's account, favored treatment of nonprofit hospitals is not so clearly in the public interest. This multiplicity of theories regarding the existence of nonprofit firms, particularly of hospitals, is mirrored in a multiplicity of theories of hospital behavior.

Models of Nonprofit Hospital Behavior

Health economics offers many descriptions of hospital behavior, but three models represent the distinctive classes of behavior. We begin with a nonprofit model that applies in principle to an entire class of nonprofit firms. We then follow with two model theories that are specific to hospitals.

THE QUALITY–QUANTITY NONPROFIT THEORY

When economists study nonprofit hospital responses to policy change, they begin by positing an objective of the hospital decision makers. Most frequently, they choose either a utility-maximization or a profit-maximization type of model. The first and most prominent example of the utility-maximizing hospital was the model proposed by Joseph Newhouse (1970); it applies to nonprofit firms in general.

For Newhouse, the hospital's objective was to maximize the utility of the decision makers. Utility of the firm has a similar meaning to the utility of a consumer; it is an index of the decision maker's preferences and can be thought of as a measure of satisfaction.

The special difficulty for the case of hospitals is to describe the complex elements and interactions of the set of hospital decision makers. Nonprofit hospitals in the United States tend to have three parties with considerable decision making authority. The trustees are nominally in charge of the hospital, but boards of trustees may include people with widely varying backgrounds, knowledge of health care, and management expertise. The trustees' decision making agent is the hospital administrator or CEO. This manager may have varying degrees of actual power and authority. Finally, the arbiters of medical decision making are the physician staff. The physicians also may exercise considerable decision making authority. We assume that this complex decision making apparatus resolves into a single utility function and describes a set of well-behaved indifference curves.

The Utility Function

Under Newhouse's construction, the hospital's preferences are defined over quantity and quality of output. Quantity of output could be measured in several ways, but in the graphical treatment we assume that it is measured by the number of cases treated by the hospital over a given time period. We further assume that there is only one type of case to be treated, though in principle there could be hundreds. Quality of output can entail many different characteristics of the care provided. Some top decision makers may value the quality or beauty of the hospital structure; others may emphasize expertise of the physician or nursing staff; others may emphasize prestige in the medical community; and still others may stress the quality of mercy or the tender loving care provided. Graphically, we shall suppose that just one index of quality exists.

This conception of the nonprofit hospital is consistent with the external-benefits account of the role of nonprofit firms. The utility derived from producing quantity and quality might arise because care to these patients entails an external benefit to the community at large and to the hospital decision makers in particular. The external benefit could take on many forms, being purely charitable in some cases or purely concerned with personal prestige and influence in others. Nevertheless, the objective of the hospital could be construed as to maximize the external benefit.

The Quantity-Quality Frontier

In any case, the hospital does not simply maximize quantity or maximize quality, but instead selects a combination of quantity and quality that maximizes utility. The hospital faces a budget constraint: It must pay its bills and cannot run a negative net revenue as a general rule. Furthermore, the nondistribution constraint on all nonprofits entails that this hospital has no incentive to choose positive net revenues as a general rule. Thus, the budget constraint effectively requires that the sum of patient-generated revenues plus donations equal the hospital's costs.

Following Newhouse, assume that all revenue sources, which are primarily patient-generated revenues, are summarized in an average revenue curve labeled $D(q_1)$ in Figure 17.2. This curve is the demand curve facing the hospital. This demand curve would in general depend on the level of quality, q_1; higher quality of care would translate into a higher demand for care. Thus, for example, $D(q_2)$ would represent the demand curve for a higher-quality level. Inasmuch as quality is costly to produce, we can assume that higher-quality levels will entail higher average costs. For example, average cost curve $AC(q_2)$ represents the average cost curve for quality level 2, a higher-quality level than for average cost curve $AC(q_1)$, the average cost curve for quality level 1.

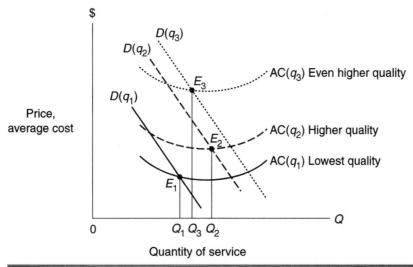

FIGURE 17.2 Hospital Average Cost Curves.

The budget constraint requires that the hospital produce where average revenue equals average cost. For example, output Q_1 satisfies the budget constraint for quality level 1. If consumers place a higher marginal valuation on the incremental quality than it costs to produce, then $D(q_2)$ will shift up by more than will $AC(q_2)$, and incremental quality will be accompanied by incremental quantity. Eventually, however, it is likely that the cost of incremental quality will increase by more than consumers' willingness to pay for it ($AC(q_3)$ constitutes a much bigger rise than $D(q_3)$). When this happens, it becomes clear that incremental quality comes at the expense of quantity of services (fewer people can afford the higher-quality services). Thus, although Q_2 exceeded Q_1, quantity Q_3 (and all further quantities) represents decreases in equilibrium quantity as trade-offs with increased quality. Tracing all these possibilities generates the quality–quantity frontier of the hospital in Figure 17.3.

FIGURE 17.3 Hospital Quality–Quantity Trade-Offs.

Maximization of Utility

Given the possibility frontier, the hospital decision makers choose the point that maximizes utility. The constrained utility maximization point occurs at a point of tangency between the frontier and the highest indifference curve attainable. In Figure 17.3, utility maximization occurs at point A.

The model also illustrates two other prior theories as special cases. On the one hand, let the hospital preferences place sole weight on quantity. Then the hospital would behave like a constrained quantity maximizer and produce at point B. This special case is similar to a theory of hospital-quantity maximization proposed earlier by Long (1964). On the other hand, let the hospital primarily value quality, and further let quality as perceived by the top decision makers be primarily the prestige of the hospital as compared to its peers. It would produce at point C. This special case is similar to a model of the hospital as a conspicuous producer as proposed by Lee (1971). A unique feature of Lee's approach, however, is that the hospital chooses production technologies that are conspicuously prestigious, such as for open heart surgery or transplants. The hospital's search for prestige may lead to socially inefficient production technologies or output qualities.

THE HOSPITAL AS A PHYSICIANS' COOPERATIVE

A different account of the nonprofit hospital is provided in theories that posit the objective of the hospital as the maximization of some pecuniary gain to the decisive set of decision makers. A prime example of this type of model is proposed by Mark Pauly and Michael Redisch (1973), who describe the not-for-profit hospital as a "physicians' cooperative." Here we begin with the assumption that the hospital is de facto controlled by the physician staff who operate the hospital so as to maximize their net incomes.

In this view of the hospital, the focus is on the "full price" of the hospital care, meaning the total charges to the patient by both the hospital and the physician. Assume that the patient pays a single bill representing the full price of the care; let donations be zero. The full price of care will be determined by consumer demand and depends on the total quantity of care offered by the physicians' cooperative. The amount of care produced and offered to patients depends in turn on the quantity of inputs chosen by the top decision makers, here the physicians. Summarize hospital inputs as capital, K, and labor, L. Let the physician input be M, which is fixed if the hospital selects a "closed staff."

Maximizing Net Revenue per Physician

The hospital is then run so as to maximize the net revenue (NR) per physician (M), or NR/M. The net revenue is the sum of all of the revenue less factor payments to nonphysician labor and payments to capital. The net revenue per physician divides that revenue over the total number of physicians, M. An increase in the number of physicians, M, initially increases revenues per physician. Eventually, revenues per physician must fall because (due to the fixed levels of nonphysician labor and capital) the percent increase in revenues (in the numerator) will be smaller than the percent change in number of physicians (in the denominator).

Figure 17.4 shows the optimal size of the staff if the physicians can limit the size of the staff, or "close" the staff. Here dollar values are on the vertical axis and the number of physicians on staff, M, is on the horizontal. The curve N denotes average physician income. The N curve starts at the origin point A (no revenue), rises to a maximum at point B, and then falls. Curve s depicts the supply curve of physicians, which is infinitely elastic, representing

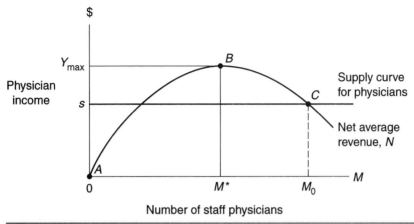

FIGURE 17.4 Maximizing Net Average Physician Revenue in a Hospital.

plausibly a case in an urban, physician-dense environment. For physicians who are on the staff, the optimal staff size would be M^*, where curve N reaches its maximum.[6]

In contrast, if the hospital has an open staff, physicians are free to enter as long as their resulting average income, N, equals or exceeds their supply price, s. The open-staff equilibrium, hence, occurs at point C, where net revenue (the demand for physicians) equals supply, s, with M_0 physicians hired. Regardless of the number of physicians on staff (either a closed-staff or an open-staff equilibrium), the hospital inputs are chosen to maximize residual income for the medical staff. If the Newhouse model can be viewed as resulting from the maximization of external benefit perceived to accrue to the community, then the Pauly–Redisch objective is the complete antithesis.

You may find that friends and acquaintances, perhaps including professionals in health care, differ from one another in various ways. One doctor may be the most intensely concerned when thinking over personal investments or purchases, while another is off to Guatemala on unpaid leave to care for hurricane victims. Might not hospital board members, physicians, and managers also differ from one another? Might not some for-profit firms lean toward charitable endeavors and might not the various nonprofit firms be a mix of the profit oriented and the community minded? Lakdawalla and Philipson (1998) develop this line of reasoning in an attempt to create a synthesis of the many past efforts at modeling. Their point of departure is simple—hospitals all seek profits but deviate from this goal in varying degrees. They explain why accurate prediction of a hospital's behavior requires knowledge of its "profit-deviating" preference.

A COMPARISON OF THE QUANTITY–QUALITY AND THE PHYSICIANS' COOPERATIVE THEORIES

It should be apparent that these two models are conceptually different. It is useful to contrast the two by comparing them on the same graph. To do so, we must make simplifying assumptions to ensure that the two models are described in a comparable

[6]The authors state that this model is similar to models used to explain the economic behavior of the former Soviet collective farm.

context. Applying the Pauly–Redisch idea of full price to both models, we represent combined (physician and hospital) revenues as a single function:

$$R = R(K, L, M_0)$$

The combined revenues depend on the quantity and quality of care produced, which in turn depend on the amounts of the inputs used. Like Newhouse, assume that the hospital/physician care is produced efficiently so that a higher quality of care requires necessarily a higher level and hence cost of inputs. Let us add that the hospital may receive additional revenues in the form of donations, D_0, and government subsidies, G_0. Let physician supply be perfectly elastic at a constant supply price, s. Constant input prices, r for capital and w for labor, complete the description. Finally, define the hospital residual, HR, revenues as the following equation:

$$HR = R(K, L, M_0) - wL - rK - sM_0 + D_0 + G_0 \qquad (17.1)$$

Under the Pauly–Redisch model, the hospital residual, HR, is usurped by the physicians on the staff. For a given level of physicians on the staff, M_0, the physicians will maximize their average incomes by maximizing HR itself.

In contrast, the Newhouse hospital will maximize utility of quantity, Q, and quality, q, subject to the constraint that the hospital residual is zero; that is, the hospital breaks even. To simplify the graphical representation, let the hospital residual function, HR, form a rounded hill.[7] The contours of that hill are shown in Figure 17.5 in a graph with quantity and quality of care on the axes. The contours have a meaning analogous to contour lines on a topographical map. For example, the contour line labeled $HR = 1$ represents the collection of all combinations of quality and quantity of care that yield a hospital residual of $1 million. Contours farther away from the maximum residual point, $HR = HR_{max}$, yield successively lower levels of hospital residual. The contour curve labeled $HR = 0$ indicates the combinations of quality and quantity that yield a zero residual.

FIGURE 17.5 Hospital Quantity-Quality Contours and Hospital Residual.

[7]For further understanding of the shapes of these isoprofit contours, see Spence (1973).

Let us begin with the Pauly–Redisch analysis of a closed hospital staff. Let the hospital physician staff be fixed at some level, M_0. The Pauly–Redisch hospital chooses the quantity–quality combination that maximizes the hospital residual, point $HR = HR_{max}$. The hospital residual then goes to the staff physicians, and these physicians will thus have maximized their average incomes. In contrast, the Newhouse hospital maximizes utility at point A, the point of tangency between the $HR = 0$ contour, representing the Newhouse budget constraint, and the highest indifference curve attainable. Thus, in the closed-staff case, the models yield very different results. As depicted, the Newhouse hospital tends to produce more quantity and quality of care. Perhaps more disturbing, under the Pauly–Redisch behavior, the physicians indirectly usurp the hospital-care residual, and this includes the donations and government subsidy as well. It is as if the nonprofit hospital is a for-profit firm in disguise. If we believed that the nonprofit hospitals behaved like this, we would likely call for an end to government tax exemptions for this nonprofit status. This helps to explain the arguments for the end of nonprofit subsidies as made strongly, for example, by Clark (1980).

Effects of Increased Competition

Before leaving the comparison of models, examine an effect of increased competition in the hospital sector. If entry were free, then all potential firms that may want to compete for hospital care patients are free to do so. Potential competitors could include alternative delivery systems as well as other hospitals. As more competitors enter the market and compete for business, the demand for care at any existing hospital will tend to fall. For our purposes, this means that competition will tend to shrink the hospital residual hill in size.

Figure 17.6 depicts a case where competition has continued until the maximum hospital residual attainable is zero. As we move away from the top of the hospital residual hill in any direction, the contours reflect negative and successively more negative residuals. The result is that the Newhouse and the Pauly–Redisch nonprofit hospital in this end result will converge in their choices of quantity and quality.

It is often agreed that the hospital industry experienced increasing competition in the 1980s. Especially noteworthy are the competition from alternative delivery systems

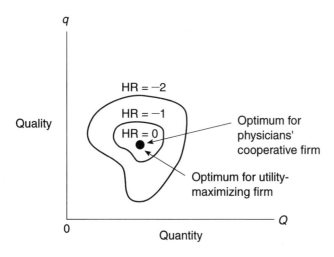

FIGURE 17.6 Convergence of Hospital Models in Long-Run Equilibrium under Free Entry.

and the competitive incentives introduced under Medicare's prospective payment system. A tendency for nonprofit hospitals to converge toward for-profitlike behavior has long been noted in theory (Newhouse, 1970), and more recently it has been proposed as a probable result of competition in the 1980s and beyond.

THE EVIDENCE: DO NONPROFIT HOSPITALS DIFFER FROM FOR-PROFIT HOSPITALS?

Inasmuch as the physicians' cooperative would choose nonphysician inputs and outputs much like a pure profit-oriented firm, we look at empirical comparisons of nonprofit and for-profit hospitals. Despite what appears to be a big difference in orientation, only a few behavioral differences are clear in theory. The nonprofit, in theory, will win at least one "contest": it will produce at a higher quality, a higher quantity, or both. The Newhouse nonprofit *could* be very quantity oriented; for example, it may strive in the extreme to provide large quantities of basic hospital care to a deserving, perhaps destitute, population. Yet another nonprofit hospital might strive single-mindedly for the highest quality of care possible (Newhouse argued that there would be a bias toward quality). These (potentially) different types of nonprofits make comparisons of average quality of all nonprofits versus for-profits difficult to interpret.

Hoerger (1991) has suggested a test that avoids this indeterminancy; it can be understood using Figure 17.5. Again, consider that increased competition shifts the nonprofit's break-even profit contour, HR = 0, inward toward the origin; with this shift, the nonprofit optimimum also moves toward the origin. At the same time, the for-profit's profit level falls, whereas the nonprofit's profit level is more or less fixed at breakeven. Hoerger concluded that the for-profit hospital would exhibit greater variability in its profit level, and the argument also suggested that the for-profit would show less variability in its quality/quantity response to changes in the economic environment.

A large, national sample of hospitals observed from 1983 to 1988 supported Hoerger's hypothesis: for-profit hospital profits were significantly more variable than those of the nonprofit hospitals. Devising a crucial test, however, is complicated by the fact that for-profit hospitals also sort themselves out geographically in distinctive patterns (for example, they are more urban than nonprofits). Mobley and Bradford (1997) show that once these geographical choices are incorporated into the analysis, differences in the variability of profits cannot be distinguished with confidence.

Geography is also the confounding issue for Norton and Staiger (1994), who measured the differences in care provided to the uninsured by nonprofit and for-profit hospitals. They found that when hospitals of each type are located in the same area, they tend to serve the same number of uninsured patients, but for-profits tend to avoid areas where many patients are uninsured. Taking this geographic location factor into account, the nonprofit hospital is more likely to serve the uninsured.

THE HARRIS MODEL

The two hospital models strongly contrast the roles of the two principal power groups in the modern hospital, the physician staff group and the trustee–administrator group. The utility-maximizing models posit this power distribution to be resolved somehow into a coherent utility function, and it is tempting to view the utility function as representing the top management as constrained by the realities of physician behavior. The Pauly–Redisch

model posits the de facto control by the physicians. In either case, there is presumably a resolution of power that occurs, perhaps even harmoniously. The hospital theory proposed by Jeffrey Harris (1977) represents an entirely different approach. The hospital, under Harris's account, is the scene of continual conflict within an organization inherently split into two parts—what Harris describes as a noncooperative oligopoly game.

The Harris model is noteworthy for two additional reasons. On the one hand, Harris is a physician with a Ph.D. in economics. He devised his account after experience as a physician in an urban hospital. As an economist, he is trained in economic organizational theories. On the other hand, Harris presents his work more informally in words and images describing experience within a hospital.

The Hospital as Two Firms

Harris proposes that the hospital's internal organization is really two separate firms interacting in a complex way. The hospital's structure has two main parts: the trustee–administrator group that serves as the supplier of inputs, and the physician staff that serves as the demanders. Like an automobile parts-and-service shop, the hospital has technical experts providing the actual service and requesting supplies from the organization. Unlike the auto shop, the physician's loyalties lie almost entirely with the patient. The physician is the patient's "hired gun."

Rather than having a predictable technological and inventory problem, the administrator has the problem of providing inputs to the physician–agent during a complicated, uncertain sequence of events. Consider Harris's account of a hypothetical case history:

> Mr. X comes to Dr. A with a fever and a cough. A chest X ray reveals a density. He is hospitalized. Penicillin is administered. Although the fever subsides with this treatment, a repeat X ray shows that the density has not disappeared. A sputum cytological examination is performed and lung cancer is diagnosed. Further studies suggest that the cancer can be removed surgically. An operation is performed. Unfortunately, massive postoperative bleeding occurs. Matched whole blood is administered. Despite this treatment, a cardiac arrest ensues and an emergency resuscitation (code call) is announced. Mr. X is transferred to Intensive Care with chest tubes and a respirator. A special contrast study (angiogram) reveals the site of bleeding. A repeat operation is performed (p. 469).

The moral of this account is that rather than being a predictable assembly-line procedure, the hospital service is unique and customized for each patient; it plays out in an unpredictable way. The physician hurries to various supply centers, demanding services on behalf of his patient, like a firefighter. The administrator supplies these services. Under the circumstances, marketlike negotiations between the supplier and demander are impossible, as are lengthy determinations of an exact price for the patient prior to treatment. The problem is not merely that the patient is usually heavily insured; instead, it is the unusual agency relationship that requires the physician to make noneconomic decisions on the patient's behalf. As Harris states,

> There is a special negative externality in an arrangement in which one makes repeated marginal decisions about life and death. This externality is so important that the physician's participation in the "market" for angiograms and code calls is explicitly foreclosed. Whether or not it is justified, this notion has an important influence on the way the hospital is organized (p. 473).

The hospital, according to Harris, solves the rationing problem with a variety of nonprice-related decision rules. "There are loosely enforced standards, rules of thumb, side bargains, cajoling, negotiations, special contingency plans, and in some cases literally shouting and screaming" (p. 478). Furthermore, the physicians often are not organized collusively as a group; rather, each is vying to establish his or her own empire.

Implications

Harris's model provides three implications. First, given the role of physicians, we can expect that the hospital's preferences for new technology will be driven by the preferences of the physician demanders. The physician–agent will tend to prefer technologies that are complementary to existing capacity and that are thus quality enhancing. Second, hospital regulation aimed primarily at the trustee–administrator group may have little effect. That is, regulation to limit hospital costs must establish incentives for and constraints on the physician–agent as well as the administrator. Third, reorganization of the hospital along product lines might make it a more effective organization. For example, reorganizing departments by cardiology, neurology, and so on may better help to integrate the physician into the decision-making apparatus.

SUMMARY ON MODELS OF HOSPITAL BEHAVIOR

While many theories of nonprofit hospital behavior exist, we have described three main types. Most commonly, hospitals are depicted in research as being either utility maximizers or profit maximizers. Of the utility-maximizing type, the Newhouse model is a prominent example, and it depicts the top hospital decision makers as choosing a best combination of quantity and quality of care. Of the profit-maximizing models, the Pauly–Redisch physicians' cooperative version is perhaps most prominent. The key feature in this type of approach is that the nonprofit hospital is depicted as effectively making choices that serve to maximize the pecuniary gain to physicians—the decisive set of decision makers. The Harris model forms a distinctive alternative, depicting the hospital as two separate firms representing somewhat opposing interests who interact in ways similar to what professional economists would term a noncooperative oligopolistic game.

The continued attempts to distinguish the theoretical models will remain a serious interest for policy if only for the importance of this issue to the nonprofit's favored status. For example, would we continue to extend tax-exempt status to the Pauly–Redisch type of nonprofit? Ironically, if we become successful in identifying nonprofit hospitals by behavioral type, we may find that hospitals of all types coexist. At present, we must be content in finding many ideas about nonprofits contained in the various theories.

WHAT CAUSES CONVERSION OF NONPROFITS INTO FOR-PROFITS?

About 7 percent of nonprofit hospitals converted into for-profits between 1970 and 1995; the rate of conversion has been increasing in recent years. Usually, conversion means the sale of the hospital assets to a profit-oriented corporation and the use of the proceeds to fund a nonprofit foundation. Although the theory of conversion is still a work in progress, several ideas recur in this new literature. Lakdawalla and Philipson (1998) explain that if hospital decision makers value profit goals and output goals, then

increases in consumer demand, which will improve profitability, will induce some nonprofits to convert. In such cases, shedding the nonprofit constraint has become more attractive. Others make essentially the same observation in noting that the secular decline in the importance of donations to nonprofit hospitals makes continued nonprofit status less important to many decision makers. A reduction of nonprofit tax benefits theoretically also erodes loyalty to the nonprofit status; the data show that tax rate changes have the corresponding effect on nonprofit market share.[8]

More idiosyncratic, individual motives may be just as important. Frequently, a conversion is motivated in part by financial distress, and the new management often succeeds in relieving the distress by providing new cash and by streamlining operations. However, case studies reveal that personal financial benefits sometimes accrue to the nonprofit decision makers who agree to the conversion. Or, in cases when the nonprofit management goals stay in place after conversion, the conversion may be motivated by the desire to gain greater access to capital; raising equity capital is possible for for-profits but violates the nondistribution constraint for nonprofits.[9]

The question of whether society gains a net benefit from these increasing conversions has come to interest health economists. At least two possible efficiency gains have been suggested: dynamic efficiency, in which better access to capital enables the rapid development of needed facilities, and efficiency of operation. Efficiency of operation may occur if new management and control permit the elimination of entrenched practices and the streamlining of operations. In addition, this type of efficiency difference should be observable in cost-efficiency studies that compare nonprofit hospitals with for-profits, a subject to which we return shortly.

The Relative Efficiency of Nonprofits versus For-Profits

Economic efficiency takes on several meanings. The "social efficiency" of a market structure requires that total social benefits net of opportunity costs be maximized. The early criticism of nonprofit market structure pointed to its tendency to overproduce—to produce to the extent that marginal cost exceeds marginal benefit. However, theoretically, the gains from the provision of underprovided public goods, the benefits from mending "contract failure," can overcome this drawback.

Other types of efficiency—scale, technical, and allocative (discussed in chapter 13)—are provided by the theoretical perfectly competitive industry under for-profit ownership. Beginning with the work of Harvey Leibenstein (1966), economists have taken more interest in the empirical side of the question: Do for-profit firms always maximize and always attain complete technical and allocative efficiency? The pursuit of such issues has been furthered by the corresponding development of econometric tools to estimate whether and how far firms fall short of best practice or frontier production. Many economists now recognize that real for-profit firms may fall short of perfection. The relative efficiency of for-profits versus nonprofits must be decided by the evidence.

Nonprofit hospitals can be of several varieties. They often (in theory) will be efficient in the production of hospital output, meaning cases treated. However, these

[8]See Gully and Santerre (1993), and Hansmann (1987), for an inside look at the effect of tax rates on nonprofit market shares.
[9]For further investigation of conversions, see also Mark (1999), Cutler and Horwitz (1998), and Goddeeris and Weisbrod (1998).

hospitals are neither in control of nor responsible for other inputs into the community's health production, such as exercise and diets, but the combination of nonprofit hospital care and the community's other health production inputs will most probably produce community health inefficiently (Ellis, 1993).

The Newhouse hospital produces the chosen quantity/quality combination efficiently but it may choose a quality in excess of its worth in the production of community health. The Pauly–Redisch hospital produces the hospital service side of care efficiently, but the physicians in control employ excessive amounts of hospital service in the production of patient care. The Harris hospital's internal competition and cross-subsidization may, despite appearances to the contrary, restore social efficiency in a previously imperfect health economy.

PROPERTY RIGHTS THEORY AND ITS APPLICATION TO NONPROFITS

Based on expense preference theory and on property rights theory, a model by H. E. Frech III (1976) argues that an essential economic problem arises because of the nondistribution constraint. Because "profit" cannot be taken out of the nonprofit firm, the opportunity cost of nonpecuniary benefits is lowered, making them more attractive to the manager.

Private property rights are important to the functioning of the firm organized for profit. This is evident as former Soviet Union and other former Eastern Bloc countries struggle toward market economies. The key property rights entail the right of the owner to decide on the employment of the firm's resources, the right to keep the residual, and the right to sell the value of any gains (that is, to sell the property rights). The firm's wealth is the market value of its assets. In theory, the market value of a firm's assets will tend to equal the present value of all future dividends.

In any for-profit firm, the day-to-day managers will make decisions for the owners. These agents for the owners probably acquire some independence and have the opportunity to act as imperfect agents. It is costly for the owners to monitor perfectly the managers, and the owners may accept some degree of departure from pure profit-maximizing behavior. The manager may find it rewarding to seek nonpecuniary gains as well as profits in any given period.

Nonpecuniary benefits could include anything other than money rewards that the manager enjoys: pleasant office space, extra staff, the firm's prestige, or even the prestige of producing high-quality and high-quantity output. Because profit making is what creates firm wealth, this behavior means that the firm will behave as if the top decision makers valued two goals, wealth and nonpecuniary benefits. Thus, the firm is a utility maximizer, but here the indifference curves are described over firm wealth and nonpecuniary benefits. The curves U_1 and U_2 in Figure 17.7 represent examples of these indifference curves for the top decision makers of the firm.

The production of nonpecuniary benefits will affect the wealth attainable by the firm. For example, if the hospital introduces an unprofitable open heart surgery capability for prestige reasons, it will find that its current profits and hence its wealth are reduced. This idea suggests that the firm will face a constraint on its choices, the constraint being the trade-off between maximum possible wealth and the level of nonpecuniary benefits. This wealth–benefits possibility frontier is shown in Figure 17.7 as curve *FF*.

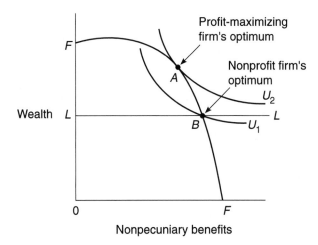

FIGURE 17.7 Optimization between Wealth and Nonpecuniary Benefits.

The For-Profit and Nonprofit Equilibria

The for-profit firm, as managed by the top decision makers, is thus really a utility maximizer over wealth and nonpecuniary benefits. The utility will be maximized in a manner common to all constrained maximization problems at a solution where the highest attainable indifference curve is reached. The for-profit utility maximization occurs in Figure 17.7 at the point of tangency labeled A.

The nonprofit firm experiences a radical attenuation of property rights. There is no property right attaching to the residual and hence to wealth. Only the manager or administrator, and perhaps some other employees, are in a position to attach or usurp the firm's wealth by funneling this wealth to themselves in subtler forms. When this occurs in money terms, we can term the payments a form of salary. Nonprofits in any industry usually are limited in the degree of salary that can be paid to managers, so that unreasonably large salaries are discouraged by regulatory agents. Thus, the most wealth a nonprofit firm can or will accrue is limited to the present value of this implied salary limit. In graphical terms, the nonprofit faces a second constraint in that wealth may not exceed that salary limit, LL, in Figure 17.7.

A nonprofit firm with similar preferences as the for-profit firm depicted will therefore maximize utility at the corner solution point labeled B. Note that at B, the nonprofit reaches the highest indifference curve attainable given its constraints—that is, indifference curve U_1. The implication of Frech's analysis is that the nonprofit will tend to choose a higher level of nonpecuniary benefits than the for-profit. If these nonpecuniary benefits entail things that are not productive, then the nonprofit will tend to be a more costly and inefficient producer than the for-profit firm.

ARE NONPROFIT HEALTH CARE FIRMS IN FACT LESS EFFICIENT?

Cost-efficiency has been compared frequently between nonprofit and for-profit hospitals, and the studies are generally of two types: nonfrontier and frontier studies.

Hospital Studies

Before the frontier techniques described in chapter 13 became widely available, comparisons of hospital performance by ownership were essentially comparisons of

actual costs made after adjusting for possibly confounding factors not considered important to the basic issue. These nonfrontier studies matched hospitals pairwise or compared carefully selected groups of hospitals. The issue of whether some or all studied firms were achieving their best, frontier practice was not addressed directly and it remained a worry to analysts. These studies usually found little if any cost efficiency differences between the nonprofits and the for-profits; occasionally, the results ran opposite to accepted theory so that the nonprofits evidenced higher efficiency levels.[10] Because the newer, frontier methods are more directly appropriate to efficiency studies conceptually, they largely replace the frontier methods beginning in the latter 1980s.

The frontier approach attempts to identify among firms in the sample the best possible practice. A firm is observed to be inefficient when it falls short of the best possible production practice frontier or above the cost frontier. Wilson and Jadlow (1982) compared nuclear medicine services in nonprofit and for-profit hospitals and found for-profits more efficient.

Frontier studies come in two types, data envelopment analysis (DEA) and stochastic frontier analysis (SFA). Though an earlier comparison study using DEA (Ozcan et al., 1992) had suggested small differences, more recent work (Burgess and Wilson, 1996b, 1998) concludes that no significant difference in efficiency can be found between nonprofit and for-profit hospitals.

This general finding in DEA studies is supported by the SFA studies. Zuckerman et al. (1994), addressing both method and empirical issues, found no differences between for-profit and nonprofit hospitals in their "whole sample" method results, though a small yet significant difference favoring the for-profits was observed in their "split sample." Later studies, including further investigation of the method issue, has thus far shown no significant difference.[11]

Such a conclusion does not warrant rejection of property rights theory or of the Frech hypothesis per se, but it does raise the question of the theory's applicability to the hospital sector. The possibility that nonprofit hospitals are of the Pauly–Redisch type is sufficient to account for this result. Cost efficiency in production may be the somewhat ironic side benefit of de facto physician control. However, if the theory does not appear to apply to nonprofit hospitals, it is nevertheless natural to ask in turn whether for-profit nursing homes differ in cost-efficiency from nonprofit homes.

Nursing Home Studies

Early studies applying nonfrontier methods consistently found higher costs in nonprofit nursing homes, a fact considered to be clear support for the property rights.[12] More recently, frontier studies have clarified some issues in efficiency analysis while offering somewhat more mixed findings. Among the DEA analyses, improved efficiency among for-profits was found on two occasions, though less than five percentage points in one of these. Other studies, including two applying stochastic methods, tended to reverse the order to find only trivial inefficiencies across the board.[13]

[10]For further study and review, see Pattison and Katz (1982); Lewin, Derzon, and Margulies (1981); Bays (1979); Sloan (1988); and Becker and Sloan (1985).

[11]See Folland and Hofler (1999), and Vitaliano and Toren (1996).

[12]Bishop (1980); Birnbaum et al. (1981), Frech and Ginsburg (1981), Borjas, Frech, and Ginsburg (1983), and Frech (1985).

[13]Nyman (1989), Sexton et al. (1989), Rosko et al. (1995), Fizel and Nunnikoven (1992), and Hofler and Rungeling (1994).

The bottom line? Many health economists would say that at this stage in frontier analysis of nursing home efficiency, the usual tests of statistical confidence—the levels of *t* values, probability values, F tests, and the like—are at best rough guides and overstate our true confidence, "we do not know yet for sure." The success of these studies has been to raise good method questions and to make us more humble about whether or not a favored theory is true.

One of the thorniest method questions is whether nonprofit homes sometimes appear to be less efficient merely because they are offering a higher quality of care. Under the theory of "contract failure," already discussed in this chapter, nonprofit nursing homes naturally should tend toward higher quality of care, a prediction consistent with mathematical modeling (Hirth, 1999). "The devil is in the details" issue may apply to the health economist's incomplete understanding of individual variables. For example, we know (Nyman and Bricker, 1989), that high occupancy rates are a significant indicator of high efficiency scores, *ceteris paribus*. We don't know clearly, however, how occupancy rates are related to quality of care and how they affect the length of waiting lists for those elderly who would like nursing care near their natural home, another aspect of quality.

FEATURE

Why Are RNs' Wages Higher in Nonprofit Nursing Homes?

Holtmann and Idson (1993) provide recent evidence to explain why registered nurses (RNs) are paid higher wages by nonprofit than by for-profit nursing homes. As described previously, nonprofits are formed in response to patients' informational limitations in assessing quality. Specifically, because of patients' difficulties in distinguishing among nursing homes of varying quality, the market will fail to produce high-quality nursing homes.

Holtmann and Idson observe, as have others, the differentially higher wages that RNs receive in the nonprofit nursing home sector. Earlier studies (for example, Borjas, Frech, and Ginsburg, 1983) attributed these differentials to the premise that because nonprofits do not distribute the residuals (the revenues less the costs), they are less interested in minimizing the costs. Holtmann and Idson propose an alternative hypothesis that nonprofits pay nurses higher wages to get higher quality.

Using sophisticated econometric analyses, the authors discover that the differential wages reflect quality-enhancing characteristics of the nurses, such as years of experience and length of tenure on the current job. Both of these reflect higher quality of care, because the provision of such care may require more stable employment relationships.

The authors then compare the quality and the property rights hypotheses. According to the property rights hypothesis, employees in nonprofit homes are paid higher wages than they could command in for-profit homes; this implies a higher return to their productivity-related attributes than in for-profit homes. However, the authors' methods show that workers in nonprofit facilities generally are compensated at a lower rate for their productivity-related attributes, and it is the fact that they have *more* of these attributes that leads to the wage differences. They view these distinctions as "strong evidence against the property-rights hypothesis that nonprofits are paying wasteful, inefficient wage premiums" (p. 73).

Conclusions

The theme of this chapter was the nonprofit firm in the health care sector. We began with a description of the nonprofit firm, noting the importance of the nonprofit constraint. We then asked the question: Why do nonprofit firms exist? We found three principal accounts of the nonprofit phenomenon. Weisbrod explained how nonprofit firms might arise to provide public goods that are neglected by the private markets and the government. Hansmann explained how nonprofit firms might be formed to reduce or eliminate a contract failure that arises because consumers may not trust the profit-motivated firm to perform faithfully certain functions, often charitable ones. Finally, Bays explained that the reason the nonprofit form might take over the hospital industry is because an interest group, the physicians, finds greater financial rewards under the nonprofit system. We noted that under both theories, the nonprofits can improve the well-being of the community, overcoming the for-profit firm's tendency to underproduce in the presence of beneficial externalities.

We then investigated three models of nonprofit hospital behavior. The Newhouse hospital is motivated by the desire to provide service to the community, often the quality of care being as important as the quantity. In contrast, the Pauly–Redisch hospital is really under the physicians' control, who use it to maximize the average physician's income. We contrasted these two hospitals as polar opposites; the Newhouse hospital model may be interpreted (though it need not be) as motivated by the good of the community, whereas the Pauly–Redisch model does not vary from monetary gain. We showed the irony that under pressure of competition, these differently motivated firms may behave essentially the same. The Harris hospital casts a different and illuminating picture of what a nonprofit hospital looks like on the inside to a physician/economist at work in the hospital. We closed with a discussion of current issues, such as conversions of nonprofits into for-profits.

Finally, the nonprofit and for-profit health care firms were contrasted regarding cost efficiency. Frech's theory makes a strong claim for the relative efficiency of for-profit firms; the nondistribution constraint of the nonprofit firms effects a lowering of the opportunity cost of nonpecuniary benefits, the "perks" that tempt managers to make inefficient choices. The data from recent efficiency studies offer little support regarding hospitals, which generally have found little if any significant difference. Nursing home studies have often suggested large and significant advantages to for-profits.

The first half of the twentieth century saw radical changes in the structure of the health care industry, particularly in the prevalence of nonprofit firms. In the latter half, we gained a better understanding of the economic factors that make nonprofits attractive, and we are beginning to understand what can make them disappear. Of the many types of nonprofits, the nonprofit hospital in the United States is one of the relatively more commercial nonprofits, receiving the lion's share of its revenues from its customers. Against this backdrop are many economists and political leaders in reemerging or developing countries who look hopefully to nonprofits as a third way. Predicting where these trends will reach by the mid twenty-first century is fruitless, yet many if not most health economists would agree that the urge to provide for others in the community, though less than the urge toward private gain, is just as persistent in human nature.

Summary

1. The defining characteristic of a nonprofit firm is the nondistribution constraint. Furthermore, nonprofits are typically tax exempt, and donations to nonprofit firms receive favorable tax treatment.
2. The Weisbrod theory for the existence of nonprofits proposes that nonprofit firms arise to fulfill unmet demands for public goods.
3. The contract failure theory for the existence of nonprofits proposes that nonprofit firms are advantageous under circumstances where it is difficult or impossible for the purchaser of the good to verify the delivery and the quality of the good.
4. The interest group theory for the existence of nonprofit hospitals proposes that physicians favor the nonprofit hospital organizations because they can exercise greater economic control within them.
5. Utility-maximizing models of nonprofit firms are exemplified by the Newhouse model, in which the hospital decision makers choose preferred combinations of quality and quantity of care subject to a break-even constraint.
6. The physicians' cooperative model in contrast depicts the hospital under de facto physician control exercised so as to maximize average physician income.
7. The Harris hospital model is distinct from both the utility-maximizing type and the income-maximizing type. Harris depicts the nonprofit hospital as the outcome of two noncooperative interacting firms represented by administrators on one side and physicians on the other. These groups often must employ nonmarket decision making in life-or-death situations.
8. Under property rights theory, the nonprofit health care firm is less efficient than its for-profit counterpart because the incentive to maximize firm wealth is attenuated by the nondistribution constraint.
9. Evidence suggests that nonprofit hospitals in the United States are not very different in economic efficiency from for-profit hospitals.

Discussion Questions

1. What is the nondistribution constraint? In what way is the nondistribution constraint circumvented in the Pauly–Redisch model? What implication does this have for the efficiency of the Pauly–Redisch nonprofit hospital?
2. If the delivery and quality of care by health care firms could be cheaply and accurately monitored by a monitoring agency, would there be any contract failure in health care remaining? Would there be any need for nonprofits in health care? Would any arise?
3. If the interest group theory applies to hospitals, why doesn't it also apply to nursing homes? Would a doctor-owned, for-profit hospital be as attractive to physicians as a nonprofit hospital?
4. Suppose that population growth expands the quality–quantity frontier of a Newhouse utility-maximizing nonprofit hospital. How would its choice of quantity and quality change? In your view, is a for-profit hospital likely to respond more quickly to population growth? Discuss.
5. Under which of the three models of hospital behavior described in this chapter does the tax-exempt status of nonprofit hospitals make the most sense? Under which the least?

6. Can we say which are the most efficient hospitals—nonprofits or for-profits? Which are the most efficient nursing homes? What qualifications apply to our present knowledge in each case? What is your view?

7. Why might information problems lead to consumer preferences for nonprofit provision of some goods and services? Reconcile your answer with the observation that most physician care, drug products, and many other services are provided by for-profit firms.

8. In what sense do nonprofits earn "profits" and need to earn "profits" to survive?

9. What are some cost advantages that nonprofits have over for-profits? Are there any disadvantages?

10. Explain the logic behind the argument that donations have characteristics of a public good.

11. Weisbrod, Bays, and Hansmann, present three different theories on the existence of nonprofit organizations. Compare and contrast them in regard to the types of firms and the ways they are financed.

Exercises

1. In Figure 17.1, if two additional voters had demand curves equal to D_5, what amount of the public good would tend to be provided by the democratic government? Which voters would be unlikely to promote a nonprofit? Which likely?

2. In Figure 17.1, suppose that Voter 5 decides that he values the public good even more than before. Will there be an increase in the amount provided through the median voter model of the voting process? Why or why not?
 Suppose that Voter 5 can bribe one of the voters to change his or her preferences. Which one will Voter 5 approach?

3. Under the physicians' cooperative model, if the supply price of physicians were to rise, how would this affect the equilibrium staff size in the open-staff case? How would it affect the optimal staff size in the closed-staff case?

4. Of the Newhouse and the physicians' cooperative models, which nonprofit hospital is likely to produce more quantity and quality in equilibrium with barriers to entry? In long-run equilibrium with free entry and exit?

5. In the property rights model graph in Figure 17.7, if strenuous regulatory activity were to lower the maximum salary level, LL, of nonprofits, how would this affect the nonprofit efficiency level?

6. Consider Figures 17.2 and 17.3. Suppose that technological improvements allow hospitals to produce quality at lower average costs. What will happen to the average cost curves in Figure 17.2? What will happen to equilibrium quality and quantity in Figure 17.3?

18

Hospitals and Long-Term Care

- Background and Overview of Hospitals
- Hospital Utilization and Costs
- Nursing Homes
- Hospice and Home Health
- Conclusions

In 1996, there were 6,201 hospitals with just over 1 million beds in the United States (Table 18.1). Hospital care dominates total health care spending, and the hospital remains at the center of a rapidly changing health economy. At the same time, the aging of the population has created a major challenge for the adequate provision of long-term care. This chapter provides an overview of the hospital and long-term care sectors. It also examines several issues that have led to some surprising and controversial results. These issues include the "medical arms race" and cost shifting for hospitals, as well as various quality, demand, and cost themes in the nursing home literature.

Background and Overview of Hospitals[1]

It often is helpful to distinguish among the many hospitals by using four criteria: length of stay, type, ownership, and size. Hospitals are categorized as short stay (usually less than 30 days) or long term (usually more than 30 days). The *community hospital* is the type with which the general public is most familiar. It consists of all nonfederal general hospitals that provide acute, short-term care. Community hospitals employed 3.6 million personnel in 1993, with registered nurses (874,000) as the largest single category.

Many community hospitals are also teaching hospitals. These are hospitals that have residency programs approved by the Accreditation Council for Graduate Medical

[1]More extensive discussions of many of the topics in this section are found in Starr (1982), Temin (1988), Jonas (1992), and Raffel and Raffel (1994).

TABLE 18.1 Hospital Data			
	1980	*1990*	*1996*
All Hospitals (beds in 1,000s)	6,965 (1,365)[a]	6,649 (1,213)	6,201 (1,062)
Federal Hospitals	359 (117)	337 (98)	290 (73)
Nonfederal Hospitals	6,606 (1,248)	6,312 (1,113)	5,911 (989)
Community	5,830 (988)	5,384 (927)	5,134 (862)
Nonprofit	3,322 (692)	3,191 (657)	3,045 (598)
For-profit	730 (87)	749 (102)	759 (109)
State–local government	1,778 (209)	1,578 (169)	1,330 (155)
Psychiatric and other long-term	702 (256)	892 (183)	768 (125)
Community Hospitals			
Size			
6–199 beds	4,120 (341)	3,730 (314)	3,634 (309)
200–499 beds	1,393 (430)	1,369 (417)	1,249 (380)
500 or more beds	317 (218)	285 (196)	251 (173)
Occupancy Rate (percent)	75.6	66.8	61.5
Admissions (per 1,000 pop.)	159	125	117
Average Length of Stay (days)	7.6	7.2	6.2
Outpatient Visits (per 1,000 pop.)	890	1,208	1,659

[a]Numbers in parentheses are beds in thousands.

Sources: U.S. Department of Commerce, *Statistical Abstract of the United States, 1998,* Tables 200 and 202; and U.S. Department of Health and Human Services (DHHS), *Health, United States, 1998,* Table 109.

Education. Other hospital types are: mental, including those treating alcoholism and other chemical dependencies; tuberculosis and other respiratory diseases; and other special (e.g., maternity, orthopedic, and rehabilitation).

Hospital ownership can be private or public (federal, state, county, or local). The former category consists of either nonprofit or proprietary (for-profit) hospitals. Table 18.1 indicates that there are 1,330 public short-stay hospitals, mainly state or local. Nonprofits dominate the remainder.

Most short-stay hospitals are relatively small with fewer than 200 beds. However, the categories consisting of hospitals that have more than 200 beds account for 64 percent of all beds. The largest hospitals usually are affiliated with university medical schools and provide tertiary care in addition to primary and secondary care. Tertiary care consists of the most complex procedures such as organ transplant surgery and open heart procedures. The typical community hospital is limited to secondary care consisting of the more common surgical and medical procedures. Primary care consists of the kinds of preventive and curative care received by patients who are not hospitalized.

HISTORY

The history of hospitals dates back to ancient Egypt and Greece. From that time, places of healing in many countries were organized by religious establishments. Illness was closely associated with a lack of faith or superstition, and care was administered by priests. Even today, it is not unusual for the afflicted to believe that they are being pun-

ished or cursed and, in some parts of the world, shamans and other "medicine men" are called upon to exorcise evil spirits.

Early hospitals in the United States were associated with the poor or with mental and infectious diseases, and medicine was practiced mainly at the home. This picture changed as more effective surgery became possible following scientific and technological advances in the last half of the nineteenth century. The modern U.S. hospital emerged at the turn of the twentieth century. In particular, important advances in antisepsis to help fight off infections greatly increased the probability of surgical success. Major advances in anesthesia, anatomy, and physiology and the invention of the X ray were also important contributors.

Two nonscientific factors helped accelerate the process. One was the rapid pace of urbanization resulting from industrialization. Sophisticated hospitals could not be supported by rural areas because of transportation problems and low population densities. Urbanization also created health problems, such as outbreaks of infectious disease that were much less common in rural areas and that required hospitalization. The second factor was a financial one. Early hospitals relied on philanthropic contributions or state and local government funds. These alone would have been inadequate to support the growing numbers and costs associated with the modern hospital. The rise of an urban middle class led to a greater ability to pay, as well as third-party payment through private insurance and workers' compensation, which originated shortly after the turn of the century.

The opening of The Johns Hopkins Hospital in Baltimore in 1885 was a significant milestone. Though few other hospitals would ultimately be able to emulate or compete with its international reputation, The Johns Hopkins Hospital introduced the latest advances in medical technology and hospital design. Through its affiliation with The Johns Hopkins University, it became a model of the teaching and research hospital.

ORGANIZATION

The typical nonprofit community hospital is governed by a board of trustees that selects the president and is responsible for approving most major decisions. The members of the board are often leading members of the community known for their ability to contribute or raise funds.[2] The president and other administrative staff are regular employees who manage the hospital.

A distinguishing feature of the hospital arises from claims that the hospital's decision-making power rests with the medical staff rather than the administrators or the board. To appreciate the significance of this phenomenon, consider that the medical staff in most hospitals is composed of admitting physicians who are not employees of the hospital. Physicians apply for staff privileges to admit patients and perform certain procedures. Because it is the physician who often has admitting privileges at many hospitals and who brings patients to the hospital, admitting physicians have considerable influence on hospital decision making by serving on many committees relating to hospital governance and patient care. Because of these arrangements, the hospital has been referred to as the

[2]These are evolving into boards with business backgrounds. Also, the roles of boards have been changing as they become more concerned with community health in managed care settings.

physician's "rent-free workshop" where the physician can direct substantial resources for patient care but is not held directly accountable for those resources. Physicians also bill separately for their services.

To deal with the conflicts and cost pressures created by the traditional system, more hospitals are now relying on permanent physician–employees who are paid salaries or combinations of salaries and bonuses, the latter driven by various incentives. As these staff physicians are no longer the driving force to admit patients, hospitals with permanent staff physicians must have other means to attract patients. The source of patients for such hospitals is often affiliation with or ownership of HMOs. Direct advertising through the broadcast or print media and purchases of physician practices also are becoming important sources of patients.

The hospital industry is going through a period of rapid change. As a result of declining inpatient utilization, many smaller hospitals have closed while others have merged or reorganized. Hospitals face considerable pressure to join networks of providers in order to participate in managed care plans and to become diversified health care centers with expanded primary care facilities. Many hospitals are concentrating resources on free-standing outpatient surgery units and other outpatient programs such as cardiac rehabilitation. Table 18.1 reveals the extent of these changes. Inpatient admissions per capita dropped 26 percent from 1980 to 1996, and the occupancy rate dropped from 76 percent to 62 percent. Over the same period, the number of outpatient visits nearly doubled.

Despite this dramatic shift to outpatient care, it is likely that the pace of hospital closings will increase and that hospitals will continuously reorganize, especially as Medicare and Medicaid budgets tighten. Governments provide more than 60 percent of hospital revenues, although this figure can go higher than 75 percent for many urban and small hospitals that rely heavily on poor and elderly patients. Proposals to reform Medicare and Medicaid also tend to be directed at reducing federal spending and invariably include reductions in hospital reimbursement rates. Thus, hospitals that disproportionately depend on Medicare and Medicaid are especially vulnerable.

Nevertheless, in an increasingly competitive, cost-conscious environment, all hospitals are under considerable pressure to respond quickly to new incentives and opportunities. For example, the Balanced Budget Act of 1997 allows hospitals to form networks to sell Medicare HMO plans directly to beneficiaries. It is too early to evaluate the effects of this change, but Congress expects that these Medicare PSOs (provider-sponsored organizations) will increase competition and bring more seniors under managed care.

REGULATION AND ACCREDITATION

Hospitals are subject to a wide variety of state and federal regulations designed to deal with quality, costs, and reimbursement. They are licensed at the state level, although licensure is often focused on the adequacy of the hospital's physical plant and other inputs. Hospitals have their own quality assurance programs but, of greater policy significance, Professional Standards Review Organizations (PSROs) were established in 1971 under federal legislation to monitor quality while limiting utilization. After considerable controversy regarding their effectiveness, these agencies were replaced in 1984 by Peer Review Organizations (PROs). PROs are awarded contracts by the Health Care Financing Administration (HCFA) to perform case-by-case peer review and to monitor Medicare utilization in hospitals and other facilities. Because PROs often are domi-

nated by physicians and hospitals, the impact of PROs has been questioned. In the mid-1990s, the HCFA adopted the position that case-by-case inspection brings only marginal improvements in quality. As a result, PROs' funding and responsibilities were reduced substantially.

Hospitals also are subject to numerous other regulations and requirements. Many of these relate to reimbursement such as Medicare's Prospective Payments System (PPS) and various forms of state rate regulation. Certificate-of-need (CON) laws have been used to limit capital spending, and hospitals are subject to antitrust laws intended to promote competition.

In addition to meeting licensure and regulatory requirements, most hospitals and many other health care facilities seek accreditation from the Joint Commission on the Accreditation of Healthcare Organizations (JCAHO). The JCAHO is a private, not-for-profit organization that was founded in 1952 and has a board dominated by representatives from physician and hospital associations. Its goal is to set standards for patient safety and quality of care. Hospitals seeking accreditation are evaluated by a visitation team, which examines hospital compliance with JCAHO standards. To maintain accreditation, the hospital must undergo an on-site review every three years. A survey of 300 hospital CEOs found that 59 percent indicated that hospitals should seek accreditation to validate and measure quality and safety; 25 percent indicated that they seek accreditation to improve quality.[3]

Many third-party payers reimburse only for care provided in accredited hospitals. Though hospitals can be evaluated by federal inspectors to qualify for Medicare and Medicaid reimbursement, JCAHO accreditation also satisfies the federal requirement. As a result of the importance of JCAHO accreditation and concerns about the accreditation process, the JCAHO has been described as "one of the most powerful and secretive groups in all of health care."[4] The potential for conflict between professional self-interests and public interests is evident. The influence of the JCAHO can be used to limit hospital competition and to protect physicians against other groups of providers by denying them access to hospitals or influence within hospitals. An example of the former emerged in one antitrust case in which osteopathic doctors successfully sued a hospital over discrimination in the awarding of staff privileges.[5]

Hospital Utilization and Costs

The relentless and rapid growth of hospital costs has served as the impetus for many forms of regulation and other policy initiatives. Table 18.2 shows the extent of the increases in total hospital costs, as well as costs per day and costs per admission. Hospital costs account for 35 percent of total health expenditures and have increased at an annual rate of 10.7 percent since 1960. Table 18.2 also shows that a minimal and dwindling share has been paid out of pocket, especially after Medicare and Medicaid were introduced in 1965. Governments now pay for 62 percent of all hospital costs compared to 38 percent in 1965.

[3] *American Hospital Association, AHA News,* September 25, 1995.
[4] "Prized by Hospitals, Accreditation Hides Perils Patients Face," *The Wall Street Journal,* October 12, 1988, p. 1.
[5] *Weiss v. New York Hospital,* 745 F.2d 786, 814 (3rd Cir. 1984).

TABLE 18.2 Hospital and Nursing Home Costs

	1960	*1970*	*1980*	*1990*	*1996*
Health Care Spending ($ billion)[a]	27	73	247	700	1,035
Hospital Care ($billion)	9.3	28	103	256	359
% of total health spending	34.5	38.2	41.5	36.7	34.6
Percent of Hospital Care Paid by					
Out of pocket	20.7	9.0	5.2	4.0	2.6
Private health insurance and other private	36.8	35.6	40.4	41.1	35.9
Government	42.5	55.4	54.4	54.9	61.5
Medicare	—	19.2	29.1	27.3	33.0
Medicaid	—	9.5	9.3	13.4	14.7
Other government[b]	42.5	26.7	16.0	14.2	13.8
Average Hospital Cost ($)					
Per day	—	—	245	687	1,006
Per stay	—	—	1,851	4,947	6,225
Nursing Home Care ($ billion)	0.8	4.2	18	51	79
% of total health spending	3.2	5.8	7.1	7.3	7.6
Percent of Nursing Home Paid by					
Out of pocket	77.9	53.5	41.8	43.1	31.4
Private health insurance and other private	6.3	5.3	4.2	5.8	7.1
Government	15.7	41.2	54.0	51.0	61.5
Medicare	—	3.4	1.7	3.4	11.4
Medicaid	—	22.3	50.0	45.4	47.8
Other government	15.7	15.5	2.3	2.2	2.3

[a]All monetary values are in nominal dollars.
[b]Includes the Department of Veterans Affairs and state and local spending.
Sources: U.S. DHHS, *Health, United States, 1998,* Tables 95, 120, and 125; and U.S. Department of Commerce, *Statistical Abstract of the United States, 1998,* Table 203.

The increase in costs is not the result of more inpatient admissions, despite a growing and aging population. As previously noted in Table 18.1, the number of hospital beds and occupancy rates have been declining. Rather, the cost per day and cost per admission and the shift to outpatient services (leaving hospitals with high fixed costs) are the main driving forces. The influence of these determinants of hospital costs is intertwined closely with numerous features of health care markets including changes in technology and reimbursement methods. These issues and many others relating to hospital costs and health system reform are developed in other chapters. In this section, we address two of the many other concerns relevant to the growth of hospital costs. The first concerns the effect of competition on costs, and the second deals with cost shifting.

COMPETITION AND COSTS

Is hospital competition inefficient and has it led to, as many analysts contend, an unproductive and costly medical arms race (MAR)? Intuitively, it would appear that having a larger number of hospitals in a given market would lead to unnecessary duplication of expensive capital equipment and unnecessary expenditures on advertising in order to attract doctors and their patients. It also may create pressure to fill beds through questionable admissions.

Game Theory and the Medical Arms Race (MAR)

Game theory is a powerful analytical tool that is being used increasingly in economics and other disciplines. The theory of games can be used to show why it may be in the best interests for each hospital to engage in a MAR even when hospitals as a whole are negatively affected. Game theory begins with a payoff matrix of the type shown in Figure 18.1. Suppose there are two large hospitals, A and B, in a market, each facing the decision of whether or not to add an expensive heart transplant unit without knowing what its rival will do. The payoff matrix shows the total profit for each hospital (with values for A's profit shown first) resulting from the four combinations of strategies. For example, if both adopt (the "northwest" cell), each hospital will have a total profit of $100 (million). If A alone adopts (the "northeast" cell), assume that it will have a significant advantage resulting in a profit of $200 (million), while B loses $50 (million).

Game theory tries to predict a solution, that is, the strategy chosen by each participant.

It is clear that both hospitals with a combined profit of $300 (million) will be better off if neither introduces the unit. However, if the hospitals cannot agree (for example, they may not trust each other or they may believe that antitrust laws preclude cooperation), game theory predicts a solution in which each hospital will adopt the unit and combined profits will be $200 (million). Why? Given the payoff matrix, each hospital has a dominant strategy. That is, regardless of what Hospital B does, A will always have a higher profit by adopting rather than not adopting, that is, $100 (million) versus −$50 (million) if B adopts and $200 (million) versus $150 (million) if B does not adopt. Similarly B's dominant strategy is to adopt and, hence, a scenario results consistent with the MAR hypothesis.[6] In addition to decisions involving the acquisition of technology and introduction of new services, game theory can provide insight into hospital advertising and other forms of nonprice competition.

Hospital B

		Adopt	Do not adopt
Hospital A	Adopt	100, 100	200, −50
	Do not adopt	−50, 200	150, 150

FIGURE 18.1 Payoff Matrix (Millions of Dollars).

[6]Students of game theory will recognize this as an example of the prisoner's dilemma and the solution as a Nash equilibrium. See McKay (1994) for other health care applications of game theory. See also Calem and Rizzo (1995) for an application of location theory to hospital quality and specialty mix decisions. It, too, raises the possibility of excessive quality competition.

Such concerns with the potential adverse consequences of hospital competition are interesting and unique. With the exception of natural monopolies resulting from economies of scale, economists usually endorse competition as being in the best interests of consumers. Evidence is substantial that higher levels of seller concentration in most markets lead to higher prices and reduced choices. Indeed, this is the premise behind federal and state antitrust laws, though the relevance of these laws to the hospital sector also has been questioned by those who support the MAR hypothesis.

Are there any features of the hospital industry that might negate the conventional wisdom? With hospitals enjoying only limited economies of scale (chapter 13), the economies of scale justification is not well supported. Instead, hospital reimbursement methods probably hold the key. Traditionally, hospitals were reimbursed by third parties on a retrospective cost basis. Higher costs generally meant higher payments to hospitals. Unlike other industries, where sellers must compete on the basis of price for customers, retrospective reimbursement meant that hospitals were largely immune from the discipline exerted by the competitive process.

This situation has changed in recent years. Hospitals as well as insurance companies must compete for their managed care business through price and quality. Hospitals also are now reimbursed by many major third-party payers on a prospective basis at rates that are independent of their actual costs. It would thus appear that hospitals have a strong financial stake in being efficient and in avoiding capital investments that are not profitable.

Economists have begun to look at the MAR hypothesis in this increasingly competitive environment. Dranove and colleagues (1992) developed and estimated a theoretical model of the number of specialized hospital services in a market. They found that increased competition increases the number of services offered, but the MAR effect is dominated by economies of scale and scope, as well as other demand and supply considerations.

Mobley and Frech (1994) also provide insight into the role of competition, although they do not deal directly with the MAR hypothesis. In their study of California hospitals during the 1980s, the authors found that demand is an important determinant of growth and survival and that increased competition forces smaller, low-quality hospitals to exit.

HOSPITAL COST SHIFTING

Hospitals provide substantial amounts of uncompensated care.[7] Most of this care is provided to uninsured indigents, but uncollectibles from incompletely insured patients are also considerable. In addition, many third-party payers place stringent limits on reimbursement rates, and proposals to reduce Medicare and Medicaid expenditures typically call for further reductions. After an initial period of generous payments under PPS, by 1993 Medicare paid only 89 percent of hospitals' costs to treat its patients, compared to 93 percent for Medicaid and 129 percent for private patients.[8]

A vital policy issue is whether or not the costs of uncompensated care and "discounts" to some third-party payers are passed on by hospitals to other patients as is often claimed. Thus, if Medicare and Medicaid cuts are passed on to others, there would

[7]Hospitals have many legal and ethical reasons for providing uncompensated care. A good review is found in Duncan (1992).
[8]Prospective Payment Assessment Commission (1995, Tables 1–8).

be no savings to society but merely a shifting of the hospital cost burden. The burden would be shifted similarly if the number of uninsured or poorly insured increases because of an increase in part-time employment in the services sector and cutbacks in fringe benefits by some employers.

Intuition suggests that these costs are shifted. After all, services must be paid for and it stands to reason that the burden for those who are not paying must be picked up by others. However, the issue may not be as simple as it first appears. To see why, we develop a model of hospital fee determination.

A variety of models of hospital behavior were examined in chapter 17 but, for simplicity, assume that hospitals maximize profits (or the undistributed residual in the case of nonprofits). Suppose also for simplicity that there are just two groups of patients: private (insured or self-pay) and Medicare. The downward-sloping demand curve for the private sector and the constant Medicare hospital reimbursement rate (R_1) per patient are shown in Figure 18.2. The private demand curve (panel A) is negatively sloped because at least some patients economize or substitute other services as their out-of-pocket obligations increase, and hospitals that raise fees lose patients to other hospitals. Assume further that R_1 covers the average variable cost (C_1) for a fixed number of Medicare patients seeking admission (i.e., Q_2 Medicare patients in panel B) but that the rate does not necessarily cover all costs. Finally, assume that the hospital is operating below capacity and that C_1 is constant over the relevant range and equal to marginal cost.[9]

FIGURE 18.2 Analysis of Changes in the Medicare Hospital Reimbursement Rate.

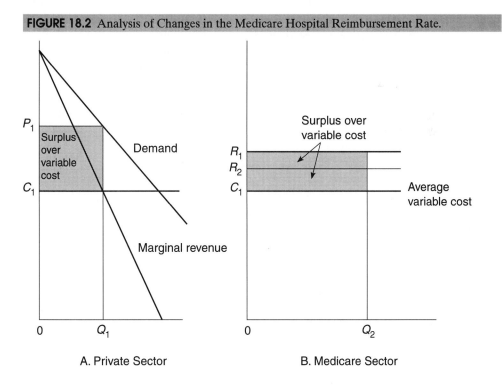

A. Private Sector B. Medicare Sector

[9]With considerable excess capacity in the U.S. hospital industry, this assumption is plausible. It is made only for convenience and does not affect the results.

If the hospital is unable to price discriminate in the private sector, it will accept Q_1 private patients (the quantity where marginal revenue equals marginal cost) and charge the price, P_1.[10] It also will accept all Medicare patients (Q_2) at the Medicare rate[11] so that the hospital treats a total of ($Q_1 + Q_2$) patients. Total revenues of ($P_1Q_1 + R_1Q_2$) produce a surplus over variable cost equal to ($P_1 - C_1$) Q_1 + ($R_1 - C_1$) Q_2.

Suppose that the Medicare reimbursement rate is lowered to R_2 but that the rate still covers the average variable and marginal costs so that the hospital continues to accept Q_2 Medicare patients. Contrary to intuition, it makes no sense to increase prices in the private sector. Hospital surpluses diminish at prices above P_1 because the hospital will lose private sector patients whose marginal revenue exceeds marginal cost. The optimal private rate remains at P_1 for the Q_1 private patients, and no cost shifting occurs.[12]

This is not the end of the story because the hospital's revenues are reduced. In the long run, revenues must cover all costs; otherwise, the hospital can not survive. If revenues exceed costs for the hospital in Figure 18.2 after the lower Medicare rate, then the private rate may be unaffected in the long run, as well. Suppose, however, that the hospital's revenues now fall short of total costs. If it cannot reduce costs, the hospital and others in the same situation may be forced out of business or forced to merge. As this happens, demand will increase for the remaining hospitals and, as a result, the private rate also could rise.

Determining the burden of lower public reimbursement is thus complex. The burden ultimately can be borne by many groups through reductions in the number of hospitals, lower compensation to hospital employees as the demand for their services diminishes, reduced access to care for those with public insurance or those receiving uncompensated care, and higher fees to the private paying groups.

A review of the limited evidence on cost shifting by Morrisey (1995) indicates that cost shifting through higher prices has taken place but that it is far from complete. One study included in his review shows that California hospitals reduced the amount of uncompensated care by 53 cents for every $1 decrease in their discounts to third parties. This would have been unnecessary if the hospitals could have shifted the costs to others. Other studies showed partial cost shifting through higher fees.[13]

HOSPITAL CLOSURES

We have already referred to some of the dramatic changes affecting hospitals. The growth of managed care and the introduction of reimbursement methods that discourage inpatient care and long lengths of stay have been major contributors to declining inpatient utilization. In response, capacity has been reduced through the sharp drop since 1980 in the number of hospitals and beds (Table 18.1). Even so, with occupancy

[10]Ideally, the hospital would like to perfectly price discriminate by charging each private patient the highest he or she is willing to pay. In this ideal case, it will admit private patients up to the intersection of the demand curve and cost curves in panel A with prices to some patients falling as low as C_1. The hospital will then capture the entire consumers' surplus consisting of the area under the demand curve and above the cost curve.

[11]With capacity limitations, it will first raise the price to eliminate those private patients whose marginal revenue is below the Medicare rate.

[12]Cost shifting could arise if the hospital was not previously maximizing profit and accepting "unprofitable" patients whose marginal revenue fell short of marginal cost. The lower Medicare rate would encourage the hospital to reduce the number of these patients by raising the private rate.

[13]Clement (1997/1998) introduced a utility-maximizing model dependent on both profits and quantity of care. Data for three intervals from the early 1980s to early 1990s supported cost shifting, but its extent diminished over time.

running at just 62 percent in 1996, excess capacity remains one of the most visible and significant characteristics of the hospital industry.

Although hospital closure can be painful to a community, the restructuring of the hospital industry should be viewed as a market response to cost-containment efforts. Nevertheless, it remains important to determine just how well the market works for this sector and, in particular, whether inefficient hospitals are more likely to close.

Cleverly (1993) examined 160 community hospitals that closed between 1989 and 1991. Most were small, located in rural areas, and had sustained progressively larger losses for several years before closing. High costs and high prices, low utilization, and little investment in new technology were common features. From the characteristics of failed hospitals, Cleverly paints a picture of the road to failure. High prices and lack of investment in technology drive patients away. With lower utilization, costs per patient increase and cash flows become negative. The deteriorating liquidity ultimately leads to closure.

Lynch and Ozcan (1994) use a more sophisticated statistical approach to study the effects of efficiency and competition on closings. They apply data envelopment analysis (DEA) to hospitals that remained open, as well as those that closed. Chapter 13 describes how DEA identifies technically efficient hospitals to create an efficiency frontier. Technical inefficiency means that a hospital is not producing the maximum sustainable output with its inputs. Its relative distance to the frontier measures the degree of inefficiency for an inefficient hospital.

Estimates for 1988, a year with a record 102 closures (70 of them were nongovernment, short-stay hospitals), found that size and occupancy are negatively associated with closure. However, the picture that emerges is not as simple or clear as the one suggested by Cleverly. Greater competition, as measured by the Herfindahl-Hirschman Index (HHI),[14] is not associated with closure although larger hospitals in less competitive markets are less likely to close.

More surprising, however, the authors found a positive relationship between technical efficiency and closure, with efficient hospitals 1.6 times more likely to close. To explain this puzzle, they argue that the administrators of hospitals that ultimately closed were downsizing more rapidly to improve efficiency than hospitals that remained open. Many were becoming efficient by the time they closed, but it was too late to save them.

The relatively large number of small, rural hospital closings has challenged policy makers to maintain access for rural populations. To prepare for unexpected influxes of patients, small hospitals have higher rates of excess capacity, and hence lower occupancy rates than larger hospitals. Various federal programs provide subsidies to these hospitals. Nevertheless, rural hospitals can increase their chances of survival by practicing good management and responding to competitive pressures. Succi and colleagues (1997) found that rural hospitals gain an advantage and reduce the threat of competition by differentiating their services. Those that offer more basic services and high-tech services compared to the market average are less likely to close.

Nursing Homes

The rapid growth of the elderly population in many countries has led to considerable interest in the problems associated with long-term care. Long-term care encompasses a

[14]The HHI, discussed in detail in chapter 21, is the sum of squares of the market shares for each hospital.

wide variety of services and arrangements used to care for the elderly and others with serious functional impairments.

In this section, we concentrate on the nursing home. Numerous economic issues have been investigated in the nursing home literature. Following some background information, we will focus on issues involving quality, cost shifting, and financing the care.

BACKGROUND AND COSTS

Traditionally, the elderly were cared for until death by their families. Hence, the nursing home is a relatively recent phenomenon. Raffel and Raffel (1994) trace its origins. The first "nursing homes" in the United States were the county poorhouses of the eighteenth and nineteenth centuries, established for invalids and those without families. Most of the patients were elderly and the conditions were dreadful. Other state and local facilities evolved and some, usually with higher standards, were sponsored by religious and fraternal groups. The Social Security Act of 1935 provided funds for patients in private nursing homes, but the major increase in funding and nursing industry growth came after the passage of Medicare and Medicaid in 1965.

In 1960, nursing home care amounted to less than $1 billion, with 78 percent coming out of pocket (Table 18.2). Twenty years later, in 1980, spending reached $18 billion with Medicaid's share at 50 percent and only 42 percent coming out of pocket. By 1996, spending had grown to $79 billion with Medicaid contributing 48 percent (another 11 percent came from Medicare) and patients or their families paying just 31 percent. Between 1963 and 1995, the nursing home population over age 65 grew from 446,000 to 1.42 million. About 64 percent of the residents are in for-profit facilities.

As suggested by these data, the burgeoning nursing home population since 1963 and growth of costs are connected closely to Medicare and Medicaid. Medicare typically covers beneficiaries who are discharged from hospitals and require skilled nursing care to help recover from an acute illness. A skilled nursing facility (SNF) provides round-the-clock nursing care and other medical supervision. Historically, Medicare reimbursed on a cost basis, but the Balanced Budget Act of 1997 mandated a shift to a prospective payment system. Medicare now pays a fixed per diem amount determined by one of 44 categories in which the patient is placed.

Medicaid, in contrast, pays for the long-term care of the poor including the nonelderly as well as elderly. It covers both skilled nursing care and intermediate (custodial care). Because Medicaid is administered by the states subject to federal requirements, eligibility requirements as well as payment methods can vary widely. In the 1980s, many states phased in prospective payment systems that distinguished only between patients in skilled and intermediate care facilities. The rates were often set too low for heavy-care patients, discouraging nursing homes from admitting them. To provide better incentives, states increasingly are adopting case-mix reimbursement systems where payment depends on a much larger classification of patient types.[15]

A 1987 legislative change created new standards that drove costs higher. All nursing homes participating in federal programs, including Medicaid-only facilities, must now meet the same standards as Medicare SNFs. Also, nursing homes participating in

[15]The difficulty of classifying patients and determining appropriate costs for each category is bound to create profit differences by patient type. Nyman and Connor (1994) found that nursing homes take advantage of these differences by engaging in selective admission. See also Davis, Freeman, and Kirby (1998).

federal programs must evaluate each resident's needs and "provide services and activities to attain or maintain the 'highest practicable level' of function (physical, mental, and psychosocial well-being)."[16] These requirements led to large increases in staffing and the use of rehabilitation services.

QUALITY OF CARE

Despite increasingly stringent state and federal requirements, the issue of quality is undoubtedly the one with which the public is most concerned. To many, nursing homes evoke powerful images of neglected and poorly treated patients. It is thus natural that health economists and other scholars have concentrated their efforts on nursing home quality.

As we have seen from those chapters that deal with quality issues, the researcher must deal with the formidable challenge of defining and measuring quality. Regulatory standards for nursing homes tend to focus on *structure,* that is, the quantity and categories of inputs used to provide care, rather than on evaluating how the care is delivered (*process*) or on outcome indicators such as patients' satisfaction or their quality of life.

It follows that the most comprehensive and readily available information on nursing homes and other health care institutions is in the form of input data—their types and costs. Scholars have used these data to examine the relationship among quality and nursing home size, ownership, expenditures, and source of payment.[17]

One would expect, other factors held constant, that there would be some positive association between size and quality as a result of economies of scale and scope. If such economies occur over some range of output, larger institutions would be able to provide the same quality of care at a lower cost, or a higher quality of care for a given level of spending per patient. Davis's (1991) review of a large number of studies, including those that used process and structure measures of quality, suggests that no clear relationship exists.

A more important issue involves quality and cost or expenditure per patient. Do "you get what you pay for" in nursing care? Using structure measures of quality, not surprisingly, most analysts find a positive relationship, but these results are not meaningful unless they are supported by studies using process or outcome measures. (If inputs represent quality, one expects a close relationship between various measures of input and quality.) Of the 18 process and outcome studies included in Davis's review of the literature, only 6 indicate a positive relationship between quality and cost or inputs, while the results in 11 are insignificant (one is negative).[18] The failure to consistently find positive relationships is troubling. It indicates that improvements are needed in measuring quality as well as in formulating the statistical models used to estimate the relationships.

A third area of interest is in the relationship between type of ownership and quality. The previous chapter discussed the concept of contract failure within the context of nursing homes. Put simply, contract failure arises when quality is not easily observable.

[16]*Health Care Financing Review,* Medicare and Medicaid Supplement, 1995, p. 84.

[17]The 1987 requirements also are creating a valuable source of information through the instruments used to collect the resident assessment data. See Zimmerman et al. (1995) for use of these data to test nursing home quality.

[18]In one of the largest studies of long-term outcomes, Porell and colleagues (1998) found little relationship between quality and facility characteristics, such as size and ownership type. They likewise found that higher RN staffing levels do not improve outcomes.

In the case of nursing homes, patients may believe that nonprofit organizations are more likely to serve their interests than ones motivated by profits. Is this view justified by the evidence? Nursing home costs per patient are higher for nonprofits so that structure measures are clear on this point. However, because analysts have not been able to detect an unambiguous positive relationship between quality and costs, it follows that they would have great difficulty in detecting any relationship between type of ownership and process or outcome measures of quality. Davis's review confirms this conclusion.

Finally, Davis also reviews the literature on quality and the proportion of public pay (Medicaid) patients. The perception is widespread that nursing homes dominated by Medicaid patients are inferior. Expenditures per resident are lower in homes with higher proportions of Medicaid patients so that structure measures unequivocally support a negative relationship between quality and the proportion of Medicaid residents in a nursing home. However, with few studies that have used process or outcome measures, further work is needed to help settle the issue.

EXCESS DEMAND

It has been widely held for many years that the nursing home industry is characterized by excess demand and that this excess demand is one of the reasons for the allegedly inferior quality of care provided to public pay patients. Economists are naturally intrigued by, and at the same time skeptical of, claims of persistent shortages of any commodity. Put simply, they believe that prices or supply will increase to eliminate the excess demand. On the other hand, chapter 15 explored the same idea within the context of shortages of nurses, and several possibilities that could explain the claim of persistent nursing shortages were examined.

To examine the possibility of excess demand for nursing home care, Figure 18.3 shows the demand and cost conditions for a representative nursing home.[19] The demand

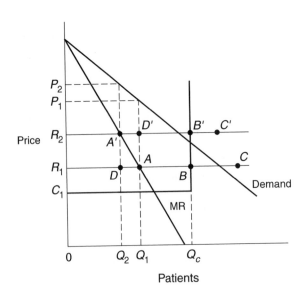

FIGURE 18.3 Analysis of Changes in the Medicaid Nursing Home Reimbursement Rate.

[19]The model is a variant of one developed by Scanlon (1980).

curve reflects only the private demand (self-pay or insured), while R_1 represents the Medicaid reimbursement rate. The segment AC along R_1 shows the number of Medicaid patients seeking admission. For simplicity, assume a constant (horizontal) marginal and average variable cost (C_1) up to the capacity level (Q_C patients) where it becomes vertical.

Under the conditions represented here, the profit-maximizing nursing home will first select all private patients whose marginal revenue exceeds R_1 and then fill the remainder of beds with Medicaid patients. The nursing home admits Q_1 private patients paying a price, P_1, and ($Q_c - Q_1$) Medicaid patients, leaving an excess demand of BC Medicaid patients.

The shortage can be reduced or even eliminated by raising the Medicaid rate. At R_2, nursing homes will raise the private fee to P_2 and substitute $A'D'$ Medicaid for AD private patients. The excess demand is reduced to $B'C'$ from BC.[20] Conversely, reductions in the Medicaid rate will lower Medicaid admissions and the private fee but increase the excess demand. Similarly, an increase in private demand resulting from higher incomes or more prevalent private long-term insurance will reduce Medicaid admissions and increase the excess demand.

One additional aspect should be considered. If the nursing home industry is profitable, and evidence suggests that it is, one would expect entry to reduce the excess demand. However, nursing homes also are subject to Certificate-of-Need (CON), and it has been argued that legislators have intentionally used CON and other restrictions to limit nursing home entry as a way of limiting Medicaid spending.[21] There is a similar theme of legislative aversion to policies that would raise the Medicaid rate which, as shown earlier, increases public spending while squeezing out private patients.

Various tests have been proposed to test the shortage hypothesis. For example, in our model, changes in reimbursement rates do not affect total utilization, just the composition between private and Medicaid patients. Any new beds are more likely to be filled by Medicaid than by private patients because that is the population for which there is excess demand. Using national data for 1969 and 1973, Scanlon's (1980) empirical tests indicate considerable excess demand for Medicaid patients. However, states may vary widely in their willingness to fund public patients, and changes may have taken place in more recent years to reduce the shortages. For example, Nyman's (1993) estimates for 1988 for Minnesota, Oregon, and Wisconsin generally do not support the shortage hypothesis.

FINANCING LONG-TERM CARE

The continuous growth of the population that will need long-term care (LTC), the requirement that patients must meet income and asset tests to qualify for nursing home benefits under Medicaid, and the budgetary problems created by the growth of Medicaid spending have led to many proposals to reform Medicaid. The need to deplete one's

[20]The rate that would eliminate the Medicaid excess demand is found by sliding the segment $A'C'$ further up the marginal revenue curve until the quantities such as $B'C'$ are eliminated. Clearly, the rate must be above R_2.

[21]CON regulations require health care providers to obtain approval from state planning agencies for capital expenditures exceeding a threshold level such as $550,000. CON was federally mandated until 1987 and then left to the states, many of which have retained some form of CON.

assets is especially irksome to the middle class. The sore point is that after paying a life-time of taxes to support Medicaid and other welfare programs, one has to become poor ("spend down") to qualify for Medicaid. As a result, a variety of proposals has been introduced to help resolve this contentious issue. These range from proposals allowing individuals to have higher incomes and retain a higher proportion of their wealth to qualify for public assistance, to proposals that would cover everyone who meets certain medical requirements.

Short and Kemper (1994) estimate the effects of a variety of plans. The least costly are proposals that create a front-end entitlement covering everyone for a limited period, for example, three to six months of care. Back-end entitlements that cover everyone after a certain waiting period of, say, one or two years of nursing home care, are more costly. The most expensive are proposals without limitations even if they have cost-sharing provisions. Short and Kemper estimate that full entitlement with a 30 percent coinsurance rate would increase overall nursing home expenditures by nearly 20 percent and public expenditures by about 80 percent (due to the overall increase in utilization and the substitution of public spending for private spending).

The alternative to greater public spending, especially in an era where many government programs are being downsized, is a strategy to encourage more private long-term coverage or home care. The market for such insurance is growing and subsidies or tax incentives could be used to encourage further growth. Allowing for tax-deductible contributions to long-term care accounts, similar to retirement plans, is one of the ideas that has been advanced.

Federal policy to contain public spending centers on two strategies: encourage home care and other potentially less costly substitutes for nursing home care, and encourage more private coverage for long-term care. The market for private long-term care (LTC) insurance is growing, and legislation passed in 1996 allows employers a 100 percent deduction on their contributions to group plans. The legislation also provides some tax relief to individuals who itemize their returns and purchase tax-qualified policies. Nevertheless, only 5 percent to 7 percent of the elderly have LTC coverage. Similarly, only 5 percent of firms with more than 1,000 workers offer a group benefit for LTC to their employees. Of those that do, the employee participation rate is low—on the order of 6 percent (Jones 1999).

Barriers to growth of private LTC insurance stem from confusion over the benefits provided by Medicare and private health plans, perceptions that such insurance is unaffordable, and perceptions that governments will somehow meet LTC needs. The low probability (about 1 percent) that an employed person will need long-term care before he or she retires, coupled with uncertainty over future premiums and medical technology, increases the difficulty of selling LTC insurance to the working population. To overcome these barriers, some analysts propose additional tax incentives by allowing all taxpayers a 100 percent tax deduction for premiums or allowing tax-deductible LTC accounts, similar to retirement accounts.

The more visible strategy to contain public spending is the federal government's emphasis on alternatives to nursing home care. Although the number of nursing home residents over age 65 increased between 1985 and 1995 (when the elderly population grew nearly 18 percent), there was a striking 8 percent drop in their use rate. Bishop (1999) estimated that a quarter million additional elders would have been in nursing homes in 1995 had the 1985 use rates continued. Where have all these patients gone?

The high rates of growth of home health care and other LTC arrangements suggest that they have at least partly filled the gap.

Hospice and Home Health

The budgetary pressure of caring for the growing elderly population in hospitals and nursing homes has promoted interest in other less-costly arrangements. Hospice and home health are two programs[22] that are perceived to be cost effective and heavily funded at the federal level.

Hospice care is intended for the terminally ill. Most hospice patients receive care in their own homes, but the use of special facilities is becoming more prevalent. An interdisciplinary team of health professionals provides individualized care that emphasizes patients' physical and emotional comfort (i.e., palliative as opposed to curative care), as well as support for family members. Hospices strive for improved quality of life in a patient's final days and death with dignity.

Medicare introduced hospice benefits in 1983, but higher reimbursement rates in 1989 accelerated growth in the number of hospices. Higher reimbursement rates will increase significantly the number of Medicare certified providers, improving access for Medicare beneficiaries. Hamilton (1993) estimated that every dollar increase in the daily rate raises the probability of certification by 1.7 percent. There were about 60,000 hospice patients at any time during 1996. With evidence that hospice programs offer savings,[23] many private insurers also have added coverage for hospice care.

Home health care, the larger and more important program, provides care to patients with acute and long-term needs including those with disabilities, those recuperating from a hospital stay, and even the terminally ill. The home care benefit was included in the initial Medicare legislation of 1965 that was extended in 1973 to certain disabled persons under 65. By 1996, about 2.4 million home health patients were on the rolls of agencies at any time, and their numbers are growing rapidly. With a doubling of patients in just four years since 1992, home health care is one of the fastest-growing components of total spending. Between 1992 and 1996, Medicare spending for home health care grew from $7.7 to $18.1 billion. Medicare and Medicaid together account for about two-thirds of the $40 billion spent on home care.[24]

The support for public funding for home health care stems from perceptions that it is much less expensive than either hospital or nursing home care. However, even though a home health visit is unquestionably far less costly than a day spent in an institution, the effect on total health spending is not entirely clear. The principal issue is the extent to which home health substitutes for "unpaid" care by family members and other caregivers, or for institutional care.[25] Policy makers are concerned that more generous

[22]Other long-term arrangements, especially for the less severely disabled, include adult day care and other community-based programs.

[23]Abou-Sayf (1991) and Stevenson (1996).

[24]National Association for Home Care (1999). To rein in this spending, the Balanced Budget Act of 1997 directed the Health Care Financing Administration to shift from a cost-based system under Medicare to a prospective payment system by October 1, 1999.

[25]Extensive literature is available on the impact of home care on hospital utilization. Hughes's (1997) meta analysis found that home care unambiguously reduces hospital days for the terminally ill. For others, the effect on hospital days is negative though not "overwhelmingly large."

public funding for home care will substitute for previously "unpaid" care without significantly increasing the overall care for patients.

To investigate substitution effects, Pezzin and colleagues (1996) developed a conceptual approach rooted in utility theory. The specifics of the model and estimation methods are beyond the scope of this chapter, but the essential elements can be described readily. Begin with a family utility function:

$$U = U(X, L, F; t)$$

where X represents private goods, L represents leisure, and F represents the disabled person's functioning. The parameter, t, reflects the family's tastes for privacy and independence.

The disabled person's functioning can be produced either at a nursing institution or in the community by combinations of home care formally purchased in the market and the informal care provided by family members and others. The family is constrained by time that it can use in three ways: care for the disabled person to increase F; work to earn income to buy market goods, X, or home and institutional care for the disabled person; and enjoy as leisure time, L. The family cannot have more of any one of three goods without giving up some of the other two.

Conceptually, the model is identical to the standard labor–leisure utility maximization problem involving a budget line and indifference curves. However, here the budget line and indifference curves are three-dimensional. The point of tangency, which can be found mathematically, indicates the optimal values of X, L, and F. It also provides the optimal combination of institutional and home care to produce F and the optimal combination of paid and informal time to produce home care.

Using data from an experiment to examine the effects of expanded public funding, the study found no reductions in the amount of informal care for married persons and only small reductions to unmarried persons. Thus, the benefits of expanded funding flow mainly to the disabled recipients, and not to the informal caregivers through more leisure time. Generous public support also affects living arrangements. It increases the probability that unmarried persons will live independently and reduces their probability of living in nursing homes or with others in shared arrangements.

The authors leave readers with a question: "Are the benefits of increased independence and the associated quality of life sufficient to justify the costs [of a generous public home health program]?" Economics alone cannot provide unequivocal answers to a normative question such as this one, but they can contribute to the policy debate through continued improvements in theory and empirical evidence.

Conclusions

Following a discussion of the history and organization of hospitals and hospital costs, we examined two economic and policy issues—the medical arms race hypothesis and cost shifting. Careful analysis indicates that both issues are far more complex than they first appear. The existing literature confirms this analysis by indicating that the common perceptions of a wasteful MAR and complete cost shifting do not accurately represent how hospital markets function.

We also examined the long-term care sector focusing on nursing homes. Three issues are emphasized: quality, especially for Medicaid patients; shortages; and financing nursing home care. We found that economic theory and empirical evidence can provide useful and sometimes surprising results. For example, no clear relationship exists between costs and quality. It is also possible to have a persistent shortage of nursing home beds without any mechanism, such as price, that would alleviate the shortage.

Finally we examined potentially less-costly alternatives to nursing homes. Home health care represents one of the fastest-growing components of health care spending. Home care does not substitute for informal care of family members and other caregivers.

Summary

1. The modern hospital evolved at the turn of the twentieth century following the invention of the X ray and significant advances in antisepsis, anesthesia, and the biological sciences.

2. Hospital spending has grown rapidly in recent decades as a result of the growth of private and public insurance and other factors. It accounts for about 35 percent of health expenditures.

3. The hospital industry is experiencing rapid change including reductions in the number of hospital beds and inpatient utilization and significant growth of outpatient services. Hospitals are facing competitive pressure to further diversify and to introduce or participate in managed care arrangements.

4. Hospitals are licensed and subject to a wide range of state and federal regulation.

5. Many analysts believe that the hospital industry is in a medical arms race resulting in unnecessary duplication of expensive technology. The limited empirical evidence does not support this view.

6. Intuitive reasoning suggests that the costs of discounts or uncompensated care to some patient groups must be passed on to other paying groups. More formal analysis leads to a richer set of results including situations where costs cannot be shifted. The empirical literature indicates that cost shifting is far from complete.

7. The nursing home population has grown dramatically since the introduction of Medicare and Medicaid. Governments pay more than 60 percent of all nursing home costs.

8. Nursing home quality has been examined through structure, process, and outcome indicators. Surprisingly, no conclusive evidence relates cost to quality or supports the view that nursing homes with higher proportions of Medicaid patients produce lower-quality care.

9. A familiar theme in the nursing home literature is one of persistent excess demand by Medicaid patients. A model of chronic excess demand is plausible, although recent evidence indicates that excess demand is not a universal phenomenon.

10. Financing the growing nursing home population is a great social challenge. Many proposals would reduce the need for patients to "spend down" their assets to qualify for public coverage.

11. The nursing home population is leveling off and use rates for the elderly are actually declining. Home health care and other alternatives are growing rapidly in number of patients and costs. They can be cost-effective alternatives to hospital and nursing home care.

Discussion Questions

1. Explain why it is often claimed that hospitals compete for doctors rather than patients. What are some of the implications of this phenomenon, assuming that it is true?
2. Even not-for-profit hospitals must earn a "profit." Evaluate this statement.
3. What is the medical arms race (MAR) hypothesis? What features of hospital markets make the presence of an unproductive MAR possible?
4. Suppose that the Medicare rate of hospital reimbursement is reduced. Explain why the costs may not be shifted to other patients in the short run.
5. How can the JCAHO limit competition?
6. Hospital costs have grown following growth of private and public insurance. Describe other factors that could account for some of the growth.
7. Explain how excess demand for nursing home beds may persist over long periods of time. How can the hypothesis be tested?
8. Nonprofits are dominant in the hospital industry while for-profits dominate the nursing home industry. Develop some possible explanations for this difference.

Exercises

1. What is a dominant strategy in game theory? Using Figure 18.1, replace the entry in the first row and second column with (125, −50). Does A have a dominant strategy? Does B? What is the solution to this game?
2. Assume that there are three groups of hospital patients (instead of two as shown in Figure 18.2): private, Medicare, and Medicaid (which has a lower fixed rate of reimbursement than Medicare). Explain how a hospital would select patients in order to maximize profits.
3. Suppose that the Medicaid reimbursement rate does not cover the variable costs of patient care. Will a profit-maximizing hospital accept Medicaid patients? If not, under what circumstances will the hospital accept such patients?
4. Assume that a patient's health can be improved by home care or institutional care. Use isoquants and isocost curves to determine the condition for efficient utilization of these two forms of care. Under what circumstances will an insurance program promote or fail to promote efficiency?

Equity, Efficiency, and Need

- Efficiency and Competitive Markets

- Deviations from the Competitive Model in the Health Care Sector

- Promoting Competition in the Health Care Sector

- An Economic Efficiency Rationale for Social Programs in Health Care Based on Externalities

- Need and Need-Based Distributions

- Economic Criticisms of Need-Based Distributions

- Horizontal Equity and Need

- Theories of Social Justice

- Conclusions

A re health care markets efficient, and are people getting the care that they need? These two questions occupy the minds of the many people who study or simply think about the state of health care in America. Efficiency questions arise because of the high costs people must pay for health care. Are these costs too high? Likewise, equity questions are raised because of the experiences of many people, certainly including the uninsured, who face barriers in obtaining health care.

Compared to Canadians and many Europeans, Americans are more likely to find experts and analysts who favor competitive market solutions to health care system problems, though many here as elsewhere argue that this approach is ill-suited to the nature of health care markets. Canadians and Europeans are more willing to use government interventions such as social insurance programs in addressing health care problems. The Clinton proposal to expand social insurance for health care died in Congress in the United States in 1994. However, Medicare reform and access for the uninsured remain issues and for many Americans equity and efficiency in the health care system remain important.

A solid grounding in these issues requires an understanding of the economics of efficiency, the departures of many health care markets from the competitive model, the role of equity concerns, and issues of social justice theory. Because of the central role of the concept of need within the realm of the health system, it also requires an investigation into the meaning of health care need. These subjects are the themes of the present chapter.

We begin by developing the simple analytics of welfare economics within the context of the Edgeworth box for exchange. We will discover that competitive, efficient, well-functioning markets can leave many in economic need.

Following an exposition of the theoretical efficiency of competition, we then identify the departures of health care markets from the model of perfect competition, and we investigate a possible efficiency rationale for social programs in health care. The nature of health care need is then featured, including some approaches found in this literature. This is followed by a discussion of contrasting theories of social justice.

Efficiency and Competitive Markets

The meaning of economic efficiency can be made fairly clear within the context of the Edgeworth box for exchange. This approach is a useful way of showing theorems that are developed in more sophisticated mathematical models.

The analysis here generates the First Fundamental Theorem of Welfare Economics and illustrates the Second Fundamental Theorem, as well. The First Theorem demonstrates that competitive markets under certain conditions are economically efficient. The second establishes the idea that any desired economically efficient outcome could in principle be achieved by competitive markets given appropriate initial endowments.

THE CONCEPT OF PARETO EFFICIENCY (OPTIMALITY)

To establish these ideas, we must define rigorously the concept of efficiency. Nearly a century ago, the economist Vilfredo Pareto defined the concept of efficiency as it is used most frequently by economists today. According to Pareto, an economically efficient (optimal) outcome in society is one under which it is impossible to improve the lot of any person without hurting someone else. Pareto efficiency also implies that no further exchanges would be found that could in principle improve the lot of everyone to some degree. An efficient economy necessarily would have exhausted all means for mutual gains.

The Edgeworth box, using a hypothetical two-person economy and showing exchanges between these two people, provides a context in which to make the idea of Pareto efficiency clear. Consider the Edgeworth box depicted in Figure 19.1. In the two-person economy depicted here, a fixed total quantity of goods is available. We assume that only two goods are available: medical care, M, and food, F. The total available quantities are $0_A M$ and $0_A F$, respectively.

Abner has preferences over food and medical care, preferences that are represented by the indifference curves sloping downward and convex to the origin, 0_A. In contrast, the indifference curves for Belinda have been inverted so that her origin is point 0_B, and higher indifference curves for her are ones to the southwest.

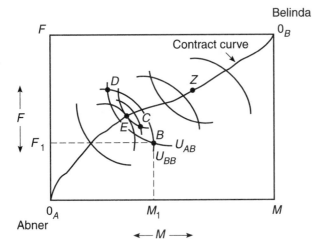

FIGURE 19.1 Edgeworth Box for Exchange; Pareto Efficient Points Lie on the Contract Curve.

To identify the concept of efficiency in this context, consider the arbitrary starting point B. Point B, like any point in the box, represents a complete distribution of the two goods between the two persons. B identifies a situation where Abner has $0_A M_1$ units of medical care and $0_A F_1$ units of food. As an exercise, identify the quantities of food and medical products owned by Belinda at point B. With this orientation, we ask the following question: Is point B an economically efficient distribution?

The answer to this question must be no. To see this fact, examine by comparison point C. Point C lies on an indifference curve that is above (to the northeast of) indifference curve U_{AB} and, therefore, C is superior to B in Abner's view. Similarly, point C lies on an indifference curve that is above (to the southwest of) indifference curve U_{BB} and, therefore, C is superior to B from Belinda's view. Because point C is attainable and improves the lot of both persons while harming neither, it follows that the original point B is not economically efficient.

Geometrically, the analysis just completed regarding point B can be repeated for any point that forms a "lens" from the indifference curves passing through it. A lens is formed by the indifference curves U_{AB} and U_{BB} from point B to point D. Whenever such a lens can be found, it will be possible to identify one or more other points superior to the initial point.

Reapplying this method of reasoning, point C is also not Pareto efficient. Pareto superior moves, where the welfare of both improves, can be made from point C. In contrast, a Pareto efficient point in the box is a point of tangency between two indifference curves, such as point E. It is impossible to move from a point of tangency without harming the lot of one of the two persons.

Each of Abner's indifference curves will have a point of tangency with one of Belinda's indifference curves. The collection of all Pareto efficient points in the box is called the *contract curve,* which is so labeled in the figure. For example, at point 0_A, Belinda has all of both goods, and even if this may be considered inequitable by many or most people, it *is* Pareto efficient.

THE IDEA OF TRADING ALONG THE BUDGET LINE

Having defined efficiency in the context of the Edgeworth box, we next ask whether the competitive market generates an efficient equilibrium in exchange. In a competitive market, each person treats prices as given and responds to prices by choosing the utility-maximizing bundle subject to his or her resource constraint. The resource constraint in the present context depends on the person's initial endowment of food and medical care. Let the initial endowment for this two-person economy be represented by ω in Figure 19.2. Either person may trade away from his or her initial endowment at the market prices. Thus, Abner's resource constraint will be represented by a budget line that passes through point ω. As with any budget line, the slope of this line is the negative of the ratio of the price of medical care to food.

Inasmuch as the slope of the budget line represents the rate at which one can trade one good for another at market prices, the steeper the budget line is in Figure 19.2, the greater the price is of medical care relative to food. For example, budget line AB represents a relatively lower price of medical care relative to food than does budget line CD.

THE COMPETITIVE EQUILIBRIUM

To find the competitive equilibrium, we must identify the offer curves of both persons. Abner's offer curve, for example, is the collection of points representing his offer for trade at each possible set of prices. To illustrate, let the prices be such that budget line AB obtains. Given budget line AB, Abner is willing to stay at point ω, the point of tangency between budget line AB and the highest indifference curve that is attainable.

FIGURE 19.2 The Intersection of Offer Curves Determines the Competitive Equilibrium.

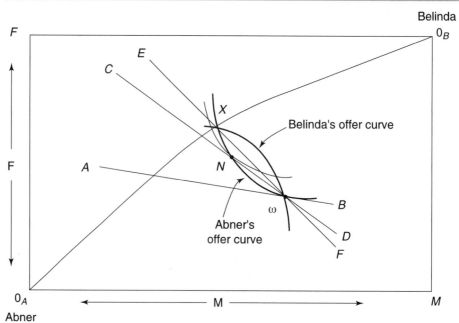

To complete Abner's offer curve, find his desired trades at other possible prices. For example, suppose the price of medical care were higher relative to food so that the steeper budget line *CD* is obtained. Given budget line *CD*, Abner's optimal trade would be from point ω to point *N*. With budget line *EF*, Abner's optimal trade is to point *X*. Connecting all such points generates *Abner's offer curve.*

The figure also shows Belinda's offer curve, beginning at endowment point ω. This offer curve is found in a similar manner and is labeled *Belinda's offer curve.* The two heavily shaded offer curves represent voluntary trades for the two parties. For trade, as in a competitive market, to be mutually voluntary, the offers of the two persons must agree. The offer curves agree only at their point of intersection labeled point *X* in the figure. Point *X* thus constitutes the competitive market equilibrium in exchange for this two-person economy, given an endowment of ω.

THE FIRST FUNDAMENTAL THEOREM OF WELFARE ECONOMICS

Is the competitive equilibrium, *X*, Pareto efficient? This is so, and it must be so of every competitive equilibrium in this context for the following reasons. The intersection of two offer curves is reached by a single price line from point ω. By construction of each offer curve, each person is at a point of tangency between the budget line and the highest attainable indifference curve. At point *X*, Abner's indifference curve (not shown) is tangent to the budget line. Likewise, at point *X*, Belinda's indifference curve (also not shown) is tangent to the budget line. Because these indifference curves are tangent to the same budget line at the same point, they must be tangent to each other. Because they are tangent to each other at point *X*, this point is Pareto efficient. The same argument applies for any competitive equilibrium; therefore, we have shown the First Fundamental Theorem in this context, namely that the perfectly competitive market equilibrium is Pareto efficient.

The theorem makes the competitive market solution attractive. If perfect competition can be achieved, then the market forces left to their own workings will generate an efficient outcome—an invisible hand solution. However, the theorem evokes several serious questions: Can competitive markets be achieved in health care? Is the context of this theorem appropriate for health care? Would the competitive market solution be equitable or would it leave too many people without adequate health care? We will address each of these questions. However, we begin this process by exploring the issue of equity within the context of the Second Fundamental Theorem.

REDISTRIBUTION OF THE ENDOWMENT

The applicability of the First Fundamental Theorem is extended somewhat by the second. The Second Fundamental Theorem states that any Pareto efficient outcome can in principle be achieved by a competitive market, given an appropriate endowment. Figure 19.3 illustrates the significance of this theorem.

In Figure 19.3, suppose that the initial endowment is ω, and suppose that this endowment results in the competitive outcome represented by point *E*. Point *E* is only one of an infinite number of Pareto efficient points. It may be an outcome that is viewed as inequitable by some members of the society. In real life, the society may have millions of members, and the analogous market outcome may even be perceived as inequitable by a majority of people.

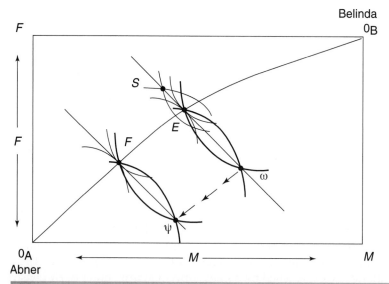

FIGURE 19.3 A Preferred Efficient Outcome May Be Achieved by an Initial Redistribution of Resources.

The Second Theorem, however, defines a central role for competitive markets, even in cases where some competitive outcomes are considered inequitable. This idea is illustrated in the figure. Suppose, for example, that society determines that outcome E is inequitable and thus rejects this particular market solution. It prefers outcomes in the vicinity of point F. By the Second Theorem, the desired outcome can be achieved by a competitive market, but it requires a different initial endowment from point ω. As shown, the endowment point ψ is a suitable point from which to achieve an equitable market outcome, point F. Seen this way, redistribution combined with competitive markets generates an outcome that is efficient and equitable. This contrasts with command systems that eschew free markets and with alternative solutions such as price discrimination.

PRICE DISCRIMINATION

An alternative method often proposed for achieving a more equitable outcome is to provide certain services to the poor at reduced, subsidized prices. It may be surprising to learn that such systems are not consistent with Pareto efficiency. Consider the proof of the efficiency of competitive markets. Here it was crucial that both parties optimizing with a given budget line achieve a point of tangency to the same budget line. If different prices for medical care are charged to the poorer person than to the richer, then the two face different slopes of their budget lines. The result would be a position such as S in Figure 19.3, a point that is not Pareto efficient.

The inefficiency of price discrimination can be understood intuitively as well as through the geometry. Consider, for example, a situation where the poor are subsidized in the purchase of bread. The poor would adapt to the subsidized price until the rate at which they were willing to trade bread for other goods was equal to the rate at which they could exchange the goods at the subsidized price. The result is that the poor would

undervalue bread in comparison to the wealthy. It would be more efficient for the poor then to buy up bread and sell it to the rich. Such a side market, which would improve efficiency in the bread example, is not possible for medical care, which is not easily transferable. Thus, subsidized prices for medical care would generate an inefficient equilibrium.

The two theorems, plus the facts regarding the inefficiency of price discrimination, suggest the superiority of income transfers as a solution to equity problems in health care markets. In Figure 19.3, the following situation takes place: by transferring initial resources between the two persons, the market is allowed to achieve an efficient outcome within the equitable range.

OKUN'S LEAKY BUCKET

The theoretical superiority of redistribution of income to programs such as price subsidies has led many analysts to favor income maintenance programs as policy tools to offset the problems of poverty, including the problems of access to health care. Income maintenance programs are government programs designed to provide cash subsidies to the poor so as to maintain their incomes at or above a preset floor. Despite continuing interest in such programs, policy makers often have hesitated to use large-scale income redistribution.

The major criticism of income maintenance can be summarized by appealing to Arthur Okun's (1975) analogy of the leaky bucket. The problem is that the act of transferring wealth from one group to another in society generates disincentives that discourage productive effort. The tax-paying group incurs a tax burden that may reduce work incentives, and the recipient group receives subsidies that may reduce incentives to work and to self-help. By analogy, when we transfer income our task is similar to transferring water in a leaky bucket. The amount of income available to be redistributed will decline as a result.

In recent decades, the federal government sponsored large-scale experiments to investigate in part the degree of work loss induced by the incentives inherent in income maintenance programs. These experiments reported reductions in work effort on average of between 5 percent and 10 percent. However, the work reduction estimates were considerably higher for certain subgroups such as "male nonheads" (meaning nonheads of families) and women. Also, results generated in an experimental situation make it difficult to predict the results if the program were to become universal and permanent.

Deviations from the Competitive Model in the Health Care Sector

Another major criticism of the applicability of our theoretical analysis concerns the question of whether health care markets are sufficiently competitive or whether they can be made to be sufficiently competitive for competitive outcomes to be obtained. Substantial differences clearly exist between most health care markets and the theoretical model of competition.

The results of the First and Second Theorems have been extended to larger and more complete models that include production. These models increase the number of

commodities and individuals, and they identify optimal results for competition in production and exchange. For the results to hold, several assumptions must apply.

THE ASSUMPTIONS UNDER PERFECT COMPETITION

First of all, the theorems apply to competitive markets. Consider the assumptions necessary for a market to be perfectly competitive: It must have free entry and exit, perfect information, a homogeneous product, and numerous buyers and sellers each with no power over price. Furthermore, the efficiency of competitive markets is derived under conditions where no significant externalities, public goods, or natural monopolies exist. Finally, the actors in the competitive markets are alternatively consumers maximizing their utility or producers maximizing their profits.

Deviations from the Competitive Assumptions

Many have criticized the applicability of the theorems to the health care sector, claiming that health care markets are typically not perfectly competitive. The health care markets depart from competition in several ways:

1. Barriers to entry exist in health care markets. Such barriers include licensure laws and health planning controls on prices and facility construction.
2. Information problems exist.
3. Often firms are few enough in number that they have some degree of monopoly power.
4. Health care services are not uniform in quality or character.
5. Externalities are prevalent in health care.
6. Motivations other than pure profit are common in health care.
7. The model depicts the operation of markets under conditions of certainty. However, health events entail a considerable degree of uncertainty.

The Role of Uncertainty

Several of the seven listed deviations need little further explanation. However, we consider three of them for extended discussion: the role of uncertainty, the role of information, and the role of externalities.

As we have seen, the uncertain nature of health status gives rise to the demand for insurance coverage among persons who are risk averse. In the present context, insurance creates problems for the efficient functioning of health care markets. Four issues should be noted

1. Insurance changes the price of care to the insured person, which in turn leads to the distortions described under price discrimination.
2. Insurance causes the price paid to suppliers to differ from the price paid by the consumer, and this distorts the efficient matching of production to consumption.
3. Large insurance companies and government programs have historically negotiated payment rates on a retrospective cost basis, thus removing price determination, at least in part, from the market.
4. In some health care markets, the average insurance coverage is so complete as to distort substantially the producer's incentives to be efficient.

The Role of Information

The efficiency results for competitive markets depend on all parties having complete information available. As we have shown elsewhere, it is particularly problematic for market functioning when information is imperfect and asymmetrically available to the parties in the market, whether it be the consumer or the provider who is relatively less informed. Potential problems of information and efficiency arise when the physician is much more informed about the appropriateness and effectiveness of treatments and techniques than the consumer is, and also when the consumer has more knowledge of his or her health status and health habits than the potential insurer does.

The Role of Externalities

Finally, health care markets are subject to prevalent externalities. A prominent externality will occur whenever participants in the market are significantly concerned about the health care received by others, not just their own health care. This externality may be difficult to internalize in private charity markets, and it arguably causes health care markets to be inefficient. Because externalities have been identified by some analysts as the most important efficiency argument for social insurance programs in health care, we develop an extended discussion in this chapter.

Promoting Competition in the Health Care Sector

If we could manipulate real-world markets as easily as we can change the assumptions of theory, then it would seem to follow from our theoretical discussion that we should promote competition in health care markets whenever possible. Often the promotion of competitive elements in health care markets will prove useful. However, further theoretical grounds exist to qualify our statements.

THE THEOREM OF THE SECOND BEST

One qualification involves the Theorem of the Second Best in welfare economics. In informal terms, consider an economy in which there is more than one departure from the conditions of perfect competition. Consider further any policy that corrects one or more of these departures from perfect competition but does not correct all of them. It has been shown under the Theorem of the Second Best that such a policy will not necessarily improve society's welfare.

An intuitive understanding of why this result is obtained can be gained by considering a frequently used example. Consider a market where there exists a pure monopolist (a departure from the conditions of perfect competition) who is also a polluter (a departure from the conditions under which competition is efficient). Basic theory shows that a monopolist will produce less output than a competitive industry would have under otherwise-similar conditions. A policy that hypothetically converts the industry to perfect competition would resolve one discrepancy but not both. Such a policy would not necessarily improve the well-being of society because both output and pollution would increase. Societal valuations of the extra output versus the extra pollution could in principle determine whether the change worsened society's well-being.

Thus, correcting some economic "wrongs" but not all of them will not necessarily improve welfare.

This classic example of the monopolist polluter illustrates the idea of the theorem, but it does not make clear its applicability to the health sector. Consider a somewhat more controversial example that applies to health. Physician licensure laws grant licensed physicians a degree of monopoly power, a distortion from the competitive conditions. At the same time, however, consumers in health have imperfect information on therapies and prices, and information asymmetrically favors the physician; this, too, is a departure from competitive conditions. If one eliminated the imperfection caused by licensure but did not simultaneously address the information problem, patient welfare could be worsened.

THE WISDOM OF PROMOTING COMPETITION IN HEALTH CARE MARKETS

It would be a misapplication of the Theorem of the Second Best, however, to conclude that all policies that improve competitive elements in health care markets are incorrect. More properly, it means that we cannot assume such policies will improve welfare. Instead, we are operating in a world of second best. We are necessarily in the world of second best because it will be impossible to convert all health care markets into the model of perfect competition. It is nevertheless the case, however, that a given competitive policy may improve the functioning of health care markets in a manner that improves society's well-being. Each policy must be considered on its own merits, not on the grounds per se that it promotes competition.

An Economic Efficiency Rationale for Social Programs in Health Care Based on Externalities

An externality occurs when someone external to the market transaction—that is, someone who is neither the buyer nor the seller—is affected directly by the transaction and not compensated. A common example in health care occurs in the case of immunization for contagious diseases. Here people outside the market transaction—people who are not presently being immunized—are affected by the immunization. This occurs because the immunized person is less likely to become a carrier of the disease. This situation is an example of a beneficial consumption externality.

In the presence of a beneficial externality, the competitive market will tend to produce an inefficiently low level of output. The Pareto efficiency definition can be transformed in terms of a single market as the condition that marginal benefits equal marginal costs in equilibrium. Individuals in a well-functioning, perfectly competitive market in theory will, for example, use medical care until the marginal benefits, measured through the demand curve, equal marginal costs, which in equilibrium will equal the price. In Figure 19.4, this leads to an efficient level of consumption, Q_m, in the absence of externalities.

When there exists a marginal external benefit to people in society, then this external benefit must be added to the marginal private benefit, which is measured by the demand curve, to determine marginal social benefit. In Figure 19.4, the marginal external benefit curve is shown as MEB. The marginal benefit to society as a whole is the verti-

The Rice Critique

Welfare economics warns that the benefits of competition require many assumptions that do not hold of the health economy. To fix one of these flaws by itself does not necessarily help society. Understanding these caveats, we noted that most health economists favor competitive markets when they do improve welfare. Thomas Rice (1998), however, makes the stronger case that too often health economists promote competition but fail to acknowledge the many market flaws.

His line of reasoning is essentially the same—that many needed assumptions are violated. However, his more extensive list illuminates additional basic issues:

1. The law of diminishing marginal returns may not hold.
2. Consumer utility may depend on factors other than goods and services.
3. Consumer tastes are not fixed but are often learned.
4. Consumers may not be rational.
5. Individuals may not be the best judges of their own well-being.
6. The Social Welfare Function depends on more than individual consumption.

These issues, recognizable to economists, could raise serious questions for the analysis we have described. For example, if the assumption of rationality fails to approximate behavior, then most microeconomic theory needs to be reevaluated.

Items 5 and 6 further show how thorny the underlying normative issues are. A normative proposition is a statement of what ought to be done, while a positive proposition is a statement of how the world actually is, was, or will be. Notice that U.S. society often makes choices that imply that individuals are not the best judges of their own well-being. Examples include helmet laws, criminalization of drugs, and mandatory retirement contributions. Wide acceptance of these limitations suggests that Rice is correct on item 5 and possibly item 6. However, controversy always arises over where to draw the line. Rice quotes Princeton economist Uwe Reinhardt (1996), who states the issue more strongly:

I, for one, believe that, if this nation is ever to have truly universal health insurance coverage and a truly humane safety net all around, an elite espousing those goals would have to impose that state of affairs on a generally confused plebs that has quite unstable, often logically inconsistent and utterly malleable preferences on the matter.

Reinhardt echoes the frustration of many health economists on this point, but many also will express concern about accepting Rice's items 5 and 6 in the process. "Plebs" here means the general populace, but it shares the same root with the word *plebiscite,* a vote of the general populace. Would health policy "impose(d)...on a generally confused plebs" pass a plebiscite?

cal sum of the MEB curve and the demand curve. The result is the marginal social benefit curve, MSB. Efficiency for society occurs at output level Q_{opt}, whereas the market would achieve an inefficiently low level of output, Q_m. Thus, on efficiency grounds alone, society may be justified in subsidizing immunizations in some way.

While the case of immunization for contagious diseases illustrates the logic and role of beneficial consumption externalities in justifying subsidies for (or possibly public

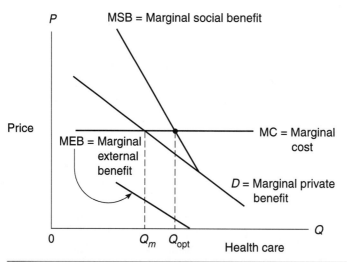

FIGURE 19.4 The Socially Efficient Equilibrium in the Presence of a Beneficial Externality.

provision of) care, such as the polio immunizations of the 1950s and 1960s, it represents a fairly minor problem and could not in itself be used to justify large social insurance programs. However, an alternative health care externality, one that we have identified elsewhere as a charitable externality, can in principle be sufficiently important to justify such programs.

This externality would occur, for example, whenever people feel that some segment of society is receiving insufficient care in the sense that the charitably minded person would be willing to pay to help these people get care. *Willing to pay* here means that they would pay if it were so arranged that their contribution would be perceived as helping the poor to acquire health care.

Such charitable feelings are probably widespread in most societies. As Pauly (1971) argued:

> The desire to eliminate the diseconomy that the presence of curable but uncured disease or injury may exert on others does appear, in general terms, to be a common characteristic of human beings. At least at some levels, most of us would be willing to give up some of our income to help a suffering fellow. Some may, of course, be immune to such feelings, but individuals may also be immune to contagious disease, and this should cause no insurmountable theoretical problems (pp. 10–11).

Although this externality has a different source than the case of immunization and is probably of more substantial importance, the economic argument is of the same form. In Figure 19.4, consider the curve MEB to measure this charitable externality. Then, as before, the efficient level of output, Q_{opt}, is greater than the market output, Q_m. Under certain circumstances, this efficiency may be sufficient grounds to intervene, for example, by providing a program of social insurance.

Need and Need-Based Distributions

If we can identify accurately the efficient allocation of health care, we nevertheless may find many people in society dissatisfied with the outcome. That is, there may be additional concerns, over and above efficiency concerns, regarding equity. In the health care literature, the concerns for equity most often center on the question of whether people are getting the health care they need. Thus, health care needs must be addressed.[1]

The task of treating the concept of health care need analytically is made difficult by the fact that need is often either undefined or variously defined. The definitions employed may take either extreme, *need* being defined maximally or minimally. For example, Culyer and Wagstaff (1993) review several definitions of health care need; they conclude that a maximal need definition is superior, defining need as:

> the expenditure required to effect the maximum possible health improvement or, equivalently, the expenditure required to reduce the individual's capacity to benefit to zero (p. 436).

In contrast, it is also common usage to treat health care need as a minimal requirement or standard of adequacy. This was the spirit of federal health planning efforts in the 1970s, which sought to control the perceived proliferation of health care in order to control costs. Health planners at the time, as well as most health cost control advocates in any era, argued implicitly that consumers were getting more health care than they really needed.

Often the discussion of needs gets disconnected from the fact that the output of health care and the distribution of health care to meet people's needs are chosen in the context of society's choices of all its public goals. We present a construction of need that brings this to mind.

Let health care needs be defined within the context of the choice of society's goals for population health status as well as in the contexts of other goals like education and defense. To illustrate, we identify in Figure 19.5 the production function for health

FIGURE 19.5 The Production Function for Health.

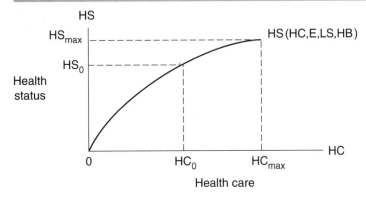

[1]This discussion and interpretation of need follow Folland (1986).

defined over the levels of a variable input, health care, given the conditions of environment, E; lifestyle, LS; and human biological endowment, HB. Here the technically maximal health status is HS_{max}. To achieve this health status level, a health care level of HC_{max} is needed. However, society may choose a lesser health status goal than the maximum achievable, using the savings to further other goals. For example, if society through its choice processes selects health status goal HS_0, then health care level HC_0 is needed.

We have described the choice of a health goal as implying a needed level of health care; that is, a level of health care "utilization." In the early 1990s, economists debated the issue of whether utilization or "access" was the superior choice for defining needs. The words "equity of access," which frequently appear in public documents in various countries, suggest an equal opportunity, especially financial opportunity (Mooney et al., 1992). For many health economists, however, "access" is difficult to define. While health care utilization is more easily measured, it is usually also the ultimate reason for our concern about access (Culyer, van Doorslaer, and Wagstaff, 1992a, 1992b).

HEALTH CARE NEEDS AND THE SOCIAL WELFARE FUNCTION

How, then, is the health status goal selected? We depict this choice using the concept of a social welfare function.

The Utility–Possibility Frontier

The Edgeworth box shows the efficient choices available to society in allocating resources among people. Yet it is also apparent that at many points on the contract curve, Abner or Belinda may be allocated few or no resources. These points are unquestionably economically efficient, yet they may be indefensible within any definition of a humane society.

Economic theory suggests that a social welfare function reflecting society's overall preferences is necessary to determine which of the efficient points is chosen.[2] We can trace out a utility–possibility frontier, *UU*, from the points in the Edgeworth box in Figure 19.1. Begin at the allocation where Belinda has everything and Abner has nothing. In Figure 19.6, we can assign Abner a utility of 0 and evaluate Belinda's utility as the intercept of the vertical axis.

We can then draw a *UU* curve by reallocating resources to Abner from Belinda as we move along the contract curve in Figure 19.1. Recall that the fundamental property of Pareto efficient distributions is that Abner's utility can come only at the expense of Belinda's utility. Therefore, the *UU* curve in Figure 19.6 must be downward sloping. The horizontal axis intercept summarizes the point at which Abner has all of the resources.

The Social Welfare Function

It is now up to society to decide which of the points on *UU* to choose. This decision must be made according to the rules by which societies operate: through debate, consensus, and maybe even dictatorial power. Economists define this as a *social welfare function*. Consider, for example, a society in which the consensus was that everyone's utility level should be exactly the same, with no variations tolerated. We would recognize this as a set of right-angled social indifference curves along a 45-degree line from

[2]The classic discussion of this problem is Bator (1957). Since our discussion concerns exchange only, we have simplified his exposition.

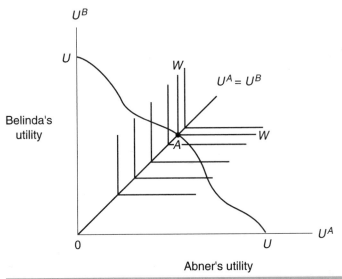

FIGURE 19.6 The Utility–Possibility Frontier and Social Welfare Maximization: Egalitarian Preferences.

the origin. The optimum allocation would be at point *A*, which is a tangency between the *WW* curve and the *UU* curve. This would indicate equal utility levels for Abner and Belinda. From point *A*, we can then return to the one point on the contract curve in Figure 19.1 in which the utility levels are equal, denoted *Z*. Picking this point leads to the unique allocation of the two goods to Abner and Belinda (although not necessarily the same amounts to each, as shown in Figure 19.1).

Many would argue that the specific social welfare function (with equal levels of utility) discussed previously would be highly questionable. Humane societies might agree that everyone should be provided with enough resources for at least a minimal standard of living; for Abner this would be U^A_{min}, and for Belinda this would be U^B_{min}. This can be characterized as two constraints on the *UU* curve in Figure 19.7. Such societies would consider no utility functions that would provide Abner with less utility than U^A_{min}: similarly for Belinda regarding U^B_{min}. Even here, however, the answer depends on the exact social welfare function chosen. Societies in which people like Belinda are most influential may have social welfare functions with social indifference curves like $W'W'$. In this case, people like Belinda would get larger shares of the resources than people like Abner. The optimum at point *B*, although providing subsistence living for citizens like Abner, would leave citizens like Belinda better off than the optimum in Figure 19.6.

The Social Welfare Function and Health Care Needs

Within this framework, we now discuss the various social choice processes that scholars and policy makers have proposed for the equitable provision of health care. Let the social welfare function of society (SW) represent the preferences of society as a whole. The function in a commonly used form may be written as follows:

$$SW = f(U_1, U_2, \ldots U_m) \tag{19.1}$$

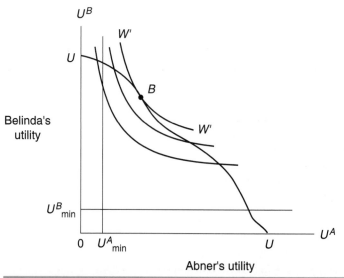

FIGURE 19.7 The Utility Frontier and Social Welfare Maximization: Preferences Favoring Belinda.

where social welfare is characterized as a function of the utility levels of each of the n persons in the society. Utility for each person as usual depends on his or her consumption of the available goods in society, including health care. In addition, we may suppose that each individual to some degree perceives an external benefit from the consumption of health care by others.

Society may be perceived to be efficient when it acts as if it were choosing among its variables to maximize the social welfare function. The choice process may be conceived graphically in Figure 19.7 as choosing the highest social indifference curve attainable given the utility–possibility frontier. The level of health care needed can be defined within this context. The health care needed by each person in society is that which maximizes SW. Social welfare will be maximized when society chooses its optimal health status goals in conjunction with optimal levels of other goals.

The social welfare function has proved flexible within health economics, because it can be used to formulate other conceptions of health equity. Some health economists who study welfare issues propose that society's health goal should be the maximization of community health and propose that the quality adjusted life years (QALYs) that remain in the life expectancy of the community be used as the measure of health. Wagstaff (1991) showed how this concept, as well as equity adjustment factors, can be incorporated into the social welfare function framework. Bleichrodt (1997) attempted to make the QALY approach more concrete by demonstrating mathematical assumptions that give the utility of the QALY interpersonal comparability, making the social welfare function a matter of simply adding up all individual utilities. This is a return to utilitarianism of the eighteenth century, but also a novel use of the social welfare function framework.

NORMAN DANIELS'S CONCEPT OF HEALTH CARE NEED

To assume that health care need is determined by the same social choice mechanism by which society makes all its choices of social goals is to treat health status like all other goals. Some analysts argue that health is special and that the health care needs have a more objective independent basis. Others argue that the standard economic conception of society's well-being is flawed. Its dependence on the inviobility of the individual's conception of his own well-being, its reliance on the Pareto principle, and its usual insistence that social choice issues depend solely on individual utilities have been criticized as "welfarism." Those making the criticism include recent Nobel economist Amartya Sen. To address the special role of health, the philosopher Norman Daniels (1985) has developed a health care needs definition and we provide an outline of his approach here. Daniels's concept of health care need has three main elements.

1. *Health care is special.* Under this view, health care can be separated from other goals. To make this separation plausible, health care must be viewed as a primary good that is special because it is central to the task of attaining or restoring a fair equality of opportunity. In this sense, it comes prior to other considerations.
2. *Species-typical functioning.* It is further argued that the human species has a range of functioning that is typical and appropriate to it. Disease here means the absence of health; health is defined as the ability to attain a functioning level typical to the species.
3. *Fair equality of opportunity.* Given the nature of society and the human species, there is a range of behavior opportunity that every person in society should have available. The range will vary somewhat from person to person inasmuch as we each have different endowments of skills and abilities. But all are entitled to their fair share.[3]

To use the *fair equality of opportunity* standard of health care need, we must imagine that there is a degree of objectivity behind its construction, and that need so constructed would be observable in common by most people. We do not solve this matter here, but instead point out what Daniels's project entails. If Daniels's view were accepted as correct, then health care need could be identified separately from the context in which other goals for society are chosen. We leave as a discussion question the issue of whether this is possible.[4]

Economic Criticisms of Need-Based Distributions

The ideas of mainstream economics often clash with need-based conceptions of the appropriate distribution of health care resources. The economic criticisms that have been leveled do not necessarily apply to each existing conception of need. The criticisms are each directed to particular conceptions of need. They can be understood as criticisms of

[3]Health economist Alan Williams (1997) promotes a similar concept in that all people should be entitled to their "fair innings" of life expectancy and health.
[4]The issue can be pursued further beginning with Daniels's stimulating and controversial book (1985) and articles (1981, 1982).

the form "if by need you mean X, then the following criticism applies. . . ." Several criticisms of this sort are found in the literature.

1. *The bottomless pit.* Health is undoubtedly subject to diminishing marginal returns in production. Thus, if the technical maximum health status goal is chosen, the marginal unit of health care will have nearly zero effect on health status. Because it is doubtful that all societal goals can be attained maximally, social welfare generally would be improved if society would reduce health care use somewhat and use the freed resources for other goals. For that matter, health care needs at or close to the technical maximum also could exhaust most of society's resources and thus constitute a bottomless pit.
2. *Needs should not be chosen independent of costs.* Society's health status goals should depend in part on the costs of health and thus on the price of health care. This is so because the costs of health care resources determine the amounts of other goods that must be given up to attain health goals. No society is wealthy enough to attain the maximum amounts of all goals, and thus health has opportunity costs.
3. *The role of scientific medicine in determining needs.* From similar reasoning, it follows that health needs cannot be determined solely on the basis of scientific medical knowledge. The role of medical experts is critical in needs analysis, inasmuch as scientific data are required to determine the medical inputs needed to attain a given health goal. However, the appropriate health status goals themselves must be chosen with knowledge of society's economic constraints and its values. In some form, the political process is required to identify the trade-offs that society is willing to incur to attain any given goal.
4. *Monotechnic needs.* Finally, Fuchs (1974) has pointed out that when needs analyses are stated in terms of needed health resources per capita, they often implicitly falsely assume that only one available technique exists for pursuing a health status goal. More plausibly, many opportunities exist for substitution, not only among health care inputs but also among health care inputs and other inputs into the production function of health.

Horizontal Equity and Need

Health care need is also a central focus in recent research attempting to answer questions about the equitable treatment of people with equal needs. Equal treatment of equals is known as *horizontal equity*. To understand the issues and findings, we draw on the work of van Doorslaer and Wagstaff (1992).

These authors define inequity by beginning with the following equations:

$$m_1 = a_p + b_p h_i \qquad \text{if poor}$$
$$m_1 = a_r + b_r h_i \qquad \text{if rich} \tag{19.2}$$

In these equations, m is medical expenditure; a_p and a_r are constant levels of expenditure when healthy for the poor and the rich, respectively; b_p and b_r are constant coefficients of health status, h_i, which equals 0 when the person is healthy and 1 when sick. (We omit random error terms depicting the minor characteristics of individuals that affect medical expenditure irrespective of need.)

Horizontal equity occurs when $a_p = a_r$ and $b_p = b_t$; that is, when the expected average spending of the rich and poor are equal both when well ($h_i = 0$) and when sick ($h_i = 1$). Does this square with your own sense of what equity means?[5]

HOW TO COMPARE HORIZONTAL EQUITY AMONG COUNTRIES

To generate a measure of the degree of inequity, the authors then calculate the standardized expenditure shares, based on equations (19.2), which are the groups' shares of total expenditure reflected by their spending. The final result is described graphically in Figure 19.8. Here the curve labeled *g* measures the cumulative standardized shares against the cumulative population arranged by income level. As shown in this hypothetical example, the poorest 20 percent of the population accounts for about 5 percent of medical expenditure, the poorest 40 percent accounts for about 11 percent of the expenditure, and so on.

If spending favors the rich, the curve will lie below the diagonal, as in this case. When spending favors the poor, the curve will lie above the diagonal. The degree of inequality is measured as the ratio of the area of the ellipsoid *A* to the total area under the diagonal.[6]

THE RESULTS

The van Doorslaer and Wagstaff results for inequity across countries are shown in Table 19.1. These data suggest that unequal use by people and income groups given

FIGURE 19.8 Standardized Expenditure Concentration Curve.

[5]Mooney et al. (1991, 1992) question whether equity means equal expenditure. An individual may differ from another because of different preferences, so even with equal access, the amount of expenditures on care will differ. Culyer, van Doorslaer, and Wagstaff (1992) respond to this objection. The interested reader is recommended these original sources.
[6]If the curve lies above the diagonal, then the inequality is measured as the ratio of the negative area of the ellipsoid to the total area under the diagonal.

TABLE 19.1	Tests of Inequality across Countries	
Country	*Measure of Inequality*[a]	*Statistically Significant*
Denmark	−0.055	Yes
Ireland	−0.076	Yes
Italy	−0.036	Yes
Netherlands	0.025	No
Spain	0.146	Yes
Switzerland	−0.043	No
United Kingdom	0.013	Yes
United States	0.028	Yes

[a]Measured at the 1 percent level of statistical significance.

Source: Reprinted from *Journal of Health Economics,* van Doorslaer, Eddy, and Adam Wagstaff, "Equity in the Delivery of Health Care: Some International Comparisons." *Journal of Health Economics* 11 (1992): 389–411, with permission from Elsevier Science.

health status is the common rule, not the exception. However, the negative numbers in the table show countries where the estimated inequality is in favor of the poorer people. Only in the Netherlands, Spain, the United Kingdom, and the United States is the distribution tending to favor the rich, although in the Netherlands the result is not statistically significant. When the elderly are left out of consideration in the United States, then the authors report that the distribution even in the United States favors the poor. While measurement and definition issues of horizontal equity may elicit disagreement, these numbers representing unequal use for a given health status across income groups are clearly defined and tell an important part of the story.

Theories of Social Justice

Inevitably, a treatment of what health care distribution is equitable and of what health care needs should be met in a society, depends on ethical theory. An ethical theory serves to identify a context and reasoning to determine what ought to be done, as opposed to mere positive analysis of what is the case. Ethical theories that serve to determine a fair or just distribution of economic resources are sometimes called theories of social justice. Seen this way, any notion of equity or need in health care, in order to be complete, must be connected to an ethical theory or perhaps to a theory of social justice.

Several theories of social justice have been proposed. It cannot be said that we have a consensus-accepted theory of social justice. Even without a consensus, however, an examination of several examples of theories of social justice helps to illuminate the issues that must be addressed if a consensus is to be achieved. We offer a brief overview of three social justice theories, along with a selection of criticisms of each theory.

UTILITARIANISM

Utilitarianism became prominent in the nineteenth century and is still current in modified forms. It can be understood as the greatest good for the greatest number. In its clas-

sical form, it identified the social optimum coincident with maximization of the sum of utilities of all persons in society. Classical utilitarianism in effect defines the social welfare function as the sum of individual utilities.

In the form of utilitarianism promoted by Jeremy Bentham in the eighteenth and nineteenth century, an individual's utility was conceived of as cardinally measurable, at least in principle, and comparable among individuals. The utilitarian ethic thus originally was conceived somewhat literally as maximization of society's total satisfaction level.

Utilitarianism captures the idea of trade-offs among goals. Under this construction, society may choose to accept some harm for a few members in return for a greater good for the many. As such, it avoids the bottomless pit criticisms mentioned earlier. Health status would not generally be maximized for every individual in society under this view.

Some Criticisms of Utilitarianism

Classical utilitarianism came to be criticized within the economics profession early in this century. Economists generally rejected the idea that utility could be cardinally measurable and comparable among people. It is viewed as unscientific to suppose that one individual's level of satisfaction could somehow be added to that of another person. Modern social welfare theory in economics has proceeded along ordinal utility lines. Utility in these theories retains the role of ranking preferences among alternatives, but the notion of a fixed quantitative measure of happiness was discarded in most modern theory.

Two other criticisms of utilitarianism help to illustrate some of the weaknesses that have been identified in the theory. One is the question of domain—that is, whose utilities are to count? Utilitarianism does not itself identify where to draw the boundaries of membership in the society. Are foreign people or noncitizens to count? If not, why not? Are animals to count? Unborn future generations? Is the utility of the fetus to count or only that of the already born?

A second criticism raised by Robert Nozick (1974) poses a similar question regarding possibly malevolent individuals in society. For example, suppose an individual, because of bigotry or sheer malevolence, gets satisfaction out of the suffering of some other group in society. Is the malevolent utility of such a person also to count?

RAWLS AND JUSTICE AS FAIRNESS

John Rawls (1971) approached the concept of social justice from a different viewpoint. Here a primary principle of justice is that social choices must be fair. It is unfair, according to Rawls, for social choices to be dominated by people with economic or political power who often have vested interests because of their circumstances in society. Instead, to be fair we should make our choices from a position divorced from arbitrary special interestedness. Such a position, it is proposed, is one from behind the "veil of ignorance."[7]

[7]Olsen (1997) notes that Rawls's maximin is one of a class of egalitarian social justice principles. It has become the most prominent. Olsen's exposition offers a diagrammatic depiction of each social justice theory prominent in health economics.

The Rawlsian veil of ignorance is a hypothetical situation in which we can think rationally but for which our particularities of self and economic situation are as yet unknown. It is as if we could somehow contemplate life in society before we are born and before we know whether we will be rich or poor, black or white, male or female, tall or short, and so on. Rawls's idea is that, so divorced from our vested interests of life, we would generally come to a consensus about principles of social justice, and specifically we would agree to the Rawlsian *maximin* principle.

Under the maximin principle, we would each reason that without knowing who we were to become in society, we would presume that we could be the person worst off. Under such circumstances, we would agree, argues Rawls, only to a system of justice in society that maximized the position of the worst off. This need not result in complete equality of incomes and resources including health care, but departures from equality would be permitted only if the lot of the worst off would improve. Health care under a Rawlsian system of social justice would presumably also be provided if the needs of the worst off were regarded as a priority.

Some Criticisms of Rawlsian Justice

Rawls's theory of justice also has drawn criticism, and we illustrate some of these criticisms. It has been pointed out that Rawls assumes that each of us behind the veil of ignorance is extremely risk averse. Suppose that an alternative situation, A, offered everyone an income of $10,000, while alternative B offered one person $9,000 but everyone else $100,000. Under the maximin principle, persons behind the veil would choose alternative A, the alternative with the higher income for the worst off. Would people really be so risk averse as to forgo even extremely good odds of a large gain?

The Rawlsian theory of justice also appears subject to the bottomless pit argument. The instance of health care provides a good example of the problem in the views of Arrow (1973):

> Thus there could easily exist medical procedures which serve to keep people barely alive but with little satisfaction and which are yet so expensive as to reduce the rest of the population to poverty (p. 251).

Despite the criticisms, Rawlsian justice provides a prominent example of a theory of social justice that entails a strong presumption in favor of equality—a presumption that permits inequalities to arise only if they contribute to the lot of the worst off.

NOZICK AND ENTITLEMENT THEORY

Finally, we describe a theory of justice that puts a premium on liberty. Robert Nozick (1974) offers a conception of justice that begins by proposing that natural rights suggest the necessity for a libertarian constraint. By a libertarian constraint, he means that any system of social organization should prohibit the coercion of others. All persons are entitled to enter into voluntary transactions, free from coercion. Property rights are acknowledged and people are entitled to keep any property received through a voluntary transaction.

From these principles, Nozick develops a justification for the existence of a minimal state. He argues that these principles of justice necessarily limit the role of the state, and in consequence, social programs beyond the minimal functions of government in providing public police protection services would not be warranted. It follows that social programs providing for health care also would not be warranted, and the health care needs of one person would not place obligations on any other person other than for what he or she voluntarily is willing to accept.

Some Criticisms of Entitlement Theory

A central focus of criticism is the assumed libertarian constraint itself. For those who do not accept the constraint as an implication or necessity of natural rights, it will be hard to see why we are not free to trade off some degree of liberty in order to make gains in efficiency. For example, the Food and Drug Administration restrictions on the availability of certain drugs represent restrictions on liberty, but at least in some cases they may be supportable on efficiency grounds. Pauly (1978) has argued, for example, that if the costs of conveying information to the public are sufficiently large, substantial efficiency gains may accrue simply by restricting access to a potentially dangerous drug. The restriction of access may in some cases require a physician's prescription; in other cases, it may require banning the drug from the market.

Members of society frequently accept rules that are expected to improve outcomes yet that restrict liberty somewhat. Wittman (1982) has discussed the potential efficiency of simple rules in day-to-day life and in sports. A traffic light restricts liberty somewhat but promotes the efficient and safe flow of traffic. If we accept the principle that liberties can be traded off to gain certain efficiencies, this raises the question of whether we must accept the libertarian constraint.

Conclusions

The three theories of social justice described here attempt to ground our understanding of the distribution of goods and services—including importantly health care—in a system of ethics. The brief review of these theories cannot account for all arguments and rebuttals and cannot resolve controversies. Those interested in ethics, as it concerns economic distribution, should consult the original sources.

The theories, however, serve to show how widely people's understanding of appropriate distributions of health care differ, and their consideration suggests that we have as yet no consensus. Nevertheless, these issues of justice are raised whenever society wishes to modify the distribution of health resources on grounds of need and equity. The issues are no less important because there is disagreement.

The meaning of efficiency is more sharply defined. Here the issues of controversy involve the degree of efficiency attainable either with existing health care markets or with health care markets as modified by new policies. The theoretical model of perfect competition generates a Pareto efficient outcome. Health care markets in practice, however, differ in many respects from those that have perfect competition. Perhaps the most notable discrepancies of actual health care markets from the theoretical model

arise because of the role of uncertainty, the problems of information, and the presence of externalities.

Perfection in either direction is not attainable. We must inevitably accept approaches to health care distribution that are second best, evaluating each proposal on its merits. While perfect competition is unattainable, proposals that improve the degree of competition in health care markets may nevertheless improve society's well-being. On the other hand, proposals for providing social insurance programs to at least some segments of the population can be supported in principle on efficiency grounds whenever substantial charitable externalities are present. Alternatively, social insurance programs may be justified on the basis of one or more systems of social justice.

Summary

1. Pareto efficiency defines a situation where it is no longer possible to make mutually beneficial changes. It is Pareto efficient to exhaust all avenues for gains that benefit someone and harm no one.
2. Under theoretical conditions of perfect competition, the competitive market is Pareto efficient. In the Edgeworth box for exchange, regardless of the initial endowment position, a competitive free exchange will lead to a Pareto efficient point, a point on the contract curve. This is the First Fundamental Theorem of Welfare Economics.
3. The Second Fundamental Theorem of Welfare Economics also is illustrated by the Edgeworth box for exchange. The theorem holds that any Pareto efficient outcome can in principle be achieved by a competitive market, given a suitable initial distribution of resources.
4. Price discrimination is Pareto inefficient. This result includes that form of price discrimination arising when a favored segment of the population is provided reduced prices for health care so as to improve access.
5. The health care sector deviates from the conditions of perfect competition in many respects. These include major issues of the role of uncertainty, the role of information, and the role of externalities.
6. The Theorem of the Second Best suggests that promoting competitive features in health care markets is not welfare enhancing per se. Nevertheless, many competitive proposals in practice may be welfare enhancing.
7. Social programs for the subsidization or provision of health care can be theoretically rationalized on grounds of efficiency as well as equity. The usual efficiency argument posits the existence of a charitable externality in health care. The presence of externalities may in principle justify market interventions.
8. Need-based distributions of health care resources tend to be based on equity grounds and usually imply a rejection of market outcomes. Health care need may be understood as health care resources required to attain a given health goal chosen by society.
9. Society's optimal choice of goals may be summarized by the social welfare function, defined over all possible combinations of the individual utilities of society members. This leads to the optimal choice by selecting the point on the utility–possibility frontier that maximizes social welfare.

10. Norman Daniels's concept of health care need is based on the fair equality of opportunity. It argues that health care needs may be identified separately from other social decisions.

11. Several need-based distributions can be criticized on economic grounds. These grounds argue that health care needs should not be (1) the technical maximum, (2) independent of cost, (3) chosen solely on technical medical criteria, or (4) monotechnic.

12. A philosophical theory of justice is needed to provide an ethical grounding for a proposed distribution. There is no present consensus on such a theory of justice.

Discussion Questions

1. At point 0_A in Figure 19.1, Belinda has all of both goods. Is this point Pareto efficient? Is it equitable? Discuss.

2. If society could clearly choose an equitable point reflecting a distribution of the two goods, is this point inevitably going to lie on the contract curve?

3. Choose an example of a health care market, and identify ways in which it differs from the perfectly competitive model. Do you think that these deviations from competition could each be repaired by appropriate policies? Discuss.

4. We describe several economic criticisms of need-based distributions. Do any of these criticisms apply to Norman Daniels's conception of health care need?

5. Speculate on how each of the three described theories of social justice would view government programs designed to provide infant and child care to the poor using tax dollars.

6. Under utilitarianism, one maximizes the total utility of society. What does this imply about the marginal utility for each person? What does it imply about the total utility for each person?

7. Suppose society determined that it must provide a minimal sustained level of health to everyone. What would this imply regarding society's expenditures on health?

8. Insufficient health care for some often is seen as a problem of insufficient income to purchase health care. Discuss two alternatives to social programs that provide health care.

Exercises

1. Prove that point *B* in Figure 19.1 is not Pareto efficient.

2. Draw an Edgeworth box of the type in Figure 19.2 but with only these details inside: the point ω and budget line *AB* through ω. Using indifference curves, depict the utility-maximizing choice for Abner. Now let the budget line rotate to *CD*, drawn to reflect a higher relative price of medical care. Again identify the utility-maximizing choice for Abner.

3. Is it possible to find a point on the contract curve that is not a competitive equilibrium?

4. Let Q_{opt} in Figure 19.4 represent the optimal level of health care in society under the external benefits rationale for social health care programs. Would members of society necessarily view Q_{opt} as the equitable amount of health care?

5. If all tax-paying members of society became "hard hearted," feeling no external benefit in the health care provided to others, then what would be the optimal health care output under the external benefit rationale in Figure 19.4?

6. In Figure 19.7, depicting the utility–possibility frontier, would society ever choose an inefficient point (inside UU) as the optimal point?

7. Suppose Fred has an income of $5,000 per year and Harry has an income of $105,000 per year. If we tax $50,000 from Harry to give to Fred, will this represent a Pareto improvement for society? Why or why not? Would this improve society under some other criteria?

Government Intervention in Health Care Markets

- Economic Rationale for Government Intervention

- Forms of Government Intervention

- Government Involvement in Health Care Markets

- Government Failure

- Competitive Strategies

- Conclusions

The material in previous chapters has revealed in part the scope of government involvement in health care delivery. We have seen that (1) government spending accounts for a substantial portion of all health care spending, (2) governments are deeply involved in producing as well as financing health care services, and (3) governments regulate the health care industries. Also, we have found that governments are at the center of most contemporary health care issues. These include major policy issues such as national health insurance and initiatives intended to control costs and increase access to care, and also less publicized issues such as those involving federal government support for education and research.

The purpose of this chapter is to provide a framework for assessing the role of governments in health care markets. We begin with the conventional approach favored by economists, which emphasizes market failure as the rationale for government intervention. This is followed by a historical review, including examples of federal, state, and local involvement in the health economy. We continue with a discussion of government failure to identify impediments in developing effective programs used. As an alternative

to regulation, we also address competitive strategies to improve health care delivery and to meet this nation's policy goals.

Economic Rationale for Government Intervention

As we have seen, efficiency is one common standard for evaluating the desirability of economic allocations. Inefficient allocations are associated with various distortions that lead to market failure. The previous chapter introduced the distortion resulting from beneficial externalities as one justification for social programs in health care.

MONOPOLY POWER

Monopoly power provides the classic example of market failure. A profit-maximizing monopolist produces to the level at which marginal revenue equals marginal cost. Because the marginal revenue lies below the demand curve, the price charged by the monopolist will exceed the marginal cost of production. It is the price-marginal cost gap that creates the welfare loss.

Figure 20.1 summarizes these standard results. With a perfectly elastic competitive supply in the long run, which also represents the industry's average (AC) and marginal costs (MC), the competitive price and quantity are P_C and Q_C. If this industry is monopolized and no changes occur in demand or costs, the profit-maximizing output is given by Q_M, where $MR = MC$. The higher monopoly price is P_M, and the welfare loss is represented by triangle ABC.

However, monopoly power need not be associated solely with pure monopoly. The monopoly model is applied commonly to markets in which one or a small number of sellers are dominant. Several health care markets seem to hold a potential for the exercise of monopoly power in health care. Examples include hospital services in markets with few hospitals, pharmaceutical products that are protected by patents, and some health insurance markets dominated by Blue Cross and Blue Shield associations.

The potential for monopoly power exists even in markets characterized by a large number of sellers, as in the markets for doctor and dental services. Licensure laws and other forms of regulation restrict entry into some professions. Furthermore, professional associations may be able to reduce price competition by setting minimum fee schedules or by inhibiting the flow of information to buyers.

Note several issues regarding monopoly power. First, some of the barriers to entry and competition result from government intervention itself. These include licensure and patent laws. Licensure is intended to ensure minimal standards of quality; patent laws are intended to promote innovative activity.

Second, monopoly power may be inevitable in some situations and does not necessarily lead to economic profits. In a small market, for example, demand may be sufficient for only one hospital to survive while it just covers costs. If, in fact, demand were to diminish, even the one existing hospital would not be able to survive unless it received subsidies or donations or it could cut its costs.

Third, the proposed cure to monopoly inefficiencies may be worse than the problems posed by the existence and exercise of monopoly power. Some have argued that direct intervention through public provision or price controls could worsen the situation because of government failure. These critics suggest that countervailing forces and

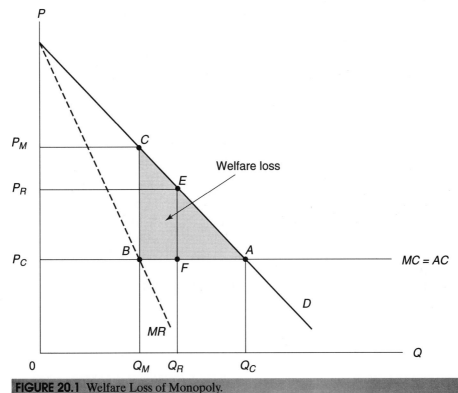

FIGURE 20.1 Welfare Loss of Monopoly.

other constraints on the full exercise of monopoly power will tend to arise in private markets, especially where antitrust laws are enforced vigorously.

In the simplest case and in the absence of government failure, price controls can theoretically reduce the welfare loss caused by monopoly. Suppose a maximum fee control of P_R is established. The monopolist's marginal revenue is constant, equal to the price, P_R, up to an output of Q_R. Because marginal revenue exceeds marginal cost up until output Q_R, the monopolist will produce at least to Q_R. Beyond Q_R, the marginal revenue is found from the usual MR curve because the monopolist would have to lower prices to attract more buyers. Marginal revenue then will be below marginal cost and eventually will become negative. The profit-maximizing output is Q_R, and the welfare loss is now reduced from area ABC to area AEF. While it thus appears in this case that price regulation can be an effective instrument in reducing prices, monopoly profits, and welfare losses, consider that a typical hospital or physician provider may produce many different services. Consider also that demand and technology are changing constantly and that it may be difficult to monitor quality. As we will discuss later, price regulation under such circumstances becomes a far more difficult task.

PUBLIC GOODS

A public good should not be confused with the public provision of a good. The postal service and garbage collection service are examples of public provision of private goods.

Such goods may be provided by government because of natural monopoly or a desire to subsidize certain users (e.g., rural postal customers). In contrast, a pure public good is one for which consumption is nonrival (i.e., consumption by one individual does not reduce someone else's consumption) and nonexcludable (i.e., a consumer cannot be excluded from consuming the good either by having to pay or through some other mechanism). National defense is used often as an example of a pure public good. Other examples of goods having some degree of publicness include highways, bridges, and parks.[1]

Market failure arises because an inefficiently small quantity of pure public goods typically will be provided without government intervention. Figure 20.2 develops this proposition. Begin with a simple case involving two persons whose demands and marginal benefits for a public good are represented by D_A and D_B. By definition, a public good is nonrival and nonexcludable. Each person must consume the identical quantity that he or she buys or that is made available. Thus, the marginal social benefits (MSB) are the sum of the two individuals' marginal private benefits. Following the classic geometric exposition developed by Samuelson (1955), this is shown as a vertical summation of

FIGURE 20.2 The Optimal Quantity of a Public Good.

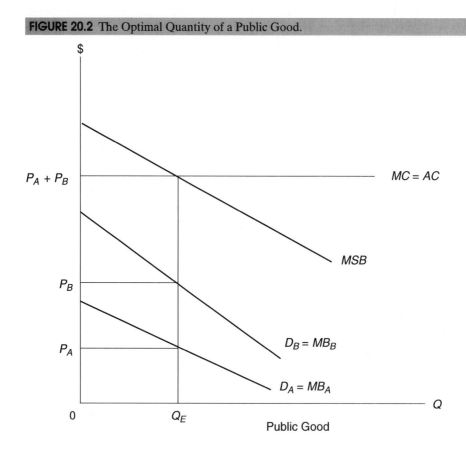

[1]Consumption of such goods tends to be nonrival but only up to some congestion point. Also, these goods are not consumed equally, and it may be feasible to exclude those who do not pay for their use.

D_A and D_B. Assuming constant costs, the efficient quantity is Q_E, where marginal social benefits are equal to the marginal costs of production MC.

Will the efficient quantity become available without government intervention? Knowing that their contributions are important, the two consumers may decide to cooperate by making voluntary contributions to fund at least some of the good. In fact, if each contributes according to his or her marginal private benefit at Q_E by paying P_A and P_B, respectively, for every unit, enough money will be collected to cover the cost of providing the optimal quantity, Q_E. It is not certain, however, whether this solution will be reached.

More realistically, public goods usually involve a large number of individuals. In principle, determining the optimal quantity, using a vertically summed marginal social benefit curve, follows the two-person example. The major difference is that these individuals are unlikely to cooperate to fund substantial amounts of the public good through voluntary contributions. Instead, more are likely to become *free riders* (i.e., make no contributions) because they cannot be excluded from consuming the good and because any voluntary contribution one makes will have a negligible impact on its availability. The predicted undersupply of public goods in private markets has led many to conclude that governments should be responsible for making them available.

Are health care services public goods? Health services provided to one person are not at the same time consumed by others. Also, those who do not pay can be excluded from receiving care. Therefore, health care services are private goods even though they may involve public provision (e.g., through the Veterans Administration) or public financing (e.g., through Medicare and Medicaid). Thus, the public goods rationale for government provision of health care is not immediately apparent.

Despite this caveat, economic theories of public goods are highly relevant to certain health care issues. Consider the following cases:

Information

Information can be thought of as an economic good that has a high degree of publicness. By obtaining information, one consumer does not reduce the information available to another. Although those who do not pay often can be excluded from receiving information, the marginal cost of providing information to another individual is often relatively small. It can thus be argued that information will be underproduced in private markets and that government intervention is needed to increase its availability.

The government may take on two distinct roles. The first is to help disseminate existing knowledge to the public. This can be achieved either through direct provision or through subsidizing private sector activities. Second, governments may expand the stock of knowledge by taking an active role in scientific research, again by direct provision or through subsidizing private sector research. The federal government has pursued both strategies.

Redistribution

Voluntary giving also has a public goods dimension. Donations help to raise lower-income persons' standards of consumption, including their consumption of health care. By letting others donate and knowing that one's contribution will have little impact on total contributions, individuals often become free riders. To help offset this effect, it can be argued that mandatory programs are needed to correct the undersupply of voluntary giving.

However, considerable disagreement can arise over the form of the redistribution. Should it be done through cash transfers to let recipients spend their additional incomes as they see fit? Or should some programs take the form of in-kind transfers (e.g., Medicaid) where the transfers must be used to purchase health care services? The many issues relating to equity and mechanisms for redistributing income are discussed in chapters 19 ("Equity, Efficiency, and Need") and 22 ("Social Insurance").

EXTERNALITIES

In contrast to pure or nearly pure public goods, another group of goods has a varying degree of publicness to it. This group is composed of those goods that have third-party effects, also known as externalities. Recall that externalities arise when a third party is affected by another party's consumption or production of a good. If a neighbor's loud music or smoke from leaves burning bothers you, a negative externality has been created.

Moreover, to be considered an externality, the effects must be transmitted outside the price system. Thus, a situation where an increase in demand for lower-cholesterol meats raises their prices, adversely affecting consumers of these products, is not an externality. The higher prices ration the supply of low-cholesterol products.

The major problem with many negative or positive externalities is that the externalities may not be reflected fully in the prices of the goods and services with which they are associated. Thus, even when competitive forces drive prices to the marginal private cost of production, social efficiency requires that marginal social benefits equal the marginal social costs. The former consists of marginal private benefits and any marginal external benefit that might exist, while marginal social costs similarly consist of marginal private costs and any marginal external costs that might exist.

With a negative externality, such as pollution, that creates a marginal external cost, a competitive market tends to overproduce relative to the socially efficient quantity. The market price will not reflect the external cost. Conversely, competitive markets tend to undersupply goods that create beneficial (positive) externalities. Marginal social benefits exceed the price at the competitive output. Positive externalities can be important in health care, as when a charitably minded person derives satisfaction from knowing that the sick, poor, or uninsured consume more health care. More tangible externalities are created when others are inoculated against communicable diseases.

The extent of the role of positive externalities should not be confused with health benefits that are largely private. Subsidies that lead to improved health are often supported on the grounds that recipients will benefit society by being more productive. However, the gains from an individual's increased productivity are largely private. Thus, the effects of the consumption of health care on productivity are not externalities.

OTHER RATIONALES FOR GOVERNMENT INTERVENTION

Several other arguments favor government intervention. An important responsibility of the federal government is to stabilize the economy through macroeconomic policies. Although macroeconomics does not usually focus on specific sectors of the economy, changes in monetary, fiscal, and debt policy can have major effects on federal and state health care programs, as well as on private health care spending through changes in taxes and interest rates.

Another distinct category involves government's role in promoting the consumption of merit goods. Merit goods are commodities thought to be good for someone regardless of the person's own preferences. Support for the arts, compulsory education, and mandated consumption of other goods are in part supported by arguments that individuals do not always know what is in their best interests. Undoubtedly, to some extent, public policy with respect to seat belts, alcohol, tobacco and drug use, and other public health issues has reflected the merit goods idea.

A final role for government involves incomplete markets. These are situations in which private markets fail to meet an existing demand. Certain insurance markets, such as those for patients with cancer, AIDS, or other preexisting conditions who seek new insurance, are sometimes suggested as examples of incomplete markets in the sense that such patients may not be able to buy insurance at *any* price. It has been proposed that government has a role in filling these gaps by providing insurance or requiring insurers to do so.

Care is needed, however, to determine whether some of these markets are truly incomplete. Is there sufficient demand by those willing to pay actuarially fair rates so that a market would emerge? Because premiums would, on average, match insurance payments, they would be very high. Are such patients seeking subsidies by having legislation guaranteeing access to insurance at lower than actuarially fair rates?

Forms of Government Intervention

Governments can adopt a variety of policies and instruments to influence the allocation of resources or the distribution of income. The principal categories relevant to health care are selective commodity taxes and subsidies, public provision of health care, transfer programs, and regulation.

COMMODITY TAXES AND SUBSIDIES

We already have established that a competitive market is inefficient when beneficial (positive) externalities result from the consumption of a commodity. Using inoculations against infectious disease as an example, we extend our previous work to show how taxes and subsidies can, in principle, correct for the externality.

Let demand, *D*, and supply, *S*, in Figure 20.3 reflect the marginal private benefits (*MPB*) and marginal private costs (*MPC*) of inoculations. *MPB* equals *MPC* at the equilibrium quantity, Q_1. However, the competitive allocation is inefficient when those who are inoculated confer a marginal external benefit (*MEB*) on others. Too little is produced at Q_1 because marginal social benefit, the vertical sum of the *MPB* and *MEB*, exceeds marginal social costs (here equal to *MPC* because there are no external costs). Pareto efficiency and the elimination of the welfare loss shown by triangle *ABC* require output Q_2 where *MSB* equals *MSC*.

The imposition of a commodity tax or subsidy provides a method of correcting for the externality. Assume for simplicity that the marginal external benefit is constant at $5 per inoculation. To correct for the externality, Congress can provide producers with a subsidy[2]

[2] A $5 subsidy provided to the consumer will shift the demand curve up by the subsidy so that the new demand mirrors *MSB* and passes through point *B*. The solution remains the same. Consumers buy quantity Q_2 at price P_1, paying P_2 net of the subsidy. It generally will be easier to administer commodity taxes and subsidies through producers than consumers.

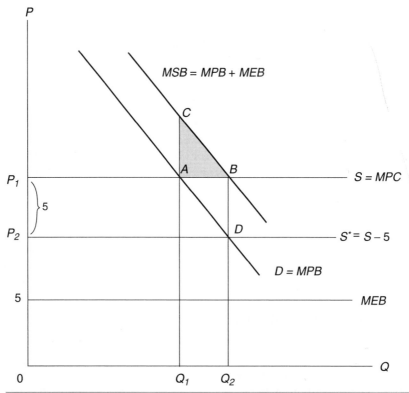

FIGURE 20.3 Using Commodity Subsidies to Correct for Positive Externalities.

of $5. The supply curve facing consumers will shift down by the amount of the subsidy to S^* because producers will need to receive $5 less than before from consumers to produce the quantities shown along the original supply, S. With the new supply, the equilibrium price paid by patients decreases to P_2 and the equilibrium quantity rises to the optimum Q_2. Governments pay producers $5Q_2$, or rectangle P_1BDP_2.

This simple example illustrates several important features of a commodity subsidy. First, the price paid by consumers will fall by the full amount of the subsidy only when the supply is perfectly elastic, as in Figure 20.3, or when the demand is perfectly inelastic. In other cases, as with a positively sloped supply, the price paid by consumers will not fall by $5. Including the subsidy, producers will receive a higher price than before. Both consumers and producers share the benefits of the subsidy even though it is paid to producers.

As the elasticity of demand increases, or elasticity of supply decreases, the equilibrium price falls by smaller amounts and the equilibrium quantity increases by larger amounts. In the long run, the competitive market supply will be highly elastic (perfectly elastic in a constant-cost industry). Thus, the benefits of a subsidy will accrue mainly to consumers in competitive markets.

Second, to achieve efficiency, decision makers need accurate estimates of both the monetary value of the externality and elasticities of demand and supply. The costs of administering taxes and the difficulties of accurate estimation are strong arguments against the use of a corrective subsidy unless the positive externality is substantial.

Finally, we note that policy makers can achieve the results described in Figure 20.3 by taxing those who are not inoculated rather than subsidizing those who are (see exercise 4). By imposing a cost on those who refuse inoculations, the opportunity cost of an inoculation is its price minus the tax. The lower effective price increases quantity. The administrative complexity of monitoring those who are or are not inoculated argues against this approach.

When consumption of a good such as smoking leads to harmful (negative) externalities, the marginal external cost must be added to the marginal private cost to determine the efficient solution. The competitive output will be greater than the optimum. To reduce consumption, price must be raised. A price increase can be achieved either through a corrective tax to shift the supply curve up or a subsidy to nonsmokers that raises the effective price of smoking.

PUBLIC PROVISION

Roads, education, water, and police and fire protection are just a few examples of the many goods and services provided by governments. Most of these goods are not pure public goods. Although national defense often serves as an example of a good that is both nonrival and nonexcludable, the same cannot be said of water, education, and most health care services. Inoculations are rival and excludable even though they may generate substantial positive externalities.

Public provision of health care is a complex process that requires a decision for each of the three basic economic questions (what? how? and for whom?) faced by every society. The "what" question relates to the types of health care to be provided (e.g., limited services such as inoculations or comprehensive health care), as well as their quantity and quality. Whether governments themselves produce the services and how they do it, or whether other arrangements such as contracting with the private sector are selected, is a part of the "how" question. The "who" question deals with the financing and distribution of the services. Will the program be created as a universal entitlement, as an entitlement for some groups, or as one with other eligibility requirements? Furthermore, should the program be "free" at the point of service and funded mainly by tax revenues or should user fees be charged? The funding mechanism could have large impacts on the resources allocated to health and on the possible redistributions as from rich to poor and young to old.

TRANSFER PROGRAMS

Cash transfer programs usually are intended to meet society's equity concerns by redistributing income. Recipients are free to spend their income in any ways they want. Social Security for the elderly and some disabled is the principal example, but income supports also are provided for the poor. Cash transfers to the poor include Temporary Assistance to Needy Families (TANF), which is funded by the federal government and administered by the states.

In-kind transfers (benefits other than cash) also redistribute income, but their main purpose is to increase a recipient's consumption of specific goods or services. Important in-kind transfers include Medicare for the elderly and food stamps, housing, and Medicaid for the poor who pass means tests. Medicare and Medicaid will be described in detail in chapter 22.

REGULATION

Governments influence the allocation of resources by establishing rules and regulations. In the extreme, governments can prohibit certain goods or activities entirely such as the production and consumption of illicit drugs. More commonly, governments regulate the form or terms under which goods are produced or consumed. Regulation can be appealing to legislators because it appears to tackle problems without incurring substantial government spending in the process. For example, regulating managed care to prevent "drive-through" deliveries appears to respond to a public concern at little direct cost to government. However, as described in chapter 12, the legislation imposes significant costs on others.

Regulation in health care markets can take many forms: licensure laws; mandates; and regulation of price, quality, and quantity of services. Several examples of regulation are provided in the following sections. Chapter 21 will focus exclusively on the principal regulatory mechanisms in health care markets.

Government Involvement in Health Care Markets

Hardly any economic activity is free of government intervention. Intervention comes mainly through three activities: provision of goods and services, redistribution, and regulation. Governments have pursued each of these activities in the health economy. Through public hospitals, the Veterans Administration, and other programs, they provide substantial amounts of health care, though this activity is overshadowed by social insurance programs for the elderly and many poor. The provision of health care and of health insurance is also the major means used to redistribute income to lower-income groups from higher-income groups. Less obvious to many is government's role as a regulator. At the federal level, the Securities and Exchange Commission (SEC), the Environmental Protection Agency (EPA), and the Occupational Safety and Health Administration (OSHA) are among the numerous regulatory agencies that affect nearly every business and working individual. In addition, various state and local requirements, such as those governing building and safety codes, may have to be met.

However, when economists and others speak of regulating or deregulating the health care industries, they are not referring to the kinds of social and commercial controls cited earlier. Rather, they are concerned with regulations that are targeted specifically at the health care industries. Government involvement in the health economy takes on many forms, some of which are developed elsewhere in this text. At this point, we only provide several examples to highlight the variety and scope of government intervention in health care markets.

SUPPORT OF HOSPITALS

As described in chapter 18, the modern hospital did not begin to emerge until the confluence of several developments in the late nineteenth century such as major improvements in anesthesia, antisepsis, and in the invention of X rays. Temin (1988) characterizes hospitals prior to this period as being more like municipal almshouses funded by taxes or voluntary contributions. Hospitals "existed for the care of marginal members of society, whether old, poor, or medically or psychologically deviant" (pp. 78–79).

In retrospect, one can argue that public support for hospitals was based on a redistribution motive and by a desire to deal with the negative externalities associated with the insane and those harboring communicable diseases such as tuberculosis. With the improvements in physicians' abilities to diagnose and to treat patients surgically, hospitals grew rapidly in the first decades of the twentieth century. Public hospitals continued to serve the poor but also focused their attention on the growing middle classes. Ultimately, patient payments and insurance became the primary sources of funds for many of these institutions.

THE HILL–BURTON ACT

Federal support for private hospitals was minimal until the passage of the Hill–Burton Act in 1946. The program was designed to expand rural health facilities by providing for matching grants to nonprofit institutions. Temin found that the Hill–Burton program contributed substantially to the rise in per-capita hospital beds between 1947 and 1970.

The Hill–Burton Act, however, also required states "to survey its hospital needs, to develop a statewide plan for the construction of public hospitals and health centers, and, finally, to construct needed hospitals and health centers."[3] This process of planning was carried a step further with the enactment of other health-planning legislation. As governments increasingly emphasized cost issues in the late 1960s, the health planning agencies that were created turned to capital expenditures controls to limit hospital growth and costs. The resulting Certificate-of-Need (CON) requirements represented a major turning point toward an increasingly regulated health care system.

THE VETERANS ADMINISTRATION AND CHAMPUS

In addition to direct subsidies for hospital construction, governments are also major providers of health care. State, county, and municipal hospitals account for approximately 20 percent of total hospital beds in the United States. The largest public provider is the Veterans Administration (VA). In 1996, the VA spent $16.4 billion for providing, among other services, hospital care for 807,000 patients and more than 29 million outpatient visits.[4] The ostensible purpose of the VA is to provide care for service-related injuries through institutions that specialize in providing and undertaking research for such care. However, a veteran may be treated for other conditions unrelated to service injuries if facilities are available and the veteran indicates an inability to afford treatment from other sources. As a result, most patients in VA hospitals are lower-income people, treated for conditions not related to their military injuries.[5]

In addition to direct care provided by the VA, the federal government finances care for retired military personnel and dependents of active-duty, deceased, and retired military personnel through CHAMPUS (Civilian Health and Medical Program for the Uniformed Services). The program has a large number of potential beneficiaries and is similar in its scope of service coverage and administration to Medicare. Because

[3]Hochban et al. (1981, p. 61).
[4]U.S. Department of Health and Human Services *Health United States* (1998).
[5]P. Feldstein (1994).

beneficiaries are encouraged to use on-base facilities with low charges, CHAMPUS finances only a relatively small portion of care for eligible beneficiaries.[6]

FOOD AND DRUG ADMINISTRATION

Various pieces of drug legislation have been promulgated, beginning with the Food and Drug Act of 1906. Legislation adopted in 1962 required considerably more testing and evidence of efficacy and, in general, gave the Food and Drug Administration (FDA) considerably more control over the introduction of new products than previously. The pharmaceutical industry's concerns are that regulatory requirements lengthen the period to FDA approval to about 10 to 12 years and raise the cost of introducing new drug products, estimated to average more than $200 million to the point of marketing.[7]

The economic issues of drug regulation pit the relative gains in drug safety and efficacy against the discouragement to innovation and the delays in availability attributable to the approval process. This and other aspects of the pharmaceutical industry are covered in depth in chapter 26.

MANDATED HEALTH INSURANCE BENEFITS

The insurance industry is regulated mainly at the state level. The state's traditional role here is to ensure financial solvency of insurance companies. However, in both auto and health insurance, the states have expanded their roles considerably. One relatively recent phenomenon in health insurance is exhibited by the proliferation of mandated insurance benefits. Such laws have grown from 48 in 1970 to about 1,000 in 1991, covering "heart transplants in Georgia, liver transplants in Illinois, hairpieces in Minnesota . . . and sperm-bank deposits in Massachusetts."[8] Such laws are often promulgated after lobbying by special interest groups who have traditionally been excluded, or after highly publicized cases involving persons who find they are not covered for heart transplants or certain expensive experimental therapies.

Gabel and Jensen (1989) found that these requirements prevent insurers from offering lower-cost alternatives that exclude the mandated benefits. This effect could be substantial for many lower-income individuals who have been priced out of the market.

TAX POLICY

Federal and state governments provide substantial tax subsidies for the consumption of health care and purchases of insurance. In particular, employer contributions to group health plans are not included in an individual's taxable income (escaping federal, state, and Social Security taxes). Individual payments for health insurance as well as many health care expenses can be itemized if they exceed threshold levels (7.5 percent of adjusted gross income in 1999).

Some have argued that the substantial reductions in the marginal cost of insurance and health care represent a major reason for the growth of insurance and consequent growth of health care spending that occurred in the 1960s and 1970s. Thus, a proposed cost-containment strategy is to reduce such subsidies. Without discussing the merits of

[6]Krizay and Wilson (1974, p. 85).
[7]DiMasi et al. (1991).
[8]"Health Insurance: States Can Help," *The Wall Street Journal,* December 17, 1991, p. A14.

this argument here, we wish only to point out that there seems to be little justification for the extensive tax subsidies. Ironically, the tax advantages are greatest to those in the highest marginal tax rates, meaning that the subsidies do not promote equity.

PUBLIC HEALTH

We have thus far focused largely on the study of personal health and health care decisions. Public health, on the other hand, deals with areas such as communicable diseases, epidemics, environmental health issues, and other activities with significant third-party health effects such as smoking and the use of drugs and alcohol.

Until the latter part of the nineteenth century, public health was a state and local responsibility. However, in 1878, the U.S. government created the Marine Hospital Service, which became the U.S. Public Health Service in 1912.[9] Despite the federal responsibilities, state and local governments spent almost 89 percent of the $39 billion spent on public health in 1997.

OTHER GOVERNMENT PROGRAMS

Numerous other channels for government involvement exist. Some are apparent—such as support for medical education and medical schools, which will influence the supply of providers. Similarly, support for health care research undertaken directly by a government agency such as the National Cancer Institutes, or undertaken by other public and private organizations, can have a substantial impact on the spread of technology and the direction of the health care system. For example, critics of the U.S. system claim that it has placed excessive emphasis on high-tech medicine at the expense of preventive medicine and that this bias stems in part from the kinds of research projects that are supported. We are hearing concerns that while support was insufficient for AIDS-related research in the early years after the discovery of the disease, support is now excessive to the detriment of those afflicted with other conditions.

Other forms of intervention are less obvious. Changes in immigration policy can affect the supply of health care personnel. Also easily overlooked is the role of the federal government as the nation's largest employer in providing fringe benefits to its employees. The Federal Employees Health Benefits Program (FEHBP) offers about 400 different insurance plans to employees and their dependents. Because of its size and its ability to experiment with alternatives, the FEHBP has the potential to influence and serve as a model for the private sector.[10]

To summarize, governments at all levels have intervened heavily in the health care sector. The intervention has taken the forms of direct provision of care, financing of health insurance (especially of Medicare and Medicaid), subsidizing of medical education and the construction of health facilities, subsidizing of purchases of health insurance through the tax structure, and the regulation of health care industries. This intervention has major effects on the total resources devoted to health care as well as on the distribution of resources within the health care industries.

Table 20.1 indicates the scope of public spending in 1997, overall as well as across health care industries. Government spending accounts for about 46 percent of total

[9]See O. Anderson (1990) for a history of public health in the United States.
[10]Moffit (1992) considers choice and competition the elements that make FEHBP a government program that works.

TABLE 20.1 National Health Expenditures, by Source of Funds and Type of Expenditure: 1997

Type of Expenditure	Total	Private					Government		
		All Private Funds	Consumer				Total	Federal	State and Local
			Total	Out of Pocket	Private Insurance	Other			
				Amount in Billions					
National Health Expenditures	1,092.4	585.3	535.6	187.6	348.0	49.7	507.1	367.0	140.0
Health services and supplies	1,057.5	571.9	535.6	187.6	348.0	36.4	485.5	351.8	133.8
Personal health care	969.0	536.7	501.0	187.6	313.5	35.6	432.4	337.3	95.1
Hospital care	371.1	142.6	125.4	12.4	113.0	17.2	228.4	185.6	42.8
Physician services	217.6	147.5	143.2	34.1	109.1	4.3	70.1	58.4	11.7
Dental services	50.6	48.4	48.1	23.9	24.3	0.2	2.3	1.3	1.0
Other professional services	61.9	48.3	43.5	24.6	18.9	4.8	13.6	10.8	2.8
Home health care	32.3	14.7	10.7	7.0	3.7	3.9	17.7	15.4	2.3
Drugs and other medical nondurables	108.9	92.9	92.9	53.0	39.9	—	16.0	9.2	6.8
Vision products and other medical durables	13.9	7.3	7.3	6.8	0.5	—	6.6	6.4	0.1
Nursing home care	82.8	31.3	29.8	25.7	4.0	1.6	51.4	34.5	16.9
Other personal health care	29.9	3.6	—	—	—	3.6	26.3	15.6	10.7
Program administration and net cost of private health insurance	50.0	35.3	34.6	—	34.6	0.7	14.7	10.4	4.3
Government public health activities	38.5	—	—	—	—	—	38.5	4.1	34.4
Research and construction	34.9	13.4	—	—	—	13.4	21.5	15.3	6.3
Research	18.0	1.5	—	—	—	1.5	16.5	13.8	2.6
Construction	16.9	11.9	—	—	—	11.9	5.0	1.4	3.6

Source: Braden, et al. (1998, Table 6).

health care spending and is concentrated on expenditures on hospital, physician, and nursing home care. However, these amounts understate the impact of public programs. By influencing levels of competition, purchases of health insurance, and the innovation and spread of technology, government activities also have substantial effects on private spending.

Government Failure

Market failure and concerns about the distribution of income can be seen as necessary conditions for government intervention. We have to ask, though, whether government can improve efficiency and better meet society's equity objectives. Many might argue that this question already has been answered. Governments around the world are heavily involved in their health economies to the point where 24 of the 29 countries that belong to the Organization for Economic Cooperation and Development (OECD) have universal health insurance coverage. The United States, with 33 percent of the population receiving government-assured coverage, has by far the lowest rate (followed by Turkey with 66 percent).[11] But even in the United States, the federal, state, and local governments still account for 46 percent of national health care spending.

Thus, the real issues are the extent and forms of government involvement. The difficulties of agreeing on objectives, choosing from many different policy instruments, and selecting the correct values of these instruments create many opportunities for "government failure." Jan Tinbergen, who shared the first Nobel Prize in Economics in 1969 with Ragnar Frisch, dealt with the process of choosing an optimum policy. In a major contribution, *On the Theory of Economic Policy,* Tinbergen (1952) formulates relationships between a government's policy instruments and its targets. His analysis highlights the interdependence of the different sectors of an economy and points to the inherent deficiency of uncoordinated policy (i.e., agricultural, trade, health, and so on) decisions.

In more contemporary work, the literature on *public choice* illustrates many of the problems in developing and implementing policy. Public choice attempts to model how decisions are made through the political process. Many models of public choice have been created. We limit our discussion to two features that are relevant to efficiency: special interest groups and bureaucratic behavior.

SPECIAL-INTEREST GROUPS

Almost all major industries and organizations establish or support special-interest groups to promote their interests. Through political contributions and their ability to harness the voting power of constituents, these groups try to pressure legislators into passing favorable laws or to vote against unfavorable proposals. Lawmakers often adopt legislation that benefits a relatively small number while harming a much larger number.

Why does this happen in a democracy with majority voting? When the benefits to a small number are substantial, such as subsidies to cheese producers, lobbies representing the cheese industry will devote a disproportionate amount of resources to influence those who shape agricultural policy. Because the harm from higher cheese prices to any person or business is relatively small or dispersed, those who are hurt do not organize

[11]Anderson and Poullier (1999).

against the policy or they become "free riders" to any organized opposition that might arise. The result is an inefficiently large public sector.[12]

Furthermore, when the beneficiaries of proposed laws are geographically concentrated, lawmakers have an incentive to engage in logrolling—the trading of votes. The senators from Wisconsin will support restrictions on steel imports in exchange for support for cheese subsidies from Pennsylvania's senators. Programs such as this are not likely to improve either allocative efficiency or the distribution of income.

BUREAUCRACY AND EFFICIENCY

Lawmakers pass legislation, but government bureaucrats are responsible for implementing programs. Do bureaucrats try to minimize the costs of their activities? Relatively little is known about the technical efficiency of the bureaucracy, but it is clear that government operations do not face the discipline of the marketplace. No income statements, balance sheets, and stock market prices are available to evaluate the success of a government program and motivate the bureaucracy, even though it is not completely immune from oversight (from legislatures, public watchdogs, and even government agencies such as the General Accounting Office). Nevertheless, the hypothesis that governments operate at lower levels of technical efficiency than the private sector is a plausible one.

Aside from the inefficiency associated with failure to minimize costs, government programs also are subject to allocative inefficiencies. That is, there may be too little or too much of a program relative to the optimum. This problem is illustrated in Figure 20.4, which shows the true marginal social benefits (MSB) and marginal social costs (MSC) of a government program to provide home health visits. The social optimum is at Q_1 visits where $MSB = MSC$. However, this allocation may not be attained for several reasons. Supporters of the program (lobbyists, legislators who support it, top bureaucrats who will run it) will be motivated by self-interests to overstate the benefits (and understate the costs). If benefits are inflated to MSB', the perceived optimum is an inefficiently large program at Q_2.

A model of bureaucratic behavior developed by Niskanen (1971) is consistent with this result, but for a different reason. There is a welfare gain, or consumer surplus shown by triangle ABC, at the efficient quantity Q_1. This means that total social benefits are greater than total social costs at Q_1. Niskanen reasoned that power and prestige motivate bureaucrats to push for large programs potentially to the point where total social benefits equal total social costs. In this limiting case, the program is expanded to Q_3 where the welfare gain at the efficient level (triangle ABC) is exactly offset by the welfare loss (triangle AEF) from the inefficient expansion.

These arguments warn us against the danger of concluding that social welfare is necessarily improved by government intervention when there is market failure. Equally serious government failure can result from inappropriate policies and high levels of technical and allocative inefficiencies.

[12]Buchanan and Tullock (1962) and Olson (1965) were pioneers in showing that the rational pursuit of self-interest traditionally associated with individuals also applies to political institutions and the public sector.

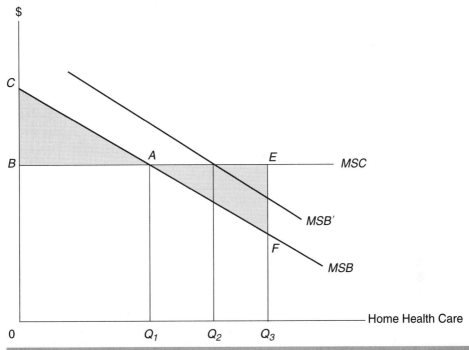

FIGURE 20.4 Overexpansion of a Government Program.

Competitive Strategies

Regardless of any changes in the direction of U.S. health care policy, governments will remain heavily involved in the financing and delivery of health care. Nevertheless, as a result of unprecedented concerns with access and costs, policy makers remain in the middle of "one of the biggest ideological battles of the 1990s: a fight over the future of the ailing American health-care system."[13] The battle is over the superiority of: (1) increased government involvement through both expanded regulation and additional government programs to provide or finance health care, or (2) an increased emphasis on market mechanisms and market forces with corresponding decreases in the use of regulatory instruments.

This controversy is not new to the academic and policy-making communities, where it is referred to as the debate over competition versus regulation. Yet, in the afterword to a special issue of the *Journal of Health Politics, Policy and Law* devoted to the controversy, editor Lawrence Brown (1988) wrote:

> it is striking that . . . fifteen years after the first flush of enthusiasm in Washington
> for a competitive approach, there still seems to be little agreement on what we
> *mean* by "competition" or a "market approach" to containing health costs (p. 361).

[13]"Health Care Choices: A Bigger Federal Role or a Market Approach," *The Wall Street Journal,* January 15, 1992, p. 1.

Those who deny the applicability of the competitive framework are most likely to favor regulatory strategies. Proponents of further regulation tend to argue that information imperfections, flawed agency relationships, and other distortions cannot be readily corrected by attempts to promote partial forms of competition. Proponents of regulation also have been strongly influenced by the rapid growth in overall health spending and in spending on Medicare, Medicaid, and other public programs. The spending record in the United States, as compared to other more highly regulated systems, has reinforced beliefs among many that health care markets do not work like most other markets. Especially widely accepted are beliefs that increases in supplies of hospital beds and physicians increase utilization of marginally necessary or even unnecessary services. There are widespread views that physicians can and do create demand and that empty beds in hospitals will be filled through physicians' discretionary decisions to admit patients.

The logical strategy to those who share these views is to increase controls limiting hospital capacity and physician supplies, and to increase monitoring of services that are being provided. We have outlined the general forms of these controls. At this point, we digress from further study of regulation to return to the question raised by Brown: What is competition in health care? Pauly (1988a) defines competition through the conditions of "free entry and potential entrants willing[ness] to offer goods and services to consumers, with no one firm large enough to have an important influence on levels of and quality" (p. 35).

From this definition, we would expect the following in a competitive health care industry: (1) elastic demands facing providers, (2) a tendency toward marginal cost pricing, (3) efficiency in production—allocative as well as technical efficiency, and (4) the availability of alternatives in terms of price, quality, and form of delivery.

Others see competition in a more limited way, largely through the form of government policy rather than the structure or performance of health care markets. A competitive health care policy is one that relies primarily on financial incentives rather than controls to achieve goals. The theoretical underpinning of this approach is the view that market participants respond to changes in prices in a predictable and substantial way. Supporters of competitive approaches also argue that even imperfections in their strategies are preferable to the distortions caused by imperfect regulation.

Under either view of competition, most forms of government intervention such as CON laws, utilization review, and mandated benefits are anticompetitive—they compel. To be more specific in the distinction between competition and regulation, consider the uninsured. From the competitive point of view, many of the uninsured are seen largely as having insufficient income to purchase insurance. Their dilemma is aggravated by mandated benefits and other requirements that drive up insurance prices. A competitive solution is to subsidize purchases of insurance for lower-income uninsureds through tax credits, and to deregulate insurers so that lower-priced options become available. Programs, on the other hand, that would provide insurance for the uninsured are seen as lacking in incentives for efficient consumer search. Bearing in mind these distinctions, we turn to several broad competitive strategies for reforming the U.S. health care system.

INCREASED COST SHARING

Martin Feldstein was the earliest and the best-known advocate of using increased cost sharing to overcome the incentives to overinsure. Furthermore, he argued that the prevalence of "first-dollar insurance" up to certain limits (often inadequate for catastrophic events) is the result of the tax preferences described previously for purchases

of insurance, especially of employer-provided group insurance. He and others have advocated a variety of plans that would involve reducing the tax subsidies and increasing patients' out-of-pocket costs to approximately 10 percent of income.[14] This would be achieved through high coinsurance rates on initial health care expenditures, but with declining coinsurance until the maximum out-of-pocket liability is reached.

The effects of coinsurance on moral hazard and demand elasticities have been described in our chapters on demand and insurance. Findings from the Rand Health Insurance Experiment support the hypotheses that consumers respond in a significant and substantial way to changes in their share of costs.

However, we have not previously considered Feldstein's hypothesis that taxes and other distortions in the insurance market have skewed purchases toward comprehensive first-dollar coverage. On this issue, Hershey and colleagues (1984) administered a questionnaire to a random sample of 480 nonunion employees of a university to see how they would choose among actuarially fair policies. Their findings indicated a preference for coverage with higher limits. But respondents were also as likely to select policies with cost-sharing features (which reduce price) as they were to select policies without those features.

Thus, to summarize, evidence shows that consumers will behave differently in circumstances where there are no tax subsidies and where there are wider choices than those usually available under group health insurance. Some consumers would opt for plans with greater cost sharing when the premiums for these plans are reduced sufficiently.

DEVELOPMENT OF ALTERNATIVE DELIVERY SYSTEMS

The dominant competitive strategy, which evolved in the 1970s, has been the promotion of delivery systems that can provide an alternative to traditional fee for service with its comprehensive first-dollar insurance coverage. The cornerstone of this strategy has been the promotion of health maintenance organizations (HMOs), preferred provider organizations (PPOs), and other forms of managed care.

As described in chapter 12, HMOs and other capitated health plans provide a comprehensive set of services for a fixed monthly premium. Typically, there is minimal (or no) cost sharing for covered ambulatory services. In exchange for expanded coverage, a patient's choice is restricted to specific providers and hospitals. Furthermore, the patient's primary care physician serves as the gatekeeper in that this physician's approval is required for referral to most specialists and nonemergency hospital admissions.

Expansion of the population covered by HMOs has been a major policy goal. The primary motive behind the HMO strategy is the view among many policy makers that the traditional form of health care delivery was the primary culprit in rising costs and unnecessary care.

HMOs tend to reduce costs primarily by reducing the rate of hospital utilization. However, the rates of increases in HMO costs have paralleled the rates of increases elsewhere—a phenomenon that limits the overall potential for cost containment. Nevertheless, federal policy continues to emphasize the HMO strategy by proposing expanded incentives for those who select prepaid, managed care systems, especially Medicare and Medicaid beneficiaries. This dichotomy between health care policy and results suggests that it is worth examining Medicare's HMO experience.

[14]For example, see M. Feldstein (1977).

MEDICARE MANAGED CARE

Though the possibility of some HMO involvement was included early in the Medicare program, the Tax Equity and Fiscal Responsibility Act (TEFRA), implemented in 1985, marked an important turning point. Under TEFRA, an HMO can contract with the Health Care Financing Administration (HCFA) to enroll Medicare beneficiaries on a prepaid capitation rate determined by 95 percent of its area's AAPCC (the average adjusted per-capita cost). This payment is based on the amount HCFA expected to pay on behalf of a beneficiary if he or she had remained in the fee-for-service sector.

This type of contract is called a TEFRA risk contract because it places the HMO at risk for costs that exceed its receipts. Though some limited risk contracts were available prior to 1985 and 52 HMOs participated in the demonstration period, most HMOs entered into cost contracts. These provided capitated payments based on actual costs up to 100 percent of AAPCC.

Immediately after TEFRA, there was a sharp increase in HMO enrollments and HMO beneficiaries. Medicare enrollments nearly doubled between June 1985 and July 1987, and the number of Medicare HMOs increased from 102 to 179.[15] Most were TEFRA risk contracts.

Using data from the demonstration period, Adamache and Rossiter (1986) found that market entry was influenced mainly by the AAPCC rate. However, despite a 14 percent increase in the AAPCC rate, 21 HMOs did not renew their risk contracts in 1988; also, HMO enrollments dropped slightly.[16]

Total enrollment in Medicare risk and cost plans increased from 5.4 percent in 1990 to 12.7 percent by the end of 1996, with enrollments doubling in just the three years between 1993 and 1996.[17] The rapid increase correlates with overall HMO enrollments, which have increased rapidly. Most of the Medicare increase is found in risk-based plans so that they now represent nearly 90 percent of Medicare's managed care beneficiaries (up from 60 percent in 1990). As a result, the determination of the appropriate capitated payments to those plans has become an increasingly important policy problem. Excessive payments provide a windfall to the plans while imposing unnecessary costs on the Medicare program. Insufficient rates can create serious problems for beneficiaries in that they create risks that HMOs will not renew their contracts with Medicare.[18]

ANTITRUST

The goal of U.S. antitrust laws is to promote competition. The Sherman Act passed in 1890 and several successive acts constitute the federal laws. These laws attempt to define the practices that constitute anticompetitive behavior and create the agencies, Department of Justice (DOJ) and Federal Trade Commission (FTC), to enforce the laws.

Until recent decades, antitrust was used sparingly in the health care sector, in part because of perceptions that the "learned professions" were immune from the federal laws. Several landmark decisions handed down by the U.S Supreme Court in the 1970s

[15]Pitt (1988).

[16]Ibid.

[17]The data on Medicare managed care are found in *Physician Payment Review Commission* (1997).

[18]A striking example emerged in 1999 when a reduction of services by 58 HMOs and the nonrenewal of contracts by 48 others forced 327,000 beneficiaries to scramble to other HMOs or switch to the traditional Medicare program.

forcefully rejected this view and led to a flurry of antitrust activity, especially cases dealing with the granting or termination of hospital staff privileges. Arrangements involving physician control over Blue Cross and Blue Shield plans, the use of relative value scales, AMA restrictions on advertising, and AMA restrictions that limited competition from other providers such as chiropractors were challenged successfully. There is general agreement that antitrust enforcement has benefited the consumer by raising the level of competition in many health care markets.

Nevertheless, the growth of managed care and this nation's preoccupation with costs and efficiency have led to many changes in the health care sector. These changes are reflected in the increasing number of hospital mergers and cooperative activities including information sharing among providers, hospital joint ventures involving expensive capital equipment, and hospital purchasing agreements. Such activities could certainly lead to more monopoly power to the detriment of the public. More detailed discussion of antitrust appears in the next chapter.

MEDICAL SAVINGS ACCOUNTS

Individual medical savings accounts (MSAs) represent a unique strategy to encourage more efficient health care utilization. Under the MSA scheme, employers or public payers make contributions to an individual's MSA, enabling the person to buy relatively low-cost insurance with high deductibles or copayments. Balances in an MSA can then be used to pay out-of-pocket costs, or the unused portion can be distributed to the individual.[19]

Those who support MSAs argue that comprehensive, tax-subsidized insurance creates substantial moral hazard and ineffective incentives for efficient consumption of care. On the other hand, the lure of a potential distribution from an MSA provides the individual with an incentive to become a prudent user of care. In principle, patients will be less likely to consume unnecessary or marginally beneficial care, and stronger market forces will help restrain prices.

After years of debate, the 1996 Kassebaum–Kennedy legislation included a provision for a demonstration with up to 750,000 MSAs to be made available to the self-employed and small firms with 50 or fewer employees. Individuals would choose plans with high deductibles and other cost-sharing features. They may put a certain percentage of the deductible into a tax-free savings account. Funds from this account are used to pay for out-of-pocket expenses or deferred for future health care needs including long-term care. Withdrawals for nonmedical purposes are taxed and penalized for those under age 65.[20]

The MSA scheme is intuitively appealing, and some analysts project considerable savings from more efficient levels of utilization (Ozanne 1996, Heffley and Miceli 1998). However any enthusiasm for MSAs must be tempered by the undesired consequences

[19]Originally developed by Stano (1981), many variations of the basic MSA concept have been proposed. Another alternative, introduced by Pauly and Goodman (1995), would provide tax credits to those who voluntarily choose a combination of catastrophic coverage and an MSA.

[20]The Medicare + Choice options established in 1997 similarly set up a pilot program allowing up to 390,000 Medicare enrollees to select a high-deductible MSA. Under the MSA option, a beneficiary's Medicare capitated payment rate is used to purchase a catastrophic insurance policy meeting certain standards including an annual deductible of no more than $6,000 for 1999. The difference between the capitated payment rate and the insurance premium is deposited in an MSA.

that may result from a system that depends on voluntary enrollments. Healthier individuals are more likely to establish MSAs. They may be able to purchase catastrophic coverage at relatively low rates and will be more likely to have funds left over in their MSA accounts. There is thus a justifiable concern that this selection phenomenon will lead to escalating premiums for the sicker populations who remain in conventional plans.

It is still too early to evaluate the limited U.S. experience. Few individuals have established MSAs—about 55,000 as of mid-1999—and a single company (the Golden Rule Group) dominates the MSA market. The complexity of the program has been cited as the primary obstacle to greater consumer and insurer participation. However, Zabinski and colleagues (1999) simulated the effects of MSAs through a model that incorporates adverse selection. Their estimates indicate the potential for spiraling comprehensive insurance premiums, as well as significant income redistributions away from the poor and families with infants. Overall, the net welfare gains of widespread MSA adoption were modest.

Fortunately, health care reforms introduced in Singapore in 1984 provide an example where theory, for the case of a mandated MSA system, has been put to a stronger test. Singapore requires all workers and the self-employed to contribute a portion of earnings to Medisave accounts.[21] The Medisave account is used to pay for hospital care and a limited amount of outpatient care (the remainder is paid out of pocket). Once Medisave balances reach a certain level, funds can be transferred for other approved uses. At death, balances become part of the deceased's estate.

Evidence indicates that hospitals have become more productive and efficient and that patients are satisfied with the quality of care. The record on cost containment is unclear. Expenditures continued to rise rapidly, although not as much as in other Asian countries.

REPRESENTATION OF THE COMPETITIVE APPROACH

The shortcomings of the existing system of health care delivery, together with the goals of the competitive approach, can be illustrated with the help of Figure 20.5. At the risk of neglecting the various market imperfections and resulting inefficiencies that we have studied, we rely on the simplicity of the demand–supply paradigm. Let S_1 and D_1 represent the existing demand and supply curves for health care. The equilibrium quantity is Q_1, and total spending is represented by the rectangle $0P_1EQ_1$.

Competitive strategies have two broad goals. The first is to reduce demand by increasing the number of patients in managed care settings who are sensitive to price and the diminishing marginal benefit associated with health care. By encouraging the use of managed care and reducing the tax subsidy for employer-provided health insurance, it is expected that demand for health services, especially the relatively less beneficial services, will diminish to D_2. The equilibrium quantity will decrease, as will prices and expenditures, though the price effect will be small where the elasticity of supply is large.

However, there is another important role for competitive strategies, which operates through effects on the supply side. Here a relaxation of regulatory, entry, and capacity controls is seen as reducing producer costs and increasing the supply of providers. At

[21]The material on Singapore is taken from Hsiao (1995) and Massaro and Wong (1995).

FIGURE 20.5 The Intended Effects of Competitive Strategies on Demand and Supply.

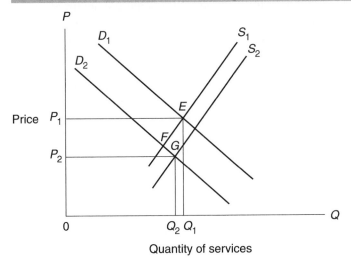

the same time, competitive pressure introduced through consumer search will push providers to become more efficient producers of care so that any given quantity of care can be provided at lower cost. These effects are represented by a rightward movement in supply to S_2.

The combined effects, if they are substantial, would lead to large decreases (from $0P_1EQ_1$ to $0P_2GQ_2$) in health care spending, as illustrated in Figure 20.5, or to reduced growth rates in spending. Of course, the predicted effects must materialize. Otherwise, the strategies would be ineffective and might even backfire. For instance, if supply does increase but prices remain rigid and large amounts of supplier-induced demand (SID) follow, then both demand and supply may increase, thereby aggravating the utilization and spending problems. For this reason, the issues of SID and the existence of independent demands that are responsive to financial incentives are seen by economists as being at the heart of the controversy.

Conclusions

This chapter emphasizes market failure as the economic rationale for government intervention. Monopoly power provides the classic example, but public goods and externalities are two additional categories that are relevant to health care. Government policies, in principle, can correct misallocations resulting from market failure. To do so, governments can use specific commodity taxes and subsidies, public provision of goods and services, transfer programs, and regulation.

Through a wide variety of programs, governments at all levels have become major players in the health economy, accounting for 46 percent of national health expenditures. However, government activities also are associated with government failure. Information deficiencies, the efforts of special interest groups, and bureaucratic behavior can lead to socially undesirable programs or inefficient levels of these programs.

Despite concerns about the effectiveness of government programs, there is no doubt that governments will continue to dominate the health economy through their various spending programs and heavy regulation.

At the same time, federal policy is promoting competitive strategies to deal especially with the cost and access concerns. The emphasis in this policy has been on an expansion of health care delivery by HMOs and other forms of managed care. With the strong political pressure to downsize the role of government, there is likely also to be continuing interest in market-driven changes to Medicare and Medicaid such as MSAs and the shifting of recipients into managed care. It remains to be seen whether such changes can break the "stalemate between halfway competition and ineffective regulation"[22] to bring meaningful reforms to the health economy.

Summary

1. Government spending accounts for about 46 percent of total health care expenditures.
2. The traditional rationale for government intervention is market failure. Sources of market failure include monopoly power, externalities, and public goods.
3. There is a public goods aspect to information and redistribution that can be used to justify a role for government in health care.
4. Commodity taxes and subsidies, public provision, transfer programs, and regulation are the principal policy instruments used by governments.
5. Regulation refers to the use of nonmarket means to affect the quality, price, or quantity of a good or service. The principal categories of regulation include fee controls and rate regulation, quantity and capacity controls, and quality controls.
6. Governments have been involved in a wide variety of activities, including the direct provision of health care, subsidizing the production of health care, the provision of social insurance, public health, and regulation of health care products and providers.
7. Government failure is associated with the many obstacles in developing and implementing policy.
8. The past two decades have witnessed a major debate over whether to rely increasingly on regulatory strategies to achieve health policy objectives or to rely increasingly on competitive strategies.
9. Competitive strategies include increased cost sharing, the promotion of alternative delivery systems, more aggressive enforcement of antitrust laws, and the establishment of medical savings accounts.

Discussion Questions

1. What is meant by market failure? What is the potential role of government in each instance of market failure found in the health care sector?
2. In what sense can information and redistribution be thought of as public goods? Explain whether private markets will oversupply or undersupply these goods.
3. What are some examples of government providing health care? Of subsidizing the production or consumption of health care? Of providing insurance for health care? Of regulating health care markets?

[22]Altman and Rodwin (1988, p. 323).

4. Why is government needed to provide a public good? Under what circumstances might the voluntary contribution model described in Figure 20.2 work reasonably well?

5. The standard monopoly-competition comparison describes the welfare loss. Develop arguments to support the view that in the real world:
 a) the welfare loss is exaggerated.
 b) the welfare loss is understated.

6. What are the major competitive strategies proposed by economists? How, for example, would elimination of the tax subsidy for employer-provided health insurance reduce spending on health care?

7. What are medical savings accounts (MSAs)? Why might MSAs decrease health care spending? What are some problems with the MSA concept?

8. The pharmaceutical industry has been subject to considerable regulation in bringing drugs to the marketplace. Discuss the benefits and costs to society from such a policy.

Exercises

1. What is meant by the welfare loss of monopoly? Who bears this loss? Determine the regulated price in Figure 20.1 that will eliminate the welfare loss. Why will it be difficult in practice to adopt this solution?

2. Suppose that the public good in Figure 20.2 is associated with increasing costs of production (i.e., where the AC is positively sloped). Will the two individuals be able to fund the optimal amount if each pays according to marginal benefits? Repeat if there are decreasing costs of production.

3. Assume a positively sloped, short-run supply curve in Figure 20.3 and a constant $5 per unit marginal external benefit. Show what happens with a $5 subsidy given to producers. Who gains the benefits of this policy?

4. Using Figure 20.3, explain how a $5 tax on those who are not inoculated will result in the efficient output. Why is this approach unlikely to work in practice?

5. Take a commodity, such as cigarettes, that is associated with negative externalities. Assume that the marginal private cost of production and the marginal external cost per unit are both constant. Graph the actual and efficient quantities. Show how a tax on producers (or consumers) can result in the efficient output. Explain whether it is possible to attain efficiency with a subsidy.

6. Instead of using MSB and MSC in Figure 20.4 to deal with problems of government failure, show the optimal and Niskanen results using a graph with total social benefits and total social costs.

7. Using a demand–supply framework, explain how increased cost sharing could lead to lower utilization and spending on health care.

21

Government Regulation— Principal Regulatory Mechanisms

- Do the Laws of Supply and Demand Apply?
- Monopoly and Regulation
- Objectives of Regulation
- Regulation of the Hospital Sector
- Prospective Payment
- The Theory of Yardstick Competition and DRGs
- Prospective Payment—Recent Evidence
- Who Does the Regulator Represent?
- Antitrust
- Conclusions

Do the Laws of Supply and Demand Apply?

We have devoted a good part of this text to the idea that conventional economic tools can play a powerful role in explaining how health care markets work. Certainly, great care is needed to account for the special features of the health economy and, where appropriate, to modify the analysis. Overall, we have found considerable empirical evidence attesting to the rationality of decision makers. Supporters of competitive strategies have faith in the power of market forces to allocate resources to their best uses among health care and other goods and within the health care markets.

It would be unwise, however, to ignore concerns about the strength of market forces. Consider this article taken from the *Wall Street Journal,* one of the nation's most

respected publications, known for its strong resistance to government intervention in the marketplace.[1]

> In a conventional market, a high-cost, low-quality producer would be doomed, or, at least, worried. But the laws of economics have been repealed in the health business. Consumers don't comparison shop and often lack the information to do so. Many hospitals compete to buy the latest technology rather than provide the lowest-cost quality care. And providers resist outsiders' attempts to gauge quality. The result: a seemingly unstoppable increase in the cost of health care.

To support this argument, the article compared cost and outcome data for coronary bypass surgery at two Pennsylvania hospitals located 38 miles apart. One hospital charged about 50 percent more than the other in 1989, but its death rate considerably exceeded the expected death rate as determined by the age and health of the patients. The death rate at the lower-priced hospital was below the expected rate.

A lack of access to such information about price and quality, lack of incentives to patients, and provider resistance to releasing mortality data were singled out as culprits. To help correct these deficiencies, a Pennsylvania agency planned to release such data on individual physician performance. The agency was quoted by the *Wall Street Journal* as saying "making such information public and encouraging employers and patients to use it is essential if the health care market is to work without major government intervention."

We have established that most health care providers (hospitals, clinics, physicians) face portions of downward demand curves; that is, they have some monopoly power. When this happens, the desirable outcomes of competitive markets become much more difficult to achieve. Using competitive markets at least implicitly as a comparison group, one can classify policies into three major categories:

1. Policies that recognize the monopoly power and try to control it. These policies include some traditional features such as utilization review, capital controls, or rate controls.
2. Policies that try to make monopolistic firms act like competitors. These policies include prospective plans for physicians such as Medicare assignment or the institution of relative value scales.
3. Policies that attempt to prevent the accumulation of monopoly power. Most antitrust policies fall into this category.

Monopoly and Regulation

As we saw in chapter 20, the fundamental story regarding regulation relates to monopoly power. In Figure 20.1, the provider faced a downward-sloping demand curve and a constant marginal cost curve. In equilibrium, price exceeded marginal cost by $(P_M - P_C)$. As a result, at least some consumers who would have willingly paid more than it cost to produce the health care service were unable to get it. The shaded triangle in Figure 20.1 represented the loss to society from monopoly.

[1]"Laws of Economics Often Don't Apply in Health Care Field," *The Wall Street Journal*, January 22, 1992, p. A1.

The consequences of real-world monopoly and production are more complex than this simple graphical account. For example, we have ignored the possibility of quality degradation under monopoly and the possibility that technological innovation may be retarded. Nevertheless, Figure 20.1 does serve to illustrate that competitive markets often will be more efficient than markets in which firms have monopoly power.

Objectives of Regulation

The early focus on regulation in the United States was found in the transportation and utilities sectors. In those sectors, concern with excessive monopoly power and natural monopoly arising from economies of scale and high capital expenditures led to the establishment of the Interstate Commerce Commission in 1888, which regulated railroads and shipping. Subsequently, other federal and state regulatory commissions were formed to regulate a variety of commodities including electricity, gas, telephone service, oil pipelines, airlines, and broadcasting.[2] The overriding objective in regulation was, and continues to be, on rate setting. Its primary goal is to limit the high price–cost margins that would otherwise be expected.

Despite concerns with possible abuse of monopoly power in certain health care markets, those favoring increased regulation do not rely on the traditional monopoly power argument. They focus on the absence of discipline in markets brought on by a lack of consumer information and the prevalence of comprehensive fee-for-service insurance.

Lack of consumer information, as discussed elsewhere, has been used to justify licensure and other quality controls as means to ensure minimal standards of care. Similarly, the role of insurance as a source of market failure was discussed earlier, emphasizing the lack of incentives to both patient and provider to shop around or otherwise conserve resources. Perhaps more importantly, we emphasized the role of traditional forms of insurance in contributing to moral hazard. Unlike other sources of market failure, market failure associated with insurance has led to regulation of fees and also to regulation of hospital revenues and costs.

HEALTH REGULATORY POLICY: AN INTRODUCTION

Regulation refers to the use of nonmarket means to address the quantity, price, or quality of the good brought to market. Because regulations typically address the quantity of services used, the quality of the services, or the amount that payers (either individuals or insurers) are charged, consider total expenditures in a given health care market.

By definition, expenditures, E, equal the price of health care, P, multiplied by the quantity of services, Q or $E = PQ$. Price of care, P, also depends on quality of care, q. Quality of care in this framework can be thought of as any aspect of a service for which someone is willing to pay extra. An example may be a private, rather than a shared, room in a hospital. Under most circumstances, the private room does not make the patient recover more quickly. However, the patient may be more comfortable with the privacy, and hence be willing to pay more for it.

The key feature of this framework is the idea that within the health economy, regulation uses nonmarket means to affect, P, Q, or q, or, of course, combinations. For ex-

[2] Some of these industries have since been deregulated.

ample, licensure requirements may raise q, which is likely to raise P. If they also restrict the supply of providers, they are further likely to raise P. Other regulations such as the Medicare Prospective Payment System may tend to decrease the amount of services, Q, used, lowering expenditures. We will address these aspects elsewhere in this chapter. The point here is that most regulations are directed toward changing price, quantity, or quality.

However, the objective of regulation is not merely to reduce spending; otherwise, rationing or even prohibiting certain services may meet this objective successfully. Rather, its goals are to promote minimal quality levels while eliminating the inefficient components of spending. The inefficiences include technical inefficiency, allocative inefficiency, and the inefficiencies associated with economies of scale and scope.

REGULATORY INSTRUMENTS IN HEALTH CARE

A variety of price, quantity, and quality controls have been introduced. Here we provide a brief overview of these controls, leaving more detailed analyses of hospital regulation for the next section.

Fee Controls and Rate Regulation

The hospital sector has been the main object of rate regulation. In his review of this subject, Sloan (1983, p. 195) defines *rate regulation* as establishing "the terms under which public and/or private insurers pay hospitals." In the 1960s and 1970s, many states adopted various mandatory or advisory forms of regulation. State approval of rate changes was generally based on hospital costs per day or per admission, or on a hospital's overall costs.

Reimbursement for hospital care was usually on a retrospective basis, determined by allowable costs that were incurred. A number of states, however, adopted prospective forms of reimbursements beginning in the 1970s. Some have been mandated at the state level while other programs are voluntary.[3] The goal of these arrangements is to remove the disincentives hospitals have to be efficient producers under cost-based retrospective reimbursement and to limit the amount of care they provide patients who are hospitalized.

Prospective reimbursement, especially once it was adopted by Medicare in 1983, marked an important turning point in regulatory efforts to contain the growth of hospital costs. Medicare's Prospective Payment System (PPS) limits hospital revenues per Medicare patient. Under PPS, hospitals are reimbursed a fixed amount per admission, determined by the patient's diagnostic condition, regardless of the hospital's actual costs. The strategy behind PPS is simple. By limiting revenues, it provides hospitals with strong disincentives to extend lengths of stay and provide unnecessary or marginal care. A detailed discussion of PPS and its effects is found later in this chapter.

Quantity and Capacity Controls

The controls on quantity tend to be indirect rather than direct, with the most prominent example being Certificate-of-Need (CON) laws. These laws required hospitals to obtain approval from planning agencies for capital expenditures in excess of various

[3]Gaumer et al. (1989) describe many of these arrangements.

threshold levels. The rationale was embedded in views that unnecessary duplication of facilities as well as the mere availability of facilities lead to higher costs (i.e., fixed costs spread out over fewer users) and to higher rates of utilization (due to access and/or physician discretion).

Utilization review (UR), although primarily directed at quality, also has been supported on the basis of its expected negative effects on quantity. To the extent that third parties choose not to reimburse for services determined to be inappropriate, UR could have a deterrent effect on the provision of questionable services.

QUALITY CONTROLS

Apart from licensure and accreditation requirements, utlization review is the primary quality assurance mechanism. Utilization review is conducted by hospitals and by Peer Review Organizations (PROs).[4] Under UR, the main questions are whether the admission and length of stay were appropriate and whether the patient received appropriate care. However, most of the work of evaluating UR has focused on costs rather than quality, so there is little evidence on quality effects.

Regulation of the Hospital Sector

Given its large and growing share of the U.S. health economy, policy makers have addressed cost inflation by regulating the hospital industry. The previous section provided a general introduction to regulation. In this section, we focus on the three major forms of hospital regulation: rate regulation, utilization review, and Certificate-of-Need. These are administered mainly at the state level.

RATE REGULATION, UTILIZATION REVIEW, AND CERTIFICATE-OF-NEED

As described previously, rate regulation defines the terms under which hospitals are reimbursed. The underlying premise has been that, due to market power, hospitals may charge rates that vary from the cost of providing the services. Prospective forms of reimbursement also are intended to deal with hospital inefficiency and incentives to overprovide care that exist under retrospective reimbursement.

Rate regulation (RR) may occur by type of service provided: on a daily (or per-diem basis), or on a per-patient or per-admission basis. The goal of rate regulation is to lower costs or at least to reduce the rate of hospital cost inflation.

Utilization review (UR) programs seek to determine whether specific services are medically necessary and whether they are delivered at an appropriate level of intensity and cost. Ermann (1988) identifies three general types of utilization review:

- *Preadmission review* examines the necessity of hospital admission before admission occurs to determine if inpatient care is necessary.
- *Concurrent review* ascertains whether patients need continuing care by means of record review.
- *Retrospective review* attempts to identify questionable patterns of care.

[4]See chapter 18 for further discussion of PROs and their predecessor, Professional Standards Review Organizations (PSROs).

Another form of UR is second-opinion surgery review. This either requires or encourages patients who are contemplating elective surgery to seek advice from a second physician. One of the key questions in analyzing the impacts of any form of utilization review is the extent to which "truly" unnecessary procedures are eliminated as opposed to the extent that the quality of care suffers.

Certificate-of-Need (CON) regulation addresses capital expenditure (either beds or other expensive hospital equipment). The general aim is to reduce excess capacity or to eliminate costly duplication of resources. An unintended impact occurs, however, if this review process reduces competition in the provision of the services. This reduction of competition, of course, could lead to increased monopoly power and to higher prices.

EMPIRICAL FINDINGS ON REGULATION

Utilization Review

The premise behind UR is to reduce unnecessary costs without adversely affecting patient health. The results of UR have been mixed. Much of the work has reviewed the Professional Standards Review Organizations (PSROs) that were established at local levels under federal laws in 1972. Two factors have led to difficulties. First, there has been a wide variation among PSROs. Some may have been quite effective, while others were not. Looking across a whole group may not provide much guidance.

Second, the PSRO program had two mandates. Cost was to be contained and quality was to be ensured. It is clear that if quality-related aspects of health care provision cost money, then these two goals may conflict with each other. Not surprisingly, empirical results have generally been inconclusive. Rosko and Broyles (1988, chapter 12) provide a review of earlier studies.

Subsequently, Wickizer, Wheeler, and Feldstein (1989) found that UR reduced admissions by 13 percent, inpatient days by 11 percent, expenditures on routine hospital inpatient service by 7 percent, expenditures on hospital ancillary services by 9 percent, and total medical expenditures by 6 percent. The same authors (1991) also find that the adoption of UR implies substitution effects (approximately $9 per insured person per year) suggests a limited, although measurable, effect.

As for concerns that patients will get less care and with less certain (and possibly less positive) outcomes, Ermann (1988) cites the lack of conclusive evidence. Dranove (1991) nevertheless argues that price competition may force those who engage in UR to focus on cost savings "at the expense of appropriateness." He concludes that "cost cutting through UR is easy. Improving the health care product through UR is not" (p. 26).

Rate Regulation

Much of the early research investigating the impact of rate regulation (RR) centered around the states of Connecticut, Massachusetts, New Jersey, New York, Maryland, and Washington, which had or adopted rate regulation through the 1970s and early 1980s. Studies investigating the impacts of RR looked at costs or changes in costs in these states, or in hospitals within these states. The typical method estimated a regression such that:

$$\log C_t - \log C_{t-1} = b(X_t - X_{t-1}) + dD + \epsilon$$

where the left-hand side reflects the change in the logarithm of hospital expenses (or the logarithm of the percent change in expenses) as a function of changes in explanatory

variables, X, and imposition of rate regulation, D. If coefficient d is negative, then all else being equal, the imposition of regulation D reduces the growth in costs.

Dranove and Cone (1985) present an interesting discussion of the impacts of rate regulation. They carefully examine the possibility of *regression to the mean.* Suppose at a given point some states have unusually high or unusually low costs. If these differences are transient due to jumps in energy or insurance costs or some form of natural disaster, then total costs would be expected to return to the mean as the transient events disappear. Laws enacted in high-cost states may appear to be successful because the effects attributed to the laws really are caused by regression of the state to the overall mean of all states. The reverse, of course, also is possible. States that were below the mean could see rising costs, even with effective regulation.

The authors estimated the foregoing difference in equation, with the following explanatory variables:

- Income—median family income
- Education—population percent with high school diploma
- Age—population percent over age 65
- Insurance—population percent insured against physician expenses
- Metro—population percent living in an urban area
- Union—population percent who are union members

and the following policy variable:

- Law—number of years the law has been in effect

They sought to explain (1) expenses per admission, (2) expenses per day, and (3) expenses per person.

The regression results are presented in Table 21.1. Multiplying each coefficient of the law variable by 100 approximates (due to the logarithmic transformation of the

TABLE 21.1	**Percentage Change in Hospital Costs**		
Variable	Expenses per Admission	Expenses per Day	Expenses per Person
Constant	0.70^a	0.72^a	0.46^a
Income	0.66^a	1.13^a	0.79^a
Education	-0.63^b	-0.69^b	0.30
Age	0.35^b	0.28	0.83^a
Insurance	−0.094	-0.26^b	−0.67
Metro	−0.016	-0.70^b	−0.33
Union	−0.11	-0.33^a	−0.57
Law	$\mathbf{-0.0132}^a$	$\mathbf{-0.0141}^a$	$\mathbf{-0.0104}^b$
Adjustment	-0.20^b	−0.005	-0.33^a
Adjusted R^2	0.46	0.50	0.52

[a]Significant at 1 percent level.
[b]Significant at 10 percent level.

Source: Reprinted from *Journal of Health Economics.* Dranove, David and Kenneth Cone, "Do State Rate Setting Regulations Really Lower Hospital Expenses?" *Journal of Health Economics* 4 (1985): 159–165, with permission from Elsevier Science.

dependent variable) the law's percentage impact. For example, those states with a regulation law exhibited approximately a 1.32 percent smaller increase in expenses per admission than other states; a 1.41 percent smaller increase in expenses/day; and a 1.04 percent smaller increase in expenses per person.

Regression to the mean does occur. Dranove and Cone suggest that mean regression made laws in New York and Massachusetts look more effective than they were (costs would have decreased anyhow). Conversely, mean regression made laws in Connecticut, New Jersey, and Washington look less effective. New Jersey, in fact, moved from 4 percentage points worse than the average rate-setting state to 4 percentage points better.

Rosko and Broyles (1988) summarize findings of restraint of cost inflation per year:

- Costs per admission rose by 1.4 percent to 8.7 percent less.
- Costs per patient day rose by 1.2 percent to 10.5 percent less.
- Expenditures per capita rose by 2.0 percent to 7.6 percent less.

Certificate-of-Need

Certificate-of-Need (CON) legislation has been studied in a variety of contexts. Salkever and Bice (1979) provided early and useful analyses of the programs. Their methods, as with others, were to predict costs using binary variables to represent the presence, comprehensiveness, and maturity of programs designed to regulate capital formation. Almost all of the studies found essentially no impact of CON on total expenditures.

Nevertheless, it is plausible to expect that other hospital inputs may increase to substitute for limits on capital expenditures. Salkever and Bice note that hospitals appear to have substituted investment for new services in place of investment in beds. Another study reported similar results, as well as increased ratios of registered nurses and licensed practical nurses per bed.[5]

Recognizing the problem of characterizing CON across states, Mayo and McFarland (1989) present a theoretically appealing examination over time within a single state. Recall that the goal of CON is to reduce capital expenditures, and thus prevent costly duplication of facilities.

One can posit three impacts of CON:

1. The intended impact on capital costs, which reduces cost by reducing capital expenditures.
2. The substitution effect in which the hospitals substitute nonregulated inputs for the regulated ones. This may offset capital cost reductions.[6]
3. The increased monopoly power of existing hospitals. If competitors are prevented from engaging in capital expenditures, then existing hospitals have increased monopoly power. Some economists also argue that incentives to innovate, and hence lower production costs, may be lost if competition is lessened.

Mayo and McFarland, in data for the state of Tennessee, find the direct effects of CON to lower hospital costs, and the indirect substitution and market concentration

[5]See Sloan and Steinwald (1980).

[6]Mayo and McFarland (1989) do not address this issue. In response to an insightful comment by K. Anderson (1991), they reestimate their cost equation (Mayo and McFarland, 1991) to allow for such a cost adjustment. Our discussion uses the restimated 1991 equation.

effects to raise them. While many studies in other states indicate no significant effect of CON, the newer theoretical and empirical models suggest the importance of modeling cost-containment policies at the hospital rather than at the regional level. Hospitals react to cost-containment policies not only by changing the costs of the services, but by adjusting the amounts of the services and the inputs into the services.

The 1990s brought new perspective to the evaluation of the traditional regulatory mechanisms. With the emergence of managed care, utilization review has become a common feature of almost all health care systems. The general concern about health care costs has made CON regulations somewhat outdated. Existing hospitals are addressing hard questions such as whether to close units rather than planning new ones. More competitive market mechanisms are impacting the physician and the hospital sector.

Two recent studies address and evaluate the more traditional regulatory mechanisms. Conover and Sloan (1998) assess the impact of CON regulation on hospital spending per capita, hospital supply, diffusion of technology, and hospital industry organization for the years 1976 through 1993. Using statistical analyses, the authors found that long-term CON programs were associated with what they termed a "modest (5 percent)" long-term reduction in acute care spending per capita, but not with significant reduction in total per-capita spending.

They view it as doubtful that CON regulations have had much effect on quality of care, either positive or negative. They suggest that CON regulations may have improved access to care but find little empirical evidence to support the suggestion.

Antel and colleagues (1995) address two major issues in measuring the impacts of the regulations over the contiguous 48 United States for the years 1968 to 1990. First, if certain economic factors persist over time (like high wage rates), they might affect state-level hospital costs and influence the states' regulatory decisions. If these factors are not accounted for properly in the analyses, it is difficult to measure the regulatory impacts accurately.

Second, they note that regulations may interact with each other. For example, hospital responses to the Medicare prospective payment system may raise costs; rate regulation may limit the cost-increasing effects of the Medicare system.

The researchers model six regulatory instruments. If regulation were effective, each of these instruments would be expected to lower costs:

1. Proportion of hospital revenue affected by *mandatory state rate-setting regulation*
2. *Certificate-of-Need* programs passed by the states in the 1960s and 1970s
3. *Legislation* in the 1970s that denied Medicare and Medicaid cost reimbursement to hospitals that were expanding capacity without prior approval by local planning agencies
4. *Professional Standards Review Organizations* to control hospital services utilization
5. Medicare *prospective payment,* beginning in 1984
6. Nixon-era *price controls* under the Economic Stabilization Act from 1971 through 1974

They examine costs per day, costs per admission, and costs per person.

Analyses of the "simple" impacts, without interaction among them, indicate that rate regulation and economic stabilization policies appear to have had substantive impacts; the other instruments did not. However, the more complex models indicate that rate regulation, which seemed reasonably effective in the simple models, appeared un-

able, alone, to control per-day, per-admission, or per-capita hospital costs. Nor was there any evidence that federal utilization controls or state and federal hospital investment restrictions lowered hospital costs. Some regulations did interact, however. For example, investment restrictions in some cases appear to have limited the cost increases associated with rate regulation.

Interestingly, the authors found the Nixon-era price regulations to have been effective in lowering costs. They conjecture that this occurred because the controls covered hospital wages and other input prices. Also, because the controls were temporary, hospitals may have had less incentive to adjust or to evade them.

Prospective Payment

The enactment of Medicare and Medicaid involved the federal government to a large degree in the reimbursement of services. The costs of these programs have increased substantially over the years, and as costs have grown, so has interest in cost-containment policies.

In this section, we focus on the Medicare program that converted the financing of Medicare hospital care to a prospective payment system based on diagnosis-related groups (DRGs). We discuss the system in the present context because its widespread use stems from its adoption by the Medicare program. However, the PPS system under DRGs has wider significance to other segments of the health sector, as well as to the regulation of industry in general. In fact, under the Balanced Budget Act of 1997, PPS is being extended to outpatient nursing home care and to home health care.

DESCRIPTION OF PPS

Understanding PPS under DRGs requires knowing what prospective payment means and what DRGs are. Prospective payment is best seen in contrast to the former retrospective reimbursement system under Medicare. Under retrospective payment, a hospital submits its bill to Medicare after the care has been given and the costs to the hospital are known. Retrospective payment allowed the hospitals to recover their expenses, as allowed by Medicare rules, regardless of whether these expenses were high or low, excessive or efficient. Under retrospective reimbursement, incentives for cost efficiency were questionable.

Prospective payment sets payment rates prior to the period for which care is given. By setting a fixed reimbursement level per admission, prospective payment provides economic incentives to conserve on the use of input resources. Hospitals that use more resources than covered by the flat rate lose the difference. Those with costs below that rate retain the difference.

The rates themselves are determined by DRGs. Under PPS, patients are admitted according to their condition under one of 495 applicable DRGs. Each DRG attempts to represent a case type that identifies patients with similar conditions and processes of care. Some of the most common DRGs, based on hospital discharges, or the most expensive, based on total charges, are shown in Table 21.2.

Each DRG is given a flat payment rate calculated in part on the basis of costs incurred for that DRG nationally. These rates are modified somewhat, in practice, to account for differences in local wages, urban versus rural location, and other factors such as whether the hospital is a teaching hospital. The rates are flat in the important sense

TABLE 21.2 Common DRGs

Five Most Common DRGs by Number of Discharges (1998)

DRG		Total Charges	Total Days	Number of Discharges	Days/ Discharge
127	Heart failure & shock	$7,152,055,390	3,919,453	727,523	5.4
089	Simple pneumonia & pleurisy age > 17 with complications or comorbidity	$5,262,937,344	3,135,115	512,593	6.1
088	Chronic obstructive pulmonary disease	$3,540,730,468	2,103,606	399,638	5.3
014	Specific cerebrovascular disorders except transient ischemic attack	$4,158,773,852	2,186,366	359,625	6.1
209	Major joint and limb reattachment procedures of lower extremity	$7,160,320,840	1,828,944	356,006	5.1
Sum		$27,274,817,894	13,173,484	2,355,385	

Five Most Expensive DRGs by Total Charges (1998)

DRG		Total Charges	Total Days	Number of Discharges	Days/ Discharge
483	Tracheostomy except for face, mouth, & neck diagnoses	$7,198,352,756	1,705,165	43,708	39.0
209	Major joint & limb reattachment procedures of lower extremity	$7,160,320,840	1,828,944	356,006	5.1
127	Heart failure and shock	$7,152,055,390	3,919,453	727,523	5.4
116	Other Perm cardiac pacemaker implant	$6,606,346,030	1,072,256	273,202	3.9
106	Coronary bypass with cardiac catheterization	$5,550,331,173	1,066,713	101,672	10.5
Sum		$33,667,406,189	9,592,531	1,502,111	
Total for all DRGs		*$171,614,021,916*	*73,589,099*	*11,912,079*	

Source: Health Care Financing Administration, http://www.hcfa.gov/stats/medpar/ss98d&s.txt. Accessed March 1, 2000.

that they are not varied or softened for hospitals that spend more than the rate, or for that matter less.

The Theory of Yardstick Competition and DRGs

Shleifer (1985) has described the theory of yardstick competition, which is a close approximation to the Prospective Payment System under DRGs. We can think of yardstick competition as the ideal form of such a system, while the actual Medicare payment system is a real-life approximation.

Shleifer describes yardstick competition in the context of markets where firms have at least some monopoly power. Because most medical providers face downward-sloping demand curves, they posses some degree of monopoly power.

Recall that monopolistic firms reduce production to outputs that are smaller than an industry made up of competitive firms would offer and correspondingly charge higher prices. Moreover, left to its own devices, secure monopoly firms lack some of the incentives to be cost efficient that rigorous competition would provide. In hospital markets in the United States prior to PPS, one of the most serious cost-efficiency *disincentives* was the retrospective payment system already discussed. Shleifer's yardstick

competition describes a regulatory scheme, much like Medicare's PPS, that restores cost-consciousness incentives.

Consider Figure 21.1 in which the hospital faces demand curve D, and where marginal and average costs equal C_0. As we have seen before, the monopoly hospital will provide Q_0 units of output and charge P_0 indicated by point M. In contrast, with retrospective reimbursement, the hospital will be paid C_0, and will produce at the intersection of demand D with C_0, at point R. A suitable competitive mechanism should give the hospital incentives to reduce costs and to price their services competitively.

Suppose the hospital knows that it could be more cost efficient if it would hire a team of efficiency experts, which is a fixed cost that is unrelated to output, and carry out their advice, which is also a fixed cost. An optimal scheme would lead the hospital to invest so as to reduce costs. The problem for yardstick competition is to set up a payment scheme so that these firms have the incentives to spend just the right amount of money and effort on reducing production costs.

What is just the right amount of expense to incur in the effort to reduce production costs? Suppose the hospital discovers that it could most likely reduce its marginal costs of production by $1 per unit of output (say, case treated) if it were to spend $1,500 on cost-reduction efforts. Suppose the hospital treats 5,000 cases per year, or 5,000 units of

FIGURE 21.1 The Impact of Yardstick Competition.

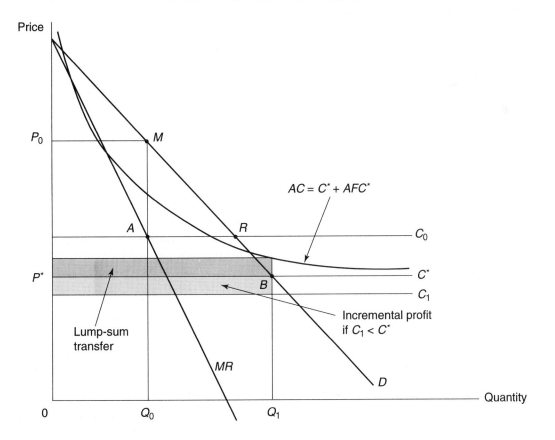

output. Would the cost-reduction effort be worth it? The example is shown in the first line of the following schedule.

	Marginal Cost of Efficiency Effort		Marginal Revenue Generated
Step (1)	$1,500	<	$1 × 5,000
Step (2)	$2,700	<	$1 × 5,000
Step (3)	$4,900	<	$1 × 5,000
Step (4)	$7,500	>	$1 × 5,000

Step (1) represents the first of four possible steps in cost reduction. Each step will reduce costs per case by $1. With step (1), reducing per-unit costs by $1 costs a total of $1,500 in cost-efficiency efforts. The extra dollar saved for every case treated generates $5,000 in extra revenue.

Clearly, this step of cost saving is worthwhile because it costs less ($1,500) than it saves ($5,000). By similar reasoning, one more step of cost saving also would be worthwhile, costing $2,700, but saving another $5,000. Step (3) is worthwhile too, but that is where we would stop. Unregulated monopolists or retrospectively reimbursed firms will not necessarily have the built-in incentives to take these three steps. It would be good to have a payment system that would induce them to do so.

How does yardstick competition provide this inducement? Return to Figure 21.1. With yardstick competition, prices at which the hospital is reimbursed are set *beforehand* at fixed rates. These rates—that is, these regulated prices—are set equal to the averages of the marginal costs of *all other* hospitals in the market.

Suppose the regulator is able to determine the marginal cost of each hospital. Consider then, Hospital 1. Recall that the cost-reduction efforts represent a fixed cost to the hospital, and the average fixed cost (graphed in Figure 21.1) must be covered by additional revenues. Hospital 1 is assigned service price C^*, equal to the average marginal cost of all of its competitors, Hospitals 2 through N, and a break-even subsidy (dark shaded area) again equal to the average of all of its competitors. With its revenue per patient now fixed prospectively, Hospital 1's incentive is to invest in cost-cutting technologies or practices.

Recall what the "yardstick competition" does. It induces the hospital to reduce its marginal costs from C_0 to some lower level and to price its output at the "average" marginal cost of its competitors. We treat the cost-cutting innovation as a fixed cost for the hospital output. As a result, the hospital's new average cost curve is the sum of the (now-lower) marginal cost C^* and the optimum average fixed cost, AFC^*. The new output occurs where C^* is equal to the demand price, or point B. The optimal output becomes Q_1, and the price falls to P^*, which equals C^*.

Suppose, fortuitously, that the hospital's new marginal cost equals C^*. Under yardstick competition, the firm will lose an amount equal to the fixed costs of reducing its marginal costs, or the dark shaded area in Figure 21.1. The yardstick pricing scheme provides a lump sum subsidy to the hospital allowing it to "break even" despite incurring the fixed costs required for its cost reducing efforts.

If the hospital has succeeded in lowering its marginal costs to C_1, which is less than C^*, then it will earn a profit equal to $Q_1 (C^* - C_1)$, the lightly shaded area. If the hos-

pital cannot lower its costs to C^*, then it will lose money in addition to the fixed costs. In either case, because the hospital's actual costs do not enter into the price that it receives, the hospital has a considerable incentive to reduce its costs.

In this model, hospitals are not subsidized for inefficient behavior. Hospitals compete, and this competition leads to the optimum solution discussed earlier.[7] Shleifer notes that it is

> essential for the regulator to commit himself not to pay attention to the firms' complaints and to be prepared to let the firms go bankrupt if they choose inefficient cost levels. Unless the regulator can credibly threaten to make inefficient firms lose money . . . cost reduction cannot be enforced (p. 327).

The model presented implicitly assumes that all firms, in this case hospitals, are the same. Shleifer, however, shows how one could construct a multiple regression model that would help generate a similar solution in the more realistic case where firms are different from each other. Furthermore, he demonstrates a closely related scheme of pricing based on average industry costs that leads to virtually the same results in the realistic case where the theoretically needed lump-sum subsidies would be difficult to calculate or difficult to pass politically.

Let us return now to DRGs as practiced. It is important to note that, consistent with Shleifer's formulation, a hospital's actual costs do not enter into the formula for its payment rate. As a result, the hospital must become a price taker in the strictest sense. If it costs the hospital more to provide the service than the DRGs allow, the hospital either loses money on the service and is forced to stop offering it, or is forced to cross-subsidize the service from other services that may be produced at costs lower than their DRGs. Thus, the cost-cutting incentives are strong.

Predictably, the inception of DRGs raised major concerns among hospitals. Those familiar with diagnoses will recognize that even as many as 495 categories imply that the thousands of diagnoses must be lumped into groupings that offer single payments appropriate to some, but not to all, conditions handled in a given DRG. This suggests the necessity of refining the DRG categories.

Shleifer, in fact, notes that some of the problems with DRGs result from the fact that not all of the sources of cost variation are considered. Medicare does not adjust payment for severity of illness. Although it would seem that the average severity of illness might be the same among hospitals, those hospitals getting the more severely ill patients might suffer financially.

ON THE EFFECTS OF MEDICARE'S PROSPECTIVE PAYMENT SYSTEM

It is clear that yardstick competition in theory and the actual Medicare Prospective Payment System in practice change firms' economic incentives considerably.[8] Results to

[7]This process is known as a Nash equilibrium. It refers to a market solution in which each firm does the best it can, given the decision of others. It is an equilibrium because once the choices are made, no firm has any motive to change its action.

[8]Hodgkin and McGuire (1994) develop a model in which the level of prospective payment affects the hospital's choice of intensity of care, which affects the demand for admissions. The model suggests that both the average payment level and the incentives created by changes in the marginal rate affect hospital utilization.

date show some clear impacts, as well as some remaining ambiguities. We examine briefly here several categories of possible effects.

Average Hospital Length of Stay

One method of cutting costs available to hospitals, in theory, is to reduce the number of days of care taken to treat a patient case. In fact, average length of stay did drop after the advent of PPS. It dropped 9 percent in the first year of PPS, and a total of 14.6 percent between 1982 and 1985.[9] The effect of PPS on length of stay is plausible and clearly established in the data. However, Newhouse and Byrne (1988) point out that this effect is found in short-term acute general care hospitals that are subject to PPS. When considering the effects of increased length of stay in other, exempted longer-stay institutions, the net result is that overall health system length of stay rose between 1981 and 1984. Even so, net cost savings are possible systemwide because exempted institutions tend to have lower daily costs.

A related item is the admission rate to short-term hospitals. Although the effect of PPS on admissions is theoretically ambiguous, several analysts had expected PPS to increase admissions to hospitals. However, since the onset of Medicare's PPS, admission rates have tended to fall rather than rise.

Access and Quality

A number of people have been concerned that the Prospective Payment System under DRGs would induce hospitals to save on costs by cutting corners, reducing quality, refusing to treat costly patients, or closing treatment units. That is, the system would reduce access to care and the quality of care. Research has addressed these issues to some extent.

One study found that use of intensive care units did not fall after PPS, allaying fears about access to needed care. Use of many diagnostic and treatment technologies did fall after PPS started, but these also fell for non-Medicare patients. A second study used statistical techniques to estimate quality changes in a sample of 729 U.S. short-term general care hospitals following Medicare's PPS. The results were negative, meaning that no evidence of quality reduction was found.[10]

DesHarnais and colleagues (1988) found no evidence of quality reductions for a sample of 646 U.S. hospitals. Also relevant to quality issues, Carroll and Erwin (1987) showed no significant difference in several major health status measures for patients being transferred from hospitals to nursing homes before and after PPS. In surveying the available evidence as of 1991, Feinglass and Holloway (1991) conclude that while evidence can be found of individual instances where access or quality has been limited because of PPS,

> to date, there is *little direct, generalizable evidence* [emphasis added] that PPS has reduced the quality of care for Medicare patients. Hospital use and mortality rates for potentially unprofitable patients such as the oldest old, minorities, self-paying, uninsured, or nursing home patients covered by both Medicare and Medicaid have decreased at the same rate as the rest of the population (p. 107).

[9]See Guterman and Dobson (1986) and Feinglass and Holloway (1991).
[10]For the two studies cited, see Sloan, Morrisey, and Valvona (1988a) and DesHarnais et al. (1987).

Severity of the Case Mix

Another observed change following the onset of Medicare's PPS has been the increase in common *case-mix indexes.* A case-mix index is a numerical measure of the assortment of patient cases treated by a given hospital, so that a higher value for the index indicates a greater average degree of complexity of the cases and consequently a greater need for input resources. Some of the increase in the indexes has probably occurred because hospitals are being more careful about which diagnosis they pick (for patients with multiple diagnoses) to categorize the patient for Medicare payment purposes. This maneuver is sometimes called "DRG-Creep."

It is difficult, however, to distinguish this as the cause of increased case complexity. In any case, it seems clear that hospital treatment practice patterns have changed following PPS. Also, it is reported that average severity of the cases treated on an inpatient basis in hospitals has increased subsequent to PPS,[11] suggesting that less severe cases are now assigned to outpatient treatment.

Financial Condition of Hospitals

Most agree that PPS puts a degree of financial stress on hospitals, particularly on those that have higher-than-usual costs. This, after all, is the way in which PPS alters financial incentives. However, hospitals that are run on the principles of yardstick competition might well increase their wealth position subsequent to PPS. In any case, at the beginning of Medicare's PPS, the fixed-payment rates proved sufficiently generous that average operating margins of hospitals were substantial, thus reducing the cost-saving incentives. Payment rates subsequently did not keep up with inflation, perhaps due to Congressional concern about hospital windfall profits, and operating margins fell steadily. By the late 1980s and extending through the early 1990s, average operating margins for the Medicare segment of patients tended to be negative.[12]

Effect on Costs

The point of this program, from Medicare's point of view, was to control costs. So the ultimate question is whether PPS succeeded. This question, however, can be addressed from at least three perspectives.[13] First, did individual hospitals respond by reducing their expenditures? Evidence indicates that they did so, at least in the first year. Zwanziger and Melnick (1988) observed that for a sample of California hospitals, those under the strongest pressure from PPS responded by reducing expenditures.

Second, did PPS reduce expenditures in Medicare's budget? Hospital savings seem likely. Medicare outlays for hospital care increased at an annual rate of 3.5 percent from 1984 to 1987, compared to 7.1 percent from 1977 to 1982, and hospital care fell as a proportion of the Medicare budget from 70 percent to 57 percent by 1988. Subsequently, PPS payments per case rose only slightly faster than the consumer price index so that by 1993, after the first ten years of PPS, Medicare's share of hospital payments remained at 28 percent despite a 23 percent growth in Medicare enrollments.

[11]See Steinwald and Dummit (1989); Feinglass and Holloway (1991); and Sloan, Morrisey, and Valvona (1988a).

[12]For further references, see Folland and Kleiman (1990), Dobson and Hoy (1988), Bromberg and Goodwin (1988), and Prospective Payment Assessment Commission (1995).

[13]For discussion, see Hadley, Zuckerman, and Feder (1989); Feinglass and Holloway (1991); Guterman and Dobson (1986); and Prospective Payment Assessment Commission (1995).

Lastly, did per-capita expenditures for society as a whole fall as a result of Medicare's PPS? This is a much more difficult question to answer. Feinglass and Holloway (1991) argue that the savings from PPS were one-time-only events, occurring in the early years of PPS. This possibility is evidenced by increasing inflation rates in the late 1980s for U.S. health care expenditures, which in real terms were outstripping the inflation rates of 1980 to 1985.

In a statistical study of the issue, Sloan, Morrisey, and Valvona (1988a) find a significant reduction in hospital patient–generated revenues per capita subsequent to PPS, but they note that the savings are found primarily in reductions in admissions, a category PPS does not provide specific incentives to reduce. They note the possibility that utilization review under Peer Review Organizations (PROs)—a utilization review effort begun along with Medicare's Prospective Payment System—could conceivably be the source of per-capita cost reductions for hospital care.[14]

Thus, on the principle question of the three, we are left somewhat in doubt. Feinglass and Holloway argue that Medicare's PPS may have had an ambiguous or negligible effect on overall societal health care costs. Many economists and policy analysts have found that when you squeeze a balloon in one place, it expands in others.

Prospective Payment—Recent Evidence

The prospective payment system was developed at least in part to address perceived cost increases in the health care sector. Yet, early analyses indicated that its effectiveness was at best mixed. It is worthwhile to examine analyses that are provided by the Medicare Payment Advisory Commission (MEDPAC) in looking at more recent trends. MEDPAC starts with the identity that costs per inpatient stay, indicated by discharge data, can be rewritten as the following equation:

$$(\text{cost/discharge}) = (\text{days/discharge})(\text{service intensity/day})(\text{cost/service unit})$$

So, a hospital stay that lasts eight days, with two treatments per day at a cost of $100 per treatment, will cost:

$$(\text{cost/discharge}) = (8 \text{ days})(2 \text{ treatments})(\$100) = \$1,600$$

It is easy to apply this formula to changes over time. Some manipulation leads to:

$$\% \text{ Change (cost/discharge)} = \% \text{ Change (days/discharge)}$$
$$+ \% \text{ Change (service/day)}$$
$$+ \% \text{ Change (cost/service)}$$

Table 21.3 provides such a decomposition. Costs are measured relative to general price inflation, so the table suggests, for example, that costs increased by 2.5 percent more per year than goods outside the hospital sector from 1985 to 1989.

The most important variable has been length-of-stay reduction, which went from an increasing factor (0.8 percent per year) to substantial decreases of −1.3 percent per year from 1989 to 1992 and −3.3 percent per year from 1992 to 1996. This was somewhat offset by increased services per day, although overall services per discharge (the sum of percentage changes in days/discharge and services/day) appear to have dropped.

[14]Shifts to outpatient care, which similarly does not provide specific cost-reduction incentives, also may occur.

TABLE 21.3 Average Annual Hospital Cost Changes

Average Annual Changes (%)

Years	Cost/ Discharge	=	Days/ Discharge	+	Services/ Day	+	Costs/ Service
1985 to 1989	**2.5**		0.8		2.2		−0.3
1989 to 1992	**1.3**		−1.3		1.4		1.3
1992 to 1996	**−2.7**		−3.3		0.9		−0.3

Source: MEDPAC (March 1999, Appendix D, Table D-1).

REGULATION OF PHYSICIAN PAYMENT

Traditionally, physicians in the United States have been paid on a fee-for-service (FFS) basis. Under FFS, each physician has a schedule of fees and expects to be reimbursed for each unit of service provided.

As commercial insurance proliferated with the growth of the Blues and other private insurance following World War II, benefit schedules generally were used to determine reimbursement. These schedules contained the maximum amounts that the insurers would pay for a particular service. If the provider charged less, the lower amount would be paid. Typically, also, individuals paid the providers' charges and were reimbursed (indemnified) by insurers according to the benefit schedule. Indemnity plans are still common in the for-profit insurance market.

UCR REIMBURSEMENT, ASSIGNMENT, AND ALTERNATIVE PAYMENT MECHANISMS

Following the introduction of Medicare in 1965, another system for reimbursing providers became more prevalent. It uses fee screens and is commonly called the usual, customary, and reasonable (UCR) payment mechanism.

The fee screens are determined by the maximum of the doctor's median charge (i.e., usual charge) and the customary fees charged by the other physicians in the area. Some criterion, such as the 80th percentile of the distribution of charges, may be selected for this cutoff. In addition, higher charges may be allowed if they are deemed reasonable in light of any unusual circumstances that would justify the higher payment. Under UCR, the maximum reimbursement is the lowest of the actual charge or the two fee screens.

Clearly, the UCR method is far more complicated and difficult to administer than the benefit schedule because it involves data collection on every provider. Supporters of this approach argue, however, that it is flexible and fair because it allows for differences across different specialty groups and market areas. Once Medicare adopted the UCR, the Blues and many other third-party payers followed. In 1975, it was estimated that approximately 130 million of 169 million persons with private coverage for physician care were subject to UCR methods.[15]

However, several concerns with UCR soon became apparent. Many critics argued that UCR is inflationary. Providers have incentives to raise their charges so that the usual and customary screens increase, resulting in an increase in future payments.

[15]See Showstack et al. (1979).

Furthermore, there is no incentive to compete by charging less than the screens. Studies of UCR generally support this view. To deal with this problem, Medicare and many Blue Shield plans introduced various mechanisms to limit the increases in the screens.

RELATIVE VALUE SCALES

Relative value scales (RVSs) were developed by state medical societies and other organizations (the California RVS, developed in 1969, was one of the most widely used). An RVS establishes a weight (or multiple) for each procedure. The weight may reflect the time needed to perform a procedure and its complexity. Although the RVS does not provide fee information, if providers adhere to the guide, the price they set for any one procedure will determine the prices charged for all other procedures.

One must recognize that any system of relative value scales depends on a set of given technologies. When, for example, the method of treating heart disease changes, the RVS for that category also must change in order to remain valid. If the technological advance causes the treatment to become cheaper, the treatment may become more profitable to the provider as long as the treatment retains its old place in the relative value scale.

Over the years, perceived inequities in Medicare's UCR system between primary care and surgical specialties led to attempts to change Medicare's physician payment system. Harvard University researchers, led by William Hsiao, undertook the task of developing a "resource-based" RVS, or RBRVS, as an alternative method of reimbursing physicians. As a result of their work, a new Medicare payment system, based on RBRVS, was phased in over a five-year period beginning in 1992.

The RBRVS (MEDPAC, 1999) has three components, corresponding to three different types of resources used to provide physicians' services:

1. Physician work, including the time, intensity of effort, skill, and risk to the patient associated with each service. On average, this accounts for 54.5 percent of the fee.
2. Practice expenses, including the cost of nonphysician staff, office space, equipment, and supplies. This accounts for 42.3 percent of the fee.
3. Professional liability insurance, accounting for 3.2 percent of the fee (for certain services, this amount is higher, accounting for 12.1 percent of the total relative value unit for spinal laminectomy [surgery], for example).

The system introduced a major restructuring of fees away from specialists and toward primary care providers. This development is supported by many in the U.S. health care community who feel that health care is improperly skewed toward the provision of specialized care. However, many who encourage the use of market-based mechanisms generally believe that the new system will reduce competition among providers who in principle will be working from similar fee schedules.

The new RBRVS was expected to produce substantial redistribution among providers. Table 21.4 compares the distribution of physician payment for selected specialties in 1991, before the inception of RBRVS, and in 1995, when the RBRVS had been in effect for three years. Although the absolute changes in shares are modest, the percentage changes indicate a substantive shift away from surgery to specialties such as internal medicine, dermatology, and urology.

In a 1997 report (PPRC, 1997), the Prospective Payment Review Commission noted that the fee schedule changed the pattern of relative payment less than originally an-

TABLE 21.4	Effect of Fee Schedule on Distribution of Physician Payments, Selected Specialties			
Share of Medicare Physician Payments				
Specialty	*1991*	*1995*	*Change*	*Percent Change*
Cardiology	8.6	8.9	0.3	3.5
Family Practice/				
General Practice	9.0	9.3	0.3	3.3
Internal Medicine	19.2	20.0	0.8	4.2
Dermatology	2.0	2.4	0.4	20.0
General Surgery	6.4	5.9	−0.5	−7.8
Orthopedic Surgery	5.1	5.1	0.0	0.0
Thoracic Surgery	2.9	2.5	−0.4	−13.8
Urology	3.9	4.3	0.4	10.3
Other Medicine	7.2	8.5	1.3	18.1

Source: PPRC (1997).

ticipated. The surgical services conversion factor (converting RBRVS to dollars) grew about 15 percent faster than the primary care and other services factor, thus offsetting changes in payments across services and specialties. Medicare's move to a single conversion factor in 1998 is expected to further redistribute payments as was originally anticipated.

Who Does the Regulator Represent?

Thus far in this chapter and elsewhere that we have addressed regulatory activities such as licensure or other quality controls, we have assumed that the regulator knows the right regulatory actions to take. Most often we treat the regulator as representing an omniscient but benevolent despot who knows what is good for the economy and regulates accordingly. Yet students of railroad regulation might argue that the railroads played major roles in influencing their regulators. Likewise, some observers believe that the American Medical Association has influenced laws on licensure and legislation on Medicare. Can the theory of regulation address issues such as these?

It can. An influential school of economists, often associated with the University of Chicago, have argued that the regulation process can be thought of as a "maximizing" process, just like many others that we have examined, in which a regulator seeks "votes" from a group of potential beneficiaries. These votes would allow the transfer of wealth, such as monopoly profits, from those who are regulated to those who benefit from the regulations.[16]

In this model, the regulator seeks supporters by imposing a percentage "tax" (rate t) on those who are regulated, with the tax receipts (tax rate, t, multiplied by the wealth of those being taxed) being transferred to the beneficiaries. A higher tax rate on those who are regulated (more stringent regulation) may win more supporters, but it also may

[16]This model follows the framework derived by Peltzman (1976).

mobilize more opponents. The successful regulator seeks a certain transfer of wealth while gathering votes to effect this transfer efficiently.

Suppose the regulator starts with a modest tax. The imposition and increase of this tax yields favorable votes for two reasons:

1. The revenues increase the probability of support from the potential beneficiaries.
2. The revenues increase the value of the transfer to the beneficiaries.

Opposition also will be heard. Those who would be regulated will oppose a transfer because it is coming from them. Their opposition will grow the higher the tax is (the more stringent the regulation is); that is, the more that is being taken from them.

The regulator's optimal tax rate in this setting occurs where the following equality holds:

Marginal benefits from regulation = Marginal costs from regulation

or,

$$
\begin{bmatrix} \text{marginal} \\ \text{increase in} \\ \text{probability} \\ \text{of support} \end{bmatrix} \times \begin{bmatrix} \text{marginal} \\ \text{product of} \\ \text{raising revenue} \\ \text{from those} \\ \text{regulated} \end{bmatrix} = \begin{bmatrix} \text{marginal} \\ \text{opposition} \\ \text{from increased} \\ \text{taxes} \end{bmatrix} \qquad \textbf{(21.1)}
$$

$$[1] \qquad \times \qquad [2] \qquad = \qquad [3]$$

This is easily seen in Figure 21.2. The initial incremental, or marginal, benefits are high because of the high number of potential beneficiaries (term 1), and because considerable wealth is available to be transferred (term 2). The initial opposition, measured

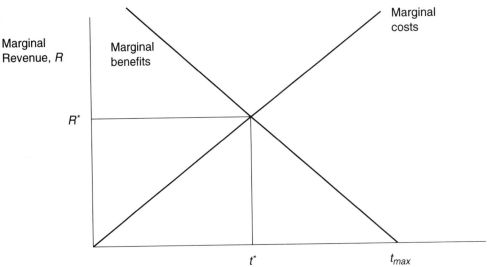

FIGURE 21.2 The Regulator's Optimum Level of Regulation.

in dollar terms, may be small because the taxes are small; that is, the regulation is not onerous.

As the tax rate rises, the marginal benefits fall for two reasons. There may be fewer supporters to attract (term 1), and the taxation or regulation may be reducing the wealth left for the beneficiaries to tax (term 2). At the same time, opposition to the tax (regulation) is growing because of the increased tax level. The regulator's optimum occurs where the marginal benefits from increasing the tax equal the marginal costs at tax rate t^* and expected marginal revenue, R^*.

Note that as long as the left-hand side of equation 21.1 is positive, the expected marginal transfer from those who are regulated to the beneficiaries increases (up to the point t_{max} in Figure 21.2). However, the successful regulator will stop short of t_{max}, because "excessive" regulation may compromise his or her majority.

Remember, also, that the potential beneficiaries seek transfers of wealth. The two terms on the left-hand side of equation 21.1 suggest that regulation will be sought if there is a large group of supporters (term 1) *or* if there is a smaller, well-organized group that perceives large expected gains (term 2). Thus, one may see regulations imposed that benefit relatively small but well-organized groups of potential gainers.

While this analysis does not negate the economic arguments in favor of regulation, it provides some sobering insights into how regulations may be implemented. Regulators may well respond to similar economic incentives as do other economic men and women. The resulting regulations, although possibly addressing issues of economic efficiency, most likely will reflect the particular preferences of the beneficiaries, moderated by the opposition of those who stand to lose under the regulations.

Antitrust

We have addressed the issues of regulating monopolistic firms, as well as trying to make them act like competitors. As third form of regulation attempts to keep monopolies from forming. This is typically referred to as antitrust policy. The discussion of federal antitrust law in the United States appropriately begins with the Sherman Act. This act was passed in 1890 and followed widespread perceptions of abuse of consumers in several industries as a result of trust arrangements. In a trust, a central board votes all the stock of the members of the trust. The best-known was the Standard Oil Trust organized by John D. Rockefeller. It was able to monopolize the markets for crude and refined oil, achieving a 90 percent share, by combining more than 100 firms into the trust.

The Sherman Act has two main sections. Section 1 specifies that "every contract, combination in the form of a trust or otherwise, or conspiracy, in restraint of trade . . . is declared to be illegal." The main target of Section 1 is price fixing and market division. Under Section 2, "every person who shall monopolize, or attempt to monopolize, . . . shall be deemed guilty of a felony."

Because enforcement of the Sherman Act was a problem, and specific antitrust practices were not stated, two additional actions by Congress strengthened the antitrust laws. The Clayton Act, first passed in 1914, addressed certain practices such as price discrimination (when the price discrimination restrains trade), interlocking directorates, mergers, and joint ventures. The Federal Trade Commission Act, also passed in 1914, created an independent agency to help enforce the laws. The act also addressed "unfair" methods of competition and "unfair" practices such as false advertising. Other legislation has

been passed since then, including the Robinson-Patman Act in 1936, which modified the price discrimination provision of the Clayton Act. The Celler-Kefauver Antimerger Amendment in 1950 focused especially on vertical mergers (a type of merger that occurs, for example, when a firm merges with the firm or firms that are used to supply its inputs).

ENFORCEMENT

The federal antitrust laws are enforced by two agencies. One, the Antitrust Division of the Department of Justice (DOJ), was formed in 1903. The DOJ alone has the power to seek criminal charges. Shortly after its creation, it launched a major wave of "trust-busting," culminating with the breakup of the Standard Oil and American Tobacco companies following court decisions in 1911.

The second agency is the Federal Trade Commission, an independent agency with exclusive jurisdiction over the FTC Act. Because the resources of the two agencies are small, they are selective about the cases they pursue. Their strategy is to deter anticompetitive behavior and clarify the application of antitrust laws by seeking precedent-setting reviews.

EXEMPTIONS

It is well-known that professional baseball and labor unions have received special exemptions from federal antitrust laws. Many other industries are at least partially exempt. These include agriculture, fishing, the many regulated industries, and national defense contractors. In addition, there are some important limits relevant to the health industries.

First, federal antitrust applies only to entities involved in interstate or foreign commerce; thus, many firms are excluded. On the surface, it would appear also that many health care providers, such as hospitals and physicians, are immune from federal antitrust because their activities affect mainly local, within-state markets. However, the courts have ruled that it is sufficient to show that the seller is receiving substantial reimbursement from Medicare (or other out-of-state payers) or purchasing supplies from out-of-state vendors. As a result of this interpretation, there is a broad applicability of federal antitrust laws to health care markets.[17]

Nevertheless, two important exemptions, though not unique to health care, are particularly important in health care antitrust. The McCarran-Ferguson Act of 1945 exempts the insurance industry to the extent that it is regulated by state law. With the monopsony power enjoyed by Blue Cross and Blue Shield in many states, a broad interpretation of this exemption would give the Blues and other insurers a free hand in exercising that power. The courts, however, have narrowed this exemption by carefully defining insurance activities and eliminating antitrust protection for the many non-insurance activities that may be undertaken by insurance companies.

The second exemption is referred to as the Noerr–Pennington doctrine. Through two decisions handed down by the Supreme Court, private parties and professional organizations have broad immunity from antitrust for lobbying activities, even where those lobbying activities lead to anticompetitive legislation. For example, lobbying ef-

[17]See *Summit Health, Ltd. v. Pinhas*, 59 U.S.L.W. 4493.

forts designed to tighten licensure requirements or limit the scope of practice allowed for other groups of providers could be protected under Noerr–Pennington *even though the legislation reduces competition.* This doctrine is especially important in health care as a result of the intense political lobbying by professional and trade associations. It is also worthwhile to note that the Noerr–Pennington doctrine is based on First Amendment Constitutional law, which provides for guarantees to freedom of speech. The fact that it is tied to Constitutional grounds gives the doctrine even more force than is usually the case regarding antitrust law.[18] First-Amendment protection also has been extended to professional advertising, which we will discuss shortly, so that advertising freedoms have a force beyond antitrust and competitive grounds.

Because the basic premise of antitrust policy points toward competition with its result of pricing at marginal cost, it is useful to address a potential criticism that relates to health insurance. Figure 21.3 revisits the issue of insurance-induced moral hazard. We find that because of coinsurance, the demand curve has rotated from D to D_1, leading the amount of medical services to increase from the optimum at Q_{opt}, where marginal benefit equals marginal cost, to Q_I. Triangle ABS represents the welfare loss due to moral hazard.

Suppose, however, that the health care is monopolistically provided. Here the monopolist optimizes where marginal cost equals marginal revenue, MR_I, and provides Q_M (at price P_M). There are now two market imperfections: the insurance-induced moral hazard, which potentially leads to an overprovision of services, and the monopoly provision of services, which potentially leads to an underprovision as noted by triangle ACT. Economic theory suggests that in the presence of an existing market imperfection (moral hazard), imposing marginal cost pricing may not be optimal.[19]

This would occur if the demand were such that point C lay to the right of point A. Imposing competition would induce more production and a larger welfare loss. As it turns out, because $Q_M < Q_{opt}$, imposing some competitive framework in the form of antitrust legislation is economically optimal if it moves the quantity provided toward level Q_{opt}.

MEASURING MONOPOLY POWER

Perhaps the most natural measure of monopoly power, yet the most difficult to implement, is a direct comparison of the price to the marginal cost. The eminent economist Abba Lerner (1943) proposed the following measure d of monopoly power.

$$d = (P - MC)/P = 1 - (MC/P)$$

where P = market price and MC = marginal cost. Clearly, in the theoretical limit under perfect competition, $d = 0$ because price equals marginal cost. Because MC is in theory less than price when monopoly exists, then d will increase and will approach 1 if MC is low relative to price.

Lerner's measure is elegant, and it captures the essence of monopolistic behavior and its economic inefficiencies very well. Unfortunately, it is difficult if not impossible in many cases to measure marginal cost, especially for the modern multiproduct firm

[18]However, even Noerr–Pennington could be negated if it is used as a "sham" to cover up intentions to harm competitors.

[19]This is known as the "theory of the second best," as referred to in chapter 19. The classic reference is Lipsey and Lancaster (1956).

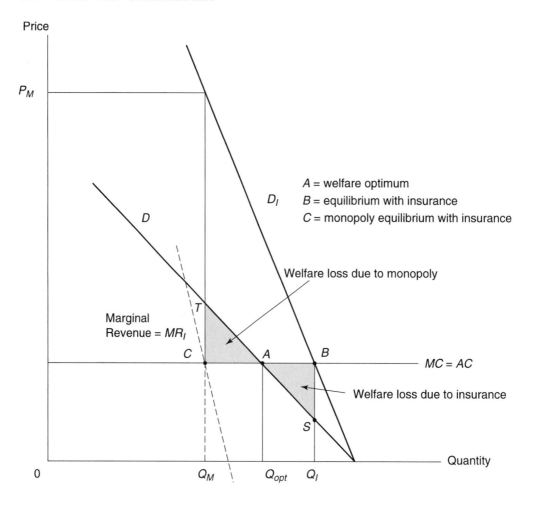

FIGURE 21.3 Welfare Optimum in the Presence of Insurance and Regulation.

with its complicated production processes. Consequently, economists also have developed other measures that may indicate market power.

Concentration Ratios

One widely used measure of market monopolization is the concentration ratio. Concentration ratios describe the percentage of total industry sales accounted for by the largest firms in an industry. The logic behind this approach is the premise that the greater the market share held by a few firms, the more likely it is that firms are colluding. The concentration ratio itself does not indicate inefficiency (as does a gap between price and marginal cost), but high concentration ratios offer a greater possibility that firms collude to engage in anticompetitive behavior.

The maximum value for a concentration ratio is 100 in the case of a monopoly. Often, the four-firm concentration ratio (i.e., share accounted for by the four largest

firms) is used. A four-firm concentration ratio of 80 percent indicates more monopoly power than, for example, a four-firm concentration ratio of 10 percent. What is useful about concentration ratios is that they are much easier to calculate than the Lerner measure, and one can readily compare these ratios. They are used, for example, to study relationships between market concentration and profitability, or to study the impact of mergers and other changes in market structure.

The Herfindahl–Hirschman Index

A second measure of market monopolization, also relatively easy to compute, is known as the Herfindahl–Hirschman Index (HHI). This index calculates the sum of the squares of the market shares, expressed as a percent, held by each firm in an industry. The maximum value is 10,000 (i.e., 100^2), and the minimum approaches zero. The HHI is considered superior to the concentration ratio because it captures the size distribution of firms in that larger firms are given more weight.[20] The HHI often is used as a screening device to measure the competitive impact of mergers and takeovers. Under the Merger Guidelines issued by the Department of Justice (DOJ) in 1984, a market with an HHI value above 1,800 is considered "highly concentrated," while one below 1,000 is considered "unconcentrated."

An economic criticism of both the concentration ratio and HHI concepts argues that such indexes in themselves say little about competitive behavior. It is possible that some industries with few firms may compete vigorously, whereas others with many firms may not.[21] It is also critical to define the relevant geographic and product markets carefully. For example, one may see many hospitals within a given state, which would imply a low concentration ratio. However, if they are separated geographically, they may have monopoly power in the relevant geographic area or in the market for a particular service if it is impractical to receive that care at an alternative location. We will see later in this chapter how the definition of the relevant market is crucial in the practice of antitrust policy.

ANTITRUST PROCEDURES

In deciding whether anticompetitive behavior should be addressed under the Clayton or Sherman Acts, the courts and the enforcement agencies go through a fairly routinized sequence of steps.[22] Using hospital mergers as an example, the steps (following Miles, 1998) are:

1. Defining the relevant product market
2. Defining the relevant geographic market
3. Identifying the competitors in the relevant product/geographic market
4. Calculating the market shares of the competitors and Herfindahl–Hirschman concentration index
5. Calculating the merging firms' post-merger share and the post-merger Herfindahl–Hirschman index, and determining the likely competitive effect of the merger
6. Considering any factors that mitigate or exacerbate anticompetitive effects

[20]To illustrate, consider one industry in which the four largest firms each have a 20 percent share of the market and another in which one firm has 50 percent while the remaining three have 10 percent each. Both industries have a four-firm concentration ratio of 80, but the second industry has a much higher HHI index.

[21]These traditional measures of concentration also do not take into account the impact on competition of actual or potential entrants. Recently formulated theories of "contestable markets" suggest that a large number of existing firms is not necessary in order to have prices pushed toward marginal costs.

[22]This presentation is drawn from Gaynor and Vogt (1999).

In defining the relevant market, analysts must find the smallest group of products for which no close substitutes exist. A product is to be included in the relevant market if buyers easily could find a substitute for it in response to a price increase of the merging firms. In addition, a supplier is to be included in the relevant market if it does produce the same product or does not produce the relevant product currently but could easily come to produce it. DOJ's 1984 Merger Guidelines say that the relevant market, both product and geographic, is the smallest market in which the sellers, acting as a cartel, could implement profitably a "small but significant and nontransitory price increase." They later go on to say that, most often, this means a 5 percent increase for a period of at least one year.

Defining the relative geographic market has become critical. If a market is defined too narrowly, the true impact of a merger on market concentration will be overestimated. Conversely, a market that is defined too broadly will lead to an underestimate of the impact on the concentration of a merger.

The relevant geographic area for antitrust purposes, as defined in the DOJ's 1984 Merger Guidelines, is the smallest area in which buyers could not switch easily to providers elsewhere in order to escape attempts to exercise monopoly power. In effect, this definition revolves around the ability of producers to raise prices above competitive levels. This ability may be approached best by measuring the price elasticity of demand facing the producers in the market. Relatively low price elasticities increase the ability of producers to raise prices. Often, however, reliable measures, or even indirect evidence, of elasticity are not available, so the courts will look at a variety of approaches.

THE ELZINGA–HOGARTY CRITERION

One common standard for determining market areas involves measurements of product flows into and out of an area—an approach consistent with the economic concept of a market. Here, the work of Elzinga and Hogarty (1978) has been influential. The authors (EH) define a geographic market as one in which the outflow of goods to other areas is relatively small and the inflow (imports) from elsewhere is also relatively small.

The logic is simple. If producers exported significant amounts elsewhere, they could not raise prices without jeopardizing their external markets. Thus, those external markets must be included. Similarly, if imports are substantial, price increases would result in substitution of more imports. Therefore, the geographic markets supplying the imports must be included. Criteria of 75 percent and 90 percent were suggested; that is, both imports and exports must be less than 25 percent (10 percent) of the product flows. To satisfy, for example, the 90 percent criterion, hospitals must provide at least 90 percent of their services to patients residing in the market, and patients residing in the market must receive no more than 10 percent of their care from hospitals located in other market areas.[23]

Despite advances made by economists in defining markets, court decisions in merger cases have been contradictory. Some cases have accepted the EH method, while others have relied on various methods including ad hoc approaches such as defining markets by the 15-mile radius around a hospital. Thus, the law remains unsettled on this important issue.

Much of the analysis has involved hospital mergers. Two fundamental reasons for hospital mergers, and concerns about them, are:

[23]In addition, the EH criteria selected, whether 75 or 90 percent, are purely arbitrary. It may be more appropriate to focus on particular groups of services by DRG, for example, rather than on aggregated measures of hospital care.

1. Hospital services technology involves large fixed costs (we see very few 10-bed hospitals), which must be spread out over a large demand.
2. Assuming two identical hospitals, without mergers, one or both would go bankrupt, leaving a monopoly anyhow.

To reiterate the economics behind the rules and practices, consider Figure 21.4. In this figure, curve AC reflects average costs, and the representative hospital's service demand is D_h. If the representative hospital equates marginal revenues and marginal costs at point A, it loses money, because P_h (determined by the demand curve) is less than average cost AC_h. The loss is indicated by the box with height $(AC_h - P_h)$.

If the hospitals are allowed to merge, the demand curve facing the single hospital shifts to the right because there are more people to serve. It also becomes less elastic because the number of competitors is reduced. As drawn, the merged hospital equates marginal revenues and marginal costs at point B and earns a profit indicated by the box with height $(P_m - AC_m)$. Note, however, that this is achieved with a higher price, because

FIGURE 21.4 Potential Impacts of Hospital Mergers.

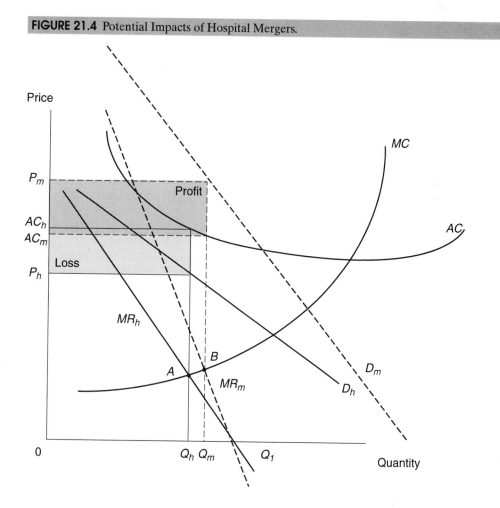

P_m exceeds P_h, and the Q_m of services provided by the newly monopolized hospital is far less than the amount $(2Q_h)$ that was provided by the two hospitals. Antitrust policy makers must address issues such as these.

Conclusions

This chapter discusses and analyzes specific regulatory mechanisms that have been introduced into the health care economy. Early regulatory mechanisms, including rate regulation, utilization review, and Certificate-of-Need programs, sought to control markets that seemed otherwise impervious to competitive forces. Rate regulation was somewhat effective in reducing expenses per admission, per day, and per capita; Certificate-of-Need regulation (addressing capital expenses) was largely ineffective; and utilization review was somewhat effective in reducing admissions, inpatient days, and expenditures. With the growth of managed care throughout the economy in the 1990s, utilization review has come to characterize almost all health delivery systems, whether they are formally regulated or not.

The imposition of prospective payment (PPS) in the 1980s can be interpreted as a form of regulation that promotes competition. We see how payment by DRG promotes a form of yardstick competition among monopolistic firms. Medicare's PPS has reduced length of stay in hospitals subject to the regulation but has not led to reduced quality of care or access to care. With the particular limitations on inpatient care, many large U.S. hospitals have come to face major financial challenges, and analysts will be monitoring governmental responses to the considerable political pressure to adjust reimbursement rates.

In the 1990s, interest in antitrust approaches toward regulation has been renewed. Regulators continue to face the trade-off between the potentially increased efficiency of larger-scale firms, at the potential cost of decreased competition and higher prices for the delivered services.

Summary

1. Economists feel that regulation often is needed when competitive market pressures are not present. One can categorize the policies as:
 - those that recognize the monopoly power and try to control it
 - those that try to make monopolistic firms act like competitors
 - those that attempt to prevent the accumulation of monopoly power
2. Regulation refers to the use of nonmarket means to affect the quality, price, or quantity of a good or service. Principal categories of regulation include fee controls and rate regulation, quantity and capacity controls, and quality controls.
3. Empirical findings on utilization review have tended to be inconclusive, although Wickizer, Wheeler, and Feldstein find that utilization review reduces admissions, inpatient days, and expenditures.
4. Studies of rate regulation suggest that this regulatory device is effective in reducing expenses per admission, per day, and per capita.
5. Studies of CON have tended to find it ineffective. Mayo and McFarland, in contrast, find that CON significantly lowered the number of beds, and consequently costs, of a single state studied.

6. The Medicare Prospective Payment System (PPS) based on DRGs predetermines a flat fee per case. Hospitals that exceed this rate suffer losses, while hospitals with case costs below the rate receive profits.

7. Medicare's PPS approximates yardstick competition. By setting the payment rates according to industry average marginal costs, yardstick competition induces the firms to choose the socially efficient level of cost-containment expenditure.

8. Medicare's PPS has reduced length of stay in hospitals subject to the regulation. It is doubtful that the regulation has led to reduced quality of care or access to care. Case-mix severity has increased post-PPS. Finally, while it is likely that the system has helped control Medicare's budget, it is unclear whether a reduction has occurred in per-capita costs.

9. Relative value scales (RVSs) originally were developed by state medical societies and other organizations as guides in establishing physician fees and reimbursement rates. The weights under the resource-based RVS (RBRVS) introduced under Medicare's physician payment reforms are determined by the inputs needed to provide procedures. These include physician work, practice expenses, and professional liability insurance.

10. Traditional economic descriptions depict regulation as a process in which the optimal policy is determined and imposed by an omniscient regulator. An alternative theory suggests that regulations result from political processes. Thus, the regulations will reflect the particular preferences of the beneficiaries, moderated by the opposition of those who stand to lose if the regulations are imposed.

11. Antitrust refers to the use of government policy or legislation aimed at deterring collusive arrangements and certain other practices that restrict competition.

12. The Lerner index is a measure of a firm's monopoly power. Concentration ratios and the Herfindahl–Hirschman index often are used to measure market monopolization.

Discussion Questions

1. Describe the major regulatory strategies that have been adopted in the United States.

2. How does prospective payment change the incentive to hospitals as compared to retrospective reimbursement? What predictions would one make as a result of the adoption of reimbursement based on DRGs?

3. Some argue that controls on some payers lead to a shift in cost to other payers (and that a one-payer system is needed). What evidence would suggest cost shifting to other third-party payers? What evidence suggests that not all the costs are shifted?

4. What is *regression to the mean?* How might this affect our evaluation of the efficacy of rate regulation?

5. CON legislation is designed to control costs by limiting capital expenditures. However, CON also may influence competition in the hospital market. Discuss at least two ways in which this might occur.

6. Under Shleifer's theory of yardstick competition, why does the firm have an incentive to reduce its costs? If all firms respond by reducing their costs, will the payment rate also subsequently fall?

7. What is the Medicare PPS program under DRGs? How has the Medicare PPS payment under DRGs affected hospital practices? Length of stay? Quality of care? Financial condition?

8. Does the Medicare PPS payment under DRGs reduce costs? Discuss.
9. Market power means that providers face downward-sloping demand curves. Give three examples of health services providers who have considerable market power. Give three examples of health services providers who have little or no market power.
10. Why is the determination of relevant markets so important to antitrust cases? Why will plaintiffs want narrow definitions and defendants want broad definitions?

Exercises

1. In Figure 20.1, suppose the demand for the good is summarized by the equation:

$$P = 100 - Q/2$$
$$MR = 100 - Q$$

and that the marginal cost equals the average costs at $10 per unit.
 a. Calculate the optimum market quantity in a competitive market. (Hint: Set price equal to marginal cost.)
 b. Calculate the quantity brought to market by the monopolist.
 c. Calculate the monopolist's profit.
 d. Calculate the deadweight loss to society from the monopoly.
2. Suppose that a hospital has a production function of the type:

$$Q = S^\alpha B^\beta$$

where Q is quantity of output, S is level of services, and B is number of beds, with α and β as parameters. The hospital buys S at price p_s and B at price p_b.
 a. If regulators force the hospital to decrease the amount of B by 10 percent, what must the hospital do to maintain quantity Q?
 b. If the hospital maintains quantity Q, what will be the effect of the regulation on total hospital expenditures? Why?
3. Suppose that Hospitals A through E have the following marginal costs for a given procedure:
 Hospital A—$1,000
 Hospital B—$1,200
 Hospital C—$800
 Hospital D—$1,700
 Hospital E—$1,300
 Calculate the yardstick price that would be assigned to each hospital. Which two hospitals will be assigned yardstick prices that do not cover their current marginal costs?
4. Suppose that the town of Greenville has three hospitals. Hospital A has a 30 percent market share, Hospital B has a 35 percent market share, and Hospital C has a 35 percent market share. Hospital A and Hospital B have proposed to merge. The government argues that the merger would constitute monopoly power, but the two hospitals disagree.
 a. Provide a clear argument in favor of the hospitals' position.
 b. Provide a clear argument in favor of the antitrust position.
5. Consider an industry with 6 firms with the following market shares.
 Firm A—40 percent
 Firm B—25 percent
 Firm C—12 percent

Firm D—12 percent
Firm E—7 percent
Firm F—4 percent
a. Compute the four-firm concentration ratio. What is the value of the HHI?
b. Suppose Firm D proposes to merge with Firm E. Calculate the new four-firm ratio and the new HHI.

22

Social Insurance

- ■ Social Insurance Policies and Social Programs
- ■ Historical Roots of Social Insurance
- ■ Medicare and Medicaid in the United States
- ■ The Effects of Medicare and Medicaid
- ■ National Health Insurance
- ■ Conclusions

Throughout this book, we have emphasized the role that markets can play in providing health care. We have also generally taken economic efficiency, provided in theory by perfectly competitive markets, as a standard against which to judge the costs and benefits of policies. In this chapter, we address instead the issues that arise when a society considers providing for health care by offering health insurance, to some significant degree, at the public's expense. Such insurance programs provided through taxes or regulations are called *social insurance programs*. Having earlier provided an overview of the rationales for social insurance in health care, we now turn to an examination of social insurance. We begin by considering the history of health care social insurance throughout the world, with some emphasis on the United States. We then examine Medicaid and Medicare and their effects, and close by examining prospects and issues for national health insurance in the United States.

Social Insurance Policies and Social Programs

We begin with a review of the types and characteristics of social insurance programs in health-related and other contexts. Social insurance programs can be discussed under five categories. While not mutually exclusive, these categories suggest distinctive aspects of the various programs. Programs of the following five types exist in the United States and in other countries.

TYPES OF PROGRAMS

1. **Poverty** The individual lacks purchasing power to buy the amounts of goods that are considered to provide the minimal standards of decent life. Programs that are directed toward persons experiencing poverty involve either the provision of cash, or more often the subsidized provisions of goods "in kind," such as rent vouchers or food stamps.

2. **Old Age** The individual has attained a certain age, generally coinciding with his or her retirement from active employment. Programs that are directed toward the elderly include income maintenance, such as Social Security, as well as services and considerations (such as old-age housing, Meals-on-Wheels) that may address the generally decreased mobility of the elderly.

3. **Disability** The person has either a temporary or permanent inability to work because of illness or has a work-related injury. Programs generally provide cash benefits. Disability programs were among the earliest social insurance programs available.

4. **Health** Programs cover illness or well-care financing and/or provide facilities for various segments of populations. In the United States, most programs are addressed to the elderly and/or poor. The individual's health care is financed either entirely or in part by the government. In other countries, governments have more direct involvement in the financing and delivery of health services for larger segments (or all) of the population.

5. **Unemployment** The person receives assistance because of a temporary loss of work due to economic considerations. Programs generally provide short-term cash benefits. In many countries, longer-term unemployment may lead into poverty-related welfare programs.

Several other definitions are useful in considering social insurance programs. Some programs, termed *entitlements,* are available to all who qualify. Food stamps, for example, are available to all households whose incomes fall below specified levels.[1] Medicaid, or financed health care for the poor (to be discussed in considerable detail later in this chapter), is also an entitlement program. Housing programs in the United States, in contrast, are not entitlements. Only limited numbers of subsidized units (on the supply side) or vouchers (on the demand side) are available.

Many programs are *means-tested;* that is, they are available only to individuals or households who meet certain income criteria. Households who receive aid for poverty-related problems may lose some or all of the aid if their incomes pass certain levels. This reduction in aid may have the unintended effect of discouraging efforts by low-income households to find jobs. This effect may occur because if poverty-related aid is reduced by a dollar for each dollar earned on the job, the job earnings are potentially taxed at rates approaching 100 percent.

[1]The determination of these specified levels may depend on income, family size, and geographic location. Such determinations often are related to political considerations.

Finally, the aid may take various forms. Often, it is tied to the purchase of certain items, such as food or housing. This procedure ensures that the people use the aid to buy items that the legislators have deemed important. Under certain circumstances, it may be more efficient to provide a cash subsidy rather than one in kind. Economists have long felt that it is cheaper, and therefore more efficient, to provide cash instead. Generally, such cash programs would make the recipient better off in his or her own eyes: Which would you prefer, $100 in cash or $100 worth of physician care? Legislators and the voting public, however, often seem to prefer that the subsidies be made in kind rather than in cash to control the purchases of those receiving the subsidies.

PROGRAM FEATURES

To characterize health-related social insurance programs in the United States and elsewhere, we discuss certain common features:

1. Contributions. These include taxes, deductibles, and coinsurance.
2. Benefits. Various benefit aspects can be discussed, including how much, who is included, and what types of treatment are included.
3. Length of coverage.
4. Means of reimbursement to providers.
5. Methods of determining payment levels to providers.

The first three items are related fundamentally to the receipt of care. The last two are related to the provision of care, as well as to the political problems involved in initiating plans.

Although supported by government, most social insurance plans are not without cost to the recipients. Many are funded by tax collections, and recipients of care often are also taxpayers. In some cases, the taxes in question may be regressive. A regressive tax is one for which lower-income people pay higher portions of their incomes to the tax than do richer people. In contrast, a progressive tax is one in which lower-income people pay lower portions of their incomes to the tax than do richer people.

Tax payments into the Social Security program have been somewhat regressive. Throughout most of the life of the program, the tax has been a constant percentage of wage income, up to some ceiling, at which point the marginal tax rate becomes zero. This means that on average, people in higher-income groups pay a smaller proportion of their income in payroll taxes; thus, the tax is regressive.[2]

To determine whether a social insurance program is redistributive in net—that is, whether it in net causes a transfer of money from the rich to the poor—one must consider not just the tax payments made but also the benefits received. For example, data for the Social Security program in the United States tend to show that Social Security is redistributive—that the poorer people in a given age group tend to gain more in net than do the rich.

In addition to tax payments, eligible recipients often must pay deductibles or coinsurance. Time costs with respect to paperwork, or waiting time for appointments or treatment, also must be considered.

[2] The Medicare tax rate is now 1.45 percent of all wage income. For 1999, the wage base for Social Security was 6.20 percent on a base salary of $72,600.

Levels of benefits and length of coverage are fairly similar to the workings of private insurance. Given the equity considerations of social insurance, political considerations may affect both. The determination of who and which treatments are covered is also important. Coverage of individuals may involve children and spouses. Coverage of treatments may mandate coverage of certain diseases (i.e., end-stage kidney disease) and exclude others (i.e., optometric or chiropractic services).

Health-related social insurance also has supply-related characteristics. Some expenses may be paid directly by the patient and may be reimbursed; others may be paid directly by the government to the provider. In some countries, all physicians who participate in the national health care program are government employees.

Historical Roots of Social Insurance

EUROPEAN BEGINNINGS

The United States and South Africa are often characterized as the only industrialized countries that lack a comprehensive health-related social insurance system. Experts identify the pioneering legislation for a system of compulsory national health insurance as that which started in Germany in 1883. National health insurance spread to other European countries at the end of the nineteenth and the early part of the twentieth centuries.

The German system and the other European systems were extensions of already-existing voluntary associations, which were often guild or mutual aid groups whose benefits to members included the pooling of insurable risks.[3] The political impetus for converting or merging voluntary local groups in a system of national coverage was often its usefulness as a stabilizing influence:

> Political discontent precipitated the introduction of social insurance in both Germany and England . . . In Germany, Bismarck introduced social rights to avoid granting wider political rights; in Britain, Lloyd George sought social rights within the context of existing rights to political participation. But both were basically defensive efforts to stabilize the political order. . . . (Starr, 1982, p. 239).

The German laws of 1883 set up a highly decentralized program covering workers in mining, transportation, construction, manufacturing, mechanical trades, and establishments using power machinery. Other countries followed. Austria (1888), Hungary (1891), Sweden (1891), Denmark (1892), and Belgium (1894) were early adopters of health insurance. With Spain's adoption of a plan in 1929, nearly every European country had enacted health insurance laws. Some were compulsory, as in Germany, but other countries, such as Belgium, Denmark, Sweden, and Switzerland, provided government subsidies to voluntary mutual funds.

The United Kingdom established its first social health insurance system in 1911. The 1911 legislation creating social insurance in Britain is of special interest because it helped to prepare for the British National Health Service that was adopted in 1946. Governmental provision of health care through a national health service system is most prominently exemplified in the Western countries by the United Kingdom.

[3]For more discussion, see Starr (1982) and Jensen and Cotter (1987).

Government provision was common in Eastern European countries and the former Soviet Union, which began its system in 1926. A more detailed examination and comparison of health insurance systems across countries are provided in chapter 23.[4]

EARLY EXPERIENCE IN THE UNITED STATES

Compared with the European countries, the United States was a latecomer to the provision of social insurance, and to the provision of governmental health insurance in particular. In the late nineteenth century and early twentieth century, the American experience was similar to that of Europe in that voluntary group purchasing arrangements, mutual benefit associations, and the like were common. However, in America the funding of these voluntary societies was not taken up by government, and from the advent of the German system in 1883 to the beginnings of the British system in 1911, governmental compulsory insurance for health care was not really an issue in the United States.

In the early years of the twentieth century, health insurance plans began to gain supporters. The American Association for Labor Legislation (AALL) supported such a plan, and the American Medical Association initially responded positively to health insurance proposals.[5] However, a political consensus was lacking, as evidenced by the fact that Samuel Gompers, president of the American Federation of Labor, opposed compulsory health insurance.

As the Great Depression approached, public attention to health issues was focused by the activities of the privately funded Committee on the Cost of Medical Care (CCMC). The most prominent recommendations of the committee supported group practice in the provision of medical care and the use of insurance, either private or tax supported, to pay for its costs. The flurry of minority reports and opposition by other groups indicated problems in achieving consensus, as stronger alliances both pro and con apparently were forming.

The major advent of social insurance legislation in the United States occurred in the midst of the Depression during the 1930s, through the Social Security program that began in 1935. Despite the social insurance thrust of the program and the reform-minded support for it, the legislation evidenced concessions to political opposition to the New Deal, including the omission of governmental health insurance. Starr notes that the omission of health insurance from the Social Security Act was by no means the Act's only conservative feature. It relied on a regressive tax and gave no coverage to some of the very poor, such as farm laborers and domestics.

The Roosevelt administration in the late 1930s investigated the needs for a national program in health care through the work of the Technical Committee on Medical Care. The committee recommended support of state-funded programs instead of a single national health insurance program. Though support seemed to gather for compulsory health insurance through the work of this committee and the succeeding National Health Conference, opposition, in part from the American Medical Association, convinced President Franklin Roosevelt to step back from such a plan.

Proponents of compulsory health insurance plans were not successful through the 1940s and 1950s. President Truman called for another national conference on health is-

[4]Gordon (1988, p. 201) provides a good overview of this topic.
[5]Much of the following material is treated in more detail by Starr (1982).

sues.[6] Truman proposed "a single health insurance system that would include all classes of the society, even those . . . not covered by Social Security" (Starr, p. 282). During the public debate over these issues, compulsory health insurance often was called *socialized medicine,* a term that greatly weakened its support during the political climate of the early years of the Cold War. Though Truman won the election in 1948, his success was never translated into a health insurance program.

THE ESTABLISHMENT OF MEDICARE AND MEDICAID

Throughout this time, however, there also was substantial and perhaps growing support for health insurance, in particular for governmental insurance aimed to support the health needs of the elderly. A compromise program sponsored by Senator Robert Kerr and Representative Wilbur Mills was passed in 1960; Kerr–Mills responded to the growing concern for unmet health insurance needs but was directed solely at the aged poor. Kerr–Mills used federal dollars to support state-based programs, but many states did not respond; three years after its passage, Kerr–Mills funding was not evenly spread because five large industrial states were receiving 90 percent of the funds.

The major social insurance programs for health care in the United States, Medicare and Medicaid, were passed during the Johnson administration. Johnson had supported health care for the aged, and by winning a landslide victory in the 1964 election, he was able to push for these programs. The political climate also had shifted somewhat in favor of such programs. Even so, the passage of the Medicare bill, in a form apparently more extensive than the President had even initially asked for, is a story of individuals interacting in a complex way. As Anderson (1990) says:

> How the bill that finally passed was put together is difficult to determine. It is unlikely that the chain of events and decisions could be reconstructed, even by the principals (p. 177).

The social insurance debate in the United States often ranged between those who believed in *voluntarism* and voluntary insurance, as won in negotiations between self-reliant industries and unions, and those who believed that only a compulsory insurance program would provide the insurance that was necessary for the larger population. The resolution of the debate in the form of Medicare and Medicaid can be said to have achieved widespread political support since the 1960s.

The fundamental concerns about Medicare and Medicaid stem from their rising costs. In the mid-1990s, with growing elderly and poor populations as well as continual health care cost inflation, the total costs of the social insurance programs were perceived by many to have grown out of control. Politicians sought to ensure that Medicare would have a sufficient trust fund to meet future needs, while balancing these needs against the increased taxes and payments for services necessary to support them.

The wider issue of social health insurance for the population as a whole cannot be said to be decided at this writing. The experience of 1993 to 1994 with the Clinton health plan, however, was a "massive political upheaval"[7] that must be studied in order to sketch possibilities for the future. The Clinton plan began with fairly positive reviews

[6]See O. Anderson (1990) for further discussion.
[7]The account in this paragraph comes from Skocpol (1995).

and public interest. Clinton was elected in 1992 on a plurality with a campaign promising health system reform. There had been signs of growing interest among the electorate in health system reform including social health insurance. The Clinton plan was drafted during January through May 1993 by a large task force made up of government officials, health policy experts, congressional staffers, and others. Many perceived the task force to be secretive. During the remainder of the year, a coalition of interests failed to form around clearly defined features of reform, while substantial interests, such as insurers, lobbied and advertised against the plan. During 1994, the plan was reworked to respond to critics. The public, however, seemed increasingly to believe that Clinton's plan would entail huge government bureaucracy, cost, and inefficiency. By the end of the summer of 1994, we had witnessed the resounding demise of the plan.

Will the U.S. government pass health reform including social health insurance in the near future? It can be said that many of the same cost and insurance issues are still with us. However, while there are new efforts for an incremental approach, the "whole cloth" approach of the early Clinton plan seems implausible for the foreseeable future.

Medicare and Medicaid in the United States

The two major health-related social insurance programs in the United States, Medicare and Medicaid, were enacted in 1965 after years of debate. Medicare is a national program that primarily provides compulsory hospital insurance to the elderly plus optional medical coverage to which nearly all elderly subscribe. In contrast, Medicaid is a program operated by the states with matching federal dollars; primarily provides health care coverage to categories of the poor.

MEDICARE

Medicare consists of two primary parts: Hospital Insurance, also known as Part A, and Supplementary Medical Insurance, also known as Part B. A third part of Medicare, sometimes known as Part C, is the Medicare+Choice program, which was established by the Balanced Budget Act of 1997 and became effective in January 1998. Beneficiaries must, however, have Medicare Part A and Part B in order to enroll in a Part C plan. When Medicare began on July 1, 1966, 19.1 million persons were enrolled in the program. In 1997, about 38 million were enrolled in one or both of Parts A and B of the Medicare program, and about 87 percent of all Medicare enrollees used some Part A and/or Part B service.

Medicare Coverage

Part A generally is provided automatically to persons age 65 and over who are entitled to Social Security or Railroad Retirement Board benefits. Similarly, those who have received such benefits based on their disability for a period of at least 24 months also are entitled to Part A benefits. Approximately 22 percent of these individuals received services covered by Part A during the year. The Part A benefits totaled $137.8 billion in 1997.

Medicare's Part A coverage includes:

- *Inpatient hospital care coverage,* requiring an initial deductible payment, plus co-payments for all hospital days following day 60 within a benefit period.

- *Skilled nursing facility (SNF) care,* which generally is covered by Part A only if it is within 30 days of a hospitalization of three or more days and certified as medically necessary.
- *Home Health Agency (HHA) care,* including care provided by a home health aide.
- *Hospice,* which is provided to those terminally ill persons with a life expectancy of six months or less and who elect to forgo standard Medicare benefits and receive only hospice care.

Supplementary Medical Insurance (Part B) benefits are available to almost all resident citizens age 65 and over. Part B coverage is optional and requires payment of a monthly premium. Part B covers physician services (in both hospital and nonhospital settings) as well as other services including clinical laboratory tests, diagnostic tests, ambulance services, and blood, which was not supplied by Part A. Almost all persons entitled to Part A also choose to enroll in Part B. In 1997, the Part B program provided benefits to about 36 million people.

Medicare+Choice (Part C) is another option whereby beneficiaries who have both Part A and Part B can choose to get their benefits through a variety of risk-based plans known as Part C of Medicare. The primary Medicare+Choice plans include *coordinated care plans,* which include Health Maintenance Organizations (HMOs), Provider-Sponsored Organizations (PSOs), Preferred Provider Organizations (PPOs), and other certified public or private coordinated care plans and entities that meet the approved, required standards as set forth in the law.

They also include medical savings accounts, which allow beneficiaries (initially up to 390,000) to enroll in a high-deductible plan (the maximum for 1999 equaled $6,000). After the deductible is paid, the MSA plan pays providers the lesser of 100 percent of specified expenses or 100 percent of the amounts that would have been payable under the original fee-for-service Medicare program. If extra money remains in the MSA, it can be used to pay for future medical needs and, subject to program rules, the remainder can be used for nonmedical purchases.

Program Financing

The Medicare Part A program is financed primarily through a mandatory payroll deduction (FICA tax). The FICA tax is 1.45 percent of earnings (paid by each employee and also by the employer) or 2.90 percent for self-employed persons. This tax is paid on all covered wages and self-employment income without limit.

The Medicare Part B program is financed through: (1) premium payments ($45.50 per month in 1999), which are usually deducted from the monthly Social Security benefit checks of those who are enrolled in Part B, and (2) through contributions from general revenue of the U.S. Treasury. Beneficiary premiums are currently set to cover 25 percent of the average expenditures for aged beneficiaries.

Beneficiary Payment Liabilities

Parts A and B beneficiaries are responsible for charges not covered by Medicare and for various cost-sharing features of the plans. These liabilities may be paid by the beneficiary, by a third party such as a private "medigap" insurance policy purchased by the beneficiary, or by Medicaid if the person is eligible. Medigap refers to private health insurance that, within limits, pays most of the health care service charges not covered by Parts A and B of Medicare.

For hospital care covered under Part A, the beneficiary's payment share includes a one-time deductible at the beginning of each benefit period ($768 in 1999). This covers the beneficiary's part of the first 60 days of each spell of inpatient hospital care. If continued inpatient care is needed beyond the 60 days, additional coinsurance payments ($192 per day in 1999) are required through the 90th day of a benefit period.

For Part B, the beneficiary's payment share includes one annual deductible (currently $100), the monthly premiums, the coinsurance payments for Part B services (usually 20 percent of the medically allowed charges), a deductible for blood, and payment for any services that are not covered by Medicare. For end-stage renal disease (ESRD) patients, Medicare Part B covers kidney dialysis and physician charges incurred by the patient and donor during the transplant and follow-up care.[8]

Medicare Summary

The Medicare program covers 95 percent of the U.S. aged population, plus many who are on Social Security because of disability. In 1997, Part A covered about 38 million enrollees at a cost of $137.8 billion, and Part B covered 36 million enrollees at a cost of $72.8 billion. Of those who were entitled to Medicare in 1997, about 87 percent used Part B services, while only 22 percent used the Part A services. The combined Part A and Part B benefit payments for all Medicare services in 1997 averaged about $6,300 per enrollee. Total Medicare disbursements for 1997 were $213.6 billion.

MEDICAID OVERVIEW

Medicaid, referring to Title XIX of the Social Security Act, is a federal–state matching entitlement program that pays for medical assistance for certain vulnerable and needy individuals and families with low incomes and resources. This program is the largest source of funding for medical and health-related services for America's poorest people. In 1996, it provided health care assistance to more than 36 million persons at a cost of $160 billion.

Within broad national guidelines established by federal statutes, regulations, and policies, each state: (1) establishes its own eligibility standards; (2)determines the type, amount, duration, and scope of services; (3) sets the rate of payment for services; and (4) administers its own program. Medicaid policies for eligibility, services, and payment vary considerably even among similar-sized and/or adjacent states, and the services provided by one state may differ considerably in amount, duration, or scope from services provided in a neighboring state.

Medicaid Eligibility

Medicaid does not provide medical assistance for all poor persons. Even under the broadest provisions of the federal statute, it does not provide health care services even for very poor persons unless they are in one of the designated groups. Low income is only one test for Medicaid eligibility for those within these groups; their resources also are tested against threshold levels (as determined by each state within federal guidelines).

States generally have broad discretion in determining which groups their Medicaid programs will cover and the financial criteria for Medicaid eligibility. To be eligible for

[8]For Part C, the beneficiary's payment share is based upon the cost-sharing structure of the specific Medicare+Choice plan selected. Each plan has its own requirements.

federal funds, however, states must provide Medicaid coverage for certain individuals who receive federally assisted income-maintenance payments, as well as for related groups not receiving cash payments. Although there is a long list, Medicaid "categorically needy" eligibility groups for which federal matching funds are provided to states include:

- Those meeting the requirements for the AFDC (Aid to Families with Dependent Children) program in effect in their state on July 16, 1996, or—at state option— more liberal criteria.
- Children under age six or pregnant women whose family income is at or below 133 percent of the federal poverty level (FPL).
- All children born after September 30, 1983, who are under age 19, in families with incomes at or below the FPL. (This feature phases in coverage so that by 2002, all such poor children under age 19 will be covered.)

The Scope and Duration of Medicaid Services

The Medicaid program allows considerable flexibility within the states' Medicaid plans. Indeed, some analysts examine varying state programs to determine how differing program features might work. However, a state's Medicaid program *must* offer medical assistance for certain basic services to most categorically needy populations, including inpatient hospital services, outpatient hospital services, prenatal care, vaccines for children, physician services, nursing facility services for persons aged 21 or older, and family planning services and supplies.

Within broad federal guidelines and certain limitations, states determine the amount and duration of services offered under their Medicaid programs. States may limit, for example, the number of days of hospital care or the number of physician visits covered. States *must* provide sufficient levels of services to achieve the purpose of the benefits, and benefits limits may not discriminate among beneficiaries based on medical diagnosis or condition.

Payment for Medicaid Services

States may impose nominal deductibles, coinsurance, or copayments on some Medicaid recipients for certain services, but certain Medicaid recipients, including pregnant women and children under age 18, are excluded from cost sharing. All Medicaid recipients must be exempt from copayments for emergency services and family planning services.

Medicaid is a cost-sharing partnership between the federal government and the states. The federal government pays a share of the medical assistance expenditures under each state's Medicaid program. That share, known as the Federal Medical Assistance Percentage (FMAP), is determined annually by a formula that compares the state's average per-capita income level with the national income average. States with higher per-capita income levels are reimbursed smaller shares of their costs. By law, the FMAP cannot be lower than 50 percent or higher than 83 percent. In 1997, the FMAPs varied from 50 percent (13 states and the District of Columbia) to 77.2 percent (Mississippi), with the average federal share among all states being 57.0 percent.

Medicaid Summary

Medicaid initially was formulated as a medical care extension of federally funded programs providing cash income assistance for the poor, with an emphasis on dependent children and their mothers, the disabled, and the elderly. Legislation in the late 1980s

assured Medicaid coverage to an expanded number of low-income pregnant women, poor children, and some Medicare beneficiaries who are not eligible for any cash assistance program. Legislative changes also focused on increased access, better quality of care, specific benefits, enhanced outreach programs, and fewer limits on services.

Most Medicaid recipients require relatively small average expenditures per person each year. The data for 1996 indicate that Medicaid payments for services for children (who constitute more than 46 percent of all Medicaid recipients) averaged only a little more than $1,000 per child.

Long-term care is an increasingly utilized provision as the population ages. Almost 50 percent of the total cost of nursing facility or home health services care for persons in the United States is paid for by Medicaid. The 1996 data show that Medicaid payments for nursing facility and home health care totaled $40.5 billion for more than 3.6 million recipients of these services—an average expenditure of more than $12,300 per long-term care recipient. With the elderly and/or disabled percentage of our population increasing faster than the younger groups, the need for long-term care is expected to increase.

The 1997 total expenditure for the nation's Medicaid program was $159.9 billion. With anticipated impacts from the Balanced Budget Act of 1997, analysts project total Medicaid outlays of $250 billion in fiscal year 2003.

THE MEDICAID–MEDICARE RELATIONSHIP

The Medicare and Medicaid programs work jointly for many beneficiaries. Medicare beneficiaries who have low incomes and limited resources also may receive help from the Medicaid program. For those eligible for full Medicaid coverage, the Medicare

FEATURE

Oregon Medicaid's Doctor-Assisted Suicide

Perhaps nowhere is the state-level autonomy in the U.S. Medicaid system more apparent than in the items that the various states choose to cover. In late February 1998, the state of Oregon's Health Services Commission voted 10 to 1 to include doctor-assisted suicide on the list of "treatments" covered for Medicaid patients, reported Peter Steinfels of the *New York Times.* This decision joined doctor-assisted suicide to other forms of "comfort care" for any "terminal illness, regardless of diagnosis."

Residents of Oregon voted twice, in 1994 and again in 1997, to legalize doctor-assisted suicide. However, neither vote dealt with the public financing of the procedure.

Dr. Alan Bates, who headed the Commission, acknowledged the divisive nature of the decision. He noted, however, that if dying people with private insurance could pay for medical help in taking their own lives, why should poor people be deprived of the same opportunity?

The federal government bars all federal support, direct or indirect, for assisted suicide. That means that Oregon must segregate carefully the medical services involved in assisting suicide and pay for them with the state's own dollars. Reporter Steinfels notes that in effect, the federal government is saying that taxpayers throughout the country should be spared "moral complicity" in Oregon's innovation.

Source: Steinfels, Peter, "Oregon Medicaid's Doctor-Assisted Suicide," *New York Times,* March 7, 1998, National/Metro Section.

health care coverage is supplemented by services that are available under their state's Medicaid program, according to eligibility category. These additional services may include, for example, nursing facility care beyond the 100-day limit covered by Medicare, prescription drugs, eyeglasses, and hearing aids. For persons enrolled in both programs, any services that are covered by Medicare are paid for by the Medicare program before any payments are made by the Medicaid program because Medicaid is always the "payer of last resort."

HCFA estimates that Medicaid provided some supplemental health coverage for 5.9 million persons who were Medicare beneficiaries for fiscal year (FY) 1995. Although they represent only 17 percent of the total Medicare enrollees, they accounted for 35 percent of the total Medicaid expenditures ($53 billion in FY 1995), including $10 billion for Medicare cost sharing, $5 billion for other acute care services and prescription drugs, and $38 billion for long-term care.

The Effects of Medicare and Medicaid

Though we can be certain about the provisions of Medicare and Medicaid, we are necessarily less certain about their effects. The effects are the more important research concern. We consider here a selection of findings on what is known about the effects of Medicare and Medicaid on:

- Health care costs
- Access to health care
- Health status

COSTS AND INFLATION

The implementation of Medicare and Medicaid coincided with a considerable increase in health care costs in the United States. While health care costs had been rising before 1965, both in simple percentage terms and in comparison to the general rate of inflation, the hospital care inflation rate increased somewhat after the implementation of Medicare and Medicaid.

The expenditure levels of the two programs increased much more rapidly than most people had expected. Table 22.1 shows the pattern of expenditures over time. As shown, the percentage increases in expenditures on both programs were in double digits for most of the years. Even accounting for the substantial rate of inflation since the late 1960s, Medicare outlays increased by a factor of 13 from 1975 to 1997, and Medicaid outlays by a factor of 12 over the same period.

Clearly, also, the populations at risk grew for both Medicare and Medicaid. The number of Medicare enrollees grew at a compounded rate of 2.3 percent—a number that included disabled enrollees beginning in 1973. This rate exceeded population growth and can be attributed in part to the aging of the population. Growth in the enrollee population often is cited as the primary reason for growth in Medicaid payments. Responding to the availability of Medicaid, which provided cost sharing for many programs, many states changed their needs standards for several types of programs, allowing more families to qualify for cash assistance. There was additional publicity for Medicaid programs, and additional states initiated Medicaid programs.

TABLE 22.1 Personal Health Expenditures under Medicare and Medicaid

	Medicare			Medicaid		
Year	Enrollment	Expend.	Percent Increase	Enrollment	Expend.	Percent Increase
1966	19.1	1.8	—	—	1.3	—
1967	19.5	4.9	167.6	—	3.2	140.8
1968	19.8	6.2	26.3	—	3.6	12.7
1969	20.1	7.1	13.3	—	4.2	17.9
1970	20.5	7.7	8.9	—	5.3	26.8
1971	20.9	8.5	10.0	—	6.7	26.6
1972	21.3	9.4	10.5	17.6	8.4	24.1
1973	23.5	10.8	15.1	19.6	9.5	13.3
1974	24.2	13.5	25.1	21.5	11.1	17.5
1975	25.0	16.4	21.6	22.0	13.5	21.4
1976	25.7	19.8	20.5	22.8	15.2	13.0
1977	26.5	23.0	16.2	22.8	17.5	15.0
1978	27.2	26.8	16.5	22.0	19.5	11.5
1979	27.9	31.0	16.0	21.5	22.4	14.7
1980	28.5	37.5	20.9	21.6	26.1	16.6
1981	29.0	44.9	19.6	22.0	30.4	16.2
1982	29.5	52.5	16.9	21.6	32.1	5.7
1983	30.0	59.8	13.9	21.6	35.3	10.0
1984	30.5	66.4	11.2	21.6	38.2	8.3
1985	31.1	72.1	8.5	21.8	41.3	7.9
1986	31.7	76.8	6.6	22.5	45.5	10.4
1987	32.4	82.7	7.6	23.2	50.4	10.7
1988	33.0	90.1	8.9	22.9	55.1	9.3
1989	33.5	102.4	13.7	23.5	62.3	12.9
1990	34.1	111.5	8.9	25.2	75.4	21.1
1991	34.8	121.1	8.6	28.3	93.9	24.6
1992	35.5	136.2	12.4	30.9	106.4	13.2
1993	36.2	148.7	9.2	33.4	121.7	14.5
1994	36.9	166.9	12.2	35.0	134.6	10.5
1995	37.5	184.2	10.4	36.3	146.1	8.6
1996	38.1	200.3	8.7	36.1	154.1	5.5
1997	38.4	213.6	6.6	33.6	159.9	3.8
1998	—	213.2	−0.2	—	—	—

Note: Percentage increases for 1967 are so large because 1966 was a partial year for the beginning of the programs. Enrollments are in millions; expenditures are in billions.

Source: HCFA Tables.

Why Spending Has Risen—Increased Coverage, Technological Improvement, and Increased Inefficiency

The increase in the population that is eligible and covered by Medicare and Medicaid clearly helps explain why program expenditures have risen, but it does not fully account for the inflationary effects that these programs could have. Newhouse (1978) suggests three ways through which insurance programs such as these could affect prices and costs, even without growth in the population served.

First, Medicare and Medicaid both tended to increase the insurance coverage of the populations eligible. An increase in insurance has expansionary effects on the demand for care.

Figure 22.1 reviews this theoretical effect. Start at point *A,* where quantity of service, Q_0, is provided at price (or cost), P_0. When the increase in insurance coverage reduces the portion of the bill paid by the eligible recipient, the demand for care rotates outward to the right from D_1 to D_2. In Figure 22.1, price rises to P_1 and quantity consumed increases to Q_1, or point *B.* Total expenditures rise from P_0Q_0 to P_1Q_1.

Newhouse explains, however, that these social insurance programs may have additional effects. He proposes that insurance coverage may induce technological improvements. If more costly technological improvements are induced by these social insurance programs, then the cost per unit of care may rise.

Finally, Newhouse proposes a third theory for the effect of insurance on costs and quantity used. This may be called the "increased inefficiency" theory. The idea is that when insurance covers a substantial portion of the health care bill, institutions such as hospitals have less incentive to control costs. It is not clear from this theory that the advent of Medicare and Medicaid, for example, would cause the level of inefficiency in hospitals to increase over time, but such a pattern is at least consistent with the theory.

The Evidence

What do we know about the patterns of health expenditure inflation subsequent to the adoption of Medicare and Medicaid, and what do we know about the sources of this inflation? One approach to answering these questions is to partition the observed rise in expenditures into its logical components: changes in population, in quantity per capita, and in the nature of services provided per visit or per admission.

The 1985 *Economic Report of the President* reported that general inflation was responsible for slightly more than half of the inflation in hospital spending between 1971 and 1981, but hospital input prices increased an additional 11.7 percent more than general inflation. Population growth was a lesser factor, contributing 7.2 percent during that

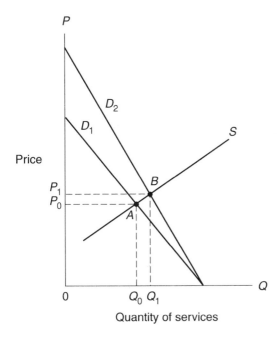

FIGURE 22.1 Cost Impact of Increased Insurance Coverage.

period, whereas growth in admissions per capita contributed 8.6 percent and, importantly, real expenses per admission, 20.8 percent. The growth in real expenses per admission is especially noteworthy because it tends to reflect technological changes.

A more recent analysis by Cutler and Meara (1997) addresses the problem more directly. These researchers found a dramatic change in medical spending over time, and disproportionately so for the very young (those less than 1 year old) and the old (those age 65 or over). From 1963 through 1987, per-person spending on infants increased by 9.8 percent per year, and per-person spending on the elderly increased by 8.0 percent per year (compared to 4.7 percent per year for the others).

Moreover, they find that essentially all of the disporportionate growth of spending for the very young and the old is accounted for by high-cost users within those groups, and that a substantial amount of high-cost medical use is associated with the increasing technological capabilities of medicine. Among infants, high-cost users are premature babies with substantial respiratory or other acute conditions. For the elderly, high-cost users are generally patients with severe cardiovascular problems or cancer.

These data are consistent with the Newhouse theories, but they do not address the theories directly.[9] It seems likely that technological change has played a substantial role. However, the evidence is not precise, and we must conclude that while we have a fairly clear understanding of how social insurance programs like these could affect price and use rates, we are not equally certain about the magnitudes of the effects.

Irrespective of the considerable costs, the predominant evidence seems to suggest that both Medicare and Medicaid have succeeded in addressing the problems of access to which they have been directed. That there was a change in health care use rates among the lower-income groups and the elderly following the beginning of Medicare and Medicaid is evident from the data.

Table 22.2 investigates two dimensions of health care access and utilization: the interval since the last physician contact, and the number of hospital discharges per 1,000 population. In 1964, just prior to the passage of Medicare and Medicaid, 69.7 percent of those aged 65 and older had seen a physician within the past year. This was 4.2 percent higher than the general population and 8.1 percent higher than the group aged 45 to 64. By 1990, those aged 65 and older were 11.4 and 12.7 percent more likely than the respective comparison groups to have seen a physician within a year.

Another measure of access for the elderly involves hospital discharges per 1,000 population. In 1964, those aged 65 and older had 190.0 compared with 146.2 for the group aged 45 to 64, or a 30 percent differential. By 1990, the differential had grown to 83.3 percent, and by 1995 to 118.1 percent.

Similar comparisons are appropriate when comparing the less affluent to the more affluent. In 1964, those with incomes less than $15,000 were 79.6 percent as likely to have seen a physician in the past year as those with incomes higher than $50,000. By 1990, they were 94.6 percent as likely.

In 1964, those with incomes less than $15,000 had 102.4 hospital discharges per 1,000, compared with 110.7 discharges for those with incomes higher than $50,000, or only 92.5 percent as many. By 1990, the lower-income people had 96.1 percent more discharges per 1,000 people, and by 1995 they had 128.4 percent as many.

[9]See Newhouse's own (1988) econometric study for further detail.

TABLE 22.2 Indirect Impacts of Medicare and Medicaid

A. Age Comparisons

Interval since last physician contact

	Percent less than 1 year			Age 65+ relative to:		
	1964	*1990*	*1995*	*1964*	*1990*	*1995*
Total	66.9	78.2	79.5	1.042	1.114	1.132
Age 45–64	64.5	77.3	79.9	1.081	1.127	1.126
Age 65+	69.7	87.1	90.0			

Hospital discharges per 1,000

	1964	*1990*	*1995*	*1964*	*1990*	*1995*
Total	109.1	91.0	86.2	1.742	2.734	3.096
Age 45–64	146.2	135.7	122.4	1.300	1.833	2.181
Age 65+	190.0	248.8	266.9			

B. Income Comparisons

Interval since last physician contact

	Percent less than 1 year			Income <$15,000 relative to:		
	1964	*1990*	*1995*	*1964*	*1990*	*1995*
Total	66.9	78.2	79.5	0.876	0.988	0.984
Income <$15,000	58.6	77.3	78.2			
Income >$50,000	73.6	81.7	83.5	0.796	0.946	0.937

Hospital discharges per 1,000

	1964	*1990*	*1995*	*1964*	*1990*	*1995*
Total	109.1	91.0	86.2	0.939	1.563	1.632
Income <$15,000	102.4	142.2	140.7			
Income >$50,000	110.7	72.5	61.6	0.925	1.961	2.284

Source: Derived from *Health United States* (1998), Tables 77 and 87.

Clearly, many other factors in the health care system have changed in the 30 plus years since the enactment of Medicare and Medicaid. One might ask whether the poor *overuse* inpatient care, seeking hospital emergency care instead of more appropriate outpatient care. Nonetheless, by these gross measures, the poor and the elderly have improved their access dramatically in the last 30 years, with no inconsiderable boost from Medicare and Medicaid.

We also can learn something about the effects of the two programs by examining data on the out-of-pocket expenditures of eligible recipients. Table 22.3 reports these figures, comparing 1966 (pre-Medicare and Medicaid) and 1984. As shown in Subtable A, out-of-pocket expenditures were reduced sharply after the programs as a percentage of total expenditure. However, expenditures out of pocket by persons age 65 or older as a percentage of income and beneficiary liabilities as a share of total health expenditures have been held fairly constant since the beginning of the programs (Subtables B and C).

These data on use rates and financial access to care, however, leave at least one question unanswered. Would we find that these social insurance programs increased access to care in a study that controlled, among other things, for the level of health status or health care need, rather than just comparing data before and after the event?

TABLE 22.3 Three Ways to Measure the Health Care Expenditure Burden for the Elderly under Medicare

Subtable A: Per-Capita Personal Health Care Expenditures for Persons 65 Years or Older, by Source of Funds: Fiscal Year 1966 and Calendar Year 1984

Source of Funds	1966		1984	
	Amount	*Percent*	*Amount*	*Percent*
Per capita	$445	100.0	$4,202	100.0
Out of pocket	237	53.2	1,059	25.2
Private insurance	71	15.9	304	7.2
Other private	5	1.1	16	0.4
Medicare	—	—	2,051	48.8
Medicaid	—	—	536	12.8
Other government	133	29.8	236	5.6

Source: Gornick et al. (1985).

Subtable B: Mean Out-of-Pocket Health Costs as a Percent of Income for Persons 65 Years of Age or Older, Selected Years, 1966–1984

Year	Mean Out-of-Pocket Expenditures	Mean Personal Income	Out-of-Pocket as a Percent of Income
1966	$ 300	$ 2,000	15
1977	690	5,592	12
1981	1,187	8,639	14
1984	1,575	10,615	15

Source: Gornick et al. (1985).

Subtable C: Estimated Beneficiary Liabilities: 1985–1994

Year	Beneficiary Liability ($ billion)	Program Payments ($ billion)	Beneficiary Share of Total Payments
1985	$13.5	$ 70.3	16.2%
1986	15.4	75.7	16.9
1987	16.8	80.5	17.2
1988	18.0	88.5	16.9
1989	17.4	99.8	14.8
1990	21.4	109.0	16.4
1991	22.7	121.2	15.8
1992	23.4	134.2	14.8
1993	30.6	149.1	17.0
1994	31.4	166.1	15.9
1995	33.2	185.2	15.2

Source: Medicare and Medicaid Guide, No. 858, June 15, 1995, Table 3-4, p. 67. MEDPAC, Report to Congress. Chapter 1, June 1999.

The answer to this question appears to be yes. Davis and Reynolds (1976) examine the effect of access to these public assistance programs in a statistical context that controls for other factors. For people with the same health status, they compare average health care use by those eligible for assistance with those low-income people not receiving assistance. Examine Table 22.4 excerpted from their study. These data indicate a fairly strong impact of improved financial access on care.

These data, however, do not resolve a perhaps more important question: Have the inequalities in use rates between the low-income and the high-income groups been reduced? The difficulty in assessing inequalities in use rates between the low-income and high-income groups lies in the fact that lower-income groups tend to be sicker. Are use rates equal after adjusting for health status?

This issue is disputed in the literature, but the relevant evidence has been reviewed by Starr (1986, pp. 117–118). He concludes that the poor show significantly lower levels of physician use at comparable levels of health and disability, and that the age-adjusted number of physician visits per 100 bed-disability days proved to be 80 percent higher among higher-income whites than among whites below the poverty level.

Before concluding the discussion on access to health care, we should identify a characteristic of access specific to the Medicaid program. Because Medicaid is state operated, as we have noted, characteristics vary somewhat across the nation. As recently as 1987, Medicaid was fundamentally restricted to children in very low-income, single-parent families. Since then, a series of legislative initiatives has extended Medicaid more broadly among children. By 1996, all pregnant women and all children under age 6 who had family incomes below 133 percent of the poverty line, and all children age 13 and younger with family incomes below 100 percent of the poverty line, were eligible for Medicaid. Coverage will continue to be phased in for all children born after September 1983 until poor children of all ages are covered.[10]

The net result is that the proportion of the child population enrolled in Medicaid increased from 15.7 percent in 1989 to 23.2 percent in 1995. For children under the age of 6, the percentage grew from 20.3 to 29.6.

Interestingly enough, at the same time that Medicaid eligibility has increased, there has been a reduction in children's private insurance coverage. There are two plausible

TABLE 22.4 Annual Predicted Utilization for Low-Income Persons by Health Status and Welfare Eligibility, Adjusted for Other Characteristics, 1969

	Health Status					
	Public Assistance Recipients			*Other Low-Income Persons*		
	Good	*Average*	*Poor*	*Good*	*Average*	*Poor*
Physician visits	4.09	4.95	7.10	2.29	3.36	5.12
Hospital admissions	0.14	0.16	0.21	0.09	0.11	0.15
Hospital days	2.40	2.72	3.47	1.18	1.42	2.04

Source: Davis and Reynolds (1976).

[10]Further discussion on this issue is contained in the *Economic Report of the President* 1998, pp. 104–109.

reasons. First, the 1990s saw a leveling off in the variety and generosity of employer-provided health insurance, affecting both low- and high-income households. To the extent that lower-income households have been affected disproportionately by changes in job-related insurance, they may have substituted Medicaid. Second, newly eligible families may have voluntarily dropped private insurance coverage in order to enroll in Medicaid.

Coincident with the expansion of Medicaid since the late 1980s, analysts have seen an increase in physician contacts for the poorest segment of the population. Table 22.5 shows the access to physicians over a 6-year period. Those in good or excellent health increased their average number of contacts by 11.1 percent, and those in fair or poor health increased their average number of contacts by 31.5 percent. Although increased federal coverage under Medicaid comes with increased state matches, Medicaid scholars have noted that unlike cash assistance welfare, health care is viewed as a "positive good" that everyone should receive. Holahan, Wiener, and Wallin (1998, p. 58) note that "declining Medicaid caseloads are matters of concern for state officials while falling cash welfare caseloads are matters of pride."[11]

HEALTH STATUS

The ultimate question regarding Medicare and Medicaid is whether or not these programs improve the health status of the eligible populations. This question is a specific application of the production function of health. Early econometric studies of the effects of health care on mortality rates suggested small and insignificant effects. The Rand Health Insurance Experiments, with their randomized format, found little or no effect on health status in most cases for increased health care consumed by people with better insurance coverage. Into the mid-1980s, the evidence seemed to weigh against the belief that health care made a significant difference in the health status of populations generally, and the insured populations in particular.

However, studies from the mid-1980s on have found important evidence to the contrary. Hadley's studies (1982, 1988) focus on the role of Medicare expenditures. He finds a significant impact of Medicare on mortality rates, and this health care provides incremental benefits that exceed the incremental costs (i.e., it is cost beneficial). Hadley also

TABLE 22.5 Average Number of Physician Contacts in Last Year for Children under Age 15 by Family Income

Family Income	Good/Excellent Health			Fair/Poor Health		
	1987–89	*1993–95*	*Percent Change*	*1987–89*	*1993–95*	*Percent Change*
Below poverty line	3.6	4.0	11.11	10.8	14.2	31.48
Poverty line to twice poverty line	3.8	3.9	2.63	15.2	16.2	6.58
Above twice poverty line	5.0	4.9	−2.00	22.6	20.7	−8.41

Source: Derived from Table 3-7, *Economic Report of the President* 1998.

[11]For a detailed look at Medicaid policies and practices in 13 states, see Holahan, Wiener, and Wallin (1998).

finds a stronger impact of Medicare expenditures for population subgroups including blacks whose lower-than-average health status has been of public concern.

Recent work also has evaluated the impacts of selected Medicaid programs. Reichman and Florio (1996) use a health production framework to evaluate race-specific effects of participation in New Jersey's HealthStart (Medicaid) program on birthweight and on newborn hospitalization costs in 1990. The results were mixed. Black participants had increased birthweights and lower hospitalization costs, but no evidence was found of improved birth outcomes or lower costs for whites.

Favorable impacts also must be measured against their incremental costs. Currie and Gruber (1996) measure the impacts of increased Medicaid eligibility (throughout the United States) for pregnant women between 1979 and 1992. Certain groups saw substantial improvements. For example, a 30-percentage-point increase in eligibility among 15- to 44-year-old women was associated with a decrease in infant mortality of 8.5 percent. However, even the most carefully targeted changes in Medicaid eligibility cost the Medicaid program $840,000 per infant life saved, raising important questions of cost effectiveness. In a similar study, Joyce (1999) finds reductions in newborn costs associated with Medicaid participation (this time in New York) to be between $100 and $300 per recipient, insufficient to offset program expenditures.

National Health Insurance

Return now to the question of broader social insurance for health care. We have noted that the United States is one of two industrialized nations without a comprehensive social insurance program for health care. Should the United States adopt national health insurance? It would seem that this issue is dead with the demise of the 1993–1994 Clinton plan. Steps toward universal coverage might be taken with limited goals in mind. Steps toward cost containment may be more palatable in the current climate. Nevertheless, health system reform is still on the agenda in the United States and many other countries. It is wise to be acquainted with the possible features of such plans.

DIFFERENT KINDS OF POSSIBLE NATIONAL HEALTH INSURANCE (NHI) PLANS

It should be clear from the discussion that a national health insurance scheme should possess several desirable aspects:

- It should provide a health "safety net" for all residents, irrespective of age or employment status.
- It should provide choice for providers and patients.
- It should provide market incentives for cost containment.
- It should be relatively easy to administer.

Unfortunately, even within this list of presumably noncontroversial goals there is considerable room for controversy. To illustrate, the *Journal of the American Medical Association* (May 1991) asked health care experts to formulate plans for health insurance reform. More than 80 proposals were submitted, and after rigorous review, the journal published 13 of them. During the 1993–1994 national debate on health reform, at least as many plans and versions of plans came before Congress.

Particular bills at particular times will vary considerably, especially when one considers the options across countries. Several features of the bills considered by Congress in 1993–1994 address questions posed by most reform efforts. Table 22.6 lists several features that appeared in the various bills including the Clinton plan. Policy makers faced a dilemma as to whether to fund national health insurance coverage by individual mandate, employer/employee mandate, or general revenues. An individual mandate is a law that requires individuals to buy health insurance for themselves, with subsidies for those who can't afford it. The subsidies usually would be funded out of general revenues. The employer/employee mandates would require taxes on wages for the employee's share. The employer's share may fall on the employee in the form of lower wages. Subsidies out of general revenues would provide for the unemployed.

People advocating a Canadian-style system seek a single-payer system with government revenues providing all of the national health insurance. A final alternative is the medical savings accounts method of payment that would allow people to set up a tax-free savings account out of which they can pay the out-of-pocket costs of their health care. Usually, these systems entail health insurance with high deductibles and coinsurance.

Some plans would define a minimum acceptable level of insurance, with people allowed to purchase more extensive coverage if desired and if they can afford it. Others would define one plan to fit all. At the beginning of the debates, many plans featured universal coverage. As support for this waned in Congress, more plans offered lesser goals for reaching the population.

Single-payer systems tend to eliminate the private insurance function and feature government as the single payer. Managed care was a central feature of the health debate because the Clinton plan featured it. Managed care is promoted under health insurance reform as a cost-saving mechanism. Finally, Congress debated whether to feature purchasing cooperatives for health insurance, compulsory or voluntary. These cooperatives were viewed as a way to provide people with a choice of health plan, whether or not their employer offers it and whether or not the person is employed.

TABLE 22.6	Alternative Features of a National Health Insurance Reform
Financing:	employer/employee mandate
	individual mandate
	general tax revenues
	medical savings accounts
Coverage of Services:	a minimum plan defined
	a standard plan for all
Coverage of People:	universal
	limited
Insurer:	private insurance companies retained
	government insurance
Managed Care:	encouraged or mandated
	not encouraged or mandated
Purchasing Cooperative:	alliances mandated
	no alliances mandated

THE COSTS OF NHI

National health insurance programs certainly cost a great deal of money, but it is important to distinguish which costs are incremental. In other words, what are the additional costs to society from the imposition of NHI?

From society's point of view, the incremental cost of NHI in the United States is the extra total expenditure on health care that would be incurred if we switched to national health insurance. Inasmuch as most people already are insured for almost all hospital care and most physician care, the extra cost of NHI would be much smaller than many people expect.

The truly incremental costs stem from several sources. First, the major reason for switching to a national health insurance plan is to extend coverage to the uninsured, perhaps some 40 million people. Pauly and colleagues (1991) estimated the incremental costs of this newly covered population at roughly $17 billion, about $459 per person, or about 3 percent of health care spending. If this amount seems low, it should be understood that the uninsured already consume more than half as much care as the insured population on average; that is, zero insurance does *not* necessarily mean zero care.

Second, the insured population will incur some incremental cost to the extent that the national health insurance proposal chosen provides greater typical coverage than people already choose to buy or have provided to them by other sources. Third, any tax-supported system of financing care necessarily entails a deadweight loss to society. This is true even if the program is of the employer-mandated type because a law forcing employers to incur expense is really a tax. The deadweight loss of a tax means that some efficiency loss will result, caused by the disincentives to work and invest.

These sources of incremental costs to society are probably the most significant. In one sense, the incremental costs are the real costs to society, whereas differences in financing methods are not as economically meaningful. It may be politically more palatable to choose a plan that does not greatly expand the government budget; employment-mandated plans may be attractive politically for this reason. It should be made clear, however, that society incurs the cost irrespective of whether it is financed through the government or mandated to employers by law.

MEDICARE AND THE FUTURE

The U.S. Medicare system will become much larger over the next quarter century. Table 22.7 displays projections of the total population and the population age 65 and older, starting in the year 2006. Although projections into the future can be risky, this one is a fairly safe bet. All of the people who will be 65 years of age in 2030 are already 34 years old. To project future populations, demographers statistically "age" the various population cohorts by predicting how many will die between now and then.[12]

Any way that one looks at things, Medicare will grow. The population in the 65-plus age category will increase by 89.6 percent between 2006 and 2030, the result of the baby boom starting in the late 1940s and extending through the early 1960s. The total population, in contrast, is projected to increase by 20.3 percent.

[12]Immigration and emigration generally provide only small adjustments at the national level.

	TABLE 22.7	Projections of Total and Over 65 Populations, 2006–2030	
Year	Total Pop.	Total (Age 65+)	Percent (Age 65+)
2006	288,269	36,591	12.7
2007	290,583	37,131	12.8
2008	292,928	37,998	13.0
2009	295,306	38,708	13.1
2010	297,716	39,408	13.2
2015	310,134	45,567	14.7
2020	322,742	53,220	16.5
2025	335,050	61,952	18.5
2030	346,899	69,379	20.0

Middle Series Projections

Source: U.S. Bureau of the Census, http://www.census.gov/population/projections/nation/nas/npas0610.txt, Accessed December 3, 1999.

Looking at the numbers slightly differently, one can see that between the years 2010 and 2015 (10 years from now), the total population is expected to grow by about 12.4 million, and the cohort of those age 65 and older is expected to grow by 6.2 million. One of every two "new" people in the country will be eligible for Medicare, and the expenses of those who receive Medicare (largely those who have retired) must be financed by those who still are working.

Marilyn Moon has studied the elderly and the Medicare system extensively.[13] She notes that in combination with the aging of the population and costly advances in medicine and technology, Medicare's share of the Gross Domestic Product will rise from 2.53 percent in 1998 to 4.43 percent in 2025.

In her June 1999 testimony before Congress, Moon stressed three principles that she viewed as integral to Medicare's role as a social insurance program:

- The universal status of the program and its consequent redistributive function
- The pooling of risks that Medicare has achieved across the sick and the healthy
- The role of government in protecting the rights of the beneficiaries

The first principle reiterates our discussion at the beginning of the chapter regarding the fundamentally redistributive nature of social insurance. Before Medicare's passage, many elderly persons could not afford insurance, and others who could not obtain it were denied coverage as poor risk. Medicare effected a wealth transfer from those who work to those who cannot, and Medicare beneficiaries need not fear losing coverage.

Second, through (close to) universal coverage of the elderly, Medicare pools risks among the healthy and the sick. With a potentially reduced (or a privatized) Medicare program, those with health problems—who disporportionately have lower incomes—would have to pay the highest prices.

Third, governmental rules have protected beneficiaries. Although governmental oversight may have its shortcomings, Moon views it as a necessary counterweight to the

[13]This section draws heavily on Moon (1999).

potential loss of essentia care than could accompany plans run and administered by private insurers.

Moon suggests that any reformed Medicare program must address improved coverage for prescription d ugs and limit the out-of-pocket costs that an individual beneficiary must pay in a give year. She also indicates that some parts of a long-term solution probably will and proba ly should include future increases in contributions from beneficiaries beyond what is lready scheduled to go into place.

She notes that unde current projections, the "date of exhaustion" of the Medicare Part A Trust Fund will b 2015. What then? Will Medicare beneficiaries find that none of their case is reimbursed? Will hospitals and clinics shut down because of lack of payment?

Clearly not. Medica e is part of a social contract in which the older part of the population receives benefits hat are paid for by the younger part of the population. The wealth behind the payn nts is the country's productive capacity and the willingness of those who are working o pay for those who no longer do so. This does not mean that the details of the progra , of the benefits, and of the financing are unimportant: Billions of dollars per year will e involved. It does mean that political consensus and the economic productivity tha supports it will enable a socially insured medical program to continue well into the t enty-first century.

Conclusions

In this chapter, we have presented a general discussion of social insurance and its application to the health c e sector. We noted that almost all modern industrialized countries provide fairly com rehensive health care social insurance, and we have reviewed the history of these dev lopments and the pattern in the United States.

Today, the major h alth care social insurance programs in the United States are Medicare and Medicai These programs increase costs in theory and have been increasingly costly in pra ice. It is clear that they have had a beneficial effect on access to care among the elde y and low-income groups, and recent studies suggest that they have a beneficial effect n health status. They leave, however, a fairly large number of the poor or uninsured thout health care coverage.

Finally, whether or ot the United States should move to a national health insurance program must refl ct the values of the public. This is true of both efficiency and equity rationales. The ficiency rationales depend on individual values expressed in willingness to pay. The quity rationales, in contrast, are a direct expression of values. Comprehensive social surance for health care in the United States would directly address and presumabl solve the widely perceived problem of providing for the uninsured, who often inclu le people in the poverty, near-poverty, and other lower-income groups.

These problems ca be addressed in many ways. We have noted the salient policy features or decision isst s in the plans considered by Congress in 1993–1994. What can economics say about th se features, whose ultimate choice or the choice of no change depends on the values the voting public? There are areas of theory and evidence in economics that shed lig on these questions. It is also useful, however, to look at health reform beyond the bor rs of the United States. We learn from each other's experience and research. We begin uch an effort by first comparing the features of health systems across countries in the ext chapter.

Summary

1. Several different types of social insurance policies and social programs exist. They are usefully grouped into poverty programs, old-age assistance, disability, health, and unemployment.
2. Program features variously include contributions, benefits, length of coverage, means of reimbursement to providers, and methods of determining payment levels to providers.
3. Social insurance originated in nineteenth-century Europe. Groups in the United States have supported health care social insurance programs throughout the twentieth century. This history led to the adoption of Medicare and Medicaid in 1965. Since then, however, the United States remains one of the few developed countries that has not adopted a comprehensive health care social insurance program.
4. Medicare is a national program that provides hospital insurance to the elderly, along with optional supplemental physician care insurance. The Balanced Budget Act of 1997 established several new categories of Medicare options.
5. Medicaid programs are funded through matching state and federal funds and run by the states. They provide health care to certain categories of the needy and are the primary providers of nursing home aid.
6. Medicare and Medicaid expenditures have increased rapidly since the programs began, due to increases in medical care prices, in the population covered, in the quantity of care per capita consumed by the population, and due to changes in the nature of the services provided.
7. Medicare and Medicaid accompanied clear improvement in access to care by the lower-income population, as evidenced by increased utilization rates by lower-income groups, both absolutely and relatively to the higher-income groups.
8. National health insurance (NHI) proposals include compulsory private insurance programs through employers and tax credits for the purchase of private insurance, as well as proposals for an all-government system.
9. From society's viewpoint, the cost of NHI is the incremental cost of additional health care purchased by people due to improved insurance coverage. Savings from successful cost controls may offset these costs.
10. With the aging of the baby boom cohort in the early twenty-first century, Medicare must determine how best to structure, provide, and finance the benefits that it is providing to this growing segment of the population.

Discussion Questions

1. In what ways does social insurance differ from private insurance?
2. Of the five types of social insurance programs described, which types describe Medicare? Which types describe Medicaid?
3. What are the similarities between Medicare and Medicaid? What are the differences?
4. What factors contributed to the historical growth in Medicare spending?
5. Describe how Medicare has affected access to care for the elderly.
6. Is health status affected by the access to health care provided through social insurance programs? Discuss the evidence.

7. What are some possible reasons that other industrially advanced countries have far more comprehensive social insurance programs for health care than does the United States?
8. Historically in the United States, what groups have supported social insurance for health care, and what groups have opposed it? Why do you think this is the case?

Exercises

1. Calculate the average tax rate for Social Security at incomes of $25,000; $50,000; $75,000; and $100,000. Do the same for Medicare. Characterize each tax as being progressive, regressive, or neutral.
2. From Table 22.1, calculate average growth rates for Medicare and Medicaid from 1972 to 1997. Which program increased more regularly? Which increased more erratically? Why?
3. Suppose that in Figure 22.1, $P_0 = 1$ and $P_1 = 1.1$. Suppose also that $Q_0 = 100,000$ and $Q_1 = 110,000$.
 - What is the effect of the increased insurance coverage on total expenditures?
 - What is the elasticity of health service supply?
 - Would the total expenditures in the presence of increased insurance be higher or lower if the supply were more elastic? (Hint: Think about how we calculate total expenditures.)
4. Table 22.5 shows the effect of enhanced Medicaid programs on children who are below the poverty line. The table shows how physician utilization has increased for the poor children.
 - Compare the levels of utilization between children who are below the poverty line and children who are above twice the poverty line. Who had more care in 1987? In 1993? Who is likely to be sicker?
 - Compare the relative amount of utilization between the two groups. What happened to these measures from 1987 to 1993? Discuss your answer.
5. Table 22.7, describing the potential Medicare burden, provides an interesting example of the marginal and average concepts that we have seen elsewhere. Column 3 provides the average proportion of the population age 65 and older.
 - Add a column that calculates the proportion of the population increase that is age 65 and older. Are its figures greater or less than the average? Why?
 - How do these figures describe the financial burden on the Medicare system?

Comparative Health Care Systems

- ■ Criticisms of the American Health Care System
- ■ Contemporary Health Care Systems
- ■ National Health Programs: Three Examples
- ■ The Canadian Health Care System
- ■ Differences in Health Care Spending across Countries
- ■ Conclusions

W e will now consider the experiences of other countries in providing large-scale health care. We undertake this study for two reasons. First, many European countries have constructed programs that predate U.S. programs by decades. There is a rich variation in programs and experiences that in itself is worth discovering. Second, and more important, the U.S. system has some gaping holes compared with the coverage extended by many other systems. Understanding the approaches used by other countries may provide important clues to assessing our own system.

Criticisms of the American Health Care System

Critics of the Medicare and Medicaid delivery systems have expressed concerns about the sizable personal liabilities involved for individuals entering hospitals under Medicare. Here are some examples of uncovered expenditures under Medicare and Medicaid. In 1999, the inpatient hospital deductible under Medicare was $768 for a stay of 1 to 60 days. Patients were required to pay $192 per day for days 61 to 90, $384 per day for days 91 to 150, and all costs for each day beyond 150 days.

Subscribers to Medicare Part B were required to pay the following:

- • a monthly premium of $45.50 in 1999
- • a $100 annual deductible
- • coinsurance payments of 20 percent of the Medicare-approved charge

- 50 percent for most outpatient mental health
- 20 percent of the first $1,500 for all physical therapy services, 20 percent of the first $1,500 for all occupational therapy services, and all charges thereafter

Overall, beneficiaries were liable for 15.2 percent of the Medicare community-based population's total spending on medical care (MEDPAC, 1999). Services such as drugs, dental care, eyeglasses, and most long-term care are not covered.[1] Are these personal liabilities under Medicare too burdensome? Certainly, some Americans think so.

Because Medicaid refers to 51 separate state programs, there are numerous variations in coverage. Holahan and Liska (1997) find that a major source of variation in Medicaid spending among states comes from their differences in coverage of their low-income populations. In 1994, less than half (46 percent) of all Americans below 150 percent of the poverty line were covered by Medicaid.

The states with the smallest coverage gaps tended to be high-income states in the Northeast. For example, Connecticut, Massachusetts, New York, Rhode Island, and Vermont all covered more than 60 percent of their low-income populations. States with the largest coverage gaps tended to be lower-income states in the South and the West. Alabama, Arkansas, Florida, Idaho, Nevada, Oklahoma, South Dakota, and Utah all covered less than 40 percent of their low-income populations.

While various health reform policies were brought forward with the aim of restructuring of the Medicaid program, the fact remains that well into the 1990s, coverage varied widely for the low-income populations, related either to a state's ability, or willingness, to match federal funds. Moreover, even in states where programs were most comprehensive, more than one-quarter of the low-income populations had no Medicaid coverage.

Aside from these gaps in the Medicare and Medicaid programs, many critics of the American system characterize its main weakness as the problem of the uninsured. More than 40 million people at any point in time go without health insurance. While this does not mean that they go *entirely* without care, the uninsured consume only half as much health care on average as those who are insured.

Lack of insurance may be a matter of choice for some, but many of those who are uninsured are severely constrained in their freedom of choice. Often they are the poor and the near poor who do not receive Medicaid. Other uninsureds often work at jobs that typically do not offer health insurance fringe benefits, or they are people who do not qualify for benefits on the job.

Still other Americans wish to control health care cost inflation. Political pressure to contain costs for public programs is considerable. In chapter 22, we discussed specific strategies, such as the Medicare Prospective Payment System under DRGs.

If the United States were to move to a national health care program, what sort of system might it be? We provide both an introduction to cross-national data on health care spending and a typology of the various systems that have been put into place.

We then examine the United Kingdom, Germany, and South Korea in more detail because their health care systems are perceived to be successful. Because of the numerous similarities between the United States and Canada, we devote an entire section

[1]Most Medicare patients' out-of-pocket liabilities are reduced substantially by private supplemental insurance (about four-fifths have Medigap coverage) or various forms of public assistance.

to Canada's national health program, and we compare its performance with that of the United States. We then present a framework for comparing different spending rates across countries.

Contemporary Health Care Systems

Many industrialized countries either provide health care directly through the government or provide publicly funded health insurance with comprehensive coverage. The origins of government programs for health care, particularly for social insurance programs, were previously explored. Rather than describe details about the health care programs of dozens of countries, we prefer to characterize the basic types of systems employed and to develop a few examples in greater detail.[2]

A TYPOLOGY OF CONTEMPORARY HEALTH CARE SYSTEMS

Consider a broad framework for describing different approaches. For this purpose, Gordon (1988) develops a useful typology of four health benefit systems.

1. *Traditional sickness insurance* is fundamentally a private insurance market approach with a state subsidy. Countries with this system include Austria, Belgium, France, Luxembourg, the Netherlands, and Germany.
2. *National health insurance* involves a national-level health insurance system. Countries with this system include Canada, Finland, Norway, Spain, and Sweden.
3. *National health services* have the state providing the health care. Countries with this system include Denmark, Greece, Italy, New Zealand, Portugal, Turkey, and the United Kingdom.
4. *Mixed systems* contain elements of both traditional sickness insurance and national health coverage. Countries with this system include Australia, Iceland, Ireland, Japan, Switzerland, and the United States.

In comparing economic data across countries, Table 23.1 shows per-capita health expenditures expressed in U.S. dollars in many countries for 1997. These figures have been adjusted for the purchasing powers of the local currencies (known as purchasing power parity). Other columns show each country's health care spending as a percent of GDP for selected years.

The countries vary substantially. Other countries (e.g., Canada, Denmark, France, Italy) spend considerably larger percentages on inpatient care than does the United States. It may surprise readers to discover that next to Switzerland, our percentage expenditures on pharmaceuticals are the lowest among all of the countries.

Several countries have lower rates of infant mortality (measured in deaths per 1,000 live births) than does the United States. Several countries also have higher life expectancies at birth than we do.

The United States is the biggest spender in the per-capita terms ($4,090). It is also the biggest spender as a share of GDP (14.0 percent by OECD figures). These figures, as well as concerns about access to health care, are the sorts of indicators that have led

[2]The Social Security system maintains an excellent data archive called *Social Security Statistics Throughout the World,* in which they describe the health, unemployment, and poverty programs of more than 100 countries. It is located at http://www.ssa.gov/statistics/ssptw97, August 7, 1999.

TABLE 23.1 Health Care Spending and Outcomes in Selected Industrial Countries

Country	GDP per Capita 1997	Per-Capita Expend. 1997	% on Inpatient Care 1996	% on Pharmac. 1996	% of GDP Spent on Health Care 1960	1990	1997	Deaths/ 1,000 Live Births 1996	Life Expectancy at Birth F 1996	M 1996
Australia	21,671	1,805	43.2	11.4	4.9	8.3	8.3	5.8	81.1	75.2
Austria	22,789	1,793	20.9	14.1	4.3	7.2	7.9	5.1	80.2	73.9
Belgium	22,902	1,747	40.5	17.9	3.4	7.5	7.6	6.0	81.0	74.3
Canada	22,606	2,095	44.5	12.5	5.5	9.2	9.3	6.0	81.5	75.4
Denmark	_..._	_..._	_..._	_..._	_..._	_..._	_..._	_..._	_..._	_..._
Finland	19,821	1,447	40.8	15.2	3.9	8.0	7.3	4.0	80.5	73.0
France	21,290	2,103	45.6	17.0	4.2	8.9	9.9	4.9	82.0	74.1
Germany	22,385	2,339	35.0	12.7	4.8	8.7	10.4	5.0	79.9	73.6
Greece	13,805	974	N/A	26.6	2.4	4.2	7.1	7.3	80.4	75.1
Ireland	18,875	1,324	N/A	9.9	3.8	6.7	7.0	5.5	78.5	73.2
Italy	20,914	1,589	46.9	17.9	3.6	8.1	7.6	5.8	81.3	74.9
Japan	23,765	1,741	N/A	20.8	N/A	6.0	7.3	3.8	83.6	77.0
Korea	14,578	587	34.4	N/A	N/A	3.9	4.0	9.0	77.4[a]	69.5[a]
Netherlands	21,450	1,825	52.4	10.9	3.8	8.3	8.5	5.2	80.4	74.7
New Zealand	17,903	1,352	N/A	16.8	4.3	7.0	7.6	7.4	79.8	74.3
Norway	24,423	1,814	N/A	9.0	2.9	7.8	7.4	4.0	81.1	75.4
Spain	15,800	1,168	45.0	20.0	1.5	6.9	7.4	5.0	81.6	74.4
Sweden	20,150	1,728	N/A	13.0	4.7	8.8	8.6	4.0	81.5	76.5
Switzerland	25,088	2,547	49.3	7.6	3.1	8.3	10.2	4.7	81.9	75.7
United Kingdom	20,139	1,347	N/A	16.5	3.9	6.0	6.7	6.1	79.3	74.4
United States	29,195	4,090	42.2	8.8	5.2	12.6	14.0	7.8	79.4	72.7

[a]Indicates 1995 data.

Source: OECD Health Data 1998.

many to question what Americans are getting for their spending. However, high expenditures may have three meanings:

- High average level of services
- High resource costs for services
- Inefficient provision of services

OECD Data and Opportunity Costs

What else do we have to keep in mind when examining large differences in health care spending across countries? The noted health economist Mark Pauly warns that OECD and other spending data may be poor measures of opportunity cost. As every economics student learns early on, it is the opportunity cost (i.e., what a nation forgoes) that matters. For example, the economic profits that might be earned by the pharmaceutical industry or physicians are included in spending, but they represent a transfer of income and are not part of opportunity costs.

Pauly (1993) developed crude measures of health care labor inputs and their opportunity costs for 17 OECD countries for 1988. In one approach, health employment is weighted, using relative income as weights, and expressed as a percent of the labor force. An alternative is based on the assumption that the opportunity cost of health workers is the same across countries. Expenditures on medical care labor are then expressed as a percent of GDP. His estimates for selected countries are shown below.

These measures paint a strikingly different picture of the United States than the one described by OECD data. Health employment is a little above the median, but medical labor expenditures are considerably below the median. Of course, the United States spends heavily on capital and other nonlabor inputs so there is some downward bias here in its relative position. Although more careful comparisons are needed, Pauly's results should be enough to warn scholars and policy makers against drawing sweeping or seemingly obvious conclusions from conventional comparative data.

Country	*Health Employment* (percent of labor force)	*Spending on Medical Care Labor* (percent of GDP)
Canada	6.39	4.89
France	8.31	6.85
Germany	7.24	6.56
Japan	3.58	3.42
Sweden	10.87	9.83
United Kingdom	5.52	5.09
United States	7.03	4.77
Median (17 countries)	6.80	7.24

Source: Pauly (1993, Exhibits 1 and 2).

In examining cross-country differences, we keep these points in mind. A high level of services reflects at least the possibility that populations have chosen to spend their incomes in this fashion. We have noted previously that higher income levels are reflected in higher consumption levels of *all* normal goods, including health care. Cross-national studies indicate a fairly substantial income elasticity for health care. U.S. expenditure levels thus reflect in part the higher per-capita income level in the United States.

National Health Programs: Three Examples

In this section, we examine the national health systems of three countries: the United Kingdom, Germany, and South Korea. In the next section, we will contrast Canada's plan, an example of a national health insurance system, with that of the United States, an example of a mixed system.

The United Kingdom is featured as an example of a national health service. Germany is important as the birthplace of compulsory insurance schemes, and it represents an example of the traditional sickness insurance. South Korea is a newcomer to the community of nations that have universal health insurance. Though that country's program has received little publicity, its mandated approach offers important insights to other countries, including the United States, that have considered or are considering a plan based on mandatory employer coverage.

THE UNITED KINGDOM—THE NATIONAL HEALTH SERVICE

Great Britain's National Health Service (NHS) was established in 1946 and provides health care to all British residents.[3] It is financed largely (about 85 percent) through general revenues, with capital and current budget filtering from the national level down to the regional, and then to the district level. The plan pays general practitioners on a capitation basis and hospital physicians largely on a salaried basis. In addition to the NHS, there is also a private sector health system. About 10 percent of Britains purchase private health insurance.

Services are not entirely free. Patients desiring private rooms pay extra, and there is a small surcharge for drug prescriptions filled outside the hospital. Dental care and eyeglasses also require patient copayments.

The general practitioner, or GP, serves as the gatekeeper to the health care system. Contrary to U.S. perceptions, GPs are not government employees. Rather, they are self-employed and receive about half their incomes from capitation contracts. They typically treat routine conditions and will refer patients to hospitals for more specialized care. The referral usually will be to a district hospital. Once at the hospital, the patients are under the care of physicians (consultants) who are allocated staffed beds and junior hospital staff to work under their direction.

As shown by the comparative data in Table 23.2, the resources available across systems can vary widely. The United States has 10 percent fewer hospital beds per capita than provided in the United Kingdom, but it has 63 percent more physicians. The United States has slightly fewer acute care nurses per bed. Germany, by comparison, has more than twice as many beds and physicians per capita as the United Kingdom, but only about 30 percent of the nursing staff per bed.

[3]The descriptive material here is taken largely from Gordon (1988) and Maynard (1990).

TABLE 23.2 Health Care Resources in Selected Countries						
	Inpatient Beds per 1,000 Population (1996)	*% of U.S.*	*Practicing Physicians per 1,000 Population (1994)*	*% of U.S.*	*Acute Care Nurses Staff/Bed (1992)*	*% of U.S.*
United States	4.1		2.6		1.57	
Korea	4.6	112.2	1.1	42.3	0.50	31.8
Germany	9.6	234.1	3.3	126.9	0.51	32.5
United Kingdom	4.5	109.8	1.6	61.5	1.65	105.1
Canada	5.1	124.4	2.2	84.6	0.84	53.5

Source: OECD Health Data 1999.

Referring to Table 23.1, we see that per-capita spending ($1,347) in the United Kingdom in 1997 was just 33 percent of the level of the United States ($4,090) and just a little less than half when expressed as a ratio to GDP (6.7 percent as opposed to 14.0 percent). How does the United Kingdom keep its health care expenditures this much lower while providing universal access to health care? Though patients have relatively easy access to primary and emergency care, specialty care is rationed through long waiting lists and a limit on the availability of new technologies. A relatively simple model is useful to illustrate this phenomenon.

A Model of Rationed Health Care and Private Markets

We can consider the practices of an NHS-type of organization diagrammatically. In panel A of Figure 23.1, we treat the supply of health services as totally price inelastic. That is, the supply curve, being a reflection of what is provided by the government,

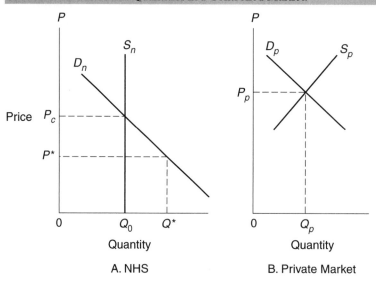

FIGURE 23.1 Prices and Quantities in a Controlled Market.

A. NHS

B. Private Market

is a vertical line. This indicates that the quantity supplied is unresponsive to the price of the services.

Furthermore, the money price of the services is set by the government at P^*, which is less than the market clearing price of P_c. Predictably, there is excess demand ($Q^* - Q_0$) at the administered price, P^*. Because most health care cannot be bought and resold, other forms of rationing, largely time related, become important. There is a legendary list of ailments for which the waiting period for treatment by the NHS is months or even years.

Again, as might be predicted, a small private market for services has developed for those who choose to enter the private market without governmental aid, either due to strong preferences for private care or due to the ability to pay more than the NHS price. Because there is excess demand at P^*, that excess demand, in part, represents people who are queued and who may wish to pay in the private sector to avoid the long waits. Those who participate in the private market, shown in panel B, will pay P_p for the quantity of services, Q_p.

Performance under the NHS and Reforms in the 1990s

On the one hand, the effect of a system such as the NHS that depends on queuing for access to care is often to postpone, or simply not provide, certain services. On the other hand, the NHS devotes considerable resources to such high-return services as prenatal and infant care. To these populations served, and to the larger public concerned with equitable provision of care to these segments of the population, the universal nature of the service is particularly beneficial.

Over the years, the United Kingdom has spent considerably less on health care than the United States and many other countries. Expenditures through the 1980s held at about 6 percent of GDP, and rose to only 6.7 percent by 1997, while U.S. expenditures have not seen these ratios since the 1960s. By most measures of mortality and morbidity, the United Kingdom does about as well. Certainly, many nonmedical factors are involved in determining disease and death rates in a population, and these factors also will vary across countries.

In addition, despite universal access to care in the United Kingdom, historically there have been considerable regional disparities in funding and in the use of health care. Evidence shows that upper-class patients have received substantially more care for a given illness than have lower-class patients.[4] Thus, even where access is universal, the results are not necessarily equal.

The NHS is extremely popular with the public and is probably the most valued piece of the British welfare state. Nevertheless, in response to perceived inefficiencies and the intellectual influence of Enthoven's (1993, 1985) proposals for "managed competition," 1991 reforms were introduced by Conservative Prime Minister Margaret Thatcher. The reforms replaced the centralized, hierarchical NHS bureaucracy with a quasi-market mechanism. A purchaser/provider split was created where "purchasers" of health care, regional health authorities and general practice fund holders, are allocated budgets to purchase services for their populations. These purchasers are distinct

[4]See Maynard (1990) for further details.

from providers—mainly hospitals. The incentives for efficiency and a responsive system come as providers compete for contracts with purchasers.

Le Grand's (1999) review of the limited evidence on the effects of the reforms on efficiency, equity, and patient choice suggests that not much of substance has changed. His explanation is:

> The incentives were too weak (e.g., purchasers could not keep any surpluses or invest them in new technology) and the constraints were too strong. Put another way, the motivations for change were relatively weak, especially when compared with the pressures for stability from outside (p. 33).

In many markets, also, there are too few hospitals to allow for meaningful competition.

In a change of policy following Tony Blair's victory in 1997, the Labour government remained committed to the purchaser/provider split. All general practitioners in the NHS participate in primary care groups (PCGs), which receive capitated funding from the government and are responsible for most health care services for their patients (about 100,000 patients per PCG). PCGs have more flexibility with their budgets than was given to its predecessors. Instead of trying to inject more supply-side competition, the new policy will focus on quality standards established through studies of clinical outcomes and cost effectiveness.

The experience of the United Kingdom's National Health Service in the area of cost containment, however, seems fairly clear. Rationed care cuts money costs. We should inquire whether their observed ability to keep costs lower holds some opportunities for the United States.

GERMANY

The German health care system is rooted in the programs laid out by Bismarck in 1883. Legislation was introduced to require workers in various occupations to enroll in sickness insurance funds. The original legislation covered only a small fraction of the population. Nevertheless, the basic approach of mandatory enrollment in autonomous sickness funds, financed by payroll taxes, was expanded and today lies at the heart of the German social insurance program.

Also at the heart of the German health system is a sense of solidarity—a sense that all citizens are concerned with the provision of equal access to health care. Germans and many Europeans speak of this as the solidarity goal (v.D. Schulenburg, 1992). Despite the many Americans who support such a goal, the base of support is not similar, so that Uwe Reinhardt (1994b) has spoken of Germany's health system as "not the American way" (p. 22).

Structure of the System

In the German system, all working persons are required to have health insurance with costs divided equally between employer and employee.[5] The employee's share is collected as a payroll tax at a rate proportional to his or her gross wages. The average contribution rate to sickness funds in 1997 was 13.6 percent. Individuals with income

[5]The following material, with some updates, is based largely on Henke (1990) and Hinrichs (1995), and on special reports by Hurst and by Schneider in the Spring 1991 issue of *Health Care Financing Review*.

beyond a given ceiling are eligible to choose the private health system, which handles about 10 percent of the population.

Approximately 88 percent of Germans have social health insurance, 10 percent have private insurance, and the remaining 2 percent, for various reasons, receive free care. The social insurance component is organized around some 500 localized sickness funds. These funds are independent and self-regulating. They pay providers directly for services provided to their members at rates that they negotiate with individual hospitals. Regional groups of funds negotiate with regional doctors' and dentists' associations for payments for ambulatory and dental care. Payment from these funds represents about 70 percent of health care spending.

The sickness funds are required by law to provide a comprehensive set of benefits. These include physician ambulatory care provided by physicians in private practice, hospital care, home nursing care, and a wide range of preventive services. Patient cost sharing is minimal. The funds, like disability insurance, also provide additional cash payments to those who are unemployed as a result of illness.

As for reimbursement, ambulatory providers are paid on a fee-for-service basis, hospitals on a prospective basis. Both public and private (including for-profit) hospitals exist, though the public hospitals account for about half the beds. Hospitals tend to use salaried physicians, and, unlike the United States, physicians in private practice generally do not have admitting privileges. Thus, many doctors have invested in elaborately equipped clinics to compete with hospitals by being able to perform a wide range of procedures.

The German experience is especially relevant to the United States. Coverage is provided through a large number of relatively small and independent plans. In this sense, the delivery of health care is similar to that found in the United States where, for the most part, large numbers of employee groups, independent insurers, and providers reach agreements without direct government intervention. Many Americans propose mandated coverage for the working uninsured. Germany relies on a mandated approach, where coverage for certain conditions is required by law. Germany also introduced cost controls similar in principle to prospective payment under the U.S. DRG mechanism.

The Role of Government

Each level of government has specific responsibilities in the German system.

- The central government passes legislation on policy and jurisdiction.
- State governments are responsible for hospital planning, managing state hospitals, and supervising the sickness funds and physician associations.
- Local governments manage local hospitals and public health programs.

Within this framework, decentralization is considerable. As we have noted, the sickness funds and physician associations have considerable administrative autonomy.

Despite this autonomy, it is apparent that government intervention is extensive and that is has been increasing steadily. Expenditures of the sickness funds grew rapidly in the 1960s and early 1970s. As a result, the Cost Containment Act of 1977 introduced a fixed budget for payments by the sickness funds to the physician associations. In essence, this program is similar to prospective payment schemes developed in the United States. However, because hospitals were excluded from this act, a series of additional acts was introduced between 1981 and 1986. Here, too, it was required that prospective budgets be negotiated between the sickness funds and hospitals.

The Health Care Reform Act of 1989 introduced more major changes. These were directed at attempts to further reduce the growth of health expenditures through means familiar to those in the United States. The changes included greater cost sharing, a strategy increasingly favored in Germany's many reform efforts. The act also attempted to control hospital costs through reductions in hospital capacity, hospital inpatient admissions, and hospital expenditures on capital equipment.

As costs continued to rise for the sickness funds at a rate faster than the rise in incomes, the call for reform continued. Figure 23.2 shows this pattern of increased expenditures. This concern led to the 1993 Health Care Reform Act. To introduce supply-side competition, the reforms also gave members the freedom to choose among a range of sickness funds whose revenues would be determined by the risks of their members. The reforms further changed the hospital payment system from a per-diem payment to a DRG-styled prospective payment basis (Henke, Murray, and Ade, 1994). Subsequent legislation in 1997 was aimed at continuing the momentum toward competition.

Performance

Despite the frequent calls for reform in Germany, as well as the recurrent complaints that the system is in crisis, the German health system has been relatively successful at controlling costs. Preceding the period of reforms, 1970 to 1977, spending increased at a 14.4 percent annual rate, but this dropped to 6.5 percent from 1977 to 1983 and to 5.1 percent from 1983 to 1989. The contribution rate of payment to the sickness funds was 13.2 percent in 1995 compared to 10.5 percent in 1975.

For a better perspective of the relative success of the German, British, Canadian, Korean, and U.S. systems in controlling inflation, examine Figure 23.3. Again, the data describe only country average trends in share of GDP spent on health care and do not identify causes. However, the data are suggestive. One notices that the upward trends in expenditures continued to the early 1990s for the United States, but the rate of increase was noticeably moderated in the other four systems.

Since 1990, the share of GDP spent on health care has risen substantially from 8.7 percent to 10.4 percent in 1997 (Table 23.1), but this apparent inability to contain costs (though still far less than the United States) is partly an artifact of Germany's reunification. The former East Germany added considerably to Germany's health care spend-

FIGURE 23.2 Annual Growth in Physician Expenditures and Income per Sickness Fund Member, Western Germany, 1985–1993.

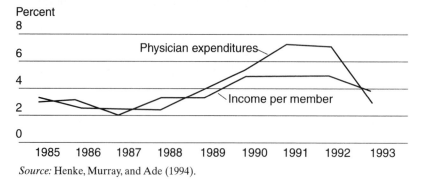

Source: Henke, Murray, and Ade (1994).

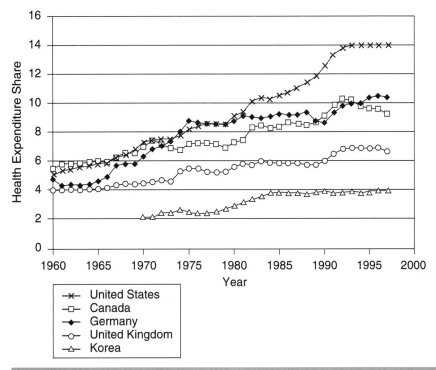

FIGURE 23.3 Health Expenditures as Percent of GDP, Five Countries.

ing without adding much GDP. The German health care system also faces additional cost pressures from having a much older population than the United States does.

Germany has achieved a favorable record along other criteria. It has a publicly funded system with virtually universal coverage but has avoided queues and extensive government intrusion. Both patient and provider have considerable autonomy.

After examining the performance of the German system, we may question whether it is the United States or Germany that has the better system. Surveys of public opinion in these two countries (Table 23.3) plus Canada help answer the subjective side of this question. While Canadians and Germans are still more satisfied with their systems, public opinion has been changing such that more Canadians and Germans are finding fault with their systems, whereas Americans' opinions have become somewhat more favorable.

The German health system faces many challenges. The German population is aging rapidly, causing a demographic change that will place severe pressure on its social security and health care programs. Hurst (1991) claims that an overemphasis is placed on high-tech medicine at the expense of preventive and long-term care. Those who have private insurance have more choice than those in the statutory programs, and similarly situated individuals may contribute different amounts to their sickness funds because the membership profiles of their respective funds are different. Hurst also is concerned about excessive regulation of the funds and lack of incentive for the funds to become efficient buyers of services.

TABLE 23.3 Ratings of Health Care Systems in the United States, Canada, and Western Germany, Selected Years

	United States			Canada			Western Germany	
	1988	1994	1998	1988	1994	1998	1990	1994
On the whole, the health care system works pretty well, and only minor changes are necessary to make it work better.	10%	18%	17%	56%	29%	20%	41%	30%
There are some good things in our health care system, but fundamental changes are needed to make it work better.	60	53	46	38	59	56	35	55
Our health care system has so much wrong with it that we need to completely rebuild it.	29	28	33	5	12	23	13	11
Not sure	1	2	4	1	—[a]	1	11	4

[a]Less than 0.5 percent.

Sources: Blendon, Robert J., et al. "Satisfaction with Health Systems in Ten Nations," *Health Affairs* 9 (1990): 185–192. Copyright © 1990 The People to People Health Foundation, Inc., All Rights Reserved. Blendon et al. (1995) for 1998 and 1994; Donelon et al. (1999) for 1998. Germany was not included in the 1998 survey.

Finally, Germany's attempt to introduce managed competition is still a work in progress. As we have seen from the U.K.'s experience, major reforms do not necessarily mean major changes to health care practice. Brown and Amelung (1999, p. 84) judge that consequences of the reforms "have so far been unspectacular," with the most visible change being the substantial drop in the number of sickness funds from about 1,000 before the 1993 reforms to 477 by early 1998.

SOUTH KOREA

Unlike the two other examples we have examined, South Korea has received little attention either in the scholarly literature or by policy makers.[6] However, the South Korean experience may provide an important example to other countries without universal health care coverage, including the United States. As recently as 1977, less than 10 percent of the South Korean population had insurance. By July 1989, however, South Korea completed the final phase of a program that introduced universal coverage to a system that maintained private provision of health care with fee-for-service reimbursement.

Structure of the System

In 1977, South Korea required all firms with more than 500 employees to establish insurance societies to provide specific health care benefits. The employee threshold was reduced in stages so that by January 1988, it included firms with fewer than five employees.

A second scheme for government employees, teachers, dependents of soldiers, and pensioners was phased in under another law. Similarly, the self-employed, farmers, fish-

[6]For more detail, see Moon (1989); G. F. Anderson (1989); Flynn and Chung (1990); and Peabody, Lee, and Bickel (1995).

ermen, and other occupational groups were phased in under a third program. Finally, low-income individuals were covered by public insurance similar to Medicaid.

The insurance is provided by insurance societies and is financed by employer contributions and payroll deductions. For example, for the employee program (class I), deductions are taken as percentages of wages or salaries. These are shared equally between employers and employees at rates ranging from 3 percent to 8 percent. The insurance societies also determine the benefits and cover a broad range of inpatient and outpatient services. The system is characterized by a relatively high coinsurance rate of 20 percent for hospital inpatient care and 30 percent to 55 percent for outpatient care.

Commensurate with the expansion of insurance and the rapid growth of South Korea's economy has been a rapid increase in utilization and costs. For example, annual outpatient visits per person for class I beneficiaries increased from 1.3 in 1977 to 6.2 in 1987; hospital inpatient cases increased from 3.0 to 6.2 per 100 persons. Spending as a share of GDP also rose from 2.8 percent of GDP in 1978, but it has stabilized in the relatively low 4 percent range in the 1990s.

Performance

South Korea's cost-containment strategies rely mainly on fee controls and high coinsurance rates. Under the fee schedules, all providers in each of three categories (comparable to community hospitals, teaching and specialty hospitals, and clinics) are reimbursed a uniform amount for an insured service. In addition to high coinsurance rates, a fixed consultation fee for each outpatient medical and dental visit was introduced in 1986 to help limit spending.

Commensurate with rapid economic development since the introduction of national health insurance, health care spending also rose rapidly. It is therefore difficult to isolate the effects of the cost-containment measures, but Jung's (1998) analysis of the effects of the 1986 copayments is revealing.

As one would expect, the copayments reduced the probability of outpatient visits. However, they had no effect on spending because patients and providers reacted rationally by offsetting the reduced contacts with more services per visit. This lesson may be valuable to the United States and other health care systems, where fixed visit copayments are being increasingly considered or adopted. Above all, the South Korean experience is a powerful demonstration to emerging industrial countries that it is possible to phase in a mandated employment-based insurance system without serious adverse effects on a nation's economy.

The Canadian Health Care System

As a result of the rapid increases in U.S. health care costs and growing concern over the large number of uninsured, many in the United States look at Canada's health system as a possible model for reform in this country. The widespread perception in the United States is that Canada has successfully developed a comprehensive and universal national health insurance program that is cost effective and highly popular.

BACKGROUND

The Canadian system of financing and delivering health care is known as Medicare, although it should not be confused with the U.S. Medicare program that has been

developed for the elderly. In Canada, each of the ten provinces and three territories administers a comprehensive and universal program that is partially supported by grants from the federal government.[7] Various criteria established by the federal government with respect to coverage must be met. Coverage must be universal, comprehensive, and portable, meaning that individuals can transfer their coverage to other provinces as they migrate across the country. There are no financial barriers to access, and patients have free choice in the selection of providers.

Canada's Medicare also should be distinguished from Britain's National Health Service. Most Canadian physicians are in private practice and have hospital admitting privileges. They are reimbursed by the provinces on a fee-for-service basis under fee schedules negotiated by the provinces and physician organizations. Hospitals are also private institutions, although their budgets are approved and largely funded by the provinces.

The Canadian system originated in the 1930s when compulsory health insurance programs were introduced by some provinces.[8] The main impetus, however, came from two sources: the federal legislation adopted in 1957 that provided cost sharing for inpatient hospital services, and the Medical Care Act of 1966 that provided cost sharing for physician care. Since 1971, every province and territory has provided universal coverage for hospital and physician care.

The extraordinary U.S. interest in Canada's approach is attributable to the fact that Canada and the United States share a long border and similar heritage in terms of language and culture; they also have similar economic institutions. The health care systems evolved similarly until the 1960s. Even as recently as 1971, both countries spent approximately 7.5 percent of their GDPs on health care.

Since 1971, however, the health care systems have moved in different directions. While Canada has had publicly funded national health insurance, the United States has relied largely on private financing and delivery (although governments have been heavily involved through Medicare, Medicaid, and numerous regulatory programs). During this period, spending in the United States has grown much more rapidly despite large groups that are either uninsured or minimally insured.

Table 23.4 provides comparative data on the two countries. Canada is geographically larger than the United States but has slightly more than one-tenth the U.S. population. Although a wealthy country, its per-capita GDP is only about 77 percent of the U.S. level. Canada has a relatively high level of social services, with public expenditures representing 43 percent of GDP compared to 32 percent for the United States. With a national health system providing universal coverage, public funds account for more than two-thirds of total health spending. However, not all services are covered (e.g., vision, dental, prescription drugs, semiprivate and private rooms), meaning that private funds account for nearly one-third—a share that has grown in recent years.

[7] Good overviews are found in Coyte (1990), Rakich (1991), and Graig (1999).

[8] There was considerable support for national health insurance in both the United States and Canada up to the late 1940s, with much of it coming from organized labor. President Truman even proposed compulsory prepaid insurance among other health reforms, but he could never put together a successful political coalition. Organized medicine in both countries was strongly opposed to the proposal and, with the start of the Cold War, the AMA was more successful than its Canadian counterpart in linking national health insurance to "socialized medicine" and the communist threat, and hence preventing its adoption. Maioni (1995) provides further discussion of this fascinating history.

TABLE 23.4 Comparative Data—Canada and the United States: 1997		
	Canada (in U.S. dollars)	*United States*
Population (millions)	30.2	276.7
Uninsured population (%)	0.0	15.7[b]
Population over 65 (%)	11.9[a]	12.6[a]
GDP ($ billions)	683	7,817
Per-capita GDP ($)	22,606	29,195
Public expenditures (% of GDP)	42.6	32.0
Per-capita health spending ($)	2,095	4,090
Health spending (% of GDP)	9.3	14.0
Percent of health spending		
Public expenditures	68.7	46.7
Inpatient care	44.5	42.2
Physicians	14.5	19.5
Inpatient beds/1000 population	5.1[a]	4.1[a]
Average length of stay (days)	12.0[a]	7.8[a]

Note: Canadian dollar values were converted to U.S. dollars using purchasing power parity indexes.
[a]indicates 1996 figures.
[b]indicates estimate.
Source: OECD Health Data (1998).

Canada has maintained substantially lower per-capita health spending and share of GDP than the United States, despite its higher bed–population ratio and relatively long lengths of stay. However, Canada's physician–population ratio is 15 percent lower and its acute care nurse staffing level is only about half the U.S. level (Table 23.2). In all, Americans spend 95 percent more per capita on health care ($4,090 vs. $2,095), although nearly 16 percent of the U.S. population goes without insurance coverage at any time. Despite lower spending, Table 23.1 shows that commonly compared health status indicators—such as infant mortality and life expectancy—are more favorable in Canada than in the United States. Finally, public opinion polls indicate that Canadians support their system much more than Americans support theirs and are concerned about any threats to it.

Given the Canadian record, health care scholars, policy makers, and politicians have shown great interest in determining the sources for its apparent success. In particular, health researchers have focused on the sources of the savings under the Canadian plan. One comparative study of per-capita spending is especially revealing.

PHYSICIAN FEES AND QUANTITY

Fuchs and Hahn (1990) provide a detailed breakdown of Canadian and U.S. expenditures by specific services, while separating their price and quantity components. In addition, the U.S. state of Iowa is compared with the Canadian province of Manitoba. Both have largely rural areas with relatively homogeneous populations. The data again have been adjusted to reflect purchasing power parity. Fuchs and Hahn estimated that per-capita spending on health care was 38 percent higher in the United States in 1985. More striking was the disparity in spending on physician services; it was 72 percent higher in

the United States, and 178 percent higher for the procedures component. (The relative ratios of Iowa to Manitoba were just slightly lower.)

Because spending is the product of prices and quantities, it seems logical to pursue differences in fees (prices) and utilization per capita (quantities). Overall, fees were 239 percent higher in the United States for 1985. Though there were variations in the ratios across service categories, U.S. fees were considerably higher in each category. The net incomes of U.S. doctors were also substantially higher than were their Canadian counterparts.

Perhaps more surprising than the fee differentials are estimates of the service volume. Despite the much higher spending per capita for physician care, the quantity of care per capita was considerably lower in the United States. Thus, the savings in Canada, at least for physician care, do not come from reduced volume of care.

WHY ARE FEES AND HOSPITAL COSTS LOWER IN CANADA?

Patients in Canada have longer lengths of stay, in part because of the greater use of Canadian hospitals for chronic long-term care. Nonetheless, after adjusting for differences in case mix between the two countries, researchers found that the cost per case-mix adjusted unit was roughly 50 percent higher in the United States.[9] Several reasons can be proposed for this phenomenon.

In Canada, unlike the United States, physician fees result from negotiation between physicians' organizations and the provincial governments, as well as from other limits on total spending. Physicians cannot evade the fee controls by charging extra (sometimes called *balance billing*) to patients who can afford it.

Hospital costs are similarly regulated by the provinces through approval of hospital budgets. Hospitals and provinces negotiate operating budgets financed by the provincial governments. The capital budget may include other sources of funding, but provinces still must approve capital expenditures. Thus, a centralized mechanism allocates resources to the hospital sector and determines the distribution of resources among hospitals.

Occupancy rates are higher in Canadian hospitals. Also, the provinces have limited the capital costs associated with expensive new technologies.

Table 23.5 provides comparisons on the availability of several relatively recent and expensive technologies among Canada, the United States, and the former West Germany. The United States has greater availability of each technology. This is particularly true for procedures such as lithotripsy and magnetic resonance imaging (MRI). Whether the data suggest overutilization in the United States or rationing in Canada or Germany is a subject to which we will return.

ADMINISTRATIVE COSTS

The centralized system of health care control in Canada has led to theories about the possible economies associated with administrative and other overhead expenses. Almost all patients in the United States are familiar with extensive paperwork and complex billing practices. For providers and third-party payers, the paperwork is more than

[9]See Newhouse, Anderson, and Roos (1988).

TABLE 23.5	Availability of Selected Technologies: Canada, West Germany, and the United States					
	Comparative Availability of Selected Medical Technologies					
	Canada (1993)		*Germany (1993)*		*United States (1992)*	
	Number of Units	*Units per Million Persons*	*Number of Units*	*Units per Million Persons*	*Number of Units*	*Units per Million Persons*
Open heart surgery	36	1.3	61	0.8	945	3.7
Cardiac catheterization	78	2.8	277	3.4	1,631	6.4
Organ transplantation	34	1.2	39	0.5	612	2.4
Radiation therapy	132	4.8	373	4.6	2,637	10.3
Extracorporeal shock wave lithotripsy	13	0.5	117	1.4	480	1.9
Magnetic resonance imaging	30	1.1	296	3.7	2,900	11.2

Source: Rublee, Dale A., "Medical Technology in Canada, Germany and the United States: An Update." *Health Affairs* 13 (1994): 113–117. Copyright © 1994 The People to People Health Foundation, Inc., All Rights Reserved.

an inconvenience; it involves major administrative expenses. Table 23.6 contains estimates of various categories of administrative expenses for 1987. The total expenses were approximately $300 more per capita in the United States than in Canada. This figure accounts for a substantial portion of the difference in per-capita spending between the countries.

Even more provocative is the direction of the trends. Woolhandler and Himmelstein (1991) note that the increases since 1983 were especially severe. For example, the authors found that administrative costs in the United States increased from 21.9 to 23.9 percent of health care spending between 1983 and 1987, while similar costs declined in Canada from 13.7 percent to 11 percent.

TABLE 23.6	Costs of Health Care Administration per Capita: Canada and the United States, 1987	
	Spending per Capita	
Cost Category	*U.S.*	*Canada*
Insurance administration	106	17
Hospital administration	162	50
Nursing home administration	26	9
Physicians' overhead and billing expenses		
Expense-based estimate	203	80
Personnel-based estimate	106	41
Total costs of health care administration		
High estimate	497	156
Low estimate	400	117

Note: All costs are expressed in U.S. dollars.

Source: Woolhandler and Himmelstein (1991, Table 1) Copyright © 1991 Massachusetts Medical Society. All rights reserved.

How Is Health Care "Rationed" in Canada?

Though there have been many claims that health care is "rationed" in Canada through longer waiting times and reduced access to services, more recent studies help identify specific differences between the U.S. and Canadian systems. The following are prominent examples of this research emphasis.

Coyte and colleagues (1994) examined waiting times for patients undergoing knee-replacement surgery in Ontario and the United States. The median waiting time after the surgery had been planned was eight weeks in Ontario versus three weeks in the United States. Overall satisfaction with the surgery was comparable at about 85 percent in both countries.

On the issue of access to technology and aggressive medical intervention, G. M. Anderson et al. (1993) compared use of coronary artery bypass surgery among several U.S. and Canadian regions. The combined age-adjusted rate for three Canadian provinces was 62 per 100,000 population, far below the rates of 113 for California and 88 for New York.

To study possible differences in inpatient physician practice patterns, Katz, McMahon, and Manning (1996) examined the use of diagnostic tests for comparable patients admitted to U.S. and Canadian hospitals with similar availability of technology. Despite the similar technologies, U.S. medical patients received 22 percent more tests (there was little difference among surgical patients) and the differences were greatest among the most expensive tests.

Elsewhere, Rouleau et al. (1993) examined patients admitted to a coronary care unit in 19 Canadian and 93 U.S. hospitals. Fifty-one percent of the Canadian patients had acute myocardial infarction (MI) compared with 35 percent of U.S. patients. This suggests that somewhat more serious cases were being treated in the Canadian hospitals. Coronary arteriography and other procedures were performed at much higher rates in the United States. Interestingly, these differences in treatment patterns had no effect on mortality or rate of reinfarction, but there was a slightly higher rate of activity-limiting angina in Canada.[10] From this evidence, the authors conclude that the threshold may be higher in Canada for hospital admission and for performing expensive diagnostic and therapeutic procedures.

Finally, Latimer and colleagues (1999) investigated end-of-life differences in the utilization of physician services between the United States and two Canadian provinces—Quebec and British Columbia. With considerable resources used to treat end-of-life patients, it would seem that rationing for this group of patients might be an inviting strategy for Canada. However, the U.S. levels of utilization for those who lived less than six months as well as those who survived longer were comparable to those found in British Columbia. Surprisingly, both were considerably below the utilization for Quebec patients.

In some instances, Canadians clearly get less health care or have to wait longer, especially for nonemergency surgery. In other instances, they get as much or more care. With little observable effect on mortality and other outcome indicators, Canadian practice patterns and case management can provide useful cost-containment information to U.S. policy makers and third-party payers.

[10]On the other hand, Marks et al. (1994) found that patients in both countries had the same functional status after 30 days, but U.S. patients showed more improvement after a year.

A CRITICAL COMPARISON

The foregoing data suggest that the Canadian system appears to be more effective than the U.S. system in several respects. Costs are lower, more services are provided, financial barriers do not exist, and health status as measured by mortality rates is superior. Canadians have longer life expectancies and lower infant mortality rates than do U.S. residents.

However, the comparisons do not tell the whole story, nor do they necessarily imply that the United States should adopt the Canadian approach. Some have argued that a system that is manageable for a population of 30 million cannot easily be adapted to a more pluralistic country with a population of nearly ten times that level.

Others point out that many Canadians are no longer confident that the provinces will be able to afford their current systems. As a result of unprecedented federal deficits, the Canadian government has reduced substantially its cash transfers to the provinces. The provinces are thus faced with the following options to cope with their increased burdens: find new sources of tax revenue, impose more stringent fee and budgetary controls on health providers, find ways to increase efficiency in health care delivery, scale back on benefits by no longer insuring some previously covered services, and impose user fees (Rathwell 1994).

Similar to the shift we have seen for the United States, the provinces have forced large reductions in hospital capacity with a corresponding substitution of outpatient care for inpatient care. However, with the exception of Ontario, the movement toward regionalization or "devolution" is their most conspicuous reaction to the fiscal constraint imposed by the federal cutbacks. Regional boards with budgetary authority have replaced centralized provincial departments. The goals of this reorganization are similar to those expected from managed care: develop an efficient, coordinated, and accountable system for the regional population. Unlike the United States, however, this goal is to be accomplished by planning rather than through the forces of competition.

It is clear that Canada, like many other countries, is facing difficult choices in finding a balance between quality and cost while maintaining the principles of its universal health care system. Canada has been able to limit spending and health care's share of GDP despite sluggish growth of its economy over most of the 1990s. To deal with the fiscal constraints, Canada is taking a different approach than one involving market reforms, and it is too early to evaluate its success. Additionally, there are serious economic considerations that we have not addressed.

Critics of the Canadian system charge that health care is rationed in the sense that all the care that patients demand, or would be provided to meet their best interests, cannot be supplied on a timely basis. As noted in the model on the British National Health Service, rationing below market price leaves some people, who would be willing to pay more, unable to purchase *any* of the good at all. Though specific estimates of such shortages are not available, the consensus is that the limits on capacity and on new technology result in longer waiting periods for hospital services.[11] The "safety valve" of a private system, as in the United Kingdom, for those who are willing to pay more is not readily available, although some Canadians (particularly those near large U.S. border cities such as Buffalo and Detroit) use the U.S. facilities for this purpose.

[11]See Rakich (1991) and Krasny and Ferrier (1991) for good discussions on this issue.

Defenders of the U.S. approach claim that the waiting and queues found in Canada would be unacceptable to many U.S. patients. There is a greater level of amenities in the United States, and the greater availability of specialized care, together with high-tech medicine, often is viewed as an indicator of superior quality. Certain population health status indicators, when used to compare the health levels of the United States and Canada, do not support this claim of higher quality in the United States, but additional quality comparison data would be useful.

Furthermore, some analysts believe that the difference in health care spending between the two countries is not nearly as great as it appears. Krasny and Ferrier (1991) suggest that the following three factors represent much of the gap:

- The failure to account for capital costs in Canadian hospitals
- The larger proportion of elderly in the United States
- The higher level of spending on research and development in the United States

Danzon (1992) also emphasizes the substantial hidden costs in public health insurance systems. These include the inefficiency (welfare loss) attributable to the taxes that are needed to raise revenues and the burdens associated with nonprice rationing.

It is of some interest to review the polled opinions of U.S. and Canadian economists on the matter. A survey found that almost all of the Canadian respondents believed that their system is far superior; U.S. respondents were divided on this issue.[12] The Canadian economists are much more willing to accept a government solution to the question of health care allocation. In contrast, many U.S. health economists argue in favor of freedom of choice for patients. They are also more likely to advocate a health system that seems to be more responsive to patient preferences and in which the patient is given incentives to choose wisely.

Though the current U.S. system has failed to achieve comparable performance to other systems in many respects, many believe that appropriate changes can be made. These changes would allow the United States to maintain a largely private system of finance and delivery, while it would preserve flexibility, choice, and higher levels of efficiency. The degree to which a synthesis of the two systems may be possible is an important health policy issue.

Differences in Health Care Spending across Countries

We have noted that different countries have different incentive systems, and, in fact, have differing shares of national product in the health care sector. Having described the systems, and having examined briefly the shares of national product in the health sector, it is appropriate now to explore why the shares differ.

A SIMPLE MODEL OF HEALTH EXPENDITURES SHARES

Consider a model of health expenditures. Let us call total expenditures on health care E. By definition, these expenditures equal the price of health care multiplied by the quantity of health care consumed, or $E = PQ$. Defining the share of national income spent on health care as s, we calculate s as the ratio of E to national income, Y, or:

$$s = PQ/Y \qquad\qquad \textbf{(23.1)}$$

[12]Feldman and Morrisey (1990, Table 7).

In this accounting framework, the share, s, can rise because either the price or quantity has risen, or because the national income has fallen. In fact, mathematically it can be shown that:

$$(\% \text{ Change})s = (\% \text{ Change})P + (\% \text{ Change})Q - (\% \text{ Change})Y \qquad \textbf{(23.2)}$$

The preceding expression is an identity, mathematically true *by definition*. Even so, it can provide useful insights. If the price of health care, P, rises by the same rate as the price of all other goods, so that Y rises at that same rate, then the health care share of national income does not change.

APPLYING THE MODEL

Rather than looking just at the percentage changes that occur, we try to examine *why* they occur. Consider, for example, that prices of health care may be related to the kind of health system the country has or to the social insurance scheme. Also consider that the quantity of health care used, Q, tends to increase when national income, Y, increases. Note also that the quantity of health care, Q, tends to be negatively related to the price of health care, P, through the demand relationship.

Consider several ideas in turn:

1. An increase in the price of health care would increase the share if there were no consumer response. The extent to which consumers reduce demand (in response to price changes) will offset the increase in prices.
2. An increase in the number of people in the population who use health care would tend to increase health care expenditures.
3. An increase in national income, Y, that is unaccompanied by an increase in demand for health care would decrease the share. However, this effect would be offset to the degree that increased national income leads to increased demand; the effect depends on the income elasticity of demand. If, in fact, a 1 percent increase in national income leads to a 1 percent increase in expenditures (that is, the income elasticity at the national level is one), then the share will be constant.

Abel–Smith (1984) suggest factors that account for the continuing increases in health expenditures. Several can be well understood, within our present context, as factors that tend to increase Q:

- Expansion in the coverage of health insurance and/or in the scope of benefits provided
- Demographic change—particularly the increasing proportion of elderly, with their higher health care costs
- Expansion of providers (including physicians and dentists) per 1,000 population, leading to larger numbers of services authorized
- Increases in hospital beds and the rebuilding of hospitals, thus reducing or removing bottlenecks and supply restrictions
- Financial incentives to authorize the use of more resources per patient

Other changes in share, s, work through changes in price, P, including the following:

- Higher relative remuneration for health sector workers, due to equal pay for women and growing unionization
- Introduction of new technologies involving both higher capital expenditures and running costs

CROSS-NATIONAL COMPARISONS: PRIVATE VERSUS PUBLIC FINANCING SYSTEMS

Pfaff (1990) examines the comparative growth of health care budget shares in the period 1960 to 1985. He notes that health care spending grew rapidly in nearly all of the Western industrialized countries until about 1975. Starting in the mid-1970s, the health care budget shares of most countries have tended to flatten out; that is, they have remained constant over time. The United States, however, has seen significant increases in its health care cost share.

Pfaff attempts to relate expenditures and budget shares across countries for the years 1975, 1980, and 1983 to numerous variables reflecting incomes, prices, costs, and demographics. Any systematic relationships between spending and these variables would provide evidence to explain changes in budget shares.

When Pfaff groups countries on the basis of their health care system, he finds that countries financed primarily by private payments, most particularly the United States, emerge with the highest expenditures, and this is not explained solely by a higher level of per-capita income. In the context of a larger study, he concludes that the dominant differences among countries in shares and expenditures are found in the mode of public or private financing. He argues that centrally funded health care systems offer more countervailing power to providers' abilities to increase P and Q than do privately funded health care systems. He also finds that copayment variables tend to be insignificant and argues that this factor casts serious doubt on the ability of market-based methods to reduce costs.

Pfaff concludes as follows:

> If this line of reasoning is accepted, a further conclusion may also be inescapable. As countries characterized by a national health service generally show lower health expenditures than those financed by contributions, and as there are no striking differences evident in the health status of the population either, the former may also be more cost-effective than the latter. Such a conclusion would *not necessarily hold* [emphasis added], however, if health status and benefits were measured not only in terms of morbidity or mortality indicators but also in terms of waiting times in ambulatory practices, delays in hospital admission, individual satisfaction of patients, etc. (p. 23).

A careful reading of Pfaff's statement here emphasizes that additional factors should be considered in choosing a health care system. A careful analyst must impute the extra time costs, as well as the possibly lower quality of care in national health service systems, before deciding conclusively on the full costs of alternative systems. The analyst also must decide whether a consumer, or a country, expresses a willingness to pay more for higher quality. Nonetheless, Pfaff's findings offer provocative evidence and encourage others to compare alternative health care delivery systems.

Goodman (1999) applies Gordon's classification of four types of health benefit systems with particular reference to health care demand per capita for the years 1980, 1985, 1990, and 1993 to 24 countries. After controlling econometrically for income, the price of health relative to other goods, and the specific years chosen, he found that the degree of health system control changed demand by the following percentages relative to traditional sickness insurance:

- National health insurance—0.6 percent lower (than sickness insurance)
- National health service—17.2 percent lower
- Mixed system—0.6 percent higher

The major impact came from the national health service category, where the state provides health care. The other two categories were statistically and substantively insignificant.

These findings must be tempered by the acknowledgement that nonmonetary costs, including waiting times for some treatments (and the inability to get some treatments at all) are not included in these calculations. Imputing money values to the (presumably) greater waiting time costs in more controlled systems would increase "full expenditures" in those countries where access to health care is more controlled by nonprice means.

Conclusions

In this chapter, we have examined a variety of health care systems found elsewhere. Variations exist in terms of financing, provider payment mechanisms, and the role of government, including the degree of centralization. The United States stands out as the country with the highest expenditures on health care.

It would appear that systems that ration their care by government provision or government insurance incur lower per-capita costs. On the other hand, in the largely private system in the United States, waiting times tend to be shorter than in rationed systems, a conclusion that follows simply from theory as well as from observation. Americans have been more dissatisfied with their health system than Canadians or Europeans have been with theirs. Which system then is best? Study of comparative systems helps to clarify the real differences and advantages from what is just opinion. The study of comparative systems suggests several features of other systems that may be worth adopting. It also suggests that cultural differences among countries may dictate that systems tailored to the local culture be different even in the long run.

Summary

1. Many characterize the main gap in the American system as the problem of the uninsured—more than 40 million people. While this does not mean that they go entirely without care, the uninsured consume only half as much health care on average as the insured. Experiences of other countries might lend useful guidance in formulating new policies.
2. A useful typology of health benefit systems provides four categories:
 - *Traditional Sickness Insurance:* the private insurance market approach, with state subsidy.
 - *National Health Insurance:* the state establishes a national-level health insurance system.
 - *National Health Service:* the state provides the health care.
 - *Mixed System:* mixed elements of the above.
3. Among all countries, the United States is by far the biggest spender in absolute per-capita terms. It is also the biggest spender as a share of GDP.
4. The United Kingdom's NHS provides relatively easy access to primary and emergency care, while elective services are rationed either through long waiting lists or

by limiting the availability of new technologies. The NHS devotes considerable resources to high-return services such as prenatal and infant care.

5. The United Kingdom reformed its health system in 1991 to include elements of competition. The United States has fewer hospital beds per capita than the United Kingdom, and fewer nurses per bed as well. Health care spending per capita in the United Kingdom, however, is only 33 percent of the U.S. level.

6. Germany manages to provide a health system that delivers universal health insurance while avoiding the queues that often trouble governmental systems. However, costs per capita have been increasing faster than the incomes per capita, a problem leading to strenuous 1993 reforms.

7. From 1977 to 1989, South Korea jumped from having just 10 percent of the population covered to universal health coverage. South Korea's cost-containment strategies rest mainly with high coinsurance rates and fee controls. Its experience demonstrates that it is possible to phase in mandated, employment-based insurance without serious adverse effects to a nation's economy.

8. Many Americans feel that Canada has successfully developed a comprehensive and universal national health insurance program that is both cost effective and popular.

9. Compared to the U.S. system, the Canadian system has lower costs, more services, universal access to health care without financial barriers, and superior health status. Canadians have longer life expectancies and lower infant mortality rates than do U.S. residents.

10. Part of the gap between U.S. and Canadian health care costs may be explained by a
 • failure to account for Canadian hospitals' capital costs
 • larger proportion of elderly in the United States
 • higher level of spending on research and development in the United States

11. National health systems appear to reduce health spending. However, careful analysis across alternative systems must impute the additional time costs, as well as the possibly lower quality of care in national health service systems, before deciding conclusively on the full costs of alternative systems.

Discussion Questions

1. Discuss the factors that may lead one nation to spend more per person on health care than another nation might spend. What are the implications of finding health care to be income elastic in cross-national studies? When health care is income elastic, will richer countries tend to have a higher or lower proportion of GDP spent on health care?

2. In countries in which there is nonprice rationing for care, waiting time costs may be substantial. How could you evaluate the economic costs of the waiting time?

3. Create a table comparing the British, German, and South Korean health care systems with respect to financing, availability, and costs of care. How do they compare with the system in the United States?

4. Suppose that the price of health care services rises and the quantity demanded falls. Under what conditions might the health care share of GDP fall? Rise?

5. It is important to compare items under the rubric of all else equal. What are some of the crucial factors that must be adjusted when comparing health expenditures across countries?

6. Distinguish between a national health insurance system and a national health service. Provide examples of each. What kind of a system does the United States have?

7. Americans are more dissatisfied with their health care system than are people in other countries. Discuss whether this is a useful indicator of the performance of a health care system.

8. A common thesis in economics is that markets are efficient unless characteristics are present that lead to market failure. What sorts of market failure in the health economy can be used to justify adoption of universal national health insurance? What kinds of government failure can be used to argue against this proposal?

9. Do countries with more comprehensive national programs for the provision of health care tend to have lower average costs than the United States? Do they have lower rates of growth in costs? Discuss.

10. Speculate about the level of technology available across countries. Do you think that better health care is available in the United States than in Canada? Do international health indices suggest this? What are the complicating issues?

Exercises

1. Consider the allocation of services in the United Kingdom's NHS, as noted in Figure 23.1. If the government raises the administered price up from P^*, trace what would happen to expenditures in the NHS and in the private sectors.

2. Define income elasticity of health care demand. If income rises by 1 percent and the income elasticity of health care demand is 0.5, does the share of income going to health care rise or fall? Why?

3. Suppose the price elasticity of health services is −0.5. What will happen to the share of health care expenditures, given a 10 percent drop in health care prices?

4. For more advanced students, Table 23.1 provides data for at least rudimentary estimates of income elasticity of health care expenditures. Estimate a regression equation of the following form:

$$Log\ (Expenditures\ per\ capita) = a + b\ log\ (GDP\ per\ capita)$$

What is the implied income elasticity of expenditures across countries?

5. From the data in Table 23.1, estimate a regression equation of the following form:

$$Log\ (Infant\ deaths\ per\ 1,000) = c + d\ log\ (Expenditures\ per\ capita)$$

What does your resulting equation say about the "effectiveness" of expenditures per capita (without adjusting for any other factors)?

Health Systems Reform

- ■ Health System Reform in International Perspective

- ■ Assuring Access to Care

- ■ Providing Care at Lower Cost

- ■ Conclusions

Health care reform is an issue that ties together countries that lack social health insurance with countries that provide universal coverage. It unites countries with competitive, pluralistic health systems with those having highly centralized, bureaucratic systems. Health care reform has two major themes:

- the provision of equitable access to care for all citizens and residents
- the attainment of lower costs, or lower rates of growth in costs

Everyone favors lower costs for a given level of services, and recently even countries with substantial welfare states have examined market reforms to address cost containment. Equity of access interests most Americans, at least those who supported a form of universal coverage during the 1993–1994 debate over the Clinton plan. In most countries, equity has dominated cost control in the policy arena, but the rising costs of the 1980s and early 1990s have made cost containment a major concern.

Reform addresses both the particular and the general. Local features of the health system must be understood by the reformers. There are also general issues, which are those faced commonly by all systems. We examine several of the general issues in this chapter. Health care must be financed, and social insurance systems must be funded by some form of taxation, thus raising the issue of tax incidence, as well as the question of whether the insurance mandated should be employer based or individual based. The common concerns about costs have raised interest in managed care and managed competition in many countries. Cost sharing has been applied in Europe and the Pacific Basin. We address the themes of access and cost containment in turn, but first consider brief histories of health system reform elsewhere.

Health System Reform in International Perspective

We review reform efforts in countries that illustrate basic approaches: the United Kingdom, the Netherlands, Germany, and Canada. European health insurance is generally provided with universal coverage. However, Europeans, too, have felt the need for reform; in fact, some countries have responded with waves of reform campaigns. Reform sometimes arrives with political turmoil and public questioning, just as in the United States.

THE UNITED KINGDOM

For Americans, the British National Health Service epitomizes alternatively a highly centralized "socialized medicine," an enviably equitable if clumsy and regimented health system, or a fine example of how a single-payer system makes possible a healthy population at modest cost. Despite its apparent success in raw data, such as life expectancy and infant mortality for low per-capita expenditure, by the 1980s, cracks in the system were becoming noticeable. Long waiting lines became commonplace, shortages of funds appeared in localities, questions were raised about quality, and accusations of overbedding were published in the press and government documents.[1]

Though many Britains still loved and supported the National Health Service, these troubles enabled Prime Minister Margaret Thatcher to call for a review of the system, which resulted in the white paper *Working for Patients,* published in 1989. In harmony with the themes of the Thatcher government, it recommended an infusion of competition, but it maintained universal coverage funded by general taxes. Vigorous protests from providers, experts, and the public did not deter the government's passage of the 1990 National Health Service and Community Care Act, which incorporated these reforms.

These sweeping reforms represent the NHS's biggest shake-up since its birth. The design instills a form of managed competition into a fundamentally bureaucratic structure. Newly identified groups of providers bid for inputs and services, with their supplier counterparts forming internal "markets." Hospital and community health systems became self-governing trusts, and district authorities became purchasers of care. This separation of purchaser and provider roles created the internal markets. A hospital now would survive only if it could attract sufficient patients.

The idea's success in getting this far politically is due in large part to the system redesigns and persuasive powers of an American health economist, Alain Enthoven, who also played a pivotal role in the American health reform debates of 1993 and 1994. The test of Enthoven's restructuring of the NHS in Britain will be whether it enlivens provider responses, reduces the ubiquitous waiting line, and, especially difficult, reduces the per-capita health care costs of one of the lowest-cost health systems in the industrialized world.

THE NETHERLANDS

The health reforms of the Netherlands also intended to instill market elements to replace government regulation, maintaining a system of social insurance that covers the entire population. In 1987, the Dekker Report led to reforms to introduce universal

[1]This and the following paragraph were particularly informed by Laurene Graig, *The Health of Nations,* 3d ed., 1999. For a further account, especially a discussion of overbedding claims, see James (1995).

insurance for a set of basic services and to allow individuals to purchase supplemental insurance beyond that (Ham and Brommels, 1994). The Dekker reform proposals also introduced "selective contracting," whereby insurance companies selectively shop for the best deals from hospitals, clinics, and other health providers. Thus, Dutch reform efforts have reflected a growing acceptance of competition in the health care marketplace.

Compared to the United Kingdom, competition has developed much more slowly in the Netherlands. "This reflects the more cautious Dutch approach to health care reform, the limited scope of competition in many parts of the country, and prevailing cultural characteristics" (Ham and Brommels, 1994, p. 112). The elections in 1994 brought a new leadership and shifted the emphasis away from market competition and toward a reemphasis on government (Graig, 1999).

GERMANY

Germany has long impressed many American analysts as a country that could maintain a well-functioning health system, provide universal access, and yet control its costs. It may be surprising to learn that many Germans see their own system differently. "As the German population ages and as medical progress and medical technology become even more widespread, the Germans . . . are searching for new ways to control costs" (Henke, Murray, and Ade, 1994).

This concern over rising costs and consequent increases in the contributions Germans must make to the "sickness funds" has created a seemingly perpetual cycle of health system reform. Their experiments with voluntary cost targets, with limits on total spending on physicians, were converted to mandatory caps in 1986. In 1989, cost sharing, such as copayments for health services, was introduced for some services and increased substantially for others (Japan and Korea also rely significantly on cost sharing in their efforts to control the rate of growth in health care costs). Still dissatisfied, Germans extended budget caps, which now are applied to many sectors within the health industry. This was the "Big Bang" in German health reform (Graig, 1999). The reform also introduced a revised payment system similar to the DRG system for Medicare in the United States. To counteract a perception of an excess of doctors— substantially more doctors per capita than in the United States—supply limit policies were introduced, such as a system of forced retirements of doctors. The 1993 reform law also introduced competition into the sickness fund system of insurers. Now, the German citizen is allowed, once a year, to choose a new insurance fund.

CANADA

Canadians have addressed reform in several ways. Hospitals are the major cost sector, and global budgets are applied to control these costs. Global budgets limit total hospital expenditures as opposed to limiting expenditures on individual patients, groups of patients, hospital input groups, or hospital cost centers. Physicians are reimbursed directly by the provincial governments, and vigorous government fee negotiation is a potential cost control measure. Ten provinces now cap physician fees (Graig, 1999). Finally, the Canadians have decentralized their health system, with the central parliament placing the system in the hands of the provinces and even subprovincial regions. This process is called "devolution." The test of reform for Canadian is greater cost control while reducing the level of complaints, particularly complaints about waiting times.

Assuring Access to Care

After this brief tour of health reforms of selected industrial countries, let us refocus on the United States, analyzing the major ideas and proposals applicable here and, in several cases, to the larger world. We now group reforms by their two main motivations: the desire to see that people who are sick get health care and the desire to control the rising cost of health care.

INDIVIDUAL VERSUS EMPLOYER MANDATES

The country that wishes to provide universal coverage for health care must choose one scheme or another to extract tax payments from its households. Schemes for employers or government to pay the bills are only mechanisms by which households ultimately pay. In the U.S. health debate, two mechanisms were featured prominently in proposals and thus contrasted: individual versus employer mandates.

Employer mandates form the backbone of the health systems in Europe, Latin America, and Asia (Krueger and Reinhardt, 1994). Under the employer mandate, the employer must procure health insurance for its employees and their dependents. While the employer nominally pays, the firm undoubtedly will pass on as much of this cost as it can to customers in the form of higher prices, or to employees in the form of lower wages. Under the individual mandate, workers are obligated to purchase health insurance for themselves and their families, either from private insurance (individually purchased) or through a group such as a work group, professional organization, or religious group. The poor are subsidized in their purchases through government taxation of the relatively well-to-do.

The issue of who pays can be developed graphically. Figure 24.1A shows the demand and supply of labor in a market in which firms do not provide their employees with insurance. The equilibrium before the employer mandate is wage, W_0, and employment level, L_0. Suppose the health insurance premium for each worker is $\$H$. By forcing the employer to pay this premium, we are adding $\$H$ to the wage bill: employers would likely subtract this from the wages they are willing to pay. To keep the problem simple, let us also assume that workers do not value this fringe benefit. The effect of the mandate then is to shift the demand curve downward by the amount of the premium.

The new demand for labor, the dotted line in Figure 24.1A, forms a new equilibrium at wage, W_1, and employment level, L_1. Thus, the result is a job loss of $(L_0 - L_1)$ and a reduction in wages of $(W_0 - W_1)$. The employee thus faces a substantial part of the burden of the mandate. The loss in wages here is less than the premium because part of the premium shock has been absorbed by a reduction in employment.

Business leaders often complain that employer mandates either will reduce profits or force firms out of business. Such responses often seem to be made, however, under the assumption that only the one firm is affected by the mandate. If all firms were made to bear the same labor costs, it is doubtful that closings would result. In the short run, firms would pay workers less, take less in profits, and raise prices to consumers. "Economists are convinced, however, that in the longer run more and more of the cost of the employer mandate would likely be shifted backward to employees . . . through smaller real (inflation-adjusted) increases in wages that would have been warranted by long-run productivity gain" (Krueger and Reinhardt, 1994, p. 44).

It is more plausible, however, that many workers will value the health insurance benefit and be attracted to the job in part because of this benefit. As a result, a lower

Are People Everywhere in the World Basically the Same?

This question takes on importance when we consider whether convergence of the world's many health systems is desirable. A local academic recently returned from a sabbatical in Germany with this story:

> My wife and I became good friends while we were in Freiburg with a German couple named Joachim and Marlene. At some point they told us, half humorously, that theirs was a 'mixed marriage.' They meant that Joachim came from Baden, while Marlene was from Schwaben, two neighboring areas that few foreigners could tell apart. Our friends, to the contrary, said these were quite different cultures, at least at one time."

Written sources support this account so far as to assert that until modern mobility arrived in Germany, the large middle contained many distinct "kingdoms." Would these different peoples desire identical health systems and reforms? Are many of the differences we observe across health systems truly the result of inefficiencies, or are they the expressions of different cultures?

That cultural differences may motivate both health care consumers and providers has been noted by many researchers. U.S. researchers are aware that ranchers in Montana have different attitudes about seeing the doctor or going to the hospital than do residents of Manhattan. The largely Mormon residents of Utah exhibit substantially better health habits than do residents of neighboring Nevada. Approaches to childbirth in France, an innovator in the reliance on midwifery, are distinct from the mix of approaches applied in Holland. If these cultural differences have consequences for health costs, are higher health costs necessarily a problem?

Three cases suggest that there may be large consequences from the differences in cultures.

U.S. patients demand the latest health technologies when a serious illness occurs or threatens. Correspondingly, the prevalence of high-tech scanners and other new diagnostic equipment is much higher in the United States, and their use has significant cost consequences. Are costs that are inflated for this reason to be considered inefficiencies or merely questions of taste?

Similarly, medical anthropologists argue that cultural differences among countries are important in both the diagnosis and treatment of common mental illnesses; historically, U.S. physicians are reported to apply the diagnosis of schizophrenia to patients much more commonly than do European physicians. Furthermore, the patient's approach to mental illness depends in important ways on his or her culture.

Lastly, a number of European countries have health systems that reflect European perceptions of illness and the human need for recuperation. Joachim and Marlene told of visiting the health spa, "the Kur," while under prescription from a physician and fully covered by the health insurance system. The "cures" are often more vigorous than might be desired by the truly idle rich. Daily regimens require vigorous and healthful activities. Yet, a proposal in the United States to offer universal access to basic health care, including access to the health spa when needed, would hardly be treated seriously.

These examples of known cultural differences regarding health and health care are all found across industrialized Western societies. Greater differences are found quickly when expanding the search to the cultures throughout the developing world. Are people everywhere basically the same, and will one ideal health system fit all? Travelers would probably agree that the answer must be "no."

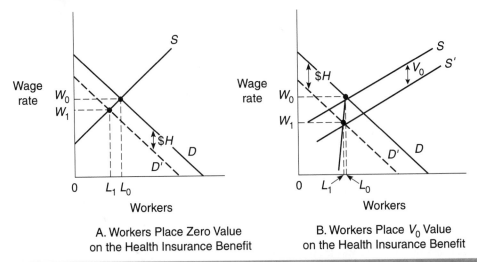

FIGURE 24.1 Impact of Employer Mandate in an Uninsured Industry.

money wage is necessary to induce workers to offer their labor than would be necessary without the benefit. This implies that the labor supply curve will shift downward by the value workers place on the health insurance. In Figure 24.1B, the depicted workers happen to value the benefit dollar for dollar as much as its cost to employers. The result is a new equilibrium with the same quantity of labor supplied after as before the benefit was provided, and the workers' wages have declined, exactly offsetting the extra health benefit cost to the employer.

When the labor supply curve is nearly vertical, representing a very inelastic labor supply, the employer's extra health benefit costs are offset by lower wage expenditures regardless of whether the laborers value the benefit highly or not at all. Most economists who study the issue probably would agree that the aggregate labor supply, at least in the long run, is nearly vertical for men and also highly inelastic for women. In this scenario, the mandate has little effect on producers, their competitive position, or their customers. Whether the program helps or harms the well-being of society under conventional economic analysis depends to a large extent simply on whether workers value their health insurance as much or more as they did their foregone wages.[2]

On appearances, the individual mandate provides the same result with a clearer pathway. The cost falls on the one to whom it is assessed. Pauly (1994b) describes an individual mandate, enforced by employers and subsidized for the poor, requiring all individuals to purchase a minimum health plan or better. He argues that this approach is "desirable for rational political decision making for citizens to be aware of what taxes they are paying to obtain benefits" (p. 23).

During the U.S. debate of 1993–1994, disputes arose frequently over the fraction that the employer pays versus the fraction paid by the individual. The presumption in these arguments is that the chosen fraction reflects the burden. Economists, however, tend to agree that the fraction chosen does not matter. Some argue that it is a political

[2]The issues of employer vs. individual mandate are elaborated by Pauly (1997).

necessity to overlook the economics, yet others insist that an open public discussion of the genuine issues would improve the quality of national debate.

SEPARATION OF HEALTH INSURANCE FROM EMPLOYMENT

In redesigning a health system, a good argument can be made for revising or replacing the prevailing system of employer-provided insurance. Change can be accomplished by either a single-payer system or an individual mandate. The benefits of employer provision are partly the result of a deception, which is possibly well meant but causes economic distortions.

The historical relationship of the two reveals a distortive beginning. During World War II, the U.S. government further froze prices and wages. Firms and markets are nevertheless dynamic and resistant to such imposed freezes. Competing for workers, firms expanded their fringe benefits, which were not subject to the freeze. In postwar years, employer contributions to health insurance were and continue to be tax exempt, providing workers with a substantial discount and thus inviting inefficiencies of overinsurance. Meanwhile, many of the unemployed, as well as many low-wage employed, go without health insurance, creating a system of substantial overinsurance for some while many are not insured at all.

The highly mobile U.S. working population also results in health insurance problems when workers change jobs. When leaving their old company's health coverage behind them, workers have little choice but to buy an individual policy or do without insurance entirely. Individual policies are often more expensive, sometimes pose administrative problems, and sometimes are a lower financial priority for people out of work. Workers, at least prior to recent legislation that addressed some of these problems, often found their preexisting conditions to be uninsurable.

To deal with these and other distortions, some economists recommend radical changes in the tax system to remove the tax subsidy that effectively ties health insurance to the workplace. Fuchs (1994, p. 11) argues: "... that if government imposes enough mandates, enough subsidies, enough surcharges, and enough controls and regulations, the tie to employment can be severed. However, such a complex system invites evasion, gaming, and litigation." Fuchs recommends a value-added tax to finance universal coverage of health insurance. It is not without controversy, but it does suggest an alternative system in which health insurance is not tied to the job.

SINGLE PAYER VERSUS MULTIPLE INSURERS

A move in the United States toward universal coverage also entails the option of a single insurer, presumably the federal government. The option of multiple insurers retains part of the status quo in the United States, where many private insurance companies provide the majority of insurance with government providing about 40 percent. The most prominent single-payer proposal discussed in the U.S. debates was a version of the Canadian system, which the Canadians call Medicare.

In principle, costs can be reduced by consolidating insurers if there are economies of scale in administration or if gains can be made from pooling the insureds. The U.S. health system has been criticized for its excessive administrative costs. Assuming that administrative savings can be achieved by switching to a government single-payer system is somewhat risky, however. The same administrative technology is available to the private sector, and if further economies were possible, it is likely that surviving private

firms would be those who merged to take advantage of the economies, provided the existing firms were not earning monopoly profits. In addition, the profits that private firm insurers gain are not a waste to the economy, but rather are a payment for capital that government also must incur.

In an example of the theory, the single-payer system reduces costs by eliminating the multiple forms and policy rules that face hospitals, clinics, and nursing homes. The United States has some 1,500 different insurers (Gauthier et al., 1992). The difficulty of coordinating many different policies falls on hospitals and physicians; it is external to the insurance company. Nevertheless, it is a real economic cost to society, and it could be reduced if the government as single payer offers fewer forms and some standardization. These are costs that increase with decentralization.

Costs of decentralization, however, could be reduced by improvements in computer technology. As claims handling becomes computerized, potential is increased for solving the problem with software that establishes interfaces between the forms and protocols of different companies. Electronic data interchange technology can link "the entire health care administration and delivery systems" (Gauthier, p. 314) through the use of cards with a magnetic strip similar to ATM cards. Common formats and standards will be widespread.

The operation of the government enterprise also raises the question of incentives. Government may fail to reduce costs because government, in most cases, lacks the discipline of the profit incentive and the discipline of market competition. The result would be higher costs rather than lower costs.

In any case, the switch to a single-payer system would largely eliminate the health insurance industry. Do the problems of the health care system warrant such a radical change, presuming these problems would be solved by the change? More modest reforms address specific problems. For example, the problem of the uninsured can be addressed by mandated coverage including subsidies for the poor. The problem of providing coverage for people with preexisting conditions can be solved through the individual mandates and, without using mandates, was addressed by recent legislation. Such approaches avoid the potential slowing effect on innovation, which has been cited as a drawback of the single-payer system. Would the rapidly changing and developing computer industry have progressed so quickly were it not for the many small startup companies? Would the single-payer system for health insurance innovate as rapidly?

A potential benefit of the single-payer system lies with the common coverage that is possible. We may worry now that some insured people have inadequate policies in terms of the depth and breadth of coverage. In contrast, the single payer could offer one policy or just a few, regulated so that each one is deemed adequate by policy makers representing the public. In contrast, the availability of many policies from many companies offers variety, tailoring policies to the individual preferences for cost-sharing features and coverage.

Issues and questions surround the choice of a single-payer versus a pluralistic system that cannot be answered with confidence. Even the claim that a single-payer, Canadian-style system would have lower administrative costs is controversial. To eliminate the insurance industry on the basis of existing knowledge would be more of a political choice and an indictment of the insurance industry than an economic choice.

Would employer-based universal health insurance make the United States uncompetitive internationally? Industry executives often respond as did "Red"

Polling, then chairman of Ford Motor at a staff meeting of President-Elect Clinton in 1992:

> ... health care costs give Japanese automakers an advantage over Ford of $500 per car. Ford spends as much on health care as it does on steel. Health care providers are our biggest suppliers.[3]

The economist, in contrast, points out two features of employer-based universal health insurance that contradict such analyses: (1) the health insurance is part of the total labor compensation package, and (2) the incidence of the implied tax falls primarily on the worker. It is the workers who demand health insurance as well as money as part of their compensation; when they bargain for it, their bargaining is evidence that they feel buying health insurance as a tax-preferred fringe benefit is worth the inevitable reduction in wages.[4] Understood as such, the workers' purchase of health insurance through the employer is just a different way of purchasing a consumption good. It is essentially the same, in this respect, as the purchase of food or housing with wages. Yet, industry executives rarely complain that the high cost of food or housing in the United States is making them uncompetitive internationally, nor do they claim conversely that the high cost of housing in Japan gives Ford a big advantage in exporting cars to that country. Meanwhile, the experts on international competitiveness generally view the United States, once again, as the world's most competitive economy. The "think tanks" that touted U.S. competitiveness were well aware of America's famously high per-capita health care costs when making their judgment.

HEALTH CARE REFORM AND INTERNATIONAL COMPETITIVENESS

When health insurance costs rise or employer-based universal coverage is mandated, the adjustments will come to wages, profits, or prices (e.g. cars). The degree to which it falls on reduced wages in theory depends on the elasticities of the labor supply and demand. We will discuss that side shortly, but first suppose that it fell entirely on the employer. To consider the ability of the firm to pass along this cost to the buyer, panels A and B of Figure 24.2 depict the demand, marginal revenue, and marginal cost curves for the firm under the alternative assumptions that A, it has some monopoly power, and B, that it faces considerable competition.

In panel A, the demand curve is downward sloping and the marginal revenue curve lies below the demand curve. If health costs cause the firm's wage bill to rise, this will affect the marginal cost of producing cars, shifting curve MC upward to MC'. In response, the equilibrium price will rise from P_0 to P_1. In this sense, part of the rise in marginal costs has been passed on to the consumer. However, suppose that the firm faces substantial competition from other U.S. car companies and from abroad so that its demand curve is flatter. The more elastic demand curve implies that the firm will lose substantial business if it raises its price. In this case, the demand curve and marginal revenue are close together. We have drawn the limiting case in Panel B where they are identical. Now note that as marginal cost rises, the prices of cars does not rise. The equilibria to compare are points K and L.

[3]See Pauly (1997, p. 28).

[4]Workers who are unaware of the trade-off do not necessarily have to know of it to practice it. When looking for a job, they will be faced with the relevant number: "We pay pretty well here, and you should take a look at our great health insurance package." If they have two or more offers, they can impose their preferences.

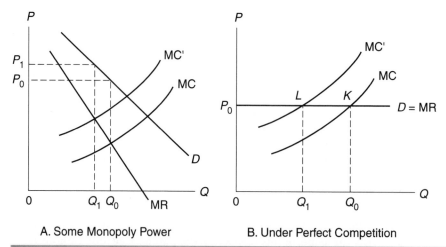

FIGURE 24.2 The Effect of a Rise in Marginal Cost on the Price of Cars.

The implication of these analyses is that the ability of the firm to pass on its health costs to the consumer depends on its elasticity of demand. If the increased car price includes hundreds of dollars of increased health costs, it is only because the firm had the power to pass these hundreds on. The more vulnerable our firms are to competition, the less ability they have to pass extra costs along to consumers. If not consumers, then who pays for them? We turn our attention now to the market for labor.

Looking back at Figure 24.1B, the labor supply shifts downward to the extent to which the laborers value the health insurance fringe benefit (at its cost in the case), with the entire incidence of the tax falling on the laborers. Making the case even stronger, were the supply curve nearly vertical, as is likely in the aggregate, then the incidence will inevitably and entirely fall on the worker.[5] The general implication of the analysis is that employer-mandated health insurance becomes a national tax borne by the worker, which will have little effect on the competitiveness of our products internationally.

Providing Care at Lower Cost

The demise of major health reform legislation in the United States in 1994 led many to conclude that sweeping reform was no longer possible politically in the near future. This led to emphasis on incremental steps to address specific problems but that avoided radical change. One proposal calls for the creation of medical savings accounts (MSAs) (Pauly, 1994b; Pauly and Goodman, 1995).

MEDICAL SAVINGS ACCOUNTS

Medical savings accounts, special accounts that individuals use only for medical purposes, address several problems. The first is the distortion caused by the current tax

[5]The labor supply curve for a single firm or even for a single industry commonly will be elastic, but for the economy as a whole, workers will have to work somewhere and empirically are unresponsive to wage changes that are widespread. However, the supply elasticities for women tend to be somewhat larger.

exclusion of employer-provided health insurance, a subsidy that increases with the worker's marginal tax rate and hence with income. Second, the subsidy is available only to those who work for someone else and only if that employer provides health insurance. Third, the bigger the policy one buys, the bigger the subsidy. Finally, the subsidy also violates the principle of horizontal equity, because it varies among people who have the same income level.

The Pauly/Goodman proposal replaces some of the current tax subsidy for health insurance with a tax credit for the purchase of insurance. The amount of the credit would be fixed irrespective of the size of the policy purchased. They also propose medical savings accounts (MSAs) and the purchase of catastrophic insurance with high deductibles.

The MSAs are savings accounts earmarked for payments of out-of-pocket expenditures for health care. The idea of MSAs is that instead of buying expensive, full-coverage policies, consumers would seek to save money by buying cheaper, high-deductible, catastrophic care coverage and then choose how to spend their leftover dollars for out-of-pocket costs under the deductible. Any money remaining in the MSA at year's end could be withdrawn and spent in any way the consumer sees fit. This feature means that the account holder has a strong incentive to buy wisely and conserve MSA money.

The tax credit would be a fixed-dollar amount contingent only on securing a basic catastrophic plan or more coverage. The credit does not increase if consumers choose to buy more extensive policies. If people choose a more expensive plan, the dollars come out of their own money. A further feature of the tax credit is that it is available to all citizens regardless of whether or not they are employees. Further, the proposed MSA contribution would occur with after-tax income: hence, it would be subject to tax just like wages and most other forms of income. MSA proposals, which come in various forms, are not without their drawbacks. Pauly projected that they would have a modest effect at best, because only a small minority of citizens would use them. His prediction has been borne out. Those who do use them, he further suggests, will see only modest gains.[6]

MANAGED CARE AND COST CONTAINMENT

Managed care, as provided by HMOs and PPOs, delivers medical services at a lower cost than fee-for-service care, the savings being achieved primarily through lower hospital use rates. Here, at least, the managed care arrangements have clearly changed the economic incentives of the decision makers. If managed care savings can be transformed into savings in per-capita costs and if managed care arrangements can be made to work in other countries and cultures, then managed care poses a significant potential for health system cost containment.

A problem with managed care is that employers who offer an HMO to their employees often pay the premium as long as the HMO premium was not higher than the fee-for-service premium. This behavior by employers creates distorted incentives for the HMO in controlling its costs. In Figure 24.3 the HMO's demand curve is essentially vertical up to the point of the fee-for-service premium and quantity of care, Q_0, at

[6]See chapter 20 for further discussion including the Kennedy–Kassenbaum demonstration and the Medicare+ Choice MSA option.

FIGURE 24.3 Demand for HMO Care When the Employer Pays Any Price up to the Fee-for-Service Price.

point A. The HMO has an incentive to control costs (as noted by average cost curves $C_1, C_2,$ and C_3), but only such that they are lower than the fee-for-service premium, P_f.

Enthoven (1993) suggests that this incentive distortion can be corrected when employers design better alternatives for their employer contributions. The employer could contribute a fixed-dollar amount for health insurance with the employee paying the full difference between plans. The greater the portion of the marginal premium paid by the employees is, the stronger the incentive is to choose lower-cost plans. For example, if the employer pays 80 percent of the premium and the employee pays the remainder, then the employee pays only 20 percent of the difference between the low (let's presume here) HMO premium and the higher fee-for-service premium.

Another problem for managed care cost-containment analysis is that younger and healthier people tend to be attracted to the HMO, which offers lower-cost care, and from their perspective, adequate levels of care. The HMO offers cost containment and the younger, healthier person contracts for it. As a result, some HMOs have an unrepresentative healthy population to serve. The members fulfill their own prophecy because of their lower health care needs, and the HMO reports annually that it has lower costs than fee for service. As such, the HMO is not necessarily reducing costs for the population as a whole because the non-HMO population will tend to represent poorer health risks and thus require more costly care.

Popular opinion among those people most concerned with health costs in the United States credits managed care with achieving the dramatic slowdown in national health expenditure growth in the latter half of the 1990s. This continues even as the public and many economists criticize the HMOs for their lapses in provision of services. The main question is whether the reduction in cost growth is only a one-time cost savings limited by the rate and level of HMO penetration—if HMO's reach their limit, then what? The public backlash against HMOs also will reduce the limit of penetration.

INTERNATIONAL PERSPECTIVE

We have addressed the issue of whether managed care savings can be transformed into cost savings for the population as a whole. Can the managed care structure be translated as well to other cultures and other countries? This is a question addressed by Harold Luft (1991).

Health care costs have been rising around the world, and there is increasing interest worldwide in reducing costs. Borrowing managed care from the United States, a "big spender" may seem unwise. However, on a case-by-case basis, elements of the U.S. system may prove effective. Can our experience with HMOs be translated to other health systems?

Luft explained that HMOs are not simple, homogeneous organizations: ". . . each HMO is a highly complex combination of economic incentives, bureaucratic structures, and personalities" (p. 172). What we know about them is limited. Economists have studied carefully a number of cases, but applying this knowledge to the broader population of HMOs may be difficult.

HMOs and other managed care arrangements organized on a prepayment basis come in a wide variety of forms. An HMO could hire physicians on a salary, contract with a preexisting group practice of physicians, or contract with physicians who maintain a fee-for-service practice. According to Luft, "Because specific social, legal, historical, political, and economic aspects of the medical care environment have shaped delivery systems such as the HMO, it is not reasonable to expect that the typical HMO could be transplanted intact to another country" (p. 173). Nevertheless, some general points can be made.

First, public risk taking can be limited with HMOs. An entitlement program requires the government to spend, without limit, bearing the risk if costs are unexpectedly high. Some risk could be transferred to the HMO, which makes a flat charge per patient.

Second, fee-for-service payment gives physicians the incentive to increase the services provided. Salaried physicians, however, have little incentive to increase patient revenues.

Third, division of labor between primary care and specialist physicians between the United States and Europe limits the export of classic HMO designs to Europe. Generalists and specialists in the United States share responsibilities and make referrals to one another, and the generalists can have hospital privileges and see patients through their hospital care. In Europe, some generalists' duties end at the hospital door. Luft argues, however, that some HMOs have developed in such environments. He cites cases where an HMO primary care group contracts with medical school-affiliated specialists, who are essentially salaried physicians taking over when appropriate at the specialist level.

Fourth, the key to HMO cost savings is the organization's wide range of medical services, both inpatient and outpatient. In this way, the HMO can receive the cost savings implied by reduced hospital use. This may be difficult to manage in systems where there are separate financing mechanisms for primary care physicians and inpatient care. As Luft (1991, p. 180) remarks. "If there were no way to shift funds from the 'hospital side' to the 'physician side,' it would be difficult to reward clinical decision makers for the development of more cost-effective practice styles."

What can we say overall? Managed care has exhibited potential for changing incentives, lowering costs, and maintaining quality. Generalizing from the existing studies to

the broad array of managed care arrangements in the United States is not yet possible. The potential for other countries is one additional step removed in that U.S. forms are not directly transplantable. Managed care nevertheless remains an intriguing if uncertain possibility for future cost containment through the reform of insurance organizations.

ETHICAL VALUES AND REFORM

Economists most often compare positive analysis (what *is*) with normative analysis (what *ought* to be). The difficulty of distinguishing between normative and positive statements illustrates the difficulty of economics as a science to make a difference in determining real-world policy. In his 1996 presidential address to the American Economics Association, Victor Fuchs addressed these issues systematically. Fuchs considered the U.S. debate over health care reform in 1993–1994 to be "shallow and inconclusive." Why does the health policy debate not have more solid economic content?

Fuchs (1996) considers three possibilities: (1) The research itself was inconclusive, (2) economists and others did not disseminate this research to a wide enough audience, and (3) the debate foundered on differences in people's ethical values. To pursue these issues, he developed and sent a questionnaire to leading health economists (46, or 88 percent, responded), leading economic theorists (44, or 63 percent, responded), and practicing physicians (42, or 89 percent, responded). The 20 statements in the questionnaire were identified by positive or normative contents by three experts who were not participants in the survey. Seven were identified as relatively value-free "positive" questions and the remaining 13 as relatively value-laden "policy-value" questions.

The responses then were tested to see if the responder groups tended to have within-group agreement. The result is that health economists were in agreement significantly for all positive questions and exhibited differences for seven out of 13 policy-value questions. Clearly, economists differ often about issues of value.

Fuchs found the health economists' agreement on positive questions to be high— higher than economists in other fields found in another recent survey—and these responses were significantly different from random chance on all seven positive questions. However, on normative questions, as is the case in many countries, health economists disagree frequently. Why is this so?

Disagreement on policy-value questions among health economists could conceivably reflect underlying disagreement on factual aspects of the policy-value questions. For example, the question "The United States should now enact some plan (national health insurance) to cover the entire population" elicited a 62–38 majority among health economists. This disagreement could result from different personal estimates of the degree of inefficiency resulting from the requirement that everyone have the same health insurance. Also plausible, however, is underlying disagreement on values, with those who agree placing a higher value on everyone having a right to care.

Fuchs's work suggests a fruitful area for future research. Its purpose would be to determine the possibilities for increasing the degree of agreement on policy issues based on further agreement on underlying positive issues. His own view is that values are the key, and that the problem is not so much that the health economists disagree about the embedded questions as that they are uncertain about them.

This insight suggests that the health policy debate in this country could improve if we are more explicit and open about value differences. Economists can help by

identifying the factual bases of policy issues and providing answers to positive questions of health economics. A further research question is to study the formation of ethical values and differences among people. Fuch's inquiry improves our understanding of past policy debacles and provides some optimism for the future.

Conclusions

Reviewing the recent history of health reforms in the United Kingdom, the Netherlands, Germany, and Canada, we found that most of the reforms have been tried somewhere in the industrialized world. These reforms can be grouped into two broad categories: assuring access to health care and controlling health care costs.

European systems generally provide universal, employer-based coverage. Reform in the United States has considered mandates to increase access, and we have examined the theory behind mandates. We found that the incidence of health premiums under employer-based systems does not depend on the fraction paid by the employer. This implies that much of the national debate on this issue has been focused on issues that most economists think irrelevant. Single-payer plans, such as that in Canada, offer theoretical economies of administration, but in practice it is more difficult to identify whether the observed cost advantages in Canada are likely to survive the translation into a reformed U.S. system. Because the incidence of the implied tax under a U.S. employer-based social insurance system is likely to fall largely on the worker, the reform has little or no theoretical effect on the economy's competitiveness and is no different from the individual mandate in this respect.

Controlling costs has been approached in many ways across countries. Strategies include a global budget, increased cost sharing, and various market incentives. The United States has left cost containment to managed care, but MSAs also have been supported. Medical savings accounts offer efficiency gains if properly designed; they substitute a tax credit payable to a special consumer account for the current tax-exempt fringe benefit approach.

Managed care achieves cost savings and may have contributed to the decline in the U.S. health cost growth rate. Their potential will continue to be limited to the extent that employers fail to offer true financial advantages to consumers who choose the low-cost health plans. American-style HMOs, the classic example of managed care, probably will not transfer unchanged to other countries because of cultural and system structure differences.

Theory and empirical evidence help clarify many questions about health reform, but it remains clear that most of these policy issues have a substantial normative component. Economics can estimate what it will cost to extend health insurance universally, but only one's values determine whether it should be done.

Summary

1. A common theme of health system reform across countries is the attempt to instill elements of competition.
2. Economic theory suggests that individual mandates and employer mandates will have similar tax incidence.
3. Advantages of the individual mandate include fine-tuning so that the subsidies could be based on low income rather than on wage.

4. Switching from the current U.S. health system to a single-payer system may save money by saving administrative work. However, such projections are risky.
5. For the entire country, labor supply is inelastic. Assuming inelastic supply, the incidence of a mandated health insurance program falls mainly on workers. International competitiveness in product markets is not affected.
6. A plan for encouraging medical savings accounts with tax credits poses the possibility of eliminating market inefficiencies now caused by the tax treatment of employer-provided health insurance.
7. The ability of managed care to control per-capita costs depends on whether consumers face incentives to choose the lower-cost plans. Managed care systems, such as HMOs, vary considerably, and they may not translate easily to other countries and other cultures.
8. Some recommend the separation of health insurance from employment in order to eliminate the inefficiency caused by the tax-exempt status of employer-provided health insurance.
9. Public disagreement on health system reform issues often may be caused by the confusion of positive issues with issues of ethical values. An opinion poll analysis suggests that differences in ethical values may be an important problem.

Discussion Questions

1. What issues are prominent in health system reforms internationally?
2. Would individual mandates for health insurance be more burdensome to the poor than employer mandates? Would lower-income groups be wise to favor one plan over the other?
3. If the national labor supply curve were elastic instead of very inelastic, how would an employer-mandated health insurance plan affect the country's international competitiveness?
4. How could a single-insurer health insurance system provide cost savings over a multiple-insurer system like that in the United States?
5. How does the medical savings account give incentives for the insured to save on care?
6. What ideas discussed in this chapter would be suitable to recommend to a country just now revising its health system? To pursue equity? To pursue cost containment?
7. What potential does managed care have to control per-capita health costs in the United States? In other countries?

Exercises

1. In Figure 24.1A, find the full per-unit cost of labor to the employer under an employer mandate. If the labor supply is perfectly inelastic, find the full per-unit cost of labor. Which of the two results is more likely in fact?
2. Suppose that a firm faces a downward-sloping demand curve and offers no health insurance to its employees. Let an employer mandate for health insurance be enacted. If this causes the firm's marginal costs to rise, will the firm pay the full cost of the health insurance out of profits? Is the mandate in fact likely to raise the firm's marginal costs?
3. In Figure 24.3, suppose the HMO sets price equal to its average cost. What is the effect on the HMO if its average cost were to rise from C_3 to C_2? What if its demand curve were to shift to the right?

25

The Health Economics of Bads

■ The Health Economics of Bads: An Introduction

■ Rationales for Public Intervention

■ Advertising Restrictions on Cigarettes and Alcohol

■ Excise Taxes and Consumption: Cigarettes and Alcohol

■ Conclusions

No discussion of the health economy can be complete without addressing one of the most prominent and controversial issues—the consumption of health bads. In a market economy, the consumer's sovereignty usually is regarded as a given: The consumer is free to choose. However, many exceptions can be found in any basically free society—cases where society encourages or discourages the consumer's desired choice. We encourage and promote use of motorcycle helmets, automobile emissions-control devices, old age pensions, and good prenatal maternal nutrition. In a similar spirit, we often discourage the purchase of alcohol, street drugs, and cigarettes.

The reason to intervene in private decisions could be paternalistic, but it also could appeal to economic efficiency. Cigarette smoking affects not merely the cigarette buyer and seller—effects that are internal to the cigarette market—but also the health of non-smokers nearby, which is an external cost. Similarly, because many health insurance companies do not distinguish between smokers and nonsmokers, perhaps because of high monitoring costs, nonsmokers may pay higher premiums than warranted by their actual health risks. The personal hazards of excessive alcohol consumption are also serious, including disability due to alcoholism and fatality due to liver disease. The external costs include possible harm to family or neighbors as well as the excessive, dangerous, and often-fatal traffic accidents due to drunk driving. Finally, when smokers and drinkers underestimate the probabilities of ill health due to their consumption, the imperfect information provides an efficiency rationale for measures such as taxes that tend to curb the behaviors.

Economists as citizens may choose one side or the other of these controversies, because their values are not determined by being economists. Economists as scientists, however, can illuminate the issues that are of interest to the public. For many people, the question is not whether to intervene in private decisions to smoke or drink, but how to do so more effectively and unobtrusively. This hinges on two economic questions. First, what is the relationship of price to demand? Second, what is the relationship of product advertising to total consumption?

The Health Economics of Bads: An Introduction

Economic reasoning is helpful to any approach to the analysis of bads such as cigarette smoking and excessive alcohol consumption. Economic models of addiction as well as market failure help determine whether intervention is justified on efficiency grounds. Alternatively, models of consumption, advertising, price, and taxation help us find relatively unobtrusive and cost-effective means to intervene, once intervention is chosen.

That cigarettes qualify as bads follows from the high death rates attributed to cigarette smoking. Deaths per capita from respiratory cancers rank highest among national death rates from malignancies and second only to categories of heart disease overall. Motor vehicle deaths are less than half this rate, and only a handful of states have HIV death rates that exceed one half of the respiratory cancer rate. Cigarette smoking is known to affect other disease categories as well, such as emphysema and heart disease. There is little doubt that getting successive generations of youth to choose never to smoke would lower average population age-adjusted mortality rates substantially. Econometric studies of the production of health commonly find cigarette consumption to be a significant and materially important predictor of mortality rates. In contrast, moderate alcohol consumption may not be medically harmful to most groups of people but substantial harm occurs with excessive consumption and inappropriate related behaviors, such as drunk driving.[1]

One economic approach is to assume that there are no grounds to intervene if the consumer chooses rationally and voluntarily, is reasonably informed of the risks, and creates no side effects for others. This view implicitly rejects all arguments not based on economic efficiency, including those grouped together as equity concerns. Furthermore, the view typically rejects other grounds as paternalistic. However, because alcohol and cigarette consumption are addictive, the issues of rationality, volition, and information take on extra weight.

MODELS OF ADDICTION

Models of addiction may posit psychological irrationality or myopia, and these begin with assumptions under which the usual economic conditions are not met. Rational addiction is a contrasting model in which it is shown that even an addictive product may be chosen voluntarily and rationally by an informed consumer. Good habits, such as listening to Mozart, or bad habits such as shooting heroin may be chosen even knowing

[1] In addition, cigarettes are implicated in low birth weights (Rosenzweig and Wolpin, 1995), and alcohol use by college age youth has been shown to reduce educational attainment (Cook and Moore, 1993).

that harmful health effects will result later in life, providing the current consumption increases the marginal utility of future consumption sufficiently. This condition is called adjacent complementarity.[2]

Rational addiction can account for behaviors of addicts commonly observed and familiar to most people, such as the phenomenon of quitting cold turkey. More useful to our purpose, the model explains how the response of consumption to price and advertising changes will differ between the short run and the long run. It generally suggests that taxation of bads, or sin taxes, will be more effective than originally thought.

Rationales for Public Intervention

Are cigarette smokers well informed of the risks of smoking so they can make rational choices? A few researchers challenged the common wisdom that smokers are ill-informed, reporting smokers' knowledge and responses to risk to be similar to that of nonsmokers.[3] At this point, however, the findings from various fields more generally suggest that smokers differ from nonsmokers on these bases.

Consider nonsmokers first. We mentioned that another route toward justifying intervention is to show that the consumption has detrimental side effects or external costs. Much then depends on the sizes of these costs. These externalities come from two principal sources: the passive smoking incurred by people nearby and all the various external costs caused by health hazards to the smoker. A Rand study led by Manning (1991) estimated the external costs at the equivalent of 33 cents per pack for a new smoker evaluated in 1995 dollars, though passive smoking costs were omitted. Viscusi (1995) also estimated the external costs per pack to be in this range, though lower than the Rand figure and near zero under some scenarios.

Because economic efficiency is only one economic criterion (the other is equity), because data issues can be disputed, and because economics is not the only basis to consider, many people will and have chosen to intervene in tobacco and alcohol use. If you decide that society should intervene, then the economic issue is how to do so. Economics offers two major tools that may be effective in curbing consumption of a targeted bad: restrictions on advertising and imposition of excise taxes. Advertising can be restricted by increasing the cost of advertising through tax code revisions, but most often the public issue is whether to restrict advertising by selective or total bans. The excise tax tool is theoretically effective to the degree that demand is more elastic for a given supply. These two principal tools of intervention form the subject of our remaining investigations. First, however, consider why we have chosen not to address the several other tools that might be used.

OTHER INTERVENTIONS

Two other potential forms of intervention are prohibitions on the consumption of the product and penalties for consumption or misuse of the product. Outright prohibition of cigarettes is unlikely to occur in the United States; memories of the Prohibition days when alcohol became illegal in the 1920s seem to point to that clear conclusion. The

[2]Becker and Murphy (1988) developed the theory of rational addiction. For additional discussion of rational addiction and adjacent complementarity, see chapter 6.
[3]Kip Viscusi has several findings of this kind (see e.g., 1995).

gangsterism and speakeasy culture of the time is not nostalgic for people who take public policy to heart. Furthermore, alcohol prohibition of that era probably was not even effective in reducing alcohol consumption (Miron, 1999).

Lesser prohibitions, however, often have been accepted and effective. These include the effect of lower speed limits on rates of fatal accidents involving alcohol, as well as bans on smoking in public places.[4] Many countries, especially in Scandinavia, apply much more severe penalties for drunk driving than the United States does. These include stiff jail sentences for alcohol offenses, offenses that many Americans regard as less serious. That legal penalties affect drunk driving behavior was shown by Mullahy and Sindelar (1994) for U.S. data in which increased fines and license revocations were highly significant in models of the individual's probability to drive drunk.

A word of caution is in order before addressing the issue of bads and advertising. The issues we will address are ones over which people differ and hold strong views. In a report on cigarettes, the Surgeon General (1989) concluded at one point that:

> There is no scientifically rigorous study available to the public that provides a definitive answer to the basic question of whether advertising and promotion affect the level of tobacco consumption. Given the complexity of the issue, none is likely to be forthcoming in the foreseeable future (pp. 516–517).

Even this conclusion is disputed by parties to both sides of the issue.

Advertising Restrictions on Cigarettes and Alcohol

Economists understand that well-intentioned interventions often have unintended consequences. Before we blame advertising for our ills, we need to inquire, more carefully than usual, into the nature of advertising.

THEORIES OF ADVERTISING

Three main theories have developed about how advertising works and what it does for or to the community. Advertising alternatively is a form of information, a tool for persuasion, or a complementary good. The first two of these represent an old battle in advertising theory with contrasting villains and heroes: Information is generally beneficial, while persuasion is at least more questionable. The most recent addition treats advertising as a complementary good.

Advertising as Information

Nelson (1974, 1970) studied the implications of advertising as information. Viewed as information, advertising can be seen to lower equilibrium prices, create better access to the market for new entrants, and provide better matches of consumer preferences with feasible consumption bundles. Informed consumers find that their dependence on or loyalty to Brand A will be weakened by their improved knowledge of alternatives.

If it is easy to opt for another brand, then the consumer has flexibility, and a flexible consumer is more likely to resist undesirable changes in the brand, such as a drop in quality or a rise in price. This greater responsiveness to price implies a more elastic

[4]See Chaloupka and Saffer (1992) and McCarthy (1993).

demand, and it makes possible lower market equilibrium prices. This theoretical result often is resisted by many laymen including physicians: How can the firm's costly advertising activity help but be passed on to consumers in the form of higher prices? The mistake is that while the price at a given output must rise, the market equilibrium quantity may change due to competition, and the equilibrium price may fall.

Advertising as a Barrier to Entry

In contrast to advertising as information, Bain (1956) argued that advertising differentiates one brand from another, creating increased brand loyalty. By making consumers more resistant to price changes and demand, advertising can result in greater market power and higher equilibrium prices.

Adding to this vision, Comanor and Wilson (1974) showed that the persuasive power of advertising may cause it to be asymmetrically effective for the incumbent versus potential new entrants. Consumers have greater experience with established firms and greater recognition of them. The next advertising dollar to be spent by the established firm will yield a greater return than the same dollar spent by the newcomer.

Advertising as a Complementary Good

Nobel laureate Gary Becker and colleague Kevin Murphy (1993) proposed a theory to account for these competing claims within a single model—one that appeals to the older theory of complements and substitutes familiar to students as well as professional economists. Let advertising be considered a good that is a complement to the good advertised. A consumer might wade through commercials with irritation during a ball game but enjoy the humorous one featuring a favorite beer. The commercial increases the consumer's marginal utility from consuming that brand, and under this theory, firm advertising will raise total consumption of the product, just as a reduction in the price of mustard will increase the consumption of hot dogs.

THE POSSIBLE EFFECTS OF BRAND SWITCHING

When an imperfectly competitive firm advertises, it potentially improves its demand in part by inducing consumers to switch brands and in part by inducing consumers to consume more product in total. However, other firms also will advertise for these purposes, and the advertising among the firms may be partially or even totally offsetting. Advertising in the industry could have little or no effect on total industry demand, but it also could have a positive effect.

Lay people often conclude mistakenly that the answer is obvious. Surely cigarette advertising must lead to more aggregate smoking or cigarette companies would not spend so much money on it. Cigarettes are among the most heavily advertised categories of product. A similar argument is made by some economists who say that the many available brands are really owned by a few companies and that the degree of brand switching (about 10 percent of smokers switch brands in a typical year) is not sufficient to justify the billions spent on advertising.[5] Sales figures confirm that 80 percent to 90 percent of U.S. cigarette sales are generated by the top four firms.

[5]Tye, Warner, and Glantz (1987).

Others argue that brand switching is a sufficient motivation for heavy advertising. Two points help explain this view: (1) the firm's decision to advertise is made ex ante with available information, and (2) the firm's decision criterion is what would happen if it did not advertise. On the one hand, the firm commits money to advertising based on the effect it expects advertising to have. The firm may not have the econometric data published later, it may not believe what is published, or admittedly, it may have better information. On the other hand, the number of smokers who actually switch on average is less relevant than the unknown number who would switch if the firm did not advertise.

INCREASED DEMAND OR BRAND SWITCHING?

To settle the question, we must examine the evidence. If we find that advertising increases total consumption, we could proceed in reverse; we could reduce consumption by restricting advertising. Studies suggest that cigarette advertising elasticities are very small. Baltagi and Levin (1986) found advertising to have no significant marginal effect on cigarette demand from 1964 to 1980.[6] More recent work, while finding a significant ad effect, generally reports small elasticities.[7] These elasticities fall between 0.1 and 0.2, and the most common result falls around 0.1. The Toxic Substance Board of New Zealand (1989), a strong advocate of advertising bans, conservatively uses an advertising elasticity of 0.07 in estimating the effect of an advertising ban.

Suppose that the true advertising elasticity were 0.1 exactly and we apply this figure to estimate the effect of a total ban on cigarette advertising. We would reduce cigarette consumption by 10 percent, which is the product of a 100 percent reduction and the 0.1 elasticity. Even this crude estimate might raise an unusual controversy: Both ban advocates and ban opponents might claim that it supports their case. The gains must be weighed against the losses, and this must depend on individual values. However, all researchers would emphasize that such estimates are crude.

The elasticity estimates often are drawn from time trends of aggregate data, sometimes aggregated to the national level. At this level, little variation in advertising expenditures is captured, and the massive advertising levels outside of the cigarette industry, though relevant to cigarette demand, usually are ignored (Saffer and Chaloupka, 1998). Also, no economist would overlook the possibility that the relationship studied might be nonlinear, as it would be if advertising were subject to the law of diminishing marginal returns. It is econometrically unsafe to extrapolate this far out of sample; thus, we are required to study the effects of actual advertising bans.

World experience with advertising bans is informative. Several countries have banned cigarette advertising outright, and the United States installed a partial ban (on broadcast media) in 1971. The effects of these bans when studied provide useful information. The picture is clear regarding the U.S. experience. The banning of cigarette advertising on television and radio at that time somewhat paradoxically may have increased cigarette consumption. Hamilton's (1972) account illustrates this peculiar history. Prior

[6]Earlier findings were essentially the same. Schmalensee (1972); Hamilton (1972); and Schneider, Klein, and Murphy (1981).

[7]McGuiness and Cowling (1975), Seldon and Doroodian (1989), and Tremblay and Tremblay (1995). A study by Roberts and Samuelson (1988) simultaneously estimates brand switching and total consumption effects, concluding for their data that total consumption effects dominated.

to the 1971 ban, an FTC ruling on the Fairness Doctrine required television and radio stations to give equal time to antismoking messages.

The result was a flurry of memorable commercials showing the harm of smoking. In one, a father appears walking in the forest with his young son. They stop to rest, lean back against a tree trunk, and the father reaches for a cigarette. His son watches in admiration as Dad lights up, but the father sees this, thinks, and stops. He gets the message, and so do we, the viewers. Hamilton argued with evidence that these antismoking messages were effective in reducing smoking in the population, while the advertising expenditures had small, if significant, marginal effects. Thus, when the ban eliminated both procigarette and the mandatory anticigarette messages at the same time, the combined effect could have increased smoking.[8]

Perhaps more important, the antismoking messages had a relatively greater effect on young, potential smokers. Lewit, Coate, and Grossman (1981) studied data on more than 6,000 youths. They found that television watching significantly increased the probability that a youth would start smoking, while the Fairness Doctrine ads reduced the probability that a youth would start smoking.

For many years, the single cross-national study of the effect of advertising bans by Hamilton (1975) showed the bans have no significant effect on cigarette consumption in the country. A later study, incorporating many new years of data and experience with bans, Laugesen and Meads (1991) reported these bans to be effective. Studying data for 1960 to 1986 and developing an index measuring the advertising restrictions, their time series estimates showed that a country banning tobacco advertising will reduce tobacco consumption by 6.8 percent, *ceteris paribus*. A recent study corroborates this result, though it warned that partial bans may invite tobacco firms to substitute advertising in unrestricted categories for banned advertising (Saffer and Chaloupka, 1998).

ADVERTISING AND ALCOHOL CONSUMPTION

Although earlier studies reported no effect of advertising on alcohol consumption, Saffer (1991) found that such advertising was a significant factor in drinking.[9] Taking a different approach, Saffer (1997) found alcohol advertising levels to be correlated positively and significantly with motor vehicle fatalities, *ceteris paribus*. He estimated that partial bans (bans on broadcast advertising) would reduce annual fatalities by 2,000 to 3,000, while a total ban could reduce fatalities by up to 10,000 nationally.

Excise Taxes and Consumption: Cigarettes and Alcohol

It is a common public misperception that taxes on products are always and fully passed on to the consumer, but this is not true. The irony is that if it were true, then cigarette and alcohol taxes would have no effect other than to raise money for the government coffers.

[8]Schneider, Klein, and Murphy (1981), with independent work on both theory and evidence, generally supported Hamilton's point. Baltagi and Levin (1986) similarly supported the basic argument. Their main difference was to conclude that the net effect of this ban was probably closer to zero.
[9]For a contrasting account, see Duffy (1995) and Nelson and Moran (1995).

By first examining the theory of excise taxation, we learn the importance of the price elasticity of demand and supply in determining the incidence of the tax and the degree to which consumption is reduced. With this understanding, we will examine the empirical knowledge regarding these elasticities.

THE CONSUMPTION-REDUCING EFFECTS OF EXCISE TAXES IN THEORY

Excise taxes form another major tool that can reduce consumption of bads in populations. Figure 25.1 depicts the supply and demand for alcoholic beverages. If a sufficient number of voters were to agree, the consumption of beer could be reduced from Q_E to Q_{E2} by imposing an excise tax increase of T dollars (recall that the tax shifts the supply curve vertically by the amount of the tax). The analysis also reveals that the tax would not fall entirely on the beer drinker, but the incidence would be shared. Assuming demand curve, D_0, because the consumer pays a higher price after the tax, we say that the incidence on the consumer is $(P_{E2} - P_E)$. Because the producer pockets the lower amount, P_{S2}, we say that the incidence on the producer is $(P_E - P_{S2})$.

The research issue is illustrated by the alternative possibility that the demand curve for beer is D_1. The alternative equilibrium is at point A, at which the reduction in consumption (not shown) is less than the original reduction, $(Q_E - Q_{E2})$. Thus, the magnitude of the reduction in quantity demanded will depend on which curve represents the true demand curve, the relatively inelastic curve, D_1, or the more elastic curve, D_0. Generally, the greater the demand elasticity in absolute value, the greater the corresponding reduction effected by the excise tax increase.

From models of the consumer's choice over bads, such as the rational addiction model, we know to distinguish between long-run and short-run effects of price changes. We also learned to distinguish youth from adult consumers, a distinction with important policy consequences.

FIGURE 25.1 The Consumption of Alcohol Is Reduced by an Excise Tax Increase.

"Mind If I Smoke?"

On a California billboard, the man's date responds to this question by asking: "Care if I die?" In a similar spirit, recent American films have depicted the inside of the tobacco industry as darkly menacing. The British news magazine, the *Economist,* ponders whether the tobacco industry has become "the new evil empire."

Meanwhile, other reports suggest that average smoking rates in the population continue to decline. The decline is also occurring among women, with an especially large drop in smoking among women of child-bearing age. Tobacco companies generally have raised cigarette prices, and in California, an unexpectedly sharp decline in cigarette sales for the first half of 1999 followed the state legislature's cigarette sales tax increase beginning the first of that year. The high level of legislative, activist, and consumer discussion and debate over tobacco continues throughout the country.

This scenario forms the backdrop for the tobacco companies' unprecedented November 1998 offer of $368 billion to the states in return for promises to limit further lawsuit activity. The American Cancer Society and the American Medical Association both gave their approval, albeit with some qualifications, and the settlement began with the highest hopes.

The legal theory applied in these contexts and to be used in future Department of Justice suits holds the tobacco companies libel for health costs incurred by the governments to provide care to cigarette-induced disease victims. The argument distinguishes cigarette issues from others involving voluntary risk taking, such as skydiving, alpine skiing, or work in risky occupations. An important legal question is whether the tobacco companies deliberately withheld critical health information.

EXCISE TAXES AND CIGARETTE CONSUMPTION IN PRACTICE

The importance of price elasticity is not lost on economists, and most econometric studies of cigarette consumption report price elasticity estimates. Over the history of these studies, the reported cigarette price elasticities in absolute value have ranged rather widely, from as low as 0.2 to occasional estimates greater than 1.0. There is no doubt that cigarette demand responds significantly to price, but the response is generally inelastic. Building on the earlier work, more recent studies find short-run price elasticities in a narrower band, typical of which is the 0.3 to 0.5 band reported by Keeler et al. (1993).[10]

The controversy over youth, tobacco, and price elasticity has taken essentially two turns. An early consensus[11] believed that youth were much more responsive to price increases and thus more accessible to the excise tax tool. This is an attractive result for anyone wishing to deter youth from taking up the smoking habit: ". . . an excise tax increase . . . might continue to discourage smoking participation by successive generations of teenagers and young adults and gradually impact the smoking levels of older age groups as the smoking-discouraged cohorts move through the age spectrum."[12] This consensus

[10]See also Tremblay and Tremblay (1995). Smokeless tobacco demand also responds to price in econometric studies, both own price and the price of substitutes (Ohsfeldt, Boyle, and Capilouto, 1998).
[11]See Lewit and Coate (1982) and Lewit, Coate, and Grossman (1981).
[12]Lewit and Coate (1982, p. 143).

was abandoned temporarily through an influential study (Wasserman et al., 1991) that found "no evidence that higher cigarette prices would have a significant impact on teenage decisions" (p. 213). The newer data, however, generally support the original consensus by finding a strong inverse relationship between age and cigarette price elasticity.[13]

As predicted by some models, such as rational addiction, estimated long-run cigarette elasticities are larger than short-run elasticities in absolute value. Chaloupka (1991) applied the rational addiction framework and estimated long-run values approximately twice as large as for the short-run. Keeler et al (1993) found them to lie in a narrow range, 0.5 to 0.6.

With the elasticity magnitudes reported in these various studies, what possible effect could excise tax increases be expected to generate? To focus the discussion, let us suppose that a tax increase has been installed of sufficient magnitude to double the price of cigarettes.[14] Assuming an elasticity of 0.4, the 100 percent price increase, by simple extrapolation, would reduce cigarette consumption by 40 percent, a substantial reduction. As we discussed earlier, where a similar extrapolation for advertising bans suggested a more modest reduction, such out-of-sample extrapolations are risky, but the example serves to illustrate the potency of the tax tool. Furthermore, the elasticity estimates for youth are so large as to double this effect for that age cohort; likewise, the larger long-run elasticities suggest the greater policy effects as time passes.

Direct measures of the effect of cigarette taxes on mortality also show the effectiveness of tax policy. Michael Moore (1995) tested tax variables in equations to predict mortality from several smoking-related diseases. Higher taxes significantly reduce mortality from lung cancer, cardiovascular disease, and asthma. He reports that a 10 percent cigarette tax hike would save 3,700 lives per year in the United States.

Although some countries have applied cigarette taxes vigorously to reduce population smoking, the United States has not done so. In 1997, the U.S. average tax rate, at 35 percent of the average price of a pack, was the lowest among 29 countries in one study. The United Kingdom, Ireland, Germany, and all of Scandinavia ranged from 70 percent to 85 percent. The U.S. federal excise tax declined in real terms since the Surgeon General's mid-1960s announcement that cigarette smoking causes cancer. Figure 25.2

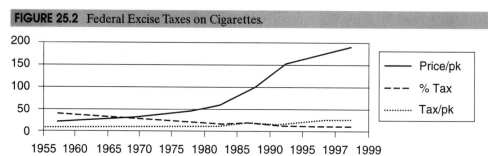

FIGURE 25.2 Federal Excise Taxes on Cigarettes.

Source: Indiana Prevention Resource Center, Indiana University, www.drugs.indiana.edu (1999), November 19, 1999.

[13]Harris and Chan (1998); Chaloupka and Pacula (1998).

[14]Recall that when the incidence of a tax is shared between demanders and sellers, then a dollar tax increase will create less than a dollar increase in the product price. Chaloupka and Warner (1999) gauge the effect of a dollar tax increase on the price of cigarettes.

reveals that the tax was reduced by allowing a nearly constant nominal tax rate to be eroded in percentage terms by the secular rise in prices per pack.

EXCISE TAXES AND ALCOHOL CONSUMPTION

The beer tax in Figure 25.1 was depicted as substantially effective in reducing consumption, but would this effect be experienced in real life? Grossman et al. (1998) find that young adults respond to beer price increases, and the elasticities range from 0.2 to 0.4 in the short run, with long-run elasticities 60 percent higher; other beer elasticity estimates have ranged even higher. Studies of wine and spirits yield elasticities ranging from 0.3 to 1.8 (Saffer and Chaloupka, 1998). The latter study also reports substantial, though inelastic, estimates for price elasticities of illicit drugs including marijuana, cocaine, and heroin. Thus taxes should have major impacts on consumption of addictive substances.

Conclusions

This chapter examines the economic nature of health bads, and it studies the potential of curbs on advertising and increased excise taxes to reduce the consumption of bads. Advertising in theory can benefit or harm society's well-being, depending on which of three theories applies to a given case. Advertising is viewed as information that generally benefits society, because it provides added information on the possible harmful effects of bads and of the potential benefits of good alternatives. When advertising is persuasive, it can increase the consumer's loyalty to a product, which can be harmful in the case of bads, yet the resulting monopoly power may partly offset this by restricting output. Finally, advertising as a complement good enhances the consumer's desire to consume the product, including those products with health risks.

Econometric estimates of the effect of advertising for cigarettes tend to report small and sometimes insignificant elasticities. These are estimates of changes at the margin. In contrast, advertising bans entail by definition large reductions in advertising levels; while previous studies have suggested insignificant effects here as well, the most recent work reports that bans have some significant effect when studied on an international basis. Related studies on alcohol advertising also report statistically significant effects.

The excise tax tool, however, appears to be more potent. Though cigarette and alcohol price elasticities are in the inelastic range, they are large enough in absolute value to have substantial potential as a curb to consumption if the public chooses to apply them. Consistent with rational addiction models, the long-run price elasticities are greater in absolute value than the short-run elasticities. Cigarette price elasticities for youth tend to be larger in absolute value than those for adults.

Summary

1. The nature of addiction, though as yet unresolved, generates behaviors that appear generally consistent with a rational addiction model. Irrational or myopic addiction provides a viable alternative model.

2. There are three contrasting theories of advertising. In one, advertising is primarily information, which leads to greater competition and possibly lower prices. The second describes advertising as a potential barrier to entry, which increases monopoly power and prices. The third describes advertising as a complement good to the good advertised; it increases marginal utility of the product.

3. The effect of advertising bans and related restrictions on advertising is suggested to have significant effects on consumption of cigarettes and alcohol. Though total effects of advertising are small in econometric studies, they are somewhat more substantial in a recent international study of total bans.
4. Excise taxes work to curb consumption in theory by increasing the price of the product. Then the effect on consumption depends on consumer responsiveness to price, which is the price elasticity.
5. Increased excise taxes on cigarettes and alcohol appear to be more potent public policy tools for curbing the consumption of bads than are advertising bans. Though estimated price elasticities are small in absolute value, they can be combined with substantial price changes to result in correspondingly large reductions in consumption.

Discussion Questions

1. Do cigarette and alcohol ads you have seen contain primarily informative content or persuasive content? What consequences would you predict from your finding?
2. Someone says: "The advertising elasticity of cigarette demand may be small, but it is big enough to warrant policy to ban cigarette advertising." What would "big enough" mean in this context?
3. What does the evidence on the effects of the partial U.S. ban on cigarette advertising suggest about the relative effectiveness of cigarette advertising versus anti-smoking advertising?
4. How does the responsiveness to cigarette advertising and price differ between youths and adults? Why is this important?
5. Explain how it is possible to advertise too little or too much.
6. Suppose it takes considerable time for the large majority of cigarette smokers to become fully informed about the fact that cigarette prices have risen all over. How would this matter to the effectiveness of a tax hike? What other effect of a cigarette tax hike may take considerable time?
7. How would an excise tax hike in Kansas be helped or harmed in its attempt to curb smoking among Kansans if the neighboring states (e.g., Missouri, Nebraska) did not also hike their cigarette excise taxes?
8. When all costs are considered, which public policy tool for curbing the consumption of bads would be the most costly to administer for a given amount of consumption reduction among consumers?

Exercises

1. If the elasticity of aggregate cigarette demand with respect to advertising were 0.15, by extrapolation what effect on cigarette consumption would be caused by a 10 percent reduction in advertising? A 50 percent reduction? A 100 percent reduction? How and why does one's confidence in prediction change over this range of reductions?
2. Suppose the price elasticity of cigarette demand is 0.4 in absolute value. If we increased the prices of cigarettes by 50 percent, what would we expect to happen to the quantity purchased? To total expenditures on cigarettes?

CHAPTER 26

The Pharmaceutical Industry

- Structure and Regulation

- The Production of Health and Substitutability

- Drug Pricing and Profits

- R&D and Innovation

- Cost Containment

- Conclusion

Prescription drugs and the pharmaceutical industry occupy important places in the health economy. Drug therapies traditionally have supplemented nutrition, sanitation, and medical care as methods for preserving health. Vaccinations for diseases such as smallpox represented early public health initiatives that saved many lives. Insulin, developed in the 1920s, prevented the certain deaths that once accompanied diabetes, and a world without antibiotics, introduced two decades later, would be unthinkable. Many among us still remember the relief following the availability of the Salk and Sabin polio vaccines in the 1950s.

In today's world, drugs are used to treat many diseases and conditions. Examples include chemotherapy for cancer, steroids for skin diseases, psychotropic drugs for mental health problems, beta-blockers for heart disease, clot busters for stroke, and protease inhibitors for AIDS. Some of these drugs represent alternatives to more invasive surgical procedures. Others are used in conjunction with surgical and radiation treatments. Still others provide treatment for conditions where no treatment was available previously.

Despite these successes, the U.S. pharmaceutical industry has come under intense media and legislative scrutiny. As shown in Table 26.1, pharmaceutical firms are among the largest and most profitable in the United States. In terms of market value, which is a measure of current and expected future profits, Merck and Pfizer ranked in the top 10 firms in 1999 and another seven appeared in the top 50. The performance of this group is especially dramatic when compared to other for-profit firms in the health sector. The

largest of these, Mckesson HBOC, has considerable revenues but enjoys only a small fraction of the profits earned by the leading pharmaceuticals.[1]

With prescription drug prices rising more quickly than prices for other health care products, the industry is a convenient target for the budgetary challenges facing patients and insurers. The introduction of new and expensive drugs, increasingly promoted through direct marketing to consumers, has only added to the expenditure burden and heightened criticism of the industry.

This burden has become especially severe for the elderly. Medicare does not cover prescription drugs for outpatient care, and the elderly suffer disproportionately from the chronic and other conditions that fuel the use of drugs.

Policy proposals to deal with these pressures range from price regulation to the expansion of Medicare to include drug benefits. Private insurance initiatives include higher patient copayments, increased emphasis on generic products, and new strategies, such as the development of drug formularies. Formularies, approved lists of drugs, were adopted by most managed care plans by the late 1990s. The patient may have difficulty in obtaining reimbursement for any drugs that are not on the list.

Pharmacoeconomics, which includes cost–benefit, cost-effectiveness, and cost–utility analyses, is playing an increasingly important role in pharmaceutical decisions, but policy must address many other questions. Of the many possible issues, this chapter selects several of more general interest to health economists. After describing the structure and regulation of the pharmaceutical industry, we focus on the following areas.[2]

1. The role of pharmaceutical products in the production of health, patient choices of drugs under various insurance schemes, and the effects of technological change on use of drugs
2. Drug pricing issues, including price discrimination by sellers and price regulation by government
3. Pharmaceutical research and the determinants of innovation
4. Cost containment through use of generic products and other measures

We conclude with recent evidence on the effects of drugs on health derived from international comparisons on drug utilization.

Structure and Regulation

In 1997, spending on prescription drugs amounted to $79 billion or 7.2 percent of national health expenditures (up from 5.4 percent in 1990 and 4.9 percent in 1980).[3] Out-of-pocket costs remained substantial at 29 percent of total drug costs, even though the patient's share stood far below the 51 percent recorded just a few years earlier in 1989.

[1]McKesson HBOC operates in drug distribution and information technology. Among 38 industries with at least four firms represented on the 1999 Fortune 500 list, pharmaceuticals ranked first in return on revenues, return on assets, and return on stockholders' equity.

[2]Other important problems, such as those dealing with measurement of drug prices and international comparisons of prices, are beyond the scope of this chapter. Excellent coverage of these and many other issues is found in Helms (1996) and Schweitzer (1996). The Pharmaceutical Research and Manufacturers of America (PhRMA 1999) also provide extensive industry information and data.

[3]Levit et al. (1998).

TABLE 26.1 Largest U.S. firms and Largest Pharmaceutical Firms Ranked by Market Value on March 15, 1999

Company	Market Value $ Billions	Revenues $ Billions	Rank	Profits $ Billions	Return on Equity (%)
1. Microsoft	418.6	14.5	109	4.49	27.0
2. General Electric	360.3	100.5	5	9.30	23.9
3. Wal-Mart	212.9	138.2	3	4.43	21.0
4. Merck*	198.9	26.9	37	5.25	41.0
5. Intel	196.7	26.3	40	6.07	26.0
6. Pfizer*	182.2	14.7	106	3.35	38.0
7. AT&T	180.1	53.6	10	6.40	21.0
8. Exxon	178.9	100.7	4	6.37	22.4
9. Coca-Cola	169.4	18.8	73	3.53	42.0
10. Cisco Systems	166.6	8.5	192	1.35	19.0
16. Bristol-Myers Squib*	129.5	18.3	77	3.14	41.5
18. Johnson & Johnson*	122.2	23.7	51	3.05	22.5
22. Eli Lilly*	105.9	10.1	160	2.10	47.4
27. American Home Products*	88.8	13.5	117	2.47	25.7
30. Schering-Plough*	84.7	8.1	200	1.76	43.9
31. Abbot Laboratories*	76.8	12.5	133	2.33	40.8
45. Warner-Lambert*	60.5	10.2	157	1.25	34.7
122. Mckesson HBOC**	17.6	20.9	59	0.15	11.0
Fortune 500 (median)	7.7	6.6		0.32	13.4

Note: The table includes all pharmaceutical firms (*) in the top 50 and the largest other health firm (**). Sales and profits are for the year ended December 31, 1998.

Source: Fortune, April 26, 1999.

With their growing share of a growing total amount, some large third-party payers have reported that their reimbursements for drugs exceed even their reimbursements for physician services. Such reports help create public perceptions that something is seriously wrong with the conduct of pharmaceutical firms and that stiff measures are needed to obtain drug costs.

With its long history of relatively high profits and rich set of features—patent protection, high research-and-development spending, intense product promotion, and heavy regulation—the pharmaceutical industry always has drawn the attention of economists in the field of industrial organization. Scholars describe levels of competition in an industry; how the competitive environment influences decisions on prices and other decision variables such as advertising, research and development (R&D), and quality; and the consequences of these decisions for socially efficient allocations of resources.

Competition

The level of competition usually holds the key to firm and industry behavior. Economists measure competition within the standard industrial classification (S.I.C.) developed by the U.S. Department of Commerce to categorize firms into meaningful industry

and product groups. The S.I.C. codes range from two to seven digits, with each successive digit representing a finer degree of classification. The "pharmaceutical preparations" industry, Code 2834, is formally defined as "establishments primarily engaged in manufacturing, fabricating, or processing drugs in pharmaceutical preparations for human or veterinary use."

The four-firm (C_4) and eight firm (C_8) concentration ratios for any selected four-digit S.I.C. codes indicate the share of industry output produced by the four or eight largest firms. These concentration ratios, shown in Table 26.2 for pharmaceuticals and several other industries, often are used to gauge competition. The pharmaceutical industry is one of the largest and most rapidly growing manufacturing industries. As measured by concentration ratios, it also appears to be much more competitive than many industries.

Another method used to measure competition is the Herfindahl–Hirschman Index (HHI). Compare Industry 1 with four firms, each with 25 percent of the market, to Industry 2, also with four firms, but where one firm has 85 percent of the market and the other three each have 5 percent. Both industries have a four-firm concentration ratio of 100 percent. However, one might guess that the one in which the leading firm has 85 percent of the market is more monopolized. The HHI incorporates differences in the size distribution of firms by squaring the market shares of each and adding them together, so that the lowest value approaches 0 (thousands of tiny firms) and the highest value approaches 10,000 (with a pure monopoly). In the example above, the respective HHIs are 2,500 and 7,300.

Table 26.2 shows that compared to other well-known industries, in addition to relatively low concentration ratios, there are a relatively large number of firms (N) and the Herfindahl–Hirschman Index (HHI) is relatively low.

Do these data indicate substantial competition? Most analysts would argue that for pharmaceuticals they could be especially misleading. Drugs in different therapeutic categories usually are not substitutes for each other. Concentration ratios for narrower drug classes are better indicators. When such data are available, they still can show considerable competition. In many cases, however, the concentration ratios will be higher,

TABLE 26.2 Concentration in Selected Manufacturing Industries: 1992

S.I.C.	Industry	C_4	C_8	HHI	N	Shipments (in $ Billions)
2834	Phamaceutical preparations	26	42	341	583	50.4
2043	Cereal breakfast foods	85	98	2,253	42	9.8
2841	Soaps and detergents	63	77	1,584	635	14.8
2851	Paints	29	43	305	1,129	15.0
2911	Petroleum refining	30	49	414	131	136.6
3571	Computer and office equipment	45	59	680	803	38.2
3674	Semiconductors	41	58	541	823	32.1
3711	Passenger cars	84	91	2,676	398	151.7
3721	Aircraft and parts	79	93	2,717	151	62.9
3861	Photographic equipment	78	83	2,408	832	22.1

Source: U.S. Bureau of the Census, "Concentration Ratios in Manufacturing," *1992 Census of Manufacturers,* Report MC92-S-2.

sometimes much higher.[4] Schweitzer (1996) illustrates with a class of drugs used to control hypertension. The top four firms controlled 91 percent of the market in 1992. Why? Patents and other barriers to entry often restrict competition.

BARRIERS TO ENTRY

A barrier to entry is any factor that impedes the entry of new firms into an industry or product market. Patent protection granted by government represents a classic example. To gain further protection, pharmaceutical firms adopt a common business strategy of surrounding a product with patents on many variations of that product.

A patent forms a legal barrier. Advertising and promotion also can create economic barriers when they successfully increase brand loyalty. Pharmaceutical promotion differs from that of typical consumer goods because pharmaceutical firms direct much of their marketing at physicians rather than patients, the end users through "detailers" who directly visit physicians' offices. Critics of this practice believe that detailing may lead to questionable financial arrangements that encourage the physician to prescribe a particular product, possibly in place of cheaper drug or nondrug substitutes.

Firms also reach physicians in other ways: by distributing samples, by direct mail, and by advertising in medical journals. Following the FDA's relaxation of rules governing advertisements through the media in 1997, the industry responded by increasing advertising in newspapers, on radio, on television, and even on freeway billboards, all aimed directly at patients. It is too early to evaluate the effects of these forms of promotion, but some physicians are raising questions about the misinformation and confusion created by the ads.[5]

As a last example of protection from competition, the regulation of drugs itself can create entry barriers. The Food and Drug Administration (FDA) approval process for a new drug is costly and time consuming. A new firm will find it difficult to marshal the financial and expert resources needed to go through the process, and especially to have a portfolio of products under development to spread risks. Only one of about 5,000 to 10,000 chemical compounds screened ultimately is approved as a drug, and of those reaching the market stage, only three of 10 products ever become profitable.[6] Not surprisingly, such odds (3 in 50,000 to 100,000 chemical compounds) create formidable deterrence to new drug development, and new pharmaceutical firms often concentrate on generic products.[7]

REGULATION

The pharmaceutical industry is one of the most heavily regulated of all industries. Governments regulate most firms for worker safety and health concerns, but pharmaceutical products are subject to further oversight by the FDA. Following a public scandal

[4]The issue of competition nevertheless remains complicated because some conditions are treated with drugs, or combinations of drugs, from different classes. For example, low-back pain, one of the most common conditions, often is treated with non-narcotic analgesics (e.g., aspirin), narcotic analgesics (e.g., Vicodin), muscle relaxants (e.g., Valium), antidepressants, and other products. The issue of competition is complicated further because most pharmaceutical companies compete internationally, and their market shares can vary widely across countries.

[5]Pharmaceutical firms also must address the formulary decisions of managed care organizations (discussed later in this chapter) rather than individual physicians, and this too is creating changes in marketing efforts.

[6]See PhRMA (1999) and Grabowski and Vernon (1994).

[7]The biotech revolution also has created hundreds of firms trying to develop new chemicals that may become blockbuster drugs (e.g., Amgen's development of Epogen, an antianemia drug, and Neupogen, an immune system stimulator).

over adulterated food products and dangerous medicines with unknown contents, the federal government introduced the Food and Drug Act of 1906. The act did nothing to prevent the public from dangerous medicines. It did not even require formal testing but dealt mainly with labeling. Requirements for testing and safety were introduced with the Federal Food, Drug, and Cosmetic Act of 1938. However, these requirements were left mainly to the drug companies.

Two events accelerated regulatory change. Exposure of questionable drug industry practices in hearings held by Senator Kefauver in 1959 was soon followed by the thalidomide tragedy. Thalidomide, a tranquilizer widely used in Europe to treat morning sickness in pregnancy, was discovered to cause severe defects in babies, who were sometimes born with deformed, flipperlike limbs. The drug was available on an experimental basis in the United States at the time. Fortunately for the United States, the number of thalidomide babies was relatively small. The FDA delayed approval and the distributor withdrew the product quickly after reports of the European experience.[8]

Although the thalidomide tragedy was averted in the United States, Congress nonetheless approved amendments in 1962 giving the FDA considerably more control over the introduction of new products. The new legislation required much more testing and extended the FDA's authority to regulate premarket testing (including generic drugs). Equally important, the legislation for the first time required evidence of efficacy.[9]

FDA review has become a lengthy, complex process. Following the discovery stage during which new chemicals are synthesized, the firm conducts preclinical animal studies involving short-term toxicity and safety tests. The drug firm next must file an application with the FDA to conduct clinical trials. If approved, the trials are conducted in three phases. Phase I begins with small groups of healthy volunteers and focuses on safety and dosage. Phase II trials involve a larger number of subjects, often several hundred who have the targeted condition, and concentrates on the drug's efficacy.[10] Stage III trials usually are conducted on thousands of patients in different settings so that safety and efficacy can be determined more precisely.

If these trials indicate safety and efficacy and the drug's safety is supported by long-term animal studies, the company submits a New Drug Application (NDA) containing all the data and results to the FDA. The FDA review usually takes more than a year. Total development time for a new product stands at about 15 years, nearly double the eight-year period in the 1960s (PhRMA, 1999).

These requirements provoke considerable controversy and provide obvious trade-offs between the goals of protecting the consumer and rapid innovation.[11] The economic approach is to weigh the gains in safety and efficacy against the cost of delaying patients

[8]Thalidomide still is marketed with a warning on pregnancy. Interest is growing in its use to treat bone cancer, inflammatory diseases, and autoimmune disorders for patients with advanced AIDS.

[9]The legislation also gave the FDA authority over the manufacturing process and extended testing requirements to include generic drugs and drugs that are similar to available products ("me-too" drugs). It also transferred regulation of drug advertising for prescription products from the Federal Trade Commission to the FDA.

[10]The terms *efficacy* or *effective*, as used by the FDA, mean that a drug has positive effects compared to a placebo. Efficacy does not imply that the product is cost effective or that it meets other economic criteria for efficiency.

[11]Some critics believe that even the current safeguards are inadequate because clinical trials are controlled by their sponsoring firms. These concerns have opened the way to federal support for "centers for education and research in therapeutics," known as CERTs, that would conduct studies on safety and cost effectiveness.

from utilizing useful products. Economists also are concerned about the potential stifling of innovation caused by regulation and their adverse effects on competition.

In a classic study of the 1962 Amendments, Peltzman (1974) found a sharp decline in new product development, especially of innovative drugs, after 1962, as well as higher prices from the decreased competition. These consequences far outweighed the benefits of reduced spending on ineffective drugs, creating a net welfare loss of about 6 percent of total drug sales.

The FDA recognized these problems and, in the mid-1970s, developed policies to accelerate the review of "important" drugs. Dranove and Meltzer (1994) found that important drugs reach the market about three years sooner than other drugs. Thus, they argue that the losses resulting from delays in the approval process have been overestimated. A 1984 act also eliminated the full range of tests for generic products that were required by the 1962 amendments.[12]

The Production of Health and Substitutability

We have seen that spending on prescription drugs is increasing rapidly and that drug firms have some monopoly power. Before we examine how that power is exercised, we turn to the role of prescription drugs in producing health and their relationship to other medical inputs. An examination of these issues is helped with the concept of a production function for health.

Recall that it is the patient's demand for health that leads to a demand for health inputs such as drugs and medical care. Consider the following production function for a patient with chronic and severe low-back pain—one of the most common reasons for physician office visits and hospitalization:

$$HS = f(D, M) \qquad\qquad \textbf{(26.1)}$$

where HS represents the individual's health status in the current period, D represents prescription drugs, and M represents all other medical inputs in this period, given existing technology and medical know-how. If no drugs or medical inputs are applied, the patient might experience considerable pain and be unable to perform many normal tasks, including work.

Assume that this patient's health can be improved by medical intervention. Suppose an individual is consuming the amount of drugs, D_1, and the amount of other medical inputs, M_1, as noted at point E of Figure 26.1. How do the drugs and the medical inputs substitute for each other?

Figure 26.1 shows three different isoquants reflecting the role of drug products and their relationship to other medical inputs. Isoquant 1 shows that drugs (e.g., narcotic analgesics or muscle relaxants) must be used in a fixed proportion to other inputs (e.g., physical therapy, counseling, and surgery in some cases). Here, inputs D and M are perfect complements with no substitutability between them.

At the other extreme, isoquant 2 reflects a production function where inputs are perfect substitutes: The marginal rate of technical substitution (*MRTS*) is constant,

[12]To expedite the review process, 1992 legislation and the Modernization Act of 1997 provide the FDA with additional resources derived from user fees levied on the industry. This has considerably reduced approval times. The 1997 act also includes many other provisions that will result in a major reorganization of the FDA.

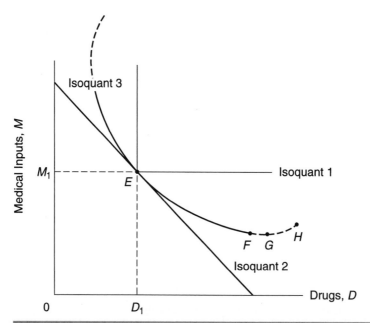

FIGURE 26.1 Substitution between Drugs and Other Medical Inputs.

meaning that drugs substitute for the other inputs at a constant rate. (Depending on the prices of each, a patient would use one or the other, but not both.) Finally, the solid portion of isoquant 3 reflects an intermediate situation where D and M can substitute for each other, but where the *MRTS* is diminishing. Fewer and fewer amounts of M are needed to substitute for a unit increase in D as more drugs are used.

In general, it seems unlikely that D and M are either perfect complements or perfect substitutes. Many conditions are likely to involve some substitutability, although its extent may vary widely among conditions and even patients. Pharmacological and other clinical studies must determine not only substitutability, but also the "uneconomic" portions of an isoquant, meaning those combinations that never should be selected.

Uneconomic combinations arise when additions of D over some range (e.g., dashed segment FG) will not benefit or harm the patient. Here, the marginal product of D is zero and the isoquant becomes horizontal. It is also possible that increases in D beyond some point may harm the patient and require more medical intervention to maintain the same health status. In this region (arc GH), the isoquant will become positively sloped. Similar logic may apply to the vertical portion of an isoquant with increases in M. Clearly, a patient will not want to be in the regions shown by the dashed segments.

LEAST-COST PRODUCTION

How will the patients and their providers choose? To abstract from the many possible levels of health that might be attained, as well as the inherent uncertainty of medical practice, assume that the patient/provider believes that it is reasonable to attain HS_1 in Figure 26.2. The rational patient seeks to find the combination of D and M on HS_1 that

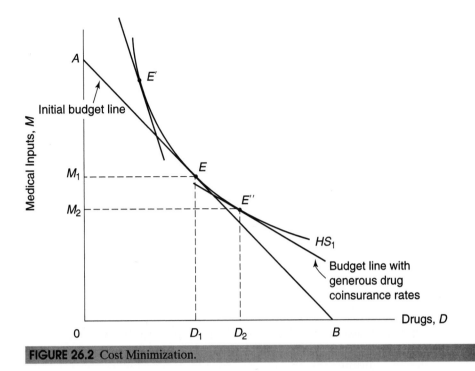

FIGURE 26.2 Cost Minimization.

minimizes spending. Without insurance coverage for either D or M, the total cost (C) of care can be written as:

$$C = P_D D + P_M M$$

or,

$$M = C/P_M - (P_D/P_M)D \tag{26.2}$$

where D and M are quantities of drugs and other inputs, and P_D and P_M are their respective prices. If, for example, $P_D = \$50$ and $P_M = \$100$, the slope of the budget line in equation (26.2) is −0.5.

The cost-minimizing combination is shown at E, where the isoquant, HS_1 is tangent to the budget line, AB. The optimal inputs are shown by D_1 and M_1, and total spending is given by these quantities multiplied by their respective prices. At E, the numerical slope of the budget line ($P_D/P_M = 0.5$) equals the MRTS, the slope of the isoquant. Suppose, for example, that $D_1 = 4$ and $M_1 = 6$, so total costs for HS_1 equal:

$$\text{Costs} = \$50 \times 4 + \$100 \times 6 = \$800$$

If prescription prices increase above $50, the budget line will become steeper and the rational patient will try to substitute more medical care by moving to the left on the isoquant to a point such as E' (and vice versa to E'' if medical care prices increase).

INSURANCE AND SUBSTITUTABILITY

Assume now that like most Americans, the patient has insurance coverage. Begin with a policy that covers a constant proportion (e.g., 80 percent) of spending on either D or

M. Out-of-pocket patient costs are $10 for each prescription (20 percent of $50) and $20 for a medical visit (20 percent of $100). Because the slope of the patient's budget line does not change, the optimal choice remains at point *E*, and the patient continues to buy four units of drugs and six visits. Total drug costs will continue to be minimized with the patient paying 20 percent ($160) and the insurer paying 80 percent ($640) of the $800 total bill.

However, *D* and *M* often are not treated uniformly under traditional health insurance. Consider a policy that pays 80 percent of medical costs but requires a deductible of only $5 (copayment) for each prescription. The patient's drug price is the $5 deductible regardless of the actual price of the medication. If the patient's out-of-pocket drug costs diminish (in our example, it is now $5/$20 = 0.25), the numerical slope of the cost-minimizing budget line diminishes. The patient will have an incentive to substitute *D* for *M* at *E″*. Continuing the example, let D_2 increase from 4 to 5 and M_2 fall from 6 to 5.75.

The patient's cost burden diminishes from $160 to $140 or:

$$(5.75 \text{ visits} \times \$100/\text{visit} \times 0.2 \text{ coinsurance rate}) + (5 \text{ units of drugs} \times \$5/\text{unit})$$

However, the total cost of care (patient plus insurer) increases from $800 to $825 ($5.75 \times 100 + 5 \times 50$). We know this is true because we already determined that *E* is the least costly combination to provide HS_1. Similarly, if prescription prices (to the insurer) increase, say to $100, the patient still pays $5 and will remain at E″ with the insurer picking up the increased drug costs. Patients have no incentive to economize by making substitutions and moving toward *E*. The higher the prescription price, the greater the distortion.[13]

TECHNOLOGICAL CHANGE

As the twentieth century drew to a close, a new category of experimental drugs, blood vessel inhibitors, generated extraordinary excitement in the medical community by fighting both cancer and heart disease. Technology often is associated with such major breakthroughs. More often, however, new drugs are similar to existing drugs, but they may produce somewhat better outcomes (if only for some patients) or reduced side effects.

A technological improvement is one where fewer inputs are needed to produce a given health outcome or where outcomes that were previously unattainable are now attainable. For example, begin with HS_1 in Figure 26.3 and let HS_1* represent all combinations of inputs with a new drug that led to the same health status as HS_1. If the cost-minimizing ratio of inputs at a given price ratio remains unchanged, so that it lies along the ray *OE* (with slope $(M/D)_0$), the innovation would represent a neutral technological change. As drawn, the new drug saves a relatively high amount of the medical input at any given price ratio; that is, drug utilization increases relative to medical care as the patient moves to *E** and substitutes *D* for *M*. As noted in the figure, the lower ratio of *M* to *D* is reflected in the less steeply sloped ray, $(M/D)_1$.

New technology can increase costs for two reasons. First, it can routinely lead to health levels that were unattainable previously (e.g. HS_2* at point *E***). It may require

[13] A similar distortion toward excessive levels of *M* and greater total costs is created when the patient's coverage excludes or limits drug benefits. Here, the savings from the reduced *M* will more than offset the additional drug spending from improved drug coverage.

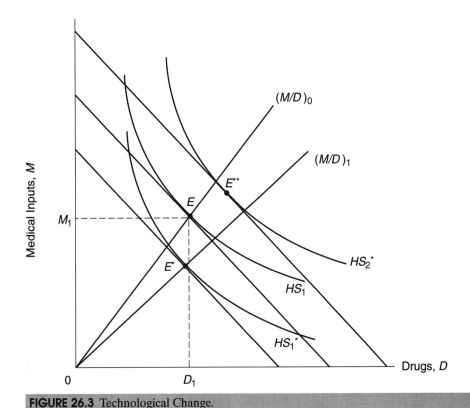

FIGURE 26.3 Technological Change.

much more drug use and possibly increased use of M, as well. When health improvements are dramatic or when drugs treat serious conditions that were not treatable previously, cost concerns are likely to be far less troublesome than those leading to only marginal improvements in health.

The second cost pressure comes from insurance. As we have seen, a patient with a constant copayment will be insulated from any price increases of the new drug. Assume that the slope of the budget line in Figure 26.3 reflects the patient's copayment of $5 and the patient moves from E to E^*. If the price of the new drug is high enough, the total cost of care at E^* could be substantially higher than total costs at the original equilibrium at E.

For conventional goods, where the consumer pays the entire price out of pocket, such technological changes will not be introduced because they will not be demanded. With insurance, the determination and elimination of cost-inefficient technology are far more difficult. A cost-inefficient drug might be marketed successfully simply because it is more convenient for the patient to reduce other services and take more medications at E^*.

Drug Pricing and Profits

Drug pricing and profitability undoubtedly generate the strongest reactions among the public and the media. News reports paint pharmaceutical companies as exploiting patients through patents and other strategies that reduce competition. Many studies have

found that pharmaceutical profits, as reported in financial statements, are consistently among the highest of all industries. Table 26.3 illustrates a study that compared 14 major industry groups. The pharmaceutical industry had the highest rate of return on equity—double the average—during the period 1980 to 1993.

This dramatic difference often is attributed to monopoly power, but the profit picture is far less clear. Conventional accounting methods treat R&D and advertising and promotion as current expenses even though, like physical investment, they provide returns in future years. Expensing can be thought of as an extreme form of accelerated depreciation. It raises rates of return by reducing taxes. When Clarkson made adjustments to capitalize and depreciate these "investments," the industry's return remained higher than average (13.3 percent versus 10.2 percent) as shown in Table 26.3, but it was well below the highest (22.5 percent for computer software).

Others argue that if drug R&D is riskier than other types of investments, a higher rate of return is needed to attract capital into the industry. Without trying to sort through all the measurement nuances, it seems reasonable to conclude that pharmaceutical firms earn above-normal rates of return but that their profitability has been exaggerated by simple accounting comparisons.

MONOPOLY PRICING

We begin with the case with a firm selling a single product (or a composite of products) at a uniform price to all buyers. Figure 26.4 shows the demand and cost conditions facing the firm. Demand is a negatively sloped curve for several reasons. Even though patients with fixed copayments are insulated from higher prices and will have a perfectly

TABLE 26.3	Accounting and Corrected Rates of Return on Equity for Selected Industries: 1980–1993	
Industry	*Accounting*	*Corrected*
Foods	17.58	14.95
Paper	9.20	8.92
Chemicals	13.43	8.46
Pharmaceuticals	24.37	13.27
Petroleum	22.03	15.81
Rubber products	12.45	9.05
Ferrous metals	−6.77	−2.91
Engines	9.22	8.26
Office machines	3.57	7.47
Electrical machines	12.26	9.93
Motor vehicles	0.07	1.54
Aerospace	10.65	9.06
Computer software	22.05	22.56
Entertainment	5.49	5.66
Average	12.32	10.19

Source: Clarkson (1996), Table 11-9, p. 257.

Price

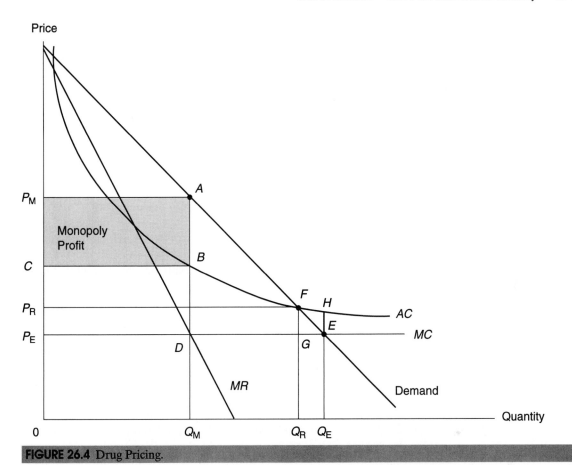

FIGURE 26.4 Drug Pricing.

inelastic demand, others have more limited coverage or no drug coverage at all. Patients with limited (or no) coverage will likely substitute generic or over-the-counter products as a drug's price rises. Some may reduce utilization by not complying with the medication regimen. The firm also must consider purchasing decisions by managed care organizations and other large buyers such as hospitals, which can be sensitive to price changes.

On the cost side, the marginal cost of manufacturing and distributing the product is usually relatively low—about half the total cost. R&D and various promotion costs are substantial. In Figure 26.4, we show the marginal cost (MC) as constant and the average cost (AC) due to high fixed costs of R&D and promotion as a downward-sloping curve. The profit-maximizing output is found where MC equals MR, resulting in P_M and Q_M. Assuming that economic profits are earned, the price must lie above average cost. Economic profits are shown by the shaded rectangle P_MABC. Consistent with the hypothesized demand and cost structures, the gap between price and the low marginal cost will be large.

The profit-maximizing model also predicts that the difference between price and marginal cost varies inversely with the elasticity of demand. Lu and Comanor (1998) examined pricing decisions on new products, and their findings support profit-maximization.

Initial (launch) prices are considerably higher for products that represent large, therapeutic gains than prices for new "me-too" drugs that are similar to available products. Why? Demand will be relatively inelastic for a product that provides significant benefits as compared to other products. Launch prices are also much higher when few branded substitutes exist. This factor similarly reduces a product's demand elasticity and requires a higher price for profit-maximization.

PRICE DISCRIMINATION

A firm may be able to increase profits beyond the level described in Figure 26.4. One of the most interesting features of the pharmaceutical industry is third-degree price discrimination where different groups of buyers are charged different prices. News stories abound about American seniors flocking to Mexico, where prices are much lower, to buy drugs. Hospitals or managed care groups often are charged less than retail pharmacies, and prices for drugs used in veterinary medicine can be much lower than prices for similar products packaged for human use.

What accounts for the wide variations in price? One explanation is straightforward. If a firm can distinguish between markets with different demand characteristics and limit arbitrage (third-party resale at lower prices in higher-priced markets), it can increase profits by charging different prices. Assume, for simplicity, that the firm described in Figure 26.4 sells only in the United States and Mexico. In Figure 26.5, its total demand is separated into the U.S. and Mexican demands. With higher incomes and better insurance, the demand is relatively inelastic in the United States. Assume further that the marginal costs of production and distribution remain constant and are equal in both countries, and that prices are not regulated in either market.

Profit maximization occurs where *MR* equals *MC* in each market, resulting in quantities Q_{US} and Q_X. Even though marginal revenue will be equal in the United States and Mexico, it can be shown that price is higher in the market with the less-elastic demand[14] (United States). Total profits must be greater than those obtained under uniform pricing.

BEHAVIOR OTHER THAN PROFIT-MAXIMIZING BEHAVIOR

Pharmaceutical firms sometimes face constraints, including governments that regulate prices or rates of return and large buyers with market power to negotiate quantity discounts (as described below). However, even in the absence of such constraints, a firm will not always try to maximize profits, at least in the short run. Despite patent protection and high development costs, an extraordinary return on a product may encourage other firms to try to develop a better or less expensive substitute. An incumbent producer will recognize this incentive and sometimes engage in strategies to deter entry. Under limit pricing, a firm reduces its price to a level that makes it less attractive for a potential entrant.

The negative publicity associated with unusually high prices also may temper a firm. The most prominent case involved the public outcry over the prices charged by

[14]A convenient formula for profit maximization is:

$$P = MC(1 + 1/E_P)$$

where E_P is the algebraic value of the price elasticity of demand. With the same *MC* in both markets, price must be higher when demand is less elastic (e.g., -2 versus -4).

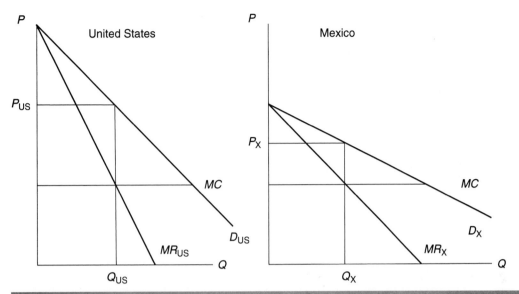

FIGURE 26.5 Price Discrimination.

Glaxo Wellcome (then known as Burroughs Wellcome) for AZT—the first promising treatment for AIDS. Because full-blown AIDS cases cause almost-certain death, the demand curve for an AIDS cure would be very price-inelastic. Hence, our earlier analyses suggest that a profit-maximizing firm could charge a considerable markup over marginal cost. Following considerable pressure from activist organizations, Glaxo Wellcome reduced prices below the $8,000 needed for a year's treatment (Hansen 1996). Nevertheless, the damage was done in the sense that the firm put itself and the pricing practices of the entire pharmaceutical research industry under a spotlight. Critics proposed price caps, using AZT and other new drug treatments costing thousands of dollars as symbols of greed.

MONOPSONY PRICING AND PRICE CONTROLS

Price discrimination is not the only possible explanation for price differentials. Prices in some foreign countries can be lower because their governments regulate prices or their national health plan serves as a monopsony buyer. Continuing with Figure 26.5, suppose that the Mexican government imposes price controls. Conceptually, it can drive price as low as the marginal cost, further increasing the price differential with the United States. Critics charge that by failing to similarly control prices, consumers in the United States are bearing the burden of the development costs and that the United States is subsidizing other countries.

Proposals have been made to limit prices in the United States or even to treat pharmaceutical firms as regulated utilities. Return to Figure 26.4. It is theoretically possible to reduce price to P_R, raising quantity to Q_R, and enable the firm to just cover its costs and earn a normal rate of return. However, the administrative complexity of regulating prices of multiproduct firms that are continuously introducing new products is enormous. Consider just the variations of a single product available in different strengths,

forms (tablet, liquid), and delivery systems (oral, intravenous, patch, inhaler). In addition, Abbott (1994) found that pharmaceutical firms are likely to set much higher introductory prices under regulation.

The complexity and potential perverse effects of regulation prompt many analysts to conclude that cost containment is better left to private initiatives. They also worry about the damaging effects of price or rate-of-return controls on innovation. Both topics will be covered later in this chapter.

Before we leave regulation, we note one more similarity between the pharmaceutical industry and regulated utilities. Observe from Figure 26.4 that we find the efficient price and quantity where price equals marginal cost. Marginal-cost pricing requires a price of P_E and a quantity of Q_E. Recall that a monopoly price is inefficient because price, an indicator of marginal benefit, exceeds marginal cost. The excess burden, or welfare loss, associated with monopoly pricing is given by triangle ADE. At P_E, however, the firm will not be able to earn even a normal rate of return unless it is given a large subsidy equal to EH per unit to cover its fixed cost. As noted above, utility rate regulation usually involves a solution like P_R, even though it too results in an excess burden (triangle EFG).

The parallel to regulated utilities can be extended to the welfare loss problem of firms selling in different markets. Energy utilities have traditionally charged big industrial users, who can substitute alternative power sources, less than residential customers, who cannot. The utilities also have incurred large fixed costs for power-generating capacity and distribution. Economists have long studied the problem of a pricing scheme that would minimize the excess burden while covering the large common costs needed to service the various markets.

The solution, known as Ramsey pricing (after the mathematical economist who developed it), would impose a higher price on markets with a less elastic demand. Returning to the example of the United States and Mexico, the logic behind Ramsey pricing is illustrated in Figure 26.6, which again describes the U.S. and Mexican demands. For global efficiency, the price must equal the marginal cost in each market. However, the revenues at this price (P_1) will cover only variable costs and not the pharmaceutical firm's research and development costs.

Should price be increased by the same amount (or by the same percentage) in each market? Suppose that an increase to P_2 in each market is sufficient to cover the fixed costs. An equal price increase will decrease quantity by a higher percentage in Mexico where the demand is more elastic. As Figure 26.6 shows, the excess burden shown by the shaded area is higher in Mexico than in the United States. The Ramsey rule requires an equal percentage reduction in quantity in both markets and thus a greater price increase for the United States. Ironically, the structure of prices under Ramsey pricing follows the pattern obtained under price discrimination where the markup over marginal cost is highest in the location where demand is least elastic.

COMPETITION AND GENERIC ENTRY

Once a patent expires, other firms are free to enter the market. Entry barriers are considerably lower than those for new-product development, and the 1984 Drug Price Competition and Patent Restoration Act further eased requirements. The act replaced the safety and efficacy testing under the 1962 amendments with much less costly bioequivalence tests. If approved, the FDA certifies a generic as "therapeutically equivalent"

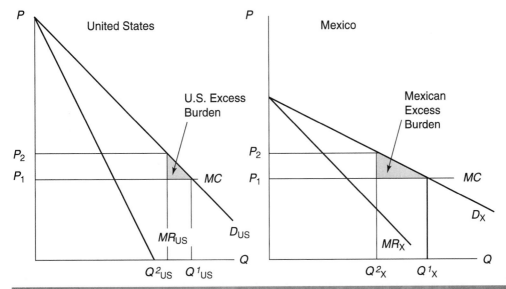

FIGURE 26.6 Ramsey Pricing.

to the branded version. The new legislation greatly increased generic applications, and as one would expect, firms target markets with the greatest opportunities. These are large markets and those where drugs are used to treat chronic conditions.[15]

What happens to prices and market shares after generic entry? Grabowski and Vernon (1992) examined 18 drugs that first experienced generic competition after the 1984 act. Generics captured one-half of their markets within two years. Surprisingly, though, as generic prices were falling, brand producers were raising theirs and widening the price gap over time. This phenomenon, corroborated by Frank and Salkever (1997), suggests that generics are not viewed as close substitutes by some patients or their providers. Pioneer firms can retain some monopoly power by capitalizing on the brand loyalty and relatively inelastic demand of this group. That is, as generics siphon off price-sensitive patients, the price-insensitive ones are left. The pioneer takes advantage of this market segmentation by raising brand-name prices for its loyal customers. (Pioneers can even introduce their own generic versions to compete in the generic segment.) We will return to the demand for generic substitutes in our section on cost containment.

R&D and Innovation

R&D expenditures for research-based pharmaceutical firms rose from $428 million in 1980 to $21 billion in 1998, a 50-fold increase (PhRMA, 1999). Over the same period, the share of sales devoted to R&D increased from 12 percent to 20 percent, the highest ratio among all major industries. Firms would not undertake these investments unless they could gain protection for their work. The patent system provides one method for providing protection.

[15]See Bae (1997) and Deutsch (1998).

A patent gives the holder the right to "to exclude others from making, using, or selling the invention." The usual term for a patent is 17 years, but there are exceptions for drug products. To counter the delays posed by the long testing and regulatory review period, a 1984 act allowed extensions for up to five years. A year earlier, Congress also passed the Orphan Drug Act, permitting extensions (and providing other benefits) for drugs designed to treat rare conditions that might otherwise not be profitable.[16]

On the one hand, patents and other legal protections such as trademarks and copyrights can lead to monopoly power, which is not in the public interest. On the other hand, a firm would be much less willing to expend millions of dollars on research if others can become free riders by mimicking its innovations. By being first, firms still would invest in R&D but at reduced levels. The question of just how much less is clearly an empirical issue.

Mansfield (1986) found that 60 percent of pharmaceutical drugs between 1981 and 1983 would not have been developed without patent protection. This figure is especially dramatic compared to the 11 other industries he sampled. The chemical industry was the only other industry with a substantial impact (30 percent) and, even more startling, the effects were either negligible (zero or 1 percent) in five others.

Although the effects of the patent system are small in most industries, it is critical to pharmaceutical innovation. We therefore turn our attention to the determinants of pharmaceutical R&D and a conceptual framework to examine the effects of FDA regulations and patent law on innovations.

INVESTMENT DECISIONS

Net present value analysis provides a simple, yet powerful approach to investment decisions. Letting R_t and C_t represent the revenues and costs in time, t, the present discounted value (*PDV*) of a project is given by:

$$PDV = \sum_{t=1}^{T} (R_t - C_t)/(1 + r)^t \qquad \textbf{(26.3)}$$

where r is the discount rate or cost of capital and T is the life of the project. Under the standard decision rule, a project is accepted if the net present value is positive. Note the similarity of equation (26.3) with the criterion used in cost–benefit analysis described in chapter 4. The principal distinction is that a firm is concerned with its own revenues and costs, not social benefits and social costs. For example, a firm's program may be helped by publicly funded basic research conducted in universities. These costs are relevant for cost–benefit analysis but not for the firm's investment decisions.

Several characteristics of pharmaceutical R&D become apparent if we break *PDV* into three components representing:

a. the research, testing, and review period (*m* years)
b. the effective period of patent protection (*n* years) after the product is launched

[16]Schweitzer describes the incentives provided by the act and how they have led to a large number of products that have been given orphan status. He argues, however, that the act does little to help populations in developing countries who suffer from diseases that are rare in the developed world. Together with the high cost of many existing drugs, the responsibilities of industrialized nations and the pharmaceutical industry to poorer nations are becoming major social and political issues. See also Arno, Bonuck, and Davis (1995) for an assessment of the act within the context of AIDS drugs.

c. the period following patent expiration (*s* years, where $m + n + s = T$).

$$PDV = \sum_{t=1}^{m} (R_t - C_t)/(1+r)^t + \sum_{t=m+1}^{m+n} (R_t - C_t)/(1+r)^t + \sum_{t=m+n+1}^{m+n+s} (R_t - C_t)/(1+r)^t$$

$$\text{\textbf{a.}} \qquad\qquad\qquad \text{\textbf{b.}} \qquad\qquad\qquad\qquad \text{\textbf{c.}} \qquad \text{(26.4)}$$

In the first component listed, **a**, the firm will not have any revenue and there will be large, negative net cash flows reflecting the high R&D costs. To offset these costs, a successful project will require even larger positive net cash flows in later years, particularly over the period represented by the second component, the effective patent life. Despite potential competition from generics and significant erosion of sales, products still may capitalize on brand recognition, marketing efforts, and new uses to remain successful after patent expiration, the last component, **c**.

This framework further tells us that regulations and testing procedures that raise costs in the first component reduce *PDV* and make an investment less attractive. Similarly, *PDV* is reduced by an increase in the length of the research, testing, and review period, because it must reduce the length of the patent protection period, **b**. Conversely, changes such as reduced regulation or fast-track laws to lower initial costs and speed up the review process as well as extensions of patent rights each serve to raise *PDV*.

Finally, the risks are important. Projects with higher risks should be discounted at a higher rate or, put another way, high-risk projects need a high rate of return to be viable. To the extent that a firm can reduce risks, for example, by supporting a portfolio of diverse projects or sharing risks through joint ventures with other firms, the discount rate, *r*, diminishes and the likelihood of investment is increased. This also suggests that large firms have an advantage over smaller firms in R&D.

R&D SPENDING

We have noted that total industry R&D spending is substantial and rising. Despite the spending, the total number of new drugs has declined substantially from a peak of 453 in the 1950s, to 235 for the next decade, and 158 for the 1970s, before increasing somewhat in the succeeding years (Deutsch, 1998). The reasons for the slowdown are not clear. However, it is clear that the cost per new drug must have risen dramatically.

Careful analyses of the drug-development process by DiMasi and colleagues (1991) at the firm level provide some startling figures for R&D costs. Focusing on the more significant innovations, the authors estimated total costs[17] at $231 million in 1987 dollars per new chemical entity that was marketed. Because there is substantial attrition as projects move to successive stages of development, about two-thirds of the cost is attributable to the preclinical phase.

How do firms recover these formidable amounts (which are much higher in current dollars)? Our understanding of the returns to investment has been aided greatly by the work of Grabowski and Vernon (1994, 1996), which follows sales over the life cycle of a product. Grabowski and Vernon found that a product has an effective patent life of about 9 to 13 years and a market life of about 20 years. Cash flows do not become positive until the third year after launch, and sales peak in the tenth or eleventh year. The

[17]The costs are computed as capitalized expected costs using a discount rate of 9 percent.

most significant finding is that a substantial portion of a company's revenue and profits are derived from a few big winners. Only the top 20 percent of new drugs have an *PDV* that is substantially positive: the *PDV* of the representative new drug is actually negative. This highly skewed distribution reinforces the firm's need for diversification by having a large number of drugs under development to reduce risks. It also suggests difficulties for smaller firms that cannot sustain a large R&D program.

FIRM SIZE AND INNOVATION

Henderson and Cockburn (1996) ask the question: "Are the research efforts of larger firms more productive than those of smaller rivals, and if so, why?" They search for evidence of the effects of size on "important" patents granted and found that the returns to size are significant. This result is not surprising, but their contribution lies in distinguishing between "economies of scale" and "economies of scope."[18]

For innovation, these concepts need clarification in that output is not easily or uniquely measured. One approach measures output through patents. Economies of scale arise if patents granted increase more rapidly than the size of an R&D program. Economies of scope will be realized if a joint program to develop different drugs is more productive than with distinct programs.

Henderson and Cockburn found that size is important and that larger programs are more productive. However, it is due more to economies of scope than to economies of scale. Little gain is achieved in increasing the size of an individual program beyond some minimal threshold level. Economies of scope arise when different research activities can share inputs, thus lowering cost. More important, spillovers of knowledge among projects raise overall productivity. The authors also found significant spillovers of information among firms.

MERGERS AND ACQUISITIONS

The pharmaceutical industry has seen a wave of megamergers and large acquisitions in recent years. Two blockbuster deals in early 2000 suggests that the merger frenzy is likely to continue. In the United Kingdom, Glaxo Wellcome and SmithKline Beecham agreed to merge to become the world's largest pharmaceutical as measured by market value. Just 1 week later, Pfizer reached a deal to acquire Warner-Lambert to become the largest U.S. pharmaceutical and the world's second largest company. Horizontal mergers (i.e., mergers between rivals within an industry) generally occur for two reasons.[19] A merger may increase the monopoly power of the merged entity, enabling it to increase prices and profits. But even without the benefit of higher prices, profits will increase if the newly formed entity can reduce costs by taking advantage of the kind of economies and externalities in R&D described above. Potential economies in marketing and administration, as well as an improved ability to complete globally, make a proposed merger even more attractive.

[18]A firm experiences economies of scale when its long-run average costs decrease with higher output. It has economies of scope if the cost of producing two or more different products is less than the costs of separate production. Earlier work, which did not distinguish between these effects, showed mixed results on the effects of firm size on innovation.

[19]A good general discussion of mergers is found in Viscusi, Vernon, and Harrington (1995). Po (1998) provides an evaluation of the recent merger phenomenon in the pharmaceutical industry.

The industry also is responding in other ways to the growing cost of R&D and conducting clinical trials. Strategic alliances among firms have risen sharply from 121 in 1986 to 635 in 1997 (PhRMA, 1999). The most ambitious involves an alliance of 10 large firms, formed in 1999, that will pool efforts to develop a fine-scale map of the human genome. Its goal is to develop new drugs that can be tailor-made to account for the large genetic variability in individuals.

In other important changes, less pharmaceutical R&D is being conducted "in house" as firms look for R&D partners to reduce costs and spread risks. As part of this trend, partnerships with contract research organizations are growing rapidly, accounting for about 10 percent of research spending by pharmaceutical and biotechnology companies (Lee, 1998). These organizations are used to conduct clinical trials and, in some cases, to provide a broad range of drug-development services.

Cost Containment

With the rapid growth in drug expenditures, there is naturally great policy interest in cost containment. President Clinton's 1993 health care reform plan included a mechanism to regulate prices through caps geared to prices in other countries and to producer costs. Despite a questionable methodology, a series of General Accounting Office reports in the early 1990s, indicating that U.S. prices were higher than prices in Canada and the United Kingdom, intensified interest in drug-price controls.

We already have addressed some of the difficulties of regulating prices for large numbers of constantly changing products. We also have addressed the problems of recovering common costs. If prices are driven toward marginal costs, R&D investment and the resulting innovation are likely to dry up to the detriment of the public's welfare. Many countries have introduced price or profit controls, discounts, and other mechanisms to try to rein in spending.[20] In the United States, Medicaid programs "discount" prices and impose restrictions on utilization. The federal government also discounts prices for drugs purchased by the Department of Veterans Affairs and other federal agencies.

Most outpatient drug purchases in the United States are paid out of pocket or by private insurance (recall that Medicare does not cover outpatient prescriptions). We therefore turn to the cost-containment efforts of the private sector, especially those introduced through managed care. These efforts include price discounting and the exercise of monopsony power, much like their public insurance counterparts. To narrow our discussion, we will describe three other strategies: higher copayments, use of generic drugs, and the adoption of drug formularies.

COPAYMENTS

A higher copayment seems simple and straightforward. It is intended to shift a larger share of the cost burden to the patient and to decrease consumption of marginally beneficial drugs. Moreover, under many current copayment plans, prescription drugs cost only a fraction of their over-the-counter substitutes.

[20]Most western European countries control either producers' prices or reimbursement rates. England has a profit control system. See Huttin (1999) for specifics.

However, a higher copayment is not a sure thing because other effects can result. Recall from Figure 26.2 that an increase in the out-of-pocket cost of a drug will decrease its use as patients substitute other inputs for drugs.

With no substitutability, use of drugs remains unchanged; only the distribution of the costs between patients and insurers is affected. If significant substitutability is possible, the total cost of care may increase as inefficient cost-minimization combinations are selected. Higher copayments work most effectively in reducing health care spending when patients are not likely to make large substitutions. Most empirical studies have found low price elasticities for drugs—approximately 0.1 to 0.3 in absolute value—and are consistent with this latter case.

However, when generic substitutes are available (multiple-source drugs), strategies involving differential copayments for brand products offer the potential for substantial shifts toward lower-priced generics without affecting overall utilization. Managed care plans are introducing tiered copayment systems where the patient pays, for example, $5 for a generic drug, $10 to $15 for a brand-name product on an approved list (formulary), and more if it is not found on the formulary. Patients and providers who consider the generic a close substitute will choose the generic.

The key question is whether there will be a large substitution toward generics? Motheral and Henderson (1999) examined two plans with tiered systems that increased brand-name copays more than copays for generics. They found little effect on total drug utilization. However, utilization of brand products decreased about 18 percent relative to a control group that had no price increases. This substitution produced substantial savings to the health plans.

GENERIC SUBSTITUTES

About 70 percent of prescriptions are written for multiple-source drugs (Hellerstein 1998), and the vast majority of the top-selling drugs have generics. With generic prices considerably below their brand-name counterparts and FDA certification of their therapeutic equivalence, one would expect little resistance to generic versions from physicians and their patients. This has not been so.

Interest in promoting generic products has a long history. Following antisubstitution laws passed by most states after World War II, prohibiting pharmacists from substituting a generic for a prescribed brand, mounting cost pressures led to reforms. In 1970, Massachusetts became the first state to legalize drug product selection and, by the end of the decade, most others followed. Despite the potential for cost saving, an early study of Michigan's substitution laws was revealing. After 1974, substitution by a pharmacist was allowed unless the doctor wrote "dispense as written" or "DAW." Relatively few prescriptions were written with this restriction. However, substitutions were given for less than 2 percent of all multiple-source prescriptions.[21]

Substitution has increased well beyond the levels of the 1970s, and generics' share of the prescription drug market reached 44 percent in 1997. Nevertheless, physicians continue to write the trade name for most prescriptions. Using 1989 survey data, Hellerstein (1998) examined multiple-source prescriptions for the eight largest drug classes. Only 29 percent of the prescriptions were written for generics. Why? Hellerstein explains

[21]Goldberg et al. (1979).

with information and agency theory. Because physicians do not gain from any cost savings, they have little incentive to invest in the information about availability of generics or their effectiveness and prices. In his empirical model, Hellerstein found that patient characteristics are not important in prescription decisions. Physician characteristics are important. In particular, physicians with a larger share of HMO and prepaid plan patients will more likely write generic prescriptions.

DRUG FORMULARIES

Managed care's strong financial interest in cost containment has led to policies that go well beyond the promotion of generics by monitoring physicians and requiring substitution. Many are using pharmacy benefit managers to negotiate discounts and improve the efficiency of their claims-processing and pharmacy operations. They are increasingly adopting other methods such as drug-utilization review programs and lower-cost, mail-order sources for prescriptions. One of the most ambitious and controversial strategies, however, involves the use of formulary committees to develop a list of approved drugs. A positive formulary restricts the choice of drugs to those on the list. A negative formulary excludes drugs on a list.

The formulary review and approval process can be elaborate, dealing not only with generic substitution but also with recommendations of different drugs that can be used to treat a condition. Ideally, the review committee will periodically review all drugs in each therapeutic class for their clinical effectiveness, safety, and cost. Mather and colleagues (1999) observe that, when properly implemented, the formulary can be an effective and well-accepted tool. If drug product decisions are based largely on cost instead of clinical outcomes, they suggest that "the health system may experience higher overall costs and the pharmacy benefit may be sharply criticized by health plan providers, enrollees, and suppliers wishing to see their products on the list" (p. 277).

The widespread adoption of formularies has elevated the importance of pharmaco-economic analyses. Pharmaceutical firms face strong pressure to provide clinical and economic data that justify their inclusion in the formulary. Formulary committee members require the skills to compare, interpret, and analyze data from many different sources, and to justify their decisions. They are under especially great pressure from both patients and providers when new and improved drugs come onto the market.

Conclusion

Our overview of the pharmaceutical industry focused on individual provider and patient decisions, firm pricing and investment decisions, and public policy issues in regulation and cost containment. Throughout, we have emphasized the use of basic economic tools to simplify and make sense of complex problems. We have neglected, however, to place some of the issues within a global context, and we will conclude with insights from international data.

It might appear from the material presented that drug spending in the United States is considerably beyond any level that could be considered reasonable or efficient. If it is, then the United States is not alone among developed countries. With an 8.8 percent share of health spending devoted to drugs, the United States stands near the bottom

Prilosec and Prozac: Why Cost Containment Is So Difficult

Generic producers often do not have the marketing ability to make significant inroads in markets with heavily promoted, brand-name products. They must also worry about the introduction of generics by brand-name companies and of new products for current brand-name products, especially of bestsellers whose patents are about to expire. Two examples involving the widely recognized products Prilosec and Prozac illustrate the challenges for generic producers and the problems of cost containment that face everyone.

Prilosec is an acid-fighting drug used to treat ulcers and severe recurrent heartburn. As the world's top-selling drug in 1998, with sales in excess of $5 billion, it has been a major "blockbuster" for its producer, Astra Pharmaceuticals. The wholesale cost for a month's supply per patient is $116 to $178. Despite much lower costs, generic substitutes and other effective products have been losing market share. Prilosec has been promoted extensively on network and cable television and in a wide range of magazines with the message: "Ask your doctor about the most prescribed acid medication in America." These ads have worked so successfully that according to the *Wall Street Journal,* Prilosec is the biggest single cost at many companies that provide drug coverage.

Prozac, developed by Eli Lilly, leads the market for antidepressants. In 1998, it ranked as the third-leading seller following Prilosec and Zocor, a cholesterol drug sold by Merck.

Prozac, which works by bolstering serotonin, a brain chemical believed to be deficient in depressed patients, has fewer side effects than the drugs it had displaced. However, Prozac's patent may expire as soon as 2001 and not later than 2004. With the huge, multibillion-dollar market for antidepressants, what will happen after Prozac's patent expires?

Lilly purchased the rights to a purified version of Prozac that will extend patent protection to 2015. It hopes to capitalize on the dominance of Prozac. But other firms are investing heavily to develop the next leader. Some analysts believe that the new drugs may not be much more effective than Prozac but will benefit patients by having fewer side effects.

Of course, any new product is likely to cost more than Prozac. Others believe that managed care will require physicians to prescribe Prozac or a generic substitute. If this scenario prevails, spending can be controlled. However, with many new products under development, the success of direct advertising to patients, and the declining stigma associated with mental health disease, a more likely scenario is that the market for antidepressants will continue to grow rapidly.

Sources: Wall Street Journal, "Son of Prozac: A New Purer Version of Top Antidepressant Is in Eli Lilly's Sights," December 7, 1998 and "Why Generic Drugs Often Can't Compete Against Brand Names," December 18, 1998; *New York Times,* "Drug Makers in Hot Race to Find the Next Prozac," October 11, 1998.

among industrial countries (see Table 23.1)[22] Many factors account for these wide variations in shares including differences in physician practice patterns, cultural attitudes toward drugs, licensure laws, and insurance and other financial arrangements (physicians are permitted to dispense drugs in some countries). All nations are dealing with the same pressures and the need to find mechanisms to promote cost-efficient use of drugs and other health care inputs. After all, the most important economic question is the value of drugs in producing health.

Fortunately, recent work is providing new and surprising results. Frech and Miller (1999) took advantage of the wide differences in drug utilization and health status across 21 OECD countries to investigate the productivity of drugs, other medical inputs, wealth, and lifestyle. They used regression analysis with alternative measures of a nation's health status as the dependent variable. Independent variables included a country's wealth, pharmaceutical spending per capita, other health spending per capita, and various lifestyle indicators.

Some of the findings are consistent with our analyses in previous chapters. Wealth, measured by per-capita GDP, showed significant and positive effects on life expectancy. A doubling of GDP has a 6 percent effect at age 40 and a 9 percent effect at age 60. Lifestyle (measured by smoking, alcohol, and consumption of animal fat) also has important effects. In particular, the consumption of animal fat, the most important lifestyle variable, has positive effects on life expectancy at birth, age 40, and age 60 up to certain levels of consumption (92, 78, and 70 grams per day, respectively). Nonpharmaceutical inputs showed no statistically significant effects at any of the three age levels.

The most interesting and surprising results relate to pharmaceutical spending per capita, with strong positive effects on life expectancy at ages 40 and 60. A doubling of drug spending increases life expectancy by 2 percent and 4 percent at these age levels, respectively. The study also estimated the lifetime pharmaceutical cost of extending life by one year. For the United States, these costs for males and females at age 40 are $21,000 and $23,000, and about $17,000 and $19,000 at age 60. Analyses of infant mortality show that drug consumption has a small, positive (harmful), but statistically insignificant effect. The consumption of animal fat, with a negative (beneficial) impact, is the most important variable.

These international comparisons support views that pharmaceuticals are extremely productive, especially as compared to other health care inputs. Pharmaceutical companies and their profits are highly visible and they make convenient targets. Although economists usually lead the charge in developing strategies to reduce inefficiencies, Frech and Miller's findings warn of the danger in focusing disproportionately on policies and measures that contain drug spending.

Summary

1. Spending on pharmaceuticals is growing rapidly. At the same time, the patient's share has diminished.
2. The pharmaceutical industry is characterized by significant barriers to entry and substantial regulation. The industry has been regulated since 1906, but 1962 legislation had the most profound effects.

[22]On a per-capita basis, where the United States spends far more on medical care than any other nation, its drug spending is similar to the levels found in several other industrial nations.

3. Pharmaceuticals substitute for health and nonhealth inputs in the production of health. A rational patient will select least-cost input combinations. Relative changes in a patient's out-of-pocket costs resulting from insurance will lead to substitution of drugs for other health care inputs or vice versa.

4. Technological change, even when the benefits are marginal, is often cost-increasing due to insurance.

5. Pharmaceutical firms earn higher-than-normal profits, but the extent of their profits is exaggerated greatly by conventional accounting data.

6. Opportunities are substantial for price discrimination. Markets, or groups of buyers, with a more inelastic demand will pay higher prices.

7. Generic products often capture a significant share of the market following patent expiration. Nevertheless, through effective marketing and promotion, trade names still can retain a monopoly premium.

8. R&D spending is substantial and a firm's profits often depend on a few big winners. Firms need to earn substantial amounts over the effective life of a patent to justify the risks.

9. Larger R&D programs are more productive than smaller programs. Economies of scope play an important role.

10. Price, rate-of-return regulation, and national formularies are used in other countries to contain costs. In the United States, higher copayments, the promotion of generic substitutes, and other managed care strategies, such as drug formularies, have been adopted.

11. Spending on drugs in the United States is not out of line as compared to other developed countries.

12. Drugs are highly productive in improving health compared to other medical inputs.

Discussion Questions

1. Explain and distinguish between the "concentration ratio" and the "HHI." What are the limitations of these measures within the context of the pharmaceutical industry?

2. Direct-to-consumer (DTC) advertising of prescription drugs is growing rapidly. List several products with which you have become familiar as a result of such advertising. Discuss the pros and cons of DTC advertising from the perspective of physicians and patients.

3. Use Figure 26.1 to explain how an isoquant can be positively sloped. Under what circumstances may a patient actually end up in the positively sloped region (e.g., at point *H*)?

4. Regulation is often proposed (and widely used in other countries) to limit prices or profits. Discuss possible adverse effects of regulating prescription prices. In light of your discussion, what accounts for the strong pressure in many countries, including the United States, to regulate prices?

5. The FDA severely restricts promotion of "off-label" uses of drugs by pharmaceutical firms even though physicians are free to, and often do, prescribe medication for conditions for which a drug has not been approved. Although this restraint is being challenged, pharmaceutical companies currently are forbidden even to inform

physicians of research about off-label uses that has been published in scientific journals. Discuss the pros and cons of the FDA's policy.
6. What are barriers to entry? Describe three potential barriers in the pharmaceutical industry. What are some consequences of these barriers?
7. There are wide differences across countries in the share of health resources spent on drugs. Describe possible economic and noneconomic factors that may contribute to the variation.

Exercises

1. Use Figure 26.2 to explain why cost minimization through a tangency between an isoquant and a budget line does not apply in cases where D and M are either perfect complements or perfect substitutes. Describe the cost-minimization process and the effects of changes in the relative prices of D and M in these special cases.
2. Assume that a patient has 80 percent coverage for medical services but no coverage for prescription drugs. An 80 percent drug benefit is added. Show graphically what will happen to the relative utilization of M and D, and total spending on health care, to attain a given health status. What happens to the amount spent on drugs (insurance plus patient amounts)? Why will total spending on health care diminish when the 80 percent drug benefit is added?
3. A pharmaceutical firm faces the following monthly demands in the U.S. and Mexican markets for one of its patented drugs:

$$Q_{US} = 300,000 - 5,000P_{US} \quad \text{and} \quad Q_X = 240,000 - 8,000P_X$$

where quantities represents the number of prescriptions. Assume that resale or arbitrage among markets is impossible and that marginal cost is constant at $2 per prescription in both markets. Monthly fixed costs are $1 million in the United States and $500,000 in Mexico.
 a. Draw the demand, marginal revenue, and marginal cost curves for each market. Estimate the profit-maximizing prices and quantities graphically and/or determine the solutions algebraically. What are the firm's total profits?
 b. Determine the quantity in each market and maximum possible total profits if the firm engages in perfect (first degree) price discrimination. Is this behavior possible?
4. Assume that the firm cannot prevent resale and is forced to set the same price in both markets. Find the price graphically and/or algebraically and show that total profits are less than those from part 3a.
5. For your answer in 3a:
 a. Calculate the price elasticity of demand in each market at the optimal price.
 b. Verify that the prices and elasticities are consistent with the profit-maximizing formula given in footnote 14.
 c. Why are both elasticities fairly close to unity? (Hint! Think about the requirement for profit maximization when marginal cost is zero.)
 d. If a firm finds that its price elasticity is numerically less than one, what advice would you have?

6. Consider only the U.S. market from problem 3. Graph solutions to parts 6a and 6b using the demand, average cost, and marginal cost curves. Also try to develop the answers algebraically.

 a. Price regulation is proposed. Find the regulated price that enables the firm to cover all its costs. Caution! There are two mathematical solutions. Which one will regulators prefer?

 b. Find also the economically efficient price (i.e., one that is consistent with marginal cost pricing). What subsidy per prescription is required to enable the firm to cover all its costs?

7. Compare your results in parts 6a and 6b with the profit-maximizing solution for the United States obtained in part 3a. Explain which of the three alternatives you would prefer if you were responsible for public policy. Be sure to consider some of the problems of regulating prices.

Glossary

Items in italics are defined elsewhere in the glossary.

Actuarially Fair Insurance under which expected payouts equal the premiums paid by beneficiaries.

Adverse Selection A situation often resulting from *asymmetric information* in which individuals are able to purchase insurance at rates that are below actuarially fair rates plus *loading costs*.

Agency Relationship A situation in which one person (agent) makes decisions on behalf of another person (principal).

Aggregate Demand (See *Market Demand*)

Allocative Efficiency (See *Efficiency*)

Alternative Delivery System (ADS) Insurance and organizational arrangements for health care delivery that are alternatives to traditional *fee-for-service* (FFS) arrangements.

Assignment (See *Participation/Assignment*)

Asymmetric Information Situations in which the parties on the opposite sides of a transaction have differing amounts of relevant information.

Average Cost Total cost represents the sum of all fixed costs and variable costs in the *short run*. Average cost equals total cost divided by the quantity of output and also equals the sum of average variable cost (AVC) and average fixed cost (AFC). In the *long run,* average total cost represents the minimum possible cost per unit of producing any given level of output when there are no fixed costs.

Balance Billing The practice of collecting from the patient the difference between the charge and the insurance reimbursement.

Barrier-to-Entry Impediments to the unrestricted flow of factors into or out of an industry or occupation (e.g., control over natural resources, licensure, patents).

Budget Constraint The line that is the collection of points representing combinations of goods that the consumer is just able to afford.

Capitation A method of reimbursement in managed care plans in which a provider is paid a fixed amount per person over a given period regardless of the amount of services rendered.

Cardinal Utility A quantitative measure of the value of a good in terms of metrically measurable utility. It is used in the study of risk and insurance.

Case-Mix Index A numerical measure of the assortment of patient cases treated by a given hospital, so that a higher value indicates a greater average degree of complexity of the cases.

Certificate-of-Need (CON) Regulations that require health care providers to obtain approval from state planning agencies for capital expenditures that exceed various threshold levels (e.g., $500,000).

Ceteris Paribus Other things being held constant.

Coefficient of Variation A measure of dispersion equal to the standard deviation divided by the mean (and sometimes multiplied by 100).

Coinsurance (Rate) The share of costs that are paid by the beneficiary of a health policy (often after some *deductible*).

Community Rating The practice of setting insurance premiums based on the utilization pattern of a broad population in a region. This approach to rate setting contrasts with *experience rating*.

Comparative Statics The analysis that calculates the level of a new equilibrium, given changed values of one or more economic parameters, such as prices or income.

611

Competition (See *Perfect Competition*)

Concentration Ratio The share of the market sales or production accounted for by a certain number of the largest firms. Often the four-firm ratio is used.

Copayment Amounts paid by the insurance beneficiary as a result of *coinsurance* and *deductibles*.

Cost–Benefit Analysis (CBA) A method of comparing the monetary value of all benefits of a social project with all costs of that project.

Cost-Effectiveness Analysis (CEA) A method that tries to find the least cost method of achieving a desired objective(s) associated with a social project.

Cost Sharing (See also *Copayment*) Methods of financing health care that require some direct payments for services by patients.

Cost Shifting Increasing revenues from some payers to offset uncompensated care costs and lower net payments from other payers.

Cross (Price) Elasticity of Demand (See also *Elasticity*) The percentage change in the quantity demanded of one good resulting from a 1 percent change in the price of another good.

Deductible The amount of health care charges for which a beneficiary is responsible before the insurer begins payment.

Demand Function The relationship between quantity demanded and price (and other independent variables such as income and tastes). One could study individual demand as well as market demand.

Depreciation The change in the value of a good over time, due to deteriorating physical characteristics or technical obsolescence.

Diagnosis-Related Groups (DRGs) A set of case types established under the *Prospective Payment System* (*PPS*) identifying patients with similar conditions and processes of care. There are currently 495 DRGs in *Medicare's Prospective Payment System*, each of which is assigned a relative weight that compares its costliness to the average for all DRGs.

Discount Rate The interest rate used when converting sums to be received at a future date to a present value.

Discounting The process of converting sums to be received at a future date to a present value.

Discrete Choice Analysis A statistical analysis in which the variable to be explained is limited among alternatives, typically to values of 0 or 1.

Economic Profit (See also *Monopoly Profit*) The return over and above that which is necessary to keep the firm from exiting the market over the *long run*. These profits are also called above *normal profits*, excess profits and supra normal profits.

Economies of Scale Situations in which the *long-run* average costs of a firm decline as output increases.

Economies of Scope Situations in which a firm can jointly produce two or more goods more cheaply than under separate production of the goods.

Edgeworth Box (in Consumption) A diagram that shows all possible allocations of fixed amounts of goods and services between two people.

Efficiency (See also *Pareto Efficiency*) Technical efficiency occurs when the firm produces the maximum possible sustained output from a given set of inputs. This idea is distinguished from allocative efficiency—situations in which either inputs or outputs are put to their best possible uses in the economy so that no further gains in output or welfare are possible. Both allocative and technical efficiency are prerequisites for *Pareto Efficiency*.

Elasticity The percentage change in some dependent variable (e.g., quantity demanded) resulting from a 1 percent change in some independent variable (e.g., price). Elasticities that exceed one in absolute value are considered elastic; elasticities less than one are inelastic.

Elasticity of Substitution (See also *Elasticity*) The percentage change in the capital–labor ratio resulting from a 1 percent change in relative factor prices.

Equilibrium Price (Quantity) The price (quantity) at which the quantity demanded and the quantity supplied are equal.

Expected Value A measure used with a probability distribution of returns. The expected value is the sum of each probability multiplied by its corresponding return.

Experience Good A good for which evaluation is difficult prior to experience or purchase.

Experience Rating The practice of setting insurance premiums for an individual or group based on historical experience or risk associated with the individual or group.

Externality A case in which a consumer (producer) affects the utility (costs) of another consumer

(producer) through actions that lie outside the price system.

Fee-for-Service (FFS) A method of payment under which the provider is paid for each procedure or service that is provided to a patient.

Fee Schedule A listing of fees by third-party payers showing the maximum amounts they will reimburse for specific services or procedures.

Firm Any entity that transforms inputs to some product or service that is sold in the marketplace.

First Fundamental Theorem of Welfare Economics The proposition that under specified conditions, competitive markets lead to *Pareto efficient* results.

Fixed Costs (TFC and AFC) Costs that do not vary with output. They are expressed either as total fixed cost (TFC) or average fixed cost (AFC).

Formulary A list of drugs developed by a managed care plan. Under a positive formulary, prescriptions on the list are covered. Under a negative formulary, prescriptions on the list are not covered.

Frontier Analysis A statistical analysis of firm efficiency that attempts to identify the best possible production practice and interprets firm inefficiency as a departure from the best possible production practice or frontier.

Galbraith Effect The effect of advertising on market demand for the product.

Game Theory A model that analyzes economic behavior as a series of strategic moves and countermoves by rival agents.

Gatekeeper The primary care provider who is responsible for coordinating a patient's care in a managed care plan. Often the gatekeeper must authorize referrals to specialists and nonemergency hospital admissions.

Gross Domestic Product (GDP) The market value of final goods and services produced within the borders of a country over a period of 1 year.

Group Insurance An insurance contract in which employees or members of a group are covered by a policy issued by their employer or group.

Group Model HMO An *HMO* organization in which the insurer contracts with group practices to provide care.

Health and Health Status (See also *Morbidity Rate* and *Mortality Rate*) The measures of the physical and emotional well-being of an individual or a defined population. Mortality and morbidity rates are often used to measure health status.

Health Care Goods and services used as inputs to produce health. In some analyses, one's own time and knowledge used to maintain and promote health are considered in addition to conventional health care inputs.

Health Care Financing Administration (HCFA) An agency of the United States Department of Health and Human Services (DHHS). HCFA is responsible for administering the financing and quality assurance programs for *Medicare* and the federal participation in *Medicaid.*

Health Maintenance Organization (HMO) A managed care plan that integrates financing and delivery of a comprehensive set of health care services to an enrolled population. HMOs may contract with or directly employ health care providers.

Herfindahl-Hirschman Index (HHI) A measure of market concentration that incorporates the size distribution of firms. It is found by summing the squares of the market shares of each firm.

Human Capital A form of intangible capital that includes the skills and other knowledge that workers have or acquire through education, training, and health care that yields valuable productive services over time.

Identification Problem In econometric analysis, the inability to distinguish between two relationships (such as demand and supply) that contain the same variables (such as price and quantity).

Income Effect (See also *Substitution Effect*) The effect on quantity demanded that results from the change in real income associated with a relative change in the price of the good or service under study.

Income Elasticity of Demand (See also *Elasticity*) The percentage change in quantity demanded resulting from a 1 percent change in income.

Indemnity Insurance Traditional health insurance often associated with *fee-for-service, fee schedules,* and, which unlike managed care, places few restrictions on choice of providers.

Independent Practice Association (IPA) Physicians in independent, solo, or small group practices, who contract with a health maintenance organization to provide services to its members.

Indifference Curve Shows all combinations of goods that provide a constant level of satisfaction (*utility*) to the individual under study.

Inefficiency (See *Efficiency* and *Pareto Efficiency*)

Infant Mortality Rate The ratio of the number of deaths in infants age 1 year or less during a year divided by the number of live births during the year.

Inferior Good (See also *Normal Good*) A good or service for which demand decreases as income increases.

Internal Rate of Return The discount rate that will equate the time streams of costs and returns of an investment. It is a measure of the profitability of an investment.

Isoquant (Isoproduct Curve) All combinations of factors of production yielding a constant level of output.

Labor–Leisure Trade-off The line that is the collection of points representing the combinations of leisure time and earnings from work that are possible for a person.

Law of Demand There is an inverse relationship between price and quantity demanded, *ceteris paribus.*

Law of Diminishing Returns After some point, the marginal product of a variable input must diminish.

Loading Costs The administrative and other costs associated with underwriting an insurance policy.

Long Run (See also *Short Run*) A period of time sufficient to permit a firm to vary all factors of production.

Long-Term Care The ongoing health and social services provided for individuals who need assistance on a continuing basis because of physical or mental disability. Services can be provided in an institution, the home, or the community, and include informal services provided by family or friends as well as formal services provided by professionals or agencies.

Luxury good A good that richer people tend to buy in greater proportions, so that its *income elasticity* is greater than one.

Managed Care Any payment or delivery arrangement used by a health plan or provider to control or to coordinate use of health services to contain health expenditures, improve quality, or both.

Managed Care Organization (MCO) A general term referring to the various health plans that use managed care arrangements and have a defined system of selected providers that contract with them. The most common are *health maintenance organizations (HMOs), preferred provider organizations (PPOs),* and *point-of-service (POS) plans.*

Mandated Benefits The coverage in health insurance policies for certain services that are mandated by state insurance statutes.

Marginal Incremental; a one unit increase.

Marginal Cost The increase in total cost resulting from a one unit increase in output.

Marginal Labor (Factor) Cost The addition to total labor (factor) costs associated with an additional unit of labor (factor of production).

Marginal Product The addition to total output resulting from an additional unit of the variable input.

Marginal Rate of Substitution The amount of one commodity given up per unit increase in another commodity while maintaining the same level of satisfaction.

Marginal Rate of Technical Substitution The amount of one factor of production given up per unit increase in another factor of production while maintaining the same level of output.

Marginal Rate of Transformation The slope of the production possibilities curve, and the rate at which society can transform one good into another.

Marginal Revenue The addition to total revenue associated with a one unit increase in output.

Marginal Revenue Product The addition to a firm's total revenue associated with employing one more unit of a variable input.

Marginal Utility The extra utility gained from consuming one more unit of a good holding others constant. Utility is a measure of the satisfaction from consuming goods.

Market Demand The total demand for a good by all consumers in the market.

Market Structure The structure relating to how an industry is organized in terms of the number and distribution of firms and how firms compete among themselves.

Medicaid The health insurance programs administered by the states for qualifying low income beneficiaries. The federal government establishes minimum standards and provides matching grants. The program became law in 1965.

Medicare The federal health insurance program established in 1965 for the elderly and other selected groups.

Medicare—Part A The Medicare Hospital Insurance that covers beneficiaries for inpatient hospital, home health, hospice, and limited skilled nursing facility services. Beneficiaries are responsible for deductibles and copayments.

Medicare—Part B The Medicare Supplementary Medical Insurance that covers Medicare beneficiaries for physician services, medical supplies,

and other outpatient treatment. Beneficiaries are responsible for monthly premiums, copayments, deductibles, and balance billing.

Medigap Policy A privately purchased insurance policy that supplements Medicare coverage and meets specified requirements set by federal statute and the National Association of Insurance Commissioners.

Monopoly Situations in which a firm faces a negatively sloped demand curve. In a pure monopoly, there is no other firm that produces a close substitute for the firm's product. Thus the demand curve facing the monopolist is the market demand curve.

Monopoly Profit (Rent) The return over and above a *normal profit* resulting from *monopoly*.

Monopsony Situations in which a firm faces a positively sloped supply curve in the product or factor market because it is the only buyer.

Moral Hazard An insurance term that represents the disincentives created by insurance for individuals to take measures that would reduce the amount of care demanded. In the health services literature, it is more commonly used to express the additional quantity of health care demanded, resulting from a decrease in the net price of care attributable to insurance.

Morbidity Rate The rate of incidence of disease in a particular population.

Mortality Rate The death rate for a particular population. The crude death rate is the ratio of deaths during a year divided by midyear population. Because age is so important, the age-adjusted mortality rate is a measure that takes into account a population's age distribution.

Necessity A good whose consumption does not vary greatly with changes in peoples' incomes. More generally, a good with an *income elasticity* less than one.

Network Model HMO A health maintenance organization made up of a network of group practices.

Nominal Value (See also *Real Value*) The money value measured in current dollars.

Nonprofit Firm A firm that is constrained by law from distributing any residual of income over costs to any party.

Normal Good (See also *Inferior Good*) A good or service for which demand increases as income increases.

Normal Return (Normal Profit) The return just sufficient to retain factors of production in an industry or an occupation in the long run. The return equal to the *opportunity cost* of a factor of production.

Nursing Facility An institution that provides skilled nursing care and rehabilitation services to injured, functionally disabled, or sick persons.

Offer Curve A set of points summarizing the amount of a good that an individual will offer for trade, given his or her preferences, endowment, and the prices of other goods.

Opportunity Cost The value of the best alternative that is forgone in order to get or produce more of the commodity under consideration.

Ordinal Utility Utility as evaluated through relative levels of satisfaction, when the particular unit of utility is not essential. Examples of ordinal numbers are 1st, 2nd, and 3rd.

Pareto Efficiency (Optimum) (See also *Efficiency*) A situation in which it is impossible to improve the level of welfare of one party without hurting the welfare level of another party. Situation in which the level of welfare of one or more parties can be improved without hurting any other party are Pareto improvements.

Participation/Assignment A situation in which a provider agrees to accept the third-party payer's payment in full thereby relieving the patient of any balance (except for applicable patient copayments).

Peer Review Organization (PRO) An organization that contracts with the Health Care Financing Administration to investigate the quality of health care furnished to Medicare beneficiaries and to educate beneficiaries and providers. PROs also conduct limited review of medical records and claims to evaluate the appropriateness of care provided.

Perfect Competition A market structure in which there are (1) numerous buyers and sellers, (2) perfect information, (3) free entry and exit, and (4) a homogeneous product.

Play or Pay Insurance proposal that would require employers to either provide minimal levels of health insurance to their employees or pay into a fund that would be used to provide coverage.

Point-of-Service (POS) Plan A managed care plan that encourages patients to select a provider in a network. Members can select nonnetwork providers but will incur higher out-of-pocket costs.

Preferred Provider Organization (PPO) An arrangement under which an enrollee is given financial

incentives (e.g., no *copayments*) to seek care from selected physicians and hospitals with which the payer has contracted.

Prepaid Group Practice (PGP) A *prepayment* arrangement under which participating providers agree to provide services to eligible enrollees in return for a fixed capitated payment.

Prepayment—Prepaid Plans Health insurance proposal that provides unlimited amounts of covered services in return for a fixed predetermined premium.

Present (Discounted) Value (PV or PDV) (See also *Discounting*) The value of a stream of returns to be received at future dates, which is discounted to the equivalent of present dollars.

Price Discrimination The sale of goods or services to different individuals at different prices.

Price Elasticity of Demand (See also *Elasticity*) The percentage change in quantity demanded resulting from a 1 percent change in price.

Price Elasticity of Supply (See also *Elasticity*) The percentage change in quantity supplied resulting from a 1 percent change in price.

Price Index An index that expresses the current prices of a group of goods relative to the prices of these goods in a base year. A price index, often used to convert *nominal values* to *real values*, shows how much prices of those goods have changed since the base year.

Production Function The relationship between the maximum output that can be produced corresponding to any combination of factor inputs.

Production Possibilities Curve (Transformation Curve) A relationship showing all combination of goods that an economy can produce with given amounts of input factors and the existing technology. The slope of the curve is the *marginal rate of transformation* showing the amount of one good that must be given up for a one unit increase in the other good.

Prospective Payment System (PPS) The method of hospital reimbursement phased in by *Medicare* beginning in 1983 under which hospitals were reimbursed a fixed amount determined by the *Diagnosis-Related Groups* of their admissions.

Public Good (Pure) A good (e.g., national defense) that no one can be prevented from consuming, nonexcludable, and that can be consumed by one person without depleting it for another, i.e., nonrival. The marginal cost of providing the good to another consumer is zero.

Rate Regulation (RR) Regulations administered largely at the state level that define the terms under which hospitals are reimbursed.

Real Value (See also *Nominal Value*) Monetary values that are adjusted for changes in the general level of prices relative to some arbitrarily selected base year.

Regression Analysis Statistical analysis that posits a linear relationship between a variable to be explained, and one or more (in multiple regression) explanatory variables, in the form $y = a + bx$.

Relative Value Scale A system that assigns relative weights to health care procedures or services. These are sometimes used as guides by providers to price their services and by third-party payers to determine reimbursement levels.

Rent (Economic Rent) The remuneration to a factor of production, over and above that amount that is necessary to induce its supply in the market.

Reputation Good A good for which consumers rely on information provided by friends, neighbors, and others.

Resource-Based Relative Value Scale (RBRVS) A relative value scale used in *Medicare* reimbursement that is based on the resources involved in providing a service.

Risk Aversion The degree to which a certain income is preferred to a risky alternative with the same expected income.

Risk Selection The enrollment choices made by health plans or enrollees on the basis of perceived risk relative to the premium to be paid.

Roemer's Law The proposed positive relationship between the availability of hospital beds and a population's utilization of those beds. It is also referred to as Say's Law for hospital beds.

Search Good A good whose characteristics can be fully evaluated upon inspection.

Second Fundamental Theorem of Welfare Economics The proposition that any *Pareto efficient* outcome can, in principle, be achieved by competitive markets, given an appropriate initial endowment.

Short Run (See also *Long Run*) Situations in which the firm is not able to vary all its inputs. There is at least one factor of production that is fixed.

Small Area Variations The large variations in the per capita rates of utilization across small, homogeneous areas for many medical and surgical procedures.

Social Insurance Government insurance programs in which eligibility and premiums are not determined by the practices common to private insurance contracts. Premiums are often subsidized and there are typically redistributions from some segments of the population to others.

Social Welfare Function A decision rule under which society ranks all possible distributions of goods and services.

Staff Model HMO A health maintenance organization (HMO) in which physicians are directly employed by the HMO.

Substitutes The substitutes in consumption are goods that satisfy the same wants (e.g., beef and chicken) so that an increase in the price of one will increase the demand for the other. Substitutes in production are alternative goods that a firm can produce (e.g., corn and soybeans for a farmer) so that an increase in the price of one will lead to a decrease in the supply of another.

Substitution Effect (See also *Income Effect*) The change in quantity demanded resulting from a relative change in commodity prices, holding real income constant.

Supplier-Induced Demand (SID) The change in demand associated with the discretionary influence of providers, especially physicians, over their patients. Demand that is provided for the self-interests of providers rather than solely for patient interests.

Target Income Hypothesis A model under which providers are thought to select a specified income level, and to adjust their amount of services provided or fees in order to reach this level.

Technical Efficiency (See *Efficiency*)

Technological Change A change in the process by which factors of production combine to produce outputs.

Theorem of the Second Best The economic theorem stating that the correction of some but not all market imperfections, in cases where there are more than one imperfection, will not necessarily improve society's welfare.

Time Costs The money value of the time lost through travel or waiting when consuming a product or service.

Uncompensated Care The care rendered by hospitals or other providers without payment from the patient or a government-sponsored private insurance program. It includes both charity care, which is provided without expectation of payment, and bad debts, for which the provider has made an unsuccessful effort to collect payment due from the patient.

Usual, Customary, and Reasonable (UCR) Reimbursement A system of insurance reimbursement under which the third-party payer restricts payment to the maximum of several limits (screens) that are established.

Utility and Utility Function Utility represents satisfaction or the level of welfare of an individual, measured in *cardinal* or *ordinal* utility terms. The utility function expresses the person's utility as a function of all possible combinations of goods and services.

Utilization Review (UR) The programs that attempt to determine whether specific services are medically necessary and delivered at an appropriate level and cost.

Variable Costs (TVC and AVC) Costs associated with variable factor(s) of production often expressed as total variable cost (TVC) or average variable cost (AVC).

Welfare A measure of an individual's or a society's level of well-being.

Welfare Loss or **Deadweight Loss** A measure of the net loss of society's welfare resulting from a misallocation of resources, usually situations in which the marginal benefits of a good are not equal to marginal costs.

Yardstick Competition A regulatory pricing policy in which an average of the marginal costs of all competing firms is used as a standard of payment to induce the firm to engage in cost-cutting innovations.

References

Abbott, Thomas A., "Price Regulation in the Pharmaceutical Industry: Prescription or Placebo?" *Journal of Health Economics* 14 (1995): 551–565.

Abel-Smith, Brian. *Cost Containment in Health Care.* (London: Bedford Square, 1984).

Abou-Sayf, Frank K. et al., "Hospice Care Can Yield Savings to HMOs, Patients," *Healthcare Financial Management* 45 (1991): 84–86.

Acton, Jan P., "Demand for Health Care among the Urban Poor with Special Emphasis on the Role of Time," in *The Role of Health Insurance in the Health Services Sector,* edited by Richard Rosett. (New York: Neal Watson, 1976).

Acton, Jan P., "Nonmonetary Factors in the Demand for Medical Services: Some Empirical Evidence," *Journal of Political Economy* 83 (1975): 595–614.

Adamache, Killard W., and Louis F. Rossiter, "The Entry of HMOs into the Medicare Market: Implications for TEFRA's Mandate," *Inquiry* 23 (1986): 349–364.

Adamache, Killard W., and Frank Sloan, "Unions and Hospitals: Some Unresolved Issues," *Journal of Health Economics* 1 (1982): 81–108.

Aigner, Dennis J., C. A. Knox Lovell, and Peter Schmidt, "Formulation and Estimation of Stochastic Frontier Production Function Models," *Journal of Econometrics* 6 (1977): 21–37.

Akerlof, George A., "The Market for 'Lemons': Qualitative Uncertainty and the Market Mechanism," *Quarterly Journal of Economics* 84 (1970): 488–500.

Albion, Mark S., and Paul W. Farris. *The Advertising Controversy: Evidence on the Economic Effects of Advertising.* (Boston: Auburn House, 1981).

Alchian Armen A., and Harold Demsetz, "Production, Information Costs, and Economic Organization," *American Economic Review* 62 (1972): 777–795.

Altman, Stuart H., and Marc A. Rodwin, "Halfway Competitive Markets and Ineffective Regulation: The American Health Care System," *Journal of Health Politics, Policy and Law* 13 (1988): 323–339.

Alvarez-Dardet, Carlos, and Maria Teresa Ruiz, "Thomas McKeown and Archibald Cochrane: A Journey through the Diffusion of Their Ideas," *British Medical Journal* 306 (May 8, 1993): 1252–1254.

Andersen, Ronald, and Lee Benham, "Factors Affecting the Relationship between Family Income and Medical Care Consumption," in *Empirical Studies in Health Economics,* edited by H. Klarman. (Baltimore: Johns Hopkins, 1970).

Anderson, Geoffrey M. et al., "Use of Coronary Bypass Surgery in the United States and Canada," *Journal of the American Medical Association* 269 (1993): 1661–1666.

Anderson, Gerard F., "Universal Health Care Coverage in Korea," *Health Affairs* 8 (1989): 24–33.

Anderson, Gerard F., and Jean-Pierre Poullier, "Health Spending, Access, and Outcomes, Trends in Industrialized Countries," *Health Affairs* 18 (1999): 178–192.

Anderson, Keith B., "Regulation, Market Structure, and Hospital Costs: Comment," *Southern Economic Journal* 58 (1991): 528–534.

Anderson, Odin W., *Health Services as a Growth Enterprise in the United States Since 1875,* 2d ed. (Ann Arbor, MI: Health Administration Press, 1990).

Anderson, Odin W., and Ellen M. Morrison, "The Worth of Medical Care: A Critical Review," *Medical Care Review* 46 (1989): 121–155.

Andreoni, James, "Impure Altruism and Donations to Public Goods: A Theory of Warm-Glow Giving," *The Economic Journal* 100 (1990): 464–477.

Antel, John J., Robert L. Ohsfeldt, and Edmund R. Becker, "State Regulation and Hospital Costs," *Review of Economics and Statistics* 77 (1995): 416–422.

Archibald, Robert, Clyde Haulman, and Carlisle Moody, "Quality, Price, Advertising and Published Quality Ratings," *Journal of Consumer Research* 9 (1983): 347–356.

Arno, Peter S., Karen Bonuck, and Michael Davis, "Rare Diseases, Drug Development, and AIDS: The Impact of the Orphan Drug Act," *Milbank Memorial Quarterly* 73 (1995): 231–252.

Arnould, Richard J., Lawrence W. Debrock, and John W. Pollard, "Do HMOs Produce Specific Services More Efficiently?" *Inquiry* 21 (1984): 243–253.

Arrow, Kenneth J. *Social Choice and Individual Values.* (New York: Wiley, 1975).

Arrow, Kenneth J., "Some Ordinalist-Utilitarian Notes on Rawls's Theory of Justice," *Journal of Philosophy* 70 (1973): 245–262.

Arrow, Kenneth J., "Uncertainty and the Welfare Economics of Medical Care," *American Economic Review* 53 (1963): 941–973.

Ash, Timothy Garton. *The Magic Lantern.* (New York: Vintage Books, 1993).

Associated Press, "Health Insurers Limit Access to New Health Advances," November 2, 1998.

Atkinson, Scott E., and Thomas Crocker, "Econometric Health Production Functions: Relative Bias from Omitted Variables and Measurement Error," *Journal of Environmental Economics and Management* 22 (1992): 12–24.

Atkinson, Scott E., and Robert Halvorsen, "The Valuation of Risks to Life," *Review of Economics and Statistics* 72 (1990): 133–136.

Auster, Richard D., and Ronald L. Oaxaca, "Identification of Supplier Induced Demand in the Health Care Sector," *Journal of Human Resources* 16 (1981): 327–342.

Auster, Richard D., Irving Leveson, and Deborah Sarachek, "The Production of Health, an Exploratory Study," *Journal of Human Resources* 4 (1969): 411–436.

Bae, Jay P., "Drug Patent Expiration and the Speed of Generic Entry," *Health Services Research* 22 (1997): 87–101.

Bain, Joe S. *Barriers to New Competition.* (Cambridge, MA: Harvard, 1956).

Baker, Laurence C., and Kenneth S. Corts, "HMO Market Penetration and the Cost of Health Care: Market Discipline or Market Segmentation," *American Economic Review* 86 (1996): 389–394.

Baker, Laurence C., and Kenneth S. Corts, "The Effects of HMOs on Conventional Insurance Premiums: Theory and Evidence," Working Paper 5356, National Bureau of Economic Research, November 1995.

Baker, Laurence C., and Joanne Spetz, "Managed Care and Medical Technology Growth," Working Paper 6894, National Bureau of Economic Research, January 1999.

Baltagi, Badi H., and Dan Levin, "Estimating Dynamic Demand for Cigarettes Using Panel Data: The Effects of Bootlegging, Taxation and Advertising Reconsidered," *Review of Economics and Statistics* 68 (1986): 148–155.

Barsky, Robert B. et al., "Preference Parameters and Behavioral Heterogeneity: An Experimental Approach in the Health and Retirement Study," *Quarterly Journal of Economics* 62 (1997): 537–579.

Bator, Francis M., "The Simple Analytics of Welfare Maximization," *American Economic Review* 47 (1957): 22–59.

Baumol, William J., "Health Care, Education and the Cost of Disease: A Looming Crisis for Public Choice," *Public Choice* 77 (1993): 17–28.

Baumol, William J., "On the Social Rate of Discount," *American Economic Review* 58 (1968): 788–802.

Baumol, William J., John C. Panzar, and Robert Willig. *Contestable Markets and the Theory of Industry.* (San Diego: Harcourt Brace Jovanovich, 1982).

Bays, Carson W., "The Determinants of Hospital Size: A Survivor Analysis," *Applied Economics* 18 (1986): 359–377.

Bays, Carson W., "Why Most Private Hospitals Are Nonprofit," *Journal of Policy Analysis and Management* 2 (1983): 366–385.

Bays, Carson W., "Specification Error in the Estimation of Hospital Cost Functions," *Review of Economics and Statistics* 62 (1980): 302–305.

Bays, Carson W., "Cost Comparisons of For Profit and Nonprofit Hospitals," *Social Science and Medicine* 13C (1979): 219–225.

Becker, Edmund R., and Frank A. Sloan, "Hospital Ownership and Performance," *Economic Inquiry* 23 (1985): 21–36.

Becker, Gary S., and Kevin M. Murphy, "A Simple Theory of Advertising as a Good or Bad," *The Quarterly Journal of Economics* 108 (1993): 941–964.

Becker, Gary S., and Kevin M. Murphy, "A Theory of Rational Addiction," *Journal of Political Economy* 96 (1988): 675–700.

Behrman, Jere R., and Barbara L. Wolfe, "Does More Schooling Make Women Better Nourished and Healthier?: Adult Sibling Random and Fixed Effects Estimates for Nicaragua," *Journal of Human Resources* 24 (1989): 644–663.

Benham, Lee, "The Effects of Advertising on the Price of Eyeglasses," *Journal of Law and Economics* 15 (1972): 421–477.

Bennefield, Robert L., "Health Insurance Coverage: 1997," *Current Population Reports,* P60–202, Washington, DC: Bureau of the Census, September 1998.

Bennefield, Robert L., "Health Insurance Coverage: 1996," *Current Population Reports,* P60–199, Washington, DC: Bureau of the Census, September 1997.

Berger, Mark C., and J. Paul Leigh, "Schooling, Self-Selection and Health," *Journal of Human Resources* 24 (1989): 433–455.

Berger, Mark C. et al., "Valuing Changes in Health Risks: A Comparison of Alternative Measures," *Southern Economic Journal* 53 (1987): 967–984.

Birnbaum, Howard et al., "Why Do Nursing Home Costs Vary?" *Medical Care* 19 (1981): 1095–1107.

Bishop, Christine E., "Where are the Missing Elders? The Decline in Nursing Home Use, 1985 and 1995," *Health Affairs* 18 (1999): 146–155.

Bishop, Christine E., "Nursing Home Cost Studies and Reimbursement Issues," *Health Care Financing Review* 1 (1980): 47–64.

Blank, David M., and George J. Stigler. *The Demand and Supply of Scientific Personnel.* (New York: National Bureau of Economic Research, 1957).

Bleichrodt, Han, "Health Utility Indices and Equity Considerations," *Journal of Health Economics* 16 (1997): 65–91.

Blendon, Robert J., Mollyann Brodie, and John Benson, "What Happened to Support for the Clinton Plan?" *Health Affairs* 14 (1995): 7–23.

Blendon, Robert J. et al., "Who Has the Best Health Care System? A Second Look," *Health Affairs* 14 (1995): 220–230.

Blendon, Robert J. et al., "Satisfaction with Health Systems in Ten Nations," *Health Affairs* 9 (1990): 185–192.

Blomquist, Glenn C., "The Value of Human Life: An Empirical Perspective," *Economic Inquiry* 19 (1981): 157–164.

Bolduc, Denis, Bernard Fortin, and Marc-Andre Fournier, "The Effect of Incentive Policies on the Practice Location of Doctors: A Multinomial Probit Analysis," *Journal of Labor Economics* 14 (1996): 703–732.

Boles, J., "Efficiency Squared: Efficient Computations of Efficiency Indexes, *Western Farm Economics Association Proceedings,* 1966: 137–142.

Bond, Ronald et al. *Staff Report on Effects of Restrictions on Advertising and Commercial Practice in the Professions: The Case of Optometry.* (Federal Trade Commission, Washington, DC: Government Printing Office, 1980).

Bopp, Kenneth D., "How Patients Evaluate the Quality of Ambulatory Medical Encounters: A Marketing Perspective," *Journal of Health Care Marketing* 10 (1990): 6–15.

Borjas, George J., H. E. Frech III, and Paul B. Ginsburg, "Property Rights and Wages: The Case of Nursing Homes," *Journal of Human Resources* 17 (1983): 232–246.

Bosmans, Nathalie, and Fabienne Fecher, "Performance of Belgian Hospitals: A Frontier Approach," *Health Economics* 4 (1995): 389–397.

Bosworth, Barry, and Gary Burtless, "Effects of Tax Reform on Labor Supply, Investment, and Saving," *Journal of Economic Perspectives* 6 (1992): 3–25.

Braden, Bradley R. et al., "National Health Expenditures, 1997," *Health Care Financing Review* 20 (1998): 83–110.

Brennan, Troyen A. et al., "Incidence of Adverse Events and Negligence in Hospitalized Patients," *New England Journal of Medicine* 324 (1991): 370–376.

Bromberg, Michael D., and Thomas C. Goodwin, "Grassroots Politics and Health Care: Effects of

Medicare Budget Cuts," *Healthcare Financial Management* 42 (1988): 20, 22, 100.

Brook, Robert H. et al., "Appropriateness of Acute Medical Care for the Elderly: An Analysis of the Literature," *Health Policy* 14 (1990): 225–242.

Brook, Robert H. et al., "Does Free Care Improve Adults' Health?: Results from a Randomized Trial," *New England Journal of Medicine* 309 (1983): 1426–1434.

Brown, Douglas M., "The Rising Price of Physicians' Services: A Correction and Extension on Supply," *Review of Economics and Statistics* 76 (1994): 389–393.

Brown, Douglas M., "Do Physicians Underutilize Aides?" *Journal of Human Resources* 23 (1988): 342–355.

Brown, Douglas M., Martin Feldstein, and Harvey E. Lapan, "The Rising Price of Physicians' Services: A Clarification," *Review of Economics and Statistics* 56 (1974): 396–398.

Brown, Kaye, and Colin Burrows, "The Sixth Stool Guaiac Test: $47 Million That Never Was," *Journal of Health Economics* 9 (1990): 429–445.

Brown, Lawrence D., "The National Politics of Oregon's Rationing Plan," *Health Affairs* 10 (1991): 28–51.

Brown, Lawrence D., "Afterward," *Journal of Health Politics, Policy and Law* 13 (1988): 361–363.

Brown, Lawrence D., and Volker E. Amelung, "'Manacled Competition': Market Reforms in German Health Care," *Health Affairs* 18 (1999): 76–91.

Browne, Mark J., and Helen I. Doerpinghaus, "Information Asymmetries and Adverse Selection in the Market for Individual Medical Expense Insurance," *Journal of Risk and Insurance* 60 (1993): 300–312.

Buchanan, James. *The Limits of Liberty.* (Chicago: University of Chicago Press, 1975).

Buchanan, James M., and Gordon Tullock. *Calculus of Consent: Logical Foundations of Constitutional Democracy.* (Ann Arbor, MI: University of Michigan Press, 1962).

Burgess, James F. Jr., and Paul W. Wilson, "Hospital Ownership and Technical Inefficiency," *Management Science* 42 (1996a): 110–123.

Burgess, James F. Jr. and Paul W. Wilson, "The Impact of Measuring Quality of Care on Hospital Efficiency Measurement," Veterans Administration, Bedford MA, 1996b.

Burgess, James F. Jr., and Paul W. Wilson, "Variation in Inefficiency in U.S. Hospitals," *INFOR* 36 (1998): 84–102.

Burstein, Philip L., and Jerry Cromwell, "Relative Incomes and Rates of Return for U.S. Physicians," *Journal of Health Economics* 4 (1985): 63–78.

Cady, John F. *Drugs on the Market.* (Lexington, MA: Lexington, 1975).

Calem, Paul S., and John A. Rizzo, "Competition and Specialization in the Hospital Industry: An Application of Hotelling's Location Model," *Southern Economic Journal* 61 (1995): 1182–1198.

Cameron, Sam, "Are Greek Smokers Rational Addicts?" *Applied Economics Letters* 4 (1997): 401–402.

Carey, Kathleen, and James F. Burgess Jr., "On Measuring the Hospital Cost/Quality Trade-Off," *Health Economics* 8(6) (1999): 509–520.

Carlson, Rick. *The End of Medicine.* (New York: Wiley Interscience, 1975).

Carr, W. John, and Paul J. Feldstein, "The Relationship of Cost to Hospital Size," *Inquiry* 4 (1967): 45–65.

Carroll, Norman V., and W. Gary Erwin, "Patient Shifting as a Response to Medicare Prospective Payment," *Medical Care* 25 (1987): 1161–1167.

Casteneda, Laura. "Viatical" Life Insurance Deals Get Tougher. *San Francisco Chronicle,* 10 March 1997, page E2.

The Center for Evaluative Clinical Studies. *Dartmouth Atlas of Health Care.* (Dartmouth Medical School, American Hospital Publications, Inc., 1996).

Chaloupka, Frank J., "Rational Addictive Behavior and Cigarette Smoking," *Journal of Political Economy* 99 (1991): 722–742.

Chaloupka, Frank J., and Rosalie Liccardo Pacula, "An Examination of Gender and Race Differences in Youth Smoking Responsiveness to Price and Tobacco Control Policies," Working Paper 6541, National Bureau of Economic Research, April 1998.

Chaloupka, Frank J., and Henry Saffer, "Clean Indoor Air Laws and the Demand for Cigarettes," *Contemporary Policy Issues* 10 (1992): 72–83.

Chaloupka, Frank J., and Kenneth E. Warner, "The Economics of Smoking," Working Paper 7047, National Bureau of Economic Research, March 1999.

Charnes, A., W. W. Cooper, and E. Rhodes, "Measuring the Efficiency of Decision Making Units," *European Journal of Operational Research* 2 (1978): 429–444.

Chernew, Michael, and Dennis P. Scanlon, "Health Plan Report Cards and Insurance Choice," *Inquiry* 35 (1998): 9–22.

Chetty, V. K., "Stochastic Technology, Production Organization and Costs," *Journal of Health Economics* 17 (1998): 187–210.

Chilingerian, Jon, "Evaluating Physician Efficiency in Hospitals: A Multivariate Analysis of Best Practices," *European Journal of Operations Research* 80 (1995): 548–574.

Chiswick, Barry R., "The Demand for Nursing Home Care: An Analysis of the Substitution between Institutional and Noninstitutional Care," *Journal of Human Resources* 11 (1976): 295–316.

Christianson, Jon B. et al., "The HMO Industry: Evolution in Population Demographics and Market Structures," *Medical Care Review* 48 (1991): 3–46.

Chung, Fwu-Ranq, "Uncertainty and Investment in Health," *Journal of Health Economics* 15 (1996): 369–376.

Clark, Derek, and Jan Abel Olsen, "Agency in Health Care with an Endogenous Budget Constraint," *Journal of Health Economics* 13 (1994): 231–251.

Clark, Robert Charles, "Does the Nonprofit Form Fit the Hospital Industry?" *Harvard Law Review* 93 (1980): 1417–1489.

Clarkson, Kenneth W., "The Effects of Research and Promotion on Rates of Return," in *Competitive Strategies in the Pharmaceutical Industry,* edited by Robert B. Helms. (Washington, DC: American Enterprise Institute, 1996, 238–268).

Clement, Jan P., "Dynamic Cost Shifting in Hospitals: Evidence from the 1980s and 1990s," *Inquiry* 34 (1997/98): 340–349.

Cleverly, William O., "More Efficient Hospitals Are Closing," *Healthcare Financial Management* 47 (1993): 82–85.

Cochrane, Archibald L. *Effectiveness and Efficiency: Random Reflections on Health Services.* (London: Nuffield Provincial Hospital Trust, 1978).

Coddington, Dean C. et al. *The Crisis in Health Care: Costs, Choices, and Strategies.* (San Francisco: Jossey-Bass, 1990).

Coffey, Rosanna M., "The Effect of Time Price on the Demand for Medical Care Services," *Journal of Human Resources* 18 (1983): 407–424.

Cohen, Harold A., "Variations in Cost among Hospitals of Different Sizes," *Southern Economic Journal* 33 (1967): 355–366.

Cohen, Joel W., and William D. Spector, "The Effect of Medicaid Reimbursement on Quality of Care in Nursing Homes," *Journal of Health Economics* 15 (1996): 23–48.

Comanor, William S., and Thomas A. Wilson, "The Effect of Advertising on Competition: A Survey," *Journal of Economic Literature* 17 (1979): 453–476.

Comanor, William S., and Thomas A. Wilson. *Advertising and Market Power.* (Cambridge, MA: Harvard, 1974).

Conover, Christopher J., and Frank A. Sloan, "Does Removing Certificate of Need Regulations Lead to a Surge in Health Care Spending?" *Journal of Health Politics, Policy and Law* 23 (1998): 455–481.

Conrad, Robert F., and Robert P. Strauss, "A Multiple–Output Multiple–Input Model of the Hospital Industry in North Carolina," *Applied Economics* 15 (1983): 341–352.

Cook, Philip J., and Michael J. Moore, "Drinking and Schooling," *Journal of Health Economics* 12 (1993): 411–429.

Cooper, Philip F., and Alan C. Monheit, "Does Employment-Related Health Insurance Inhibit Job Mobility?" *Inquiry* 30 (1993): 400–416.

Corman, Hope, and Michael Grossman, "Determinants of Neonatal Mortality Rate in the U.S.: A Reduced Form Model," *Journal of Health Economics* 4 (1985): 213–236.

Corman, Hope, Theodore J. Joyce, and Michael Grossman, "Birth Outcome Production Function in the United States," *Journal of Human Resources* 22 (1987): 339–360.

Cowing, Thomas G., and Alphonse G. Holtmann, "Multiproduct Short-Run Hospital Cost Functions: Empirical Evidence and Policy Implications from Cross-Section Data," *Southern Economic Journal* 49 (1983): 637–653.

Cowing, Thomas G., Alphonse G. Holtmann, and Susan Powers, "Hospital Cost Analysis: A Survey and Evaluation of Recent Studies," *Advances in Health Economics and Health Services Research* 4 (1983).

Coyte, Peter C., "Canada," in *Advances in Health Economics and Health Services Research, Supplement 1: Comparative Health Systems,* edited by Jean-Jacques Rosa. (Greenwich, CT: JAI Press, 1990).

Coyte, Peter et al., "The Relationship between Variations in Knee Replacement Utilization Rates and the Reported Prevalence of Arthritis in Ontario, Canada," *Journal of Rheumatology* 24 (1997): 2403–2412.

Coyte, Peter C. et al., "Waiting Times for Knee-Replacement Surgery in the United States and Ontario," *New England Journal of Medicine* 331 (1994): 1068–1071.

Cropper, Maureen L. et al., "The Health Benefit of Air Pollution Control in New Delhi," *American Journal of Agricultural Economics* 79 (1997): 1625–1629.

Cropper, Maureen L. et al., "The Determinants of Pesticide Regulation: A Statistical Analysis of EPA Decision Making," *Journal of Political Economy* 100 (1992): 175–197.

Culyer, A. J., "The United Kingdom: Effective, Efficient, Equitable?" *Journal of Health Politics, Policy and Law* 17 (1992): 667–688.

Culyer, A. J., "The Normative Economics of Health Care Finance and Provision," *Oxford Review of Economic Policy* 5 (1989): 34–58.

Culyer, A. J., and Adam Wagstaff, "Equity and Equality in Health and Health Care," *Journal of Health Economics* 12 (1993): 431–457.

Culyer, A. J., Eddy van Doorslaer, and Adam Wagstaff, "Access, Utilisation and Equity: A Further Comment," *Journal of Health Economics* 11 (1992a): 207–210.

Culyer, A. J., Eddy van Doorslaer, and Adam Wagstaff, "Utilisation as a Measure of Equity by Mooney, Hall, Donaldson and Gerard," *Journal of Health Economics* 11 (1992b): 93–98.

Currie, Janet, and Nancy Cole, "Welfare and Child Health: The Link between AFDC Participation and Birth Weight," *American Economic Review* 83 (1993): 971–985.

Currie, Janet, and Jonathan Gruber, "Saving Babies: The Efficacy and Cost of Recent Changes in the Medicaid Eligibility of Pregnant Women," *Journal of Political Economy* 104 (1996): 1263–1296.

Custer, W. S., and R. J. Willke, "Teaching Hospital Costs: The Effect of Medical Staff Characteristics," *Health Services Research* 25 (1991): 831–857.

Cutler, David M., and Jill R. Horwitz, "Converting Hospitals from Not-for-Profit to For-Profit Status: Why and What Effects?" Working Paper 6672, National Bureau of Economic Research, August 1998.

Cutler, David M., and Ellen Meara, "The Medical Costs of the Young and Old: A Forty Year Perspective," Working Paper 6114, National Bureau of Economic Research, July 1997.

Cutler, David M., and Sarah J. Reber, "The Trade-off between Competition and Adverse Selection," *Quarterly Journal of Economics* 113 (1998): 433–466.

Cutler, David M., Mark McClellan, and Joseph P. Newhouse, "Price and Productivity in Managed Care Insurance," Working Paper 6677, National Bureau of Economic Research, August 1998.

Cutler, David M. et al., "Pricing Heart Attack Treatments," Working Paper 7089, National Bureau of Economic Research, April 1999.

Daniels, Norman. *Just Health Care.* (Cambridge: Cambridge University Press, 1985).

Daniels, Norman, "Equity of Access to Health Care: Some Conceptual and Ethical Issues," *Milbank Memorial Fund Quarterly/Health and Society* 60 (1982): 51–81.

Daniels, Norman, "Health Care Needs and Distributive Justice," *Philosophy and Public Affairs* 10 (1981): 146–179.

Danzon, Patricia M., "Hidden Overhead Costs: Is Canada's System Really Less Expensive?" *Health Affairs* 11 (1992): 21–43.

Davis, Karen, and Roger Reynolds, "The Impact of Medicare and Medicaid on Access to Medical Care," in *The Role of Health Insurance in the United States Health Services Sector,* edited by Richard Rosett. (New York: Neal Watson, 1976).

Davis, Mark A., "On Nursing Home Quality: A Review and Analysis," *Medical Care Review* 48 (1991): 129–166.

Davis, Mark A., James W. Freeman, and Eric C. Kirby, "Nursing Home Performance under Case-Mix Reimbursement: Responding to Heavy-Care Incentives and Market Changes," *Health Services Research* 33 (1998): 815–834.

de Lissovoy, Gregory et al., "Preferred Provider Organizations One Year Later," *Inquiry* 24 (1987): 127–135.

Deloitte and Touche, "U.S. Hospitals and the Future of Health Care," 1999.

DesHarnais, Susan, James Chesney, and Steven Fleming, "Trends in Regional Variations in Hospital Utilization and Quality during the First Two Years of the Prospective Payment System," *Inquiry* 25 (1988): 374–382.

DesHarnais, Susan et al., "The Early Effects of the Prospective Payment System on Inpatient Utilization and the Quality of Care," *Inquiry* 24 (1987): 7–16.

Despotakis, Kostas A., "Economic Performance of Flexible Functional Forms," *European Economic Review* 30 (1986): 1107–1143.

Deutsch, Larry, L., "Pharmaceuticals: The Critical Role of Innovation," in *Industry Studies,* 2d ed., edited by Larry L. Deutsch. (Armonk, NY: M.E. Sharpe, 1998).

Diehr, Paula et al., "What Is Too Much Variation: The Null Hypothesis in Small-Area Analysis," *Health Services Research* 24 (1990): 741–771.

DiFranza, Joseph R. et al., "RJR Nabisco's Cartoon Camel Promotes Camel Cigarettes to Children," *Journal of the American Medical Association* 266 (December 11, 1991): 3149–3153.

DiMasi, Joseph A. et al., "Cost of Innovation in the Pharmaceutical Industry," *Journal of Health Economics* 10 (1991): 107–142.

Dobson, Allen, and Elizabeth W. Hoy, "Hospital PPS Profits: Past and Prospective," *Health Affairs* 7 (1988): 126–129.

Donabedian, Avedis. *The Definition of Quality and Approaches to Its Assessment.* (Ann Arbor, MI: Health Administration Press, 1980).

Donabedian, Avedis, "Evaluating the Quality of Medical Care," *Milbank Memorial Fund Quarterly/ Health and Society* 44 (1966): 166–203.

Donelan, Karen et al., "The Cost of Change: Public Discontent in Five Nations," *Health Affairs* 18 (1999): 206–216.

Dor, Avi, "Non-Minimum Cost Functions and the Stochastic Frontier: On Applications to Health Care Providers," *Journal of Health Economics* 13 (1994): 329–334.

Dorfman, Robert, and Peter O. Steiner, "Optimal Advertising and Optimal Quality," *American Economic Review* 44 (1954): 826–836.

Douglas, Stratford, and Govind Hariharan, "The Hazard of Starting Smoking: Estimates from a Split Population Duration Model," *Journal of Health Economics* 13 (1994): 213–230.

Dranove, David, "A Problem with Consumer Surplus Measures of the Cost of Practice Variations," *Journal of Health Economics* 14 (1995): 243–251.

Dranove, David, "The Five Ws of Utilization Review," American Enterprise Institute Conference on Health Policy Reform, October 1991.

Dranove, David, "Demand Inducement and the Physician/Patient Relationship," *Economic Inquiry* 26 (1988): 281–298.

Dranove, David, and Kenneth Cone, "Do State Rate Setting Regulations Really Lower Hospital Expenses?" *Journal of Health Economics* 4 (1985): 159–165.

Dranove, David, and David Meltzer, "Do Important Drugs Reach the Market Sooner?" *RAND Journal of Economics* 25 (1994): 402–423.

Dranove, David, and Paul Wehner, "Physician-Induced Demand for Childbirths," *Journal of Health Economics* 13 (1994): 61–73.

Dranove, David, and William D. White, "Agency and the Organization of Health Care Delivery," *Inquiry* 24 (1987): 405–415.

Dranove, David, Carol J. Simon, and William D. White, "Determinants of Managed Care Penetration," *Journal of Health Economics* 17 (1998): 729–745.

Dranove, David, Mark Stanley, and Carol Simon, "Is Hospital Competition Wasteful?" *RAND Journal of Economics* 23 (1992): 247–262.

Drummond, Michael F. et al. *Methods for the Economic Evaluation of Health Care Programmes,* 2d ed. (New York: Oxford University Press, 1997).

Dubos, Rene. *The Mirage of Health.* (London: George Allen and Unwin, Ltd., 1960).

Duffy, Martyn, "Advertising in Demand Systems for Alcoholic Drinks and Tobacco: A Comparative Study," *Journal of Policy Modeling* 17 (1995): 557–577.

Duncan, R. Paul, "Uncompensated Hospital Care," *Medical Care Review* 49 (1992): 265–330.

Dunn, Daniel L. et al, "Economies of Scope in Physicians' Work: The Performance of Multiple Surgery," *Inquiry* 32 (1995): 87–101.

Dyck, Frank J. et al., "Effect of Surveillance on the Number of Hysterectomies in the Province of Saskatchewan," *New England Journal of Medicine* 296 (1977): 1326–1328.

Eakin, B. Kelly, and Thomas J. Kniesner, "Estimating a Non-Minimum Cost Function for Hospitals,"

Southern Economic Journal 54 (January 1988): 583–597.

Easley, David, and Maureen O'Hara, "The Economic Role of the Nonprofit Firm," *Bell Journal of Economics* 14 (1983): 531–538.

Economic Report of the President, transmitted to the Congress, February 1985. (Washington, DC: United States Government Printing Office, 1985).

Eddy, David M., "Clinical Decision Making; From Theory to Practice," *Journal of the American Medical Association* 263 (January 19, 1990): 441–443.

Eisenberg, J. M. *Doctors' Decisions and the Cost of Medical Care.* (Ann Arbor, MI: Health Administration Press, 1986).

Elixhauser, Anne, ed., "Health Care Cost–Benefit and Cost Effectiveness Analysis (CBA/CEA)," *Medical Care* 31 (1993): JS1–JS150.

Elixhauser, Anne et al., "Health Care CBA and CEA from 1991 to 1996: An Updated Bibliography," *Medical Care* 36 (1996): MS1–MS9.

Ellis, Randall P., "Creaming, Skimping and Dumping: Provider Competition on the Intensive and Extensive Margins," *Journal of Health Economics* 17 (1998): 537–555.

Ellis, Randall P., "Hospital Cost Function Estimation When Firms May Not Try to Minimize Total Costs," mimeo. (Boston: Boston University, 1993).

Ellis, Randall P., and Thomas G. McGuire, "Cost Sharing and Patterns of Mental Health Care Utilization," *Journal of Human Resources* 21 (1986): 359–380.

Ellis, Randall P., and Thomas G. McGuire, "Provider Behavior under Prospective Reimbursement," *Journal of Health Economics* 5 (1986): 129–151.

Elzinga, Kenneth G., and T. F. Hogarty, "The Problem of Geographic Market Definition Revisited: The Case of Coal," *Antitrust Bulletin* 23 (1978): 1–18.

Enthoven, Alain C., "The History and Principles of Managed Competiton," *Health Affairs* 10 (1993): 24–48.

Enthoven, Alain C., "National Health Service: Some Reforms That Might Be Politically Feasible," *The Economist* 22 (1985): 61–64.

Ermann, Danny, "Hospital Utilization Review: Past Experience, Future Directions," *Journal of Health Politics, Policy and Law* 13 (1988): 683–704.

Ernst, Richard L., and Donald E. Yett. *Physician Location and Specialty Choice.* (Ann Arbor, MI: Health Administration Press, 1985).

Escarce, José J., "Externalities in Hospitals and Physicians Adoption of a New Surgical Technology: An Exploratory Analysis," *Journal of Health Economics* 15 (1996): 715–734.

Escarce, José J., "Would Eliminating Differences in Physician Practice Style Reduce Geographic Variations in Cataract Surgery Rates?" *Medical Care* 12 (1993): 1106–1118.

Escarce, José J., "Explaining the Association between Surgeon Supply and Utilization," *Inquiry* 29 (1992): 403–415.

Escarce, José J., and Mark V. Pauly, "Physician Opportunity Costs in Physician Practice Cost Functions," *Journal of Health Economics* 17 (1998): 129–151.

Escarce, José J. et al., "Diffusion of Laparoscopic Cholecystectomy among General Surgeons in the United States," *Medical Care* 33 (1995): 256–271.

Eskin, Gerald J., "A Case for Test Marketing Experiments," *Journal of Advertising Research* 15 (1975): 27–33.

Eskin, Gerald J., and Penny H. Barron, "Effect of Price and Advertising in Test-Market Experiments," *Journal of Marketing Research* 14 (1977): 499–508.

Evans, Robert G., "Supplier-Induced Demand; Some Empirical Evidence and Implications," in *The Economics of Health and Medical Care,* edited by Mark Perlman. (London: Macmillan, 1974).

Evans, Robert G., "Behavioral Cost Functions for Hospitals," *Canadian Journal of Economics* 4 (1971): 198–215.

Fare, Rolf, and C. A. Knox Lovell, "Measuring the Technical Efficiency of Production," *Journal of Economic Theory* 19 (1978): 150–62.

Farmer, Paul, and Edward Nardell, "Editorial: Nihilism and Pragmatism in Tuberculosis Control," *American Journal of Public Health* 88 (1998): 1014–1015.

Farrell, M. J., "The Measurement of Productive Efficiency," *Journal of the Royal Statistical Society* 120: series A, part 3 (1957): 253–281.

Feinglass, Joe, and James J. Holloway, "The Initial Impact of the Medicare Prospective Payment System on U.S. Health Care: A Review of the Literature," *Medical Care Review* 48 (1991): 91–115.

Feinstein, Jonathon S., "The Relationship between Socioeconomic Status and Health: A Review of

the Literature," *Milbank Quarterly* 71 (1993): 279–322.

Feldman, Roger et al., "Effect of HMOs on the Creation of Competitive Markets for Hospital Services," *Journal of Health Economics* 9 (1990): 207–222.

Feldman, Roger, and Bryan Dowd, "A New Estimate of the Welfare Loss of Excess Health Insurance," *American Economic Review* 81 (1991): 297–301.

Feldman, Roger, and Bryan Dowd, "Is There a Competitive Market for Hospital Services?" *Journal of Health Economics* 5 (1986): 277–292.

Feldman, Roger, and J. Begun, "Effects of Advertising: Lessons from Optometry," *Journal of Human Resources* 13 (Supplement 1978): 247–262.

Feldman, Roger, and Michael A. Morrissey, "Health Economics: A Report on the Field," *Journal of Health Politics, Policy and Law* 15 (1990): 627–646.

Feldman, Roger, and Richard M. Scheffler, "The Union Impact on Hospital Wages and Fringe Benefits," *Industrial Labor Relations Review* 35 (1982): 196–206.

Feldman, Roger et al., "The Effect of Premiums on the Small Firm's Decision to Offer Health Insurance," *Journal of Human Resources* 32 (1998): 635–658.

Feldman, Roger et al., "Effects of HMOs on the Creation of Competitive Markets for Hospital Services," *Journal of Health Economics* 9 (1990): 207–222.

Feldstein, Martin S., "The High Cost of Hospitals—and What to Do About It," *The Public Interest* 48 (1977): 40–54.

Feldstein, Martin S., "The Welfare Loss of Excess Health Insurance," *Journal of Political Economy* 81 (1973): 251–280.

Feldstein, Martin S., "Hospital Cost Inflation: A Study of Nonprofit Price Dynamics," *American Economic Review* 61 (1971): 853–872.

Feldstein, Martin S., "The Rising Price of Physicians' Services," *Review of Economics and Statistics* 52 (1970): 121–133.

Feldstein, Martin S. *Economic Analysis for Health Service Efficiency.* (Amsterdam: North-Holland, 1967).

Feldstein, Paul J. *Health Care Economics,* 4th ed. (Albany, NY: Delmar, 1994).

Feldstein, Paul J., "The Emergence of Market Competition in the U.S. Health Care System. Its Causes, Likely Structure, and Implications," *Health Policy* 6 (1986): 1–20.

Finkler, Merton D., and David D. Wirtschafter, "Cost-Effectiveness and Data Envelopment Analysis," *Health Care Management Review* 18 (1993): 81–88.

Fisher, Elliott S. et al., "Hospital Readmission Rates for Cohorts of Medicare Beneficiaries in Boston and New Haven," *New England Journal of Medicine* 331 (1994): 989–995.

Fizel, John L., and Thomas S. Nunnikhoven, "Technical Efficiency of For-Profit and Non-Profit Nursing Homes," *Managerial and Decision Economics* 13 (1992): 429–439.

Flexner, Abraham. *Medical Education in the United States and Canada, Bulletin No. 4.* (New York: Carnegie Foundation for the Advancement of Teaching, 1910).

Flynn, Marilyn L., and Yong-Soon Chung, "Health Care Financing in Korea: Private Market Dilemmas for a Developing Nation," *Journal of Public Health Policy* 2 (1990): 238–253.

Fogel, Robert W., "Nutrition and the Decline in Mortality Since 1700: Some Additional Preliminary Findings," Working Paper 1802, National Bureau of Economic Research, 1986.

Folland, Sherman T., "A Critique of Pure Need: An Analysis of Norman Daniels's Concept of Health Care Need," *International Journal of Social Economics* 17 (1990): 36–45.

Folland, Sherman T., "Health Care Need, Economics and Social Justice," *International Journal of Social Economics* 13 (1986): 98–116.

Folland Sherman, and Richard A. Hofler, "A Problem Concerning the Sensitivity of Hospital Frontiers to Plausible Changes in the Economist's Model," mimeo. (Rochester, MI: Oakland University, January 1999).

Folland, Sherman T., and Robert Kleiman, "The Effect of Prospective Payment under DRGs on the Market Value of Hospitals," *Quarterly Review of Economics and Business* 30 (1990): 50–68.

Folland, Sherman T., and Miron Stano, "Small Area Variations: A Critical Review of Propositions, Methods, and Evidence," *Medical Care Review* 47 (1990): 419–465.

Folland, Sherman T., and Miron Stano, "Sources of Small Area Variations in the Use of Medical

Care," *Journal of Health Economics* 8 (1989): 85–107.

Fontana, John P., "Hospital Marketing Is Here to Stay," *Hospital Topics* 62 (1984): 12–13.

Foster, Stuart A., and Wilpen L. Gorr, "Federal Health Policy and the Geographic Diffusion of Physicians: A Macro-Scale Analysis," *Policy Sciences* 25 (1992): 117–134.

Fournier, Gary M., and Melayne M. McInnes, "Medical Board Regulation of Physician Licensure: Is Excessive Malpractice Sanctioned?" *Journal of Regulatory Economics* 12 (1997): 113–126.

Fournier, Gary M., and Jean M. Mitchell, "Hospital Costs and Competition for Services: A Multiproduct Analysis," *Review of Economics and Statistics* 74 (1992): 627–634.

Fox, William F., and Richard A. Hofler, "Using Homothetic Composed Error Frontiers to Measure Water Utility Efficiency," *Southern Economic Journal* 53 (1986): 461–477.

Frank, Richard G., and David S. Salkever, "Generic Entry and the Pricing of Pharmaceuticals," *Journal of Economics and Management Strategy* 6 (1997): 75–90.

Frank, Richard G., and David S. Salkever, "Nonprofit Organizations in the Health Sector," *Journal of Economic Perspectives* 8 (1994): 129–144.

Frank, Richard G., and W. Pete Welch, "The Competitive Effects of HMOs: A Review of the Evidence," *Inquiry* 22 (1985): 148–161.

Frech, H.E. III. *Competition & Monopoly in Medical Care.* (Washington, DC: AEI Press, 1996).

Frech, H. E. III, "The United States, Advances in Health Economics and Health Services Research Supplement 1: Comparative Health Systems." (Greenwich, CT: JAI Press, 1990: 43–75).

Frech, H. E. III, "The Property Rights Theory of the Firm: Some Evidence from the U.S. Nursing Home Industry," *Zeitschrift Fur Staatswissenschaft* 141 (1985): 146–166.

Frech, H. E. III, "The Property Rights Theory of the Firm: Empirical Results from a Natural Experiment," *Journal of Political Economy* 84 (1976): 143–152.

Frech, H. E. III, and Paul B. Ginsburg, "Competition among Health Insurers, Revisited," *Journal of Health Politics, Policy and Law* 13 (1988): 279–291.

Frech, H. E. III, and Paul B. Ginsburg, "The Cost of Nursing Home Care in the United States: Government Financing, Ownership, and Efficiency," in J. van der Gaag and Marc Perlman, Eds., *Health, Economics, and Health Economics* (Amsterdam: North-Holland, 1981).

Frech, H. E. III, and Paul B. Ginsburg, "Optimal Scale in Medical Practice: A Survivor Analysis," *Journal of Business* 47 (1974): 23–36.

Frech, H.E. III, and Richard D. Miller, Jr. *The Productivity of Health Care and Pharmaceuticals.* (Washington, DC: American Enterprise Institute, 1999).

Frech, H.E. III, and Lee R. Mobley, "Resolving the Impasse on Hospital Scale Economies: A New Approach," *Applied Economics* 27 (1995): 286–296.

Frech, H.E. III, and Lee R. Mobley, "The Demsetz Hypothesis and Hospital Markets: An Empirical Analysis," Working Papers in Economics 5-96, Department of Economics, University of California, Santa Barbara, CA, 1996.

Frenk, Julio, "Editorial: Medical Care and Health Improvement: The Critical Link," *Annals of Internal Medicine* 129 (1998): 419–420.

Friedman, Bernard, and Claudia Steiner, "Does Managed Care Affect the Supply and Use of ICU Services?" *Inquiry* 36 (1999): 68–77.

Friedman, Milton, and Simon Kuznets. *Income from Independent Professional Practice.* (New York: National Bureau of Economic Research, 1945).

Fries, James F., "The Compression of Morbidity: Near or Far?" *Milbank Quarterly* 67 (1990): 208–232.

Fries, James F., "Aging, Natural Death, and the Compression of Morbidity," *New England Journal of Medicine* 303 (1980): 130–136.

Fuchs, Victor R., "Economics, Values, and Health Care Reform," Presidential Address to the American Economic Association, *American Economic Review* 86 (1996): 11–24.

Fuchs, Victor R., "The Clinton Plan: A Researcher Examines Reform," *Health Affairs* 13 (1994): 102–114.

Fuchs, Victor R., "Time Preference and Health: An Exploratory Study," in *Economic Aspects of Health,* edited by Victor R. Fuchs. (Chicago: The University of Chicago Press, 1982: 93–120).

Fuchs, Victor R., "Economics, Health, and Post-Industrial Society," *Milbank Memorial Fund Quarterly/Health and Society* 57 (1979): 153–182.

Fuchs, Victor R., "The Supply of Surgeons and the Demand for Operations," *Journal of Human Resources* 13 (Supplement 1978): 35–56.

Fuchs, Victor R. *Who Shall Live?* (New York: Basic Books, Inc., 1974).

Fuchs, Victor R., "The Contribution of Health Services to the American Economy," in *Essays in the Economics of Health and Medical Care,* edited by Victor R. Fuchs. (New York: National Bureau of Economic Research, 1972).

Fuchs, Victor R., and James S. Hahn, "How Does Canada Do It? A Comparison of Expenditures for Physicians' Services in the United States and Canada," *New England Journal of Medicine* 323 (1990): 884–890.

Fuchs, Victor R., and Marcia J. Kramer, "Determinants of Expenditures for Physicians' Services in the United States 1948–68," Publication No. (HSM) 73-3013, National Bureau of Economic Research, National Center for Health Services Research and Development, DHEW, December 1972.

Gabel, Jon, and Dan Ermann, "Preferred Provider Organizations: Performance, Problems, and Promise," *Health Affairs* 4 (1985): 24–40.

Galbraith, John K. *The Affluent Society.* (Boston: Houghton Mifflin, 1958).

Garbacz, Christopher, "Smoke Detector Effectiveness and the Value of Saving a Life," *Economic Letters* 31 (1989): 281–286.

Garber, Alan M., and Charles E. Phelps, "Economic Foundations of Cost-Effectiveness Analysis," *Journal of Health Economics* 16 (1997): 1–31.

Gastonis, Constantine, "The Long Debate on the Sixth Guaiac Test: Time to Move on to New Grounds," *Journal of Health Economics* 9 (1990): 495–497.

Gaumer, Gary L., "Regulating Health Professionals: A Review of the Empirical Literature," *Milbank Memorial Fund Quarterly/Health and Society* 62 (1984): 380–416.

Gaumer, Gary L. et al., "Effects of State Prospective Reimbursement Programs on Hospital Mortality," *Medical Care* 27 (1989): 724–736.

Gauthier, Anne K. et al., "Administrative Costs in the U.S. Health Care System: The Problem or the Solution?" *Inquiry* 29 (1992): 308–320.

Gaynor, Martin, and Mark V. Pauly, "Compensation and Productive Efficiency in Partnerships: Evidence from Medical Group Practice," *Journal of Political Economy* 98 (1990): 544–573.

Gaynor, Martin, and Solomon Polachek, "Measuring Information in the Market: An Application to Physician Services," *Southern Economic Journal* 60 (1994): 815–831.

Gaynor, Martin, and William B. Vogt, "Antitrust and Competition in Health Care Markets," in *Handbook of Health Economics,* by Anthony J. Culyer and Joseph P. Newhouse. (Amsterdam: North-Holland, 1999).

Gegax, Douglas, Shelby Gerking, and William Schulze, "Perceived Risk and the Marginal Value of Safety," *Review of Economics and Statistics,* 73 (1991): 589–596.

Gerdtham, Ulf-G. et al., "An Econometric Analysis of Health Care Expenditure: A Cross-Section Study of the OECD Countries," *Journal of Health Economics* 11 (1992): 63–84.

Gertler, Paul J., "Subsidies, Quality, and the Regulation of Nursing Homes," *Journal of Public Economics* 38 (1989): 33–52.

Gertler, Paul J., and Donald M. Waldman, "Quality-Adjusted Cost Functions and Policy Evaluation in the Nursing Home Industry," *Journal of Political Economy* 100 (1992): 1232–1256.

Gibson, Robert M., and Marjorie Smith Mueller, "National Health Expenditures, Fiscal Year 1976," *Social Security Bulletin* 40 (1977): 3–32.

Gillum B. S., E. J. Graves, and E. Wood, National Hospital Discharge Survey: Annual Summary, 1995. National Center for Health Statistics. *Vital Health Statistics* 13 (1998).

Glick, Peter, and David E. Sahn, "Health and Productivity in a Heterogeneous Urban Labor Market," *Applied Economics* 30 (1998): 203–216.

Goddeeris, John H., "Economic Forces and Hospital Technology: Lessons from the United States Experience," *International Journal of Technology Assessment in Health Care* 3 (1987): 223–240.

Goddeeris, John H., "Insurance and Incentives for Innovation in *Medical Care,*" *Southern Economic Journal* 51 (1984a): 530–539.

Goddeeris, John H., "Medical Insurance, Technological Change, and Welfare," *Economic Inquiry* 22 (1984b): 56–67.

Goddeeris, John H., and Thomas P. Bronken, "Benefit–Cost Analysis of Screening," *Medical Care* 23 (1985): 1242–1255.

Goddeeris, John H., and Burton A. Weisbrod, "Conversion from Nonprofit to For-Profit Legal Status: Why Does It Happen and Should Anyone Care?" *Journal of Policy Analysis and Management* 17 (1998): 215–233.

Gold, Marthe R. et al., (eds). *Cost Effectiveness in Health and Medicine.* (New York: Oxford University Press, 1996).

Goldberg, Lawrence G., and Warren Greenberg, "The Effect of Physician-Controlled Health Insurance," *Journal of Health Politics, Policy and Law* 2 (1977): 48–78.

Goldberg, Theodore et. al., "Evaluation of Economic Effects of Drug Product Selection Legislation," *Medical Care* 17 (1979): 411–419.

Goldman, Dana et al., "Redistributional Consequences of Community Rating," *Health Services Research* 32 (1997): 71–86.

Goldstein, Gerald S., and Mark V. Pauly, "Group Insurance as a Local Public Good," in *The Role of Health Insurance in the Health Services Sector,* edited by R. Rossett. (New York: Neal Watson, 1976).

Goodman, Allen C., "New Estimates of Cross-National Health Expenditures: Income and Price Elasticities," Wayne State University, Detroit, Michigan, 1999.

Goodman, Allen C., "Estimation of Offset and Income Effects on the Demand for Mental Health," *Inquiry* 26 (1989): 235–248.

Goodman, Allen C., and Miron Stano, "HMOs and Health Externalities: A Local Public Good Perspective," *Public Finance Review* 28 (May 2000): 247–269.

Goodman, Allen C., Miron Stano, and John M. Tilford, "Applications and Extensions of the Grossman Health Care Model," *Southern Economic Journal* 65 (1999): 791–806.

Goodman, Clifford S., "Healthcare Technology Assessment: Methods, Framework, and Role in Policy Making," *American Journal of Managed Care* 4 (1998: Special Issue): SP200–SP213.

Goodman, John C., Health insurance: States can help, *Wall Street Journal,* 17 October 1991: A14.

Gordon, Margaret S. *Social Security Policies in Industrial Countries.* (Cambridge: Cambridge University Press, 1988).

Gornick, Marian et al., "Twenty Years of Medicare and Medicaid: Covered Populations, Use of Benefits, and Program Expenditures," *Health Care Financing Review, Annual Supplement* 6 (1985): 13–59.

Grabowski, Henry G., and John M. Vernon, "Prospects for Returns to Pharmaceutical R&D under Health Care Reform," in *Competitive Strategies in the Pharmaceutical Industry,* edited by Robert B. Helms. (Washington, DC: American Enterprise Institute, 1996, 194–207).

Grabowski, Henry G., and John M. Vernon, "Brand Loyalty, Entry, and Price Competition in Pharmaceuticals after the 1984 Drug Act," *Journal of Law and Economics* 35 (1992): 331–350.

Grabowski, Henry G., and John M. Vernon, "Returns to R&D on New Drug Innovations in the 1980s," *Journal of Health Economics* 13 (1994): 383–406.

Graddy, Elizabeth, "Interest Groups or the Public Interest—Why Do We Regulate Health Occupations?" *Journal of Health Politics, Policy and Law* 16 (1991): 25–49.

Graig, Laurene A. *Health of Nations: An International Perspective on U.S. Health Care Reform,* 3d ed. (Washington, DC: Congressional Quarterly, Inc., 1999).

Grannemann, Thomas W., Randall S. Brown, and Mark V. Pauly, "Estimating Hospital Costs: A Multiple-Output Analysis," *Journal of Health Economics* 5 (1986): 107–127.

Green, Lee A., and Mark P. Becker, "Physician Decision Making and Variation in Hospital Admission Rates for Suspected Acute Cardiac Ischemia," *Medical Care* 32 (1994): 1086–1097.

Grosskopf, Shawna, and Vivian Valdmanis, "Measuring Hospital Performance: A Non-Parametric Approach," *Journal of Health Economics* 6 (1987): 89–107.

Grossman, Michael. *The Demand for Health: A Theoretical and Empirical Investigation.* [New York: Columbia (for the National Bureau of Economic Research), 1972a].

Grossman, Michael, "On the Concept of Health Capital and the Demand for Health," *Journal of Political Economy* 80 (1972b): 223–255.

Grossman, Michael, and Theodore J. Joyce, "Unobservables, Pregnancy Resolutions, and Birth Weight Production Functions in New York

City," *Journal of Political Economy* 98 (1990): 983–1007.

Grossman, Michael, Frank J. Chaloupka, and Ismail Sirtalan, "An Empirical Analysis of Alcohol Addiction: Result from the Monitoring the Future Panels," *Economic Inquiry* 36 (1998): 39–48.

Grossman, Sanford, and Joseph E. Stiglitz, "Information and Competitive Price Systems," *American Economic Review* 66 (1976): 246–253.

Grytten, Jostein, and Rune Sørensen, "Supplier Inducement in a Public Health Care System," *Journal of Health Economics* 14 (1995): 207–229.

Gully, O. David, and Rexford E. Santerre, "The Effect of Tax Exemption on the Market Share of Nonprofit Hospitals," *National Tax Journal* 46 (1993): 477–486.

Guterman, Stuart, and Allen Dobson, "Impact of Medicare Perspective Payment System for Hospitals," *Health Care Financing Review* 7 (1986): 97–114.

Haas-Wilson, Deborah, "Consumer Information and Providers' Reputations: An Empirical Test in the Market for Psychotherapy," *Journal of Health Economics* 9 (1990): 321–333.

Hadley, Jack, "Medicare Spending and Mortality Rates of the Elderly," *Inquiry* 25 (1988): 485–493.

Hadley, Jack. *More Medical Care, Better Health?* (Washington, DC: Urban Institute, 1982).

Hadley, Jack, and Stephen Zuckerman, "The Role of Efficiency in Hospital Rate Setting," *Journal of Health Economics* 13 (1994): 335–340.

Hadley, Jack, Stephen Zuckerman, and Judith Feder, "Profits and Fiscal Pressure in the Prospective Payment System," *Inquiry* 26 (1989): 354–365.

Hall, Thomas D., and Cotton M. Lindsay, "Medical Schools: Producers of What? Sellers to Whom?" *Journal of Law and Economics* 23 (1980): 55–80.

Ham, Chris, and Mats Brommels, "Health Care Reform in the Netherlands, Sweden, and the United Kingdom," *Health Affairs* 13 (1994): 106–119.

Hamilton, James L., "The Effect of Cigarette Advertising Bans on Cigarette Consumption," *Proceedings of the Third World Conference on Smoking and Health.* (Washington, DC: U.S. DHEW, 1975).

Hamilton, James L., "The Demand for Cigarettes: Advertising, the Health Scare, and the Cigarette Advertising Ban," *Review of Economics and Statistics* 54 (1972): 401–411.

Hamilton, Vivian, "The Medicare Hospice Benefit: The Effectiveness of Price Incentives in Health Care Policy," *Rand Journal of Economics* 24 (1993): 605–624.

Hanke, Steve H., and Richard A. Walker, "Benefit–Cost Analysis Reconsidered: An Evaluation of the Mid-States Project," *Water Resources Research* 10 (1974): 898–908. Reprinted in *Public Expenditure and Policy Analysis,* 2d ed., edited by Robert H. Haveman and Julius Margolis. (Chicago: Rand-McNally, 1977).

Hansen, Ronald W., "Costs and Benefits of Cost–Benefit Analysis in Pharmaceutical Promotion and Utilization Decisions," in *Competitive Strategies in the Pharmaceutical Industry,* edited by Robert B. Helms. (Washington, DC: American Enterprise Institute, 1996, 322–336).

Hansen, W. Lee, "Shortages and Investment in Health Manpower," in *The Economics of Health and Medical Care: Proceedings of the Conference on the Economics of Health and Medical Care May 10–12, 1962.* (Ann Arbor, MI: University of Michigan, 1964).

Hansmann, Henry B., "The Effect of Tax Exemption and Other Factors on the Market Share of Nonprofit Versus For-Profit Firms," *National Tax Journal* 40 (1987): 71–82.

Hansmann, Henry B., "The Role of Nonprofit Enterprise," *Yale Law Journal* 89 (1980): 835–901.

Harrington, Charlene, James H. Swan, and Leslie A. Grant, "Nursing Home Bed Capacity in the States, 1978–86," *Health Care Financing Review* 9 (1988): 81–97.

Harris, Jeffrey E., "The Internal Organization of Hospitals: Some Economic Implications," *Bell Journal of Economics* 8 (1977): 467–482.

Harris, Jeffrey E., and Sandra W. Chan, "The Continuum-of-Addiction: Cigarette Smoking in Relation to Price among Americans," *electronic Health Economics Letters* 2 (1998): 3–12.

Havighurst, Clark C., "The Questionable Cost-Containment Record of Commercial Health Insurers," in *Health Care in America,* edited by H. E. Frech III. (San Francisco: Pacific Research Institute for Public Policy, 1988).

Hay, Joel W., and Gerard Anderson, "The Hospital Services Market: A Disequilibrium Analysis," *Southern Economic Journal* 54 (1988): 656–665.

Hay, Joel W., and Michael J. Leahy, "Physician-Induced Demand: An Empirical Analysis of the Consumer Information Gap," *Journal of Health Economics* 1 (1982): 231–244.

Headen, Alvin E., Jr., "Wages, Returns to Ownership, and Fee Responses to Physician Supply," *Review of Economics and Statistics* 72 (1990): 30–37.

Health Insurance Association of America, *Source Book of Health Insurance Data,* various years.

Heffley, Dennis R., and Thomas J. Miceli, "The Economics of Incentive-Based Health Plans," *Journal of Risk and Insurance* 65 (1998): 445–465.

Hellerstein, James K., "The Importance of the Physician in the Generic Versus Trade-Name Prescription Decision," *RAND Journal of Economics* 29 (1998): 108–136.

Helms, Robert B., ed. *Competitive Strategies in the Pharmaceutical Industry,* American Enterprise Institute, Washington, DC, 1996.

Henderson, Rebecca, and Iain Cockburn, "Scale, Scope, and Spillovers: The Determinants of Research Productivity in Drug Discovery," *RAND Journal of Economics* 27 (1996): 32–59.

Henke, Klaus-Dirk, Margaret A. Murray, and Claudia Ade, "Global Budgeting in Germany: Lessons for the United States," *Health Affairs* 13 (1994): 7–21.

Henke, Klaus-Dirk, "The Federal Republic of Germany," in *Advances in Health Economics and Health Services Research, Supplement 1: Comparative Health Systems,* edited by Jean-Jacques Rosa. (Greenwich, CT: JAI Press, 1990).

Hershey, John C. et al., "Health Insurance under Competition: Would People Choose What Is Expected?" *Inquiry* 21 (1984): 349–360.

Hill, Steven C., and Barbara L. Wolfe, "Testing the HMO Competitive Strategy: An Analysis of Its Impact on Medical Care Resources," *Journal of Health Economics* 16 (1997): 261–286.

Hinrichs, Karl, "The Impact of German Health Insurance Reforms on Redistribution and the Culture of Solidarity," *Journal of Health Politics, Policy and Law* 20 (1995): 653–687.

Hirsch, Barry T., and Edward Schumacher, "Union Wages, Rents, and Skills in Health Care Labor Markets," *Journal of Labor Research* 19 (1998): 125–147.

Hirsch, Barry T., and Edward Schumacher, "Monopsony Power and Relative Wages in the Labor Market for Nurses," *Journal of Health Economics* 14 (1995): 443–476.

Hirshleifer, Jack, and Amihai Glazer. *Price Theory and Applications,* 5th ed. (Upper Saddle River, NJ: Prentice Hall, 1992).

Hirth, Richard A., "Consumer Information and Competition between Nonprofit and For-Profit Nursing Homes," *Journal of Health Economics* 18 (1999): 219–240.

Hitiris, Theo, and John Posnett, "The Determinants and Effects of Health Expenditure in Developed Countries," *Journal of Health Economics* 11 (1992): 173–181.

Hochban, Jacquelyn et al., "The Hill-Burton Program and Changes in Health Services Delivery," *Inquiry* 18 (1981): 61–69.

Hodgkin, Dominic, and Thomas G. McGuire, "Payment Levels and Hospital Response to Prospective Payment," *Journal of Health Economics* 13 (1994): 1–29.

Hodgson, Thomas A., "Cigarette Smoking and Lifetime Medical Expenditures," *Milbank Quarterly* 70 (1992): 81–125.

Hoerger, Thomas J., "Profit Variability in For-Profit and Not-for-Profit Hospitals," *Journal of Health Economics* 10 (1991): 259–289.

Hofler, Richard, and Sherman Folland, "Technical and Allocative Inefficiencies of United States Hospitals under a Stochastic Frontier Approach," Working Paper No. 92-1, Rochester, Michigan, 1992.

Hofler, Richard A., and Brian Rungeling, "U.S. Nursing Homes: Are They Cost Efficient?" *Economics Letters* 44 (1994): 301–305.

Holahan, John, and Liska, David "Variations in Medicaid Spending among States," *Assessing New Federalism: Issues and Options for States, A-3.* (Washington, DC: Urban Institute, January 1997).

Holahan, John, Joshua Wiener, and Susan Wallin, "Health Policy for the Low-Income Population: Major Findings from the *Assessing the New Federalism* Case Studies." (Washington, DC: Urban Institute, November 1998).

Holtmann, Alphonse G., "Theories of Non-Profit Institutions," *Journal of Economic Surveys* 2 (1988): 29–45.

Holtmann, Alphonse G., "A Theory of Non-Profit Firms," *Economica* 50 (November 1983): 439–449.

Holtmann, Alphonse G., and Todd L. Idson, "Wage Determination of Registered Nurses in Proprietary and Nonprofit Nursing Homes," *Journal of Human Resources* 28 (1993): 55–79.

Hornbrook, Mark C., and Alan C. Monheit, "The Contribution of Case-Mix Severity to the Hospital Cost–Output Relation," *Inquiry* 22 (1985): 259–271.

Hsiao, William C., "Medical Savings Accounts: Lessons from Singapore," *Health Affairs* 14 (1995): 260–266.

Hsiao, William C., "Resource-Based Relative Value Scale: An Option for Physician Payment," *Inquiry* 24 (1987): 360–361.

Hsiao, William C., Daniel L. Dunn, and Diana K. Verrilli, "Assessing the Implementation of Physician-Payment Reform," *New England Journal of Medicine* 328 (1993): 928–933.

Hughes, Susan L. et al., "Impact of Home Care on Hospital Days: A Meta Analysis," *Health Services Research* 32 (1997): 415–432.

Hurd, Richard W., "Equilibrium Vacancies in a Labor Market Dominated by Nonprofit Firms: The 'Shortage of Nurses,'" *Review of Economics and Statistics* 55 (1973): 234–240.

Hurst, Jeremy, W., "Reform of Health Care in Germany," *Health Care Financing Review* 12 (1991): 73–86.

Hurwitz, Mark A., and Richard E. Caves, "Persuasion or Information? Promotion and the Shares of Brand Name and Generic Pharmaceuticals," *Journal of Law and Economics* 31 (1988): 299–320.

Huttin, Christine, "Drug Price Divergence in Europe: Regulatory Aspect," *Health Affairs* 18 (1999): 245–249.

Iglehart, John K., "An Interview with Leonard D. Schaeffer," *Health Affairs* 14 (1995): 131–142.

Illich, Ivan. *Medical Nemesis.* (New York: Bantam Books, 1976).

Ingbar, Mary Lee, and Lester D. Taylor. *Hospital Costs in Massachusetts.* (Cambridge, MA: Harvard, 1968).

Ippolito, Pauline M., and Richard A. Ippolito, "Measuring the Value of Life Saving from Consumer Reactions to New Information," *Journal of Public Economics* 25 (1984): 53–81.

Jacobson, Peter D., Lousie E. Parker, and Ian D. Coulter, "Nurse Practitioners and Physician Assistants as Primary Care Providers in Institutional Settings," *Inquiry* 35 (1998/99): 432–446.

James, John H., "Reforming the British National Health Service: Implementation Problems in London," *Journal of Health Politics, Policy and Law* 20 (1995): 653–687.

Jensen, Gail A., and Kevin D. Cotter, "Choice of Purchasing Arrangements in Insurance Markets," manuscript, Department of Economics, Wayne State University, November 1987.

Jensen, Gail A., and Allen C. Goodman, "The Economics of Gynecology and Obstetrics," in *Practical Strategies in Obstetrics and Gynecology,* edited by Scott B. Ransom. (New York: W. B. Saunders, 1999): 719–733.

Jensen, Gail A., and Michael A. Morrisey, "Mandated Benefit Laws and Employer-Sponsored Health Insurance," Washington, DC: Health Insurance Association of America, 1999 (Report).

Jensen, Gail A., and Michael A. Morrisey, "Group Health Insurance: A Hedonic Price Approach," *Review of Economics and Statistics* 72 (1990): 38–44.

Jensen, Gail A., and Michael A. Morrisey, "The Role of Physicians in Hospital Production," *Review of Economics and Statistics* 68 (1986): 432–442.

Jensen, Gail A. et al., "The New Dominance of Managed Care: Insurance Trends in the 1990s," *Health Affairs* 16 (1997): 125–136.

Joesch, Jutta M., Thomas M. Wickizer, and Paul J. Feldstein, "Does Competition by Health Maintenance Organizations Affect the Adoption of Cost-Containment Measures by Fee-for-Service Plans?" *American Journal of Managed Care* 4 (1998): 832–838.

Johnston, Jack, "Advertising and the Aggregate Demand for Cigarettes: A Comment," *European Economic Review* 14 (1980): 117–125.

Jolin, Leanne D. et al., "U.S. Medical School Finances," *Journal of the American Medical Association* 266 (1991): 985–990.

Jonas, Steven. *An Introduction to the U.S. Health Care System,* 3d ed. (1st and 2d editions by Milton Roemer). (New York: Springer Publishing Co., 1992).

Jondrow, J. et al., "On the Estimation of Technical Inefficiency in the Stochastic Frontier Production Function Model," *Journal of Econometrics* (1982): 233–238.

Jones, Chuck, "Despite Tax Break, Group LTC Market Stalls," *Life Association News* 94 (1999): 32–35.

Jones, Robert F. et al., "Review of U.S. Medical School Finances, 1996–1997," *Journal of the American Medical Association* 280 (1998): 813–818.

Jorgenson, Dale W., "Capital Theory and Investment Behavior," *American Economic Review* 53 (1963): 247–259.

Joskow, Paul L., "The Effects of Competition and Regulation on Hospital Bed Supply and the Reservation Quality of the Hospital," *Bell Journal of Economics* 11 (1980): 421–447.

Joyce, Theodore, "Impact of Augmented Prenatal Care on Birth Outcomes of Medicaid Recipients in New York City," *Journal of Health Economics* 18 (1999): 31–67.

Joyce, Theodore, Andrew D. Racine, and Naci Mocan, "The Consequences and Costs of Maternal Substance Abuse in New York City: A Pooled Time-Series, Cross-Section Analysis," *Journal of Health Economics* 11 (1992): 297–314.

Juba, David A., *Price Setting in the Market for Physicians' Services: A Review of the Literature,* U.S. Department of Health, Education and Welfare, Health Care Financing Administration, HEW Publication No. (HCFA) 03012 9–79, GPO 1979.

Jung, Ki-Taig, "Influence of the Introduction of a Per-Visit Copayment on Health Care Use and Expenditures: The Korean Experience," *Journal of Risk and Insurance* 65 (1998): 35–56.

Kaestner, Robert, Theodore Joyce, and Hassan Wehbeh, "The Effect of Maternal Drug Use on Birth Weight: Measurement Error in Binary Variables," *Economic Inquiry* 34 (October 1996): 617–629.

Kamien, Morton I., and Nancy L. Schwartz. *Market Structure and Innovation.* (Cambridge: Cambridge University Press, 1982).

Kaplan, Robert M., and John P. Anderson, "A General Health Policy Model: Update and Applications," *Health Services Research* 23 (1988): 203–235.

Katz, Steven J., Lawrence F. McMahon, and Willard G. Manning, "Comparing the Use of Diagnostic Tests in Canadian and U.S. Hospitals," *Medical Care* 34 (1996): 117–125.

Keeler, Emmett B., and John E. Rolph, "The Demand for Episodes of Treatment in the Health Insurance Experiment," *Journal of Health Economics* 7 (1988): 333–367.

Keeler, Emmett B., Willard G. Manning, Jr., and Kenneth B. Wells, "The Demand for Episodes of Mental Health Services," *Journal of Health Economics* 7 (1988): 369–392.

Keeler, Theodore E. et al., "Taxation, Regulation, and Addiction: A Demand Function for Cigarettes Based on Time-Series Evidence," *Journal of Health Economics* 12 (1993): 1–18.

Kenkel, Donald S., "The Demand for Preventive Medical Care," *Applied Economics* 26 (1994): 313–325.

Kessel, Reuben, "Price Discrimination in Medicine," *Journal of Law and Economics* 1 (1958): 20–53.

Kessides, Ioannis N., "Advertising, Sunk Costs, and Barriers to Entry," *Review of Economics and Statistics* 68 (1986): 84–95.

Klausen, Liv Marit, Trand E. Olsen, and Alf Erling Risa, "Technological Diffusion in Primary Health Care," *Journal of Health Economics* 13 (1994): 439–452.

Kniesner, Thomas J., and John Leeth, "Compensating Wage Differentials for Fatal Injury Risk in Australia, Japan, and the United States," *Journal of Risk and Insurance* 4 (1991): 75–90.

Kooreman, Peter, "Nursing Home Care in the Netherlands: A Nonparametric Efficiency Analysis," *Journal of Health Economics* 13 (1994): 301–316.

Kooreman, Peter, "Data Envelopment Analysis and Parametric Frontier Estimation: Complementary Tools," *Journal of Health Economics* 13 (1994): 345–346.

Krasny, Jacques, and Ian R. Ferrier, "A Closer Look at Health Care in Canada," *Health Affairs* 10 (1991): 152–158.

Krizay, John, and Andrew Wilson. *The Patient as Consumer.* (Lexington, MA: Lexington, 1974).

Krueger, Alan B., and Uwe E. Reinhardt, "The Economics of Employer Versus Individual Mandates," *Health Affairs* 13 (1994): 34–53.

Kwoka, John E. Jr., "Advertising and the Price and Quality of Optometric Services," *American Economic Review* 74 (1984): 211–216.

Labelle, Roberta, Gregg Stoddard, and Thomas Rice, "A Re-Examination of the Meaning and Importance of Supplier-Induced Demand," *Journal of Health Economics* 13 (1994): 347–368.

Lakdawalla, Darius, and Tomas Philipson, "Nonprofit Production and Competition," Working Pa-

per 6377, National Bureau of Economic Research, January 1998.

Lalonde, Marc, *A New Perspective on the Health of Canadians,* Office of the Canadian Minister of National Health and Welfare, Ottawa, 1974.

Lamberton, C. E., W. D. Ellington, and K. R. Spear, "Factors Determining the Demand for Nursing Home Services," *Quarterly Review of Economics and Business* 26 (1986): 74–90.

Lambin, J. J. *Advertising, Competition and Market Conduct in Oligopoly over Time.* (Amsterdam: North-Holland, 1976).

Lane, Julia, and Stephan Gohmann, "Shortage or Surplus: Economic and Noneconomic Approaches to the Analysis of Nursing Labor Markets," *Southern Economic Journal* 61 (1995): 644–653.

Langwell, Kathryn M., and Lyle M. Nelson, "Physician Payment Systems: A Review of History, Alternatives and Evidence," *Medical Care Review* 43 (1986): 5–58.

Latimer, Eric A., Diana Verrilli, and W. Pete Welch, "Utilization of Physician Services at the End of Life: Differences between the United States and Canada," *Inquiry* 36 (1999): 90–100.

Laugesen, Murray, and Chris Meads, "Tobacco Advertising Restrictions, Price, Income, and Tobacco Consumption in OECD Countries, 1960–1986," *British Journal of Addiction* 86 (1991): 1343–1354.

Lave, Judith R., and Lester B. Lave, "Hospital Cost Functions," *American Economic Review* 60 (1970): 379–395.

Lawrence, David, "Nonprofit Versus For-Profit Health Plans," *Health Affairs* 15 (1996): 237–238.

Le Grand, Julian, "Competition, Cooperation or Control? Tales from the British National Health Service," *Health Affairs* 18 (1999): 27–39.

Lee, Dwight R., "Why Workers Should Want Mandated Benefits to Lower Their Wages," *Economic Inquiry* 34 (1996): 401–407.

Lee, Maw L., "A Conspicuous Production Theory of Hospital Behavior," *Southern Economic Journal* 38 (1971): 48–58.

Lee, Robert H., and Jack Hadley, "Physicians' Fees and Public Medical Care Programs," *Health Services Research* 16 (1981): 185–203.

Lee, Roger I., and Lewis W. Jones, *The Fundamentals of Good Medical Care.* Publication of the Committee on the Costs of Medical Care. (Chicago: University of Chicago, 1933).

Lee, T. Y., "Contract Research Organizations," *Drug Information Journal* 32 (1998): 1259S-1263S.

Lee, Young Hoon, and Peter Schmidt, "A Production Frontier Model with Flexible Temporal Variation in Technical Efficiency," in Harold O. Fried, C. A. Knox Lovell et al., *Measurement of Production Efficiency.* (New York: Oxford University Press, 1993).

Leffler, Keith B., "Persuasion or Information? The Economics of Prescription Drug Advertising," *Journal of Law and Economics* 24 (1981): 45–74.

Leffler, Keith B., "Physician Licensure: Competition and Monopoly in American Medicine," *Journal of Law and Economics* 21 (1978): 165–186.

Leffler, Keith B., and Cotton M. Lindsay, "Student Discount Rates, Consumption Loans, and Subsidies to Professional Training," *Journal of Human Resources* 16 (1981): 468–476.

Legnini, Mark W. et al., "Changes in Connecticut Hospital Use Rates: Have Small-Area Variations Been Affected?" *Inquiry* 27 (1990): 51–60.

Lehner, Laura A. and James F. Burgess, "Teaching and Hospital Production: The Use of Regression Estimates," *Health Economics* 4 (1995): 113–125.

Leibenstein, Harvey. *General X-Efficiency Theory and Economic Development.* (New York: Oxford University Press, 1978).

Leibenstein, Harvey, "Aspects of the X-Efficiency Theory of the Firm," *Bell Journal of Economics* 6 (1975): 580–606.

Leibenstein, Harvey, "Allocative Efficiency vs. 'X-Efficiency,'" *American Economic Review* 56 (1966): 392–415.

Leigh, J. Paul, "Gender, Firm Size, Industry, and Estimates of the Value-of-Life," *Journal of Health Economics* 6 (1987): 255–273.

Lerner, Abba P., "The Concept of Monopoly and the Measurement of Monopoly Power," *Review of Economic Studies* 11 (1943): 157–175.

Lerner, Arthur N., "Federal Trade Commission Antitrust Activities in the Health Care Services Field," *Antitrust Bulletin* (1984): 205–224.

Levit, Katherine et al., "Health Spending in 1998: Signals of Change," *Health Affairs* 19 (2000): 124–132.

Levit, Katherine et al., "National Health Expenditures in 1997: More Slow Growth," *Health Affairs* 17 (1998): 99–110.

Levit, Katherine R. et al., "National Health Expenditures, 1993," *Health Care Financing Review* 16 (1994): 247–294.

Lewin, Lawrence, Robert Derzon, and Rhea Margulies, "Investor-Owneds and Nonprofits Differ in Economic Performance," *Hospitals* 55 (July 1, 1981): 52–58.

Lewin, Lawrence, Timothy J. Eckels, and Linda B. Miller, "Setting the Record Straight: The Provision of Uncompensated Care by Not-for-Profit Hospitals," *New England Journal of Medicine* 318 (1988): 1212–1215.

Lewis, Karen, "Comparison of Use by Enrolled and Recently Disenrolled Populations in a Health Maintenance Organization," *Health Services Research* 19 (1984): 1–22.

Lewit, Eugene M., and Douglas Coate, "The Potential for Using Excise Taxes to Reduce Smoking," *Journal of Health Economics* 1 (1982): 121–145.

Lewit, Eugene M., Douglas Coate, and Michael Grossman, "The Effects of Government Regulation on Teenage Smoking," *Journal of Law and Economics* 24 (1981): 545–569.

Lichtenberg, Frank R., "Pharmaceutical Innovation, Mortality Reduction, and Economic Growth," Working Paper 6569, National Bureau of Economic Research, May 1998.

Linet, Martha S. et al., "Residential Magnetic Field Exposures and Childhood Acute Lymphoblastic Leukemia," *New England Journal of Medicine* 337 (July 3, 1997): 1–7.

Link, Charles, and John Landon, "Monopsony and Union Power in the Market for Nurses," *Southern Economic Journal* 41 (1975): 649–659.

Linn, Margaret W., Lee Gurel, and Bernard S. Linn, "Patient Outcome as a Measure of Quality of Nursing Home Care," *American Journal of Public Health* 4 (1977): 337–344.

Linnerooth, Joanne, "The Value of Human Life: A Review of the Models," *Economic Inquiry* 17 (1979): 52–74.

Lipsey, Richard G., and Kelvin Lancaster, "The General Theory of the Second Best," *Review of Economic Studies* 24 (1956): 11–32.

Liu, Gordon G., "Birth Outcomes and the Effectiveness of Prenatal Care," *Health Services Research* 32 (1998): 805–823.

LoGerfo, James P. et al., "Rates of Surgical Care in Prepaid Group Practices and the Independent Setting: What Are the Reasons for the Differences?" *Medical Care* 17 (1979): 1–10.

Long, Millard F., "Efficient Use of Hospitals," in *The Economics of Health and Medical Care,* edited by Selma J. Mushkin. (Ann Arbor, MI: University of Michigan, 1964).

Long, Stephen H., Russell F. Settle, and Charles W. Wrightson Jr., "Employee Premiums, Availability of Alternative Plans, and HMO Disenrollment," *Medical Care* 26 (1988): 927–938.

Lovell, C. A. Knox, and Shelton S. Schmidt, eds. *The Measurement of Productive Efficiency.* (Oxford: Oxford University Press, 1993).

Lu, John Z., and William S. Comanor, "Strategic Pricing of New Pharmaceuticals," *Review of Economics and Statistics* 80 (1998): 108–117.

Luft, Harold S., "Health Maintenance Organizations and the Rationing of Medical Care," *Milbank Memorial Fund Quarterly/Health and Society* 60 (1982): 268–306.

Luft, Harold S. *Health Maintenance Organizations: Dimensions of Performance.* (New York: John Wiley & Sons, 1981).

Luft, Harold S., "How Do Health-Maintenance Organizations Achieve Their "Savings"?" *New England Journal of Medicine* 298 (1978): 1336–1343.

Luft, Harold S. et al., "Does Quality Influence Choice of Hospital?" *Journal of the American Medical Association* 263 (1990): 2899–2906.

Lynch, James, and Drue Schuler, "Consumer Evaluation of the Quality of Hospital Services from an Economics of Information Perspective," *Journal of Health Care Marketing* 19 (1990): 16–22.

Lynch, Janet R., and Yasar A. Ozcan, "Hospital Closure: An Efficiency Analysis," *Hospital and Health Services Administration* 39 (1994): 205–220.

Maddala, G. S. *Limited Dependent and Qualitative Variables in Econometrics.* (Cambridge: Cambridge University Press, 1983).

Madrian, Brigitte C., "Employment-Based Health Insurance and Job Mobility: Is There Evidence of Job-Lock?" *Quarterly Journal of Economics* 109 (1994): 27–54.

Magnusson, Jon, "Efficiency Measurement and the Operationalization of Hospital Production," *Health Services Research* 31 (1996): 21–37.

Maioni, Antonia, "Nothing Succeeds Like the Right Kind of Failure: Postwar National Health Insurance Initiatives in Canada and the United States," *Journal of Health Politics, Policy and Law* 20 (1995): 5–30.

Manning, Willard G. et al. *The Costs of Poor Health Habits.* (Cambridge, MA: Harvard University Press, 1991).

Manning, Willard G. et al., "Health Insurance and the Demand for Medical Care: Evidence from a Randomized Experiment," *American Economic Review* 77 (1987): 251–277.

Manning, Willard G. et al., "A Controlled Trial of the Effect of a Prepaid Group Practice on Use of Services," *New England Journal of Medicine* 310 (1984): 1505–1510.

Mansfield, Edwin, "Patent Innovation: An Empirical Study," *Management Science* 32 (1986): 173–181.

Marder, William D., and Stephen Zuckerman, "Competition and Medical Groups: A Survivor Analysis," *Journal of Health Economics* 4 (1985): 167–176.

Mark, Tami L., "Analysis of the Rationale for, and Consequences of, Nonprofit and For-Profit Ownership Conversions," *Health Services Research* 34 (1999): 83–101.

Mark, Tami L., "Psychiatric Hospital Ownership and Performance: Do Nonprofit Organizations Offer Advantages in Markets Characterized by Asymmetric Information?" *Journal of Human Resources* 31 (1996): 631–649.

Marks, Daniel B. et al., "Use of Medical Resources and Quality of Life after Acute Myocardial Infarction in Canada and the United States," *New England Journal of Medicine* 331 (1994): 1130–1135.

Massaro, Thomas A., and Yu-Ning Wong, "Positive Experience with Medical Savings Accounts in Singapore," *Health Affairs* 14 (1995): 267–271.

Mather Dell, B., "Incorporating Clinical Outcomes and Economic Consequences into Drug Formulary Decisions: A Practical Approach," *American Journal of Managed Care* 5 (1999): 277–285.

Mauldon, Jane, "The Effect of Marital Disruption on Children's Health," *Demography* 27 (1990): 431–446.

Maynard, Alan, "The United Kingdom," in *Advances in Health Economics and Health Services Research, Supplement 1: Comparative Health Systems,* edited by Jean-Jacques Rosa. (Greenwich, CT: JAI Press, 1990: 1–26.

Mayo, John W., and Deborah A. McFarland, "Regulation, Market Structure, and Hospital Costs: Reply," *Southern Economic Journal* 57 (1991): 535–538.

Mayo, John W., and Deborah A. McFarland, "Regulation, Market Structure, and Hospital Costs," *Southern Economic Journal* 55 (1989): 559–569.

McCarthy, Patrick S., "The Effect of Higher Rural Interstate Speed Limits in Alcohol-Related Accidents," *Journal of Health Economics* 12 (1993): 281–299.

McCarthy, Thomas R., "The Competitive Nature of the Primary-Care Physician Services Market," *Journal of Health Economics* 4 (1985): 93–117.

McGuinness, Tony, and Keith Cowling, "Advertising and the Aggregate Demand for Cigarettes," *European Economic Review* 6 (1975): 311–328.

McGuire, Thomas G., and Mark V. Pauly, "Physician Response to Fee Changes with Multiple Payers," *Journal of Health Economics* 10 (1991): 385–410.

McKay, Niccie L., "The Prisoner's Dilemma: An Obstacle to Cooperation in Health Care Markets," *Medical Care Review* 51 (1994): 179–204.

McKeown, Thomas. *The Modern Rise of Population.* (New York: Academic Press, 1976).

McKinlay, John B., and Sonja M. McKinlay, "The Questionable Contribution of Medical Measures to the Decline of Mortality in the United States in the Twentieth Century," *Milbank Memorial Fund Quarterly/Health and Society* 55 (1977): 405–428.

McLaughlin, Catherine G., "The Dilemma of Affordability: Health Insurance for Small Business," in *American Health Policy: Critical Issues for Reform,* edited by Robert B. Helms. (Washington, DC: AEI Press, 1993, 152–166).

McLaughlin, Catherine G., "Market Responses to HMOs: Price Competition or Rivalry?" *Inquiry* 25 (1988): 207–218.

McLaughlin, Catherine G., and Wendy K. Zellers, "Small Business and Health Care Reform," The University of Michigan School of Public Health, 1994.

McPherson, Klim et al., "Small-Area Variations in the Use of Common Surgical Procedures: An International Comparison of New England, England, and Norway," *New England Journal of Medicine* 307 (1982): 1310–1313.

Medicare and Medicaid, Prospective Payment Assessment Commission: Medicare and the Health System, Report to Congress (Chicago: Commerce Clearing House, Inc., 1991).

Medicare Payment Advisory Commission (MEDPAC), *Report to Congress: Selected Medicare Issues,* June 1999, ch. 1, p. 6.

Medicare Payment Advisory Commission, *Report to Congress, Medicare Payment Policy,* March 1999: ch. 7, app. D.

Miles, J. J. *Health Care and Antitrust Law.* (St. Paul, MN: West Group, 1998).

Miller, Rebecca S., Harry S. Jonas, and Michael E. Whitcomb, "The Initial Employment Status of Physicians Completing Training in 1994," *Journal of the American Medical Association* 275 (1996): 708–712.

Miller, Robert H., and Harold S. Luft, "Does Managed Care Lead to Better or Worse Quality of Care?" *Health Affairs* 16 (1997): 7–25.

Miller, Robert H., and Harold S. Luft, "Managed Care Plan Performance Since 1980: A Literature Analysis," *Journal of the American Medical Association* 271 (May 18, 1994): 1512–1519.

Mills, Edwin S. *Studies in the Structure of the Urban Economy.* (Baltimore: Johns Hopkins, 1972).

Mills, Edwin S., and Bruce W. Hamilton. *Urban Economics,* 5th ed. (New York: Harper Collins, 1994).

Miron, Jeffrey A., "The Effect of Alcohol Prohibition on Alcohol Consumption," Working Paper 7130, National Bureau of Economic Research, May 1999.

Mitchell, Janet B., and Jerry Cromwell, "Impact of All-or-Nothing Assignment Requirement under Medicare," *Health Care Financing Review* 4 (1983): 59–78.

Mitchell, Janet B., and Jerry Cromwell, "Physician Behavior under the Medicare Assignment Option," *Journal of Health Economics* 1 (1982): 245–264.

Mobley, Lee Rivers, and W. David Bradford, "Behavioral Differences among Hospitals: Is It Ownership, or Location?" *Applied Economics* 29 (1997): 1125–1138.

Mobley, Lee R., and H. E. Frech III, "Firm Growth and Failure in Increasingly Competitive Markets: Theory and Application to Hospital Markets," *Journal of the Economics of Business* 1 (1994).

Moffit, Robert E., Surprise, a government health plan that works, *Wall Street Journal* 2 April 1992, sec. A14.

Monroe, Kent B., "Buyers Subjective Perceptions of Price," *Journal of Marketing Research* 10 (1973): 70–80.

Montgomery-Karp, Beverly, "Market Demands Call for New Treatment," *Advertising Age* 54 (September 26, 1983): M9–11.

Moon, Marilyn, "The Value of Social Insurance," testimony to the Committee on Finance, United States Senate, May 27, 1999.

Moon, Ok-Ryun, "The National Health Insurance Policy Issues in Korea," *Korean Journal of Public Health* 42 (1989): 98–114.

Mooney, Gavin et al., "Reweighing Heat: Response to Culyer, van Doorslaer and Wagstaff," *Journal of Health Economics* 11 (1992): 199–205.

Mooney, Gavin et al., "Utilisation as a Measure of Equity: Weighing Heat?" *Journal of Health Economics* 10 (1991): 475–480.

Moore, Gordon T., "Will the Power of the Marketplace Produce the Workforce We Need?" *Inquiry* 31 (1994): 276–282.

Moore, Michael J., "Death and Tobacco Taxes," Working Paper 5153, National Bureau of Economic Research, June 1995.

Moore, Michael J., and W. Kip Viscusi, "Doubling the Estimated Value of Life: Results Using New Occupational Fatality Data," *Journal of Policy Analysis Management,* 7 (1988): 476–490.

Morrisey, Michael A., "Introduction," in *Managed Care and Changing Health Care Markets,* edited by Michael A. Morrisey. (Washington, DC: AEI Press, 1998, 1–23).

Morrisey, Michael A., "Movies and Myths: Hospital Cost Shifting," *Business Economics* 30 (1995): 22–25.

Motheral, Brenda R., and Rochelle Henderson, "The Effect of a Copay Increase on Pharmaceutical Utilization, Expenditures, and Treatment Continuation," *American Journal of Managed Care,* 5 (1999): 1383–1394.

Mott, Peter D., "Hospital Utilization by Health Maintenance Organizations: Separating Apples from Oranges," *Medical Care* 24 (1986): 398–406.

Mueller, Curt D., and Alan C. Monheit, "Insurance Coverage and the Demand for Dental Care," *Journal of Health Economics* 7 (1988): 59–72.

Mullahy, John, and Jody Sindelar, "Do Drinkers Know When to Say When? An Empirical Analysis of Drunk Driving," *Economic Inquiry* 22 (1994): 383–394.

Mullahy, John, and Jody L. Sindelar, "Alcoholism, Work, and Income," *Journal of Labor Economics* 11 (1993): 494–520.

Mushkin, Selma J. *Biomedical Research: Costs and Benefits.* (Cambridge, MA: Ballinger, 1979).

Mwabu, Germano, Martha Ainsworth, and Andrew Nyamete, "Quality of Medical Care and Choice of Medical Treatment in Kenya: An Empirical Analysis," *Journal of Human Resources* 28 (1993): 838–862.

National Association of Home Care, "Basic Statistics about Hospice," www.nahc.org/consumer/hpcstats, 1999.

Naylor, C. David, "Health Care in Canada: Incrementalism under Fiscal Duress," *Health Affairs* 18 (1999): 9–26.

Nelson, Jon P., and John R. Moran, "Advertising and U.S. Alcoholic Beverage Demand: System-Wide Estimates," *Applied Economics* 27 (1995): 1225–1236.

Nelson, Phillip, "Advertising as Information," *Journal of Political Economy* 82 (1974): 729–754.

Nelson, Phillip, "Information and Consumer Behavior," *Journal of Political Economy* 78 (1970): 311–329.

Neuhauser, Duncan, and Ann M. Lewicki, "What Do We Gain from the Sixth Stool Guaiac?" *New England Journal of Medicine* 293 (1975): 226–228.

Newbold, Paul. *Statistics for Business and Economics,* 4th ed. (Upper Saddle River, NJ: Prentice-Hall, 1995).

Newhouse, Joseph P., "Frontier Estimation: How Useful a Tool in Health Economics?" *Journal of Health Economics* 13 (1994): 317–322.

Newhouse, Joseph P., "Has the Erosion of the Medical Marketplace Ended?" *Journal of Health Politics, Policy and Law* 13 (1988): 263–277.

Newhouse, Joseph P., *The Economics of Medical Care.* (Reading, MA: Addison-Wesley, 1978a).

Newhouse, Joseph P., "The Structure of Health Insurance and the Erosion of Competition in the Medical Marketplace," in *Competition in the Health Care Sector: Past, Present and Future,* edited by W. Greenberg. (Germantown, MD: Aspen Systems, 1978b).

Newhouse, Joseph P., "Medical-Care Expenditures: A Cross-National Survey," *Journal of Human Resources* 12 (1977): 115–125.

Newhouse, Joseph P., "Toward a Theory of Nonprofit Institutions: An Economic Model of a Hospital," *American Economic Review* 60 (1970): 64–74.

Newhouse, Joseph P., and Daniel J. Byrne, "Did Medicare's Perspective Payment System Cause Length of Stay to Fall?" *Journal of Health Economics* 7 (1988): 413–416.

Newhouse, Joseph P., and Lindy J. Friedlander, "The Relationship between Medical Resources and Measures of Health: Some Additional Evidence," *Journal of Human Resources* 15 (1980): 200–218.

Newhouse, Joseph P., and Charles E. Phelps, "New Estimates of Price and Income Elasticities of Medical Care Services," in *The Role of Health Insurance in the Health Services Sector,* edited by Richard Rosett. (New York: Neal Watson, 1976).

Newhouse, Joseph P., Geoffrey Anderson, and Leslie L. Roos, "Hospital Spending in the United States and Canada: A Comparison," *Health Affairs* 7 (1988): 6–16.

Newhouse, Joseph P. et. al. *Free for All? Lessons from the RAND Health Insurance Experiment.* (Cambridge MA: Harvard University Press, 1993).

Newhouse, Joseph P. et al., "Are Fee-for-Service Costs Increasing Faster Than HMO Costs?" *Medical Care* 23 (1985): 960–966.

Newhouse, Joseph P. et al., "How Have Location Patterns Affected the Availability of Medical Services?" Publication R-2872–HJK/HHS/RWJ, Rand, Santa Monica, CA, May 1982.

Niskanen, William A. *Bureaucracy and Representative Government.* (Chicago: Aldine, Etherton, 1971).

Norton, Edward C., and Douglas O. Staiger, "How Hospital Ownership Affects Access to Care for the Uninsured," *RAND Journal of Economics* 25 (1994): 171–185.

Nozick, Robert. *Anarchy, State, and Utopia.* (New York: Basic Books, 1974).

Nyman, John A., "Testing for Excess Demand in Nursing Home Markets," *Medical Care* 31 (1993): 680–693.

Nyman, John A., and Robert A. Connor, "Do Case-Mix Adjusted Nursing Home Reimbursements Actually Reflect Costs? Minnesota's Experience," *Journal of Health Economics* 13 (1994): 145–162.

Nyman, John A., and Daniel L. Bricker, "Profit Incentives and Technical Efficiency in the Production of Nursing Home Care," *Review of Economics and Statistics* 71 (1989): 586–594.

Nyman, John A. et al., "Changing Physician Behavior: Does Medical Review of Part B Medicare Claims Make a Difference?" *Inquiry* 27 (1990): 127–137.

O'Brien, Jack, Borje O. Saxberg, and Howard L. Smith, "For-Profit or Not-for-Profit Nursing Homes: Does It Matter?" *The Gerontologist* 23 (1983): 341–348.

Office of National Cost Estimates, "National Health Expenditures, 1990," *Health Care Financing Review* 13 (1991): 29–54.

Office of National Cost Estimates, "National Health Expenditures, 1988," *Health Care Financing Review* 11 (1990): 1–41.

Ohsfeldt, Robert L., Raymond G. Boyle, and Eli I. Capilouto, "Tobacco Taxes, Smoking Restrictions, and Tobacco Use," Working Paper 6486, National Bureau of Economic Research, March 1998.

Okun, Arthur. *Efficiency and Equity: The Big Trade-off.* (Washington, DC: Brookings, 1975).

Olkin, Ingram, and Jerome Sacks, "Cross-Disciplinary Research in the Statistical Sciences," Hayward, CA: Institute of Mathematical Statistics, September 1988.

Olsen, Jan Abel, "But *Health* Can Still Be a Necessity . . .," *Journal of Health Economics* 12 (1993): 187–191.

Olsen, Jan Abel, "Theories of Justice and Their Implications for Priority Setting in Health Care," *Journal of Health Economics* 16 (1997): 625–639.

Olson, Mancur. *The Logic of Collective Action: Public Goods and the Theory of Groups.* (New York, Schocken Books, 1965).

Oregon Health Services Commission, State of Oregon, Prioritization of Health Services: A Report to the Governor and Legislature, May 1991.

Ozanne, Larry, "How Will Medical Savings Accounts Affect Spending?" *Inquiry* 33 (1996): 225–236.

Ozcan, Yasar A., Roice D. Luke, and Cengiz Haksever, "Ownership and Organizational Performance: A Comparison of Technical Efficiency across Hospital Types," *Medical Care* 30 (1992): 781–794.

Parker-Pope, Tara, Antismoking sentiment flares in Europe's smoke-filled cafes, *Wall Street Journal,* 28 August 1995, sec. B1.

Parkin, David, Alistair McGuire, and Brian Yule, "Aggregate Health Care Expenditures and National Income: Is Health Care a Luxury Good?" *Journal of Health Economics* 6 (1987): 109–128.

Pattison, Robert, and Hallie Katz, "Investor-Owned and Not-for-Profit Hospitals: A Comparison Based on California Data," *New England Journal of Medicine* 309 (1982): 347–353.

Paul, Chris, "Physician Licensure and the Quality of Medical Care," *Atlantic Economic Journal* 12 (1984): 18–30.

Pauly, Mark V. *Health Benefits at Work: An Economic and Political Analysis of Employment-Based Health Insurance.* (Ann Arbor, MI: The University of Michigan Press, 1997).

Pauly, Mark V. *An Analysis of Medical Savings Accounts: Do Two Wrongs Make a Right?* (Washington, DC: American Enterprise Institute for Public Policy Research, 1994).

Pauly, Mark V., "Making a Case for Employer-Enforced Individual Mandates," *Health Affairs* 13 (1994b): 21–33.

Pauly, Mark V., "Editorial: A Re-Examination of the Meaning and Importance of Supplier-Induced Demand," *Journal of Health Economics* 13 (1994a): 369–372.

Pauly, Mark, V., "U.S. Health Care Costs: The Untold True Story," *Health Affairs* 12 (1993): 154–159.

Pauly, Mark V., "A Primer on Competition in Medical Markets," in *Health Care in America,* edited by H. E. Frech III. (San Francisco: Pacific Research Institute for Public Policy, 1988a).

Pauly, Mark V., "Is Medical Care Different? Old Questions, New Answers," *Journal of Health Politics, Policy and Law* 13 (1988b): 227–237.

Pauly, Mark V., Doctors and Their Workshops (Chicago: University of Chicago Press, 1980).

Pauly, Mark V., "Is Medical Care Really Different?" in *Competition in the Health Care Sector,* edited by Warren Greenberg. (Germantown, MD; Aspen Systems, 1978).

Pauly, Mark V. *Medical Care at Public Expense: A Study in Applied Welfare Economics.* (New York: Praeger, 1971).

Pauly, Mark V., "The Economics of Moral Hazard: Comment," *American Economic Review* 58 (1968): 531–537.

Pauly, Mark V., and John C. Goodman, "Tax Credits for Health Insurance and Medical Savings Accounts," *Health Affairs* 14 (1995): 126–139.

Pauly, Mark V., and Michael Redisch, "The Not-for-Profit Hospital as a Physician's Cooperative," *American Economic Review* 63 (1973): 87–100.

Pauly, Mark V., and Mark A. Satterthwaite, "The Pricing of Primary Care Physicians' Services: A Test of the Role of Consumer Information," *Bell Journal of Economics* 12 (1981): 488–506.

Pauly, Mark V. et al., "A Plan for 'Responsible National Health Insurance,'" *Health Affairs* 10 (1991): 5–25.

Payne, Abigail A., "Does the Government Crowd-Out Private Donations? New Evidence from a Sample of Non-Profit Firms," *Journal of Public Economics* 69 (1998): 323–345.

Peabody, John W., Sung-Woo Lee, and Stephen R. Bickel, "Health Care for All in the Republic of Korea: One Country's Experience with Implementing Universal Health Care," *Health Policy* 31 (1995): 29–42.

Pear, Robert, Policy changes fail to fill gaps in health coverage, *New York Times,* 9 August 1998, sec. A1, A18.

Peden, Edgar A., and Mark S. Freeland, "Insurance Effects on U.S. Medical Spending (1960–1993)," *Health Economics* 7 (1998): 671–687.

Peltzman, Sam, "Toward a More General Theory of Regulation," *Journal of Law and Economics* 19 (1976): 211–248.

Peltzman, Sam, *Regulation of Pharmaceutical Innovation: The 1962 Amendments,* American Enterprise Institute, Washington, DC, 1974.

Pernick, Martin S., "The Cultural Ecology of Health: Science, Values, and Society in the History of American Medicine," manuscript of book in progress, 1991.

Petroshius, Susan M., and Kent B. Monroe, "Effect of Product Line Pricing Characteristics on Product Evaluations," *Journal of Consumer Research* 13 (1987): 511–519.

Pezzin, Lilliana E., Peter Kemper, and James Reschovsky, "Does Publicly Provided Home Care Substitute for Family Care?" *Journal of Human Resources* 31 (1996): 650–676.

Pfaff, Martin, "Differences in Health Care Spending across Countries: Statistical Evidence," *Journal of Health Politics, Policy and Law* 15 (1990): 1–67.

Pharmaceutical Research and Manufacturers of America (PhRMA), *Pharmaceutical Industry Profile 1999,* www.phrma.org/publications/industry/profile99/index.html.

Phelps, Charles E., "Welfare Loss from Variations: Further Considerations," *Journal of Health Economics* 14 (1995): 253–260.

Phelps, Charles E. *Health Economics.* (New York: Harper Collins, 1992).

Phelps, Charles E., "Induced Demand—Can We Ever Know Its Extent?" *Journal of Health Economics* 5 (1986): 355–365.

Phelps, Charles E., and Cathleen Mooney, "Correction and Update on 'Priority Setting in Medical Technology Assessment,'" *Medical Care* 30 (1992): 744–751.

Phelps, Charles E., and Stephen T. Parente, "Priority Setting in Medical Technology and Medical Practice Assessment," *Medical Care* 28 (1990): 703–723.

Phlips, Louis. *The Economics of Imperfect Information.* (Cambridge: Cambridge University Press, 1988).

Physician Payment Review Commission, *The Medicare Fee Schedule,* PPRC Basics, September 1997, no. 5.

Physicians' Medicare Fee Schedules. (Chicago, IL: Commerce Clearing House, 1990, 1992).

Picone, Gabriel, Martin Uribe, and R. Mark Wilson, "The Effect of Uncertainty on the Demand for Medical Care, Health Capital and Wealth," *Journal of Health Economics* 17 (1998): 171–185.

Pindyck, Robert S., and Daniel L. Rubinfeld, *Microeconomics,* 4th ed. (Upper Saddle River, NJ: Prentice Hall, 1998).

Pitt, Laura. *1988 January Update of Medicare Enrollments in HMOs.* (Excelsior, MN: InterStudy, 1988).

Pitt, Mark M., "Estimating the Determinants of Child Health When Fertility and Mortality Are Selective," *Journal of Human Resources* 32 (1997): 129–58.

Po, Alain Li Wan, "Mega-Mergers in the Pharmaceutical Industry: In Whose Interests?" *Pharmacoeconomics* 14 (1998): 349–355.

Politzer, Robert M., Charles A. Yesalis, and Jerald M. Katzoff, "The Hidden Supply of Foreign Medical Graduates," *Medical Care* 27 (1989): 1046–1057.

Pollard, Michael R., and Robert F. Leibenluft, *Antitrust and the Health Professions,* Office of Policy and Planning, Federal Trade Commission, 1981.

Porell, Frank et al., "A Longitudinal Analysis of Nursing Home Outcomes," *Health Services Research* 33 (1998): 835–865.

Portney, Paul R., "Housing Prices, Health Effects and Valuing Reduction in Risk of Death," *Journal of Environmental Economic Management* 8 (1981): 72–78.

President, The President's Comprehensive Health Reform Program, February 6, 1992.

Prospective Payment Assessment Commission, *Annual Report to Congress,* April 11, 1997.

Prospective Payment Review Commission, *Annual Report to Congress,* April 5, 1995.

Prospective Payment Review Commission, *Medicare Prospective Payment and the American Health Care System, Report to Congress,* June 24, 1991. (Chicago, IL: Commerce Clearing House, Inc., 1991).

Quick, Jonathan D., M. R. Greenlick, and K. L. Roghmann, "Prenatal Care and Pregnancy Outcome in an HMO and General Population: A Multivariate Cohort Analysis," *American Journal of Public Health* 71 (1981): 381–390.

Raffel, Marshall W., and Norna K. Raffel. *The U.S. Health System: Origins and Functions,* 4th ed. (Albany, NY: Delmar, 1994).

Rakich, Jonathon S., "The Canadian and U.S. Health Care Systems: Profiles and Policies," *Hospital and Health Services Administration* 36 (1991): 25–42.

Rathwell, Tom, "Health Care in Canada: A System in Turmoil," *Health Policy* 24 (1994): 5–17.

Rawls, John. *A Theory of Justice.* (Cambridge: Belnap Press of the Harvard University Press, 1971).

Register, Charles A., and Edward R. Bruning, "Profit Incentives and Technical Efficiency in the Production of Hospital Care," *Southern Economic Journal* 53 (1987): 899–914.

Reichman, Nancy E., and Maryanne J. Florio, "The Effects of Enriched Prenatal Care Services on Medicaid Birth Outcomes in New Jersey," *Journal of Health Economics* 15 (1996): 455–476.

Reinhardt, Uwe E., "Germany's Health Care System: It's Not the American Way," *Health Affairs* 13 (1994a): 22–24.

Reinhardt, Uwe W., "Planning the Nation's Health Workforce: Let the Market In," *Inquiry* 31 (1994b): 250–263.

Reinhardt, Uwe E., "Economists in Health Care: Saviors, or Elephants in a Porcelain Shop?" *American Economic Review* 79 (1989): 337–342.

Reinhardt, Uwe E., "A Production Function for Physician Services," *Review of Economics and Statistics* 54 (1972): 55–65.

Renn, Steven C. et al., "The Effects of Ownership and System Affiliation on the Economic Performance of Hospitals," *Inquiry* 22 (1985): 219–236.

Rhee, Sang-O et al., "USMGs Versus FMGs: Are There Performance Differences in the Ambulatory Setting?" *Medical Care* 24 (1986): 248–258.

Rice, Dorothy, *Estimating the Cost of Illness,* U.S. Public Health Service Publication No. 947–6. (Washington, DC: GPO, May 1966).

Rice, Thomas. *The Economics of Health Reconsidered.* (Chicago: Health Administration Press, 1998).

Rice, Thomas H., "The Impact of Changing Medicare Reimbursement Rates on Physician-Induced Demand," *Medical Care* 21 (1983): 803–815.

Rice, Thomas H., and Roberta J. Labelle, "Do Physicians Induce Demand for Medical Service?" *Journal of Health Politics, Policy and Law* 14 (1989): 587–600.

Ried, Walter, "QALYs Versus HYEs—What's Right and What's Wrong: A Review of the Controversy," *Journal of Health Economics* 17 (1998): 607–625.

Rifkind, Basil M. et. al., "Distribution of High Density and Other Lipoproteins in Selected LRC Prevalence Study Populations: A Brief Survey," *Lipids* 14 (1979): 105–112.

Rizzo, John A., "Physician Advertising Revisited," *Medical Care* 26 (1988): 1238–1244.

Rizzo, John A., and David Blumenthal, "Is the Target Income Hypothesis an Economic Heresy?" *Medical Care Research and Review* 53 (1996): 243–266.

Rizzo, John A., and David Blumenthal, "Physician Labor Supply: Do Income Effects Matter?" *Journal of Health Economics* 33 (1994): 433–453.

Rizzo, John A., and John H. Goddeeris, "The Economic Returns to Hospital Admitting Privileges," *Journal of Health Politics, Policy and Law* 23 (1998): 483–513.

Rizzo, John A., and Richard J. Zeckhauser, "Income Targets, Loss Aversion, and Physicians' Behavior," Working Paper, October 1998.

Rizzo, John A., and Richard J. Zeckhauser, "Advertising and the Price, Quantity, and Quality of Primary Care Physician Services," *Journal of Human Resources* 27 (1992): 381–421.

Rizzo, John A., and Richard J. Zeckhauser, "Advertising and Entry: The Case of Physician Services," *Journal of Political Economy* 98 (1990): 476–500.

Roberts, Mark J., and Larry Samuelson, "An Empirical Analysis of Dynamic, Nonprice Competition in an Oligopolistic Industry," *Rand Journal of Economics* 19 (1988): 200–220.

Rochaix, Lise, "Information Asymmetry and Search in the Market for Physicians' Services," *Journal of Health Economics* 8 (1989): 53–84.

Roemer, Milton I., "Bed Supply and Hospital Utilization: A National Experiment," *Hospitals, J.A.H.A.* 35 (1961): 988–993.

Roemer, Milton I., and William Shonick, "HMO Performance: The Recent Evidence," *Milbank Memorial Fund Quarterly/Health and Society* 51 (Summer 1973): 271–317.

Romeo, Anthony A., Judith L. Wagner, and Robert H. Lee, "Prospective Reimbursement and the Diffusion of New Technologies in Hospitals," *Journal of Health Economics* 3 (1984): 1–24.

Roos, N. P., and L. L. Roos, Jr., "Surgical Rate Variations: Do They Reflect the Health or Socioeconomic Characteristics of the Population?" *Medical Care* 20 (1982): 945–958.

Rosenzweig, Mark R., and T. Paul Schultz, "Estimating a Household Production Function: Heterogeneity, the Demand for Health Inputs, and Their Effects on Birth Weight," *Journal of Political Economy* 91 (1983): 723–746.

Rosenzweig, Mark R., and Kenneth I. Wolpin, "Sisters, Siblings, and Mothers: The Effect of Teen-Age Childbearing on Birth Outcomes in a Dynamic Family Context," *Econometrica* 63 (1995): 303–326.

Rosett, Richard N., and Lien-fu Huang, "The Effect of Health Insurance on the Demand for Medical Care," *Journal of Political Economy* 81 (1973): 281–305.

Rosko, Michael D., and Robert W. Broyles. *The Economics of Health Care.* (New York: Greenwood, 1988).

Rosko, Michael D. et al., "The Effects of Ownership, Operating Environment, and Strategic Choices on Nursing Home Efficiency, *Medical Care* 33 (1995): 1001–1021.

Rossiter, Louis F., and Gail R. Wilensky, "Identification of Physician-Induced Demand," *Journal of Human Resources* 19 (1984): 231–244.

Rossiter, Louis F., and Gail R. Wilensky, "A Reexamination of the Use of Physician Services: The Role of Physician-Initiated Demand," *Inquiry* 20 (1983): 162–172.

Rotfeld, Herbert J., and Kim B. Rotzoll, "Advertising and Product Quality: Are Heavily Advertised Products Better?" *Journal of Consumer Affairs* 10 (1976): 37–47.

Rouleau, Jean L. et al., "A Comparison of Management Patterns after Acute Myocardial Infarction in Canada and the United States," *New England Journal of Medicine* 328 (1993): 779–784.

Rublee, Dale A., "Medical Technology in Canada, Germany, and the United States: An Update," *Health Affairs* 13 (1994): 113–117.

Ruffin, Roy J., and Duane E. Leigh, "Charity, Competition, and the Pricing of Doctors' Services," *Journal of Human Resources* 8 (1973): 212–222.

Russell, Louise B. *Educated Guesses: Making Policy about Medical Screening Tests.* (Berkeley, CA: University of California Press, 1994).

Russell, Louise B., "The Diffusion of Hospital Technologies: Some Econometric Evidence," *Journal of Human Resources* 12 (1977): 482–502.

Russell, Louise B. et al., "The Role of Cost-Effectiveness in Health and Medicine," *Journal of the American Medical Association* 276 (1996): 1172–1177.

Saffer, Henry, "Alcohol Advertising and Motor Vehicle Fatalities," *Review of Economics and Statistics* 79 (1997): 431–442.

Saffer, Henry, "Alcohol Advertising Bans and Alcohol Abuse: An International Perspective," *Journal of Health Economics* 10 (1991): 65–79.

Saffer, Henry, and Frank Chaloupka, "Demographic Differentials in the Demand for Alcohol and Illicit Drugs," Working Paper 6432, National Bureau of Economic Research, February 1998.

Safriet, Barbara J., "Impediments to Progress in Health Care Workforce Policy: License and Practice Laws," *Inquiry* 31 (1994): 310–317.

Salkever, David S., and Thomas W. Bice. *Hospital Certificate-of Need Controls: Impact on Investment, Costs, and Use.* (Washington: American Enterprise Institute, 1979).

Salop, Stephen C., "Information and Monopolistic Competition," *American Economic Review* 66 (1976): 240–245.

Salvatore, Dominick. *Schaum's Outline Series: Microeconomic Theory,* 2d ed. (New York: McGraw-Hill, 1983).

Samuelson, Paul A., "Diagrammatic Exposition of the Theory of Public Expenditure," *Review of Economics and Statistics* 37 (1955): 350–356.

Sassone, Peter G., and William A. Schaffer. *Cost-Benefit Analysis: A Handbook.* (New York: Academic Press, 1978).

Satterthwaite, Mark A., "Consumer Information, Equilibrium Industry Price, and the Number of Sellers," *Bell Journal of Economics* 10 (1979): 483–502.

Scanlon, William J., "A Theory of the Nursing Home Market," *Inquiry* 17 (1980): 25–41.

Schaefer, Mark E., "Demand Versus Need for Medical Services in a General Cost Benefit Setting," *American Journal of Public Health* 65 (1975): 293–295.

Schaeffer, Leonard D., "Rebuttal on Nonprofit/For Profit Debate," *Health Affairs* 15 (1996): 238–239.

Scheffler, Richard M., "The United Mine Workers' Health Plan: An Analysis of the Cost-Sharing Program," *Medical Care* 22 (1984): 247–254.

Scherer, F. Michael. *Innovation and Growth: Schumpeterian Perspectives.* (Cambridge, MA: MIT, 1984).

Schieber, George J., and Jean-Pierre Poullier, "International Health Spending: Issues and Trends," *Health Affairs* 10 (1991): 106–116.

Schieber, George J., and Jean-Pierre Poullier, "Overview of International Comparisons of Health Care Expenditures," *Health Care Financing Review* 10 (Annual Supplement 1989): 1–7.

Schmalensee, Richard. *The Economics of Advertising.* (Amsterdam: North-Holland, 1972).

Schmalensee, Richard, "A Model of Advertising and Product Quality," *Journal of Political Economy* 86 (1978): 485–503.

Schmidt, P. and R. Sickles, "Production Frontiers and Panel Data," *Journal of Business and Economic Statistics* 2 (1984): 367–374.

Schneider, Lynne, Benjamin Klein, and Kevin M. Murphy, "Governmental Regulation of Cigarette Health Information," *Journal of Law and Economics* 24 (1981): 575–612.

Schneider, Markus, "Health Care Cost Containment in the Federal Republic of Germany," *Health Care Financing Review* 12 (1991): 87–101.

Schneyer, Solomon, J. Steven Landefeld, and Frank H. Sandifer, "Biomedical Research and Illness: 1900–1979," *Milbank Memorial Fund Quarterly/Health and Society* 59 (1981): 44–58.

Schultz, T. Paul, "Introduction: Symposium on Investments in Women's Human Capital and Development," *Journal of Human Resources* 28 (1993): 689–693.

Schwartz, Joel, and Dockery, Douglas W., "Increased Mortality in Philadelphia Associated with Daily Air Pollution Concentrations," *American Review of Respiratory Diseases* 145 (1992): 600–604.

Schwartz, Michael et al., "Small Area Variations in Hospitalization Rates: How Much You See Depends on How You Look," *Medical Care* 32 (1994): 189–201.

Schwartz, William B., "In the Pipeline: A Wave of Valuable Medical Technology," *Health Affairs* 13 (1994): 70–79.

Schwartz, William B., and Daniel N. Mendelson, "Eliminating Waste and Inefficiency Can Do Little to Contain Costs," *Health Affairs* 13 (1994): 224–238.

Schweitzer, Stuart O. *Pharmaceutical Economics and Policy.* (New York: Oxford University Press, 1996).

Scitovsky, Anne A., "Changes in the Costs of Treatment of Selected Illnesses, 1971–1981," *Medical Care* 23 (1985): 1345–1357.

Scitovsky, Anne A., and Nelda McCall, "Changes in the Costs of Treatment of Selected Illnesses, 1951–1964–1971," National Center for Health Services Research, DHEW Publication No. (HRA) 77–3161, 1977.

Seldon, Barry J., and Khowsrow Doroodian, "A Simultaneous Model of Cigarette Advertising: Effects on Demand and Industry Response to Public Policy," *Review of Economics and Statistics* 71 (1989): 673–677.

Seldon, Barry J., Chulho Jung, and Roberto J. Cavazos, "Market Power among Physicians in the U.S., 1983–1991," *Quarterly Review of Economics and Finance* 38 (1998): 799–824.

Sexton, Thomas R. et al., "Evaluating Managerial Efficiency of Veterans Administration Medical Centers Using Data Envelopment Analysis," *Medical Care* 27 (1989): 1175–1185.

Shain, Max, and Milton I. Roemer, "Hospital Costs Relate to the Supply of Beds," *Modern Hospital* 92 (1959): 71–73.

Shalit, Sol S., "A Doctor-Hospital Cartel Theory," *Journal of Business* 50 (1977): 1–20.

Sherman, H. David, "Hospital Efficiency Measurement and Evaluation," *Medical Care* 22 (1984): 922–935.

Shleifer, Andrei, "A Theory of Yardstick Competition, *Rand Journal of Economics* 16 (1985): 319–327.

Short, Pamela F., and Peter Kemper, "Nursing Home Financing Reform: How Would It Affect Expenditures for Nursing Home Care?" *Inquiry* 31 (1994): 141–152.

Shortell, Stephen M., "A Model of Physician Referral Behavior: A Test of Exchange Theory in Medical Practice," Chicago: Center for Health Administration Studies, 1973.

Shortell, Stephen M., Robin R. Gillies, and David A. Anderson, "The New World of Managed Care: Creating Organized Delivery Systems," *Health Affairs* 13 (1994): 46–64.

Showalter, Mark H., and Norman K. Thurston, "Taxes and Labor Supply of High-Income Physicians," *Journal of Public Economics* 66 (1997): 73–97.

Showstack, Jonathon A. et al., "Fee-for-Service Physician Payment: Analysis of Current Methods and Evidence," *Inquiry* 16 (1979): 230–246.

Sickles, Robin C., and Abdo Yazbeck, "On the Dynamics of Demand for Leisure and the Production of Health," *Journal of Business & Economic Statistics* 16 (1998): 187–197.

Siegel, Joanna E. et al., "Recommendations for Reporting Cost-Effectiveness Analyses," *Journal of the American Medical Association* 276 (1996): 1339–1341.

Silver, Morris, "An Economic Analysis of Variations in Medical Expenses and Work-Loss Rates," in *Empirical Studies in Health Economics,* edited by H. Klarman. (Baltimore: Johns Hopkins, 1970).

Simon, Carol J., David Dranove, and William White, "The Effect of Managed Care on the Incomes of Primary and Specialty Physicians," *Health Services Research* 33 (1998): 549–569.

Simon, Carol J., and David W. Emmons, "Physician Earnings at Risk: An Examination of Capitated Contracts," *Health Affairs* 16 (1997): 120–126.

Sindelar, Jody, "The Declining Price of Health Insurance," in *Health Care in America,* edited by H. E. Frech III. (San Francisco: Pacific Research Institute for Public Policy, 1988).

Sinjay, Ugur A., and Claudia R. Campbell, "Scope and Scale Economies in Merging Hospitals Prior to Merger," *Journal of Economics and Finance* 19 (1995): 107–123.

Skinner, Jonathon, "What Do Stochastic Cost Functions Tell Us about Inefficiency?" *Journal of Health Economics* 13 (1994): 323–328.

Skocpol, Theda, "The Rise and Resounding Demise of the Clinton Plan," *Health Affairs* 14 (1995): 66–87.

Sloan, Frank A., "Property Rights in the Hospital Industry," in *Health Care in America,* edited by H. E. Frech III. (San Francisco: Pacific Research Institute for Public Policy, 1988).

Sloan, Frank A., "Rate Regulation as a Strategy for Hospital Cost Control: Evidence from the Last Decade," *Milbank Memorial Fund Quarterly/ Health and Society* 61 (1983): 195–221.

Sloan, Frank A., and Edmund R. Becker, "Internal Organization of Hospitals and Hospital Costs," *Inquiry* 28 (1981): 224–239.

Sloan, Frank A., and A. Bruce Steinwald, "Effects of Regulation on Hospital Costs and Input Use," *Journal of Law and Economics* 23 (1980): 81–109.

Sloan, Frank A., Roger D. Feldman, and A. Bruce Steinwald, "Effects of Teaching on Hospital Costs," *Journal of Health Economics* 3 (1983): 1–28.

Sloan, Frank A., Michael A. Morrisey, and Joseph Valvona, "Effects of the Medicare Prospective Payment System on Hospital Cost Containment: An Early Appraisal," *Milbank Quarterly* 66 (1988a): 191–219.

Sloan, Frank A., Michael A. Morrisey, and Joseph Valvona, "Medicare Prospective Payment and the Use of Medical Technologies in Hospitals," *Medical Care* 26 (1988b): 837–853.

Sloan, Frank A. et al., "The Demise of Hospital Philanthropy," *Economic Inquiry* 28 (1990): 725–743.

Sloan, Frank A. et al., "Diffusion of Surgical Technology: An Exploratory Study," *Journal of Health Economics* 5 (1986): 31–61.

Smith, Francis B. *The Retreat of Tuberculosis 1850–1950.* (London: Croom Helm, 1988).

Smith, James P., "Socioeconomic Status and Health," *American Economic Review* 88 (1998): 192–196.

Smith, Sheila et al., "The Next Ten Years of Health Spending: What Does the Future Hold?" *Health Affairs* 17 (1998): 128–140.

Sonnenfeld, Sally T. et al., "Projections of National Health Expenditures through the Year 2000," *Health Care Financing Review* 13 (1991): 1–27.

Sørenson, Rune, and Jostein Grytten, "Competition and Supplier Induced Demand in a Health Care System with Fixed Fees," *Health Economics* 8 (1999): 497–508.

Spence, A. Michael, "Monopoly, Quality, and Regulation," *Bell Journal of Economics* 6 (1975): 417–429.

Stano, Miron, "A Further Analysis of the Physician Inducement Controversy," *Journal of Health Economics* 6 (1987): 227–238.

Stano, Miron, "An Analysis of the Evidence on Competition in the Physician Services Markets," *Journal of Health Economics* 4 (1985): 197–211.

Stano, Miron, "Individual Health Accounts: An Alternative Health Care Financing Approach," *Health Care Financing Review* 3 (1981): 117–125.

Stano, Miron, and Sherman Folland, "Variations in the Use of Physician Services by Medicare Beneficiaries," *Health Care Financing Review* 9 (1988): 51–58.

Stano, Miron et al., "The Effects of Physician Availability on Fees and the Demand for Doctors' Services," *Atlantic Economic Journal* 13 (1985): 51–60.

Starr, Paul, "Health Care for the Poor: The Past Twenty Years," in *Fighting Poverty: What Works and What Doesn't,* edited by Sheldon Danziger and Daniel Weinberg. (Cambridge: Harvard, 1986).

Starr, Paul. *The Social Transformation of American Medicine.* (New York: Basic Books, 1982).

Steinberg, Richard, "Voluntary Donations and Public Expenditures in a Federalist System," *American Economic Review* 77 (1987): 24–36.

Steinberg, Richard, "Charitable Giving as a Mixed Public/Private Good: Implications for Tax Policy," *Public Finance Quarterly* 14 (1986): 415–431.

Steinberg, Richard, "The Revealed Objective Functions of Nonprofit Firms," *Rand Journal of Economics* 17 (1986): 508–526.

Steinfels, Peter, Oregon Medicaid's doctor-assisted suicide, *New York Times,* 7 March 1998, national/metro Sec.

Steinwald, A. Bruce, and Laura A. Dummit, "Hospital Case-Mix Change: Sicker Patients or DRG Creep?" *Health Affairs* 8 (1989): 35–47.

Stevenson, Carolyn, "Hospice Care: A Look at Cost-Effectiveness," *Employee Benefit Plan Review* 51 (1996): 49–50.

Stigler, George J., "The Theory of Economic Regulation," *Bell Journal of Economics* 2 (1971): 3–21.

Stigler, George J., "The Economics of Information," *Journal of Political Economy* 69 (1961): 213–225.

Stiglitz, Joseph E. *Economics of the Public Sector,* 2d ed. (New York: Norton, 1988).

Strauss, John et al, "Gender and Life-Cycle Differentials in the Patterns and Determinants of Adult Health," *Journal of Human Resources* 28 (1993): 791–837.

Strumwasser, Ira et al., "The Triple Option Choice: Self-Selection Bias in Traditional Coverage, HMOs and PPOs," *Inquiry* 26 (1989): 432–441.

Succi, Melissa J., Shoou-Yih Lee, and Jeffrey A. Alexander, "Effects of Market Position and Competition on Rural Hospital Closures," *Health Services Research* 31 (1997): 679–699.

Sullivan, Daniel, "Monopsony Power in the Market for Nurses," *Journal of Law and Economics* 32 (1989): S135–S179.

Surgeon General of the United States. *Reducing the Health Consequences of Smoking: 25 Years of Progress, Executive Summary.* U.S. Department of Health and Human Services, Public Health Service, Office on Smoking and Health, Rockville, MD, 1989.

Svorny, Shirley, "Should We Reconsider Licensing Physicians?" *Contemporary Policy Issues* 10 (1992): 31–38.

Tamblyn, R. et al., "Association between Licensing Examination Scores and Resource Use and Quality of Care in Primary Care Practice," *Journal of the American Medical Association* 280 (1998): 989–996.

Telser, Lester G., "Advertising and Competition," *Journal of Political Economy* 72 (1964): 537–562.

Temin, Peter, "An Economic History of American Hospitals," in *Health Care in America: The Political Economy of Hospitals and Health Insurance,*

edited by H. E. Frech III. (San Francisco: Pacific Research Institute for Public Policy, 1988).

Tengs, Tammy O. et al., "Five Hundred Life-Saving Interventions and Their Cost-Effectiveness," *Risk Analysis* 15 (1995): 369–390.

Teplensky, Jill D. et al., "Hospital Adoption of Medical Technology: An Empirical Test of Alternative Models," *Health Services Research* 30 (1995): 437–466.

Thomas, Lewis. *The Lives of a Cell.* (New York: Viking, 1974).

Thornton, James, "The Labor Supply Behavior of Self-Employed Solo Practice Physicians," *Applied Economics* 30 (1998): 85–94.

Thornton, James, and B. Kelly Eakin, "The Utility-Maximizing Self-Employed Physician," *Journal of Human Resources* 32 (1997): 98–128.

Tinbergen, Jan. *On the Theory of Economic Policy.* (Amsterdam: North-Holland Pub. Co., 1952).

Torrance, George W., "Preferences for Health Outcomes and Cost–Utility Analysis," *American Journal of Managed Care* 3 (1997 Supplement): S8–S20.

Toxic Substances Board, *Health or Tobacco: An End to Tobacco Advertising and Promotion,* Department of Health, Wellington, New Zealand, May 1989.

Tremblay, Carol Horton, and Victor J. Tremblay, "The Impact of Cigarette Advertising on Consumer Surplus, Profit, and Social Welfare," *Contemporary Economic Policy* 13 (1995): 113–124.

Trigg, Andrew B., and Nick Bosanquet, "Tax Harmonisation and the Reduction of European Smoking Rates," *Journal of Health Economics* 11 (1992): 329–346.

Tumlinson, Anne et al., "Choosing a Health Plan: What Information Will Consumers Use?" *Health Affairs* 16 (1997): 229–238.

Tye, Joe B., Kenneth E. Warner, and Stanton A. Glantz, "Tobacco Advertising and Consumption: Evidence of a Causal Relationship," *Journal of Public Health Policy* 8 (1987): 492–508.

United Nations, "World Population from Year 0 to Stabilization," http://www.*gopher.undp.org:70/00/ ungophers/popin/wdtrends/histor,* 1996.

U.S. Department of Commerce. *Statistical Abstract.* Washington, DC, various years.

U.S. Department of Health and Human Services. *1997 Social Security Statistics Throughout the World.* Washington, DC, 1997, http://www.ssa.gov/ statistics/ssptw97.

U.S. Department of Health and Human Services, Agency for Health Care Policy and Research. *The 50 Most Frequent Diagnosis-Related Groups (DRGs), Diagnoses, and Procedures: Statistics by Hospital Size and Location.* DHHS Publication No. (PHS) 90–3465, September 1990.

U.S. Department of Health and Human Services, Public Health Service. *Health United States,* various years.

U.S. Department of Health and Human Services, Public Health Service. *Seventh Report to the President and Congress on the Status of Health Personnel in the United States.* DHHS Publication No. HRS-P-OD-90-1, March 1990.

U.S. Department of Health and Human Services. *Report of the Expert Panel on Population Strategies for Blood Cholesterol Reduction.* NIH Publication No. 90-3046, November 1990.

U.S. Department of Labor, Bureau of Labor Statistics. *Occupational Outlook Handbook,* 1990–91 edition. April 1990.

v. D. Schulenburg, J. Matthias, "Germany: Solidarity at a Price," *Journal of Health Politics, Policy and Law* 17 (1992): 715–738.

Valdez, R. Burciaga et al., "Consequences of Cost-Sharing for Children's Health," *Pediatrics* 75 (1985): 952–961.

Valdmanis, Vivian G., "Ownership and Technical Efficiency of Hospitals," *Medical Care* 28 (1990): 552–561.

van de Ven, Wynand P.M.M., and Rene C.J.A. van Vliet, "Consumer Information Surplus and Adverse Selection in Competitive Health Insurance Markets: An Empirical Study," *Journal of Health Economics* 14 (1995): 149–169.

van Doorslaer, Eddy, and Adam Wagstaff, "Equity in the Delivery of Health Care: Some International Comparisons," *Journal of Health Economics* 11 (1992): 389–411.

van Lear, William, and Lynette Fowler, "Efficiency and Service in the Group Home Industry," *Journal of Economic Issues* 21 (1997): 1039–1050.

Vehorn, Charles L., J. Steven Landefeld, and Douglas P. Wagner, "Measuring the Contribution of

Biomedical Research to the Production of Health," *Research Policy* 11 (1982): 3–13.

Vick, Sandra, and Anthony Scott, "Agency in Health Care. Examining Patients' Preferences for Attributes of the Doctor–Patient Relationship," *Journal of Health Economics* 17 (1998): 587–605.

Viscusi, W. Kip, "Cigarette Taxation and the Social Consequence of Smoking," *Tax Policy and the Economy* 9 (1995): 51–101.

Viscusi, W. Kip, "Promoting Smokers' Welfare with Responsible Taxation," *National Tax Journal* 57 (1994): 547–558.

Viscusi, W. Kip, "The Value of Risks to Life and Health," *Journal of Economic Literature* 31 (1993): 1912–1946.

Viscusi, W. Kip, "Age Variations in Risk Perceptions and Smoking Decisions," *Review of Economics and Statistics* 73 (1991): 577–588.

Viscusi, W. Kip, John M. Vernon, and Joseph E. Harrington Jr. *Economics of Regulation and Antitrust,* 2d ed. (Cambridge, MA: MIT Press, 1995).

Vita, Michael G., "Exploring Hospital Production Relationships with Flexible Functional Forms," *Journal of Health Economics* 9 (1990): 1–21.

Vital Statistics, World Health Organization, various years.

Vitaliano, Donald F., "On the Estimation of Hospital Cost Functions," *Journal of Health Economics* 6 (1987): 305–318.

Vitaliano, Donald F., and Mark Toren, "Hospital Cost and Efficiency in a Regime of Stringent Regulation," *Eastern Economic Journal* 22 (1996): 161–175.

Vitaliano, Donald F., and Mark Toren, "Cost Efficiency in Nursing Homes: A Stochastic Frontier Approach," *Journal of Health Economics* 13 (1994): 281–300.

Wagstaff, Adam, "QALYs and the Equity-Efficiency Trade-Off," *Journal of Health Economics* 10 (1991): 21–41.

Wagstaff, Adam, "Estimating Efficiency in the Hospital Sector: A Comparison of Three Statistical Cost Frontier Models," *Applied Economics* 21 (1989): 659–672.

Wagstaff, Adam, and Guillem Lopez, "Hospital Costs in Catalonia: A Stochastic Frontier Analysis," *Applied Economics* 3 (1996): 471–474.

Waid, Mary Onnis, "Brief Summaries of Medicare & Medicaid, as of June 25, 1998," http://www.hcfa.gov/medicare/ormedmed.htm., September 1, 1999.

Waldmann, Robert J., "Income Distribution and Infant Mortality," *Quarterly Journal of Economics* 107 (1992): 1283–1302.

Warner, Kenneth E., and Linda M. Goldenhar, "The Cigarette Advertising Broadcast Ban and Magazine Coverage of Smoking and Health," *Journal of Public Health Policy* 10 (1989): 32–42.

Warner, Kenneth E. et al., "Promotion of Tobacco Products: Issues and Policy Options," *Journal of Health Politics, Policy and Law* 11 (1986): 367–392.

Wasserman, Jeffrey et al., "The Effects of Excise Taxes and Regulations on Cigarette Smoking," *Journal of Health Economics* 10 (1991): 43–64.

Wedig, Gerard J., "Health Status and the Demand for Health: Results on Price Elasticities," *Journal of Health Economics* 7 (1988): 151–163.

Weinstein, M. A., "The Sum of Values from a Normal and a Truncated Normal Distribution," *Technometrics* 6 (1964): 104–105.

Weinstein, Milton C. et al., "Recommendations of the Panel on Cost-Effectiveness in Health and Medicine," *Journal of the American Medical Association* 276 (1996): 1253–1258.

Weisbrod, Burton A., "The Health Care Quadrilemma: An Essay on Technological Change, Insurance, Quality of Care, and Cost Containment," *Journal of Economic Literature* 29 (1991): 523–552.

Weisbrod, Burton A. *The Nonprofit Economy.* (Cambridge, MA: Harvard, 1988).

Weisbrod, Burton A., "Toward a Theory of the Voluntary Non-Profit Sector in a Three-Sector Economy," in *Altruism, Morality, and Economic Theory,* edited by Edmund S. Phelps. (New York: Russell Sage Foundation, 1975).

Weisbrod, Burton A., "Costs and Benefits of Medical Research: A Case Study of Poliomyelitis," *Journal of Political Economy* 79 (1971): 527–544.

Wells, William, John Burnett, and Sandra Moriarity. *Advertising: Principles and Practice.* (Upper Saddle River, NJ: Prentice Hall, 1989).

Wennberg, John E., "Population Illness Rates Do Not Explain Population Hospitalization Rates," *Medical Care* 25 (1987): 354–359.

Wennberg, John E., "Dealing with Medical Practice Variations: A Proposal for Action," *Health Affairs* 3 (1984): 6–32.

Wennberg, John E., and F. J. Fowler, "A Test of Consumer Contribution to Small Area Variations in Health Care Delivery," *Journal of the Maine Medical Association* 68 (1977): 275–279.

Wennberg, John E., and Alan Gittelsohn, "Variations in Medical Care among Small Areas," *Scientific American* 246 (1982): 120–134.

Wennberg, John E., and Alan Gittelsohn, "Small Area Variations in Health Care Delivery," *Science* 182 (1973): 1102–1108.

Wennberg, John E., B. A. Barnes, and M. Zubkoff, "Professional Uncertainty and the Problem of Supplier-Induced-Demand," *Social Science and Medicine* 16 (1982): 811–824.

Wennberg, John E., Jean L. Freeman, and William J. Culp, "Are Hospital Services Rationed in New Haven or Overutilized in Boston?" *The Lancet* 1 (1987): 1185–1189.

Wennberg, John E. et al., "Hospital Use and Mortality among Medicare Beneficiaries in Boston and New Haven," *New England Journal of Medicine* 321 (1989): 1168–1173.

Wennberg, John E. et al., "Changes in Tonsillectomy Rates Associated with Feedback and Review," *Pediatrics* 59 (1977): 821–826.

Wickizer, Thomas M., and Paul J. Feldstein, "The Impact of HMO Competition on Private Health Insurance Premiums, 1985–92," *Inquiry* 32 (1995): 241–251.

Wickizer, Thomas M., John R. C. Wheeler, and Paul J. Feldstein, "Have Hospital Inpatient Cost Containment Programs Contributed to the Growth in Outpatient Expenditures?" *Medical Care* 29 (1991): 442–451.

Wickizer, Thomas M., John R. C. Wheeler, and Paul J. Feldstein, "Does Utilization Review Reduce Unnecessary Hospital Care and Contain Costs?" *Medical Care* 27 (1989): 632–647.

Wildasin, David E. *Urban Public Finance.* (London: Harwood Academic Publishers, 1986).

Wilensky, Gail R., and Louis F. Rossiter, "Economic Advantages of Board Certification," *Journal of Health Economics* 2 (1983): 87–94.

Williams, Alan, "Intergeneration Equity: An Exploration of the 'Fair Innings' Argument," *Health Economics* 6 (1997): 117–132.

Williamson, Oliver E. *The Economics of Discretionary Behavior: Managerial Objectives in the Theory of the Firm.* (Upper Saddle River, NJ: Prentice Hall, 1964).

Wilson, George W., and Joseph M. Jadlow, "Competition, Profit Incentives, and Technical Efficiency in the Provision of Nuclear Medicine Services," *Bell Journal of Economics* 13 (1982): 472–482.

Wittink, Dick R., "Advertising Increases Sensitivity to Price," *Journal of Advertising Research* 17 (1977): 27–33.

Wittman, Donald, "Efficient Rules in Highway Safety and Sports Activity," *American Economic Review* 72 (1982): 78–90.

Wolfe, Barbara L., "Health Status and Medical Expenditures: Is There a Link?" *Social Science and Medicine* 22 (1986): 993–999.

Wolfe, Barbara L., and Jere R. Behrman, "Women's Schooling and Children's Health: Are the Effects Robust with Adult Sibling Control for the Women's Childhood Background?" *Journal of Health Economics* 6 (1987): 239–254.

Wolfe, John R., and John H. Goddeeris, "Adverse Selection, Moral Hazard, and the Wealth Effects in the Medigap Insurance Market," *Journal of Health Economics* 10 (1991): 433–459.

Wolinsky, Frederick. *The Sociology of Health: Principles, Practitioners, and Issues.* (Belmont, CA: Wadsworth, 1988).

Woods, Robert, and P. R. Andrew Hinde, "Mortality in Victorian England: Models and Patterns," *Journal of Interdisciplinary History* 18 (1987): 27–54.

Woolhandler, Steffie, and David U. Himmelstein, "The Deteriorating Administrative Efficiency of the U.S. Health Care System," *New England Journal of Medicine* 324 (1991): 1253–1258.

Wyszewianski, Leon, John R. C. Wheeler, and Avedis Donabedian, "Market-Oriented Cost-Containment Strategies and Quality of Care," *Milbank Memorial Fund Quarterly/Health and Society* 60 (1982): 518–550.

Yett, Donald E. *An Economic Analysis of the Nurse Shortage.* (Lexington, MA: Lexington Books, 1975).

Zabinski, Daniel et al., "Medical Savings Accounts: Microsimulation Results from a Model with Adverse Selection, *Journal of Health Economics* 18 (1999): 195–218.

Zeckhauser, Richard J., and D. Marks, "Sign-Posting Selected Product Information and Market Function," manuscript, John F. Kennedy School of Government, 1989.

Zimmerman, David R. et al., "Development and Testing of Nursing Home Quality Indicators," *Health Care Financing Review* 16 (1995): 107–127.

Zuckerman, Stephen, Jack Hadley, and Lisa Iezzoni, "Measuring Hospital Efficiency with Frontier Cost Functions," *Journal of Health Economics* 13 (1994): 255–280.

Zwanziger, Jack, and Adam Meirowitz, "Strategic Factors in Hospital Selection for HMO and PPO Networks," in *Managed Care and Changing Health Markets,* edited by Michael A. Morrisey. (Washington, DC: AEI Press, 1998).

Zwanziger, Jack, and Glen A. Melnick, "The Effects of Hospital Competition and the Medicare PPS Program on Hospital Cost Behavior in California," *Journal of Health Economics* 7 (1988): 301–320.

Name Index

Subject Index